DB2® for z/OS® Version 8 DBA Certification Guide

IBM Press Series—Information Management

ON DEMAND COMPUTING BOOKS

On Demand Computing
Fellenstein

Autonomic Computing
Murch

Grid Computing
Joseph and Fellenstein

Business Intelligence for the Enterprise
Biere

DB2 BOOKS

DB2 Express: Application Development and Deployment
Yip, Cheung, Gartner, Liu, and O'Connell

DB2 Universal Database v8.1 Certification Exam 703 Study Guide
Sanders

The Official Introduction to DB2 for z/OS
Sloan

High Availability Guide to DB2
Eaton and Cialini

DB2 Universal Database v8.1 Certification Exams 701 and 706 Study Guide
Sanders

Integrated Solutions with DB2
Cutlip and Medicke

DB2 Universal Database v8.1 Certification Exam 700 Study Guide
Sanders

DB2 for Solaris: The Official Guide
Bauch and Wilding

DB2 Universal Database v8 Handbook for Windows, UNIX, and Linux
Gunning

Advanced DBA Certification Guide and Reference for DB2 Universal Database v8 for Linux, UNIX, and Windows
Snow and Phan

DB2 Universal Database v8 Application Development Certification Guide, Second Edition
Martineau, Sanyal, Gashyna, and Kyprianou

DB2 Universal Database v8 for Linux, UNIX, and Windows Database Administration Certification Guide, Fifth Edition
Baklarz and Wong

DB2 SQL Procedural Language for Linux, UNIX, and Windows
Yip, Bradstock, Curtis, Gao, Janmohamed, Liu, and McArthur

DB2 Universal Database for OS/390 Version 7.1 Certification Guide
Lawson and Yevich

DB2 Version 8: The Official Guide
Zikopoulos, Baklarz, deRoos, and Melnyk

DB2 UDB for OS/390: An Introduction to DB2 OS/390
Sloan and Hernandez

MORE BOOKS FROM IBM PRESS

The Inventor's Guide to Trademarks and Patents
Fellenstein

WebSphere and Lotus: Implementing Collaboration Solutions
Lamb and Laskey

IBM WebSphere: Deployment and Advanced Configuration
Barcia, Hines, Alcott, and Botzum

IBM WebSphere System Administration
Williamson, Chan, Cundiff, Lauzon, and Mitchell

Developing Quality Technical Information, Second Edition
Hargis, Carey, Hernandez, Hughes, Longo, Rouiller, and Wilde

Enterprise Messaging Using JMS and IBM WebSphere
Yusuf

Enterprise Java Programming with IBM WebSphere, Second Edition
Brown, Craig, Hester, Pitt, Stinehour, Weitzel, Amsden, Jakab, and Berg

IBM Press

DB2® for z/OS®
Version 8 DBA
Certification Guide

DB2® Information Management Software

Susan Lawson

PRENTICE HALL
Professional Technical Reference
Upper Saddle River, New Jersey 07458
www.phptr.com

Note to U.S. Government Users — Documentation related to restricted rights — Use, duplication, or disclosure is subject to restrictions set forth in GSA ADP Schedule Contract with IBM Corp.

Publisher: John Wait
Editor in Chief: Don O'Hagan
Acquisitions Editor: Jeffrey Pepper
IBM Consulting Editor: Susan Visser
IBM Editorial Board: Tara Woodman, Ellice Uffer
Editorial Assistant: Mary Kate Murray
Marketing Manager: Robin O'Brien
Publicist: Heather Fox
Cover Designer: Alan Clements
Managing Editor: John Fuller
Project Editor: Lara Wysong
Copy Editor: Evelyn Pyle
Indexer: Ted Laux
Compositor: ContentWorks
Manufacturing Buyer: Carol Melville

Published by Pearson Education, Inc.
Publishing as Prentice Hall Professional Technical Reference
Upper Saddle River, NJ 07458

Library of Congress Cataloging-in-Publication Data

Lawson, Susan.
  DB2® for z/OS® version 8 DBA certification guide / Susan Lawson.
    p. cm.
  Includes bibliographical references and index.
  ISBN 0-13-149120-2 (hardback : alk. paper)
  1. Electronic data processing personnel—Certification. 2. Database
management—Examinations—Study guides. 3. IBM Database 2. 4. z/OS. I.
Title.

  QA76.3.L3895 2004
  005.75'65—dc22

                                                        2004020381

Prentice Hall PTR offers excellent discounts on this book when ordered in quantity for bulk purchases or special sales. For more information, please contact: U.S. Corporate and Government Sales, 1-800-382-3419, corpsales@pearsontechgroup.com. For sales outside of the U.S., please contact: International Sales, international@pearsoned.com.

ISBN   0-13-149120-2

Printed in the United States of America

First Printing, October 2004

To my husband, Alex,
who has put up with my work and
travel schedule for all these years

CONTENTS _____

Foreword   xv

Preface   xix

Acknowledgments   xxi

P A R T 1   DB2 Family and DB2 for z/OS Environment   1

C H A P T E R 1   **Product Overview**   3

DB2 and the On-Demand Business   4
DB2 Universal Database   5
DB2 Middleware and Connectivity   9
DB2 Application Development   12
DB2 Administration   16
Data Management Tools   19
Summary   21
Additional Resources   21

CHAPTER 2   **Environment**   **23**

z/OS   24
Address Spaces   24
Security   33
Parallel Sysplex Support   33
DFSMS   33
Interfaces   33
Installation and Migration   36
System Parameters   41
Commands   50
Utilities   53
Catalog and Directory   57
Distributed Data   63
Subsystem Pools   68
Summary   70
Additional Resources   71

CHAPTER 3   **DB2 Access and Security**   **73**

Subsystem Access   74
Data Set Protection   76
Access to DB2 objects   77
Multilevel Security   94
Auditing   95
Summary   98
Additional Resources   99

PART II   **Structured Query Language**   **101**

CHAPTER 4   **Database Objects**   **103**

Understanding Data Structures   104
Managing Database Objects   108
Creating Database Objects   110
Database Design and Implementation   160
Summary   175
Additional Resources   176

CHAPTER 5 **Retrieving and Manipulating Database Objects** **177**

Data Retrieval 178
Data Modification 200
Summary 208
Additional Resources 209

CHAPTER 6 **Advanced SQL Coding** **211**

Subqueries 211
Unions 215
Joins 217
Nested and Common Table Expressions 229
CASE Expressions 231
Row Expressions 233
OLAP and Star Joins 233
Predicates and Filtering 236
Summary 241
Additional Resources 241

PART III **Database Administration** **243**

CHAPTER 7 **Maintaining Data** **245**

Data Movement 245
Data Maintenance 260
Gathering Statistics 281
Real-Time Statistics 287
Statistics Usage 290
Resolving Restrictive and Advisory States 299
Summary 304
Additional Resources 304

CHAPTER 8   **Recovery and Restart**   **305**

Database Recovery Concepts   305
Logging   307
Image Copies   309
Data Recoveries   318
Disaster Recoveries   327
System-Level Backup and Recovery   330
DB2 Restart   332
Summary   333
Additional Resources   334

PART IV   Developing Applications with DB2   **335**

CHAPTER 9   **Data Sharing**   **337**

Data Sharing Components   339
Maintaining Data Integrity   345
Performance and Processing Costs   351
Movement to Data Sharing   353
Recovery Considerations   357
Summary   360
Additional Resources   360

CHAPTER 10   **Using SQL in an Application Program**   **361**

Delimiting SQL in a Program   362
Table and View Definitions   362
Host Variables and Structures   363
SQL Execution Validation   368
Cursors   375
Dynamic SQL   384
Summary   385
Additional Resources   385

CHAPTER 11 **Binding an Application Program** 387

Precompiling 388
Binding 389
Plan or Package Ownership 402
Summary 403
Additional Resources 403

CHAPTER 12 **Application Program Features** 405

Commit, Rollback, and Savepoint Operations 405
Global Transactions 413
Global Temporary Tables 413
Fetch for Limited Rows 418
Multirow Fetch and Multirow Insert 419
Identity Columns 420
Sequence Objects 423
Summary 426
Additional Resources 426

PART V **Advanced Functions and Performance** 427

CHAPTER 13 **Stored Procedures** 429

Benefits of Using Stored Procedures 430
Writing Stored Procedures 431
Defining Stored Procedures 438
Execution Environments 440
SQL Procedure Language 445
Developing SQL Stored Procedures 446
DB2 Development Center 447
Summary 447
Additional Resources 448

CHAPTER 14   **Accessing Distributed Data**   **449**

Distributed Data   450
Coding Methods for Distributed Data   455
Programming Considerations   462
Remote Query Performance   466
Summary   467
Additional Resources   468

CHAPTER 15   **Object-Relational Functionality**   **469**

Triggers   469
Object-Relational Extensions   482
Large Objects   496
Summary   506
Additional Resources   506

CHAPTER 16   **Locking and Concurrency**   **507**

Locking Data   508
Avoiding Locks   519
Claims and Drains   520
Locking Issues and Problems   522
Designing for Concurrency   525
Summary   528
Additional Resources   528

CHAPTER 17   **SQL Optimization and Performance**   **529**

Access Paths and Optimization   529
Designing Indexes and SQL for Performance   553
Summary   560
Additional Resources   560

CHAPTER 18   **DB2 Monitoring and Tuning**   **561**

Overview of Performance and Tuning   562
Database Monitoring   565
Using Traces to Solve Problems in DB2   566
Memory Tuning   586

Summary   598
Additional Resources   598

APPENDIX A **DDL for the DB2CERT Database**   **599**

APPENDIX B **IBM Certified Database Administrator for DB2 UDB Version 8 for z/OS**   **605**

DB2 UDB V8 Family Fundamentals: 700 Exam   606
DB2 UDB V8 for z/OS Database Administration: 702 Exam   607

APPENDIX C **702 Sample Exam**   **611**

Questions   611
Answers and Chapter References   623

Bibliography   **627**

Index   **629**

FOREWORD

DB2 Universal Database for z/OS has changed a lot over the past few years, with significant growth in the applications and in the size of the data. Some of the growth reflects the increasing volume and complexity of applications. More of the growth has come from new applications, the Web, and vendors. The use of DB2 has changed as well. The initial query, or decision-support, applications began relatively small and simple, but have grown from megabytes to gigabytes to terabytes and continue to grow in size and complexity. There is not much terror in a terabyte any more. Business-intelligence applications have added many options for data mining, online analytical processing, and complex analytics.

We have partnered with many application vendors that have grown rapidly, especially SAP, PeopleSoft, and Siebel. These applications are extremely demanding for a database management system, and they also require a close partnership to provide the best in scalability and availability. We work across the middleware stack of IBM software brands from DB2, Tivoli, WebSphere, Rational, and Lotus. In the past few years, major acquisitions of Informix, Rational, and Candle have enriched our options. We also work with a much larger group of vendors for business intelligence, application development, and database management tools.

Traditional online transaction processing has changed dramatically. Batch work has increased in volume and in the need to be run concurrently. The batch and utility windows have been closing, so that batch has become a sequence of transactions in many situations, and the utilities must run online with other work. The applications have increased in complexity.

In some ways, e-business is very simple. Customers want the best of everything, and they want it now. If yours is not the best or if your site is slow or down, the competition is only a mouse click away. The demands on e-business applications are similar. They must be fast, flexible, scalable, and easy to use. Data management for Web transactions has evolved from simple transactions, accessing a few files in one database management system, to much more complicated, federated access. One Web click can drive a dozen transactions across several machines in different time zones to improve the end user experience.

The Web has also changed the rules for scalability and for availability. As long as employees were providing access, the pattern of use was relatively predictable. Twelve or 18 hours a day were adequate, and the usage peak might be double the average load. The peak load can be a factor of ten and is much less predictable, with billions of potential users in every time zone. Automated search engines, Web devices, and Web appliances can provide trillions of requesters who want your information. Data is retained longer and has more uses. Disk storage continues to grow at an astonishing compound rate of 90 percent per year. At that rate, the current 1-terabyte database will become 24 terabytes in five years.

Improving the business process is important for being competitive. We need to provide fast response to the Web users, but we also need to use the data to find ways to improve our business. Collecting, organizing, and understanding information about how to improve are crucial for a competitive business. I view the process as a cycle, with the e-transaction processing providing information to the business intelligence, and the business intelligence providing process improvements back to the e-transaction processing. Thus, the improvements continue in a cycle. SAP, PeopleSoft, and Siebel have all added business intelligence to their applications to complete the cycle.

DB2 began with a design to handle online transaction processing, batch, and query work. DB2 has grown with the demands for large volumes, higher performance, improved availability, and better concurrency. Over the past decades, that design has been expanded to handle more diverse work even as the volumes and work loads grew. We have added many improvements for optimization and parallel processing. We have found ways to make dynamic SQL more static and static SQL more dynamic. We have new options to index the information. So that's all we need to do in DB2: provide the best of everything; deliver fast; make the information very usable; make the application fun to use; be able to scale, provide concurrent access, and respond immediately; be available 24 hours a day, 365.25 days a year, 100 percent of the time, without increasing costs; and use the information from the click stream to improve the business.

We are not there yet, but DB2 UDB for z/OS version 8 provides a giant step in the right direction. For continuous availability, the options have improved, with more online utilities, improved techniques for backup and recovery, and online schema evolution. The range of options for scalability and performance has improved, allowing much larger volumes of data and logs, using more memory more effectively, and reducing times dramatically with the optimization improvements, materialized query tables, and multirow operations. Programmer productivity has improved with many additions to SQL. It is much easier to port an application from UNIX or Windows with all the improvements. Ease of safe use has improved with a range of security enhancements.

Building a high-performance, high-availability application and database requires a lot of skill, teamwork, knowledge, and experience. Although they have shown that they can build large, high-volume applications, our customers have also learned some hard lessons. It's much easier to learn in a class or from a book than when angry customers and your boss are waiting. Using design and tuning lessons for another product or another version can be part of the problem, not the solution. Susan Lawson is experienced with large, complex DB2 data sharing applications that need both high performance and high availability. She has worked with very large tables and demanding applications. As you read this book, you will see that her experience and judgment show.

Most of the complex and interesting questions do not have a simple answer. The simple answer to the complex problem is generally wrong. Experts know the right answer: It depends.

Perhaps the management would like a simple, certain answer. Sometimes, the pressure is so great that we oversimplify and give a simple answer, even though it's not correct. But although "It depends" is completely correct, that response is also completely useless. We must go on to explain the problem and the issues: State what the response depends on and the range of possibilities. You will find that Susan understands and explains what it depends on.

—Roger Miller
DB2 UDB for z/OS Strategist

PREFACE

The purpose of this book is to serve as a self-study guide for the certification test required to become an IBM Certified Database Administrator (DBA) for DB2 Universal Database (UDB) version 8. In order to become certified, you must pass two exams:

1. 700—IBM DB2 UDB Version 8 Family Fundamentals
2. 702—IBM DB2 UDB Version 8 for z/OS Database Administration

In order to become an IBM Certified Database Administrator, you need to be familiar with the fundamentals of all DB2 platforms. This book covers DB2 UDB for z/OS, especially the topics on the 702 exam. If you are planning to become certified or would like an additional reference for information about DB2 for z/OS version 8, this book is for you. If you are interested in becoming an IBM Certified Professional, you will want to review the sample questions in Appendix C. For details on the other platforms, such as UNIX and Linux, and details needed for the 700 exam, refer to the other certification guide: *DB2 Universal Database Version 8 for Linux, UNIX and Windows Database Administration Certification Guide, fifth edition*, by George Baklarz and Bill Wong (Prentice Hall PTR, 2003).

The book is divided into five implicit sections.

1. Chapters 1–3 discuss the family of DB2 products, the DB2 z/OS environment, and access controls.
2. Chapters 4–6 cover the Structured Query Language (SQL), and its use, such as database objects creation, manipulation, and retrieval, as well as all DB2 database objects.

3. Chapters 7–9 describe common administration tasks and recovery issues. Chapter 9 also covers the architecture and implementation of data sharing in a parallel sysplex environment.

4. Chapters 10–12 provide an introduction to application development for DBAs and some of the additional considerations for application development.

5. Chapters 13–18 cover such topics as locking; advanced functions, such as stored procedures; and other object-relational extensions. Performance and optimization are covered in detail in Chapters 17 and 18.

This book can be used as a self-study guide to help you prepare for the DB2 Universal Database V8 for z/OS DBA certification exam or simply as a guide to DB2 Universal Database V8 for z/OS. For information about the DB2 UDB family or other DB2 platforms, refer to the other certification books. For detailed information about the exams, refer to Appendix C.

ACKNOWLEDGMENTS

Acknowledgments go to Dan Luksetich and John Maenpaa of YL&A, who provide their expertise and knowledge to this book and to our daily work. Also, special thanks to Roger Miller and Willie Favero of IBM for their reviews of the book and to Susan Visser and Melissa Montoya of IBM for their help and support. Finally, a special thank you to Kathy Komer for her help and insight with many parts of the book.

DB2 Family and DB2 for z/OS Environment

CHAPTER 1

Product Overview

- DB2 Universal Database
- DB2 middleware, connectivity, and information integration
- DB2 application development
- DB2 administration
- DB2 data management tools

This chapter introduces you to the DB2 Universal Database (DB2 UDB) family of products for z/Series, UNIX, and Intel platforms. DB2 has the ability to store all types of electronic information: traditional relational data, as well as structured, semistructured, and unstructured information; documents and text in many languages; graphics and images; audio and video; information specific to operations, such as engineering drawings, maps, insurance claims forms, numerical control streams; and any type of electronic information. This chapter provides you with information about the various DB2 and related information-management products from IBM. A description of each DB2 product is provided to illustrate some of its features and functions. Products are discussed based on features for version 8 levels of function.

The DB2 family of database products providing information management is an important part of IBM's e-business software portfolio. The e-business Application Framework provides an open blueprint on how to build e-business applications. Popular IBM e-business tools include WebSphere Studio for developing Java programs or components, Rational Suite and XDE for system analysis and design, and Tivoli software for distributed systems management. As for application server software, IBM offers several types of servers, depending on the business requirement, from message queuing with WebSphere MQ to Java-based transaction processing with WebSphere Application Server. Several other products use the WebSphere Application Server infrastructure: WebSphere MQ, WebSphere Host Access Transformation Services (HATS), WebSphere Portal, and WebSphere Business Integration Server Foundation. The most popular IBM software servers are its database servers: specifically, the DB2 family.

The DB2 family executes on pervasive devices and Intel, Linux, UNIX, midrange, and mainframe servers. Supported operating environments include Windows 2000/2003/NT/XP, Linux, AIX, Hewlett-Packard's HP-UX, Sun Microsystems' Solaris, OS/400, VSE/VM, OS/390, and z/OS. The DB2 code base is optimized for each platform to ensure maximum performance. The SQL API is common to all platforms, which allows applications written on one platform to access data on any platform. Internally, DB2 on iSeries, VSE/VM, and z/OS differs from DB2 on the UNIX and Intel platforms, but it is the common SQL API that enables applications to work together. The DB2 code base on Intel and UNIX platforms is the same. DB2 provides seamless database connectivity, using the most popular network communications protocols.

The DB2 family of database products is part of the IBM DB2 software brand. With respect to leveraging IBM information assets, this group of products has expanded to include Informix, U2, Cloudscape, and IMS database products, as well as a variety of tools and new products in the areas of business intelligence, information integration, and content management. With IBM's recent acquisition of Candle, this group of products could expand in the future.

DB2 AND THE ON-DEMAND BUSINESS

As a core component of IBM's e-business cycle, DB2 is a catalyst for delivering applications that directly impact a company's operations. The three phases of the e-business cycle are transform, build, and run. Transform is the process that takes a business to an e-business; common applications in this area include electronic commerce, enterprise resource planning (ERP), customer relationship management (CRM), and supply chain management (SCM). DB2 as the database is part of the transform phase. Build is the process of exploiting the integrated Java and multimedia features of DB2. Run is the part of the e-business cycle that ensures performance and scalability; this is especially important with companies using the Internet, new Internet-based companies, and the challenges faced by these companies.

Today's companies face four main business challenges: continuous change, rigorous competition, financial pressures, and unpredictable threats. These challenges cause demands to go beyond e-business and create the need for an on-demand operating environment. An on-demand operating environment requires a set of integration and infrastructure-management capabilities that businesses, customers, and partners can use, in a modular and incremental manner, to enable the transformation to e-business on demand. Integration includes business modeling, process transformation, application and information integration, access, collaboration, and business process management. Implementation of these capabilities allows companies to further integrate their people, processes, and information. Infrastructure management includes such areas as availability, security, optimization, business service management, and resource virtualization. Implementation of these functions allows companies to create greater optimization and simplification of their infrastructures.

Focusing on the database, we see business challenges manifest through unpredictable workloads with less problem tolerance, business partners of all types with evolving language standards, increased real-time decision making, continuous growth in size and form of data, and skyrocketing systems complexity. Successful management of the integration and infrastructure is critical. Successful e-business and success in the on-demand world of today will, to a significant degree, be determined by the level of success in meeting the information challenges at the database level.

DB2 UNIVERSAL DATABASE

The DB2 UDB family consists of many platforms that can coexist in a distributed environment.

- **DB2 UDB for z/OS.** This relational database management system, the largest of the DB2 family, often serves as an enterprise server handling many e-business, business intelligence, and mission-critical systems. This offering is used most often to support the very largest databases. The zSeries is IBM's largest hardware platform.
- **DB2 UDB for Linux, UNIX, and Windows.** This full-function database offering is scalable from single processors to symmetric multiprocessors and to massively parallel clusters. The *Enterprise Server Edition* is often used to build e-business applications and to support large departmental applications. This offering has many connectivity options and can share data with third-party databases and DB2 on heterogeneous platforms. It is used most often to support very large databases. Popular applications include supporting large data warehouses and Internet applications. DB2 UDB *Enterprise Server Edition* Database Partitioning Feature (DPF) can exploit clusters or massively parallel hardware architectures. The *Workgroup Server Edition and Workgroup Server Unlimited Edition* is often used for small business and departmental computing or for applications that do not need access to remote databases on the OS/400, VSE/VM, or z/OS platforms. The *Personal Edition*, a full-function database offering, is for standalone use and will not accept remote database requests. Personal Edition is available on Windows and Linux. *Personal Developer's Edition* is a full-function database for standalone use, primarily by application developers. Finally, *Express Edition*, a full-function database offering, is specifically for the support of small to medium-size businesses, with the database running on one or two processors.
- **DB2 Everyplace.** This mobile computing offering can be embedded into devices and appliances and used as a local independent database, or it can give mobile workers access to DB2 data sources in the enterprise through handheld devices when a connection is available. The database runs on a variety of mobile and embedded platforms, including Palm OS, Microsoft Windows CE/Pocket PC, Symbian, embedded Linux, QNX Neutrino, Microsoft Win32, and Linux.

DB2 UDB for z/OS

The DB2 for z/OS relational database management system is the foundation of many e-business, business intelligence, CRM, ERP applications, and mission-critical systems and is the primary focus of this certification guide. DB2 for z/OS is the largest member of the DB2 family, often serving as an enterprise server handling many of the largest applications in the world. The operating environment provided by z/OS is IBM's largest and most powerful, providing the most scalable and available platform.

DB2 for z/OS delivers large data capacity, high transaction performance, and extensive connectivity. DB2 supports transactions arising from Web servers, CICS (Customer Information Control System), IMS (Information Management System) transaction management, MVS (Multiple Virtual System) batch jobs, and via distributed connections from remote clients on numerous platforms.

Significant enhancements in SQL (Structured Query Language) and optimization permit DB2 UDB for z/OS to remain a premiere choice for application development. Leading Java and XML technologies provide the infrastructure for Web-based applications. The following are examples of recent enhancements.

- Breaking the limits in virtually all dimensions of database management, virtual-storage addressing has expanded from 31-bit to full 64-bit addressing. Table name sizes have expanded from 18 to 128 characters; VIEW and ALIAS names, from 18 to 128 characters; column name sizes, from 18 to 30 characters; SQL statement length, from 32KB to 2MB; and tables in a join, from 15 to 225.
- Enhanced SQL for DB2 UDB for z/OS includes support for common table expressions, Multirow INSERT and FETCH, GET DIAGNOSTICS, dynamic scrollable cursors, CURRENT PACKAGE PATH, materialized query tables, XML (Extensible Markup Language) publishing and Unicode SQL, and multiple CCSIDs in a single SQL statement.
- Unicode enhancements deliver globalization capability and also enhance Java applications, including catalog data conversion to Unicode format and Unicode within SQL statements and literals.
- Enhancements for continuous availability include online schema evolution, system-level point in time recovery, and partitioning.
- Version 8 delivers the new Universal Java Drivers, providing a consistent Java interface across the DB2 family. The Java drivers support the JDBC/SQLJ 3.0 standard, savepoints, and connection-pooling enhancements.

DB2 UDB for Linux, UNIX, and Windows

The DB2 database is used for the development and deployment of critical e-business, business intelligence, content management, enterprise resource planning, and customer relationship

management. To improve manageability, DB2 greatly reduces the complexity of data management by eliminating, simplifying, and automating many tasks traditionally associated with maintaining a database. Some of these advances are the first implementation of the Self-Managing
and Resource Tuning (SMART) project and the first steps toward making full autonomic computing a reality for database implementations.

DB2 provides a strong foundation of information-integration technologies, including federation,
replication, Web services, and XML. With DB2's built-in capabilities, you can query, update,
and replicate data across DB2 and Informix Dynamic Server data sources. DB2 provides rich
type support for spatial data, text data, and flat files via DB2 Spatial Extender, DB2 Net Search
Extender, and DB2 Data Links Manager, respectively.

The connection concentrator reduces memory consumption on the database server by allowing
transactions from remote clients to be concentrated, or multiplexed, across a small number of
persistent database connections. DB2 also has improved performance of databases with multiple
partitions, multidimensional data clustering, faster page cleaners, user-maintained MQTs (materialized query tables) , support for 64-bit Windows and 64-bit Linux, and new, streamlined application drivers (ODBC, OLE DB, JDBC, and SQLJ) and new client architecture.

DB2 Enterprise Server Edition

DB2 Enterprise Server Edition (DB2 ESE) is fully Web enabled, scalable from single processors
to symmetric multiprocessors and to massively parallel clusters, and supports unstructured data,
such as image, audio, video, text, spatial, and XML with its object-relational capabilities. Applications for DB2 Enterprise Server Edition can scale upward and execute on massively parallel
clusters or can scale downward with applications executing on single-user database systems.
The ESE scalability, reliability, and availability provide the ideal foundation for building data
warehouses, transaction processing, or Web-based solutions, as well as a back end for packaged
solutions, such as ERP, CRM, or SCM. Additionally, ESE offers connectivity and integration for
other enterprise DB2 and Informix data sources. DB2 ESE is available on Windows NT/2000/
2003/XP (test/development only), Linux, and UNIX (AIX, Solaris, and HP-UX). DB2 ESE is
ideal for large or midsized servers and includes DB2 Connect, which allows for connections to
iSeries- or zSeries-based DB2 databases.

DB2 ESE can be installed on any number of processors on a single symmetric multiprocessing
(SMP) box or on multiple boxes. DB2 ESE also can have data partitioned within a single server,
across multiple data servers, or within a large SMP machine with the DPF (database partitioning
feature).

DB2 Workgroup Server Edition

DB2 Workgroup Server Edition (DB2 WSE) is designed for use in a LAN (local area network)
environment, providing support for both remote and local clients. DB2 WSE includes DB2

Extenders, which provide the ability to manipulate data outside of conventional rows and columns; DB2 WSE is available on the Windows (NT/2000/2003/XP), AIX, Solaris, HP-UX, and Linux platforms. DB2 Workgroup Edition can also be installed on symmetric multiprocessing (SMP) machines with up to four processors. DB2 WSE is the database server designed for deployment in a departmental or small-business environment that involves a small number of internal users. The WSE licensing model provides an attractive price point for smaller installations while still providing a full-function database server.

Another option is the DB2 Workgroup Server Unlimited Edition (WSUE), which offers a simplified per-processor licensing model for deployment in a departmental or small-business environment that has Internet users or whose number of users makes per-processor licensing more attractive than the WSE licensing model.

DB2 Personal Edition and Personal Developer's Edition
DB2 Personal Edition (PE) is a full-function database that enables a single user to create databases on the workstation on which it is installed. DB2 PE can be used as a remote client to a DB2 server, as it also contains the DB2 client components. The DB2 PE product is often used by end users requiring access to local and remote DB2 databases or by developers' prototyping applications that will be accessing other DB2 databases.

DB2 PE includes graphical tools, as do all of the other products, via the DB2 Administration Client component, which enable a user to administer, tune for performance, access remote DB2 servers, process SQL queries, and manage other servers from a single workstation. Personal Edition is available on Windows (98/NT/2000/XP) and Linux.

DB2 Personal Developer's Edition provides an extensive toolkit for building DB2 applications. These tools focus on maximizing programmer productivity by providing support for major application frameworks popular with both Java and Microsoft application programmers. Enhancements include SQL enhancements, enhanced drivers for applications written to ADO, ODBC, OLE DB, DB2 CLI, JDBC, and SQLJ programming interfaces; enhanced support for XML, industry-leading Web Services support; the new Development Center; new plug-ins for WebSphere Studio integrated development environment; and new add-ins for Microsoft Visual-Studio development products (VisualBasic, Visual C++, and InterDev).

DB2 UDB Express Edition
DB2 Universal Database Express Edition is the lowest-priced full-function relational database specifically designed to meet the needs of small and medium-size businesses. DB2 UDB Express Edition is available on Windows and Linux (32-bit Intel) platforms with one or two CPUs. Its self-tuning, self-managing, and self-configuring capabilities increase reliability while

reducing complexity and required skills. The full-function DB2 Universal Database Express Edition allows seamless upgrades to other scalable DB2 UDB Editions as business needs grow. DB2 Express Edition is also configurable by business partners for transparent installation within their application

DB2 Everyplace

DB2 Everyplace is a tiny database of about 200K that can be embedded into devices and appliances or be used as a local independent database of the mobile device or query information on remote servers when a connection is available. DB2 Everyplace is also a complete development environment that includes the tools needed to build, deploy, and support applications. DB2 Everyplace includes security features, such as table encryption, secure data synchronization, and advanced indexing techniques for performance. This database can comfortably run, with multi-threaded support, on a wide variety of handheld devices, with support for Palm OS, Microsoft Windows CE/Pocket PC, any Microsoft Windows 32-bit operating system, Symbian, QNX Neutrino, Java 2 Platform Micro Edition (J2ME) devices, and embedded Linux distributions, such as BlueCat Linux.

DB2 Everyplace integrates with WebSphere Everyplace Access and WebSphere Everyplace Server. The DB2 Everyplace Sync Server provides the bidirectional or unidirectional synchronization of data and applications between DB2 Everyplace client devices and enterprise data sources.

DB2 MIDDLEWARE AND CONNECTIVITY

DB2 is a very open database and provides a variety of options for connecting to DB2 and non-DB2 databases.

- **DB2 client code** is required on workstations for remote users to access a DB2 database or on servers for remote programs or applications to access a DB2 database.
- **DB2 Connect** provides support for applications executing on UNIX and Intel platforms to transparently access DB2 databases on the OS/400, VSE/VM, z/OS, and Linux on zSeries environments. Note that DB2 Connect is not required to access DB2 databases on UNIX or Intel platforms.
- **DB2 Information Integrator** integrates data and content sources across the enterprise, based on the SQL programming model product, which allows DB2 clients to access, join, and update tables from heterogeneous databases, such as Sybase, Informix, and Microsoft SQL Server.
- **DB2 Information Integrator for Content (EIP)** integrates data and content sources across and beyond the enterprise, based on the content programming model.

DB2 Universal Database Clients

The DB2 product enables clients that are used by applications or workstations to communicate with DB2 servers. There are three types of DB2 clients.

1. **DB2 runtime client** enables workstations running a variety of platforms to access DB2 databases. It includes basic connectivity only—nothing more and nothing less. If you need to establish connectivity to a remote DB2 server or DB2 Connect Gateway, which helps you access DB2 on a mainframe or host system, such as DB2 UDB for z/OS, the runtime client provides this.

2. **DB2 administration client** provides the ability for workstations from a variety of platforms to access and administer DB2 databases through the Command Center, Control Center, or Configuration Assistant. Additional tools are included for monitoring and general administration: the Replication Center. A DB2 administration client has all the features of the DB2 runtime client and also includes all the DB2 administration tools, documentation, and support for thin clients.

3. **DB2 application development client** provides the tools and environment you need to develop applications that access DB2 servers. You can build and run DB2 applications with a DB2 application development client. Of course, because this is a DB2 client, it also gives users the power of connectivity and includes the functions of the preceding two clients.

The DB2 clients are supported on a variety of platforms, including Windows, AIX, HP-UX, Linux, and Solaris.

DB2 Connect

DB2 Connect provides connectivity to IBM mainframe databases for e-business and other applications running under various UNIX and non-UNIX operating systems. DB2 Connect has several connection solutions. DB2 Connect Personal Edition provides direct connectivity to zSeries or iSeries databases; DB2 Connect Enterprise Edition provides indirect connectivity that allows clients to access host databases through the DB2 Connect server. DB2 Connect Unlimited Edition is an additional solution that makes product selection and licensing easier.

DB2 Connect forwards SQL statements submitted by application programs to DB2 for z/OS, DB2 for VSE and VM, or DB2 for iSeries database servers. DB2 Connect can forward almost any valid SQL statement. DB2 Connect fully supports the common IBM SQL, as well as the DB2 Universal Database for z/OS, DB2 for VSE and VM, and DB2 for iSeries implementations of SQL.

DB2 Connect implements the Distributed Relational Database Architecture (DRDA) to reduce the cost and complexity of accessing data stored in DB2 for iSeries, DB2 UDB for z/OS, DB2 for VSE and VM, and other DRDA-compliant database servers. By fully exploiting DRDA, DB2 Connect offers a well-performing, low-cost solution with the system-management characteristics that customers require. In the DB2 Connect environment, the DB2 Connect workstation can function only as an application requester on behalf of application programs.

DB2 Connect allows clients to access data stored on data servers that implement the DRDA. The target database server for a DB2 Connect installation is known as a DRDA application server. The most commonly accessed DRDA application server is DB2 for z/OS. The database application must request the data from a DRDA application server through a DRDA application requester. DB2 Connect provides the DRDA application requestor functionality. The DRDA application server accessed using DB2 Connect could be any DB2 server on z/OS, VM and VSE, or iSeries.

A distributed request is a distributed database function that allows applications and users to submit SQL statements that reference two or more DBMSs or databases in a single statement, such as a join between tables in two DB2 for z/OS subsystems. DB2 Connect provides support for distributed requests across databases and DBMSs. You can, for example, perform a UNION operation between a DB2 table and an Oracle view. Supported DBMSs include DB2 UDB for Linux, UNIX, and Windows; DB2 for z/OS and DB2 for iSeries; and Oracle. Distributed request provides location transparency for database objects. Distributed request also provides compensation for DBMSs that do not support all the DB2 SQL dialect or certain optimization capabilities. Operations that cannot be performed under such a DBMS such as recursive SQL are run under DB2 Connect.

Multisite update, also known as distributed unit of work (DUOW) and two-phase commit, is a function that enables your applications to update data in multiple remote database servers and with guaranteed integrity. A distributed transaction can update any mix of supported database servers. For example, your application can update several tables in DB2 Universal Database on Windows, a DB2 for z/OS database, and a DB2 for iSeries database, all within a single transaction. DB2 products, including DB2 Connect, provide comprehensive support for multisite updates. This support is available for applications developed using regular SQL, as well as applications that use transaction monitor (TP monitor) products that implement the X/Open XA interface specification.

DB2 Information Integrator

DB2 Information Integrator provides integrated, real-time access to structured and unstructured information as if it were a single database, regardless of where it resides. The federated server lets users create an abstract relational view across diverse data, use existing reporting and development tools, and use cost optimizations for SQL. The replication server lets users manage data movement strategies, including distribution and consolidation models, and monitor synchronization processes.

Supported data sources include DB2 UDB, Informix, MS SQL Server, Oracle, Sybase, Teradata, ODBC, and others. Supported content sources include WebSphere MQ Message Queues, Lotus Notes, XML, Web Services, MS Excel Spreadsheets, and others. DB2 Information Integrator acts as middleware for access to heterogeneous data sources. With a single SQL statement, an application can transparently access, join, and update data located across multiple data sources. The access can be done without needing to know the location of the data or the specifics of the SQL dialects for the data source.

DB2 Information Integrator for Content (EIP)

DB2 Information Integrator for Content, formerly named Enterprise Information Portal, is an information-integration infrastructure that gives applications access to information sources from inside and outside the enterprise. From a Web browser or a portal, knowledge workers can concurrently access data and content from multiple sources, expanding the reach of their analysis and improving their productivity. DB2 Information Integrator for Content provides a federated search, direct connectors, and simultaneous access across the multiple repositories, workflow integration and Web crawling, and information mining.

Users can personalize data queries and search extensively for very specific needs across traditional and multimedia data sources. Developers can more rapidly develop and deploy portal applications with the information-integration application development toolkit.

DB2 APPLICATION DEVELOPMENT

DB2 offers a rich application development environment that allows developers to build databases supporting requirements for e-business and business intelligence applications. Many of these tools are integrated with the database; the major tools, especially those that can be used with DB2 for z/OS, are reviewed next.

- **DB2 Application Development Client** is used for creating, testing, and debugging stored procedures on local and remote DB2 servers.
- **DB2 Extenders** enable the SQL API to access unstructured data types, including text, image, audio, video, and XML.
- **DB2 Cube Views** provide OLAP support in DB2 UDB, including features and functions that improve the relational database's ability for managing and deploying multidimensional data across the enterprise.
- **DB2 OLAP Server** provides the ability to build online analytical processing (OLAP) cubes using DB2 as the relational data store; a higher-end version of the DB2 OLAP Server is available to handle larger numbers of users.

- **DB2 Data Warehouse Edition** provides the ability to build data marts/warehouses by automating the processes involved in managing, refreshing, moving, and transforming data, including the ability to define the star schema model.
- **QMF** provides an integrated, powerful, and reliable query and reporting tool set for DB2 data. An optional QMF for Windows is available.

DB2 Application Development Client

The Application Development Client provides many tools for development, including business intelligence (Data Warehouse Center and Information Catalog Center), command line tools (Command Center, Command Line Processor, Command Window), Development Center, Control Center, Replication Center, Task Center, Information Center, and monitoring tools (Health Center, Memory Visualizer, Event Analyzer). DB2 Development Center is the successor to the DB2 version 7 Stored Procedure Builder. In a nutshell, the DB2 Development Center is a rapid iterative development environment for building stored procedures (SPs), user-defined functions (UDFs), structured data types, and much more. This tool was rewritten to allow for concurrent task execution, flexible docking, enhanced scalability, and higher productivity. This integrated development environment (IDE) can stand on its own or be embedded into WebSphere Studio Application Developer or any of the Microsoft Visual Studio development products. As a result, developers can build DB2 business logic *without* leaving their favorite IDE.

Some of the Development Center features are:

- Support for the entire family of DB2 server operating systems, including z/OS, OS/400, UNIX, and Windows
- Support for developing SQL and Java stored procedures, SQL scalar and table user-defined functions; MQSeries, OLE DB, and XML table functions; and structured data types for Enterprise JavaBeans (EJB) methods and properties
- Support for viewing live database tables, views, triggers, SPs, and UDFs, as well as the ability to test SPs and UDFs written in any language
- Enhanced round-trip debugging of SQL SPs with variable-value change support, using an integrated SQL debugger

The Development Center can work as a Microsoft Visual Studio plug-in or with Microsoft Visual Basic or IBM WebSphere Studio Application Developer or it can stand alone. The DB2 Development Center supports the entire DB2 family from a single development environment and has facilities for debugging and deploying stored procedures.

DB2 Extenders

The DB2 Extenders can take your database applications beyond traditional numeric and character data to images, XML, videos, voice, spatial objects, complex documents, and more. You can use the extenders to bring all these types of data into a database and work with them, using SQL.

- **XML Extender** provides new data types that let you store XML documents in DB2 databases and adds functions that help you work with these XML documents while in a database. You can store entire XML documents in DB2 or store them as external files managed by the database. This method is known is *XML Columns.* You can also decompose an XML document into relational tables and then recompose that information to XML on the way out of the database. Thus, your DB2 database can strip the XML out of a document and simply take the data, or the DB2 database can take data and create an XML document from it. This method is known as *XML columns.* In DB2 version 7, the XML Extender was a free, separately installable product. In DB2 version 8, it is built into the DB2 installation as a component.
- **DB2 Net Search Extender** helps businesses that need fast performance when searching for information in a database. This extender is likely to be used in Internet applications, which need excellent search performance on large indexes and scalability of concurrent queries. In DB2 version 8, the Text Information Extender has merged with the Net Search Extender.
- **DB2 Spatial Extender** allows you to store, manage, and analyze spatial data, such as the location of geographic features, in DB2, along with traditional data for text and numbers. The DB2 Spatial Extender extends the function of DB2 with a set of advanced spatial data types that represent geometries, such as points, lines, and polygons; it also includes many functions and features that interoperate with those new data types.
- **Text, Audio, Image, and Video Extenders** allow you to extend the relational database to use nontraditional forms of data, such as text, songs, pictures, and movies. With these extenders, you can work with data via SQL

DB2 Cube Views

DB2 Cube Views, the latest generation of OLAP support in DB2 UDB, includes features and functions that improve the relational database's ability for managing and deploying multidimensional data across the enterprise. With DB2 Cube Views, the database becomes multidimensionally aware by including metadata support for dimensions, hierarchies, attributes, and analytical functions; analyzing the dimensional model and recommending aggregates—MQTs, also known as summary tables—that improve OLAP performance; adding OLAP metadata to the DB2 catalogs; providing an OLAP foundation that will speed deployment and improve performance; and simplifying the exploitation of advanced DB2 technologies, such as summary table management and analytical functions. DB2 Cube Views improves DB2 query performance by enabling the

DB2 optimizer to rewrite incoming queries to take advantage of the MQTs that DB2 Cube Views recommends, loading cubes, performing drill-through queries and ad hoc analysis directly to the relational tables in DB2, and enhancing all queries that use aggregate data.

DB2 OLAP Server

DB2 OLAP Server can be used for developing analytic applications for fast, intuitive, multidimensional analysis, allowing users to ask questions in an intuitive business language. The server can process multidimensional requests that calculate, consolidate, and retrieve information from a multidimensional database, a relational database, or both. Create your own applications or have turnkey solutions built for you with the many applications, tools, and solutions from providers that support DB2 OLAP Server. Perform analysis such as "Display the profit of my highest- and lowest-performing products last quarter in my domestic sales regions."

DB2 OLAP includes both features of the two main types of OLAP: MOLAP (multidimensional OLAP) and ROLAP (relational OLAP). MOLAP is known for its performance and ability to deliver answers to users very quickly. ROLAP is known for its scalability and ability to give users access to very detailed drill-down data when required. Additionally, DB2 OLAP integrates the popular Hyperion Essbase OLAP products with the e-business-ready IBM DB2 UDB relational database and combines powerful multidimensional analysis with a comprehensive set of built-in financial, mathematical, and statistical functions.

DB2 Warehouse Edition

DB2 Warehouse Edition (DWE) has two versions: Enterprise and Standard. DB2 Data Warehouse Enterprise Edition includes and extends the powerful DB2 Enterprise Server Edition (ESE) and is designed for enterprise-wide data warehouses with unlimited scalability. The DB2 Data Warehouse Standard Edition includes and extends DB2 Workgroup Edition and is limited to four CPUs (DB2 UDB Workgroup Edition licensing).

DB2 has been steadily progressing toward supporting business intelligence functions inside the database. The latest release of DB2 DWE enables customers and partners to perform mining; online analytic processing; extract, transform, and load (ETL); and advanced analytics, with a single, unified engine operating on common data structures within a consolidated data warehouse. This release combines a carefully selected set of IBM products to provide the essential infrastructure needed to extend the enterprise data warehouse as a platform for business intelligence.

The analytics include SQL; advanced statistical functions, such as correlation, covariance, and standard deviation; a complete family of linear regression functions; and sliding-windows functions and smooth-moving average and equiheight histograms. Ad hoc capabilities include materialized query tables that cache prejoined aggregates for fast reuse by common queries, patented multidimensional clustering index and table structure that speeds OLAP queries, star join optimizer algorithms that enable faster star schema queries, and an aggregate-aware cost-based optimizer with adjustable optimization levels for query performance.

Query Management Facility (QMF)

QMF is a tightly integrated, powerful, and reliable query and reporting tool set for DB2 databases on distributed and host platforms. With QMF, you can execute queries, format reports, and build procedures to perform multiple activities. QMF stores the queries, forms, and procedures in its own database, so you can reuse them. QMF provides an environment that is easy for a novice to use but powerful enough for an application programmer.

In short, QMF also allows you to do the following:

- Easily build queries and reports via a quick-start interface
- Leverage a Java-based query capability to launch queries from your favorite Web browser
- Integrate query results with desktop tools, such as spreadsheets and personal databases
- Rapidly build data-access and update applications
- Fully exploit DB2 performance, SQL syntax, and advanced database performance techniques, such as static SQL

DB2 QMF has been enhanced with new data-visualization, solution-building, Web-enablement, and solution-sharing capabilities. This includes support for the DB2 Universal Database version 8 functionality, including IBM DB2 Cube Views, long names, Unicode, and enhancements to SQL. Also, visual data appliances, such as executive dashboards, offer visually rich interactive functionality and interfaces specific to virtually any type of information request.

DB2 ADMINISTRATION

Several DB2 tools are available to help with administration of the subsystem environment and database objects. Some of these tools are optional and Windows based. Following are some of the major tools, especially those that can be used with DB2 for z/OS.

- **DB2 Customization Center** provides a workstation-based graphical user interface (GUI) for the installation and migration of DB2.
- **DB2 Administration Client** provides a workstation-based tool for managing and administering databases.
- **Visual Explain** provides the user with a graphical tool to analyze the access paths that DB2 chooses for SQL queries or statements.
- **DB2 Estimator** provides a facility for estimating the performance of applications and SQL.

DB2 Customization Center

The z/OS Managed System Infrastructure for Setup (msys for Setup) is a framework that various z/OS products use to simplify their setup. The DB2 Customization Center uses this framework and simplifies the task of installing or migrating a DB2 subsystem in a z/OS environment. A workstation interface is used for the tasks. A set of wizards guides you through setting the parameters (DSNZPARMs) and provides defaults and recommendations wherever possible. The appropriate setup and configuration can then be submitted. The workstation interface can be used to view or update subsystem parameters and other information.

The DB2 Customization Center can be used to complete such tasks as

- Installing a new DB2 version 8 subsystem
- Cloning a DB2 version 8 subsystem
- Adding a new data sharing member to an existing version 8 data sharing group
- Migrating a subsystem from version 7 to version 8
- Turning off new-function mode or falling back to version 7
- Remigrating an existing subsystem or data sharing member to version 8 compatibility mode
- Modifying subsystem parameter values for an existing version 8 subsystem or data sharing member

DB2 Administration Client

This client enables workstations from a variety of platforms to access and administer DB2 databases through the Command Center, the Control Center, or the Configuration Assistant. The Control Center supports the entire DB2 family, including z/OS, and can be used as a single point of entry for controlling the entire DB2 family. You can use the Control Center to display database objects and their relationships to one another. The Control Center's GUI allows you to easily manage local and remote servers from a single workstation. You can also launch other tools, such as DB2 Warehouse Center, DB2 Visual Explain, Command Center, Development Center, Information Center, Configuration Assistant, and more.

Visual Explain

DB2 Visual Explain lets you graphically analyze the access paths that DB2 chooses for your SQL queries or statements. The graph of the access path is displayed on a Windows workstation, eliminating the need to manually interpret the plan table output. This tool offers suggestions for improving the performance of your SQL queries or statements. You can change an SQL statement and dynamically explain it to see whether the access path is improved by the change. You can also use this tool to browse through the current values of subsystem parameters.

Visual Explain issues DRDA queries through a DB2 client on the workstation to get needed information. DB2 Visual Explain helps database administrators and application developers to

- Graphically see the access path for a given SQL statement
- View statement cost in milliseconds and service units
- Tune SQL statements for better performance
- View the current values for subsystem parameters
- View catalog statistics for tables and indexes
- Generate custom reports

DB2 Estimator

DB2 Estimator is an easy-to-use, standalone tool for estimating the performance of DB2 z/OS and OS/390 applications. It can be run on PCs that support Microsoft Windows (98/NT/2000/XP). It supports simple table sizing up to a detailed performance analysis of an entire DB2 application. DB2 Estimator saves time and lowers costs by allowing you to investigate the impact of new or modified applications on your production system before you implement them. DB2 Estimator provides such information as

- Elapsed time for an SQL statement that fetches N rows
- Processor resources used during an N-way join
- Impact of adding and dropping an index from a table
- System support ability for an anticipated increase in workload
- Effects of doubling processor resources on transaction response time
- Storage required for a new table and its indexes
- Index support for predicates
- Effect on performance of doubling table size
- Ability of the application to complete within a batch window
- Execution time of utility jobs
- Effects of data compression
- Effects of data sharing
- Effects of triggers

DB2 Estimator lets you change your definitions easily to help you evaluate alternative designs. By comparing the cost and performance of these designs, you can determine which design provides the optimum cost/performance ratio before you invest valuable time and resources coding your application or creating a real database. DB2 Estimator helps you build more efficient databases by building a model of your system, based on your data knowledge, with reasonable access paths for your SQL statements. If DB2 information is available through DB2 Explain and/or DB2 Performance Monitor, you can tune the model by overriding the model assumptions.

You can also import table, index, and SQL statements from your DB2 database to DB2 Estimator and then modify them to suit your modeling requirements.

DATA MANAGEMENT TOOLS

IBM has made a commitment to delivering a quality set of data management tools designed to perform at the level today's systems require. In many cases, third-party tools that perform similar functions are available also.

The tools are divided into six categories: database administration, performance management, recovery management, replication management, application management, and database utilities. The following tools are available for use with DB2 UDB for z/OS.

- **DB2 Administration Tool** provides a comprehensive set of functions to efficiently and effectively manage DB2 environments.
- **DB2 Object Comparison Tool** maximizes system availability by keeping production and test catalogs in sync.
- **DB2 Performance Monitor** helps you get optimum performance from your database management system and provides useful support for resolving critical performance issues.
- **DB2 Buffer Pool Analyzer** helps database administrators manage buffer pools more efficiently by providing information about the buffer pools and the behavior of the objects in them.
- **DB2 Performance Expert** gives a comprehensive view that consolidates data, reports, analyzes, and recommends changes on DB2 performance-related information.
- **DB2 Query Monitor** provides the ability to monitor queries and to quickly pinpoint and resolve problems without going through large amounts of output.
- **DB2 SQL Performance Analyzer** gives you the ability to estimate the costs of database queries prior to execution.
- **DB2 Recovery Expert** significantly speeds up and simplifies the access to and recovery of databases throughout an enterprise.
- **DB2 Archive Log Accelerator** reduces overhead associated with database log management and managing increases in archive log growth.
- **DB2 Change Accumulation Tool** provides the ability to quickly restore database objects by setting the scope and specificity of image copy creation.
- **DB2 Log Analysis Tool** allows the monitoring of database changes and the ability to audit table activity and to produce specific reports of activity.
- **DB2 Object Restore** allows for the restoration of dropped objects and all related dependencies automatically.
- **DB2 DataPropagator** provides replication capabilities for DB2 databases and is integrated in DB2 on the UNIX and Intel platforms.

- **DB2 RepliData** provides the ability to operate multisite replica databases.
- **DB2 Information Integrator Classic Federation** provides Web and distributed applications with read/write connectivity to mainframe databases.
- **DB2 Bind Manager** helps reduce the time and cost of connecting new application programs to a database.
- **DB2 Data Archive Expert** enables the archiving of seldom-used data to a less costly storage medium without any programming.
- **DB2 Path Checker** identifies the potential effects of performing a bind on one or many programs.
- **DB2 Table Editor** is a multiplatform tool that provides a variety of ways for users to quickly and easily update, create, and delete data across multiple DB2 database platforms.
- **DB2 Test Database Generator** rapidly populates application and testing environments by creating test data from scratch or existing data sources.
- **DB2 Web Query Tool** lets end users access, create, share, and execute SQL queries through their browsers against multiple IBM DB2 databases.
- **IBM Data Encryption for IMS and DB2 Databases** enables the protection of sensitive and private data at the DB2 table level.
- **DB2 Utilities Suite V8** provides DB2 operational utilities and DB2 diagnostic and recovery utilities, such as COPY, LOAD, UNLOAD, REORG, RECOVER, RUNSTATS, REBUILD INDEX, MERGECOPY, CHECK DATA, CHECK INDEX, MODIFY, and others.
- **DB2 High Performance Unload** offers sequential reading and the capability to access your DB2 data at top speed.
- **DB2 Automation Tool** continuously and automatically coordinates the execution of DB2 tools, enabling you to realize the full potential of your DB2 system.

Several of the preceding tools are also available for distributed versions of DB2.

- **DB2 Recovery Expert** provides simplified, comprehensive, and automated recovery to minimize outage duration.
- **DB2 Performance Expert** integrates performance monitoring, reporting, buffer pool analysis, and a performance warehouse function into one tool. A *single* system overview is provided that monitors all subsystems and instances across many different platforms in a consistent way.
- **DB2 High Performance Unload** quickly and efficiently unloads and extracts data from DB2 for movement across enterprise systems.
- **DB2 Web Query Tool** connects all your users directly to multiple enterprise databases, securely and simultaneously, regardless of database size, hardware, operating system, or location.
- **DB2 Table Editor** quickly and easily accesses, updates, and deletes data across multiple DB2 database platforms.

SUMMARY

The DB2 family of products covers a wide range of platforms, allowing users to choose the best-performing platform for the job. DB2 is a very scalable product that can scale from the smallest platforms to the largest z/OS platform. IBM provides a comprehensive set of tools in many categories to support and use DB2. Many of these tools are included with the base product itself, and others are available for optional purchase.

ADDITIONAL RESOURCES

www.ibm.com/software/data/db2

www.ibm.com/software/data/db2imstools

2

DB2 Environment

- z/OS
- Address spaces
- Installation and migration
- System parameters
- Commands
- Utilities
- Catalog and directory
- Distributed data
- Subsystem pools

DB2 operates as a formal subsystem of z/OS. DB2 utilities run in the batch environment, and applications that access DB2 resources can run in the batch, TSO (Time Sharing Option), USS (UNIX System Services), IMS (Information Management System), or CICS (Customer Information Control System) environment. IBM provides attachment facilities to connect DB2 to each of these environments.

This chapter looks at the subsystem architecture that supports DB2 and the attachments available. This chapter also looks briefly at the installation process of the DB2 subsystem and the subsystem parameters known as DSNZPARMs, as well as how to execute the utilities and various commands.

DB2 also has the ability to access other DB2 subsystems and other relational databases. This chapter takes a look at the methods for doing this.

z/OS

The IBM zSeries family of enterprises servers use z/OS, the next generation of operating system replacing OS/390. The core of z/OS is the base control program MVS. Open-standard application server functions that support scalable, secure e-business applications are integrated with the MVS base.

The z/OS platform can provide scalable, secure processing for various types of workloads in a high-performance environment, such as stock trading. The applications can be batch, OLTP (Online Transaction Processing), or DSS (Decision Support Systems). The major strengths of this environment are availability, flexibility, manageability, reliability, scalability, and security.

The DB2 database management system operates as a formal subsystem of the z/OS operating system. DB2 processes can be executed in various address space regions within z/OS, such as IMS or CICS. Because it is required for DB2 version 8, z/OS provides a new architecture that supports a 64-bit operating system. Thus, the z/OS platform can support many diverse applications with increased availability, scalability, and security.

ADDRESS SPACES

The address spaces used in the operation of DB2 are

- System services address space (SSAS)
- Database services address space (DSAS)
- Internal resource lock manager (IRLM)
- Distributed Database Facility (DDF)
- Stored procedure address space (SPAS)
- Allied address spaces

Figure 2-1 shows the relationship among the address spaces DB2 uses.

The *system services address space,* also called the Data System Control Facility (DSCF) address space, is the DSN1MSTR address space. The following subcomponents execute in the SSAS:

- General command processor
- Subsystem support
- Agent services manager
- Storage manager

- Message generator
- Initialization procedures
- Instrumentation facilities
- System parameter manager
- Recovery manager
- Recovery log manager
- Group manager
- Distributed transaction manager

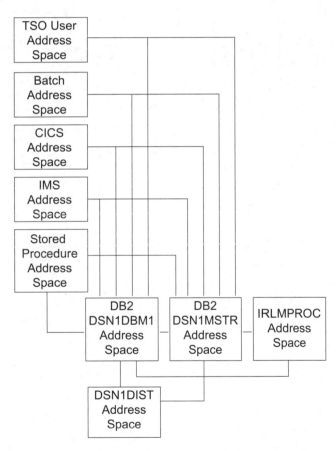

Figure 2-1   Relationship between DB2 users and DB2-related address spaces

This is critical, as it manages most of the activities in DB2. The *database services address space,* also called the Advanced Database Management Facility (ADMF) address space, is the DSNDBM1 address space. The following subcomponents execute in the DSAS:

- Service controller
- Data manager
- Large-object manager (LOBM)
- Data space manager
- Relational data system (RDS)
- Stored-procedures manager
- Utilities (work with associated code in an allied address space)
- Buffer manager

The DBM1 address space uses memory for several operations in DB2. The following output from a DB2 Performance Monitor report shows the DB2 objects that use memory in the DBM1 address space:

```
DBM1 STORAGE STATISTICS (MB)
------------------------------------
TOTAL GETMAINED STORAGE
  VIRTUAL BUFFER POOLS
  EDM POOL
  COMPRESSION DICTIONARY
  CASTOUT BUFFERS
TOTAL VARIABLE STORAGE
  TOTAL AGENT SYSTEM STORAGE
  TOTAL AGENT LOCAL STORAGE
  RDS OP POOL
  RID POOL
  PIPE MANAGER SUB POOL
  LOCAL DYNAMIC STMT CACHE CTL BLKS
LOCAL DYNAMIC STMT CACHE STMT POOL
BUFFER & DATA MANAGER TRACE TBL
VIRTUAL POOL CONTROL BLOCKS
TOTAL FIXED STORAGE
TOTAL GETMAINED STACK STORAGE
STORAGE CUSHION
TOTAL DBM1 STORAGE
TOTAL NUMBER OF ACTIVE USER THREADS
TOTAL STORAGE FOR ALL THREADS
NUMBER OF PREFETCH ENGINES
NUMBER OF DEFERRED WRITE ENGINES
NUMBER OF CASTOUT ENGINES
NUMBER OF GBP WRITE ENGINES
NUMBER OF P-LOCK/NOTIFY EXIT ENGINES
```

Each DB2 subsystem has its own internal resource lock manager. The IRLM controls access to the application data and is used by DB2 as the lock manager to ensure the integrity of the data.

The Distributed Data Facility allows client applications running in an environment that supports Distributed Relational Database Architecture (DRDA) to access DB2 data. The DDF also allows for one DB2 subsystem to access data on another DB2 subsystem. Other relational database servers can be accessed if they support DRDA. TCP/IP and SNA (Systems Network Architecture) are the supported network protocols.

DDF permits up to 150,000 distributed concurrent threads to be attached to a single DB2 subsystem at a time. The following resource managers execute in the DDF services address space:

- Data communications resource manager (DCRM)
- Distributed data interchange services (DDIS)
- Distributed relational data system manager (DRDS)
- Distributed transaction manager (DTM)

The stored-procedure address space (DSN1SPAS) is established by DB2. SPAS provides an isolated environment in which to execute stored procedures.

> **N O T E** To create new stored procedures in version 8 it is recommended that you use WLM (Workload Manager) address spaces.

The Workload Manager (WLM) component of z/OS manages address spaces for the execution of stored procedures and user-defined functions. These address spaces are called application environments. When an application calls a stored procedure or external user-defined function, DB2 schedules this work with WLM to run in a WLM-managed application environment. Each DB2 subsystem may have many defined application environments.

The *allied address spaces* communicate with DB2. The SPASs operate as allied address spaces. The following subcomponents execute in allied address spaces:

- Attachment facilities: call attachments, CICS, IMS, recoverable resource manager services, TSO
- Message generator (standalone only)
- Subsystem support
- Utilities: DDAS; standalone

Address Space Priority

To establish the z/OS address space dispatching priorities, the IRLM address space should be placed above IMS, CICS, and DB2, with DB2's MSTR and DBM1 address spaces placed above CICS. The following is a recommended priority listing:

- MVS monitor with IRLM capabilities
- IRLM
- DB2 performance monitors
- DBM1
- MSTR
- WLM-managed application environments
- CICS

If the IRLM address space is not at the top of the dispatching priorities, DB2 locks will not get set and released without causing excessive wait time (see Chapter 16 for information on DB2 locks). A warning message will be issued if the IRLM is not above DBM1 at DB2 start-up.

It is important to pay attention to the dispatching recommendations of the vendors of the various performance monitors. Each vendor has one or more address spaces and always recommends specific dispatching priorities. If a performance monitor that can analyze problems in the IRLM is being used, dispatching IRLM higher than a DB2 and/or MVS monitor could be a problem. If a performance monitor can't get dispatched ahead of IRLM, you will not be able to find or analyze the problem.

Attachments

Attachment facilities provide the interface between DB2 and other environments. Only one attachment can be active within a program at any given time. Five attachment facilities can be used, depending on the environment in which the program will execute. The attachments are

- Customer Information Control System (CICS)
- Information Management System (IMS)
- Call Attach Facility (CAF)
- Resource Recovery Manager Services Attachment Facility (RRSAF)
- Time Sharing Option (TSO)

Each program runs in an allied address space. The DB2 attachment facility modules are called by the program, execute within the allied address space, and establish communication with the DB2 address spaces. When initialized, the attachment modules make the link to DB2, and agent control blocks are created in the DSNMSTR address space to control the program's DB2 processing.

When a program issues an SQL statement, the attachment modules are given control. The attachment programs prepare the request for DB2 and pass the request over to the DB2 address space. Results are passed back to the attachment programs, and any results are copied into the application storage areas.

Call Attach Facility

The DB2 Call Attach Facility is used for application programs that run under TSO or z/OS batch. The CAF is an alternative to the DSN command processor and provides greater control over the execution environment.

With the CAF, your application program can establish and control its own connection to DB2. Programs that run in z/OS batch, TSO foreground, and TSO background can use CAF.

IMS batch applications too can access DB2 databases through CAF, although that method does not coordinate the commitment of work between the IMS and DB2 systems. It is recommended that you use the DB2 Data Language/I batch support for IMS batch applications.

Programs using CAF can

- Access DB2 from address spaces where there is no TSO, CICS, or IMS
- Access the Instrumentation Facility Interface (IFI)
- Access DB2 from multiple tasks within an address space
- Control the connection to DB2 explicitly
- Connect to DB2 implicitly, using a default subsystem ID and plan name
- Receive a signal from DB2 on start-up or shutdown.

The Call Attach Facility is being slowly replaced by the more powerful RRS (resource recovery services) attachment facility.

Customer Information Control System

CICS is an application server that provides online transaction management for applications. You can use the CICS attachment facility to connect to DB2 from this environment. CICS facilitates access to DB2 data from the CICS environment. A CICS application can access both DB2 and CICS data; in the event of a failure, CICS coordinates the recovery between DB2 and CICS.

Once the DB2 subsystem has been started, DB2 can be operated from a CICS terminal. DB2 and CICS can be started independently of each other. The connection can also be made automatic. Figure 2-2 shows the relationship between DB2 and CICS. The CICS attachment facility manages multiple connections to DB2, called threads, that can be reused for improved performance.

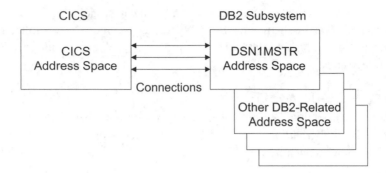

Figure 2-2   Relationship of DB2 to CICS

Information Management System

The IMS database computing system includes a hierarchical database manager, a transaction manager, and middleware products for access to the IMS databases and transactions. In order to connect to DB2, you can use the IMS attachment facility, which receives and interprets requests for access to DB2 data via exit routines in the IMS subsystems. IMS can connect automatically to DB2 without operator intervention. You can make DB2 calls from IMS applications by using embedded SQL statements. DB2 also provides the database services for IMS-dependent regions with the IMS attachment facility. An IMS batch environment has support for DL/1 batch jobs to have access to both IMS (DL/1) and DB2 data.

IMS will also coordinate recoveries between DB2 and IMS in the event of a failure. You also have the option to include DB2 in the IMS Extended Recovery Facility (XRF) recovery scenario. Figure 2-3 shows the relationship between IMS and DB2.

Resource Recovery Services Attachment Facility

RRSAF is a DB2 subcomponent that uses z/OS transaction management and resource recovery manager services to coordinate resource commitment between DB2 and all other resource managers that also use z/OS RRS in a z/OS subsystem.

An application program can use the RRSAF attachment facility to connect to and use DB2 to process SQL statements, commands, or IFI calls. Programs that run in z/OS batch, TSO foreground, and TSO background can use RRSAF.

RRSAF uses z/OS transaction management and resource recovery manager services (z/OS RRS). With RRSAF, you can coordinate DB2 updates with updates made by all other resource managers that also use z/OS RRS in a z/OS system.

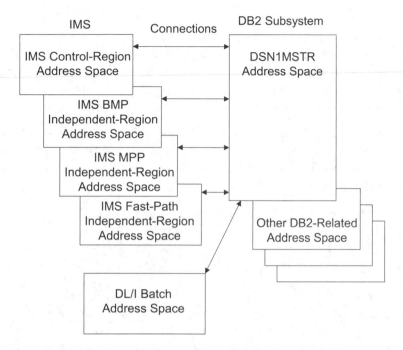

Figure 2-3   Relationship between DB2 and IMS

Programs that use RRSAF can

- Run under UNIX system services, TSO, or batch
- Use dynamic and static SQL Statements
- Sign on to DB2 with an alternative user ID
- Access DB2 from one or more tasks in an address space
- Use the IFI
- Control the exact state of the DB2 connection
- Capture DB2 start-up and termination events

Programs using RRSAF can be run from almost every environment available under z/OS. The programs can be invoked from the command prompt in TSO, from a shell prompt under UNIX system services, and, like any non-DB2 program using the PGM specification, on the EXEC card in Job Control Language (JCL).

Each task control block (TCB) can have only one connection to DB2. Using RRSAF, this connection can be switched between tasks within the address space. It is also possible to directly connect to multiple DB2 susbystems and switch between them during execution, although this would limit the ability to move subsystems to alternate systems in a sysplex.

Time Sharing Option

TSO allows interactive time-sharing capabilities from local and remote terminals. The TSO attachment facility is used by the majority of TSO applications. TSO controls programs, also allowing noninteractive batch program execution. In order to connect to DB2, you can use the TSO CAF or the RRS (resource recovery services). Historically, the TSO attachment facility has been the most commonly used connection for TSO interactive and batch applications.

Using TSO, you can bind application plans and packages and execute several online functions of DB2. Figure 2-4 shows the relationship between DB2 and TSO. Application programs and databases can be created, modified, and maintained via the TSO attach. You can run in either the foreground or batch when accessing DB2.

Access to two command processors is allowed when using TSO:

- DSN command processor
- DB2 Interactive (DB2I)

The DSN command processor runs as a TSO command processor using the attachment facility. This command processor provides an alternative method for executing programs in a TSO environment that accesses DB2. This processor can be invoked from the foreground by issuing a TSO command or from batch by invoking the TMP (terminal monitor program) from an MVS batch job, passing the commands in the SYSTSIN data set to TMP. When DSN is running and DB2 is up, you can issue DB2 or DSN commands (covered later in this chapter).

The DB2I comprises ISPF panels that allow for an interactive connection to DB2 and invokes the DSN command processor behind the scenes. With this processor, you can invoke utilities, issue commands, and run SQL statements. DB2I is discussed in more detail later in this chapter.

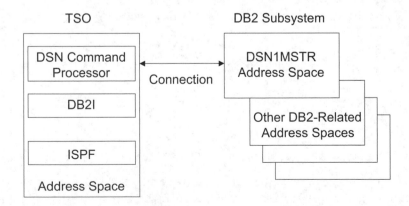

Figure 2-4   Relationship between DB2 and TSO

SECURITY

You can add security to your DB2 subsystem by using the Resource Access Control Facility (RACF). RACF is a component of the SecureWay Security Server for z/OS. Other, equivalent security packages are available on the market.

Use of RACF will prevent unauthorized users from having access to the system. RACF can be used to protect a variety of resources in DB2 and to check the identity of DB2 users. An exit routine that runs as an extension to DB2 is part of the Security Server and can also provide central control authorization to DB2 objects.

For more information on security options, refer to Chapter 3.

PARALLEL SYSPLEX SUPPORT

DB2 has the ability to run in a parallel sysplex environment. This environment is required to support DB2 data sharing (refer to Chapter 9 for more details), allowing us to configure an environment in which several processors can share data and the DB2 subsystems can have concurrent read/write access to this data. A parallel sysplex environment also gives us flexibility for adding new processors for added throughput, seamlessly routing workload away from failed processors, and balancing diverse work across multiple processors.

DFSMS

DFSMS (Data Facility Storage Management Subsystem) can be used to manage DB2 data sets automatically and to reduce the amount of administrative work for database and systems administrators. SMS facilitates allocation and movement of data, better availability and performance management, and automated space management. Most important is the aspect of performance improvements, as performance goals can be set for each class of data, thereby reducing the need for manual tuning. This environment also uses the cache provided by the storage hardware.

INTERFACES

A variety of ways to interface with DB2 are available, such as with programs using TSO, CAF, CICS, and so on. Two of the most common interfaces provided with the DB2 product are DB2 Interactive (DB2I) and Sequential Processing Using File Input (SPUFI).

DB2 Interactive

The interactive program DB2I can be used to run application programs and to perform many DB2 operations by entering values on panels. DB2I runs under TSO, using ISPF (Interactive System Productivity Facility) services. To use DB2I, follow the local procedures for logging on to TSO, and enter `ISPF`. Each operation is controlled by entering the parameters that describe it on the panels provided. DB2 also provides help panels to

- Explain how to use each operation
- Provide the syntax for and examples of DSN subcommands, DB2 operator commands, and DB2 utility control statements

The following tasks can be performed using DB2I:

- Execute SQL statements using SPUFI
- Perform a DCLGEN (Declarations Generator)
- Prepare a DB2 program
- Invoke the DB2 precompiler
- Execute BIND/REBIND/FREE commands
- RUN an SQL program
- Issue DB2 commands
- Invoke DB2 utilities
- Change DB2I defaults

An example of the DB2I menu is shown in Figure 2-5.

Figure 2-6 shows the defaults for DB2I. These defaults can be changed. Some of the parameters that can be changed are the DB2 subsystem on which to run the requests, application language of choice, number or rows returned to the session, and what string delimiter to use.

```
                       DB2I PRIMARY OPTION MENU

  ===>

  Select one of the following DB2 functions and press ENTER.

    1   SPUFI                 (Process SQL Statements)
    2   DCLGEN                (Generate SQL and source language declarations)
    3   PROGRAM PREPARATION   (Prepare a DB2 application program to run)
    4   PRECOMPILE            (Invoke DB2 precompiler)
    5   BIND/REBIND/FREE      (BIND, REBIND, or FREE plans or packages)
    6   RUN                   (RUN an SQL program)
    7   DB2 COMMANDS          (Issue DB2 commands)
    8   UTILTIES              (Invoke DB2 utilities)
    D   DB2I DEFAULTS         (Set global parameters)
    X   EXIT                  (Leave DB2I)

  Press : END to exit        HELP for more information
```

Figure 2-5   DB2I menu

```
                        DB2I DEFAULTS PANEL 1

Command ===> _

Change defaults as desired:

1   DB2 NAME.............  ===> DSN       (Subsystem Identifier)
2   DB2 CONNECTION RETRIES ===> 0         (How many retries for DB2 connection)
3   APPLICATION LANGUAGE... ===> COB2     (ASM, C, CPP, COBOL, COB2, IBMCOB,
                                            FORTRAN, PLI)
4   LINES/PAGE OF LISTING. ===> 60        (A number from 5 to 999)
5   MESSAGE LEVEL......... ===> I         (Information, Warning, Error, Severe)
6   SQL STRING DELIMITER.. ===> DEFAULT   (DEFAULT or ' or ")
7   DECIMAL POINT......... ===> .         (. or , )
8   STOP IF RETURN CODE >= ===> 8         (Lowest terminating return code)
9   NUMBER OF ROWS........ ===> 20        (For ISPF Tables)
10  CHANGE HELP BOOK NAMES? ===> NO       (YES to change HELP data set names)


Press : ENTER to process  END to cancel   HELP for more information
```

Figure 2-6 DB2I defaults screen

Sequential Processing Using File Input

SPUFI is a DB2I menu option that allows you to execute SQL statements interactively with DB2. The options on the main menu are as follows.

- **Input data set name** is the data set that contains one or more SQL statements that are to be executed. The data set needs to exist before SPUFI can be used.
- **Output data set name** is the data set that will receive the output from the SQL statement that is executed. This data set does not have to exist before execution.
- **Change defaults** allows for changing control values and characteristics of the output data set and the format of SPUFI settings.
- **Edit input** allows for editing the SQL statements.
- **Execute** indicates whether to execute the SQL statement in the input file.
- **Autocommit** tells DB2 whether to make the changes to the data permanent.
- **Browse output** allows for browsing of the query output.
- **Connect location** specifies the name of the application server to receive the queries.

SPUFI allows you to have multiple queries in one input data set member for execution. The queries can be stacked by using a ; between the statements. Without an explicit COMMIT statement, all the SQL statements are considered a unit of work.

After the SQL has been executed, SPUFI displays both the SQLCODE and the SQLSTATE. Figure 2-7 shows the main screen for SPUFI.

```
SPUFI                              SSID: DSN
===>

Enter the input data set name:      (Can be sequential or partitioned)
  1  DATA SET NAME ... ===>         ISPF.SQL(RECURS1)
  2  VOLUME SERIAL ... ===>         (Enter if not cataloged)
  3  DATA SET PASSWORD ===>         (Enter if password protected)

Enter the output data set name:     (Must be a sequential data set)
  4  DATA SET NAME ... ===>         OUTPUT.DATA

Specify processing options:
  5  CHANGE DEFAULTS   ===> YES     (Y/N - Display SPUFI defaults panel?)
  6  EDIT INPUT ...... ===> YES     (Y/N - Enter SQL statements?)
  7  EXECUTE ........  ===> YES     (Y/N - Execute SQL statements?)
  8  AUTOCOMMIT ...... ===> YES     (Y/N - Commit after successful run?)
  9  BROWSE OUTPUT ... ===> YES     (Y/N - Browse output data set?)

For remote SQL processing:
 10  CONNECT LOCATION  ===>


PRESS:  ENTER to process    END to exit         HELP for more information
```

Figure 2-7 SPUFI panel

INSTALLATION AND MIGRATION

Installation is the process of preparing DB2 to operate as a z/OS subsystem. *Migration* is the process of upgrading to a more current release of DB2. Both processes require the same steps. This book does not cover the details of each migration step; if you require more information, refer to the *DB2 Version 8 z/OS Installation* manual.

Before you begin installing or migrating, plan the amount of direct-access storage and virtual storage you need. Planning and coordinating with other DB2 subsystems is essential if you plan to install the DDF. For more information, refer to the *IBM DB2 for z/OS Version 8 Installation Guide*. Review what values are needed for the parameters on the installation and migration panels.

Another option for installation is to use the msys (Managed System Infrastructure) for Setup DB2 Customization Center. This reduces the complexity of configuring a DB2 subsystem when installing, migrating to compatibility mode, or enabling new function mode, or enabling data sharing. The msys for Setup workplace provides a GUI tool similar to Windows Explorer, that is used to manage z/OS products. The msys for Setup management directory stores configuration data for all systems.

The DB2 Customization Center can be added to the msys for Setup workplace. When refreshed, it pulls the current DB2 and z/OS settings. These settings can be reviewed and/or changed. An update can be performed to apply the changes. If a CLIST (command list) was previously used to customize a DB2 subsystem, this can be cloned by specifying the name of the output member generated by the CLIST and then performing a refresh to obtain the information.

Once in the DB2 Customization Center, the parameter values can be copied from one DB2 to another. The tasks executed during the update process are equivalent to those performed by the DB2 installation Job Control Language (JCL) jobs. If you wish to have JCL jobs configure DB2 on the host, the DB2 Customization Center can also generate an output member to be used as input to the CLIST.

For more information on the msys for Setup DB2 Customization Center, refer to the *z/OS Managed System Infrastructure for Setup Users Guide.*

DB2 provides a set of tools that automate the process of installing or migrating. These tools include most of the JCL needed to install and migrate the product. This JCL constitutes the *installation and migration job*s. Each of these jobs helps you perform a task when installing or migrating.

DB2 also includes the installation CLIST (command list) to help tailor the installation and migration jobs. This CLIST, also called the *migration CLIST*, or simply the *CLIST*, contains the code necessary to tailor the jobs to your needs. With the Interactive Systems Productivity Facility (ISPF) and Interactive Systems Productivity Facility/Program Development Facility (ISPF/PDF), you can use a series of ISPF panels to pass parameter values to the CLIST. The CLIST uses these values to tailor the installation and migration jobs.

DB2 also provides a set of sample programs and procedures that help you determine whether DB2 is functioning correctly. Because it is distributed as object code, DB2 requires few assemblies. An assembly to specify DB2 initialization parameters must be performed but requires only a few seconds.

DB2 allows you to specify many subsystem characteristics during DB2 operation, thereby providing the ability to defer decisions about DB2 characteristics until after the install or migration. Some of these decisions include authorizing users, defining databases and tables, and tuning DB2.

DB2 allows for updating most of the install options without requiring you to reinstall or remigrate. Defaults can be accepted for certain options; after acquiring experience with DB2, you can tailor them to the needs of a particular environment.

New with version 8 is the Managed System Infrastructure for Setup (msys for Setup), which is a z/OS tool that addresses the difficulties in maintaining z/OS. It can help manage all installation and customization tasks for DB2. It can be used with the DB2 Customization Center to update DB2 parameters and generate output that can be used as input to the installation CLIST.

High-Level Overview

The following procedures need to be performed for both installing and migrating DB2.

1. If using distributed data, install Virtual Telecommunication Access Method (VTAM) and, optionally, TCP/IP.
2. If planning implementation in a data sharing parallel sysplex environment, examine the additional considerations for the parallel sysplex installation before installing or migrating DB2 to data sharing.
3. Load the DB2 libraries (do the SMP/E steps).
4. Execute the additional jobs if you plan to use DB2's call level interface (CLI) or DB2 for z/OS Java Edition. (Refer to the *IBM DB2 ODBC Guide and Reference* or the *Application Programming Guide and Reference for JAVA*.)
5. Customize the installation or migration jobs.
6. Install or migrate DB2.
7. Connect the DB2 attachment facilities.
8. Prepare DB2 for use.
9. Verify installation or migration.

Version 8 Migration Considerations

Version 8 migration is different from all previous DB2 release migrations. You can upgrade only to V8 from V7. Also, the migration process has three modes.

1. **In compatibility (COMPAT) mode (CM)**, you install the new DB2 software and do some catalog updates, but no new functions are available to customers when you start DB2. Fallback to prior releases is still possible during this mode. DB2 members in a data sharing group can be migrated one by one to this mode (mix V7/V8).
2. **In enable new-function mode (ENFM)**, you make extensive changes to the catalog. For the most part, fallback to version 7 is impossible unless a complete restore of the subsystem is performed. To begin this mode, all DB2 members in data sharing have to running in be V8 COMPAT mode.
3. **In new-function mode (NFM)**, you are fully on DB2 V8 and have all new features. Fallback to version 7 is impossible. All DB2 data sharing members have to be in ENFM mode before you can migrate them.

The three modes of migration provide

- **Reduced risk.** During CM, customers can do extensive testing of their existing applications; if fallback needs to occur from CM to V7, you guarantee that no new features are used.

- **More control over doing the migration.** Fallback is allowed without users experiencing too many errors (force the fallback SPE).
- **Customer control of new-function usage.** Full control is provided over the migration process (timing) and when new functions can be used.

Compatibility Mode

In compatibility mode, you will run the MIGRATE CLIST to generate jobs, with the fallback SPE applied to all members in the data sharing group. Then start DB2 with V8 software, and run the DSNTIJTC job. Many updates are made during this mode to header pages in the directory, Boot Strap Data Set (BSCS), and Shared Communication Area (SCA). Coded Character Set Identifier (CCSID) updates are also performed at this time.

At this point, DB2 uses V8 code internally, 64-bit addressing (only virtual pools), and Unicode for parsing SQL. The V8 catalog is still in Extended Binary Coded decimal interchange format, and full fallback to V7 is allowed. To prevent BIND failures if someone tries to use new V8 features, you can use precompiler option NEWFUN=NO. While running in this mode, users have virtually no new V8 functions available.

The data sharing group permits members to be a mix of V7 and V8 in CM. However, it is best to keep the coexistence period short.

Enable New-Function Mode

Only a few new functions are available in this mode. During ENFM, a restructuring of the DB2 catalog is performed. The DSNTIJNE reorganizes 17 catalog table spaces and one directory table with extra functions (CATENFM). In a data sharing environment, this is a groupwide event because one catalog is shared by all members. It is recommended that this migration period be kept short for all members in the data sharing group.

> **N O T E**   If you do not have BP8K0, BP16K0, and BP32K buffer pools allocated, it is best to create them in compatibility mode.

> **N O T E**   At this point, fallback to version 7 is not possible.

During this mode (CATEFNM), many catalog changes are made, such as changing almost every CHAR(8) and CHAR(18) column to VARCHAR(18) and VARCHAR(128) so that DB2 can accept long names, and changing the catalog to use Unicode.

> **N O T E**   Unicode ordering is different from EBCDIC.

An online REORG of most of the catalog and one directory table space must also occur during this mode. The DSNTIJNE job is then executed in several steps, which include the following actions:

- ENFM0000. Terminate any pending DSNENFM.* utilities.
- ENFM0001. Update catalog for new mode (for every table space(18)).
- ENFMnnnn0. Test for conversion, do DDL Alters (* exclusive locking *).
- ENFM00001. Delete old data sets.
- ENFM00003. Define new data sets.
- ENFM00007. REORG and fix. Change record formats, page sizes, and encoding to Uni-code; create new V8 indexes; inline image copy; and switch.
- ENFM0009. Delete old data sets.

New-Function Mode

At this time, the subsystem is a true V8 system, with all functions available. The DSNTIJNF job signals the end of ENFM (CATENFM COMPLETE), DSNTIJNG builds a new DSNHDECP module (specifies whether to use new functions), and DSNHDECM specifies NEWFUN=YES. The new V8 IVP sample jobs can be run, including all the new functions.

In order to see the mode that DB2 is in during the migration process, you can use the -DISPLAY GROUP command. The attribute for the MODE will give you this information. Values in the MODE field are as follows:

- C = compatibility
- E = enabling new function
- N = new function

The following output shows the result of a -DISPLAY GROUP command showing new-function mode:

```
DSN7100I  +DSN8 DSN7GCMD
 *** BEGIN DISPLAY OF GROUP(........) GROUP LEVEL(...) MODE(N)
                    PROTOCOL LEVEL(2)  GROUP ATTACH NAME(....)
 -------------------------------------------------------------
 DB2                                    DB2 SYSTEM   IRLM
 MEMBER    ID  SUBSYS CMDPREF   STATUS  LVL NAME     SUBSYS IRLMPROC
 --------  --- ----   --------  ------- --- --------  ----   --------
 ........   0 DSN8    +DSN8     ACTIVE  810 P390      BRLM   BRLMPROC
 -------------------------------------------------------------
 *** END DISPLAY OF GROUP(........)
 DSN9022I  +DSN8 DSN7GCMD 'DISPLAY GROUP ' NORMAL COMPLETION
```

SYSTEM PARAMETERS

DSNZPARMs

At installation time you supply values for the DB2 DSNZPARM parameters via the install panels. Table 2-1 lists all the DSNZPARMs, along with a description of each, the allowable values, and whether they can be changed online.

Table 2-1   DSNZPARMs

Parameter	Description	Acceptable Values (defaults are in boldface)	Online Updatable
ABEXP	EXPLAIN processing	**YES**, NO	Yes
ABIND	Autobind	**YES**, NO	Yes
ACCUMACC	DDF/RRSAF accumulated data	NO, 2–65,535 **10**	Yes
AGCCSID	ASCII-coded character set (graphic)	**0**–65,533	—
ALCUNIT	Allocation units	**BLK**, TRK, CYL	Yes
ALL/dbname	Start names	**ALL**, space names	—
AMCCSID	ASCII-coded character set (mixed)	**0**–65,533	—
APPENSCH	Application encoding	ASCII, **EBCDIC**, Unicode, CCSID	—
ARCPFX1	Copy 1 prefix	1–34 characters	Yes
ARCPFX2	Copy 2 prefix	1–34 characters	Yes
ARCRETN	Retention period	**0**–**9,999**	Yes
ARCWRTC	WTOR route code	1–16 **1,3,4**	Yes
ARCWTOR	Write to operator	NO, **YES**	Yes
ARC2FRST	Read Copy 2 archive	**NO**, YES	Yes
ASCCSID	ASCII-coded character set (single byte)	**0**–65,533	—
ASSIST	Assistant	**YES**, NO	No
AUDITST	Audit trace	**NO**, YES, list, *	No
AUTH	Use protection	**YES**, NO	No

continues

Table 2-1   DSNZPARMs (Continued)

Parameter	Description	Acceptable Values (defaults are in boldface)	Online Updatable
AUTHCACH	Plan authorization cache	0–4,096 **3,072**	Yes
BACKODUR	Backout duration	0–255 **5**	No
BINDNV	Bind new package	**BINDADD**, BIND	Yes
BLKSIZE	Block size	8,192–28,672 **24,576**	Yes
BMPTOUT	IMS BMP Timeout	1–254 **4**	Yes
CACHEDYN	Cache dynamic SQL	NO, **YES**	Yes
CACHEPAC	Package authorization cache	0–2M **32K**	No
CACHERAC	Routine authorization cache	0–2M **32K**	No
CATALOG	Catalog alias	1–8 characters **DSNCAT**	Yes
CDSSRDEF	Current degree	**1**, ANY	Yes
CHARSET	CCSID used	**ALPHANUM**, KATAKANA (if SCCSID = 930 or 5,026)	—
CHKFREQ	Checkpoint frequency	200–16M records (**500K**), or 1–60 minutes	Yes
CHGDC	Drop support	**1**,2,3	Yes
CMTSTAT	DDF threads	ACTIVE, **INACTIVE**	No
COMPACT	Compact data	**NO**, YES	Yes
COMPAT	IBM service	OFF	—
CONDBAT	Maximum remote connected	0–25,000 **10,000**	Yes
CONTSTOR	Contract thread storage	**NO**, YES	Yes
COORDNTR	Coordinator	**NO**, YES	No
CTHREAD	Maximum users	1–2,000 **200**	Yes
DBACRVW	DBADM can create view for other authid	YES, **NO**	Yes
DBPROTCL	Database protocol	**DRDA**, Private	Yes
DATE	Date format	**ISO**, USA, EUR, JIS, LOCAL	—
DATELEN	Local date length	**0**, 10 –254	—
DDF	DDF start-up option	**NO**, AUTO, COMMAND	No
DEALLCT	Deallocate period	**0**–1,439 minutes, 0–59 seconds, NOLIMIT	Yes

Table 2-1 DSNZPARMs (Continued)

Parameter	Description	Acceptable Values (defaults are in boldface)	Online Updatable
DECARTH	Decimal arithmetic	DEC15, DEC31, 15, 31	—
DECDIV3	Minimum divide scale	**NO**, YES	No
DECIMAL	Decimal point	**,** .	—
DEFLANG	Language default	ASM, C, CPP, COBOL, COB2, **IBMCOB**, FORTRAN, PL1	—
DEFLTID	Unknown authid	**IBMUSER**, or authid	No
DELIM	String delimiter	**DEFAULT**, ", '	—
DESCSTAT	Describe for static	NO, **YES**	Yes
DISABSCL	SQLWARN1 and 5 for nonscrollable cursors	**NO**, YES	—
DLDFREQ	Level ID update frequency	0–32,767 **5**	Yes
DLITOUT	DL/I batch timeout	1–254 **6**	Yes
DSHARE	Data sharing	**YES**, NO, blank	No
DSMAX	Data set maximum	1–**100,000**	Yes
DSQLDELI	Dist SQL string delimiter	', ''	—
DSSTIME	Data set stats time	1–1,440 **5**	Yes
DSCVI	Vary DS control interval	**YES**, NO	—
DYNRULES	Use for dynamic rules	**YES**, NO	—
EDMBFIT	Algorithm for free chain search	YES, **NO**	Yes
EDMDBDC	EDM DBD cache	**5,000**–2,097,152K	Yes
EDMPOOL	EDMPOOL storage size	1K–2,097,152K **32,768**	Yes
EDMSTMTC	EDM statement cache size	0–1,048,576K **5,000**	Yes
EDPROP	Drop support	**1**, 2, 3	Yes
ENSCHEME	Default encoding scheme	**EBCDIC**, ASCII	—
EVALUNC	Predicate evaluation with UR and RS	YES, **NO**	Yes
EXTRAREQ	Extra blocks requester	0–**100**	Yes
EXTRASRV	Extra blocks server	0–**100**	Yes
EXTSEC	Extended security	NO, **YES**	Yes

continues

Table 2-1 DSNZPARMs (Continued)

Parameter	Description	Acceptable Values (defaults are in boldface)	Online Updatable
GCCSID	EBCDIC coded character set (graphic byte)	0–65,533	—
GRPNAME	Group name	1–8 characters **DSNCAT**	No
HOPAUTH	Authorization at hop site	**BOTH**, RUNNER	No
IDBACK	Maximum batch connect	1–2,000 **50**	Yes
IDFORE	Maximum TSO connect	1–2,000 **50**	Yes
IDTHTOIN	Idle thread timeout	0–9,999 **120**	Yes
IDXBPOOL	Default buffer pool for user indexes	**BP0**–BP*x*	Yes
IMMEDWRI	Immediate write	NO, YES, **PH1**	Yes
IRLMAUT	Autostart	**YES**, NO	No
IRLMPRC	Procedure name	**IRLMPROC**, IRLM proc name	No
IRLMRWT	Resource timeout	1–3,600 **60**	No
IRLMSID	Subsystem name	**IRLM**, IRLM name	No
IRLMSWT	Time to autostart	1–3,600	Yes
IXQTY	Index space default size	**0**–4,194,304	Yes
LBACKOUT	Postpone backward log processing	**AUTO**, YES, NO	No
LC_CTYPE	Locale LC_CTYPE	Valid locale 0–50 characters	—
LEMAX	Maximum LE Tokens	0–50, **20**	No
LOBVALA	User LOB value storage	1–2,097,152 **10,240**	Yes
LOBVALS	User LOB value storage	1–510,002 **2,048**	Yes
LOGAPSTG	Log apply storage	1–100M **100**	No
LRDRTHLD	Long-running reader threshhold	0–1,439 minutes	Yes
MAINTYPE	Current maintenance types for MQTs	NONE, **SYSTEM**, USER, ALL	Yes
MAXARCH	Recording maximum	10–**1,000**	No
MAXDBAT	Maximum remote active	0–1,999 **200**	Yes
MAX_NUM_CUR	Maximum open cursors	0–99,999 **500**	Yes

Table 2-1 DSNZPARMs (Continued)

Parameter	Description	Acceptable Values (defaults are in boldface)	Online Updatable
MAXKEEPD	Maximum kept dynamic statements	0–65,535 **5000**	Yes
MAXRBLK	RID pool size	0, 16K–1,000,000K **calculated**	Yes
MAXRTU	Read tape units	1–99 **2**	Yes
MAX_ST_PROC	Maximum number of stored procedures	0–99,999 **2,000**	Yes
MAXTYPE1	Maximum Type 1 inactive	**0**–MAX REMOTE CON	Yes
MCCSID	EBCDIC coded character set (mixed byte)	**0**–65,533	—
MEMBNAME	Member name	1–8 characters **DSN1**	No
MGEXTSZ	Optimize extent sizing	YES, **NO**	Yes
MINDVSCL	Minimum scale for decimal division	**NONE**, 3, 6	—
MINRBLK	Number of RID lists for each RID map	**1**, *n*	—
MINSTOR	Thread management	YES, **NO**	Yes
MIXED	Mixed data	**NO**, YES	—
MON	Monitor trace	**NO**, YES	No
MONSIZE	Monitor size	**8K** to 1M	No
NPGTHRSH	Use of index after table growth	**0**, –1, *n*	Yes
NUMLKTS	Locks per table space	0–50,000 **1,000**	Yes
NUMLKUS	Locks per user	0–100,000 **10,000**	Yes
OFFLOAD	Offload active logs online	NO, **YES**	—
OJPERFEH	Disable outer join performance enhancements		Yes
OPTPREF		**ON**, OFF	—
OPTHINTS	Optimization hints	**NO**, YES	Yes
OUTBUFF	Output buffer	40K–400MB **400K**	No
PADIX	Pad index by default	YES, **NO**	Yes
PADNTSTR	Pad null-terminated strings	YES, **NO**	Yes

continues

Table 2-1   DSNZPARMs (Continued)

Parameter	Description	Acceptable Values (defaults are in boldface)	Online Updatable
PARAMDEG	Degree of parallelism	**0**–no upper limit	Yes
PARTKEYU	Allow partitioning keys to be updated	**YES**, NO, or same	Yes
PCLOSEN	Read-only switch checkpoints	1–32,767 **5**	Yes
PCLOSET	Read-only switch time	1–32,767 **10**	Yes
POOLINAC	Pool thread timeout	0–9,999 **120**	Yes
PRIQTY	Primary quantity	**Blank**, 1–9,999,999	Yes
PROTECT	Archive logs protected with RACF	**NO**, YES	Yes
PTASKROL	Include accounting traces for parallel tasks	**YES**, NO	Yes
QUIESCE	Quiesce period	0–999 **5**	Yes
RECALL	Recall database	**YES**, NO	No
RECALLD	Recall delay	0–32,767 **120**	Yes
REFSHAGE	Current refresh age	**0**, ANY	Yes
RELCURHL	Release locks	**YES**, NO	Yes
RESTART/DEFR	Restart or defer	**RESTART**, DEFER	—
RESYNC	Resync interval	1, **2**–99	Yes
RETLWAIT	Retained lock timeout	**0**–254	Yes
RETVLCFK	Varchar from index	**NO**, YES	Yes
RGFCOLID	Registration owner	1–8 characters **DSNRGCOL**	No
RGFDBNAM	Registration database	1–8 characters **DSNRGFDB**	No
RGFDEDPL	Control all applications	**NO**, YES	No
RGFDEFLT	Unregistered DDL default	APPL, **ACCEPT**, REJECT	No
RGFESCP	ART/ORT escape character	Nonalphanumeric character	No
RGFFULLQ	Require full names	**YES**, NO	No
RGFINSTL	Install DD control support	**NO**, YES	No
RGFNMORT	OBJT registration table	1–17 characters **DSN_REGISTER_OBJT**	No

Table 2-1 DSNZPARMs (Continued)

Parameter	Description	Acceptable Values (defaults are in boldface)	Online Updatable
RGFNMPRT	APPL registration table	1–17 characters **DSN_REGISTER_APPL**	No
RLF	RLF autostart	**NO**, YES	No
RLFAUTH	Resource Authid	**SYSIBM**, or authid	Yes
RLFERR	RLST access error	**NOLIMIT**, NORUN,1–50,000,000	Yes
RLFERRD	RLST access error	**NOLIMIT**, NORUN,1–50,000,000	Yes
RLFTBL	RLST name suffix	**01**, 2 alphanumeric characters	Yes
ROUTCDE	WTO route codes	**1**, 1–14 route codes	No
RRULOCK	U lock for RR/RS	**NO**, YES	Yes
SCCSID	EBCDIC coded character set (single byte)	**0**–65,533	—
SECQTY	Secondary quantity	Blank, CLIST calculated, 1–9,999,999	Yes
SECLCACH			
SEQCACH	Sequential cache	**BYPASS**, SEQ	Yes
SEQPRES	Utility cache option	**NO**, YES	Yes
SITETYP	Site type	**LOCALSITE**, RECOVERYSITE	No
SJMXPOOL	Star join maximum pool	0–1,024 **20**	Yes
SJTABLES	Number of tables in star join		Yes
SMFACCT	SMF accounting	NO, **YES(1)**, list (1–5,7,8), *	No
SMFSTAT	SMF statistics	**YES (1,3,4)**, NO, list(1–5) , *	No
SMSDCFL	SMS data class for file table space	**Blank**, 1–8 characters	Yes
SMSDCIX	SMS data class for index table space	**Blank**, 1–8 characters	Yes
SPRMEDX			Yes
SPRMLTD	Size threshhold for compression	**10**	—
SQLDELI	SQL string delimiter	**Default**, ', "	—
SRTPOOL	Sort pool size	240K–64,000K	Yes

continues

Table 2-1   DSNZPARMs (Continued)

Parameter	Description	Acceptable Values (defaults are in boldface)	Online Updatable
SSID	Subsystem name	**DSN**, *SSID*	—
STARJOIN	Enabling star join	**Disable**, enable, 1, 2–32,768	Yes
STATHIST	Collect historical statistics	SPACE, **NONE**, ALL, ACCESSPATH	Yes
STATSINT	Time to write RTS stats	1–1,440 minutes **30**	Yes
STATROLL	Run stats aggregates partition-level statistics	YES, **NO**	Yes
STATIME	Statistics time	1–1,440 minutes **30**	Yes
STDSQL	Standard SQL language	**NO**, YES	—
STORMXAB	Maximum abend count	**0**–225	Yes
STORPROC	DB2 procedure name	1–8 characters **ssnmSPAS**	No
STORTIME	Timeout value	5–1,800 seconds **180**	Yes
SUPERRS	Suppress logrec recording during soft errors	**YES**, NO	Yes
SVOLARC	Single volume	YES, **NO**	Yes
SYNCVAL	Statistics sync	**NO**, 0–59	Yes
SYSADM	System administrator 1	**SYSADM** or authid	Yes
SYSADM2	System administrator 2	**SYSADM** or authid	Yes
SYSOPR1	System operator 1	**SYSOPR** or authid	Yes
SYSOPR2	System operator 2	**SYSOPR** or authid	Yes
TBSBPOOL	Default buffer pool for user data	**BP0** – BPx	Yes
TCPALVER	TCP/IP already verified	**NO**, YES	Yes
TCPKPALV	TCP/IP keep alive	ENABLE, DISABLE, 1–65,524 **120**	Yes
TIME	Time format	**ISO**, JIS, USA, EUR, LOCAL	—
TIMELEN	Local time length	0, 8–254	—
TRACLOC	Size of local trace table	**16** (4K bytes)	
TRACSTR	Trace autostart	NO, YES (1–3), list (1–9)	No
TRACTBL	Trace size	4–396K **64K**	No

Table 2-1 DSNZPARMs (Continued)

Parameter	Description	Acceptable Values (defaults are in boldface)	Online Updatable
TRKRSITE	Remote tracker site usage	**NO**, YES	No
TSQTY	Define allocation for table space	**0**–4,194,304	Yes
TSTAMP	Timestamp archives	**NO**, YES	Yes
TWOACTV	Number of active copies	**2**, 1	No
TWOARCH	Number of archive copies	**2**, 1	No
TWOBSDS	Number of BSDSs	**YES**, NO	—
UGCCSID	Unicode CCSID (graphic)	1,208	—
UIFCIDS	Unicode IFCIDS	YES, **NO**	Yes
UMCCSID	Unicode CCSID (mixed)	1,208	—
UNIT	Device Type 1	**TAPE** or any device	Yes
UNIT2	Device Type 2	Device or unit name	Yes
URCHKTH	UR check frequency	0–255	Yes
URLGWTH	UR log write check	**0–1,000K**	Yes
USCCSID	Unicode CCSID (single byte)	1,208	—
UTIMOUT	Utility timeout	1–254	Yes
VOLTDEVT	Temporary unit name	**SYSDA**, valid name	Yes
WLMENV	WLM environment	Valid name, 1–18 characters	Yes
XLKUPDT	X Lock for searched U/D	YES, **NO**	Yes

After installation, these DSNZPARMs can be changed without your having to go back through the installation process. You can do this by changing the DSNTIJUZ member and reassembling and bouncing the DB2 subsystem, or performing an online change, for them to take effect.

Online DSNZPARMs

DB2 also allows for about 123 of the most popular DSNZPARMs to be dynamically changed without your having to stop and restart the DB2 subsystem and thereby cause an unwanted outage. The advantage to changing DSNZPARMs dynamically is to be able to tailor parameters to the current workload. For example, an approved change to the Environmental Descriptor Manager pool size can be implemented sooner without a DB2 outage. It may also be desirable to change not only buffer pool size but also EDM pool size and checkpoint frequency for overnight batch processing.

The DSNZPARM member is changed dynamically in its entirety by activating a different DSNZPARM member. The `-SET SYSPARM` command is used from a z/OS console, a DSN session under TSO, a DB2I panel, a CICS or IMS terminal or via an application or product using the Instrumentation Facility. The issuer must have SYSADM, SYSCTRL, or SYSOPR authority; for more on these authorities, refer to Chapter 3. The following forms of the `SET SYSPARM` statement can be used for controlling dynamic DSNZPARM settings:

```
-SET SYSPARM LOAD (modname)
Loads the named parameter module
Default is DSNZPARM

-SET SYSPARM RELOAD
Last named subsystem parameter module is loaded into storage

-SET SYSPARM STARTUP
Loads the initial parameters from DB2 startup
```

COMMANDS

Commands in the DB2 environment are divided into the following categories:

- The DSN command and its subcommands
- DB2 commands
- IMS commands
- CICS Attachment Facility Commands
- MVS IRLM commands
- TSO CLISTs

This chapter considers only the DSN commands and the DB2 commands.

DSN Commands

DSN, the DB2 command processor, executes as a TSO command. All subcommands except SPUFI run under DSN in either the foreground or the background. All subcommands except END also run under DB2 Interactive (DB2I). SPUFI runs only in the foreground under ISPF. The DSN commands/subcommands and their functions are listed in Table 2-2.

Table 2-2 DSN Commands/Subcommands

Command/Subcommand	Function
ABEND	Causes the DSN session to terminate with an X'04E'
BIND	Builds an application package or plan
DB2 command	Executes a DB2 command
DCLGEN (declarations generator)	Produces declarations for tables or views
DSN	Starts a DSN session
END	Ends a DSN session
FREE	Deletes an application package or plan
REBIND	Updates an application package or plan
REBIND TRIGGER PACKAGE	Updates an application trigger package
RUN	Executes an application program
SPUFI	Executes the SQL processor using file input
*	Comment

DB2 Commands

The command START DB2 can be issued only from a z/OS console or Authorized Program Facility (APF) passing it to the console. All other DB2 commands can be issued from the following:

- APF authorized program
- CICS terminal
- DB2I panel
- IFI application program
- IMS terminal
- TSO terminal session
- z/OS console or z/OS application program

An application program may use the DB2 Instrumentation Facility Interface to issue DB2 commands. DB2 commands issued from an MVS console are not associated with any secondary authorization IDs. The DB2 commands and their functions are listed in Table 2-3.

Table 2-3 DB2 Commands

Command	Function
`-ALTER BUFFERPOOL`	Alters attributes for the buffer pools
`-ALTER GROUPBUFFERPOOL`	Alters attributes for the group buffer pools
`-ALTER UTILITY`	Alters parameter values of the `REORG` utility
`-ARCHIVE LOG`	Enables a site to close a current active log and open the next available log data set
`-CANCEL THREAD`	Cancels processing for specific local or distributed threads
`-DISPLAY ARCHIVE`	Displays information about archive-log processing
`-DISPLAY BUFFERPOOL`	Displays information about the buffer pools
`-DISPLAY DATABASE`	Displays status information about DB2 databases
`-DISPLAY DDF`	Displays information regarding the status and configuration of the DDF
`-DISPLAY FUNCTION SPECIFIC`	Displays statistics about external user-defined functions
`-DISPLAY GROUP`	Displays information about the data sharing group to which a DB2 subsystem belongs and which mode DB2 is operating in
`-DISPLAY GROUPBUFFERPOOL`	Displays status information about DB2 group buffer pools
`-DISPLAY LOCATION`	Displays status information about distributed threads
`-DISPLAY LOG`	Displays log information and status of the offload task
`-DISPLAYPROCEDURE`	Displays status information about stored procedures
`-DISPLAY RLIMIT`	Displays status information about the resource limit facility (governor)
`-DISPLAY THREAD`	Displays information about DB2 threads
`-DISPLAY TRACE`	Displays information about DB2 traces
`-DISPLAY UTILITY`	Displays status information about a DB2 utility
`-MODIFY TRACE`	Changes the trace events associated with a particular active trace
`-RECOVER BSDS`	Reestablishes dual-bootstrap data sets
`-RECOVER INDOUBT`	Recovers threads left in doubt
`-RECOVER POSTPONED`	Completes backout processing for units of recovery left incomplete during an earlier restart
`-RESET GENERICLU`	Purges information stored by VTAM in the coupling facility

Table 2-3   DB2 Commands (Continued)

Command	Function
-RESET INDOUBT	Purges information displayed in the in-doubt thread report generated by the -DISPLAY THREAD command
-SET ARCHIVE	Controls the allocation of tape units and the deallocation time of the tape units for archive-log processing
-SET LOG	Modifies the checkpoint frequency
-SET SYSPARM	Loads the subsystem parameters specified in the command
-START DATABASE	Makes the specified database available for use
-START DB2	Initializes the DB2 subsystem; can be issued only from an MVS console
-START DDF	Starts the Distributed Data Facility
-START FUNCTION SPECIFIC	Activates a stopped external function
-START PROCEDURE	Activates the definition of stopped or cached stored procedures
-START RLIMIT	Starts the resource limit facility (governor)
-START TRACE	Initiates DB2 trace activity 300
-STOP DATABASE	Makes specified databases unavailable for applications
-STOP DB2	Stops the DB2 subsystem
-STOP DDF	Stops the Distributed Data Facility
-STOP FUNCTION SPECIFIC	Stops the acceptance of SQL statements for specified functions
-STOP PROCEDURE	Stops the acceptance of SQL CALL statements for stored procedures
-STOP RLIMIT	Stops the resource limit facility (governor)
-STOP TRACE	Stops trace activity
-TERM UTILITY	Terminates execution of a utility

A DSN9022I message indicates the normal end of DB2 command processing. A DSN9023I message indicates the abnormal end of DB2 command processing.

UTILITIES

DB2 utilities either execute within the subsystem (online) or standalone and run outside the subsystem (offline). The activities performed by the utilities—loading and reorganizing data, recovering data and indexes, rebuilding indexes, gathering statistics, quiescing data, and repairing data—are discussed in detail in Chapters 7 and 8.

Executing Utilities

The most common way to execute the DB2 utilities is to create JCL with the appropriate control cards. The utilities must be executed on the subsystem where the objects reside. (Chapter 9 provides more information on how to do so in a data sharing environment.) However, other options for utility execution are available, as discussed next.

DB2I

The DB2I has a panel that can be used to generated and run utilities. This option does not require a great deal of JCL knowledge, and the jobs can be saved for future execution and editing. Figure 2-8 gives an example of the DB2I panel for DB2 utilities.

```
DB2 UTILITIES                        SSID: DSN
===>

Select from the following:

 1 FUNCTION ===> EDITJCL             (SUBMIT job, EDITJCL, DISPLAY, TERMINATE)
 2 JOB ID   ===> TEMP               (A unique job identifier string)
 3 UTILITY  ===>                     (CHECK DATA, CHECK INDEX, CHECK LOB,
                                      COPY, DIAGNOSE, LOAD, MERGE, MODIFY,
                                      QUIESCE, REBUILD, RECOVER, REORG INDEX,
                                      REORG LOB, REORG TABLESPACE, REPORT,
                                      REPAIR, RUNSTATS, STOSPACE, UNLOAD)
 4 STATEMENT DATA SET ===> UTIL

Specify restart or preview option, otherwise enter NO.

 5 RESTART  ===> NO                  (NO, CURRENT, PHASE or PREVIEW)

 6 LISTDEF? (YES|NO) ===>            TEMPLATE? (YES|NO) ===>

 * The data set names panel will be displayed when required by a utility.

PRESS:  ENTER to process    END to exit    HELP for more information
```

Figure 2-8   DB2 utilities panel

DSNU Command

A DB2 online utility can be executed by invoking the DSNU CLIST command under TSO. The CLIST command generates the JCL data set required to execute the DSNUPROC procedure and execute online utilities as batch jobs. When you use the CLIST command, you need not be concerned about details of the JCL data set.

The CLIST command will create a job to perform one utility operation. The command can be issued for each utility operation necessary; then the issuer can edit and merge the outputs into one job or step.

Control Center

Utility execution is also supported in the DB2 Control Center, which also supports utility wild-carding: the ability to execute utilities against a list of objects matching a specified pattern of matching characters. A utility procedure could be created that would permit running, with one command, a mixture of several utilities against several objects, making maintenance much easier for the DBA. The Control Center also supports restarting utilities from the last committed phase or the last committed point. This support is available only for utilities started in the Control Center. The restart is accessible through the Display Utility dialog.

Support is also available for utility IDs. The Tools Settings notebook has an option to create a utility ID template using a variety of variables, such as USERID and UTILNAME. Before execution of the utility, the utility ID can be edited to make it more meaningful. The execution of utilities from the Control Center requires the DSNUTILS stored procedure described below.

DSNUTILS and DSNUTILU

DSNUTILS is a DB2-supplied stored procedure for executing utilities from a local or remote application via an SQL CALL statement. The client application calls in DSNUTILS with appropriate parameters. DSNUTILS then analyzes them to create a SYSIN stream and allocate all necessary data sets. After the data sets are allocated, DSNUTILS calls DSNUTILB, which then executes the appropriate utility. The utility statements are then processed, and DSNUTILS retrieves the data (execution results) in the SYSPRINT file, puts the data in the SYSIBM.SYSPRINT temporary table, and then opens a cursor on the table and passes control back to the client application. The client application then fetches all rows from the result set. Figure 2-9 shows this flow.

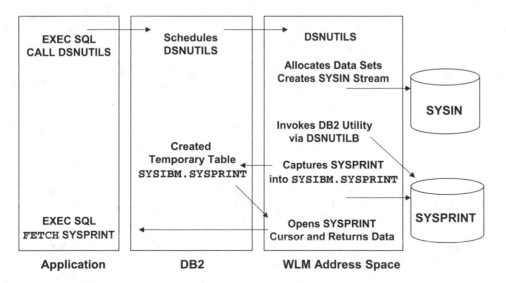

Figure 2-9 Execution of DSNUTILS

DB2 for z/OS Version 8 also includes the new DSNUTILU stored procedure which provides the same functions as DSNUTILS, but allows the control cards to be specified in Unicode (UTF-8).

Chapter 13 has more information on stored procedures.

Utility Templates

Some DB2 utilities produce data sets as a by-product or as an end result of utility execution. These data sets are referenced on utility control statements by a set of data definition (DD) name keywords and are specified in detail on the corresponding JCL DD cards.

These DD cards must be coded for each utility, as required, and maintained over time as the structure of data changes. Database administrators establish data set policies, refer to them on utility control statements, and let DB2 utilities administer those policies at execution time. Many DB2 utilities will accept a *template* construct instead of DD cards to dynamically allocate utility data sets.

Templates contain

- The data set naming convention
- DFSMS parameters
- DASD or TAPE allocation parameters

A TEMPLATE can be specified in the SYSIN data set, preceding the utility control statement that references it, or in one or more TEMPLATE data sets. The TEMPLATE data set DD name is specified on the OPTIONS utility control statement by TEMPLATEDD(*ddname*) and applies to all subsequent utility control statements until the end of input or until DB2 encounters a new OPTIONS TEMPLATEDD(*ddname*) specification. The default TEMPLATE data set DD name is SYSTEMPL.

TEMPLATE data sets may contain only TEMPLATE utility control statements. Any TEMPLATE defined within SYSIN overrides another TEMPLATE definition of the same name found in a TEMPLATE data set.

With this functionality, database administrators can standardize data set allocation and the utility control statements that refer to those data sets. This functionality reduces the need to customize and alter utility job streams.

> **N O T E**   Templates cannot be used with the REPAIR utility.

The TEMPLATE specification can be used for both DASD and TAPE data set allocation, including support for data set stacking on tape and Generation Data Group (GDG) base definition. TEMPLATE syntax also allows user-specified DASD SPACE parameters. If the SPACE keyword is not specified, the size of the data set will be estimated on the basis of formulas that vary by utility and by data set.

The TEMPLATE statement required for a COPY example might look something like this:

```
TEMPLATE TMP1
DSNAME(DB2.&TS..D&JDATE..COPY&ICTYPE.&LOCREM.&PRIBAK.)
VOLUMES(Vol1,Vol2,Vol3)
TEMPLATE TMP2
DSNAME(DB2.&TS..D&JDATE..COPY&ICTYPE.&LOCREM.&PRIBAK.)
VOLUMES(Vol4,Vol5,Vol6)
LISTDEF PAYROLL INCLUDE TABLESPACE CERTTS.*
INCLUDE INDEXSPACE CERTTS.*IX
EXCLUDE TABLESPACE CERTTS.TEMP*
EXCLUDE INDEXSPACE CERTTS.TMPIX*
COPY LIST PAYROLL ...COPYDDN(TMP1,TMP1)RECOVERYDDN(TMP2,TMP2)
```

Database administrators can check their utility control statements without execution, using the PREVIEW function. In PREVIEW mode, DB2 expands all TEMPLATE data set names appearing in the SYSIN DD, as well as any from the TEMPLATE DD that are referenced on a utility control statement. DB2 then prints the information to the SYSPRINT data set to halt execution. You can specify PREVIEW either as a JCL PARM or on the OPTIONS PREVIEW utility control statement.

For more information on templates and the DB2 utilities, refer to the *IBM DB2 UDB for z/OS Version 8 Utility Guide and Reference.*

Displaying Utilities

Utilities can be displayed in order to see important runtime information about the jobs. This includes jobs running in a data sharing group. The output has information about the

- Type of utility
- How much of the processing the utility has completed
- Status of the utility
- Member on which the utility is executing
- Phase the utility is in

CATALOG AND DIRECTORY

The DB2 catalog and directory act as central repositories for all information about the support and operations of DB2 objects, authorizations, and communications. The catalog comprises several DB2 tables and can be accessed via SQL. The catalog contains details about DB2 objects obtained from the DDL (Data Definition Language) when an object is created or altered or from

DCL (Data Control Language) when an authorization is granted on an object or a group of objects. The DB2 catalog also contains information about communications with other DB2 and non-DB2 databases through the use of the communications database (CDB), which contains information about VTAM and TCP/IP addresses.

Table 2-4 lists the DB2 catalog tables and the types of information in each. (Descriptions of all the columns in the DB2 catalog tables can be found in detail in Appendix D of the *IBM DB2 for z/OS Version 8 SQL Reference Manual*.)

Table 2-4 DB2 Catalog Tables

Table Name (SYSIBM.table)	Information Contents
IPLIST	Allows multiple IP addresses to be specified for a given LOCATION. Insert rows into this table when you want to define a remote DB2 data sharing group. Rows can be inserted, updated, and deleted.
IPNAMES	Defines the remote DRDA servers DB2 can access using TCP/IP. Rows in this table can be inserted, updated, and deleted.
LOCATIONS	Contains a row for every accessible remote server. The row associates a LOCATION name with the TCP/IP or SNA network attributes for the remote server. Requesters are not defined in this table. Rows in this table can be inserted, updated, and deleted.
LULIST	Allows multiple LU (Logical Unit) names to be specified for a given LOCATION. Insert rows into this table when you want to define a remote DB2 data sharing group. The same value for the LUNAME column cannot appear in both the SYSIBM.LUNAMES table and the SYSIBM.LULIST table. Rows in this table can be inserted, updated, and deleted.
LUMODES	Each row of the table provides VTAM with conversation limits for a specific combination of LUNAME and MODENAME. The table is accessed only during the initial conversation-limit negotiation between DB2 and a remote LU. This negotiation is called *change-number-of-sessions* (CNOS) processing. Rows in this table can be inserted, updated, and deleted.
LUNAMES	The table must contain a row for each remote SNA client or server that communicates with DB2. Rows can be inserted, updated, or deleted.
MODESELECT	Associates a mode name with any conversation created to support an outgoing SQL request. Each row represents one or more combinations of LUNAME, authorization ID, and application plan name. Rows in this table can be inserted, updated, and deleted.
SYSAUXRELS	Contains one row for each auxiliary table created for a LOB column. A base table space that is partitioned must have one auxiliary table for each partition of each LOB column.

Table 2-4   DB2 Catalog Tables (Continued)

Table Name (SYSIBM.table)	Information Contents
SYSCHECKDEP	Contains one row for each reference to a column in a table check constraint.
SYSCHECKS	Contains one row for each table-check constraint.
SYSCHECKS2	Contains one row for each table-check constraint created in or after version 7.
SYSCOLAUTH	Records the UPDATE or REFERENCES privileges that are held by users on individual columns of a table or view.
SYSCOLDIST	Contains one or more rows for the first key column of an index key. Rows in this table can be inserted, updated, and deleted.
SYSCOLDIST_HIST	Contains rows from SYSCOLDIST. Whenever rows are added or changed in SYSCOLDIST, the rows are also written to the new history table. Rows in this table can be inserted, updated, and deleted.
SYSCOLDISTSTATS	Contains zero or more rows per partition for the first key column of a partitioning index or DPSI (Data Partitioned Secondary Index). Rows are inserted when RUNSTATS scans index partitions of the partitioning index. No row is inserted if the index is nonpartitioning. Rows in this table can be inserted, updated, and deleted.
SYSCOLSTATS	Contains partition statistics for selected columns. For each column, a row exists for each partition in the table. Rows are inserted when RUNSTATS collects either indexed column statistics or nonindexed column statistics for a partitioned table space. No row is inserted if the table space is nonpartitioned. Rows in this table can be inserted, updated, and deleted.
SYSCOLUMNS	Contains one row for every column of each table and view.
SYSCOLUMNS_HIST	Contains rows from SYSCOLUMNS. Whenever rows are added or changed in SYSCOLUMNS, the rows are also written to the new history table. Rows in this table can be inserted, updated, and deleted.
SYSCONSTDEP	Records dependencies on check constraints or user-defined defaults for a column.
SYSCOPY	Contains information needed for recovery.
SYSDATABASE	Contains one row for each database, except for database DSNDB01.
SYSDATATYPES	Contains one row for each distinct type defined to the system.
SYSDBAUTH	Records the privileges held by users over databases.
SYSDBRM	Contains one row for each DBRM of each application plan.
SYSDUMMY1	Contains one row. The table is used for SQL statements in which a table reference is required, but the contents of the table are not important.

continues

Table 2-4   DB2 Catalog Tables (Continued)

Table Name (SYSIBM.*table*)	Information Contents
SYSFIELDS	Contains one row for every column that has a field procedure.
SYSFOREIGNKEYS	Contains one row for every column of every foreign key.
SYSINDEXES	Contains one row for every index.
SYSINDEXES_HIST	Contains rows from SYSINDEXES. Whenever rows are added or changed in SYSINDEXES, they are also written to the new history table. Rows in this table can be inserted, updated, and deleted.
SYSINDEXPART	Contains one row for each nonpartitioning index and one row for each partition of a partitioning index or a DPSI.
SYSINDEXPART_HIST	Contains rows from SYSINDEXPART. Whenever rows are added or changed in SYSINDEXPART, they are also written to the new history table. Rows in this table can be inserted, updated, and deleted.
SYSINDEXSTATS	Contains one row for each partition of a partitioning index. Rows in this table can be inserted, updated, and deleted.
SYSINDEXSTATS_HIST	Contains rows from SYSINDEXSTATS. Whenever rows are added or changed in SYSINDEXSTATS, they are also written to the new history table. Rows in this table can be inserted, updated, and deleted.
SYSJARCLASS_SOURCE	Auxiliary table for SYSIBMSYSCONTENTS.
SYSJARCONTENTS	Contains Java class source for installed JAR (Java Archive).
SYSJARDATA	Auxiliary table for SYSIBMSYSOBJECTS.
SYSJAROBJECTS	Contains binary large object representing the installed JAR.
SYSJAVAOPTS	Contains build options used during INSTALL_JAR.
SYSKEYCOLUSE	Contains a row for every column in a unique constraint—primary key or unique key—from the SYSIBM.SYSTABCONST table.
SYSKEYS	Contains one row for each column of an index key.
SYSLOBSTATS	Contains one row for each LOB table space.
SYSLOBSTATS_HIST	Contains rows from SYSLOBSTATS. Whenever rows are added or changed in SYSLOBSTATS, they are also written to the new history table. Rows in this table can be inserted, updated, and deleted.
SYSPACKAGE	Contains a row for every package.
SYSPACKAUTH	Records the privileges that users hold over packages.
SYSPACKDEP	Records the dependencies of packages on local tables, views, synonyms, table spaces, indexes and aliases, functions, and stored procedures.

Table 2-4 DB2 Catalog Tables (Continued)

Table Name (SYSIBM.table)	Information Contents
SYSPACKLIST	Contains one or more rows for every local application plan bound with a package list. Each row represents a unique entry in the plan's package list.
SYSPACKSTMT	Contains one or more rows for each statement in a package.
SYSPARMS	Contains one row for each parameter of a routine or multiple rows for table parameters—one for each column of the table.
SYSPKSYSTEM	Contains zero or more rows for every package. Each row for a given package represents one or more connections to an environment in which the package could be executed.
SYSPLAN	Contains one row for each application plan.
SYSPLANAUTH	Records the privileges that users hold over application plans.
SYSPLANDEP	Records the dependencies of plans on tables, views, aliases, synonyms, table spaces, indexes, functions, and stored procedures.
SYSPLSYSTEM	Contains zero or more rows for every plan. Each row for a given plan represents one or more connections to an environment in which the plan could be used.
SYSRELS	Contains one row for every referential constraint.
SYSRESAUTH	Records CREATE IN and PACKADM ON privileges for collections, USAGE privileges for distinct types, and USE privileges for buffer pools, storage groups, and table spaces.
SYSROUTINEAUTH	Records the privileges that users hold on routines. (A routine can be a user-defined function, a cast function, or a stored procedure.)
SYSROUTINES	Contains one row for every routine. (A routine can be a user-defined function, a cast function, or a stored procedure.)
SYSROUTINES_OPTS	Contains one row for each generated routine, such as one created by the DB2 Development Center tool, that records the build options for the routine. Rows in this table can be inserted, updated, and deleted.
SYSSCHEMAAUTH	Contains one or more rows for each user granted a privilege on a particular schema in the database.
SYSSEQUENCEAUTH	Records the privileges that users hold over sequences.
SYSSEQUENCES	Contains one row for each identity column.
SYSSEQUENCESDEP	Records the dependencies of identity columns on tables.
SYSSTMT	Contains one or more rows for each SQL statement of each DBRM.

continues

Table 2-4   DB2 Catalog Tables (Continued)

Table Name (SYSIBM.*table*)	Information Contents
SYSSTOGROUP	Contains one row for each storage group.
SYSSTRINGS	Contains information about character conversion. Each row describes a conversion from one coded character set to another.
SYSSYNONYMS	Contains one row for each synonym of a table or a view.
SYSTABAUTH	Records the privileges that users hold on tables and views.
SYSTABCONST	Contains one row for each unique constraint—primary key or unique key—created in DB2 for OS/390 version 7 or later.
SYSTABLEPART	Contains one row for each nonpartitioned table space and one row for each partition of a partitioned table space.
SYSTABLEPART_HIST	Contains rows from SYSTABLEPART. Rows are added or changed when RUNSTATS collects history statistics. Rows in this table can be inserted, updated, and deleted.
SYSTABLES	Contains one row for each table, view, or alias.
SYSTABLES_HIST	Contains rows from SYSTABLES. Rows are added or changed when RUNSTATS collects history statistics. Rows in this table can be inserted, updated, and deleted.
SYSTABLESPACE	Contains one row for each table space.
SYSTABSTATS	Contains one row for each partition of a partitioned table space. Rows in this table can be inserted, updated, and deleted.
SYSTABSTATS_HIST	Contains rows from SYSTABSTATS. Rows are added or changed when RUNSTATS collects history statistics. Rows in this table can be inserted, updated, and deleted.
SYSTRIGGERS	Contains one row for each trigger.
SYSUSERAUTH	Records the system privileges that users hold.
SYSVIEWDEP	Records the dependencies of views on tables, functions, and other views.
SYSVIEWS	Contains one or more rows for each view.
SYSVOLUMES	Contains one row for each volume of each storage group.
USERNAMES	Uses each row in the table to carry out one of the following operations: • Outbound ID translation • Inbound ID translation and "come from" checking Rows in this table can be inserted, updated, and deleted.

Catalog Consistency Queries

Consistency queries can be executed as part of the migration process to ensure that the data in the catalog is correct. These queries are found in the data set *prefix*.SDSNSAMP(DSNTESQ). These queries test such logical relationships as ensuring that all indexes are created on tables that exist.

The SQL statements can be executed from SPUFI or from a dynamic SQL program, such as DSNTEP2. The queries can be executed on the catalog tables or on copies of the catalog. RUNSTATS should be run on the catalog or the copies to ensure the best performance. In some cases, the queries will perform better when executed on the copies, using the extra indexes as defined for some of the tables.

Following is an example of a catalog consistency query that checks whether all table spaces belong to a defined database. This query will find all the SYSTABLESPACE databases that do not have corresponding rows in SYSDATABASE. The desired—expected—result is to have no rows returned.

```
SELECT DBNAME, NAME
    FROM SYSIBM.SYSTABLESPACE TS
    WHERE NOT EXISTS
      (SELECT *
          FROM SYSIBM.SYSDATABASE DB
          WHERE DB.NAME = TS.DBNAME);
```

DB2 Directory

The DB2 directory is used to store information about the operation and housekeeping of the DB2 environment. This directory, unlike the DB2 catalog, cannot be accessed by using SQL. The DB2 directory contains information required to start DB2; activities and utilities in the DB2 environment do the updating and deleting of table entries in the DB2 directory. The DB2 directory contains five tables: a description of each is given in Table 2-5.

DISTRIBUTED DATA

Using DB2's Distributed Data Facility (DDF) provides access to data held by other data management systems or to make your DB2 data accessible to other systems. A DB2 application program can use SQL to access data at other database management systems (DBMSs) other than the DB2 at which the application's plan is bound. This DB2 is known as the *local DB2*. The local DB2 and the other DBMSs are called *application servers*. Any application server other than the local DB2 is considered a *remote server*, and access to its data is a distributed operation.

Table 2-5 DB2 Directory Tables

Directory Table	Information Contents
SPT01	Referred to as the skeleton package table (SKPT), this table contains information about the access paths and the internal form of the SQL for a package at bind time. Entries are made into this table during bind time (BIND PACKAGE), and entries are deleted when a package is freed (FREE PACKAGE). This table is loaded into memory at execution time, along with the SCT02 table described next.
SCT02	Referred to as the skeleton cursor table (SKCT), this table contains information about access paths and the internal form of the SQL for an application plan. Entries in this table are made when a plan is bound (BIND PLAN) and deleted when a plan is freed (FREE PLAN). This table is also loaded into memory at execution time.
DBD01	Information about DBDs (database descriptors), which are internal control blocks, is kept in this table. Each DB2 database has one DBD for its objects: table spaces, indexes, tables, referential integrity constraints, and check constraints. Updates to this table are made when a database is created or updated. This information is accessed by DB2 in place of continually using the DB2 catalog, permitting faster, more efficient access to this information. The information in the DBD01 directory table is also contained in the DB2 catalog.
SYSLGRNX	Referred to as the log range table, this table contains information from the DB2 logs about the RBA (relative byte address) range for updates. This allows DB2 to efficiently find the RBAs needed from the DB2 logs for recovery purposes. A row is inserted every time a table space or a partition is opened or updated and is updated when the object is closed.
SYSUTILX	This system utilities table stores information about the execution of DB2 utilities, including the status and the steps during execution. This information is used when a utility needs to be restarted. Information in this table is added when a utility is started, and the entry is removed when the execution has ended.

DB2 provides two methods of accessing data at remote application servers: DRDA and DB2 private protocol access. For application servers that support the two-phase commit process, both methods allow for updating data at several remote locations within the same unit of work.

The location name of the DB2 subsystem is defined during DB2 installation. The CDB records the location name and the network address of a remote DBMS. The tables in the CDB are part of the DB2 catalog.

Distributed Relational Database Architecture

With DRDA, the recommended method, the application connects to a server at another location and executes packages that have been previously bound at that server. The application uses a CONNECT statement, a three-part name or, if bound with DBPROTOCOL(DRDA), an alias to access the server.

Queries can originate from any system or application that issues SQL statements as an *application requester* in the formats required by DRDA. DRDA access supports the execution of dynamic SQL statements and SQL statements that satisfy all the following conditions.

- The static statements appear in a package bound to an accessible server.
- The statements are executed using that package.
- The objects involved in the execution of the statements are at the server where the package is bound. If the server is a DB2 subsystem, three-part names and aliases can be used to refer to another DB2 server.

DRDA access can be used in application programs by coding explicit CONNECT statements or by coding three-part names and specifying the DBPROTOCOL (DRDA) bind option. For more on bind options, refer to Chapter 11.

DRDA access is based on a set of DRDA protocols. (These protocols are documented by the Open Group Technical Standard in *DRDA Volume 1: Distributed Relational Database Architecture (DRDA)*.) DRDA communication conventions are invisible to DB2 applications and allow a DB2 to bind and rebind packages at other servers and to execute the statements in those packages.

For two-phase commit using SNA connections, DB2 supports both presumed-abort and presumed-nothing protocols that are defined by DRDA. If you are usingTCP/IP, DB2 uses the sync point manager defined in the documentation for DRDA Level 3.

DB2 Private Protocol

With private protocol, the application must use an alias or a three-part name to direct the SQL statement to a given location. Private protocol works only between application requesters and servers that are both DB2 for z/OS subsystems.

A statement is executed using DB2 private protocol access if it refers to objects that are not at the current server and is implicitly or explicitly bound with DBPROTOCOL (PRIVATE). The *current server* is the DBMS to which an application is actively connected. DB2 private protocol access uses *DB2 private connections*. The statements that can be executed are SQL INSERT, UPDATE, and DELETE and SELECT statements with their associated SQL OPEN, FETCH, and CLOSE statements.

In a program running under DB2, a *three-part name* or an *alias* can refer to a table or a view at another DB2. The location name identifies the other DB2 to the DB2 application server. A three-part name consists of a location, an authorization ID, and an object name. For example, the name NYSERVER.DB2USER1.TEST refers to a table named DB2USER1.TEST at the server whose location name is NYSERVER.

Alias names have the same allowable forms as table or view names. The name can refer to a table or a view at the current server or to a table or a view elsewhere. For more on aliases, refer to Chapter 4.

> **N O T E**   Private protocol does not support many distributed functions, such as TCP/IP or stored procedures. The newer data types, such as LOB or user-defined types, are also not supported by private protocol. It is not the recommended method to use and is no longer being enhanced or supported from version 8 forward.

Communications Protocols

DDF uses TCP/IP or SNA to communicate with other systems. Setting up a network for use by database management systems requires knowledge of both database management and communications. Thus, you must put together a team of people with those skills to plan and implement the network.

TCP/IP

Transmission Control Protocol/Internet Protocol (TCP/IP) is a standard communication protocol for network communications. Previous versions of DB2 supported TCP/IP requesters, although additional software and configuration were required. Native TCP/IP eliminates these requirements, allowing gatewayless connectivity to DB2 for systems running UNIX System Services.

SNA

System Network Architecture (SNA) is the description of the logical structure, formats, protocols, and operational sequences for transmitting information through and controlling the configuration and operation of the networks. It is one of the two main network architectures used for network communications to the enterprise servers.

VTAM

DB2 also uses Virtual Telecommunications Access Method (VTAM) for communicating with remote databases. This is done be assigning two names for the local DB2 subsystem: a location name and a logical unit (LU) name. A *location name* distinguishes a specific database management system in a network, so applications use this name to direct requests to the local DB2 subsystem. Other systems use different terms for a location name. For example, DB2 Connect calls this the *target database name*. DB2 uses the DRDA term, *RDBNAM,* to refer to non-DB2 relational database names.

Communications Database

The DB2 catalog includes the communications database (CDB), which contains several tables that hold information about connections with remote systems. These tables are

- SYSIBM.LOCATIONS
- SYSIBM.LUNAMES
- SYSIBM.IPNAMES
- SYSIBM.MODESELECT
- SYSIBM.USERNAMES
- SYSIBM.LULIST
- SYSIBM.LUMODES

Some of these tables must be populated before data can be requested from remote systems. If this DB2 system services only data requests, the CDB does not have to be populated; the default values can be used.

When sending a request, DB2 uses the LINKNAME column of the SYSIBM.LOCATIONS catalog table to determine which protocol to use.

- To receive VTAM requests, a LUNAME must be selected in installation panel DSNTIPR.
- To receive TCP/IP requests, a DRDA port and a resynchronization port must be selected in installation panel DSNTIP5. TCP/IP uses the server's port number to pass network requests to the correct DB2 subsystem. If the value in the LINKNAME column is found in the SYSIBM.IPNAMES table, TCP/IP is used for DRDA connections. If the value is found in the SYSIBM.LUNAMES table, SNA is used.
- If the same name is in both SYSIBM.LUNAMES and SYSIBM.IPNAMES, TCP/IP is used to connect to the location.

> **N O T E** A requester cannot use both SNA and TCP/IP to connect to a given location. For example, if SYSIBM.LOCATIONS specifies a LINKNAME of LU1, and if LU1 is defined in both the SYSIBM.IPNAMES and SYSIBM.LUNAMES tables, TCP/IP is the only protocol used to connect to LU1 from this requester for DRDA connections. For private protocol connections, the SNA protocols are used. If private protocol connections are being used, the SYSIBM.LUNAMES table must be defined for the remote location's LUNAME.

SUBSYSTEM POOLS

In the DBM1 address space are many objects critical to the operation of DB2. Here, we take a brief look at buffer pools and the RID, EDM, and Sort pools. For tuning information about the performance or use of these pools, refer to Chapter 17.

Buffer Pools

Buffer pools are database objects used to cache database data pages in memory. If an object's data page is placed in a buffer pool, physical input/output (I/O) access to disks will be avoided. Buffer pools can be assigned to cache only a particular table space's data, that is, within the table space definition.

Buffer pools are areas of virtual storage that temporarily store pages of table spaces or indexes. When a program accesses a row of a table, DB2 places the page containing that row in a buffer. When a program changes a row of a table, DB2 must eventually write the data in the buffer back to disk, normally at either a checkpoint or a write threshold. The write thresholds are either vertical—at the page set level—or horizontal—at the buffer pool level. Storage for buffer pools is backed by memory in the DBM1 address space. Prior to version 8, this was limited to 2GB and dataspaces and hiperpools were used to provide more storage. Version 8 has a large area of real addressable memory provided by 64-bit addressability. With 64-bit support DB2 can address up to 16 exabytes (less some operating system overhead). This allows buffer pools to mainly exist in real memory with up to a total of 1TB for all buffer pools in the susbystem.

Up to 80 virtual buffer pools are available. This allows for

- Fifty 4K-page buffer pools (BP0–BP49)
- Ten 32K-page buffer pools (BP32K–BP32K9)
- Ten 8K-page buffer pools
- Ten 16K-page buffer pools

Buffer pools take their space in the DBM1 address space. A single buffer pool can be up to 1TB, but the total of all buffer pools in the subsystem is also 1TB. As mentioned previously, up to 80 buffer pools can be defined. Creating a buffer pool is easily done via an −ALTER BUFFERPOOL command. The following example shows how to create a 3,000-page buffer pool with a sequential threshold of 50 percent:

```
-ALTER BUFFERPOOL (BP3) VPSIZE(3000) VPSEQT(50)
```

(Fifty percent of the buffer pool can be used for sequentially processed pages and 50 percent for randomly processed pages.) For more information on tuning these parameters, refer to Chapter 17.

Each buffer pool can have a different size and different parameter settings. These parameters control such activities as writing changed pages to disk. Changes to the buffer pool sizes and thresholds are also done via the -ALTER BUFFERPOOL command.

Environmental Descriptor Manager Pool

The EDM pool contains many items, including the following:

- EDM DBD cache
  - DBDs (database descriptors)
- EDM pool
  - SKCTs (skeleton cursor tables)
  - CTs (cursor tables, or copies of the SKCTs)
  - SKPTs (skeleton package tables)
  - PTs (package tables, or copies of the SKPTs)
  - Authorization cache block for each plan, except one with CACHESIZE set to 0
- EDM statement cache
  - Skeletons of dynamic SQL for CACHE DYNAMIC SQL

If the pool is too small, you will see increased I/O activity in the following DB2 table spaces, which support the DB2 directory: DSNDB01.DBD01, DSNDB01.SPT01, and DSNDB01.SCT02.

The impact of having too little memory for the statement cache for dynamic SQL is a small hit ratio, causing extra CPU for the full prepares and I/O on the catalog. The main goal for the EDM pool is to limit the I/O against the directory and catalog. If the pool is too small, response times will increase because of the loading of the SKCTs, SKPTs, and DBDs and repreparing the dynamic SQL statements because they could not remain cached.

By correctly sizing the EDM pool, you can avoid unnecessary I/Os from accumulating for a transaction. A SKCT, SKPT, or DBD that has to be reloaded into the EDM pool is additional I/O. This situation can occur if the pool pages are stolen because the EDM pool is too small. Pages in the pool are maintained on an LRU (least recently used) queue, and the least recently used pages are stolen, if required. In version 8, the DBD cache and dynamic statement cache sizes are separately configurable. EDM pool structures are mainly located above the 2GB bar.

Row Identifier Pool

The RID pool is used for storing and sorting RIDs for such operations as

- List prefetch
- Multiple index access
- Hybrid joins
- Enforcing unique keys while updating multiple rows

The optimizer looks at the size of the RID pool for prefetch and RID use. The full use of the RID pool is possible for any single user at runtime. Runtime can result in a table space scan if not enough space is available in the RID. For example, if you want to retrieve 10,000 rows from a 100,000,000-row table and no RID pool is available, a scan of 100,000,000 rows would occur, at any time and without external notification. The optimizer assumes that physical I/O will be less with a large pool.

The size is set with an installation parameter (128 KB–10,000 MB). The RID pool is created at start-up time, but no space is allocated until RID storage is needed. It is then allocated above the 16MB line in 16KB blocks as needed, until the maximum size you specified on installation panel DSNTIPC is reached. Some of the RID pool, 25 percent, is located below the 2GB bar and the remainder is located above the 2GB bar.

Sort Pool

At startup, DB2 allocates a sort pool in the private area of the DBM1 address space. DB2 uses a special sorting technique, called a tournament sort. During the sorting processes, this algorithm commonly produces logical work files called runs, which are intermediate sets of ordered data. If the sort pool is large enough, the sort completes in that area. More often than not, the sort cannot complete in the sort pool, and the runs are moved into the DSNDB07 work files that are used to perform sorts. These runs are later merged to complete the sort. When DSNDB07 is used for holding the pages that make up the sort runs, you could experience performance degradation if the pages get externalized to the physical work files, as they will have to be read back in later in order to complete the sort.

The sort pool size is also defined by a DSNZPARM and is currently 240KB to 128MB, with a 2MB default.

SUMMARY

This chapter examined most of the components that make up the DB2 environment. The operating systems for DB2 on a zSeries enterprise server are based on the core operating system of MVS. Within this structure, several address spaces make up the environment, and each address space is allocated certain functions. The main components of DB2 and all its managers are in the DBAS and SSAS. The IRLM communicates with DB2 and provides the internal lock manager.

Across the environment are security services, as a total umbrella to provide many levels of security. The highest level is the component called Security Server, which houses RACF.

DB2I and SPUFI are only two of several interfaces to DB2 but provide most of the direct interface to DB2 for DBAs and developers. SPUFI is used as a method of submitting batches of SQL statements, and DB2I as a real-time interface.

The installation process, performed from TSO or the msys for Setup DB2 Customization Center, is focused primarily on picking options for the many DSNZPARMs, the configuration parameters for DB2. More than 123 parameters can be modified online, without taking an outage.

The DB2 environment has six categories of commands and many utilities. The DSN commands and the DB2 commands are used the most.

The DB2 catalog and directory comprise the control repository for the environment. There are a large number of catalog tables, populated primarily by SQL DDL and DCL, for every object creation and modification.

We briefly examined the distributed networks architecture of SNA and TCP/IP and looked at how DRDA provides the services on top of those layers. Other subsystems objects, such as the buffer pools, the EDM pool, the RID pool, and the Sort pool, were discussed in terms of how DB2 uses them. These objects will be revisited in Chapter 17.

ADDITIONAL RESOURCES

IBM DB2 UDB for z/OS Version 8 Installation Guide (GC18-7418)

IBM DB2 UDB for z/OS Version 8 Utility Guide and Reference (SC18-7427)

IBM DB2 UDB for z/OS Version 8 Administration Guide (SC18-7413)

IBM DB2 UDB for z/OS Version 8 SQL Reference (SC18-7426)

Open Group Technical Standard in DRDA Volume 1: Distributed Relational Database Architecture (DRDA)

www.opengroup.com for information on DRDA

SNA LU 6.2 Peer Protocols Reference

CHAPTER 3

DB2 Access and Security

- Subsystem access
- Data set protection
- Access to DB2 objects
- Multilevel security
- Auditing

Security is an important consideration whenever data is stored in a relational database management system. This chapter discusses various methods of controlling data access. Access to data within DB2 is controlled at many levels, including subsystem, database objects, and application plan/packages. Authentication of user IDs and passwords is discussed. Groups of typical database users, such as database administrators, system administrators, transactional processing personnel, and decision support users are configured. Each of these database user types may require different access privileges. Another topic discussed is how to perform auditing, which allows you to monitor access and manipulation of data. Figure 3-1 shows several routes from a process to DB2 data, with controls on every route.

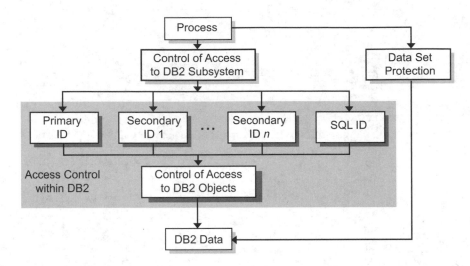

Figure 3-1   DB2 data access control

SUBSYSTEM ACCESS

Whether a process can gain access to a specific DB2 subsystem can be controlled outside of DB2. A common procedure is to grant access only through RACF or a similar security system. DB2 address spaces and profiles for access to DB2 from various environments are defined as resources to RACF. These profiles are identified by the subsystem and the environment. Environments include

- MASS for IMS
- SASS for CICS
- DIST for DDF
- RRSAF for RRSAF
- BATCH for TSO, CAF, utilities, DB2 SPAS

Each request to access DB2 is associated with an ID. RACF checks that the ID is authorized for DB2 resources and permits or refuses access to DB2. The RACF system provides several advantages of its own. For example, RACF can

- Identify and verify the identifier associated with a process
- Connect those identifiers to RACF group names
- Log and report unauthorized attempts to access protected resources

Local DB2 Access

A local DB2 user is subject to several checks even before reaching DB2. For example, if you are running a program that accesses DB2 under TSO and using the TSO log-on ID as the DB2 primary authorization ID, that ID was verified with a password when the user logged on to TSO. When the user gains access to DB2, a user-written or IBM-supplied exit routine called by DB2 can check the authorization ID further, change it, and associate it with secondary IDs. In providing these services, DB2 can use the services of an external security system.

Remote Access

A remote user is also subject to several checks before reaching your DB2 subsystem. You can use RACF or a similar security subsystem to control access from remote subsystems and clients.

RACF also provides the ability to

- Verify an identifier associated with a remote attachment request and check it with a password.
- Generate *Pass Tickets* on the sending side. PassTickets can be used instead of passwords. A PassTicket lets a user gain access to a host system without sending the RACF password across the network.

> **NOTE** DB2's communications database does allow some control of authentication in that you can cause IDs to be translated before sending them to the remote system. For more information about accessing DB2 and the CDB, refer to Chapter 2.

IMS and CICS Security

Access to DB2 can also be controlled from within IMS or CICS.

- IMS terminal security lets you limit the entry of a transaction code to a particular logical terminal (LTERM) or group of LTERMs in the system. To protect a particular program, you can authorize a transaction code to be entered only from any terminal on a list of LTERMs. Alternatively, you can associate each LTERM with a list of the transaction codes that a user can enter from that LTERM. IMS then passes the validated LTERM name to DB2 as the initial primary authorization ID. IMS can also use RACF or another security product for identification and authentication. LTERM usage is less popular.
- CICS transaction code security works with RACF to control the transactions and programs that can access DB2. Within DB2, you can use the ENABLE and DISABLE options of the bind operation to limit package access to specific CICS subsystems.

Kerberos Security

Kerberos security is a network security technology developed at the Massachusetts Institute of Technology. DB2 for z/OS can use Kerberos security services to authenticate remote users. With Kerberos security services, remote end users access DB2 when they issue their Kerberos name and password. This same name and password are used for access thoughout the network, so a separate MVS password to access DB2 is not necessary.

The Kerberos security technology does not require passwords to flow in readable text, making it secure even in client/server environments. This flexibility is possible because Kerberos uses an authentication technology that encrypts tickets that contain authentication information for the end user.

DB2 support for Kerberos security requires RACF or the functional equivalent. The Network Authentication and Privacy Service provides Kerberos support and relies on a security product, such as RACF, to provide registry support.

> **N O T E**   You can use Kerberos security only if you have RACF.

DATA SET PROTECTION

The data in a DB2 subsystem is contained in data sets, which might be accessed without going through DB2 at all. If the data is sensitive, you want to control that access route.

If RACF or a similar security system is being used to control access to DB2, the simplest means of controlling data set access outside of DB2 is to use RACF for that purpose also. That means defining RACF profiles for data sets and permitting access to them for certain DB2 IDs.

If the data is very sensitive, you may want to consider encrypting it for protection against unauthorized access to data sets and backup copies outside DB2. You can use DB2 edit procedures or field procedures to encrypt data, and those routines can use the Integrated Cryptographic Service Facility (ICSF) of MVS. Use of these routines to encrypt data only protects that data from inappropriate access outside of DB2. Any data retrieval using an SQL statement would access encrypted data values.

Data compression is not a substitute for encryption. In some cases, the compression method does not shorten the data, leaving it uncompressed and readable. If you both encrypt and compress data, compress it first to obtain the maximum compression, and then encrypt the result. When retrieving, take the steps in reverse order: Decrypt the data first, and then decompress the result. Many encryption algorithms compress data before encrypting it. DB2 also provides built-in functions to encrypt and decrypt data values where each column or row could use a different encryption phrase or password.

ACCESS TO DB2 OBJECTS

An individual process can be represented by a primary authorization identifier (ID), possibly one or more secondary IDs, and an SQL ID. The use of IDs is affected by the security and network systems and by the DB2 connections made.

DB2 controls access to objects by assigning privileges and authorities to either primary or secondary IDs. Ownership of an object carries with it a set of related privileges over the object. An ID can own an object it creates or can create an object to be owned by another ID. Creation and ownership have separate controls. We look at how privileges, authorities, and ownership work together to provide security for access to DB2 objects.

Executing a plan or a package exercises implicitly all the privileges that the owner needed when binding it. Hence, granting the privilege to execute can provide a finely detailed set of privileges and can eliminate the need to grant other privileges separately.

> **N O T E**   You can use RACF access control to supplement or replace the DB2 GRANT and REVOKE operations.

Explicit Privileges and Authorities

One way of controlling access within DB2 is by granting, not granting, or revoking explicit privileges and authorities to authorization IDs. A privilege allows a specific operation, sometimes on a specific object. An explicit privilege has a name and is held as the result of an SQL GRANT or REVOKE statement. The authorities group these privileges together. Both privileges and authorities are held by authorization IDs.

> **N O T E**   When installing or updating DB2, the entire system of control within DB2 can be disabled by setting USE PROTECTION to NO DB2. If protection in DB2 is disabled, any user who gains access can do anything, but no GRANT or REVOKE statements are allowed.

Authorization IDs

Every process that connects to or signs on to DB2 is represented by a set of one or more DB2 short identifiers called authorization IDs. Authorization IDs can be assigned to a process by default procedures or by user-written exit routines.

Primary Authorization ID

A primary authorization ID is assigned to every process. A process will have only one primary authorization ID, and it is normally used to uniquely identify a process.

Secondary Authorization ID

A secondary authorization ID is optional and can hold additional privileges. Secondary authorizations are often used for groups, such as RACF groups. A primary authorization ID can be associated with multiple secondary authorization IDs.

> **N O T E**   A new user who is added to an RACF group is visible the next time he or she logs on to TSO.

Current SQL ID

Either the primary ID or the secondary ID can be the current SQL ID at any given time. Either the primary or secondary ID is designated as the current SQL ID. You can change the value of the SQL ID during your session. If DB2EXPT is your primary or one of your secondary authorization IDs, you can make it your current SQL ID by issuing the SQL statement:

```
SET CURRENT SQLID ='DB2EXPT';
```

An ID with SYSADM authority can set the current SQL ID to any string of up to 8 bytes, whether or not it is an authorization ID or associated with the process that is running.

Explicit Privileges

Several explicit privileges can be granted to a primary or a secondary authorization ID, allowing that ID the privilege of performing a particular task. When some privileges are granted, they also provide an inherited authority; for example, if CREATEDBA is granted to an ID, that ID will become DBADM (database administrator authority) over the database it creates.

The privileges are grouped into several categories:

- Table
- Plan
- Package
- Collection
- Database
- Subsystem
- Use
- Schema
- Distinct type
- Routine

Table 3-1 lists the available privileges that can be granted to a primary or secondary authorization ID and the type of use associated with the privilege.

> **N O T E**   Additional privileges are available for statements, commands, and utility jobs.

Table 3-1   Privilege Categories and Functions

Privilege	Function
Table	
ALTER	ALTER TABLE: to change the table definition
DELETE	DELETE: to delete rows
INDEX	CREATE INDEX: to create an index on the table
INSERT	INSERT: to insert rows
REFERENCES	ALTER or CREATE TABLE: to add or remove a referential constraint referring to the named table or to a list of columns in the table
SELECT	SELECT: to retrieve data from the table
TRIGGER	CREATE TRIGGER: to define a trigger on a table
ALL	SELECT, UPDATE, DELETE, and UPDATE
Plan	
BIND	BIND, REBIND, and FREE PLAN: to bind or free the plan
EXECUTE	RUN: to use the plan when running the application
Package	
BIND	The BIND, REBIND, and FREE PACKAGE subcommands and the DROP PACKAGE statement: to bind or free the package and, depending on the installation option, BIND NEW PACKAGE: to bind a new version of a package
COPY	The COPY option of BIND PACKAGE: to copy a package
EXECUTE	Inclusion of the package in the PKLIST option of BIND PLAN
ALL	All package privileges
Collection	
CREATE IN	Naming the collection in the BIND PACKAGE subcommand
Database	
CREATETAB	The CREATE TABLE statement: to create tables in the database
CREATETS	The CREATE TABLESPACE statement: to create table spaces in the database
DISPLAYDB	The DISPLAY DATABASE command: to display the database status

continues

Table 3-1   Privilege Categories and Functions (Continued)

Privilege	Function
DROP	The DROP and ALTER DATABASE statements: to drop or alter the database
IMAGCOPY	The QUIESCE, COPY, and MERGECOPY utilities: to prepare for, make, and merge copies of table spaces in the database; the MODIFY utility: to remove records of copies
LOAD	The LOAD utility: to load tables in the database
RECOVERDB	The RECOVER, REBUILD INDEX, and REPORT utilities: to recover objects in the database and report their recovery status
REORG	The REORG utility: to reorganize objects in the database
REPAIR	The REPAIR and DIAGNOSE utilities, except REPAIR DBD and DIAGNOSE WAIT: to generate diagnostic information about, and repair data in, objects in the database
STARTDB	The START DATABASE command: to start the database
STATS	The RUNSTATS and CHECK utilities: to gather statistics and check indexes and referential constraints for objects in the database
STOPDB	The STOP DATABASE command: to stop the database
Subsystem	
ARCHIVE	The ARCHIVE LOG command: to archive the current active log; the DISPLAY ARCHIVE command: to give information about input archive logs; the SET LOG command: to modify the checkpoint frequency specified during installation; and the SET ARCHIVE command: to control allocation and deallocation of tape units for archive processing.
BINDADD	The BIND subcommand with the ADD option: to create new plans and packages
BINDAGENT	The BIND, REBIND, and FREE subcommands, and the DROP PACKAGE statement: on behalf of the grantor, to bind, rebind, or free a plan or a package or to copy a package. The BINDAGENT provides separation of duties, with relatively weak security. A bind agent with the EXECUTE privilege might be able to gain all the authority of the grantor of BINDAGENT.
BSDS	The RECOVER BSDS command: to recover the bootstrap data set
CREATEALIAS	The CREATE ALIAS statement: to create an alias for a table or a view name
CREATEDBA	The CREATE DATABASE statement: to create a database and have DBADM authority over it
CREATEDBC	The CREATE DATABASE statement: to create a database and have DBCTRL authority over it

Table 3-1 Privilege Categories and Functions (Continued)

Privilege	Function
CREATESG	The CREATE STOGROUP statement: to create a storage group
CREATETMTAB	The CREATE GLOBAL TEMPORARY TABLE statement: to define a created temporary table
DISPLAY	The DISPLAY ARCHIVE, DISPLAY BUFFERPOOL, DISPLAY DATABASE, DISPLAY LOCATION, DISPLAY LOG, DISPLAY THREAD, and DISPLAY TRACE commands: to display system information
MONITOR1	Receive trace data that is not potentially sensitive
MONITOR2	Receive all trace data
RECOVER	The RECOVER INDOUBT command: to recover threads
STOPALL	The STOP DB2 command: to stop DB2
STOSPACE	The STOSPACE utility: to obtain data about space usage
TRACE	The START TRACE, STOP TRACE, and MODIFY TRACE commands: to control tracing
Use	
USE OF BUFFERPOOL	A buffer pool
USE OF STOGROUP	A storage group
USE OF TABLESPACE	A table space
Schema	
CREATEIN	Create distinct types, user-defined functions, triggers, and stored procedures in the designated schemas
ALTERIN	Alter user-defined functions or stored procedures; specify a comment for distinct types, user-defined functions, triggers, and stored procedures in the designated schemas
DROPIN	Drop distinct types, user-defined functions, triggers, and stored procedures in the designated schemas
Distinct Type	
USAGE ON DISTINCT TYPE	A distinct type

continues

Table 3-1   Privilege Categories and Functions (Continued)

Privilege	Function
Routine	
EXECUTE ON FUNCTION	A user-defined function
EXECUTE ON PROCEDURE	A stored procedure

Granting and Revoking Privileges

The privileges in Table 3-1 must be granted to an authorization ID. The GRANT and REVOKE statements are part of the DCL.

In order to grant DB2EXPT the ability to select data from a particular table, we must execute the following SQL statement:

```
GRANT SELECT ON DB2CERT.TEST_TAKEN TO DB2EXPT
```

To grant DB2EXPT the ability to bind packages to the CERTCL collection, we would execute the following statement:

```
GRANT BIND ON PACKAGE CERTCL.* TO DB2EXPT
```

To grant DB2EXPT the ability to bind new packages to the CERTCL collection, we would execute the following statements:

```
GRANT CREATE IN COLLECTION CERTCL TO DB2EXPT
GRANT BINDADD TO DB2EXPT
```

To grant everyone the ability to select, update, insert, or delete data from a particular table, we could execute the following SQL statement:

```
GRANT ALL ON DB2CERT.TEST_TAKEN TO PUBLIC
```

> **NOTE**   The keyword PUBLIC allows any user to have the privilege granted.

To take away everyone's priviledge to delete data from a particular table, we must execute the following SQL statement:

```
REVOKE DELETE ON DB2CERT.TEST_TAKEN FROM PUBLIC
```

Revoking a privilege from a user can also cause that privilege to be revoked from other users. This is called a *cascade revoke*.

Related and Inherited Privileges

DB2 has defined sets of related privileges that are identified by *administrative authorities*. This grouping makes it easier to administrate authority; instead of having to grant several individual privileges to an ID, one can simple grant the administrative authority, which includes all applicable privileges.

Some privileges are inherited with object ownership.

Authorities

An *administrative authority* is a set of privileges that often cover a related set of objects (see Table 3-2). Authorities often include privileges that are not explicit, have no name, and cannot be specifically granted. An example is the ability to terminate any utility job, which is included in the SYSOPR authority.

Table 3-2   Administrative Authorities

Authorization	Capabilities	Privileges
Installation SYSADM	Assigned during DB2 installation. This ID has all the privileges of SYSADM, as well as the following. • Authority is *not* recorded in the DB2 catalog, which need not be available to check installation SYSADM authority. (The authority outside the catalog is crucial: If the catalog table space SYSDBAUT is stopped, for example, DB2 cannot check the authority to start it again. Only an installation SYSADM can start it.) • This can be revoked only by changing the module that contains the subsystem initialization parameters—typically, DSNZPARM. • Those IDs can also run the CATMAINT utility, access DB2 when the subsystem is started with ACCESS(MAINT), start databases DSNDB01 and DSNDB06 when they are stopped or in restricted status, run the DIAGNOSE utility with the WAIT statement, and start and stop the database containing the application registration table (ART) and object registration table (ORT).	All privileges of all the authorities

continues

Table 3-2   Administrative Authorities (Continued)

Authorization	Capabilities	Privileges
SYSCTRL	Almost complete control of the DB2 subsystem but *cannot* access user data directly unless granted the privilege to do so. Designed for administering a system containing sensitive data, SYSCTRL can • Act as installation SYSOPR—when the catalog is available—or DBCTRL over any database • Run any allowable utility on any database • Issue a COMMENT ON, LABEL ON, or LOCK TABLE statement for any table • Create a view for itself or others on any catalog table • Create tables and aliases for itself or others • Bind a new plan or package, naming any ID as the owner Without additional privileges, it *cannot* • Execute DML (Data Manipulation Language) statements on user tables or views • Run plans or packages • Set the current SQL ID to a value that is not one of its primary or secondary IDs • Start or stop the database containing the ART and ORT • Act fully as SYSADM or as DBADM over any database • Access DB2 when the subsystem is started with ACCESS(MAINT) Note: SYSCTRL authority provides relatively weak security.	System privileges: • BINDADD • BINDAGENT • CREATEDBC • CREATESG • BSDS • CREATETMTAB • CREATEALIAS • CREATEDBA • MONITOR1 • MONITOR2 • STOSPACE Privileges on all tables: • ALTER INDEX • REFERENCES • TRIGGER Privileges on catalog tables: • SELECT • UPDATE • INSERT • DELETE Privileges on all plans: BIND Privileges on all packages: • BIND • COPY Privileges on all collections: • CREATE IN Privileges on all schemas: • CREATE IN • DROPIN • ALTERIN Use privileges on • BUFFERPOOL • TABLESPACE • STOGROUP

Table 3-2   Administrative Authorities (Continued)

Authorization	Capabilities	Privileges
SYSADM	Includes SYSCTRL, as well as access to all data. SYSADM can • Use all the privileges of DBADM over any database • Use EXECUTE and BIND on any plan or package and COPY on any package • Use privileges over views that are owned by others • Set the current SQL ID to any valid value, whether it is currently a primary or a secondary authorization ID • Create and drop synonyms and views for others on any table • Use any valid value for OWNER in BIND or REBIND • Drop database DSNDB07 • Grant any of the preceding privileges to others • Drop or alter any DB2 object, except system databases, issue a COMMENT ON or LABEL ON statement for any table or view, and terminate any utility job, but SYSADM cannot specifically grant those privileges	All privileges held by SYSCTRL and DBADM Plan privileges: EXECUTE Package privileges: • BIND • COPY • FREE Routine privileges: EXECUTE Distinct type privileges: USAGE
SYSOPR	• Issue most DB2 commands except ARCHIVE LOG, START DATABASE, STOP DATABASE, and RECOVER BSDS • Ability to terminate any utility job • Ability to execute the DSN1SDMP utility	Privileges: • DISPLAY • STOPALL • RECOVER • TRACE Privileges on routines: • START DISPLAY • STOP

continues

Table 3-2   Administrative Authorities (Continued)

Authorization	Capabilities	Privileges
Installation SYSOPR	Assigned during DB2 installation. Privileges in addition to SYSOPR: • Authority is not recorded in the DB2 catalog, which need not be available to check installation SYSOPR authority. • The authority can be revoked only by changing the module that contains the subsystem initialization parameters—typically, DSNZPARM. • Access DB2 when the subsystem is started with ACCESS(MAINT). • Run all allowable utilities on the directory and catalog databases (DSNDB01 and DSNDB06). • Run the REPAIR utility with the DBD statement. • Start and stop the database containing the ART and ORT. • Issue dynamic SQL statements that are not controlled by the DB2 governor. Issue a START DATABASE command to recover objects that have LPL (Logical Page List) entries or group buffer pool recovery-pending status. These IDs cannot change the access mode.	All privileges held by SYSOPR System privileges: ARCHIVE STARTDB (cannot change access mode)
PACKADM	Has all package privileges on all packages in specific collections or on all collections, as well as the CREATE IN privilege on those collections. If the installation option BIND NEW PACKAGE is BIND, PACKADM also has the privilege to add new packages or new versions of existing packages.	Privileges on a collection: CREATE IN Privileges on all packages in the collection: • EXECUTE • BIND • COPY
DBMAINT	Granted for a specific database, in which the ID can create certain objects, run certain utilities, and issue certain commands. Can use the TERM UTILITY command to terminate all utilities except DIAGNOSE, REPORT, and STOSPACE on the database.	Privileges on one database: • CREATETAB • STARTDB • CREATETS • STATS • DISPLAYDB • STOPDB • IMAGCOPY

Table 3-2   Administrative Authorities (Continued)

Authorization	Capabilities	Privileges
DBCTRL*	In addition to DBMAINT privileges, it can also run utilities that can change the data.	All privileges held by DBMAINT on a database Privileges on one database: • DROP LOAD • RECOVERDB REORG • REPAIR
DBADM	In addition to the privileges held by DBCTRL over a specific database, DBADM has privileges to access any of its tables through SQL statements. Can also drop and alter any table space, table, or index in the database and issue a COMMENT ON, LABEL ON, or LOCK TABLE statement for any table. If the value of field DBADM CREATE VIEW on installation panel DSNTIPP was set to YES during DB2 installation, a user with DBADM authority can create a view for another user ID on any table or combination of tables and views in a database.	All privileges held by DBCTRL on a database Privileges on tables and views in one database: • ALTER • INSERT • DELETE • SELECT • INDEX • UPDATE • REFERENCES • TRIGGER

*   DBCTRL authority is a good way to give a DBA all the necessary privileges needed, without the ability to access the data itself.

Granting and Revoking Authorities

The authorities in Table 3-2 must be granted to an authorization ID. As with privileges, this can be done via the GRANT and REVOKE statements.

In order to grant DB2EXPT DBADM authority on the DB2CERT database, the following statement must be issued:

```
GRANT DBADM ON DATABASE DB2CERT TO DB2EXPT
```

In order to remove PACKADM authority from DB2EXPT, the following statement must be issued:

```
REVOKE PACKADM FROM DB2EXPT
```

WITH GRANT Option

If an authority is granted with the WITH GRANT option, the holder can grant the privileges contained in that authority to others. In order to grant DB2EXPT DBADM authority on the DB2CERT database and allow DB2EXPT to give this authority to others, the following statement must be issued:

```
GRANT DBADM ON DATABASE DB2CERT TO DB2EXPT WITH GRANT OPTION
```

> **N O T E**   If the DBADM authority is ever revoked from DB2EXPT, any ID that has been granted DBADM from this ID will also be automatically revoked. This is the primary reason why administrative authorities should be given to a role or group, rather than an individual authority.

Ownership

Implicit privileges are included with ownership of an object. When you create DB2 objects, except for plans and packages, which are bound by issuing SQL CREATE statements in which you name the object, you establish ownership. The owner implicitly holds certain privileges over it.

> **N O T E**   The privileges inherent in the ownership of an object cannot be revoked.

Unqualified Objects

The qualifier (or schema name) of tables, views, indexes, and aliases is the same as the owner. Synonyms are always unqualified. The schema name of stored procedures, user-defined functions, distinct types, triggers, and sequences may be different from the owner. If an object name is unqualified, how ownership of the object is established depends on the type of object. Ownership of tables, views, indexes, aliases, and synonyms with unqualified names is established differently from ownership of user-defined functions, stored procedures, distinct types, sequences, and triggers with unqualified names. This section describes how ownership is established for each group of objects.

If the name of a table, view, index, alias, or synonym is unqualified, you establish the object's ownership in one of two ways. If the CREATE statement was issued dynamically, via SPUFI or QMF, the owner of the created object is the current SQL ID of the issuer. That ID must have the privileges needed to create the object.

If the CREATE statement was issued statically, via execution of a plan or package that contains it, the ownership of the created object depends on the option used for the bind operation. The plan or package can be bound with the OWNER option.

- With the QUALIFIER option only, the qualifier is the owner of the object. The QUALIFIER option allows the binder to name a qualifier to use for all unqualified names of tables, views, indexes, aliases, or synonyms that appear in the plan or package.
- With the OWNER option only, the owner is the owner of the object.
- If neither option is specified, the binder of the plan or package is implicitly the object owner.

> **N O T E** The plan or package owner must have all required privileges on the objects designated by the qualified names.

Explicitly establishing the ownership of a user-defined function, stored procedure, distinct type, sequence, or trigger can be done in the following ways.

- If the CREATE statement is issued dynamically, the owner of the created object is the current SQL ID of the issuer. That ID must have the privileges needed to create the object.
- If the CREATE statement is issued statically—by running a plan or package that contains it—the owner of the object is the plan or package owner. The OWNER bind option can be used to explicitly name the object owner. If the OWNER bind option is used, the binder of the package or plan is implicitly the object owner.

Qualified Objects

If an object name is qualified during creation, establishing ownership of the object depends, again, on the type of object. For tables, views, indexes, aliases, or synonyms created with a qualified name, the qualifier becomes the owner of the object, subject to these restrictions for specifying the qualifier.

- If you issue the CREATE statement dynamically and have no administrative authority, the qualifier must be your primary ID or one of your secondary IDs.
- If the CREATE statement is issued statically and if the owner of the plan or package that contains the statement has no administrative authority, the qualifier can be only the owner. However, if the owner has at least DBCTRL authority, the plan or package can use any qualifier for a table or an index. If the owner has SYSADM or SYSCTRL authority, the plan or package can also use any qualifier for a view or an alias.

N O T E   If your current SQL ID has at least DBCTRL authority, you can use any qualifier for a table, index, view, or alias. If the current SQL ID has at least DBCTRL authority, the qualifier ID does not need any privileges. Otherwise, the SQL ID must have any additional privileges needed to create the object. If the current SQL ID does not have at least DBCTRL authority, the qualifier ID must hold all the necessary privileges.

Schema Name

If you create a distinct type, user-defined function, stored procedure, trigger, or sequence with a qualified name, the qualifier will be the *schema name,* which identifies the schema to which the object belongs. You can think of all objects that are qualified by the same schema name as a group of related objects. But this qualifier does not identify the owner of the object. You establish ownership of a distinct type, user-defined function, stored procedure, trigger, or sequence in these ways.

- If the CREATE statement is issued dynamically, the owner of the created object is your current SQL ID. That ID must have the privileges needed to create the object.
- If the CREATE statement is issued statically—by running a plan or package that contains it—the owner of the object is the plan or package owner. The OWNER bind option can be used to explicitly name the object owner. If the OWNER bind option is not used, the binder of the package or plan is the implicit object owner.

If the schema name is omitted during the creation of one of these objects, DB2 will determine the schema name using the following methods.

- If the CREATE statement is issued dynamically, the schema name of the created object is your current SQL ID.
- If the CREATE statement is issued statically, by running a plan or package that contains it, the schema name of the object is the plan or package qualifier. The QUALIFIER bind option can be used to explicitly name the object qualifier. If the QUALIFIER bind option is not specified, the owner is used.

For more information on schemas, refer to Chapter 15.

Privileges of Ownership by Object

Table 3-3 shows the privileges inherited with ownership of an object.

Table 3-3   Inherited Privileges

Object Type	Implicit Privileges of Ownership
Storage group	• ALTER or DROP the storage group • Name it in the USING clause of a CREATE INDEX or CREATE TABLESPACE statement
Database	• DBCTRL or DBADM authority over the database, depending on the privilege (CREATEDBC or CREATEDBA) used to create it
Table space	• ALTER or DROP the table space • Name it in the IN clause of a CREATE TABLE statement
Table	• ALTER or DROP the table or any indexes on it • Use LOCK TABLE, COMMENT ON, or LABEL on it • CREATE an index or view on the table • SELECT or UPDATE any row or column • INSERT or DELETE any row • Use of the LOAD utility for the table • Define referential constraints on any table or set of columns • CREATE a trigger on the table
Index	ALTER or DROP the index
View	• DROP, COMMENT ON, or LABEL the view or SELECT any row or column • UPDATE any row or column • INSERT or DELETE any row, if the view is not read-only
Synonym	USE or DROP the synonym
Package	BIND, REBIND, FREE, COPY, EXECUTE, or DROP the package
Plan	BIND, REBIND, FREE, or EXECUTE the plan
Alias	DROP the alias
Distinct type	USE or DROP a distinct type
User-defined functions	EXECUTE, ALTER, DROP, START, STOP, or DISPLAY a user-defined function
Stored procedure	EXECUTE, ALTER, DROP, START, STOP, or DISPLAY a stored procedure
Sequence	Use (USAGE), ALTER, COMMENT ON, or DROP

Plan or Package Ownership

An application plan or a package can take many actions, all of them requiring one or more privileges, on many tables. The owner of the plan or package must hold every required privilege. Another ID can execute the plan or package if it has only the EXECUTE privilege. In that way, another ID can exercise all the privileges used in validating the plan or package but only within the restrictions imposed by the SQL statements in the original program.

The executing ID can use some of the owner's privileges, within limits. If the privileges are revoked from the owner, the plan or the package is invalidated. It must be rebound, and the new owner must have the required privileges.

If an attempt to execute the plan or package occurs prior to the rebind (and automatic rebinds are permitted), DB2 will attempt to rebind the plan/package; if the owner does not have the privileges at that time, the plan/package will be marked inoperative.

The BIND and REBIND subcommands create or change an application plan or a package. On either subcommand, use the OWNER option to name the owner of the resulting plan or package.

If the OWNER option is used:

- Any user can name the owner using their primary or any of their secondary IDs.
- An ID with the BINDAGENT privilege can name the grantor of that privilege.
- An ID with SYSCTRL or SYSADM authority can name any authorization ID on a BIND command but not on a REBIND command.

If the OWNER option is omitted:

- BIND: primary ID becomes the owner
- REBIND: previous owner retains ownership

Unqualified Names

A plan or a package can contain SQL statements that use unqualified table view and alias names. For static SQL, the default qualifier for those names is the owner of the plan or package. However, you can use the QUALIFIER option of the BIND command to specify a different qualifier.

For plans or packages that contain static SQL, using the BINDAGENT privilege and the OWNER and QUALIFIER options gives you considerable flexibility in performing bind operations. For plans or packages that contain dynamic SQL, the DYNAMICRULES behavior determines how DB2 qualifies unqualified object names.

For DML statements with unqualified distinct types, user-defined functions, stored procedures, and trigger names in dynamic SQL statements, DB2 finds the schema name to use as the qualifier by searching schema names in the CURRENT PATH special register. For static statements, the PATH bind option determines the path that DB2 searches to resolve unqualified distinct types, user-defined functions, stored procedures, sequences, and trigger names.

However, an exception exists for ALTER, CREATE, DROP, COMMENT ON, GRANT, and REVOKE statements. For static SQL, specify the qualifier for these statements in the QUALIFIER bind option. For dynamic SQL, the qualifier for these statements is the authorization ID of the CURRENT SQLID special register.

Plan Execution Authorization

The owner of the plan or package must have authorization to execute all static SQL statements embedded in the plan or package. These authorizations do not need to be in place when the plan or package is bound; nor do the objects that are referred to need to exist at that time.

A bind operation always checks whether a local object exists and whether the owner has the required privileges on it. Any failure results in a message. To choose whether the failure prevents the bind operation from completing, use the VALIDATE option of BIND PLAN and BIND PACKAGE and also the SQLERROR option of BIND PACKAGE. If you let the operation complete, the checks are made again at runtime. The corresponding checks for remote objects are always made at runtime. Authorization to execute dynamic SQL statements is also checked at runtime. The authorization ID used for this check is determined by the DYNAMICRULES bind option. In order to include a package in a plan's PKLIST, the owner will need to be given execute authority on the package.

For more information on plans and packages, refer to Chapter 11.

Catalog Table Information for Object Access

Table 3-4 contains information about privileges and authorities being held on various objects in the DB2 subsystem.

Table 3-4   DB2 Privileges and Authorities

DB2 Catalog Table	Information
SYSIBM.SYSCOLAUTH	Updating column authority
SYSIBM.SYSDBAUTH	Database privileges
SYSIBM.SYSPLANAUTH	Plan privileges
SYSIBM.SYSPACKAUTH	Package privileges
SYSIBM.SYSRESAUTH	Buffer pool, storage group, collection, table space, and distinct type usage privileges
SYSIBM.SYSROUTINEAUTH	User-defined functions and stored procedure privileges
SYSIBM.SYSSCHEMAAUTH	Schema privileges
SYSIBM.SYSTABAUTH	Tables and views privileges
SYSIBM.SYSUSERAUTH	System authorities

Views

Views can be used to control what data a user can see: certain columns, certain rows, or even a combination. Using views is another way to further restrict access to data. A view is created that allows users to see only certain columns or rows; users are allowed access to the view, not to the base table.

The following example allows the user of the view to see test scores for candidates who took the test at test center 001.

```
CREATE VIEW TEST01
AS
SELECT SCORES
FROM DB2CERT.TEST_TAKEN
WHERE TCID = 001
```

MULTILEVEL SECURITY

Multilevel security permits a more granular scheme of setting security, combining hierarchical and categorical security schemes. Multilevel security can be used to prevent individuals from accessing data at a higher security level or viewing declassifying data.

DB2 z/OS version 8 supports multilevel security at row level. DB2 restricts individual user access to a specific set of rows in a table. This security method requires z/OS 1.5 RACF.

Security enforcement is automatically performed at statement runtime. New security checks are performed that are difficult to express using SQL views or queries. Multilevel security does not rely on special views or database variables, and the controls are consistent and integrated across the system.

User security classification is maintained in the RACF security database only. The DB2 tables must have a new column, defined as AS SECURITY LABEL, added to support this security. This column will contain the security label, and every row will have a specific security label. The values will match security label definitions. For each row accessed, DB2 calls the RACF Security Exit to check authorization. If access is allowed, then normal data access occurs. When data access is not allowed, the data is not returned and there is no indication that the data was omitted from the query's result set. The security label values are cached to reduce overhead.

Version 8 has a new method of feeding external security information into SQL statements. DB2 now has built-in session variables. The variables are set by the connection/sign-on exit. A new built-in function called GETVARIABLE() can be used to retrieve value for a variable. The security label can be retrieved by this function by requesting the contents of the SYSIBM.SECLABEL session variable. The contents of this variable can be used in views, triggers, stored procedures, functions, and constraints to enforce security policies. The following example uses the function in a view:

```
CREATE VIEW MY_DATA AS
        SELECT *
          FROM SHARED_DATA
          WHERE COL_OWNER
            = GETVARIABLE(SYSIBM.SECLABEL)
```

AUDITING

Two fundamental auditing questions are

1. Who is privileged to access what objects?
2. Who has accessed the data?

Answers to the first question are found in the DB2 catalog, which is a primary audit trail for the DB2 subsystem. Most of the catalog tables describe the DB2 objects, such as tables, views, table spaces, packages, and plans. Several other tables—those with the characters AUTH in their names—hold records of every grant of a privilege or authority on different types of object. Every record of a grant contains the name of the object, the ID that received the privilege, the ID that granted it, the time of the grant, and other information. You can retrieve data from catalog tables by writing SQL queries.

The audit trace is another primary audit trail for DB2. The trace can record changes in authorization IDs for a security audit and changes that are made to the structure of data, such as dropping a table, or data values, such as updating or inserting records, for an audit of data access. The trace also allows you to audit access attempts by unauthorized IDs, the results of GRANT and REVOKE statements, the mapping of Kerberos security tickets to RACF IDs, and other activities of interest to auditors.

The DB2 audit trace can tell who has accessed data. When started, the audit trace creates records of actions of certain types and sends them to a named destination, usually SMF.

Some of the types of information that can be obtained by the audit trace records are

- The ID that initiated the activity
- The location of the ID that initiated the activity, that is, whether the access was initiated from a remote location
- The type of activity and the time the activity occurred
- The DB2 objects that were affected
- Whether access was denied
- Who owns a particular plan and package

> **N O T E**   The trace can also determine which primary ID is
> responsible for the action of a secondary ID, when that information
> might not appear in the catalog.

Whether it is from a remote location or the local DB2, the request can be audited. The authorization ID on a trace record for a remote request is the ID that is the final result of any outbound translation (on remote system), inbound translation (on local system), or activity of an authorization exit routine; that is, it is the same ID to which you have granted access privileges for your data. Requests from your location to a remote DB2 are audited only if an audit trace is active at the remote location. The output from the trace appears only in the records at that location where the data resides.

Trace Details

The audit trace does not record everything. The changed data is recorded in the DB2 log. If an agent or a transaction accesses a table more than once in a single unit of recovery, only the first access is recorded, and then only if the audit trace is started for the appropriate class of events.

Some utilities are not audited. The first access of a table by LOAD is audited, but access by COPY, RECOVER, and REPAIR is not. Access by standalone utilities, such as DSN1CHKR and DSN1PRNT, is not audited. For more information on these utilities, refer to Chapter 7.

> **N O T E**   Everything comes at a cost. Auditing does have some
> overhead and can produce more data than necessary.

When the trace is started, the events to audit are chosen by giving one or more numbers to identify classes of events. Table 3-5 shows the available classes and the events they include. For additional information on trace classes, refer to Chapter 18.

Table 3-5   Classes Available for Audit and Events Included

Class	Events Traced
1	Access attempts that DB2 denies because of inadequate authorization. This class is the default.
2	Explicit GRANT and REVOKE statements and their results. The class does not include implicit grants and revokes.
3	CREATE, ALTER, and DROP operations affecting audited tables and their results. The class includes the dropping of a table caused by DROP TABLESPACE or DROP DATABASE and the creation of a table with AUDIT CHANGES or AUDIT ALL. ALTER TABLE statements are audited only when they change the AUDIT option for the table.

Table 3-5   Classes Available for Audit and Events Included (Continued)

Class	Events Traced
4	Changes to audited tables. Only the first attempt to change a table, within a unit of recovery, is recorded. (If the agent or the transaction issues more than one COMMIT statement, the number of audit records increases accordingly.) The changed data is not recorded; only the attempt to make a change is. If the change is not successful and is rolled back, the audit record remains; it is not deleted. This class includes access by the LOAD utility. Accesses that are caused by attempted deletions from a parent table to a dependent table are also audited. The audit record is written even if the delete rule is RESTRICT, which prevents the deletion from the parent table. The audit record is also written when the rule is CASCADE or SET NULL, which can result in deletions cascading to the dependent table.
5	All read accesses to tables that are identified as AUDIT ALL. As in class 4, only the first access within a DB2 unit of recovery is recorded, and references to a parent table are audited.
6	The bind of static and dynamic SQL statements of the following types: • INSERT, UPDATE, DELETE, CREATE VIEW, and LOCK TABLE statements for audited tables. Except for the values of host variables, the entire SQL statement is contained in the audit record. • SELECT statements to tables that are identified as AUDIT ALL. Except for the values of host variables, the entire SQL statement is contained in the audit record.
7	Assignment or change of an authorization ID, through an exit routine (default or user written) or a SET CURRENT SQLID statement, through either an outbound or an inbound authorization ID translation or because the ID is being mapped to an RACF ID from a Kerberos security ticket.
8	The start of a utility job and the end of each phase of the utility.
9	Various types of records that are written to IFCID 0146 by the IFI WRITE function.

Auditing Specific IDs

The audit trace can be started for a particular plan name, a particular primary authorization ID, or a combination of both. Having audit traces on at all times can be useful for tracking the activity of IDs with SYSADM authority, for example, because they have complete access to every table. If you have a network of DB2 subsystems, you might need to trace multiple authorization IDs for those users whose primary authorization ID may be translated several times.

Starting/Stopping the Trace

In order to start the audit trace, execute the following command:

```
-START TRACE (AUDIT)CLASS (4,6) DEST (GTF)LOCATION (*)
COMMENT ('Trace data changes; include text of dynamic DML statements.')
```

This example starts a trace that audits data changes and includes the text of any dynamic SQL. In order to stop this trace, simply issue the following command:

```
-STOP TRACE (AUDIT)CLASS (4,6) DEST (GTF)
```

This command simply stops the last trace started. If more than one trace is executing, the -DISPLAY TRACE command can be using to identify a particular trace by a number. For more information on DB2 commands, refer to Chapter 2.

> **N O T E**   The audit trace can be set up to start automatically when DB2 is started. This can be controlled by options on the panel DSNTIPN when DB2 is installed. This option allows you to set AUDIT TRACE to NO, YES, or a list of audit trace classes.

Auditing a Table

In order for the audit trace to be effective, you must first choose whether to audit the activity on a table, specifying an option of the CREATE and ALTER statements. The following example shows how to indicate that you wish to audit changes:

```
CREATE TABLE DB2CERT.TEST_TAKEN
(CID SMALLINT NOT NULL
   ....
IN DB2CTDB.CERTTS
AUDIT CHANGES
```

The options are AUDIT CHANGES | ALL | NONE. The default is NONE, or no auditing. In order to turn auditing off at the table level, you simply do an ALTER with AUDIT NONE.

> **N O T E**   You cannot audit auxiliary tables or catalog tables.

SUMMARY

This chapter discussed a number of topics relating to accessing data: security with the subsystem, with data sets, and within DB2. Subsystem security is handled in a number of ways, such as via IMS, CICS, Kerberos, and RACF. Securing access at the data set level also needs to be considered in some situations, as DB2 stores its data in individual data sets that can be accessed outside of DB2.

After discussing primary and secondary authorization IDs and how they are assigned, we talked about several of the authorization levels within DB2: SYSADM, SYSCNTL, DBADM, DBCNTL, PACKADM, and so on. We looked at the types of privileges each authority possesses.

Ownership of objects also comes with inherited authorities and privileges that can also be granted to other authorization IDs.

We examined the granting and revoking of database object privileges, using the GRANT and REVOKE SQL statements. Finally, we discussed the DB2 audit trace. This trace allows one to carefully monitor critical tables to see who is manipulating the data or, in some very sensitive cases, who is simply trying to access the data.

All of these levels of security can work together in order to keep data and subsystem safe.

ADDITIONAL RESOURCES

IBM DB2 UDB for z/OS Version 8 Administration Guide (SC18-7413)

IBM DB2 UDB for z/OS Version 8 SQL Reference (SC18-7426)

IBM z/OS Security Server Network Authentication Server Administration

IBM z/OS Security Server Network Authentication Server Programming

IBM DB2 UDB for z/OS Version 8 Command Reference (SC18-7416-00)

IBM DB2 UDB for z/OS Version 8 Utility Guide and Reference (SC18-7427-00)

Planning for Multilevel Security (GA22-7509)

DB2 UDB for z/OS Version 8 RACF Access Control Module Guide Reference (SA22-7938)

Structured Query Language

4

Database Objects

- Understanding data structures
- Managing database objects
- Creating database objects: data types, tables and table spaces, aliases and synonyms, constraints, views, materialized query tables, indexes, databases, storage groups, and sequence objects
- Database design and implementation

D B2 is a relational database that consists of one or more tables made up of rows and columns. The tables are created and accessed using the industry-standard Structured Query Language. Data in these tables is accessed via content, not location. This chapter looks at the structures in a DB2 subsystem and those that make up a DB2 database.

Many of these objects can be directly referenced from an SQL statement; therefore, it is important to understand their purpose. SQL is divided into three major categories.

1. DDL (Data Definition Language) is used to create, modify, or drop database objects.
2. DML (Data Manipulation Language) is used to select, insert, update, or delete database data (records).
3. DCL (Data Control Language) is used to provide data object access control.

As SQL has evolved, many new statements have been added to provide a more complete set of data access methods. The use of DDL to create database objects is discussed later in this chapter.

UNDERSTANDING DATA STRUCTURES

A database is an organized collection of related objects. SQL is used throughout the database industry as a common method of issuing database queries. SQL is considered a language, composed of statements, functions, and data types. An SQL statement is used to access database objects using relational operations. Before examining the SQL language, you need to understand some DB2 terminology. This chapter will be referring to the basic data structures, or objects, that are defined for each DB2 database. These objects include

- Tables: data types, aliases, and synonyms
- Views
- Materialized query tables
- Indexes: keys
- Table spaces
- Index spaces
- Sequence objects
- Databases
- Storage groups

Figure 4-1 shows the relationship among the DB2 objects.

A *table* is an unordered set of data records. It consists of columns and rows. Each column is based on a data type. Once created and populated with data, tables are referenced in the FROM clause of the SQL SELECT statements or in automatic query rewrite. Tables are of four types:

1. Permanent (base) tables
2. Auxiliary tables
3. Temporary—declared or global—tables
4. Materialized query tables (MQTs)

This chapter discusses only tables created with a DDL statement. These tables are created using the CREATE TABLE, CREATE AUXILIARY TABLE, or CREATE GLOBAL TEMPORARY TABLE statement, and each is a logical representation of the way the data is physically stored on disk. This chapter also discusses how to define MQTs, but their use and the declared temporary tables will be discussed in Chapter 6.

Data types are used to define the type of data that will occupy each column in a DB2 table, and to provide the length of a column. Data that does not match the data type defined to the column will not be allowed in that column. Data types may be string, numeric, date, time, row IDs, LOB (large object), and user defined. Depending on the data type, the length can be fixed or varying. Data types can be categorized as built in or user defined.

Data types that are defined by DB2 are referred to as built in. User-defined data types allow you to define your own type of data to be stored in the column. These user-defined data types are based on existing built-in data types.

An *alias* is a pointer to another table and is a substitute for the three-part name of a table or a view. An alias can be qualified by an owner ID, and the table referenced can be on the local site or on a remote site. Aliases are often used in place of any three-part named table in order to

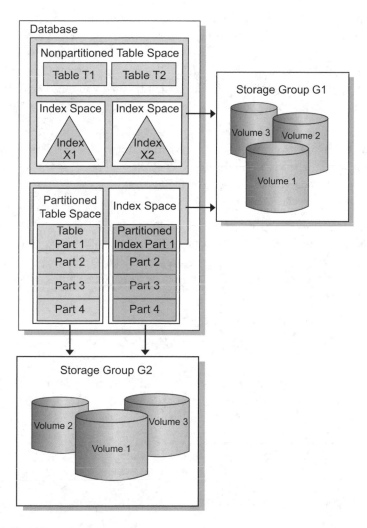

Figure 4-1 A hierarchy of DB2 structures

make the references portable, as DB2 on z/OS is the only server that supports three-part name syntax. Aliases are not dropped if the table they point to is dropped.

Synonyms are used to refer to a table using a different name or to refer to another owner's table as if you were the owner. A synonym, a private pointer to a table, can be referenced only by its owner and is not allowed to be qualified.

Unlike an alias, a synonym can be used to refer only to a table in the same subsystem in which it was defined. If the table is dropped, so too is the synonym.

Views are alternative ways of viewing data in one or more base tables or other views. A view is not a physical object and does not store data. Rather, a view is a DB2 catalog entry that, when accessed, executes an SQL statement that retrieves data from other tables or views. Views can be used to limit access to certain kinds of data, create customized views of data for users, or allow for alterations of tables without affecting application programs. Views can be read only if necessary, or they can be updatable, insertable, or deleteable. Using views has some restrictions.

Materialized query tables (MQTs) are objects created to allow whole or parts of each query to be precomputed and then use computed results to answer future queries. MQTs provide the means to save the results of prior queries and then reuse the common query results in subsequent queries. This helps avoid redundant scanning, aggregating, and joins.

Indexes are ordered sets of pointers associated with a table. Indexes can be created on permanent tables or on declared temporary tables. The index is based on the values of one or more columns in the table. The index values can be either ascending or descending. Each table can have one or more indexes, and indexes can also be used to enforce uniqueness in the data values and clustering sequence. Indexes are used to improve performance when accessing data. If an index is used, large scans of data can be avoided.

Indexes are physical objects that are created in index spaces, which are data sets like those that support the table spaces. The index space is automatically created in the same database as the table on which it is defined.

Indexes are either partitioned or nonpartitioned. A partitioned index is created on a partitioned table space and can be primary or secondary. A nonpartitioned index is used on tables defined in segmented, simple table spaces or as an alternative index on a partitioned table space.

> **N O T E**   The maintenance overhead of indexes will negatively impact the performance of INSERT, UPDATE, and DELETE statements.

Many keys can be defined on a table. A *key* is a named ordered set of columns on one table. A composite key is one made of several columns. Each key will play a particular role for a given table.

Table spaces are objects that consist of one or more data sets used to store DB2 data. Tables are created in table spaces, which can have one or many tables, depending on the type of table space defined.

Table spaces are of four types: simple, segmented, partitioned, and LOB. Both simple and segmented table spaces allow for multiple tables, but only segmented table spaces should be used, owing to the many performance issues.

- Simple table spaces can contain one or more tables; however, the rows of the tables are not kept on separate pages, which can cause concurrency and space usage issues.
- Segmented table spaces can contain one or more tables, and the space is divided into same-size segments. Each segment contains rows from only one table.
- Partitioned table spaces divide the data into several separate data sets, or partitions. A partitioned table space can have only one table. Up to 4,096 partitions of up to 64GB each are allowed. Each partition can have different characteristics, such as volume placement and free space.
- LOB table spaces are required to hold large-object data and are associated with the table space that holds the logical LOB column.

When an index is created, an index space also is created. An *index space* is a set of virtual storage access method (VSAM) linear data sets that hold index data. These index spaces are implicitly associated with the database that contains the table on which the index is defined.

A *sequence object* is a user-defined object that generates a sequence of numeric values according to the specifications in which it was created. These standalone objects provide an incremental counter generated by DB2.

Databases in DB2 for z/OS are collections of table spaces and index spaces. The database on the z/OS platform does not have any physical storage characteristics but acts more like an umbrella over all its dependent objects. This database allows for defaults to be established for the table space and indexes within in.

Storage groups are used to define a list of disk volumes to DB2 for its use when creating physical objects, such as table spaces and index spaces. The storage may be allocated when the tables are loaded with data or when they are created. Storage groups are created using DDL.

MANAGING DATABASE OBJECTS

SQL DDL is used to create, modify, or delete objects in a database. The DDL contains four main SQL statements:

- CREATE
- ALTER
- DROP
- DECLARE

The CREATE Statement

CREATE <database object>

The CREATE statement is used to define database objects. Database objects are used for various purposes. Some database objects are used to define a condition or relationship (index, trigger); others are a logical representation of the data as it is physically stored on disk (table, table space). The following database objects can be created with the CREATE statement:

- Alias
- Auxiliary table (LOBs)
- Database
- Distinct type (user-defined data type)
- Function (user-defined functions)
- Global temporary table
- Index
- Materialized query table
- Procedure (stored procedures)
- Sequence object
- Storage groups (stogroups)
- Synonym
- Table
- Table space
- Trigger
- View

The creation of any database object using DDL results in an update to the DB2 system catalog tables. Special database authorities or privileges are required to create database objects (refer to Chapter 3).

The ALTER Statement

```
ALTER <database object>....
```

The ALTER statement allows you to change some characteristics of database objects. Any object being altered must already exist in the database. The following database objects can be altered:

- Database
- Function
- Index
- Procedure
- Sequence object
- Storage group
- Table
- Table space

Every time you issue a DDL statement, the system catalog tables will be updated. The update will include a creation or modification timestamp and the authorization ID of the creator (modifier).

The DROP Statement

```
DROP <database object>
```

The DROP statement is used to remove definitions from the system catalog tables and hence the database itself. Because the system catalog tables cannot be directly deleted from, the DROP statement is used to remove data records from these tables. Database objects can be dependent on other database objects, so the act of dropping an object will result in dropping any object that is directly or indirectly dependent on that object. Any plan or package that is dependent on the object deleted from the catalog on the current server will be invalidated. You can drop any object created with the CREATE <database object> and temporary tables created with the DECLARE <table> statements.

The DECLARE Statement

```
DECLARE <database object>
```

The DECLARE statement is very similar to the CREATE statement except that one of the objects it can create is a temporary table. Temporary tables are used only for the duration of an application or stored procedure, or connection. The table does not cause any logging or contention against the system catalog tables and is very useful for working with intermediate results. The creation of a temporary table will not result in any update to the system catalog tables, so locking, logging, and other forms of contention are avoided with this object. This table must be placed into an existing TEMP database. The TEMP database should have several segmented table spaces created within it. A single declared table cannot span table spaces.

Declared tables can be dropped and altered, but no other database objects, such as views or triggers, can be created to act against them. Temporary tables do allow for the specification of a partitioning key.

Once a table is declared, it can be referenced like any other SQL table. For more information on declared temporary tables, refer to Chapter 12.

CREATING DATABASE OBJECTS

Let's look in detail at some of the objects that can be created: data types, tables, table spaces, views, materialized query tables, indexes, sequence objects, databases, and storage groups.

Data Types

Data types are used to specify the attributes of the columns when creating a table. DB2 supplies various data types; others are created by the users.

DB2-Supplied Data Types

When the database design is being implemented, any of the DB2-supplied data types can be used. Data is stored in DB2 tables consisting of columns and rows. Every DB2 table is defined by using columns, which must be one of the built-in DB2 data types or user-defined data types. Every DB2-supplied data type belongs to one of these major categories:

- Numeric
- String (binary, single byte, double byte)
- Date/time

The valid built-in DB2 data types are listed in Table 4-1.

Table 4-1 Built-In Data Types

Data	Data Type	DB2 Data Type
Signed numeric types: Exact	Binary integer: 16-bit	SMALLINT
	Binary integer: 32-bit	INTEGER
Signed numeric types: Decimal	Packed	DECIMAL
Signed numeric types: Approximate	Floating-point single-precision	REAL
	Floating-point double-precision	DOUBLE

Table 4-1   Built-In Data Types (Continued)

Data	Data Type	DB2 Data Type
Date/time types	Time	TIME
	Timestamp	TIMESTAMP
	Date	DATE
String types: Character	Fixed length	CHAR
	Varying length	VARCHAR CLOB
String types: Graphic	Fixed length	GRAPHIC
	Varying length	VARGRAPHIC DBCLOB
	Varying-length binary	BLOB
String Types: Binary	Varying length	BLOB
Row identifier		ROWID

Numeric Data Types.   These data types are used to store various numeric types and precisions. The precision of a number is the number of digits used to represent its value. The data is stored in the DB2 database, using a fixed amount of storage for all numeric data types. The amount of storage required increases as the precision of the number increases.

Numeric values should not be enclosed in quotation marks. If quotation marks are used, the value is treated as a character string. Even if a field contains numbers in its representation, a DB2 numeric data type should be used to represent the data only if arithmetic operations should be allowed.

Six DB2 data types can be used to store numeric data: SMALLINT, INTEGER, DECIMAL/ NUMERIC, FLOAT (REAL or DOUBLE), REAL, and DOUBLE.

- **Small integer (SMALLINT).** A small integer uses the least amount of storage in the database for each value. An integer does not allow any digits to the right of the decimal. The data value range for a SMALLINT is –32,768 to 32,767. The precision for a SMALLINT is five digits to the left of the decimal. Two bytes of database storage are used for each SMALLINT column value.
- **Integer (INTEGER).** An INTEGER takes twice as much storage as a SMALLINT but has a greater range of possible values. The value range for an INTEGER data type is –2,147,483,648 to 2,147,483,647. The precision for an INTEGER is ten digits to the left of the decimal. Four bytes of database storage are used for each INTEGER column value.

- **Decimal (DECIMAL/NUMERIC).** A DECIMAL or NUMERIC data type is used for numbers with fractional and whole parts. The DECIMAL data is stored in a packed format. The precision and scale must be provided when a decimal data type is used. The precision is the total number of digits—from 1 to 31—and the scale is the number of digits in the fractional part of the number. For example, a DECIMAL data type to store currency values of up to $1 million requires a definition of DECIMAL(9,2). The terms NUMERIC, DECIMAL, or DEC can all be used to declare a decimal or numeric column. A DECIMAL number takes up $p/2 + 1$ bytes of storage, where p is the precision used. For example, DEC(8,2) takes up 5 bytes of storage ($8/2 + 1$), whereas DEC(7,2) takes up only 4 bytes (truncate the division of $p/2$).
- **Single-precision floating-point (REAL/FLOAT).** A REAL data type is an approximation of a number. The approximation requires 32 bits, or 4 bytes of storage. To specify a single-precision number using the REAL data type, its length must be defined between 1 and 24, especially if the FLOAT data type is used, as it can represent both single-precision and double-precision and is determined by the integer value specified.
- **Double-precision floating-point (DOUBLE/FLOAT).** A DOUBLE or FLOAT data type is an approximation of a number. The approximation requires 64 bits, or 8 bytes of storage. To specify a double-precision number using the FLOAT data type, its length must be defined between 25 and 53.

You must also be aware of the range limits of the data types and the corresponding application programming language when you are manipulating these numeric fields. Some data values are of the integer type by nature, such as the number of test candidates. A number representing a number of people count not contain fractional data—numbers to the right of the decimal. On the other hand, some values require decimal places to accurately reflect their value, such as test scores. These two examples should use different DB2 data types to store their values (SMALLINT and DECIMAL, respectively).

String Data Types.   The seven string data types are CHAR; VARCHAR; CLOB; GRAPHIC, VARGRAPHIC, and DBCLOB; and BLOB.

> **N O T E**   The syntaxes of LONG VARCHAR, and LONG VARGRAPHIC are still supported, but the alternative syntaxes of VARCHAR(integer) and VARGRAPHIC(integer) are preferred. DB2 will translate the LONG definitions into the other format prior to defining the table. Therefore, only the VARCHAR() and VARGRAPHIC() definitions should be used.

1. **Fixed-length character strings (CHAR).** Fixed-length character strings are stored in the database, using the entire defined amount of storage. If the data being stored always has the same length, a CHAR data type should be used.

Using fixed-length character fields can potentially waste disk space within the database if the data is not using the defined amount of storage. However, overhead is involved in storing varying-length character strings. The length of a fixed-length string must be between 1 and 255 characters. If you do not supply a value for the length, a value of 1 is assumed.

2. **Varying-length character strings (VARCHAR).** Varying-length character strings are stored in the database, using only the amount of space required to store the data and a 2-byte prefix to hold the length. In the example we develop, the individual names are stored as varying-length strings (VARCHAR) because each person's name has a different length, up to a maximum length of 30 characters.

If a varying-length character string is updated and the resulting value is larger than the original, it may not fit on the same page, and the row will be moved to another page in the table, leaving a marker in the original place. These marker data records are known as indirect-reference rows. Having too many of these records can cause significant performance degradation, as multiple pages (I/Os) are required to return a single data record.

A VARCHAR column must fit on one database page. This means that a 4KB page would allow a VARCHAR up to 4,046 characters long, defined as VARCHAR(4046); an 8KB page would be up to 8,128 characters long, and so on, up to a 32KB page with the maximum column length of 32,704 bytes. This means that for this table, you must create a table space that can accommodate the larger page size, and you must have sufficient space in the row to accommodate this string.

> **NOTE** Character strings on the z/OS platform are stored in the database without a termination character. Depending on the non-z/OS development environment, a null terminator may or may not be appended to the end of a character string when the data is stored or retrieved.

> **NOTE** Updates to variable-character fields can cause the row length to change and may cause indirect references.

3. **Character large object (CLOB).** CLOB is a varying-length single-byte character set (SBCS) or multibyte character set (MBCS) character string stored in the database. CLOB columns are used to store greater than 32KB of text. The maximum size for each CLOB column is approximately 2GB (2 gigabytes minus 1 byte). Because this data type is of varying length, the amount of disk space allocated is determined by the amount of data in each record. Therefore, you should create the column specifying the length of the longest string.

NOTE The FOR BIT DATA clause can be used following a character string column definition. During data exchange, code page conversions are not performed. Rather, data is treated and compared as binary (bit) data.

4. **Double-byte character strings (GRAPHIC).** The GRAPHIC data types represent a single character using 2 bytes of storage. The GRAPHIC data types include GRAPHIC (fixed length, maximum 127 DBCS characters), VARGRAPHIC (varying length, maximum 32,704 DBCS characters for 32KB pages), and DBCLOB.

5. **VARCHAR** data types exceeding 255 bytes are similar to CLOB data types. (Both types have usage restrictions.)

6. **Double-byte character large objects (DBCLOB).** DBCLOBs are varying-length character strings that are stored in the database, using 2 bytes to represent each character. A code page is associated with each column. DBCLOB columns are used for large amounts (> 32KB) of double-byte text data, such as Japanese text. The maximum length should be specified during the column definition, because each data record will be variable in length.

7. **Binary large objects (BLOB).** BLOBs are variable-length binary strings. The data is stored in a binary format in the database. Restrictions apply when using this data type, including the inability to sort using this type of column. The BLOB data type is useful for storing nontraditional relational database information. The maximum size of each BLOB column is approximately 2GB. Because this data type is of varying length, the amount of disk space allocated is determined by the amount of data in each record, not by the defined maximum size of the column in the table definition.

Traditionally, large unstructured data was stored somewhere outside the database. Therefore, the data could not be accessed using SQL. Besides the traditional database data types, DB2 implements data types that will store large amounts of unstructured data. These data types are known as large objects (LOBs). Multiple LOB columns can be defined for a single table. DB2 provides special considerations for handling these large objects. You can choose not to log the LOB values, to avoid large amounts of data being logged.

A LOG option can be specified during the CREATE TABLESPACE statement for each AUXILIARY TABLE holding LOB column data, to avoid logging any modifications. To define a LOB column greater than 1GB, you must specify the LOG NO option.

In a database, you may choose to use BLOBs for the storage of pictures, images, or audio or video objects, along with large documents. BLOB columns will accept any binary string without regard to the contents. To manipulate textual data that is greater than 32KB in length, you use a CLOB data type. For example, if each test candidate were required to submit his or her resume, it could be stored in a CLOB column along with the rest of the candidate's information. Many SQL functions can be used to manipulate large character data columns.

> **N O T E** Support of LOB data types requires a special table space, an auxiliary table, and an auxiliary index.

Date and Time Data Types. Three DB2 data types are specifically used to represent dates and times.

1. The DATE data type is stored internally as a packed string of 4 bytes. Externally, the string has a length of 10 bytes (MM-DD-YYYY). This representation can vary and is dependent on the country code.
2. The TIME data type is stored internally as a packed string of 3 bytes. Externally, the string has a length of 8 bytes (HH-MM-SS). This representation may vary.
3. The TIMESTAMP data type is stored internally as a packed string of 10 bytes. Externally, the string has a length of 26 bytes (YYYY-MM-DD-HH-MM-SS-NNNNNN).

From the user perspective, these data types can be treated as character or string data types. Every time you need to use a date/time attribute, you will need to enclose it in quotation marks. However, date/time data types are not stored in the database as fixed-length character strings.

> **N O T E** The internal format of date, time, and timestamps is not at all similar to the external format returned via SQL. For example, the internal format of TIMESTAMP is 10 bytes, but the external format is 26 characters.

DB2 provides special functions that allow you to manipulate these data types. These functions allow you to extract the month, hour, or year of a date/time column. The date and time formats correspond to the site default. Therefore, the string that represents a date value will change, depending on the default format. In some countries, the date format is DD/MM/YYYY; in other countries, it is YYYY-MM-DD. You should be aware of the default format used by your site to use the correct date string format. If an incorrect date format is used in an SQL statement, an SQL error will be reported. Scalar functions will return date, time, and timestamp columns in formats other than the default.

As a general recommendation, if you are interested in a single element of a date string—say, month or year—always use the SQL functions provided by DB2 to interpret the column value. By using the SQL functions, you can make your application more portable.

> **N O T E**   TIMESTAMP fields use the most storage but contain the most accurate time, as they include microseconds.

> **N O T E**   Timestamps cannot be guaranteed to be unique, as the granularity is only to microseconds, and it is possible for two events to ask the system timer for the timestamp within 1 microsecond. The 8-byte system clock is unique, however, as it appends the time value with additional bits.

All date/time data types have an internal and an external format. The external format is always a character string. Three date/time data type formats are available in DB2.

1. Date string (DATE). A number of valid methods can be used to represent a DATE as a string. Any of the string formats shown in Table 4-2 can be used to store dates in a DB2 database. When the data is retrieved, using a SELECT statement, the output string will be in one of these formats or can be returned in any format specified.

Table 4-2 Date String Formats

Standard	String Format
International Standards Organization (ISO)	YYYY-MM-DD
IBM USA Standard (USA)	MM/DD/YYYY
IBM European Standard (EUR)	DD.MM.YYYY
Japanese Industrial Standard (JIS)	YYYY-MM-DD

Additionally, DB2 has many scalar functions to return date information, such as

- DATE
- DAY
- DAYOFMONTH
- DAYOFWEEK
- DAYOFWEEK_ISO
- DAYOFYEAR
- JULIAN_DAY
- MONTH
- QUARTER
- WEEK
- WEEK_ISO
- YEAR

2. Time string (`TIME`). A number of valid methods exist for representing a time as a string. Any of the string formats in Table 4-3 can be used to store times in a DB2 database. When data is retrieved, the external format of the time will be one of the formats shown in Table 4-3.

Table 4-3   Time String Formats

Standard	Format
International Standards Organization ISO	HH.MM.SS
IBM USA Standard USA	HH:MM AM or PM
IBM European Standard EUR	HH.MM.SS
Japanese Industrial Standard JIS	HH:MM:SS

Additionally, DB2 has many scalar functions to return time information, such as

- HOUR
- MINUTE
- SECOND
- TIME

3. Timestamp string (`TIMESTAMP`). The timestamp data type has a single default external format. Timestamps have an external representation of YYYY-MM-DD-HH.MM.SS.NNNNNN (year-month-day-hour-minute-seconds-microseconds). However, several scalar functions can manipulate the output format, especially the TIMESTAMP_FORMAT function, which returns any type of string, up to 255 characters, based on a user-defined template.

Additionally, DB2 has several scalar functions to return timestamp information besides all those listed for DATE and TIME, such as

- MICROSECOND
- TIMESTAMP
- TIMESTAMP_FORMAT

Special Data Types
Some special data types in DB2 can be used to support special processing, such as random-number and sequential-number generation and the ability to create data types.

ROWID.   A ROWID is a value that uniquely identifies a row in a table. A ROWID column enables writing queries that navigate directly to a row in the table. ROWID column values are generated by DB2 unless supplied, but they must be unique. If a value is supplied, it must be a valid DB2-generated value. The internal format is 17 bytes and contains bit data. The external length is 40 bytes. If a ROWID column is used in a query, the access path is referred to as

`'Direct Row Access'` because the row is directly accessed without a scan of the index or the table space. This type of access is shown as a `'D'` in the `ACCESS_PATH` column in the `PLAN_TABLE`. For more information on the `PLAN_TABLE` and access paths, refer to Chapter 17.

Identity Column. Columns can be populated with values if no value was supplied by the user. It is also possible to have DB2 generate sequence numbers or other values as part of a column during record insertion.

In the majority of applications, a single column within a table represents a unique identifier for that row. Often, this identifier is a number that gets sequentially updated as new records are added. DB2 has a feature that automatically generates this value on behalf of the user. The following example shows a table definition with the `EMP_NO` field automatically being generated as a sequence.

```
CREATE TABLE EMPLOYEE
    (EMPNO INT GENERATED ALWAYS AS IDENTITY,
     NAME CHAR(10));

INSERT INTO EMPLOYEE(NAME) VALUES 'SMITH';
INSERT INTO EMPLOYEE(NAME) VALUES 'LAWSON';

SELECT * FROM EMPLOYEE;
EMPNO       NAME
----------- ----------
1           SMITH
2           LAWSON
```

If the column is defined with `GENERATED ALWAYS`, the `INSERT` statement cannot specify a value for the `EMPNO` field. By default, the numbering will start at 1 and increment by 1. The starting and increment values can be modified as part of the column definition:

```
CREATE TABLE EMPLOYEE
    (EMPNO INT GENERATED ALWAYS AS
        IDENTITY(START WITH 100, INCREMENT BY 10)),
     NAME CHAR(10));

INSERT INTO EMPLOYEE(NAME) VALUES 'SMITH';
INSERT INTO EMPLOYEE(NAME) VALUES 'LAWSON';

SELECT * FROM EMPLOYEE;
EMPNO NAME
----------- ----------
      100 SMITH
      110 LAWSON
```

In addition, the default value can be GENERATED BY DEFAULT, which means that the user has the option of supplying a value for the field. If no value is supplied, using the DEFAULT keyword, DB2 will generate the next number in sequence.

One additional keyword (CACHE) is available as part of IDENTITY columns. You can decide how many numbers DB2 should "pregenerate." This can help reduce catalog contention, as DB2 will store the next *n* numbers in memory rather than go back to the catalog tables to determine which number to generate next.

Identity columns are restricted to numeric values—integer or decimal—and can be used in only one column in the table definition. Table 4-4 describes the values used for identity column definition.

```
CREATE TABLE EMPLOYEE
  (EMPNO INT GENERATED ALWAYS AS IDENTITY,
  NAME CHAR(10),
  SALARY INT,
  BONUS INT,
  PAY INT);
INSERT INTO EMPLOYEE(NAME, SALARY, BONUS, PAY) VALUES
('SMITH',20000,2000,22000);
INSERT INTO EMPLOYEE(NAME, SALARY, BONUS, PAY) VALUES
('LAWSON',30000,5000,35000);

SELECT * FROM EMPLOYEE;


EMPNO      NAME         SALARY        BONUS         PAY
-------    ----------   -----------   -----------   ----------
1          SMITH        20000         2000          22000
2          LAWSON       30000         5000          35000
```

The EMPNO is generated as an IDENTITY column.

Table 4-4 Identity Column Values

Value	Description
GENERATED	DB2-generated values for the column. This column must specify GENERATED if the column is to be considered an identity column or if the data type is a ROWID or a distinct type that is based on a ROWID.
ALWAYS	DB2-generated value for the column when a row is inserted into the table.
BY DEFAULT	DB2-generated value for the column when a row is inserted into the table unless a value is specified. This is recommended only when using data propagation.

continues

Table 4-4   Identity Column Values (Continued)

Value	Description
AS IDENTITY	Specifies that the column is an identity column for the table. A table can have only one identity column. AS IDENTITY can be specified only if the data type for the column is an exact numeric type with a scale of zero: SMALLINT, INTEGER, DECIMAL with a scale of zero, or a distinct type based on one of these types. An identity column is implicitly not null.
START WITH n	A numeric constant that provides the first value for the identity column. The value can be a positive or negative value that could be assigned to the column. No nonzero digits are allowed to the right of the decimal point. The default is 1.
INCREMENT BY n*	A numeric constant that provides the interval between consecutive values of the identity column. This value can be any positive or negative value that is not 0, and the default is 1. With a positive value, the sequence of values for the identity column will ascend; if it is negative, the sequence of identity column values will descend.
CACHE n*	Provides the number of values of the identity column sequence that DB2 preallocates and keeps in memory. The default is 20. If a system fails, all cached identity column values will never be used. The value specified for CACHE also represents the maximum number of identity column values that may be lost during a system failure. With a data sharing environment, each member has its own range of consecutive values to use. For instance, if using CACHE 30, susbystem DB2T may get values 1 to 30, and subsystem DB2U may use values 31 to 60. The values that are assigned might not be in the order in which they were requested, if transactions from different members generate values for the same identity column.
NO CACHE*	Specifies that caching is not to be used. Use NO CACHE to guarantee that the identity values are generated in the order in which they are requested for non-affinity transactions in a data sharing environment.
CYCLE*	Specifies whether the identity column should continue to generate values after reaching either the maximum or minimum value of the sequence. If the column values are ascending, it will start with the lowest value. If the column values are descending, it will start with the highest value. The MAXVALUE and MINVALUE are used to determine these ranges. Note that when CYCLE is in effect, duplicate values can occur. If a unique index exists, an error will occur.

Table 4-4   Identity Column Values (Continued)

Value	Description
MAXVALUE*	Specifies the maximum value that can be generated for the identity column. The value can be positive or negative but must be greater than the MINVALUE.
MINVALUE*	Specifies the minimum value that is generated for the identity column. The value can be positive or negative but must be less than the MAXVALUE.
RESET WITH*	Allows for the identity column values to be reset.

*   As of version 8, ALTER can be used on these values.

> **N O T E**   If the data needs to be unloaded and reloaded while preserving previously generated numbers, the GENERATED option can be altered.

Using identity columns has some restrictions. Identity columns cannot be specified on a table that has an edit procedure defined. An identity column cannot be defined with the FIELDPROC clause or the WITH DEFAULT clause. When updating an identity column, you cannot update the value of an identity column that is defined as GENERATED ALWAYS. If you are doing an ALTER table to add an identity column to a table that is not empty, the table space that contains the table is placed in the REORG pending state. When the REORG utility is executed, DB2 will generate the values for the identity column for all existing rows, and the REORG pending status will be removed. The values are guaranteed to be unique, and their order is determined by the system.

When creating another table using the LIKE clause—creating a table with the columns/ attributes of another table—you have some options in order to pick up identity column attributes. For an identity column, the newly created table will inherit only the data type of the identity column. No other column attributes are inherited unless the INCLUDING IDENTITY COLUMN ATTRIBUTES clause is used.

Distinct Types.   Distinct types allow a user to extend the data types that DB2 understands in a database. The distinct types can be created based on an existing data type or another distinct type. Distinct types are used to define further types of data being represented in the database. If columns are defined using different distinct types based on the same base data type, these columns cannot be directly compared. This is known as *strong typing*. DB2 provides this strong data typing to avoid end user mistakes during the assignment or comparison of different types of real-world data. For more information on how to create and use distinct types, refer to Chapter 15.

Null-Value Considerations

A null value represents an unknown state. Therefore, when columns containing null values are used in calculations, the result is unknown. All the data types discussed previously support the presence of null values. During the table definition, you can specify that a valid value must be provided. This is accomplished by adding a phrase to the column definition. The CREATE TABLE statement can contain the phrase NOT NULL following the definition of each column. This will ensure that the column contains a known data value.

Special considerations are required to properly handle null values when coding a DB2 application. DB2 treats a null value differently from other data values. To define a column not to accept null values, add the phrase NOT NULL to the end of the column definition.

In the following example, DB2 will not allow any null values to be stored in the c1 column:

```
CREATE TABLE t1 (c1 CHAR(3) NOT NULL)
```

In general, avoid using nullable columns unless they are required to implement the database design. Another factor to consider is overhead storage. An extra byte per nullable column is necessary if null values are allowed.

> **NOTE** Relational databases allow null values. It is important to remember that they can be appropriate for your database design.

When you insert a row into a table and omit the value of one or more columns, those columns may be populated using either a null value—if the column is defined as nullable—or a defined default value—if you have so specified. If the column is defined as not nullable, the insert will fail unless the data has been provided for the column.

DB2 has a defined default value for each DB2 data type, but you can provide a default value for each column. The default value is specified in the CREATE TABLE statement. By defining your own default value, you can ensure that the data value has been populated with a known value.

In the following example, all the INSERT statements that omit the DEPT column will populate the column with the default value of 10. The COMM column is defined as default. In this case, you can choose at insert time between null or the default value of 15. To ensure that the default value is being used during an INSERT operation, the keyword DEFAULT should be specified in the `VALUES` portion of the `INSERT` statement. The following example shows two examples of inserting a record with user-defined default values:

```
CREATE TABLE STAFF
(ID SMALLINT NOT NULL,
NAME VARCHAR(9),
DEPT SMALLINT NOT NULL WITH DEFAULT 10,
JOB CHAR(5),
YEARS SMALLINT,
SALARY DECIMAL(7,2),
COMM DECIMAL(7,2) NOT NULL WITH DEFAULT 15);
```

In this case, both of the following statements will have the same result:

```
INSERT INTO STAFF
VALUES(360,'Lawson',DEFAULT, 'SE',8,20000,DEFAULT);

INSERT INTO STAFF (ID,NAME,JOB,YEARS,SALARY)
VALUES(360, 'Lawson', 'SE',8,20000,);
```

The result is

```
ID      NAME       DEPT   JOB    YEARS   SALARY     COMM
------  ---------  ------ -----  ------  ---------  ---------
360     Lawson       10   SE      8        20000.00  15.00
1 record(s) selected.
```

Selecting the Correct Data Type

Knowledge of the possible data values and their usage is required to be able to select the correct data type. Specifying an inappropriate data type when defining the tables can result in wasted disk space, improper expression evaluation, and performance problems. Table 4-5 provides a brief checklist for data type selection.

Table 4-5   Data Type Selection

Usage	Data Type
Is the data variable in length?	VARCHAR
If the data is variable in length, what is the maximum length?	VARCHAR
Do you need to sort, or order, the data?	CHAR, VARCHAR, NUMERIC
Is the data going to be used in arithmetic operations?	DECIMAL, NUMERIC, REAL, DOUBLE, FLOAT, INTEGER, SMALLINT

continues

Table 4-5 Data Type Selection (Continued)

Usage	Data Type
Does the data element contain decimals?	DECIMAL, NUMERIC, REAL, DOUBLE
Is the data fixed in length?	CHAR
Does the data have a specific meaning beyond DB2 base data types?	DISTINCT TYPE
Is the data larger than what a character string can store? Do you need to store nontraditional data?	CLOB, BLOB, DBCLOB

Remember that you need to create page sizes that are large enough to contain the length of a row in a table. This is particularly important for tables with large character columns. When using character data types, the choice between CHAR and VARCHAR is determined by the range of lengths of the columns. For example, if the range of column length is relatively small, use a fixed CHAR with the maximum length. This will reduce the storage requirements and could improve performance.

Unicode Support in DB2

Unicode support is another very important enhancement. Support for Unicode will help with support across multinational boundaries. The Unicode encoding scheme allows for the representation of code points and characters of various geographies and languages. Unicode is a fixed-length character-encoding scheme that includes characters from most of the world's languages. Unicode characters are usually shown as U+xxxx, where xxxx is the hexadecimal code of the character. Each character is 16 bits wide, allowing for support of 65,000 characters. The normal support provided is the UCS-2/UTF-8 standard. With UCS-2 or Unicode encoding, ASCII and control characters are also 2 bytes long, and the lead byte is 0. Because extraneous NULLs may appear anywhere in the string, this could be a problem for programs that expect ASCII. UTF-8 is a transformation algorithm used to avoid the problem for programs that rely on ASCII code. UTF-8 transforms fixed-length (2-byte) UCS characters into variable-length byte strings. ASCII characters are represented by single-byte codes, but non-ASCII characters are 2 to 4 bytes long. UTF-8 transforms UCS-2 characters to a multibyte code set.

The UCS-2 code page is being registered as code page 1200. When new characters are added to a code page, the code page number does not change. Code page 1200 always refers to the current version of Unicode/UCS-2 and has been used for UCS-2 support in DB2 UDB on many of the other platforms. UTF-8 has been registered as CCSID (Coded Character Set Identifier) 1208 (code page 1208) and is used as the multibyte code page number for DB2's UCS-2/UTF-8 support.

DB2 UDB supports UCS-2 as a new multibyte code page. CHAR, VARCHAR, LONG VARCHAR, and CLOB data is stored in UTF-8; GRAPHIC, VARGRAPHIC, LONG VARGRAPHIC, and DBCLOB, in UCS-2.

As a default, databases are created in the code page of the application creating them. Alternatively, UTF-8 can be specified as the CODESET name with any valid two-letter TERRITORY code:

```
CREATE DATABASE dbname USING CODESET UTF-8 TERRITORY US
```

A UCS-2 database allows connection from every single-byte and multibyte code page supported. Code page character conversions between a client's code page and UTF-8 are automatically performed by DB2. Data in graphic string types is always in UCS-2 and does not go through code page conversions. Although some client workstations have a limited subset of UCS-2 characters, the database allows the entire repertoire of UCS-2 characters.

All supported data types are also supported in a UCS-2 database. In a UCS-2 database, all identifiers are in multibyte UTF-8. Therefore, it is possible to use any UCS-2 character in identifiers in which DB2 allows the use of a character in the extended character set. This feature will also allow UCS-2 literals to be specified either in GRAPHIC string constant format, using the G'...' or N'....' format, or as a UCS-2 hexadecimal string, using the UX'...' or GX'....' format.

Tables

Tables consist of columns and rows that store an unordered set of data records. Tables can have constraints to guarantee the uniqueness of data records, maintain the relationship between and within tables, and so on.

Table Constraints

A constraint is a rule that the database manager enforces. Constraints are of three types:

1. **Unique constraint.** Ensures the unique values of a key in a table. Any changes to the columns that comprise the unique key are checked for uniqueness.
2. **Referential constraint.** Enforces referential constraints on insert, update, and delete operations. It is the state of a database in which all values of all foreign keys are valid.
3. **Check constraint.** Verifies that changed data does not violate conditions specified when a table was created or altered.

Unique Constraints. A *unique constraint* is the rule that the values of a key are valid only if they are unique within the table. Each column making up the key in a unique constraint must be defined as NOT NULL. Unique constraints are defined in the CREATE TABLE statement or the ALTER TABLE statement, using the PRIMARY KEY clause or the UNIQUE clause. When used, the table is marked as unavailable until you explicitly create an index for any key specified as UNIQUE or PRIMARY KEY, unless processed by the schema processor, in which case DB2 will implicitly create all necessary indexes.

A table can have any number of unique constraints; however, a table cannot have more than one unique constraint on the same set of columns. The enforcement of the constraint is through the unique index. Once a unique constraint has been established on a column, the check for uniqueness during multiple row updates is deferred until the end of the update: deferred unique constraint. A unique constraint can also be used as the parent key in a referential constraint.

Referential Constraint.   Referential constraint, or integrity, allows you to define required relationships between and within tables. The database manager maintains these relationships, which are expressed as referential constraints, and requires that all values of a given attribute or table column also exist in another table column. Figure 4-2 shows an example of the referential integrity (RI) between two tables. This constraint requires that every employee in the EMPLOYEE table must be in a department that exists in the DEPARTMENT table. No employee can be in a department that does not exist.

- A *unique key* is a set of columns in which no two values are duplicated in any other row. Only one unique key can be defined as a primary key for each table. The unique key may also be known as the *parent key* when referenced by a foreign key.
- A *primary key* is a special case of a unique key. Each table can have only one primary key. In this example, DEPTNO and EMPNO are the primary keys of the DEPARTMENT and EMPLOYEE tables.
- A *foreign key* is a table column or set of columns that refer to a unique key or primary key of the same or another table. A foreign key is used to establish a relationship with a unique key or a primary key and enforces referential integrity among tables. The column WORKDEPT in the EMPLOYEE table is a foreign key because it refers to the primary key, column DEPTNO, in the DEPARTMENT table.

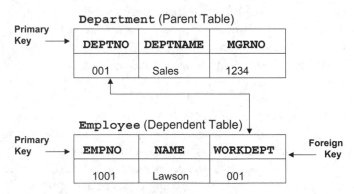

Figure 4-2   Referential integrity between two tables

A parent key is a primary key or unique key of a referential constraint. A *parent table* is a table containing a parent key that is related to at least one foreign key in the same or another table. A table can be a parent in an arbitrary number of relationships. In this example, the DEPARTMENT table, which has a primary key of DEPTNO, is a parent of the EMPLOYEE table, which contains the foreign key WORKDEPT.

A dependent table contains one or more foreign keys. A dependent table can also be a parent table. A table can be a dependent in an arbitrary number of relationships. For example, the EMPLOYEE table contains the foreign key WORKDEPT, which is dependent on the DEPARTMENT table that has a primary key.

A referential constraint is an assertion that non-null values of a designated foreign key are valid only if they also appear as values of a unique key of a designated parent table. The purpose of referential constraints is to guarantee that database relationships are maintained and that data entry rules are followed.

Enforcement of referential constraints has special implications for some SQL operations that depend on whether the table is a parent or a dependent. The database manager enforces referential constraints across systems based on the referential integrity rules: the INSERT, DELETE, and UPDATE rules. However, only the DELETE rules are explicitly defined.

The INSERT rule is implicit when a foreign key is specified. You can insert a row at any time into a parent table without any action being taken in the dependent table. You cannot insert a row into a dependent table unless a row in the parent table has a parent key value equal to the foreign key value of the row that is being inserted, unless the foreign key value is null. If an INSERT operation fails for one row during an attempt to insert more than one row, all rows inserted by the statement are removed from the database.

When you delete a row from a parent table, the database manager checks whether any dependent rows in the dependent table match foreign key values. If any dependent rows are found, several actions can be taken. You determine which action will be taken by specifying a DELETE rule when you create the dependent table.

- RESTRICT or NO ACTION prevents any row in the parent table from being deleted if any dependent rows are found. If you need to remove both parent and dependent rows, delete dependent rows first.
- CASCADE automatically deletes the row from the dependent table when the parent row is deleted.
- SET NULL sets the value of the foreign key to NULL, provided that it allows nulls. Other parts of the row will remain unchanged.

The database manager prevents the update of a unique key of a parent row. When you update a foreign key in a dependent table and the foreign key is defined with the NOT NULL option, it must match a value of the parent key of the parent table.

Check Constraints.   Table-check constraints enforce data integrity at the table level. Once a table-check constraint has been defined for a table, every UPDATE and INSERT statement will involve checking the restriction, or constraint. If the constraint is violated, the data record will not be inserted or updated, and an SQL error will be returned.

A table-check constraint can be defined at table creation time or later, using the ALTER TABLE statement. The table-check constraints can help implement specific rules for the data values contained in the table by specifying the values allowed in one or more columns in every row of a table. This can save time for the application developer, as the validation of each data value can be performed by the database and not by each of the applications accessing the database.

When a check constraint is created or added, DB2 performs a syntax check on it. A check constraint cannot contain host variables or special registers. The check constraint's definition is stored in the system catalog tables: specifically, the SYSIBM.SYSCHECKS and SYSIBM.SYSCHECKDEP tables.

You can define a check constraint on a table by using the ADD CHECK clause of the ALTER TABLE statement. If the table is empty, the check constraint is added to the description of the table. If the table is not empty, what happens when you define the check constraint depends on the value of the CURRENT RULES special register, which can be either STD or DB2. If the value is STD, the check constraint is enforced immediately when it is defined. If a row does not conform, the table-check constraint is not added to the table, and an error occurs. If the value is DB2, the check constraint is added to the table description, but its enforcement is deferred. Because some rows in the table might violate the check constraint, the table is placed in check-pending(CHKP) status. The best way to remove the CHKP status is to run the CHECK DATA utility. For more information on the CHKP status and the CHECK DATA utility, refer to Chapter 7.

The ALTER TABLE statement that is used to define a check constraint will fail if the table space or partition that contains the table is in a check-pending status, the CURRENT RULES special register value is STD, and the table is not empty. To remove a check constraint from a table, use the DROP CONSTRAINT or DROP CHECK clauses of the ALTER TABLE statement. You must not use DROP CONSTRAINT on the same ALTER TABLE statement as DROP FOREIGN KEY, DROP CHECK, or DROP.

The following example adds a check constraint to a table that checks to be sure that JOB is valid:

```
ALTER TABLE EMPLOYEE
ADD CONSTRAINT check_job
CHECK (JOB IN ('Engineer','Sales','Manager'));
```

> **N O T E** It is a good idea to appropriately label every constraint—triggers, table check, or referential integrity. This is particularly important for diagnosing errors that might occur.

As check constraints are used to implement business rules, you may need to change them from time to time. This could happen when the business rules change in your organization. No special command is used to change a check constraint. Whenever a check constraint needs to be changed, you must drop it and create a new one. Check constraints can be dropped at any time, and this action will not affect your table or the data within it.

When you drop a check constraint, you must be aware that data validation performed by the constraint will no longer be in effect. The statement used to drop a constraint is the ALTER TABLE statement. The following example shows how to modify the existing constraint. After dropping the constraint, you have to create it with the new definition:

```
ALTER TABLE EMPLOYEE DROP CONSTRAINT check_job;

ALTER TABLE EMPLOYEE
ADD CONSTRAINT check_job
CHECK (JOB IN ('OPERATOR','CLERK'));
```

Creating Tables

The CREATE TABLE statement allows you to define a new table. The definition must include its name and the attributes of its columns. The definition may include other attributes of the table, such as its primary key or check constraints. The RENAME TABLE statement can change the name of an existing table.

Once the table is defined, column names and data types cannot be modified. However, new columns can be added to the table. Be careful when adding new columns, as default data values will be used for existing records.

A table can have a maximum of 750 columns. This maximum will *not* vary depending on the data page size on the z/OS. DB2 supports 4KB, 8KB, 16KB, and 32KB data page sizes. Table 4-6 shows the maximum number of columns in a table and maximum length of a row by page size.

> **N O T E** If an EDITPROC was defined on a table, the maximum row sizes shown in Table 4-6 will decrease by 10 bytes in each case.

> **N O T E** If the table is a dependent table in a referentially intact structure, the maximum number of columns is 749.

Table 4-6   Maximum Table Columns and Row Lengths

	4KB Page	8KB Page	16KB Page	32KB Page
Maximum columns	750	750	750	750
Maximum row length (bytes)	4,056	8,138	16,330	32,714

Tables are always created within a table space. Users can specify the table space name in which the table will be created, or DB2 will create one implicitly. In the following example, DB2 will implicitly create a table space in the HUMANDB database, because no table space name was provided. The name of the table space will be derived from the table:

```
CREATE TABLE DEPARTMENT
(DEPTNUMB SMALLINT NOT NULL,
DEPTNAME VARCHAR(20),
MGRNO SMALLINT,
PRIMARY KEY(DEPTNUMB))
IN DATABASE HUMANDB;
```

> **N O T E** Indexes will have their own index spaces created when they are created.

After a table is created, user data can be placed into the table by using one of these methods:

- INSERT statement
- LOAD utility
- DSN1COPY

> **N O T E** The LOG NO option is available only for LOB table spaces.

> **N O T E** If you need a temporary table that is used only for the duration of a program, use the DECLARE GLOBAL TEMPORARY TABLE statement instead. This will result in no catalog contention, minimal logging, and no lock contention.

Following are sample CREATE TABLE statements. This example creates two tables. The definition includes unique constraints, check constraints, and referential integrity. In this example, the following conditions apply.

- The DEPARTMENT table has a primary key that consists of column DEPTNUMB.
- The EMPLOYEE table has a check constraint saying that JOB should be Sales, Mgr, or Clerk.
- The default value is defined for the column HIREDATE in the EMPLOYEE table.
- The EMPLOYEE table has a primary key that consists of the column ID.
- A referential constraint is defined between the DEPARTMENT table and the EMPLOYEE table.
- The EMPLOYEE table is created in the HUMANTS table space in the HUMANDB database.

```
CREATE TABLE DEPARTMENT
(DEPTNUMB SMALLINT NOT NULL,
DEPTNAME VARCHAR(20),
MGRNO SMALLINT,
PRIMARY KEY(DEPTNUMB))
IN HUMANDB.HUMANTS;

CREATE TABLE EMPLOYEE
   (ID SMALLINT NOT NULL,
NAME VARCHAR(9) NOT NULL,
   DEPT SMALLINT,
   JOB CHAR(5) CHECK (JOB IN('SALES','MGR','CLERK')),
   HIREDATE DATE WITH DEFAULT CURRENT DATE,
   SALARY DECIMAL(7,2),
   COMM DECIMAL(7,2),
CONSTRAINT UNIQUEID PRIMARY KEY(ID),
FOREIGN KEY(DEPT) REFERENCES DEPARTMENT(DEPTNUMB)
ON DELETE RESTRICT)
IN HUMANDB.HUMANTS;
```

Auxiliary Tables

LOB data is not stored in the table in which it is defined. The defined LOB column holds information about the LOB, whereas the LOB itself is stored in another location. The normal place for this data storage is a LOB table space defining the physical storage that will hold an auxiliary table related to the base column and table.

Because the LOB is stored in a separate table, one performance consideration might be that if you have a large variable-character column in use—that is infrequently accessed—you may be able to convert it to a LOB so that it is kept separately, and this could speed up table space scans on the remaining data because fewer pages would be accessed.

Null is the only supported default value for a LOB column; if the value is null, it will not take up space in the LOB table space. The following examples show how to create a base table with a LOB and an auxiliary table to support it:

```
CREATE TABLE DB2USER1.CANDIDATE
  (CID            CANDIDATE_ID    NOT NULL,
   ...
   CERT_APP      CHAR(1) NOT NULL WITH DEFAULT,
   PHOTO          BITMAP,
   PRIMARY KEY (CID);
   IN DB2CERT.CERTTS;

CREATE AUX TABLE CAND_PHOTO
   IN DB2CERT.CERTPIC
   STORES DB2USER1.CANDIDATE
   COLUMN PHOTO;
```

Copying a Table Definition

It is possible to create a table using the same characteristics of another table or a view. This is done through the CREATE TABLE LIKE statement. The name specified after LIKE must identify a table or a view that exists at the current server, and the privilege set must implicitly or explicitly include the SELECT privilege on the identified table or view. An identified table must not be an auxiliary table. An identified view must not include a column that is considered to be a ROWID column or an identity column.

The use of LIKE is an implicit definition of n columns, where n is the number of columns in the identified table or view. The implicit definition includes all attributes of the n columns as they are described in SYSCOLUMNS, with a few exceptions such as identity attributes, unless the INCLUDING IDENTITY clause is used.

The implicit definition does not include any other attributes of the identified table or view. For example, the new table will not have a primary key, foreign key, or check constraint. The table is created in the table space implicitly or explicitly specified by the IN clause, and the table has any other optional clause only if the optional clause is specified.

Following is an example of the CREATE LIKE statement:

```
CREATE TABLE NEW_DEPT LIKE DEPARTMENT
IN DATABASE HUMANDB
```

Modifying a Table

After you create a table, you can use the ALTER TABLE statement to modify existing tables. The ALTER TABLE statement modifies existing tables by

- Adding one or more columns to a table
- Adding or dropping a primary key
- Adding or dropping one or more unique or referential constraints
- Adding or dropping one or more check-constraint definitions
- Altering the data type length—increase only within numeric or character data types
- Altering the data type from CHAR to VARCHAR or VARCHAR to CHAR
- Altering identity column attributes
- Enable auditing of the table

> **N O T E**   If a primary key is dropped, the dependents will no longer have foreign keys.

The following example shows how to add a check constraint to the DEPARTMENT table:

```
ALTER TABLE DEPARTMENT ADD CHECK (DEPTNUM > 10)
```

The next example shows how to change a data type of a column. We assume in this example that the data type was originally CHAR and was less than 30.

```
ALTER TABLE DEPARTMENT ALTER COLUMN NAME CHAR(35)
```

> **N O T E**   With a change such as increasing the size of a data type column, we must not forget to relay this information to the application programmer, as this may impact code, that is, host variable definitions.

Removing a Table

When you want to remove a table, issue a DROP TABLE statement:

```
DROP TABLE EMPLOYEE
```

> **N O T E**   Any objects that are directly or indirectly dependent on this table are deleted or made inoperative—for example, indexes, triggers, and views. Whenever a table is deleted, its description is deleted from the catalog, and any packages that reference the object are invalidated.

Sequence Objects

A sequence object is a user-defined object that generates a sequence of numeric values according to the specifications in which it was created. Sequence objects provide an incremental counter generated by DB2 and are similar to identity columns. An identity column can be thought of as a special kind of sequence object; however, the sequence column is separate from the table. Sequence objects support many of the same attributes as identity columns, such as INCREMENT BY, CACHE, CYCLE, RESTART WITH, MINVAL, and MAXVAL.

Sequence object values can be used by applications for a variety of reasons and have several benefits:

- No waits for incrementing values
- Standalone sequential number-generating object—not tied to a table
- Ascending or descending number generation
- Useful for application porting from the other DBMSs
- Can help to generate keys that can be used to coordinate keys across multiple tables (RI or application related)

Creating Sequence Objects

The sequence name is made up of two parts: the 128-byte schema name and the 128-byte identifier. Sequence objects are created using a new CREATE SEQUENCE statement, and all attributes are completely user defined or defaults. The values in the sequence object can be of any exact numeric data type. The starting value is defined with a START WITH value and advances with INCREMENT BY, ascending or descending. The values can be cached and are generated in the order of request.

The following example shows the creation and simple use of a sequence object:

```
CREATE SEQUENCE ACCOUNT_SEQ
    AS INTEGER
    START WITH 1
    INCREMENT BY 10
    CYCLE
    CACHE 20
```

Using Sequence Objects

Some additional advantages of using sequence objects over other methods of number generation include the use of the NEXT VALUE FOR and PREVIOUS VALUE FOR expressions. The short terms NEXTVAL and PREVVAL can be used as synonyms for NEXT VALUE and PREVIOUS VALUE, respectively. NEXTVAL FOR generates and returns the next value for the sequence object. PREVVAL FOR generates and returns the previous value for the sequence object. These statements can be used with the following:

- SELECT and SELECT INTO
- An INSERT statement within the SELECT clause of fullselect
- UPDATE statement within the SET clause (searched or positioned)
- SET host variable
- VALUES or VALUES INTO
- CREATE PROCEDURE, FUNCTION, TRIGGER

The following examples show use of these statements; assume that ACCT_SEQ is START WITH 10 INCREMENT BY 10.

SELECT NEXTVAL FOR ACCT_SEQ	→ Returns 10
SELECT NEXTVAL FOR ACCT_SEQ	→ Returns 20
COMMIT	
SELECT PREVVAL FOR ACCT_SEQ	→ Returns 20

UPDATE ACCOUNTS	
SET ACCT_NO = NEXTVAL FOR ACCT_SEQ	→ Returns 30

INSERT INTO ACCOUNTS (ACCT_NO)	
VALUES(NEXTVAL FOR ACCT_SEQ)	→ Returns 40

As you can see, using sequence objects instead of identity columns has many benefits. Table 4-7 provides a short comparison of the two.

Table 4-7 Sequence Objects versus Identity Columns

Sequence Objects	Identity Columns (with V8 features)
Standalone sequence objects created at user request	Internal sequence objects generated/maintained and populated by DB2
Used for whatever purpose users choose and can have more than one	Associated with a particular table and can have only one
Can have many and populate as many table columns as necessary	Can have only one per table
CYCLE used to wrap around and repeat with no uniqueness consideration	CYCLE may have a problem if a unique index is on the identity column and duplicates are created

continues

Table 4-7 Sequence Objects versus Identity Columns (Continued)

Sequence Objects	Identity Columns (with V8 features)
When used to populate a table, can later be updated	Cannot be updated if GENERATED ALWAYS used
ALTER the sequence object attributes; COMMENT and GRANT/REVOKE privileges	ALTER TABLE only; if adding an identity column to a populated table, it will be put in REORG-pending status.
DROP a sequence object	Cannot be removed from a table.*
Supports NEXT VALUE FOR EXPRESSION and PREVIOUS VALUE FOR EXPRESSION	Must use ID_VAL_LOCAL and returns only most recent values in that user's commit scope

* If future designs would benefit more from sequence objects than identity columns, careful consideration should be made when choosing to use identity columns. If they are defined on populated tables and you want to remove them, the table must be dropped and recreated. This could be a big problem for large tables in a high-availability environment.

Both identity columns and sequence objects have their place. Given that they both accomplish the same objective—generating sequence numbers—it is up to you to choose which one would work best for you. That determination will depend on the flexibility you need with the generated numbers and how the applications will be using them.

Modifying Sequence Objects
Sequence objects can be altered to change

- Whether to cycle the generated sequence values
- The MAXVALUE or MINVALUE
- The starting value
- The increment value
- Whether to cache the values

N O T E You cannot change/alter the data type or length of the values generated by a sequence object. In order to do this, you would need to drop and recreate the sequence object.

Removing Sequence Objects
Sequence objects can be removed by using the DROP statement:

```
DROP SEQUENCE <sequence-name>
```

Table Spaces

Data is stored in table spaces, which comprise one or many VSAM data sets.

Types of Table Spaces

Types of table spaces may be simple, segmented, partitioned, or LOB.

Simple Table Space.   Simple table spaces are the default but normally not the optimal. More than one table can be in a simple table space. If several tables are in the table space, rows from different tables can be interleaved on the same page; therefore, when a page is locked, rows of other tables may potentially be locked.

Segmented Table Space.   Normally, if a table is not partitioned, a segmented table space is used. A segmented table space organizes its pages into segments, with each segment containing the rows of only one table. Segments can be 4 to 64 pages each, with each segment having the same number of pages. When using a segmented table space to hold more than one table, make sure that the tables have similar characteristics in all categories, including size, volatility, locking needs, compression, and backup/recovery strategies. Some guidelines for how many tables to have in a segmented table space, based on the number of pages in the table space, are listed in Table 4-8.

Table 4-8   Table Page Thresholds

Number of Pages	Table Space Design
> 100,000	Consider partitioning
> 10,000	One-table segmented table space
> 128 to < 10,000	Multiple-table segmented table spaces
< 128	Multiple-table segmented table spaces

Using segmented table spaces has several advantages. Because the pages in a segment contain rows from only one table, locking interference with other tables will not occur. In simple table spaces, rows are intermixed on pages: If one table page is locked, it can inadvertently lock a row of another table just because it is on the same page. When you have only one table per table space, this is not an issue. Other benefits of having a segmented table space for one table follow.

- If a table scan is performed, the segments belonging to the table being scanned are the only ones accessed; empty pages will not be scanned.
- If a mass delete or a DROP table occurs, segment pages are available for immediate reuse after the commit, and it is not necessary to run a REORG utility.

- Mass deletes are much faster for segmented table space and produce less logging.
- The COPY utility will not have to copy empty pages left by a mass delete.
- When inserting records, some read operations can be avoided by using the more comprehensive space map of the segmented table space.
- By being able to safely combine several tables in a table space, you can reduce the number of open data sets necessary, which reduces the amount of memory required in the subsystem.

SEGSIZE tells DB2 how large to make each segment for a segmented table space and determines how many pages are contained in a segment. SEGSIZE will vary, depending on the size of the table space. Recommendations are listed in Table 4-9.

NOTE A segmented table space is a single data set and is limited to 2GB.

Table 4-9 Recommendations for Table Segment Size

Number of Pages	SEGSIZE
28 or less	4 to 28
28 to 128	32
128 or more	64

The following example shows how to create a segmented table space with a segment size of 32:

```
CREATE TABLESPACE CERTTS
IN DB2CERT
USING STOGROUP CERTSTG
PRIQTY 52
SECQTY 20
ERASE NO
LOCKSIZE PAGE
BUFFERPOOL BP6
CLOSE YES
SEGSIZE 32;
```

NOTE ALTER cannot be used on the SEGSIZE parameter.

Partitioned Table Space.   Partitioning a table space has several advantages. For large tables, partitioning is the only way to store large amounts of data. Partitioning also has advantages for tables that are not large. DB2 allows defining up to 4,096 partitions of up to 64GB each. (However, total table size is limited to 128TB (terabytes) and the number of partitions is dependent on the DSSIZE specified.) Nonpartitioned table spaces are limited to 64GB of data.

You can take advantage of the ability to execute utilities on separate partitions in parallel. This also gives you the ability to access data in certain partitions while utilities are executing on others. In a data sharing environment, you can spread partitions among several members to split workloads. You can also spread your data over multiple volumes and need not use the same storage group for each data set belonging to the table space. This also allows you to place frequently accessed partitions on faster devices. The following example shows how to create a partitioned table space with two partitions:

```
CREATE TABLESPACE CERTTSPT
IN DB2CERT
USING STOGROUP CERTSTG
    PRIQTY 100
    SECQTY 120
    ERASE NO
NUMPARTS 2
(PART 1
 COMPRESS YES,
 PART 2
 FREEPAGE 20)
ERASE NO
LOCKSIZE PAGE
CLOSE NO;
```

> **NOTE** It is possible to use the ALTER statement to change the partitioning-key ranges for rebalancing. A REBALANCE option on the REORG utility allows for this as well.

Many designs are outgrowing the bounds of V7 partitioned table spaces and need to add partitions. In the past, this process could be rather cumbersome. In version 8, this can be done by using the ALTER statement:

```
ALTER TABLE table1 ADD PARTITION
```

DB2 picks the partition number, based on the next-available partition. If the partitions are storage group (stogroup) defined, the data set is allocated for table space and partitioning index with a PRIQTY value picked up from the previous partition. You may need to alter the table space to give new parameters to better suit the new partition, that is, primary allocations and free space. If your underlying data sets are VCAT defined, the data set will need to be defined first, before the ALTER is performed. The new partitions will be available immediately after the ALTER. In order for this to take place, the table space will have to be stopped and then started again. A small outage will occur in order to take advantage of this.

All affected plans, packages, and cached SQL statements are invalidated because SQL may be optimized to read certain partitions, and the new number of partitions may change the access path. If the table space is defined as LARGE, the limit is 64 partitions. If using DSSIZE, the number of the partitions is limited, based on the chosen DSSIZE and the page size. See Figure 4-12 later in this chapter.

Dealing with the archiving of data or rolling of partitions often involves a large outage and a lot of previous planning. Even though tables can support up to 4,096 partitions, some limitations exist; supporting that much historical data in the primary table space may not be desirable.

Partitions can be rotated in order to move the first partition to last. Doing so will allow moving the lowest logical partition to the last logical partition and specifying the new partition values for enforcing the values of the last partition. The RESET option allows a partition to be reset, at which time the data is deleted, which can impact the performance of the feature and the availability of the data. Before the rotation, the partition holds the oldest data; afterward, it will hold the newest data. The REUSE option allows extents to be kept, and the data set will not be physically deleted. Following is an example of how to rotate partitions:

```
ALTER TABLE table1 ROTATE PARTITION FIRST TO LAST ENDING AT ('2004-03-31')
```

As mentioned, the data is deleted from old partitions. Depending on the size of the partition, the logging impacts of the deletes may become a performance issue. You may want to consider unloading the partition prior to ALTER by using the old tried-and-true method of LOAD...PART x REPLACE, using a dummy SYSREC. This will help lessen the duration of the outage during the rotating of the partitions.

During the rotate, a DBD lock will be taken as the DDL completes. All activity will be quiesced immediately when the ALTER is issued.

Another issue is the fact that all keys for deleted rows must be deleted from nonpartitioning indexes (NPIs). If multiple NPIs are on a table, the scans must be performed serially to perform the deletes.

If a physical DB2-enforced referential integrity relationship or triggers exist, deletes will be a row at a time. Again, in this situation, you may want to consider an unload of the data first. But if a DELETE RESTRICT relationship is in place, the rotate may not work.

The `ALTER TABLE ROTATE` can change partition order. To account for this, the `LOGICAL_PART` column has been added to the `SYSTABLEPART` and `SYSCOPY` tables. This change will also be visible in the `-DISPLAY DATABASE` output.

Figure 4-3 shows the `ALTER` statement of the three-partition `CUSTOMER` table. In this example, we are rotating off the first physical partition (P1) and now the last logical partition (P3).

ALTER Table CUSTOMER; ROTATE Partition First to Last Ending at 02/29/2004; RESET

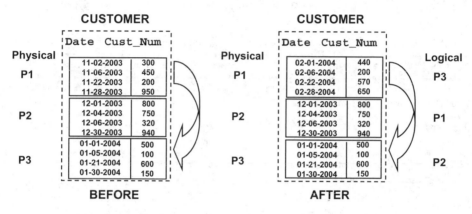

SYSIBM.SYSTABLES – Customer – PARTITION = 1, LOGICAL_PART = 3

Figure 4-3   Rotating partitions

In order to have a partitioned table in the DB2 releases prior to version 8, a partitioning index defined to give DB2 the limit keys for each partition was required. This partitioning index was also required to be the clustering index. Version 8 does not require a partitioning index to be defined on the partitioned table. The ability to partition is handled by the table creation, not the index. The following example uses the `CREATE TABLE` statement to handle the partitioning of a table:

```
CREATE TABLE ACCOUNTS
    (ENTER_DATE   DATE,
     ACCOUNT   INTEGER,
     STATUS CHAR(3))
    IN TSP1
        PARTITION BY (ENTER_DATE)
            (PARTITION 1 ENDING AT ('2002-02-28'),
             PARTITION 2 ENDING AT ('2002-03-31'));
```

The PART VALUES clause could also be used instead of the PARTITION ENDING AT clause; however, PARTITION ENDING AT is preferred.

Once a partitioned table has been created, it is ready to be used. Creating a separate partitioning index with the VALUES keyword is not required and not allowed. The information about the limit keys for the partitions will be stored in SYSTABLES, SYSCOLUMNS, and SYSTABLEPART.

Using table-controlled partitioning instead of index-controlled partitioning is recommended. Table-controlled partitioning is a replacement for index-controlled partitioning. Table 4-10 lists the differences between the two partitioning methods.

Table 4-10   Differences between Table-Controlled and Index-Controlled Partitioning

Table-Controlled Partitioning	Index-Controlled Partitioning
A partitioning index is not required; a clustering index is not required.	A partitioning index is required; a clustering index is required.
Multiple partitioned indexes can be created in a table space.	Only one partitioned index can be created in a table space.
A table space partition is identified by both a physical partition number and a logical partition number.	A table space partition is identified by a physical partition number.
The high-limit key is always enforced.	The high-limit key is not enforced if the table space is nonlarge.

The change from index-controlled partitioning to table-controlled partitioning can occur when any of the following are used:

- DROP partitioning index
- ALTER INDEX NOT CLUSTER
- ALTER TABLE ADD PART
- ALTER TABLE ALTER PART ROTATE
- ALTER TABLE ALTER PART *partno*
- CREATE INDEX PARTITIONED
- CREATE INDEX VALUES, with no CLUSTER keyword

LOB Table Space.   A LOB table space needs to be created for each column—or each column of each partition—of a base LOB table with a LOB column. This table space will contain the auxiliary table. The LOB table space has a structure that can be up to 4,000TB in size. This is a storage model used only for LOB table spaces. This linear table space can be up to 254 data sets, which can be up to 64GB each. The LOB table space is implemented in the same fashion as pieces are implemented for NPIs, as discussed later in this chapter. We can have 254 partitions of

64GB each, for a total of 16TB, and we will have one for each LOB column, up to 254 partitions, or a possible 4,000TB. See Figure 4-4.

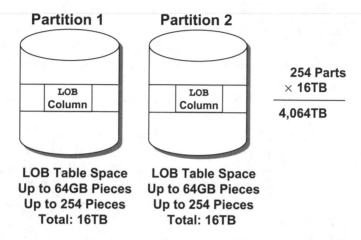

Figure 4-4   Physical LOB storage: table with a LOB column up to 254 partitions

Partitioned base tables can each have different LOB table spaces. A LOB value can be longer than a page in a LOB table space and can also span pages. Following is an example of creating a LOB table space:

```
CREATE LOB TABLESPACE CERTPIC
   IN DB2CERT
   USING STOGROUP CERTSTG
       PRIQTY 3200
       SECQTY 1600
   LOCKSIZE LOB
   BUFFERPOOL BP16K1
   GBPCACHE SYSTEM
   LOG NO
   CLOSE NO;
```

> **N O T E**   If a database is not explicitly defined for a LOB table space, it defaults to DSNDB04.

Creating Table Spaces

The CREATE TABLESPACE statement is used to define a simple, segmented, or partitioned table space on the current server. A large number of parameters with significant options are used in defining table spaces, depending on the type of table space. The major table space parameters follow.

- DSSIZE specifies that the maximum size of any partition in a partitioned table space can exceed the 2GB limit, up to a size of 64GB.
- LOB specifies that the table space is a LOB table space, used to hold only LOB values.
- USING specifies whether storage groups or a user-defined table space is being defined. USING STOGROUP specifies that DB2 will manage the data sets and that PRIQTY and SECQTY will be used to define the allocations for the data sets. USING VCAT specifies that the data sets will be user defined.
- FREEPAGE and PCTFREE specify the amount of free space to be left when a table space is loaded or reorganized.
- GBPCACHE is used in data sharing to specify which pages of a table space or a partition are written to the group buffer pools.
- NUMPARTS specifies the number of partitions in a partitioned table space, with a maximum of 4096 allowed.
- SEGSIZE specifies the number of pages in a segment for segmented table spaces.
- BUFFERPOOL specifies which buffer pool the table space is assigned to. A default buffer pool can be set with DSNZPARM TBSBPOOL.
- LOCKSIZE specifies the size of locks used within the table space and in certain cases can specify the threshold at which lock escalation occurs. The allowable lock sizes are ANY, TABLESPACE, TABLE, PAGE, ROW, and LOB.
- MAXROWS specifies the maximum number of rows allowed on a page, up to a maximum of 255.
- LOCKPART specifies whether selective partition locking is to be used when locking a partitioned table space.
- COMPRESS specifies whether data compression is used for rows in the table space or partition.
- TRACKMOD specifies whether DB2 tracks modified pages in the space map pages in the table space or partition.

Page Sizes.   Four page sizes, listed in Table 4-9, are available for use.

Table 4-11   Table Page Sizes

Buffer Pool	Pages
BP0–BP49	4KB
BP8K0–BP8K9	8KB
BP16K0–BP16K9	16KB
BP32K–BP32K9	32KB

The 8KB, 16KB, and 32KB pages are comprised of 4K control intervals (CIs), unless the DSVCI DSN2PARM is set to YES. Index page sizes are only 4KB pages, and work file (DSNDB07) table space pages are only 4KB or 32KB. The page size is defined by the buffer pool chosen for the table space; that is, BP8K0 supports 8KB pages.

Better hit ratios can be achieved with the larger page sizes, and they have less I/O because more rows can fit on a page. For instance, for a 2,200-byte row—perhaps for a data warehouse—a 4KB page would be able to hold only one row, but if an 8KB page were used, three rows could fit on a page, one more than if 4KB pages were used, and one less lock would be required.

DSSIZE. Depending on the DSSIZE and the page size, the number of partitions a table space can have has limitations. Table 4-12 shows these limits.

Table 4-12 DSSIZE and Partition Limitations

DSSIZE	4K	8K	16K	32K
4GB	4,096	4,096	4,096	4,096
8GB	2,048	4,096	4,096	4,096
16GB	1,024	2,048	4,096	4,096
32GB	512	1,024	2,048	4,096
64GB	256	512	1,024	2,048

Free Space. The FREEPAGE and PCTFREE clauses are used to help improve the performance of updates and inserts by allowing free space to exist on table spaces or index spaces. Performance improvements include improved access to the data through better clustering of data, less index page splitting, faster inserts, fewer row overflows, and a reduction in the number of REORGs required. Some tradeoffs include an increase in the number of pages—and therefore more auxiliary storage needed—fewer rows per I/O and less efficient use of buffer pools, and more pages to scan.

As a result, it is important to achieve a good balance for each individual table space and index space when deciding on free space, and that balance will depend on the processing requirements of each table space or index space. When inserts and updates are performed, DB2 will use the free space defined, and by doing so can keep records in clustering sequence as much as possible. When the free space is used up, the records must be located elsewhere, and this is when performance can begin to suffer. Read-only tables do not require any free space, and tables with a pure insert-at-end strategy generally don't require free space. Exceptions to this are tables with VARCHAR columns and tables using compression and that are subject to updates.

The FREEPAGE amount represents the number of full pages inserted between each empty page during a LOAD or REORG of a table space or an index space. The tradeoff is between how often reorganization can be performed and how much disk space can be allocated for an object. FREEPAGE should be used for table spaces so that inserts can be kept as close to the optimal page as possible. For indexes, FREEPAGE should be used for the same reason, except improvements would be in terms of keeping index page splits near the original page instead of placing them at the end of the index. FREEPAGE is useful when inserts are sequentially clustered.

PCTFREE is the percentage of a page left free during a LOAD or a REORG. PCTFREE is useful when you can assume an even distribution of inserts across the key ranges. It is also needed in indexes to avoid all random inserts causing page splits.

Compression.   Using the COMPRESS clause of the CREATE TABLESPACE and ALTER TABLESPACE SQL statements allows for the compression of data in a table space or in a partition of a partitioned table space.

> **N O T E**   Indexes and LOB table spaces are not compressed.

In many cases, using the COMPRESS clause can significantly reduce the amount of Direct Access Storage Device (DASD) space needed to store data, but the compression ratio achieved depends on the characteristics of the data. Compression allows us to get more rows on a page and therefore see many of the following performance benefits, depending on the SQL workload and the amount of compression:

- Higher buffer pool hit ratios
- Fewer I/Os
- Fewer getpage operations
- Reduced CPU (central processing unit) time for image copies

Using compression also has some considerations for processing cost.

- Compressing data can result in a higher processor cost, depending on the SQL workload. However, if you use IBM's synchronous data compression hardware, processor time is significantly less than if you use the DB2-provided software simulation or an edit or field procedure to compress the data.
- The processor cost to decode a row by using the COMPRESS clause is significantly less than the cost to encode that same row. This rule applies regardless of whether the compression uses the synchronous data compression hardware or the software simulation built into DB2.
- The data access path DB2 uses affects the processor cost for data compression. In general, the relative overhead of compression is higher for table space scans and less costly for index access.

The following example shows a table space created with compression:

```
CREATE TABLESPACE CERTTSPT
IN DB2CERT
USING STOGROUP CERTSTG
    PRIQTY 100
    SECQTY 120
    ERASE NO
COMPRESS YES
ERASE NO
LOCKSIZE PAGE
```

Modifying Table Spaces

After you create a table space, the ALTER TABLESPACE statement enables you to modify existing table spaces. The ALTER TABLESPACE statement modifies many of the table space parameters, such as

- Change the buffer pool assignment.
- Change the lock size or the lock escalation threshold.
- Change the specifics for a single partition.
- Change any of the space definitions.
- Turn compression off and on.
- Change how pages are cached in group buffer pools.
- Change logging for LOB table spaces.
- Rotate partitions.
- Add partitions.
- Change the USING VCAT.

> **NOTE** If ALTER is used on the USING VCAT, the table space must be stopped first.

In the following example, ALTER TABLESPACE is used to change the buffer pool assignment and size of the locks used:

```
ALTER TABLESPACE DB2CERT.CERTTS
    BUFFERPOOL BP4
    LOCKSIZE ROW
```

Removing Table Spaces

When you want to remove a table space, use the DROP TABLESPACE statement to delete the object. This will remove any objects that are directly or indirectly dependent on the table space.

This statement will also invalidate any packages or plans that refer to the object and will remove its descriptions and all related data from the catalog.

```
DROP TABLESPACE DB2CERT.CERTTS
```

Views

Views are logical tables created using the CREATE VIEW statement. Once a view is defined, it can be accessed using DML statements, such as SELECT, INSERT, UPDATE, and DELETE, as if it were a base table. A view is a temporary table, and the data in the view is available only during query processing.

With a view, you can make a subset of table data available to an application program and validate data that is to be inserted or updated. A view can have column names that are different from those of corresponding columns in the original tables. The use of views provides flexibility in the way the application programs and end user queries look at the table data.

A sample CREATE VIEW statement is shown in the following example. The original table, EMPLOYEE, has columns named SALARY and COMM. For security reasons, this view is created from the ID, NAME, DEPT, JOB, and HIREDATE columns. In addition, we are restricting access on the column DEPT. This definition will show the information only of employees who belong to the department whose DEPTNO is 10.

```
CREATE VIEW EMP_VIEW1
(EMPID,EMPNAME,DEPTNO,JOBTITLE,HIREDATE)
   AS SELECT ID,NAME,DEPT,JOB,HIREDATE FROM EMPLOYEE
   WHERE DEPT=10;
```

After the view has been created, the access privileges can be specified. This provides data security, as a restricted view of the base table is accessible. As we see in this example, a view can contain a WHERE clause to restrict access to certain rows or can contain a subset of the columns to restrict access to certain columns of data.

The column names in the view do not have to match the column names of the base table. The table name has an associated schema, as does the view name. Once the view has been defined, it can be used in such DML statements as SELECT, INSERT, UPDATE, and DELETE, with restrictions. The database administrator can decide to provide a group of users with a higher-level privilege on the view than the base table.

A view is an alternative way to look at data in one or more tables. A view is an SQL SELECT statement that is executed whenever the view is referenced in an SQL statement. Because it is not materialized until execution, such operations as ORDER BY, the WITH clause, and the OPTIMIZE FOR clause have no meaning.

WITH CHECK OPTION

If the view definition includes conditions, such as a WHERE clause, and the intent is to ensure that any INSERT or UPDATE statement referencing the view will have the WHERE clause applied, the view must be defined using WITH CHECK OPTION. This option can ensure the integrity of the data being modified in the database. An SQL error will be returned if the condition is violated during an INSERT or UPDATE operation.

The following example is of a view definition using the WITH CHECK OPTION, which is required to ensure that the condition is always checked. You want to ensure that the DEPT is always 10. This will restrict the input values for the DEPT column. When a view is used to insert a new value, the WITH CHECK OPTION is always enforced.

```
CREATE VIEW EMP_VIEW2
(EMPID,EMPNAME,DEPTNO,JOBTITLE,HIREDATE)
    AS SELECT ID,NAME,DEPT,JOB,HIREDATE FROM EMPLOYEE
    WHERE DEPT=10
WITH CHECK OPTION;
```

If the view in this example is used in an INSERT statement, the row will be rejected if the DEPTNO column is not the value 10. It is important to remember that no data validation occurs during data modification if the WITH CHECK OPTION is not specified. If the view in the previous example were used in a SELECT statement, the conditional—WHERE clause—would be invoked, and the resulting table would contain only the matching rows of data. In other words, the WITH CHECK OPTION does not affect the result of a SELECT statement. The WITH CHECK OPTION must not be specified for read-only views.

Read-Only Views

A read-only view allows no inserts, updates, or deletes. A view is considered read-only if

- The first FROM clause identifies more than one table or view, a table function, or a read-only view, a nested or common table expression, or a system-maintained MQT.
- The outer SELECT contains a GROUP BY or HAVING clause
- The outer SELECT contains a column function or DISTINCT
- It contains a subquery with the same table as the outer SELECT

Modifying and Removing a View

In order to modify a view, you simply drop and recreate it. You cannot alter a view's attributes, but you can regenerate it. To remove a view, you simply use the following:

```
DROP VIEW EMP_VIEW2
```

Materialized Query Tables (MQTs)

Prior to V8, decision-support queries were difficult and expensive. They typically operated over a large amount of data that might have to scan or process terabytes of data and possibly perform multiple joins and complex aggregations. With these types of queries, traditional optimization was failing, and performance was less than optimal.

The use of materialized query tables, which used to be known as automatic summary tables on non-mainframe platforms, allows you to precompute whole or parts of each query and then use computed results to answer future queries. MQTs provide the means to save the results of prior queries and then reuse the common query results in subsequent queries. This helps avoid redundant scanning, aggregating, and joins. MQTs are useful for data warehouse–type applications.

MQTs do not completely eliminate optimization problems; rather, MQTs move optimization issues to other areas. Some challenges include finding the best MQT for expected workload, maintaining the MQTs when underlying tables are updated, recognizing usefulness of MQT for a query, and determining to use the MQT for a query. Most of these types of problems are addressed by OLAP tools, but MQTs are the first step.

Defining MQTs

MQTs work with two tables: a source table and a materialized query table. The source table is the base table, view, table expression, or table function. The materialized query table is the table used to contain materialized data derived from one or more source tables in a FULLSELECT and is similar to creating a view. However, a view is logical, whereas an MQT contains materialized data of the query result. You could refer to an MQT as a "materialized view."

MQTs are created with the CREATE TABLE statement, and the columns of the MQT can be explicitly specified or derived from the fullselect associated with the table. MQTs are physically stored as are declared temporary tables. The following is an example of the syntax used to create an MQT:

```
CREATE TABLE SALESMQT (CUSTID, STOREID, LOCID, MTH) AS (
    SELECT CUSTID, STOREID, LOCID, MTH, COUNT(*)
    FROM SALES
    GROUP BY CUSTID, STOREID, LOCID, MTH)
DATA INITIALLY DEFERRED
REFRESH DEFERRED
MAINTAINED BY SYSTEM
ENABLE QUERY OPTIMIZATION
```

This example creates an MQT called SALESMQT.

MQT Options

The option `DATA INITIALLY DEFERRED` states that when a materialized query table is created, it will not be populated immediately by the fullselect defined in the DDL. The `REFRESH DEFERRED` option says that the data in the MQT is not refreshed immediately when its based tables are updates. The MQT can be refreshed at any time by using the `REFRESH TABLE` statement. The `REFRESH TABLE` command can also be used for the initial population of the MQT. The `REFRESH TABLE` statement deletes all rows with a mass delete on the MQT and then executes the fullselect in the MQT definition to recalculate the data from the base tables. It then inserts the calculated result into the MQT and updates the catalog for the refresh timestamp and cardinality of the MQT. This is all performed in a single commit scope. Following is an example of the how to refresh `SALESMQT`:

```
REFRESH TABLE SALESMQT;
```

The `MAINTAINED BY SYSTEM` option indicates that the MQT is system maintained and that you will need to use the SQL statement `REFRESH TABLE` to perform this. This option does not allow for user updates by `LOAD`, `INSERT`, `UPDATE`, or `DELETE` and thus is by nature read-only.

The `MAINTAINED BY USER` option indicates that the MQT is user maintained by either triggers or batch updates. This option allows for user updates via `LOAD`, `INSERT`, `UPDATE`, or `DELETE`, and it can also be updated by the `REFRESH TABLE` statement, which can use `EXPLAIN` if necessary.

`ENABLE FOR QUERY OPTIMIZATION` allows the DB2 optimizer to choose the MQT for use during the processes of establishing an access path. Optimization is discussed further in Chapter 17.

Indexes

An *index* is a list of the locations of rows, sorted by the contents of one or more specified columns. Indexes are typically used to improve the query performance, but can also serve a logical data design purpose. For example, a unique index does not allow the entry of duplicate values in columns, thereby guaranteeing that no rows of a table are the same. Indexes can be created to specify ascending or descending order by the values in a column. The indexes contain a pointer, known as a *row identifier (RID)*, to the physical location of the rows in the table.

Indexes are created for three main purposes:

1. To ensure uniqueness of values
2. To improve query performance
3. To ensure a physical clustering sequence

More than one index can be defined on a particular base table, which can have a beneficial effect on the performance of queries. However, the more indexes there are, the more the database manager must work to keep the indexes up to date during UPDATE, DELETE, and INSERT operations. Creating a large number of indexes for a table that receives many updates can slow down processing. Some of the most important parameters of the CREATE INDEX statement are listed in Table 4-13.

> **N O T E**   Indexes are also stored in underlying VSAM data sets, as are table spaces. In order to make a correlation between the index that you or DB2 created, you can look in the INDEXSPACE column in the SYSINDEXES catalog table.

Table 4-13 CREATE INDEX Parameters

Parameter	Function
TYPE 2	Specifies a type 2 index. The TYPE 2 clause is not required. A type 2 index is always created.
UNIQUE	Prevents the table from containing two or more rows with the same value of the index key.
USING clause	Specifies whether storage groups or a user-defined index space is being defined. • USING STOGROUP specifies that DB2 will manage the data sets and that a PRIQTY and a SECQTY will define the allocations for the data sets. • USING VCAT specifies that the data sets will be user defined and that no space allocations are defined in this statement.
FREEPAGE and PCTFREE	Specify the amount of free space to be left when an index space is built or reorganized.
GBPCACHE	Used in data sharing to specify which pages of an index space are written to the group buffer pools.
DEFINE	Specifies whether to create the underlying data sets.
CLUSTER	Specifies whether it is a clustering index.
PARTITIONED	Specifies whether the index is partitioned: primary or secondary.
PART	Identifies the partition number.

Table 4-13 CREATE INDEX Parameters (Continued)

Parameter	Function
PARTITION BY RANGE	Specifies the partitioning index for the table to determine the partitioning scheme for the data in the table.
BUFFERPOOL	Specifies which buffer pool the table space is assigned to. A default buffer pool can be assigned with DSNZPARM IDXBPOOL.
PIECESIZE	Identifies the size of the pieces—data sets—used for a nonpartitioning index.
NOT PADDED	Allows for an index with a VARCHAR column to not be padded with blanks, reducing the size of the index and allowing it to be used for index-only access.
COPY	Specifies whether the index can be image copied.

Type 2 indexes are created by default. Type 2 indexes have no locking and do not have subpages. Type 1 indexes should not be used and, as of version 8, are not supported.

An index can be defined with the DEFINE NO option (DEFINE YES is the default). This is done to specify an index and defer the physical creation. The data sets will not be created until data is inserted into the index. This option is helpful in order to reduce the number of physical data sets.

Clustering Index

It is generally important to control the physical sequence of the data in a table. The CLUSTER option is used on one, and only one, index on a table and specifies the physical sequence. If not defined, the first index defined on the table in a nonpartitioned table space is used for the clustering sequence. The best clustering index is the one that supports the majority of the sequential access to the data in the table.

> **N O T E**   When the CLUSTER keyword is used, the index is called the *explicit* clustering index. If no index is defined with the CLUSTER keyword, the index DB2 chooses for clustering is called the *implicit* clustering index.

In defining table spaces, one option is called MEMBER CLUSTER. When this option is specified, the clustering sequence specified by the clustering index is ignored. In that case, DB2 will locate the data on the basis of available space when an SQL INSERT statement is used. This option is used mainly in a data sharing environment to avoid excessive p-lock (physical lock) negotiation on the space map when inserts are coming in by the clustering index on multiple members.

The clustering index can also be changed. `ALTER` can be used to change whether an index is the clustering index. For instance, the following syntax changes an index to not be the clustering index:

```
ALTER INDEX CUSTIX NO CLUSTER
```

After the `NO CLUSTER` alter index is completed, the inserts will still occur by the implicit clustering index. A new clustering index needs to be defined, or `ALTER` can be used on an existing index to become the new clustering index, as shown in the following syntax:

```
ALTER INDEX CUSTIX2 CLUSTER
```

When the new clustering index is defined, inserts will occur by the new index. Obviously, for performance reasons, it is wise to perform a `REORG` right after the `ALTER` to specify the new clustering index so that the inserts can now occur by the new clustering index.

Partitioned Index

Partitioned indexes are of two types: primary and secondary. If the keys in the index match the limit-key columns, or subset of columns, in the partitioned table, the index is considered a primary partitioned index; if not, it is considered a secondary partitioned index. This will be reflected in `SYSIBM.SYSINDEXES`.

```
CREATE UNIQUE PARTITIONED INDEX DB2USER1.TESTCNTX
  ON DB2USER1.TEST_CENTER
   (TCID ASC)
  USING STOGROUP CERTSTG
  PRIQTY 512
  SECQTY 64
  ERASE NO
  CLUSTER
  BUFFERPOOL BP3
  CLOSE YES;
```

A partitioned index is made up of several data sets. Each partition can have different attributes; that is, some may have more free space than others.

Unique and Nonunique Indexes

A *unique index* guarantees the uniqueness of the data values in a table's columns. The unique index can be used during query processing to perform faster retrieval of data. The uniqueness is enforced at the end of the SQL statement that updates rows or inserts new rows. The uniqueness is also checked during the execution of the `CREATE INDEX` statement. If the table already contains rows with duplicate key values, the index is not created. An example of creating a unique index follows:

```
CREATE UNIQUE INDEX DB2USER1.TESTIX
  ON DB2USER1.TEST
   (NUMBER ASC)
  USING STOGROUP CERTSTG
  PRIQTY 512
  SECQTY 64
  ERASE NO
  CLUSTER
```

A *nonunique index* can improve query performance by maintaining a sorted order for the data. Depending on how many columns are used to define a key, you can have an *atomic*, or single-column, key or a *composite key*, which is composed of two or more columns.

The following are types of keys used to implement constraints.

- A *unique key* is used to implement unique constraints. A unique constraint does not allow two different rows to have the same values on the key columns.
- A *primary key* is used to implement entity-integrity constraints. A primary key is a special type of unique key. A table can have only one primary key. The primary-key column must be defined with the NOT NULL option.
- A *foreign key* is used to implement referential integrity constraints. Referential constraints can reference only a primary key or a unique constraint. The values of a foreign key can have values defined only in the primary key or unique constraint they are referencing or null values. (A foreign key is not an index; although an index can be created to improve access to rows using the foreign key columns.)

> **N O T E** DB2 uses unique indexes and the NOT NULL option to maintain primary and unique key constraints.

Unique Where Not Null Index

This is a special form of a unique index. Normally, in a unique index, any two null values are taken to be equal. Specifying WHERE NOT NULL will allow any two null values to be unequal.

Null Values and Indexes

It is important to understand the difference between a primary key and a unique index. DB2 uses two elements to implement the relational database concept of primary and unique keys: unique indexes and the NOT NULL constraint. Therefore, unique indexes do not enforce the primary key constraint by themselves, as they can allow a null value. Null values are unknown, but when it comes to indexing, a null value is treated as equal to all other null values, with the exception of the UNIQUE WHERE NOT NULL INDEX. You cannot insert a NULL value twice if the column is a key of a unique index, because it violates the uniqueness rule for the index.

Nonpartitioning Indexes

NPIs are used on partitioned tables and are not the same as the clustered partitioning key, which is used to order and partition the data. Rather, NPIs are for access to the data.

NPIs can be unique or nonunique. Although you can have only one clustered partitioning index, you can have several NPIs on a table, if necessary. NPIs can be broken apart into multiple pieces, or data sets, by using the PIECESIZE clause on the CREATE INDEX statement. Pieces can vary in size from 254KB to 64GB; the best size will depend on how much data you have and how many pieces you want to manage. If you have several pieces, you can achieve more parallelism on processes, such as heavy INSERT batch jobs, by alleviating the bottlenecks caused by contention on a single data set. The following example shows how to create an NPI with pieces:

```
CREATE UNIQUE INDEX DB2USER1.TESTCN2X
  ON DB2USER1.TEST_CENTER
   (CODE ASC)
  USING STOGROUP CERTSTG
  PIECESIZE 512K;
```

Data-Partitioned Secondary Indexes

The new DPSI index type provides many advantages over the traditional NPIs for secondary indexes on a partitioned table space in terms of availability and performance. We can now choose to partition a table without a partitioning/clustering index. So now you can choose to cluster by a different index if it better fits your data and processing requirements. This can be accomplished through a DPSI.

The partitioning scheme of the DPSI will be the same as the table space partitions, and the index keys in x index partition will match those in x partition of the table space. Figure 4-5 shows how a DPSI is physically structured. The CUST_NUMX index is a DPSI.

A DPSI provides the following benefits:

- Clustering by a secondary index
- Ability to easily drop partitions
- Ability to easily rotate partitions
- Efficient utility processing on secondary indexes
- Ability to reduce overhead in data sharing (affinity routing)

Although partition independence is furthered, some queries may not perform as well with DPSIs. If it has predicates that reference partitioning column values in a single partition and

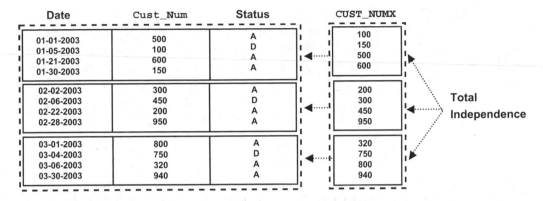

Figure 4-5 DPSI physical layout

therefore are restricted to a single partition of the DPSI, the query will benefit from this new organization. The queries will have to be designed to allow for partition pruning through the predicates in order to accomplish this. However, if it references only columns in the DPSI, the predicate may not perform very well because it may need to probe several partitions of the index. Figure 4-6 shows how applications will need to code predicates for DPSIs.

Another limitation to using DPSIs is the fact that they cannot be unique and may not be the best candidates for ORDER BYs.

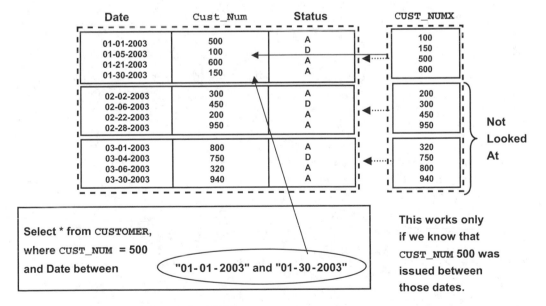

Figure 4-6 Coding predicates for DPSIs

LOB Indexes

An index must be created on an auxiliary table for a LOB. The index itself consists of 19 bytes for the ROWID and 5 bytes for the RID. Therefore, the index is always unique. No LOB columns are allowed in the index. The following example shows the CREATE statement for an auxiliary index:

```
CREATE INDEX DB2CERT.PHOTOIX
  ON DB2USER1.CAND_PHOTO
  USING VCAT DB2USER1
  COPY YES;
```

> **N O T E**   No columns are specified, because the auxiliary indexes have implicitly generated keys.

General Indexing Guidelines

Indexes consume disk space. The amount of disk space will vary, depending on the length of the key columns and whether the index is unique or nonunique. The size of the index will increase as more data is inserted into the base table. Therefore, consider the disk space required for indexes when planning the size of the database. Some of the indexing considerations include the following.

- Primary and unique key constraints will always create a unique index.
- It is usually beneficial to create indexes on foreign-key constraint columns.
- It is beneficial to always create a clustering index.

Modifying an Index

The ALTER INDEX statement allows you to change many of the characteristics on the index, such as

- Add a column to the index
- Change the buffer pool assignment
- Change the specifics for a single partition
- Change any of the space definitions
- Change whether the index is to be copied
- Change the clustering index
- Change to not pad an index if it contains a VARCHAR

The following example shows how to change the buffer pool assignment for an index:

```
ALTER INDEX TESTCN2X BUFFERPOOL BP1;
```

Removing an Index

When you want to remove an index, issue the following statement:

```
DROP INDEX TESTCN2X;
```

Databases

A database is a collection of table spaces, index spaces, and the objects with them. A couple of types of databases are used for special purposes.

- A WORKFILE database holds the DB2 work files used for sorting and other activities.
- A TEMP database holds temporary tables as defined by a DECLARE TEMP statement. (Refer to Chapter 7 for more information on declared temporary tables.)

For these special databases, you can also specify which data sharing member they are for, as each member must have its own. You can also specify the coding scheme for the data in the database (ASCII, CCSID, EBCDIC, Unicode).

Creating a Database

Following is an example of the creation of the DB2CERT database. The BUFFERPOOL parameter lets us specify that any objects created in this database without a buffer pool assigned will default to buffer pool BP7. INDEXBP has the same purpose but provides a default buffer pool for indexes.

```
CREATE DATABASE CERTTS
STOGROUP CERTSTG
BUFFERPOOL BP7
INDEXBP BP8;
```

Modifying a Database

The default buffer pools, encoding scheme, and the storage group can be changed for a database. The following is an example ALTER DATABASE:

```
ALTER DATABASE DB2CERT
BUFFERPOOL BP4;
```

Removing a Database

It is very easy to remove a database: a simple DROP statement, provided that all the appropriate authorities are in place. When a database is dropped, all dependent objects are dropped as well.

```
DROP DATABASE DB2CERT;
```

Storage Groups

Storage groups are used to list the DASD volumes that will be used to store the data. Storage groups can contain one or many volumes and can work with or without SMS (system-managed storage). If table spaces or index spaces are defined using a storage group—identified in the USING clause in the CREATE INDEX and CREATE TABLESPACE statements—they are considered to be DB2 managed, and DB2 will create them, allowing you to specify the PRIQTY and SECQTY for the data set allocations. Otherwise, they are considered to be user managed and must be defined explicitly through the IDCAMS utility.

To create a storage group, do the following:

```
CREATE STOGROUP CERTSTG
VOLUME(*) VCAT DB2USER1;
```

> **NOTE** The asterisk (*) in this example indicates that SMS will manage the volumes to be used.

We can add or remove volumes within a storage group. This is done via ALTER:

```
ALTER STOGROUP CERTSTG ADD VOL1;
```

Storage groups can be removed by using the DROP statement. This can be done only if no table spaces or index spaces are using it.

```
DROP STOGROUP CERTSTG;
```

DATABASE DESIGN AND IMPLEMENTATION

Figure 4-7 shows the many facets to work on when implementing a DB2 relational database. A couple of general design steps need to be performed: development of a logical model and development/implementation of a physical model.

Logical Design

Logical design is the process of determining entities, entity attributes, relationships among entities, degrees of the relationships, and representing them in a fully keyed, normalized data model or entity relationship diagram. The normalized data model can then be used to define the tables needed for the relational database. Performing the logical design also involves identifying primary keys and foreign keys.

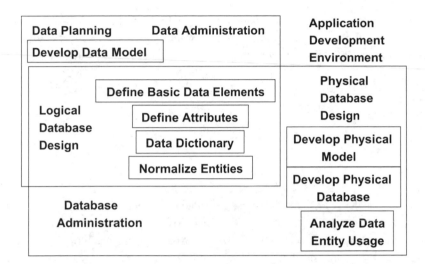

Figure 4-7   Designing relational database applications

A data model is a graphic, conceptual model that identifies the entity types of the business and the business interactions among the entities. The data model provides a static rather than dynamic view of data, which appears as if frozen in time. Two basic approaches to designing a data model follow.

1. A bottom-up approach produces a composite, or global, view of the data in the organization, based on the combination of many users' views of the problem requirements, not the inherent structure of the data. This approach does not reflect all the business activities most often used in data analysis.

2. A top-down approach produces an organizational view of the data before the application views are identified. This approach takes into account the business activities of the entire organization, independent of any particular application.

A logical data model has three basic components: entities, attributes, and relationships.

Entities

An entity is an object about which we store data for the purpose of answering a query or making a decision. An entity may be a person, place, or thing—event—of interest to the enterprise or application. Occurrences of an entity are uniquely identified by one or more attributes that make up the key to the data entity. An entity is often named with a singular noun, such as Customer. In addition, an association (relationship) between two or more data entities represents an action and may be defined in an English sentence: subject, verb. This interaction is directional:

- One to one
- One to many
- Many to many
- Zero to one
- Zero to many

Attributes

Attributes are the values, or characteristics, associated with an entity. Every occurrence of an entity has associated attributes. Attributes can be represented as a field. Domains are also used to give specific property of an object. An attribute that has attributes should be considered as a possible entity. Attributes are the data items required to make process work. When identifying attributes, consider such characteristics as data type, size, how used, and entities to which related.

Normalization.   Normalization is the process of nonloss decomposition of data relations and is performed during logical database design. Normalization promotes the formalization of simple ideas, such as "Domains must contain atomic values (single value)." The concept of functional dependence plays a key role. It is a helpful tool for physical design but is not an absolute and does not result in a physical design (final table design). Many process considerations must be accounted for before a physical design is done.

Some of the advantages of a normalized design may include

- By forcing the storage of nonkey information in a single place, minimizing the amount of space required to store data
- By storing data items only once, where possible, minimizing the risk of data inconsistencies within the database
- By storing data in only one place, where possible, minimizing several types of possible update and delete errors
- By focusing on the properties of the data rather than on how the applications will use the data, maximizing the stability of the data structures

Some of the objectives of data normalization are

- Eliminating all data "anomalies," such as UPDATE, INSERT, and DELETE
- Avoiding redundancy of data
- Avoiding potential inconsistency among data
- Preserving all relevant information
- Maintaining maximum flexibility in the database design
- Accommodating changes easily
- Providing nonloss decomposition of data elements

Depending on the interpretation of the relational model, the normal forms may vary but in general number five. We look only at three, as most normalized designs are in the third normal form.

Figure 4-8 shows the first normal form (1NF), which has the following characteristics.

- For any specific value of the unique indentifier (unique key), each attribute of the data entity has only one value.
- No repeating groups or arrays are present.
- Every attribute has a unique meaning and name.
- The data entity contains atomic values.
- The data entity must not group several data fields as a single value for a column.
- The data entity's true relational table satisfies 1NF.
- The design will still be a high degree of redundancy.

Not in First Normal Form:

Customer

ID	City	Date	Amount	Date	Amount	Date	Amount
202Smith	Chicago	2/90	20.00	3/90	40.00	4/90	22.00

Solution:

Customer

Number	Name	City
202	Smith	Chicago

Payment

Customer Number	Date	Amount
202	2/9	20.00

Figure 4-8 First normal form

Figure 4-9 shows the second normal form (2NF), which has the following characteristics.

- The data relation must first be in 1NF.
- Every nonkey attribute must be fully dependent on the primary key.
- No data elements will be dependent on a component of the primary key.
- The design does not allow nonkey attributes to be assigned to entities in which a part of the primary key can determine the nonkey attributes.

Not in Second Normal Form:

Line Item

INV_NBR	LINE_NB	CUST_NM	CUST_CTY	ITEM	AMT
175	1	Lawson	Springfield	123	500.00
175	2	Lawson	Springfield	5445	100.00

Solution:

Invoice

INV_NBR	NAME	CITY
175	Lawson	Springfield

Line Item

INV_NBR	LINE_NB	ITEM	AMT
175	1	123	500.00
175	2	544	100.00

Figure 4-9   Second normal form

Figure 4-10 shows the third normal form (3NF), which has the following characteristics.

- The data relation must first be in 2NF.
- No data elements are dependent on other nonkey data elements.
- Every nonkey attribute is nontransitively dependent on the primary key.
- This form is considered to be optimal for most tables.

Not in Third Normal Form:

Invoice

INV_NBR	NAME	CITY
175	Smith	Chicago

Solution:

Invoice

INV_NBR	NAME
175	Smith

Customer

CUST_NAME	CITY
Smith	Chicago

Figure 4-10   Third normal form

Anomolies.   The introduction of data anomalies into a database design can lower productivity in application design and create useless data. Anomolies need to be eliminated in order to

- Achieve semantic clarity
- Increase productivity and data consistency
- Create a design that requires the least amount of knowledge to achieve results

Anomalies can cause

- Integrity problems, such as duplication and inconsistencies
- A loss of conceptual clarity
- Unnecessary programming complexity
- Questionable growth and stability

Figure 4-11a shows what an update anomaly is and a problem that could result. Figure 4-11b shows how a normalized design would fix the issue.

If an attribute's value changes, it must be changed in multiple places.

Customer Order

PK

Order #	Order_Cost	Customer #	Customer_Name	Phone
1001	600.00	400	Joe Smith	555-1212
1002	150.00	540	Sam Jones	555-4444
1003	749.00	390	Harry Harris	555-1111
1004	22.00	489	Mary Mitchell	555-9990
1005	100.00	489	Mary Mitchell	555-9990

What if Mary Mitchell changes her name?

(a)

Order Table

PK

Order #	Order_Cost	Customer #
1001	600.00	400
1002	150.00	540
1003	749.00	390
1004	22.00	489
1005	100.00	489

Customer Table

PK

Customer #	Customer_Name	Phone
400	Joe Smith	555-1212
540	Sam Jones	555-4444
390	Harry Harris	555-1111
489	Mary Mitchell	555-9990

It would now have to be changed only once.

(b)

Figure 4-11 **(a)** Update anomaly; **(b)** Normalized design to solve update anomaly

Physical Design

The physical-data model is similar to the logical-data model except that the objects are identified as physical objects ready to be implemented in a DB2 environment. All elements on the logical model should transform into an object on the physical model. At this point, the model should be normalized.

Following are some general guidelines for transforming a logical model to a physical one:

- Creating a physical table for each entity
- Defining a unique index for each primary key
- Defining a nonunique index for each foreign key
- Defining other nonunique and unique indexes
- Documenting processing needs to be considered before implementation

Performance and DBMS specifics must still be considered afterward.

Example Implementation

The best way to understand data type selection is to design a database and implement the design by using DB2. This example implementation creates a database that can be used to schedule and track the results of a certification program. This database will be used to illustrate many aspects of SQL and DB2 features. Many examples from this database will be used throughout this book.

> **NOTE** This database was developed in the *DB2 Universal Database V8 for Linux, UNIX, and Windows Database Administration Certification Guide, Fifth Edition*, published by Prentice Hall, and can be referenced in that publication to observe implementation differences between DB2 z/OS and the DB2 UNIX, Windows, and Linux platforms.

This database will be used to schedule test candidates' exams; following candidates' completion of the test, the database will contain the candidates' test scores. The database and its application will need to perform eight tasks:

1. Insert/update/delete testing center information
2. Insert/update/delete test information
3. Insert/update/delete test candidate information
4. Guarantee a uniquely identified test name, regardless of the test number
5. Schedule a candidate to take a test
6. Update candidate test scores once exams have been completed
7. Determine which candidates qualify for certification
8. Generate various reports on the candidates and tests

The database will be named DB2CERT. The data to be stored in the DB2CERT database can easily be grouped into three reference tables; a fourth table is used to relate the other tables. The primary relationship can be defined as *a test candidate takes a specific test at a test center*.

Figure 4–12 shows the relationships within the problem domain. The rectangles represent the base tables: CANDIDATE, TEST_CENTER, and TEST. The fourth table is a relationship table called TEST_TAKEN.

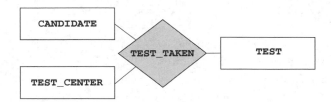

Figure 4-12   Tables for the DB2CERT database

DB2CERT Database Table Descriptions

The following tables will be used in the DB2CERT database.

- The CANDIDATE table stores information about each test candidate for the DB2 Certification Program. The candidate's name, address, ID, and phone number will be stored in this table. A data record represents a single test candidate, a person.
- The TEST_CENTER table stores information about the test centers where a candidate can take a DB2 Certification exam. The test center name, address, number of seats at the test center, test center ID, and its phone number will be stored in this table. A data record represents a single test center location.
- The TEST table stores information about each of the DB2 Certification exams. The test name, type, test ID, cut score—passing percentage—and the length of each test will be stored in this table. A data record represents a single test. Our example has three tests; therefore, this table has only three data records. A test name must be uniquely identified.
- The TEST_TAKEN table associates the records from the other three tables. It serves the dual purposes of scheduling tests and tracking each test result. The candidates' test scores, date taken, start time, and seat number will be stored in this table. This will be the most active of the four tables, as each candidate must take multiple exams to become certified; each test taken will have a corresponding data record in this table.

Once the tables and their relationships have been defined, the following should be defined:

- User-defined data types
- Columns or attributes for the tables
- (Optional) primary keys (PK) for the tables
- (Optional) unique keys for the tables
- (Optional) foreign keys—referential constraints—for the tables
- (Optional) table-check constraints for the tables
- (Optional) triggers for the database

Figure 4-13 shows the database design. The rectangles represent the entities, or tables. The columns, or attributes, are listed by the entities. Note that some of the columns are derived columns; that is, they represent a concept, not a physical attribute of an object. The derived columns (such as TOTALTAKEN on TEST) are included in the model because their values will be populated by the database, using a constraint mechanism.

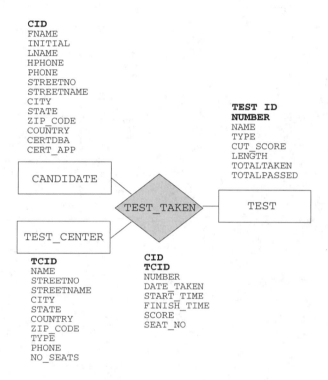

Figure 4-13   Entities and attributes

We must map the attributes shown in Figure 4-13 as DB2-supported data types or distinct types. To demonstrate some of the powerful features of DB2, we have decided to create distinct types for many of the attributes.

It is beneficial to have a primary key defined for each table to ensure uniqueness of the data records. The attributes that are bolded will be used as primary keys. We will also create unique keys to illustrate their use.

Earlier, we mentioned that the DB2CERT database will have four tables. However, the design shown in Figure 4-14 has only three tables defined, shown as rectangles.

An implied table is defined in the relationship *candidate takes a test*. A table is required to store each occurrence of a candidate taking a certification test.

A restriction will be imposed on the candidates: They can take the test only once on any given day. A candidate can take different tests on the same day but not the same test. With this restriction in place, we will define a primary key for the TEST_TAKEN table as a composite key including NUMBER (test ID), CID (candidate ID), and DATE_TAKEN (the date of the test). By defining the primary key as a combination of these three values, this constraint can be enforced.

Figure 4-14 shows the entity relationship diagrams for the Certification database.

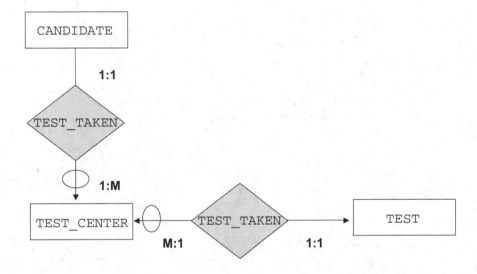

Figure 4-14   DB2 Certification database entity basic relationship

Figure 4-15 shows the RI relationships between the tables in the Certification database.

The diamond shapes are used to describe the relationships between the tables, including the parent/child relationship. For example, the CANDIDATE and the TEST_TAKEN table have a one-to-many relationship because a single candidate can take many tests. This relationship is shown by denoting the values of 1 and M (many) on the appropriate side of the diamond.

The database design shown in Figure 4-14 is just one type of diagramming technique. A logical database design can be represented in a number of ways, but it should not absolutely dictate the physical implementation of the database. It has been included it here because it will be used in many of the SQL statements throughout the rest of the book.

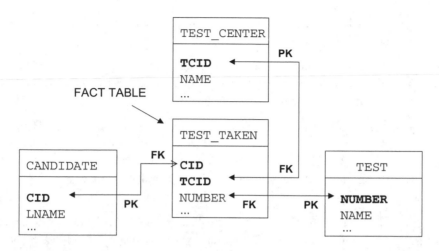

Figure 4-15   DB2 Certification database referential integrity

Defining Distinct Types

Distinct types must exist in the database before they can be referenced in a CREATE TABLE statement. We created a numeric distinct type of MINUTES; a character distinct type of PHONE; and a binary large object distinct type of BITMAP.

```
CREATE DISTINCT TYPE phone AS CHAR(10) WITH COMPARISONS;
CREATE DISTINCT TYPE bitmap AS BLOB(INT) WITH COMPARISONS;
CREATE DISTINCT TYPE minutes AS SMALLINT WITH COMPARISONS;
```

Defining Tables and Columns

Designing a database involves many considerations, only a few of which are discussed in this book. Using the database design in Figure 4-13, we can start creating database objects.

The first step in creating a database is to issue the run a CREATE DATABASE statement, such as the following:

```
CREATE DATABASE CERTTS
STOGROUP CERTSTG
BUFFERPOOL BP7
INDEXBP BP8;
```

Once the database has been created, dependent physical objects can be created. Distinct (user-defined) data types can also be created. Tables can then be created. (If explicit table spaces are to be used, they will need to be created first, but for this example, we will assume they already exist. Refer to Appendix A for more table space CREATE methods.)

The database design has a number of attributes shown. Each of these attributes will be a column in the table definitions. Every DB2 table contains one or more columns. The tables and their corresponding columns are given names.

Data is placed in a DB2 table by using the SQL statement INSERT or UPDATE. (The LOAD utility is also an option.) Usually, it is desirable for each column, or data value, to have a value. Sometimes, no value is provided for a column during the INSERT statement. If the column is defined as NOT NULL, the INSERT statement will fail. If a default value is defined, it will be stored.

The table being created in the following DDL is called DB2USER1.CANDIDATE and contains 15 columns. Each column is given a name and a data type. Two distinct data types are being used in the DB2USER1.CANDIDATE table. These data types are PHONE and BITMAP. In addition, constraints are defined for the valid values for some of the columns. For example, the null constraint is specified for all the columns except HPHONE, WPHONE, INITIAL, and PHOTO.

```
CREATE TABLE DB2USER1.CANDIDATE (
    CID CHAR(9) NOT NULL,
    LNAME VARCHAR(30) NOT NULL,
    FNAME VARCHAR(30) NOT NULL,
    INITIAL CHAR(1),
    HPHONE PHONE,
    WPHONE PHONE,
    STREETNO VARCHAR(8) NOT NULL,
    STREETNAME VARCHAR(20) NOT NULL,
    CITY VARCHAR(30) NOT NULL,
    PROV_STATE VARCHAR(30) NOT NULL,
    CODE CHAR(6) NOT NULL,
    COUNTRY VARCHAR(20)) NOT NULL,
    CERT_DBA CHAR(1) NOT NULL WITH DEFAULT 'N',
    CERT_APP CHAR(1) NOT NULL WITH DEFAULT 'N',
    PHOTO BITMAP, PRIMARY KEY (CID))
IN DB2CERT.CERTTS;
```

Keys

Keys are a special set of columns defined on a table. They can be used to uniquely identify a row or to reference a uniquely identified row from another table. Keys can be classified either by the columns they comprise or by the database constraint they support. See the discussion earlier in this chapter on types of keys.

Defining Primary Keys.   It is sometimes beneficial to define a primary key for each of your DB2 tables to guarantee the uniqueness of a column value or group of column values (composite key). In the previous CREATE statement, the primary key for the table candidate is defined as the column CID (candidate ID). By specifying this column as a primary key, DB2 will create a system-unique index if one does not already exist.

Let us look at the other tables representing the tests and the test centers. In the following CREATE statements, the TEST and TEST_CENTER tables are shown. These tables each have a primary key defined. In our example, the primary-key constraint was given a name (UNIQUE_TEST and UNIQUE_CENTER) for referencing purposes. If a constraint name is not provided, DB2 will assign a system-generated name to the constraint.

```
CREATE TABLE DB2USER1.TEST (
NUMBER CHAR(6) NOT NULL,
NAME VARCHAR(50) NOT NULL,
TYPE CHAR(1) NOT NULL,
CUT_SCORE DECIMAL(6,2) NOT NULL,
LENGTH MINUTES NOT NULL,
TOTALTAKEN SMALLINT NOT NULL,
TOTALPASSED SMALLINT NOT NULL,
CONSTRAINT UNIQUE_TEST PRIMARY KEY(NUMBER),
CONSTRAINT UNIQUE_TEST_NAME UNIQUE (NAME)
CONSTRAINT TEST_TYPE CHECK (TYPE IN ('P','B')))
IN DB2CERT.CERTTS

CREATE TABLE DB2USER1.TEST.CENTER (
    TCID CHAR(6) NOT NULL,
    NAME VARCHAR(40) NOT NULL,
    STREETNO VARCHAR(8) NOT NULL,
    STREETNAME VARCHAR(20) NOT NULL,
    CITY VARCHAR(30) NOT NULL,
    PROV_STATE VARCHAR(30) NOT NULL,
    COUNTRY VARCHAR(20) NOT NULL,
    CODE CHAR(6) NOT NULL,
    TYPE CHAR(1) NOT NULL,
    PHONE PHONE NOT NULL,
    NO_SEATS SMALLINT NOT NULL,
    CONSTRAINT UNIQUE_CENTER PRIMARY KEY (TCID))

IN DB2CERT.CERTTS
    PARTITION BY (TCID)
  . (PARTITION 1 ENDING AT ('300'),
    PARTITION 2 ENDING AT ('500'));
```

Note that the TEST_CENTER table is a partitioned table that is partitioned by TCID.

Defining Unique Keys.   Unique keys can be used to enforce uniqueness on a set of columns. A table can have more than one unique key (index) defined. The TEST table definition uses a unique constraint (UNIQUE_TEST_NAME) on column NAME to ensure that a test name is not used twice. The column NUMBER too has a primary-key constraint to avoid duplicate test numbers.

Having unique constraints on more than one set of columns of a table is different from defining a composite unique key that includes the whole set of columns. For example, even if we define a composite primary key on the columns NUMBER and NAME, a test name may still be duplicated using a different test number.

> **N O T E**   A unique index needs to always be created for primary—if one does not already exist—or unique-key constraints, unless using the schema processor. If you define a constraint name, it will be used to name the index; otherwise, a system-generated name will be used for the index.

Defining Foreign Keys.   A foreign key is a reference to the data values in another table. Foreign keys have various types of constraints. Let us look at the remaining table in the DB2 Certification database and, in particular, its foreign-key constraints. We have one composite primary key defined and three foreign-key constraints.

The primary key is defined as the columns CID, TCID, and NUMBER on the TEST_TAKEN table. The foreign-key constraints will perform the following.

- If a record in the CANDIDATE table is deleted, all matching records in the TEST_TAKEN table will be deleted (DELETE CASCADE).
- If a test center in the TEST_CENTER table is deleted, all the matching records in the TEST_TAKEN table will be deleted (DELETE CASCADE).
- If a test in the TEST table is deleted and matching records are in the TEST_TAKEN table, the DELETE statement will result in an error (DELETE RESTRICT).

> **N O T E**   A foreign-key constraint always relates to the primary or unique constraint of the table in the references clause.

```
CREATE TABLE DB2USER1.TEST_TAKEN (
    CID CANDIDATE_ID NOT NULL,
    TCID CENTER_ID NOT NULL,
    NUMBER TEST_ID NOT NULL,
    DATE_TAKEN DATE NOT NULL WITH DEFAULT,
    START_TIME TIME NOT NULL,
```

```
    FINISH_TIME TIME NOT NULL,
    SCORE SCORE,
    SEAT_NO CHAR(2) NOT NULL,
 CONSTRAINT NUMBER_CONST
 PRIMARY KEY (CID,TCID,NUMBER),
 FOREIGN KEY (CID)
 REFERENCES DB2CERT.CANDIDATE ON DELETE CASCADE,
 FOREIGN KEY (TCID)
 REFERENCES DB2CERT.TEST_CENTER ON DELETE CASCADE,
 FOREIGN KEY (NUMBER)
 REFERENCES DB2CERT.TEST ON DELETE RESTRICT)
IN DB2CERT.CERTTS
```

Defining parent/child relationships between tables is known as declarative referential integrity because the child table refers to the parent table. These constraints are defined during table creation or by using the ALTER TABLE SQL statement. DB2 will enforce referential constraints for all INSERT, UPDATE, and DELETE activity.

> **N O T E**   This database implementation created only the tables and distinct types. The complete DDL for the storage group, databases, table spaces, tables, and indexes can be found in Appendix A.

SUMMARY

In this chapter, we concentrated on the SQL Data Definition Language (DDL). DDL is used to create, modify, and remove database objects. DDL has three main statements: CREATE, ALTER, and DROP. If you want to use a DB2 database, you may need to learn DDL first to create some database objects. A DB2 database has many kinds of objects. Some of them are created by a DB2 command; some, by DDL statements.

We focused primarily on data types, tables, views, and indexes among the database objects created by DDL. A data type is used to specify the attribute of columns in a table. DB2 has two kinds of data types: built-in data types and distinct data types. The data type is a DB2-supplied data type and falls into three main categories: numeric; string, including large object (LOB); and date-time.

The distinct type enables you to create your application-oriented data type based on the built-in data type.

We also looked at DB2 support for Unicode.

A table consists of columns and rows, and stores an unordered set of records. Each column has a data type as one of the attributes. A table itself can have some rules, called *constraints*, to guarantee the uniqueness of records or to maintain the relationship between and within tables. Constraints help application programmers evaluate the records or maintain the consistency between the tables. A view may also reduce some application development workload. A logical table is created and is based on the physical table or other views. A view can be created to limit access to sensitive data while allowing more general access to other data. An index is one of the most important objects for performance. It can also be used to guarantee the uniqueness of each record. We also covered some of the options in the CREATE and ALTER statements.

ADDITIONAL RESOURCES

IBM DB2 UDB for z/OS SQL Reference (SC18-7426-00)

IBM DB2 UDB for z/OS Version 8 Administration Guide (SC18-7413-00)

IBM DB2 UDB for z/OS V8 Technical Preview (SG24-6871-00)

DB2 Universal Database V8 for Linux, UNIX, and Windows Database Administration Certification Guide, Fifth Edition (Prentice Hall, 2003)

Retrieving and Manipulating Database Objects

- Data retrieval: Basic SELECT statements
- Data modification: INSERT, UPDATE, and DELETE

hapter 4 discussed the definitions of various database objects, using the Data Definition Language (DDL). In this chapter, we start manipulating the database objects, using the portion of SQL known as Data Manipulation Language (DML). We populate (insert) data into the database and retrieve the data, using many powerful methods. Depending on their sophistication, the database users can use SQL to query the database. The majority of the SQL statements within a DB2 application involve DML statements. Therefore, application developers must understand the various methods of inserting, updating, and retrieving data from the database.

We start with simple retrieval statements and gradually introduce more complex methods of data manipulation. The DB2 Certification database will be used for most of the examples. The four main DML SQL statements we consider are SELECT, INSERT, UPDATE, and DELETE.

DATA RETRIEVAL

SQL is based on mathematical principles—specifically, on set theory and relational algebra. The data is stored in the database as unordered sets of data records. SQL is a set-oriented language, and many of its language elements are directly related to relational algebraic terms, such as *permutation, projection, restriction,* and *join.*

A set of data is represented in a DB2 database as a table or a view and is stored in a DB2 table without regard to order. To retrieve data in a particular order, an ORDER BY phrase must be added to a SELECT statement. Similarly, if the data is to be grouped, a GROUP BY phrase must be added to the statement.

Let's review the DB2USER1 database design defined in the previous chapter and manipulate data, using various SQL statements. Each of the three main tables—CANDIDATE, TEST, and TEST_CENTER—represents a set of records that correspond to a test candidate (person), a test, and a test center (location).

An associative table, known as the TEST_TAKEN table, is used to reflect the relationships among the three main tables. The TEST_TAKEN table is used to schedule the test candidates and to maintain their test scores.

> **N O T E**   The longest SQL statement is 2MB.

> **N O T E**   Remember that to execute any operation, the user must have the necessary privileges.

Retrieving the Entire Table

The most basic of all retrieval commands involves the SELECT statement, with no operators other than the name of the table. The following SQL statement retrieves all the candidates who have taken a DB2 Certification exam. The information requested is contained in the table TEST_TAKEN:

```
SELECT * FROM DB2USER1.TEST_TAKEN
```

In this example, using an asterisk (*) for column selection, the columns will be returned to the user in the order in which they are defined in the table.

SQL is a data access language that consists of language statements and clauses. Its many optional clauses can be used to modify the output. The output of a SELECT statement is known as a *result set,* or *result table.* The results from the SELECT statement are shown next:

```
CID TCID NUMBER DATE_TAKEN START_TIME FINISH_TIME SCORE PASS_FAIL SEAT_NO
--- ---- ------ ---------- ---------- ----------- ----- --------- -------
111 TX01 500    01/01/2000 11:30:00   12:30:00    65    Y         1
111 TX01 501    02/02/2000 10:30:00   11:45:00    73    Y         1
111 TX01 502    03/03/2000 12:30:00   13:30:00    67    Y         1
222 TR01 500    01/01/2000 14:00:00   15:30:00    55    N         2
222 TR01 502    01/02/2000 09:00:00   10:15:00    53    N         2
222 TR01 502    02/18/2000 10:00:00   11:30:00    75    Y         2
333 TX01 500    03/01/2000 11:30:00   13:00:00    82    Y         2
333 TX01 501    12/29/2000 14:00:00   -           -     -         1
333 TX01 502    03/02/2000 14:00:00   14:30:00    92    Y         1
9 record(s) selected.
```

In SQL, the * is used to indicate that all columns of a table are being referenced. In this example, the SQL statement refers to all the columns defined for the DB2USER1.TEST_TAKEN table. If the table is altered and a new column is added to the table definition, the result set contains the new column.

> **N O T E**   Adding a new column to an existing table will result in default values being populated for the existing rows.

Because the output of the SQL statement using the * character varies according to the table definition, it is recommended that you specify in the SELECT statement all the column names you want to see. We could have obtained the same result as the statement using SELECT * with the following SQL statement:

```
SELECT CID, TCID, NUMBER,DATE_TAKEN,START_TIME,
FINISH_TIME,SCORE,SEAT_NO
FROM DB2USER1.TEST_TAKEN;
```

> **N O T E**   The * character is used to refer to all the columns defined for a table. The order of the columns in the result table is the same order as specified in the CREATE TABLE or CREATE VIEW statement.

What is returned to the user is known as the result set. If the result set is large, it is advisable to filter the data, using a WHERE predicate.

Because it describes the location—table or view—of the data, the FROM clause is required for the SELECT SQL statement. Our example references a single table called

DB2USER1.TEST_TAKEN. The SELECT and FROM clauses are required in all data-retrieval statements. The list of columns following the SELECT keyword is referred to as the *select list*.

Projecting Columns from a Table

Projection is a relational operation that allows you to retrieve a subset of the defined columns from a table. The next example restricts the output from the SELECT command so that only the candidate ID, test center, and test number attributes from the TEST_TAKEN table are shown:

```
SELECT CID,TCID,NUMBER FROM DB2USER1.TEST_TAKEN
```

The output of this SELECT statement follows:

```
CID TCID NUMBER
--- ---- ------
111 TX01 500
111 TX01 501
111 TX01 502
222 TR01 500
222 TR01 502
222 TR01 502
333 TX01 500
333 TX01 501
333 TX01 502
9 record(s) selected.
```

The order of the columns in the result table will always match the order in the select list. The order of the columns as they were defined in the CREATE TABLE or CREATE VIEW statement is ignored when a select list is provided in the SQL statement. In this example, the order of the columns is similar to that in the CREATE TABLE statement, as the CID column was defined prior to the TCID and NUMBER columns.

Changing the Order of the Columns

Permutation is the relational operation that allows you to change the order of the columns in your result table. Permutation is used every time you select columns in an order different from the order defined in the CREATE TABLE statement. For example, to display the test center ID prior to the candidate IDs and the test number, you could execute the following:

```
SELECT TCID,CID,NUMBER FROM DB2USER1.TEST_TAKEN
```

The result of this SELECT statement specifies a select list in a different order from that defined in the table definition:

```
TCID CID NUMBER
---- --- ------
TX01 111 500
TX01 111 501
TX01 111 502
TR01 222 500
TR01 222 502
TR01 222 502
TX01 333 500
TX01 333 501
TX01 333 502
9 record(s) selected.
```

> **N O T E** We refer to the output of a SELECT statement as the result table because the output of all SELECT statements can be considered a relational table.

Restricting Rows from a Table

Restriction is a relational operation that filters the resulting rows of a table. Restriction can be accomplished through the use of *predicates* defined in an SQL WHERE clause. To restrict the result set, we need to add a WHERE clause to the SQL statement.

> **N O T E** A predicate is a condition placed on the data. The result of the condition is TRUE, FALSE, or UNKNOWN.

The WHERE clause specifies conditions, or predicates, that must be evaluated by DB2 before the result table is returned to the end user. Many valid types of predicates can be used. In the following example, the equality (=) predicate is used to restrict the records to only those candidates who have taken a DB2 Certification test at the test center TR01:

```
SELECT TCID,CID FROM DB2USER1.TEST_TAKEN
WHERE TCID ='TR01'
```

The WHERE clause also accepts other comparison operators, such as greater than (>), less than (<), greater than or equal to (>=), less than or equal to (<=), and not equal to (<>). This statement is an example of a *basic predicate*. A basic predicate compares two values. In addition, more complex predicates, such as LIKE, BETWEEN, and IN, are also valid and will be discussed later.

Predicate Evaluation for Distinct Types

If the column length was defined as a *distinct type*, in order to make a comparison in the WHERE clause valid using this column, a casting function needs to be used. This is not mandatory if the comparison is to a literal or host variable, but is demonstrated as follows:

```
SELECT NUMBER, LENGTH FROM DB2USER1.TEST
WHERE LENGTH=CAST(60 AS DB2CERT.MINUTES)
```

Predicate evaluation requires that the data types be compatible, that is, the same data type or a compatible data type. We can accomplish the data type conversion, or cast, by using either the CAST expression or a casting function. (Refer to Chapter 15 for more information on casting for distinct types.)

> **N O T E**   Although not always mandatory, casting is recommended to ensure that compatible data types are compared, including length and scale. This allows DB2 to resolve these issues as indexable or stage 1 rather than as stage 2 predicates. For more information on stage 1 and stage 2 predicates refer to Chapter 6.

Using Multiple Conditions to Restrict Rows

It is possible to combine multiple conditions, or predicates, in a single SQL statement. The predicates can be combined by using Boolean operators, such as the AND or OR operators. These operators allow you to combine multiple conditions in a single SQL statement. The order of the predicate evaluation will not affect the result set, known as *set closure*.

The next example retrieves the records for the test candidates who took a test at test center TR01 and achieved a score greater than 65. The SQL statement uses multiple predicates. The rows that satisfy the predicates are known as the *qualifying rows*.

```
SELECT TCID,CID,SCORE
FROM DB2USER1.TEST_TAKEN
WHERE TCID='TR01'
AND SCORE > 65
```

Selecting Columns from Multiple Tables

Two operations—Cartesian product and join—combine columns from multiple tables in a single SQL statement.

Cartesian Product

A *Cartesian product* is a relational operation that merges all the values from one table with all the values from another table. This operation is not used frequently, because the result table can be very large. The number of rows in the result table is always equal to the product of the number of rows in the qualifying rows for each of the tables being accessed.

> **N O T E**   The DB2 optimizer may choose to use a Cartesian product of unrelated tables if this is deemed to be an efficient method of accessing multiple tables. An example is two single-row tables that are joined with a large table. The cross-product of 1 × 1 = 1; thus, the large-table access is deferred as late as possible, with a potential increase in the restrictive predicates that can be applied without incurring the overhead of a large Cartesian result. This method of table access is typical in processing queries against a star schema data model.

The following example is a Cartesian product of all test numbers and test names from the TEST table, with all candidates from the TEST_TAKEN table. First, select from the TEST table:

```
SELECT NUMBER, NAME FROM DB2USER1.TEST;

NUMBER NAME
------ ----------------------------------------------------
500 DB2 Fundamentals
501 DB2 Administration
502 DB2 Application Development
3 record(s) selected.
```

Next, select all the candidates from the TEST_TAKEN table:

```
SELECT CID,TCID FROM DB2USER1.TEST_TAKEN;

CID TCID
--- ----
222 TR01
222 TR01
222 TR01
111 TX01
111 TX01
111 TX01
333 TX01
333 TX01
333 TX01
9 record(s) selected.
```

Then combine the two tables to form a Cartesian product result table:

```
SELECT DB2USER1.TEST_TAKEN.NUMBER,CID,TCID
FROM DB2USER1.TEST_TAKEN,DB2USER1.TEST;

NUMBER CID TCID
------ --- ----
500 111 TX01
501 111 TX01
502 111 TX01
500 222 TR01
502 222 TR01
502 222 TR01
500 333 TX01
501 333 TX01
502 333 TX01
500 111 TX01
501 111 TX01
502 111 TX01
500 222 TR01
502 222 TR01
502 222 TR01
500 333 TX01
501 333 TX01
502 333 TX01
500 111 TX01
501 111 TX01
502 111 TX01
500 222 TR01
502 222 TR01
502 222 TR01
500 333 TX01
501 333 TX01
502 333 TX01
27 record(s) selected.
```

Two tables are referenced in the FROM clause of this query. The tables are separated by commas. The WHERE clause contains no relationship expression. This type of query results in a Cartesian product.

The result table is a representation of all possible combinations of the input tables. The TEST table has 3 rows, and the TEST_TAKEN table has 9 rows. Therefore, the SELECT statement shown earlier returns 27 rows. Note the first column name in this query. It is necessary to fully qualify the column name by providing the schema name and table name with the column name because this column exists in both the TEST table and TEST_TAKEN table. In this case, we needed to specify that the number column is to be retrieved from the DB2USER1.TEST_TAKEN table and not from the DB2USER1.TEST table.

By adding a predicate to a Cartesian product SQL query, the result table can represent a more useful representation of the data. In the next example, the query returns all of the tests that were taken by the candidate whose ID is 111:

```
SELECT DB2USER1.TEST_TAKEN.NUMBER,CID,TCID
FROM DB2USER1.TEST_TAKEN,DB2USER1.TEST
WHERE CID='111'

NUMBER CID TCID
------ --- ----
500 111 TX01
500 111 TX01
500 111 TX01
501 111 TX01
501 111 TX01
501 111 TX01
502 111 TX01
502 111 TX01
502 111 TX01
9 record(s) selected.
```

Join

Adding a WHERE clause to your query does not always provide the desired result. In the preceding example, you want to know all the tests that were taken by the candidate whose ID is 111, and the query returns nine rows. But we know from previous queries that the candidate took only three tests. The query in this example has a WHERE clause to filter out the candidate whose ID is 111 from the TEST_TAKEN table, but there was no filter on the TEST_CENTER table. Therefore, the result of the query would always be a multiple of the number of testing centers. Usually, when multiple tables are referenced, you should include a cross-table relationship, using a table merge, or join, method, as shown in the following example:

```
SELECT DB2USER1.TEST_TAKEN.NUMBER,CID,TCID
FROM DB2USER1.TEST_TAKEN,DB2USER1.TEST
WHERE CID= '111'
AND DB2USER1.TEST_TAKEN.NUMBER=DB2USER1.TEST.NUMBER;

NUMBER CID TCID
------ --- ----
500 111 TX01
501 111 TX01
502 111 TX01
3 record(s) selected.
```

We will examine table join methods further in the next section.

To avoid data redundancy, the database tables should be normalized. Following a normalization process, a number of related tables will exist. To satisfy some of the required queries, the tables must be reconstructed. The tables are reconstructed temporarily, using a table join strategy to produce a single-result table.

The result tables in the previous examples usually provided candidate ID numbers and not the complete name of the test candidates. The candidate IDs are stored in the TEST_TAKEN table, and the full names are stored in the CANDIDATE table. To obtain the name of a candidate, the data must be retrieved from the CANDIDATE table, using a relationship, or join, strategy.

Consider an example that will list the names and phone numbers of candidates who were registered to take a DB2 Certification test in 2000. To accomplish this, we need to select data from two tables: DB2USER1.CANDIDATE and DB2USER1.TEST_TAKEN.

Let's retrieve a list of candidate names, phone numbers, and IDs from the CANDIDATE table. The candidate names were stored in multiple columns to allow for easy retrieval by last name:

```
SELECT FNAME,INITIAL,LNAME,HPHONE,CID
FROM DB2USER1.CANDIDATE;
```

The output of this example follows. Pay special attention to the values in the CID column. It will be used as the join column in the next example:

```
FNAME           INITIAL      LNAME          HPHONE        CID
--------        -------      ----------     ----------    ---
Susan           M            Lawson         1115551234    111
Dan                          Luksetich      2226543455    222
John            H            Maenpaa        4442314244    333
Jeremy                       Peck           5552143244    444
4 record(s) selected.
```

Now, let's retrieve the ID numbers of those candidates who were registered to take the test in 2000:

```
SELECT DISTINCT CID FROM DB2USER1.TEST_TAKEN
WHERE YEAR(DATE_TAKEN) = 2000;

CID
---
222
111
333
3 record(s) selected.
```

The candidate IDs in the TEST_TAKEN table must correspond to a candidate ID in the CANDIDATE table because of the declarative referential integrity constraints. The parent table in the relationship is the CANDIDATE table, and the child, or dependent, table is the TEST_TAKEN table.

The result table from the preceding query does not include test candidate 444, who did not have a test scheduled for 2000. We need to join the two result tables, based on the candidate ID values. This column is known as the *join column*.

> **N O T E** Query performance can significantly improve if the join columns are appropriately indexed.

The following single query will satisfy the end user requirement:

```
SELECT DISTINCT FNAME,INITIAL,LNAME,HPHONE
FROM DB2USER1.TEST_TAKEN,DB2USER1.CANDIDATE
WHERE YEAR(DATE_TAKEN) = 2000
AND DB2USER1.TEST_TAKEN.CID=DB2USER1.CANDIDATE.CID;
```

A table join requires a predicate that includes an expression based on columns from the tables referenced in the FROM clause. This is known as a *join predicate*. The FROM clause has not changed from the Cartesian product examples. The only difference is in the join predicate (TEST_TAKEN.CID = CANDIDATE.CID).

> **N O T E** An alternative form of the FROM clause for joins involves explicitly coding the JOIN keyword between the tables, rather than using a comma, and coding the join predicates in the ON clause rather than in the WHERE clause. This method of coding is covered in more detail in Chapter 6.

The table names needed to be explicitly stated because a column named CID is in both of the referenced tables. When multiple tables are being accessed in a single query, any selected columns that occur in more than one table must be qualified with the table name.

> **N O T E** An error will occur if the columns being referenced are ambiguous or not properly qualified.

A maximum of 225 base tables can be in a single SQL statement; however, you are limited to 15 tables in a join (the FROM clause).

> **N O T E**   The 15-table limit can be increased by updating the
> macro SPRMMXT to a value greater than 15.

> **N O T E**   The kind of join operation shown in the preceding
> example is also known as an *inner join*. An inner join displays only
> the rows that are present in both of the joined tables.

Using Correlation Names

If each of the columns needed to be fully qualified with the table name, such as
tableschema.tablename.columnname, the queries would become very large and cumbersome to work with. Fortunately, an easier way exists to qualify the ambiguous columns resulting from a multitable SELECT statement.

The columns can be qualified using a *correlation name*. A correlation name is a temporary alias for the tables referenced in an SQL statement. We rewrite the previous query using correlation names as follows:

```
SELECT DISTINCT FNAME,INITIAL,LNAME,HPHONE
FROM DB2USER1.TEST_TAKEN TT, DB2USER1.CANDIDATE C
WHERE YEAR(DATE_TAKEN) = 2000
AND TT.CID = C.CID;
```

The correlation name immediately follows the name of the table as stated in the FROM clause. In this example, the correlated name for the TEST_TAKEN table is TT, and the correlated name for the CANDIDATE table is C.

> **N O T E**   For readability, correlation names can be optionally
> prefixed with the AS keyword, such as DB2USER1.CANDIDATE
> AS C.

The correlated names are accessible within the SQL statement only. Following the execution of the SQL statement, the correlation name is no longer defined. Once a correlation name has been defined, it can be referenced in the rest of the query instead of the table name. However, the table name can still be referenced.

> **N O T E**   Use simple, easy-to-remember correlation names.
> Table initials are good candidates for correlation names.

Sorting Your Output

We have been retrieving data from one or more tables. The order of the result table has not been specified in any of the SQL statements. Therefore, the data is retrieved in an undetermined order if the SQL statement contains no ORDER BY clause.

> **N O T E** The only guaranteed way to return data in the required sequence is with the ORDER BY clause. Any data retrieval that is currently returned in sequence without this clause is based purely on the data retrieval method at the time. Any future access path execution may not return the data in the same sequence.

The following example produces a list of the test candidates in alphabetical order by last name for the candidates who have taken a DB2 Certification test at the TR01 test center:

```
SELECT LNAME,INITIAL,FNAME
FROM DB2USER1.CANDIDATE C,DB2USER1.TEST_TAKEN TT
WHERE C.CID=TT.CID
AND TCID='TR01'
ORDER BY LNAME;
```

This example contains a new clause: ORDER BY. After the ORDER BY clause, you can list the columns that will specify the sort order and the type of sort.

> **N O T E** Appropriate indexing may allow DB2 to avoid sorting the data to match the ORDER BY clause. If the data is already sequenced via the index, DB2 may choose to use the index and avoid sorting the data. DB2 cannot avoid a sort for an ORDER BY involving columns from more than one table. Where possible, include columns from only one table in the ORDER BY to give DB2 greater opportunity for sort avoidance.

The SQL can be modified so that the output is changed to descending order by last name and a secondary order column on the first name in ascending order:

```
SELECT LNAME,FNAME,HPHONE
FROM DB2USER1.CANDIDATE C,DB2USER1.TEST_TAKEN TT
WHERE C.CID=TT.CID
AND TCID= 'TR01'
ORDER BY LNAME DESC, FNAME;
```

In this example, the DESC keyword that follows the LNAME column indicates that the result table should be in descending order based on the last name. More than one record can have the same last name. This situation is quite common. A second column specified in the ORDER BY clause, fname, has no keyword specifying the sort sequence. Therefore, the default ordering sequence (ascending) is used.

The next example contains three columns: LNAME, FNAME, and HPHONE. You can reference the column that should be used to sort the data by using the column name or by specifying its position in the select list. Using the column position is useful when the column in the select list is made up of derived, or calculated, columns that have no explicit name:

```
SELECT LNAME,FNAME,HPHONE
FROM DB2USER1.CANDIDATE C,DB2USER1.TEST_TAKEN TT
WHERE C.CID=TT.CID
AND TCID='TR01'
ORDER BY 1 DESC, 2;
```

In this example, the sort order is specified using the column position. Therefore, the query result is exactly the same as in the previous example.

You can also assign an alternative column name using column renaming. The assigned name can then be referenced in the ORDER BY clause, and it appears as the column heading where appropriate.

> **N O T E**   Although useful, coding a column position rather than a column or renamed column in the ORDER BY clause may lead to a different sequence if another column that alters the column positioning is inadvertently added to the query.

> **N O T E**   The *order by* clause must succeed all subselects in the *fullselect* statement. The only clauses that can succeed the *order by* clause are the for *read-only*, *optimize-for*, *isolation*, and *update* clauses.

Derived Columns

In some cases, you will need to perform calculations on the data. SQL has some basic built-in mathematical and string functions. Mathematical operations include standard addition, subtraction, multiplication, and division.

The calculation can be defined in the WHERE clause of the SQL statement or the select list. Suppose that you need to calculate a passing rate for a DB2 test. The passing rate is defined as the percentage of candidates passing the test (`totalpassed*100/totaltaken`). The following SQL statement will accomplish this for us for test number 500:

```
SELECT NUMBER, TOTALPASSED*100/TOTALTAKEN
FROM TEST
WHERE NUMBER='500';
```

In this example, the second column of the output list is a calculated column. Remember that you must use the column position if you want to use this calculated column for the ORDER BY clause unless you name it, as we now discuss.

> **N O T E**   Occasionally, the results of a derived column may not display as expected. The example using `totalpassed*100/totaltaken` will result in a value of 66 being retrieved. As both the `totalpassed` and `totaltaken` columns are integers, the final result is also an integer, and the fractional part is discarded. If this is not your desired result, you should use other functions, such as `decimal`, to change the way the calculation is performed or displayed.

You can specify a column name for any expression. When you provide the derived—calculated—column with a name, the ORDER BY clause can reference the derived name to allow for a more readable SQL statement.

The following SQL calculates the percentage of people passing the DB2 Certification exams and orders the output in descending order of the passing rate:

```
SELECT NUMBER,TOTALPASSED*100/TOTALTAKEN AS PASSEDRATE
FROM TEST
ORDER BY PASSEDRATE DESC;
```

The AS clause is used to rename the default name of an element in the select list. In this example, we are giving the name of `PassedRate` to the result of the division of column `totalpassed` by column `totaltaken`. The named column is used in the query to specify the column that should be used for sorting the output.

> **N O T E**   The AS keyword is optional, although it should be added for readability. Without the AS clause, it may be unclear whether the intention was to rename a column or whether a comma was missed between two retrieved columns.

DB2 Functions

DB2 provides various types of functions. For example, two types of functions are scalar and column functions. (A third type of function, called a *table function*, is discussed in Chapter 15.)

- *Scalar functions*, also known as row functions, provide a result for each row of the result table. A scalar function can be used any place an expression is allowed.
- *Column functions*, also known as vector or aggregate functions, work with a group of rows to provide a result. The group is specified using a FULLSELECT and optionally grouped using the GROUP BY clause.

This section describes some of the SQL functions provided with DB2. SQL functions are categorized by their implementation type. The functions either are built in or are extensions of DB2 and are known as user-defined functions (UDFs).

Built-in functions are defined within the SQL standards and are provided by DB2. These functions can be either scalar or column functions.

Scalar functions are applied to each row of data, and a per row result is provided. A scalar function could be used to retrieve only the first three digits of telephone numbers for each candidate. The function used is called SUBSTR. The arguments for this function include a string data type column, a beginning offset, and length. The output data type and attribute of the function depend on the input data type and attribute. The following example retrieves the telephone area code for the column wphone:

```
SELECT LNAME, SUBSTR(CHAR(WPHONE),1,3)
FROM DB2USER1.CANDIDATE;
```

The SUBSTR function is a scalar function. SUBSTR returns a character string of three characters. The result string corresponds to the first three characters of the wphone column. This function is known as a string function because it works with any string data type. If we wanted to give the output column a meaningful name, we could provide an alias, as was done for calculated columns.

In the preceding example, the substring starts from the beginning of the string because we indicate 1 as the second parameter of the function. The length of the resulting string is indicated in the third argument. In our example, the length is 3. Note that the data type of the wphone column is phone, so a casting function is used to convert the phone data type to the CHAR data type.

The following query will provide the month when the exam was taken. The input for this function is a DATE string, and the output is an integer:

```
SELECT FNAME, MONTH (DATE_TAKEN)
FROM CANDIDATE C, TEST_TAKEN TT
WHERE C.CID=TT.CID;
```

Column functions provide a single result for a group of qualifying rows for a specified table or view. Many common queries can be satisfied using column functions if they include common tasks, such as finding the smallest value, the largest value, or the average value for a group of data records. The following example obtains the maximum total passed of any of the DB2 Certification exams:

```
SELECT MAX(TOTALPASSEd) FROM TEST;
```

If a WHERE clause were added to this example, the maximum would represent the maximum value for the qualifying rows, as the predicate is used to filter the data prior to the application of the MAX function.

This next example calculates the average of the number of seats for all the test centers. Note that the column function AVG is used in this example:

```
SELECT AVG(noseats) FROM TEST_CENTER;
```

DB2 provides many more built-in functions. If you are interested in calculating statistical information, you can use statistical functions, such as VARIANCE, STDDEV, or a sampling of these functions.

> **N O T E**   MAX and MIN functions can be either column or scalar functions, depending on the input arguments.

UDFs are not defined within the SQL standards, because they are extensions of the current SQL. These functions can be developed by a DB2 administrator or application developer. UDFs can be either scalar or table functions but not usually column functions. Once the UDFs have been created, they can be invoked by any end user with the proper privileges. For more information about UDFs, refer to Chapter 15.

Grouping Values

Many queries require some level of aggregated data, which in SQL is accomplished through the use of the GROUP BY clause. GROUP BY conceptually rearranges the table represented by the FROM clause into partitions such that within any one group, all rows have the same value for the GROUP BY field.

> **N O T E**   GROUP BY does not imply ORDER BY.

The following SQL statement obtains the average number of seats for each country:

```
SELECT COUNTRY, AVG(NOSEATS) FROM TEST_CENTER
GROUP BY COUNTRY;
```

This SQL statement obtains the average number of seats per country, and the GROUP BY clause tells DB2 to group together the rows that have the same values in the columns indicated in the GROUP BY list. In our example, we are grouping countries into subsets. As the subsets are created, DB2 calculates the average of each of those groups, or subsets: in this case, by each country.

When you combine column functions and other elements, such as column names, scalar functions, or calculated columns, you must use the GROUP BY clause. In this case, you must include every element that is not a column function in the GROUP BY list. The only elements that can be omitted in the GROUP BY list are constant values.

The next SQL statement obtains a list that includes the average cut score and minimum total passed for the DB2 Certification exams. The result is then grouped by the type of exam, as follows:

```
SELECT TYPE, AVG(CUT_SCORE),
MIN(TOTALPASSED)
FROM TEST
GROUP BY TYPE
```

> **N O T E** Appropriate indexing can allow DB2 to avoid a sort to group the data rows to match the GROUP BY clause.

It is possible to sort the output of the previous example by using an ORDER BY clause.

> **N O T E** GROUP BY may, but this is not guaranteed to, return data in the same order as an ORDER BY and is based on the access path. The only way to guarantee data sequence is with an ORDER BY.

Restricting the Use of Sets of Data

So far, we have discussed how to restrict output, based on row conditions. With SQL, it is also possible to restrict that output by using column functions and the GROUP BY clause. Suppose that you want a list of all the test centers that have administered more than five DB2 Certification exams. To make it easier to understand, let's first get the number of tests that have been taken in each test center:

```
SELECT TCID, COUNT(*) FROM TEST_TAKEN GROUP BY TCID
```

We use the COUNT column function to get the total number of tests that have been taken in each test center. Using an asterisk (*) with the COUNT function indicates that you want the number of rows in a table that meet the criteria established in the SQL statement. In this example, we are grouping by TCID because we have a number of occurrences for all the test centers in the TEST_TAKEN table. The TEST_TAKEN table has an entry for every DB2 Certification exam that has been taken. Finally, the output is restricted to only those test centers that have administered more than four exams:

```
SELECT TCID FROM TEST_TAKEN
GROUP BY TCID HAVING COUNT(*) > 4;
```

This example introduces the HAVING clause, which is equivalent to the WHERE clause for groups and column functions. The HAVING clause will restrict the result set to the groups that meet the condition specified in it. In our example, only the test centers that have administered more than four DB2 Certification exams will be displayed.

Eliminating Duplicates

When you execute a query, you might get duplicate rows in the answer set. SQL provides a special clause to remove the duplicate rows from your output. The following SQL statement generates a list of names and phone numbers for all the candidates who have taken a test. In the following example, we eliminate the duplicate rows from our output list, using the DISTINCT clause:

```
SELECT DISTINCT FNAME,WPHONE,HPHONE
FROM CANDIDATE C,TEST_TAKEN TT
WHERE C.CID=TT.CID;
```

The DISTINCT clause can also be used with the COUNT function. When you use DISTINCT inside a COUNT function, the duplicate entries for a particular column will not be counted. The following example allows you to count how many test centers have candidates registered:

```
SELECT COUNT(DISTINCT TCID) FROM TEST_TAKEN;
```

This example provides the number of test centers that are registered in the TEST_TAKEN table. Remember that all the candidates who have registered for DB2 Certification exams are stored in this table. Make sure that you understand how COUNT(*), COUNT(colname), and COUNT(DISTINCT colname) differ. They are very similar in syntax but differ in function.

> **N O T E** COUNT(*) returns a count of all rows that qualify
> against the WHERE clause. COUNT(colname) returns a count of
> all rows that qualify against the WHERE clause, with null occurrences
> of colname removed. COUNT(DISTINCT colname) counts
> distinct occurrences of colname, with nulls removed.

Searching for String Patterns

SQL has a powerful predicate—LIKE—that allows you to search for patterns in character string columns. Suppose that you want to generate a list of the candidates whose first name starts with the letter G:

```
SELECT FNAME,LNAME,WPHONE,HPHONE FROM CANDIDATE
WHERE FNAME LIKE 'G%' ORDER BY LNAME,FNAME;
```

In this query, we use a *wildcard character* with the LIKE predicate. In SQL, the percent character (%) is a substitute for zero or more characters. The search string G% can be substituted with such names as George, Gary, Ginger, and so on. (Because the percent character can substitute zero or more characters, the search string can also be a single letter *G*.)

The percent character can be used any place in the search string and as many times as you need it. The percent sign is not case sensitive, so it can take the place of uppercase or lowercase letters. However, the constant characters included in your search string are case sensitive.

Another wildcard character used with the LIKE predicate is the underline character (_). This character substitutes one and only one character. The underline character can take the place of any character but cannot be substituted for an empty character.

> **N O T E** If the pattern needs to search for occurrences of the
> wildcard characters % and _ as their values, the ESCAPE clause is
> used to specify a character that precedes the percent or underscore
> in the pattern.

The previous SQL can be modified to include all candidates' names and the telephone numbers for those candidates whose name has the letter *A* as its second letter:

```
SELECT FNAME,LNAME,WPHONE,HPHONE FROM CANDIDATE
WHERE FNAME LIKE '_A%' ORDER BY LNAME,FNAME;
```

This example uses two wildcard characters that work with the LIKE predicate. The search string in this example can include such names as Paul, Gabriel, or Natalie. (The first character may be any character, the lowercase letter *a* is the second character in the string, and the string ends with any number of characters.)

> **N O T E** When the pattern in a `LIKE` predicate is a fixed-length host variable, the correct length must be specified for the string to be returned. `'G%'` assigned to an 8-byte variable (`LIKE :variable`) will search for all occurrences of `'G%          '` (*G*, followed by any character, followed by six blank characters). To find rows that begin with a *G*, `'G%%%%%%%'` should be assigned to the fixed-length variable.

Searching for Data in Ranges

SQL also offers a range operator, which is used to restrict rows that are in a particular range of values. Consider the requirement to list those candidates whose scores in the DB2 Certification exam are between 60 and 75:

```
SELECT DISTINCT FNAME,LNAME,WPHONE,HPHONE
FROM CANDIDATE C, TEST_TAKEN TT
WHERE C.CID=TT.CID
AND SCORE BETWEEN 60 AND 75
```

The `BETWEEN` predicate includes the values that you specify for searching your data. An important fact about the `BETWEEN` predicate is that it can work with character ranges as well.

In addition to the score requirement, this example modifies the SQL to include only those candidates whose last name begins with a letter between *B* and *G*:

```
SELECT DISTINCT FNAME,LNAME,WPHONE,HPHONE
FROM CANDIDATE C, TEST_TAKEN TT
WHERE C.CID=TT.CID
AND SCORE BETWEEN 60 AND 75
AND LNAME BETWEEN 'B' AND 'GZ'
```

In this example, the second `BETWEEN` predicate contains character values. We need to specify the GZ value to include all the possible names that start with the letter *G*. This was done assuming that the letter *Z* is the last possible value in the alphabet.

> **N O T E** The arguments of the `BETWEEN` clause are not interchangeable; the first must specify the low value; the second, the high value. `BETWEEN 1 AND 2` will return all values within the range (inclusive of 1 and 2). `BETWEEN 2 AND 1` will return zero rows.

Searching for Null Values

Null values represent an unknown value for a particular occurrence of an entity. We can use a null value if we don't know a particular value of a column. Let's say that we want a list of all those candidates whose score is not yet input. This condition is represented with a null value:

```
SELECT FNAME,LNAME,WPHONE,HPHONE
FROM CANDIDATE C, TEST_TAKEN TT
WHERE C.CID=TT.CID AND SCORE IS NULL;
```

The IS predicate is used to search for the null value in this example. Remember that the null value means *unknown*. Because it has no particular value, it can't be compared with other values. You can't use conditional operands, such as equal (=) or greater than (>), with null values.

Searching for Negative Conditions

The BETWEEN, IS, and LIKE predicates always look for the values that meet a particular condition. These predicates can also be used to look for values that don't meet a particular condition.

The NOT predicate can be used to look for the opposite condition, combined with the LIKE, BETWEEN, and IS predicate, to accomplish negative searches, as shown in the following example. This example has a LIKE predicate combined with the NOT predicate. We want a list of those candidates whose last names do not start with the letter *S*:

```
SELECT DISTINCT FNAME,LNAME,WPHONE,HPHONE FROM CANDIDATE
WHERE LNAME NOT LIKE 'S%'
ORDER BY LNAME,FNAME;
```

The next example has a BETWEEN predicate combined with the NOT predicate. We want a list of those candidates whose score, in any test, is not in the range 60 to 75:

```
SELECT DISTINCT FNAME,LNAME,WPHONE,HPHONE
FROM CANDIDATE C, TEST_TAKEN TT
WHERE C.CID=TT.CID
AND INTEGER(SCORE) NOT BETWEEN 60 AND 75;
```

In this example, the NOT predicate will exclude all the values that are in the range 60 to 75.

Negation can also be applied to the null value. This SQL statement produces a report that searches for those candidates who have a seat number assigned. This is expressed with a NOT NULL value:

```
SELECT DISTINCT FNAME,LNAME,WPHONE,HPHONE
FROM CANDIDATE C, TEST_TAKEN TT
WHERE C.CID=TT.CID AND SEAT_NO IS NOT NULL;
```

> **N O T E** The NOT operator can also be used to negate the standard comparison operators: =, <, <=, >, and >=.

> **N O T E** When dealing with nulls, NOT or negation may not return the opposite of the positive logic. For example, WHERE SEAT_NO = 1 will return only the rows for seat number 1. Any value other than 1 is discarded, as these rows are FALSE, including nulls, as these are UNKNOWN. WHERE SEAT_NO <> 1 excludes rows where the seat number is 1 and also discards nulls because these are UNKNOWN.

Searching for a Set of Values

In SQL, it is possible to establish a restriction condition based on a set of values. Suppose that you need a list of the test centers that have candidates registered for the DB2 Fundamentals test and for the DB2 Application Development test. This can be queried with the following statement:

```
SELECT DISTINCT NAME,PHONE
FROM TEST_CENTER TC, TEST_TAKEN TT
WHERE TC.TCID=TT.TCID
AND (NUMBER = '500' OR NUMBER ='502');
```

To simplify building multiple OR conditions when multiple values for the same column are being compared, you can rewrite the statement, using the IN clause:

```
SELECT DISTINCT NAME,PHONE
FROM TEST_CENTER TC, TEST_TAKEN TT
WHERE TC.TCID=TT.TCID
AND NUMBER IN ('500','502');
```

The IN clause is used to denote a set of values. In this example, we use a constant set of values.

You can also use the NOT predicate with the IN clause. In this case, the condition will be true when a value is not present in the set of values provided to the IN clause. You can use as many values as you wish in the IN clause, within the defined limits of the size of a SQL statement.

Advanced Selection Functionality

Chapter 6 looks at more of the functionality and power of the SELECT statement. The following topics are covered:

- Subqueries
- Inner and outer joins

- Nested table expressions
- CASE expressions
- Table functions
- Row expressions
- Unions

DATA MODIFICATION

So far, we have discussed basic SELECT statements. The SELECT statement allows you to retrieve data from your database tables and assumes that data has been previously loaded into the tables. Now, we concentrate on getting data into the database tables by using SQL. Three main statements can be used to add and change data stored in a DB2 database table: the INSERT, UPDATE, and DELETE SQL statements.

To perform these operations, you must have the required privileges on the tables being accessed. Usually, these privileges are more strictly enforced, as they can allow the end user to modify data records.

Inserting Data Records

To initially populate a DB2 table with data, you can use the INSERT statement to store one data record at a time. The statement can be targeted to insert data directly into a base table, or a view can be used instead. If a view is being used as the target, remember that it is the base table where the data is being stored.

Every row that is populated using the INSERT statement must adhere to table-check constraints, data type validation, dynamic (trigger) constraints, and referential integrity constraints. An SQL error will occur if any of these conditions is violated during the processing of the INSERT statement.

> **N O T E**   Remember that you must have the necessary view or table privileges to perform an INSERT statement.

The first example is a simple INSERT statement. This statement will insert the data for the DB2 Data Propagation (#508) exam into the TEST table:

```
INSERT INTO DB2USER1.TEST
(NUMBER, NAME, TYPE, CUT_SCORE, LENGTH,
TOTALTAKEN, TOTALPASSED) VALUES
('508','DB2 DATA PROPAGATION','P',NULL,90,0,0);
```

In this example, we specify all the column names and their corresponding values for this data record. Following the VALUES portion of the statement, we include all the data values for this record.

In the VALUES clause, the number and order of the inserted elements must match the number and order of the column names defined in the INSERT statement. However, the order of the columns doesn't have to match the order in which they are defined in the table. For those columns that don't require a value, you can indicate null or default values. In this example, we use the null value for the cut_score column.

> **N O T E**   The number of elements following the VALUES clause must match the number of names in the INSERT column list.

Depending on your column definition, the DEFAULT value can cause to be inserted a system-defined default, a user-defined default, or null. Be aware that if the column doesn't accept nulls (NOT NULL) and wasn't defined as WITH DEFAULT, you will receive an error message when using the DEFAULT value. The reason is that the default value for those columns not using the WITH DEFAULT option is the null value.

When you want to insert values into all the columns of a table, you do not have to provide the column names in the INSERT statement. This example is shown next.

```
INSERT INTO DB2USER1.TEST VALUES
('508','DB2 DATA PROPAGATION','P',DEFAULT,90,79,11);
```

This method will work only if you specify a value for all the columns in a table. If you miss one of the columns of the table, DB2 will not allow you to insert the row into the table. The DEFAULT keyword used in this example will insert the default value for the CUT_SCORE column.

> **N O T E**   Remember that, depending on the column definition, the default value could be a user-defined default value, a system-defined default value, or null.

Inserting Data into Specific Columns

Sometimes, you need to add data to specific columns. Every column that is not included in the INSERT statement will receive its default value.

This operation can be accomplished only if the omitted columns accept nulls or have a default value definition. This means that you must specify a value for the columns defined as NOT NULL. This restriction excludes columns defined as NOT NULL WITH DEFAULT.

Let's insert a row into the TEST_TAKEN table. In the following example, we insert data only for the columns CID, TCID, NUMBER, and SEAT_NO:

```
INSERT INTO DB2USER1.TEST_TAKEN
(CID,TCID,NUMBER,SEAT_NO)
VALUES('888','TR01','508','1');
```

Remember that columns defined using WITH DEFAULT but not listed in the INSERT statement will receive the null value or a default value.

> **N O T E**   The TEST_TAKEN table has some referential integrity with other tables. If you want to insert a record into a TEST_TAKEN table, the appropriate values should be inserted into the other three tables in advance.

Inserting a Set of Values

Using SQL, you can insert the result of a SELECT statement into a different table. The SQL statement that generates the resulting set must follow these rules.

- The number of columns from the SELECT statement must equal the number of columns in the INSERT column list.
- The data type of each of the columns in the SELECT list must be compatible with the data type of those columns in the INSERT list.
- Column names can be omitted from the INSERT list only if values are inserted into all the columns in the table.
- Only columns defined to allow null or defined as NOT NULL WITH DEFAULT can be omitted from the INSERT list.

In some situations, it might be useful to create tables that are duplicates of others so that you can do multiple calculations against them. The next example uses a table called TEST_PASSED, which is a copy of the TEST_TAKEN table. This new table will be used to extract the information about those candidates who have passed any of the DB2 Certification exams.

```
INSERT INTO DB2USER1.TEST_PASSED
(CID,TCID,NUMBER,
DATE_TAKEN,START_TIME,FINISH_TIME,
PASS_FAIL,SCORE,SEAT_NO)
    (SELECT CID,TCID,NUMBER,
        DATE_TAKEN,START_TIME,FINISH_TIME,
        PASS_FAIL,SCORE,SEAT_NO
        FROM DB2USER1.TEST_TAKEN
        WHERE PASS_FAIL='P');
```

The select list used in the fullselect in the preceding example can also be substituted by a select asterisk (*). This is possible because the TEST_PASSED table has the same column structure as the TEST_TAKEN table. However, to keep this query isolated from future table modifications, you should use the select list instead of the asterisk.

You can also use a table expression to insert values into a table or view, using the INSERT clause.

Inserting Large Amounts of Data

Using the SELECT or VALUES statements to insert data into a table can be very useful. However, it is not recommended to load large amounts of data into a table using the INSERT statement, as the transaction logging overhead can become unmanageable. DB2 provides the LOAD utility, which is designed to move large amounts of data into a table.

Updating Data Records

So far, we have looked at the INSERT statement as a method of moving data into your DB2 table. You may wish to update only a column with values for a group of data records. An SQL UPDATE statement can be used to specify the column and its new values. A table or a view can be referenced as the target for the UPDATE statement.

> **N O T E**   Remember that you must have the correct privileges in order to perform the UPDATE operation.

The UPDATE statement can be used in two forms:

- **Searched update.** This type of UPDATE statement is used to update one or more rows in a table. It requires a WHERE clause to establish the update condition: which rows are to be updated.
- **Positioned update.** This kind of UPDATE statement is always embedded into a program and uses *cursors* to update the row where the cursor is positioned. As the cursor is repositioned using the FETCH statement, the target row for the UPDATE statement changes.

We focus on searched updates in this chapter. Similar to the INSERT statement, all the database constraint mechanisms are enforced during an UPDATE statement. Specific update constraint triggers and referential integrity (RI) constraints could be different from the insert constraints. For example, the following is a transaction that updates candidate ID 888's exam day for the DB2 Fundamentals certification exam:

```
UPDATE DB2USER1.TEST_TAKEN
SET DATE_TAKEN=DATE_TAKEN + 3 DAYS
WHERE CHAR(CID) ='888'
AND NUMBER='500';
```

In this example, the *labeled duration* operation is used to add 3 days to the original date.

It is important that you provide the proper WHERE clause to avoid updating unintended data records. In this example, we needed to specify the predicate NUMBER='500' to avoid changing the date for any of the other tests that the candidate can be scheduled for.

> **N O T E**   DB2-labeled durations for date-time data types include years, months, days, hours, minutes, seconds, and microseconds.

The UPDATE statement can also be used with fullselects. In this case, the fullselect must return a row with exactly the same number of columns and compatible data types of the row that will be updated. Observe that this fullselect must return only one row.

Let's use a SELECT statement to update a row to set the new value. Candidate ID 888 decides to take the DB2 Fundamentals test today in the Toronto, Canada, test center.

```
UPDATE DB2USER1.TEST_TAKEN
SET (DATE_TAKEN,TCID)=
(SELECT CURRENT DATE,TCID FROM DB2USER1.TEST_CENTER
WHERE SUBSTR(CITY,1,7)='TORONTO'
AND COUNTRY='CANADA')
WHERE CID= '888' AND NUMBER='500';
```

In this example, we update two columns in the same operation. These columns are indicated in the parentheses following the SET clause.

After indicating which columns are going to be updated, we use a SELECT statement to retrieve the current date (today) and the test center ID for the test center in Toronto, Canada. Note the last WHERE clause in the statement will restrict the rows that will be updated.

> **N O T E**   If you forget to update the WHERE clause in a searched update, all the data in your table will be updated.

The SQL statement that will update the DATE_TAKEN and TCID columns is known as a *row fullselect*. This name is given because it returns only one row. Observe that the scalar fullselect can be considered a special case of a row fullselect.

> **N O T E**   CURRENT DATE is a DB2 special register that gives the system date. Some others include CURRENT TIME, CURRENT TIMESTAMP, CURRENT PACKAGESET, and USER (the authorization ID).

Sometimes, you need to update a large number of rows of a particular table. This can be accomplished by issuing a searched update. However, this also could allocate a large amount of transactional log space. You can accomplish updates by using positioned updates, where you can easily control the commit frequency.

Removing Data

Many methods are available to remove data from a DB2 database. To remove all the data within a database, use the DROP DATABASE command. This may remove more data than you intended because the entire database, including its configuration, will be physically removed.

It is also possible to remove data by using the DROP TABLESPACE or DROP TABLE statements. These statements are usually issued only by the SYSADM or DBADM, as they will remove large amounts of data. If you wish to remove all of the data records from a table, it is easier and quicker to perform the DROP TABLE statement. Even easier, and less destructive, is using the LOAD utility, with the REPLACE option specifying an empty input file.

> **N O T E**   A mass delete from a segmented table space limits logging and improves performance by merely updating the space map pages to indicate the deletion rather than deleting each data row.

If the table is dropped, it must be recreated before any data can be populated again in the table.

To remove a single data record or a group of records from a table, use the DELETE statement. The syntax of the DELETE statement is different from that of the SELECT and INSERT statements because individual columns cannot be deleted; only rows can be deleted.

The DELETE statement can also be used with views. However, restrictions apply on the type of views that can be used within a DELETE statement.

> **N O T E**   Remember that you must have the necessary privileges over a table to perform the DELETE operation.

In general, two kinds of DELETE statements are

- **Searched delete.** This DELETE statement is used to delete one or multiple rows from a table. It can use a WHERE clause to establish the delete condition.
- **Positioned delete.** This DELETE operation is always embedded into a program. It uses *cursors* to delete the row where the cursor is positioned.

This section focuses on the searched delete.

The following SQL statement deletes candidates who don't have a telephone number loaded into the table. We use a searched delete to accomplish this task:

```
DELETE FROM DB2USER1.CANDIDATE
WHERE HPHONE IS NULL
AND WPHONE IS NULL;
```

This example uses a WHERE clause to delete the data that meets a specific criterion. To verify the result of the DELETE statement, you can issue a SELECT statement with the same WHERE clause. If the DELETE was successful, the SELECT will return an empty set.

A delete can also become more sophisticated by using subselects. The next SQL statement deletes all the candidates who took the DB2 Certification exams in February of any given year:

```
DELETE FROM DB2USER1.CANDIDATE
WHERE CID IN (SELECT CID FROM DB2USER1.TEST_TAKEN
WHERE MONTH(DATE_TAKEN)=2);
```

In this example, we use a subselect to retrieve the CID values of the candidates who took a DB2 Certification exam in February. This list will be used to search for the candidates we want to delete.

You can delete all the rows in a table if you don't specify a search condition in your DELETE statement. You must be aware of the implications of this type of statement.

However, this is not the only way to delete all the rows in a table. You can also delete them if all the rows meet the search condition.

Deleting all the rows in a table by using a DELETE statement may not be the most efficient method. This kind of statement can consume a lot of log space when your tables are large.

View Classification

Now that we have examined various SQL DML statements, let's take a closer look at views. We have already discussed creating views. Now we'll examine the various types of views. Views are classified by the operations they allow but are generally referred to as either read-only or non-read-only (updatable) views. The referential and check constraints are treated independently. They do not affect the view classification.

For example, you may not be able to insert a value into a table, because of a referential constraint. If you create a view using that table, you also can't insert that value using the view. However, if the view satisfies the rules for a non-read-only view, it will still be considered an insertable, updatable, or deleteable view because the insert restriction is located on the base table, not on the view definition.

Read-Only Views

Depending on how it is defined, a view can be read-only or can be the object of an INSERT, UPDATE, or DELETE. A view is read-only if one of the following statements is true of its definition.

- The first FROM clause identifies more than one table or view a table function, a common or nested table expression, or an MQT.
- The first SELECT specifies the keyword DISTINCT.
- The outer fullselect contains a GROUP BY clause.
- The outer fullselect contains a HAVING clause.
- The first SELECT clause contains a column function.
- The view contains a subquery such that the base object of the outer fullselect and of the subquery is the same table.
- The first FROM clause identifies a read-only view.

A read-only view cannot be the object of an INSERT, UPDATE, or DELETE statement. A view that includes GROUP BY or HAVING cannot be referred to in a subquery of a base predicate. Following is an example of a read-only view:

```
CREATE VIEW READ_ONLY_VIEW
(NAME,WORK_PHONE,HOME_PHONE)
AS
SELECT DISTINCT FNAME,WPHONE,HPHONE
FROM DB2USER1.CANDIDATE C, DB2USER1.TEST_TAKEN TT
WHERE C.CID=TT.CID;
```

The view is read-only, as it uses the DISTINCT clause and the SQL statement involves more than one table.

Non-Read-Only Views

A view must meet the rules listed earlier to be considered a non-read-only view. Following is an example of a view that can be used for a DELETE statement:

```
CREATE VIEW DELETABLE_VIEW
(TCID,CID,NUMBER,DATE_TAKEN,START_TIME,SEAT_NO,SCORE)
AS
SELECT TCID,CID,NUMBER,DATE_TAKEN,
START_TIME,SEAT_NO,SCORE
FROM DB2USER1.TEST_TAKEN
WHERE TCID='TR01';
```

A view that can be the object of an UPDATE statement is a special case of a non-read-only view, as at least one of its columns must be updatable. A column of a view can be updated when all of the following rules are true.

- The view is not a read-only view.
- The column resolves to a column of a base table.
- The FOR READ ONLY or FOR FETCH ONLY option is not specified.

Even though the following view definition uses constant values that cannot be updated, it is a non-read-only view, and at least you can update one of its columns. Therefore, it can be the object of an UPDATE statement:

```
CREATE VIEW UPDATABLE_VIEW
(TCID,CID,NUMBER,CURRENT_DATE,CURRENT_TIME,SEAT_NO,SCORE)
AS
SELECT TCID,CID,NUMBER,CURRENT DATE,
CURRENT TIME,SEAT_NO,SCORE
FROM DB2USER1.TEST_TAKEN
WHERE TCID='TX01';
```

A view can be the object of an INSERT statement when all its columns are updatable. Also, all the columns that do not have a default value must be specified in the INSERT statement. The row being inserted must contain a value for each column in the view definition. The following is a view that can be used to insert rows:

```
CREATE VIEW INSERTABLE_VIEW
(TEST_NUMBER,TEST_NAME,TOTAL_TAKEN)
AS
SELECT NUMBER,NAME,TOTALTAKEN FROM DB2USER1.TEST;
```

This view would appear to allow inserts. However, an attempt to insert the view will fail because some columns in the base table don't accept null values. Some of these columns are not present in the view definition. When you try to insert a value using the view, DB2 will try to insert a NULL into a NOT NULL column. This action is not permitted.

> **N O T E**   Remember, the constraints defined on the base table are independent of the operations that can be performed using a view.

SUMMARY

This chapter discussed the Data Manipulation Language (DML), which has four primary statements: SELECT, UPDATE, INSERT, and DELETE. These statements enable all database object data manipulation.

The knowledge of basic SQL is mandatory for a DB2 database administrator and application developer. However, SQL is very powerful language, and the level of SQL will vary, depending on the user's primary activity.

In this chapter, we covered many of the basic functions of SQL statements, including how to

- Retrieve rows
- Sort the result set
- Restrict the result with some conditions
- Retrieve rows from more than one table at a time
- Add a row to a table
- Remove a record
- Change the value of the table

If you are a business analyst, you may expect more analytical, statistical information from DB2. DB2 supports very powerful SQL functions for various business needs. We talk about some advanced SQL in the next chapter.

ADDITIONAL RESOURCES

IBM DB2 UDB for z/OS Version 8 SQL Reference (SC18-7426-00)

IBM DB2 UDB for z/OS Version 8 Application Programming and SQL Guide (SC18-7415)

DB2 Universal Database V8 for Linux, UNIX, and Windows Database Administration Certification Guide, Fifth Edition (Prentice Hall, 2003)

Advanced SQL Coding

- Subqueries
- Unions
- Joins
- Nested and common table expressions
- Case expressions
- Row expressions
- OLAP and star joins
- Predicates and filtering

This chapter covers some the more advanced DB2 SQL features. The discussion begins with the constructs of subqueries, unions, and joins. Then we examine nested and common table expressions, the CASE expression with its if-then-else logic, row expressions, and OLAP features. Efficient query coding also requires a knowledge of how DB2 processes predicates. We look at how predicates are classified and data is filtered during query processing.

SUBQUERIES

A subquery, an SQL statement specifying a search condition, contains either a subselect or a fullselect and is used inside another SQL statement. A subquery can include search conditions of its own. Each search condition can also contain subqueries. Any SQL statement can contain a hierarchy of subqueries. The SQL query block that contains subqueries is at a higher level than the subqueries it contains. This is important for how columns are referenced between levels.

A subquery can contain search conditions that reference not only columns of the tables identified by its FROM clause but also columns of tables identified at any higher level. The reverse, however, is not true. A query at a higher level cannot reference columns from a subquery, although outer query columns can be compared to the resultant columns from a subquery. Within a subquery, a reference to a column of a table from a higher level is called a *correlated reference,* or correlation predicate.

When specified in a search condition, many operands can be used. They are generally categorized as single-result, IN list, or existence subqueries.

> **N O T E**   Quantified predicates are another form and compare one or more values to a collection of values by preceding the comparison operator (=, >, <, and so on.) with ANY, SOME, or ALL. To avoid confusion, quantified predicates are ignored in this text.

The following example demonstrates a single-result subquery to return the test center with the highest number of seats:

```
SELECT TCID,NAME,NOSEATS
FROM TEST_CENTER
WHERE NOSEATS =
(SELECT MAX(NOSEATS) FROM TEST_CENTER)
```

The subquery can return only one result: either a null, if no qualifying rows are in the subquery table, or a value representing the maximum value of the column noseats in the TEST_CENTER table. This value is compared to the outer table rows, and only those rows that equal the maximum value for noseats are returned.

This type of subquery is known as a *noncorrelated subquery*; the subquery and the outer query have no correlation. The subquery is independent of the outer query and returns a single result to the outer query merely for comparison.

To demonstrate an IN list subquery, consider the difficulty of producing a report on the number of DB2 Certification exams if the name and the number of the exams are unknown. The following example produces a report that includes the names and phone numbers of all the test centers that have candidates registered for the DB2 Certification exams. The search string DB2 is used to find the numbers of the DB2 Certification program exams:

```
SELECT DISTINCT NAME,PHONE
FROM TEST_CENTER TC, TEST_TAKEN TT
WHERE TC.TCID=TT.TCID
AND NUMBER IN
(SELECT NUMBER FROM TEST
WHERE NAME LIKE 'DB2%')
```

In this example, the subquery appears as part of the IN clause. In the subquery, we are retrieving all the numbers for those tests that have DB2 in their names. Note that you will never see the subquery output. The subquery merely creates a list of values that will be used later by the outer SELECT statement.

Both previous examples have demonstrated a noncorrelated subquery. The most common forms of noncorrelated subqueries are the single-result and the IN list subqueries.

> **N O T E**   The third alternative, an EXISTS subquery, is generally not coded for a noncorrelated subquery. Because it returns a TRUE or FALSE, an EXISTS subquery will be either true for every row of the outer table or false for every row of the outer table.

In contrast, a query in which the subquery references values of the immediate outer SELECT or any subselect at a higher level is a correlated subquery. The most common forms are the single-result and the EXISTS correlated subquery. Whereas the noncorrelated subquery is evaluated once and a result is returned to the outer query, the correlated subquery is potentially evaluated once for every outer row.

> **N O T E**   The IN subquery is generally not coded for a correlated subquery, due to the potential for the IN list to be built numerous times.

As with the noncorrelated example, a single-result correlated subquery will return a single result for every execution. The difference is that a noncorrelated subquery is executed once rather than many times.

Consider a query to return the highest score for each test and the associated details. The following correlated subquery returns the desired result:

```
SELECT C.FNAME, TT.NUMBER, TT.DATE_TAKEN, TT.SCORE
FROM TEST_TAKEN TT, CANDIDATE C
WHERE C.CID = TT.CID
AND TT.SCORE =
(SELECT MAX(TT2.SCORE)
 FROM TEST_TAKEN TT2
 WHERE TT2.NUMBER = TT.NUMBER)

FNAME   NUMBER    DATE_TAKEN SCORE
------  --------  ---------- -----
Dan        501    02/02/2004    73
Susan      500    03/01/2004    82
Susan      502    03/02/2004    92
  3 record(s) selected.
```

The test number for each outer row is passed to the subquery, and the maximum score for that test is returned to the outer query for comparison. If the maximum score equals the score of the current row, that row is returned. If not, the row is discarded. It is possible for the outer query to return more than one row for each test if more than one person achieves the maximum score.

The next example demonstrates an EXISTS subquery in which we rewrite the previous noncorrelated IN list SQL example as a correlated subquery. This query produces a report that includes the names and phone numbers of all the test centers that have candidates registered for the DB2 Certification exams. To match the problem description to the query, the problem description can be rewritten as follows: Produce a report that includes the names and phone numbers of all test centers at which a candidate is registered for the DB2 Certification exams:

```
SELECT NAME,PHONE
FROM TEST_CENTER TC
WHERE EXISTS
(SELECT * FROM TEST T, TEST_TAKEN TT
WHERE T.NAME LIKE 'DB2%'
AND    T.NUMBER = TT.NUMBER
AND    TT.TCID=TC.TCID)
```

> **N O T E**   As with standard WHERE clause predicates, the reverse condition can be achieved by prefixing the condition with the NOT keyword, such as NOT EXISTS or NOT IN. Remember, however, that a null will not qualify against either an IN or a NOT IN condition.

Note that the WHERE clause in the subquery in this example references a table that is listed in the outer FROM clause.

The EXISTS subquery will return a TRUE or a FALSE to the outer query. If TRUE, the outer row is considered to be a match, and the row is returned to the application. The correlated EXISTS subquery will terminate after the first TRUE condition is found or when a FALSE can be determined, as the requirement is to return only a TRUE or FALSE condition, not to list how many occurrences match.

> **N O T E**   DB2 prunes the SELECT list for EXISTS subqueries, so it is not important for access path or performance what columns are listed in the subquery select list of an EXISTS subquery. Therefore, whether you specify SELECT * or SELECT 1, DB2 will still return a TRUE or FALSE and will not retrieve all columns as an outer query would if SELECT * were specified.

UNIONS

The UNION operation lets you combine the results of two or more SQL statements into one answer set. You can combine many tables or SQL statements by using the UNION (or UNION ALL) operator; the only restriction is that every table or SQL statement must have the same type, number, and order of columns. The term used to describe this is that they must be UNION compatible.

Suppose that you want to combine the minimum and maximum scores for each DB2 Certification program exam on different output rows and add a string constant that indicates which values are the maximum and minimum:

```
SELECT NUMBER,'MINIMUM:', MIN(SCORE)
FROM TEST_TAKEN
GROUP BY NUMBER
UNION
SELECT NUMBER,'MAXIMUM:', MAX(SCORE)
FROM TEST_TAKEN
GROUP BY NUMBER
ORDER BY NUMBER,2
```

The UNION operator shows you the results of two or more separate queries as a single result. In our example, the first query calculates the minimum score of the TEST_TAKEN table. The second query calculates the maximum score value. Both queries have the same type, order, and number of columns.

In the previous example, the two SQL statements are very similar. However, you can combine very different queries by using the UNION operator, but remember the restriction about the resulting rows.

The UNION operator removes duplicate rows from the resulting set. However, you will sometimes need to list all the rows processed by your SQL statements or when duplicates are not possible. SQL provides you with an operator clause that allows you to keep all the rows involved in a UNION operation. This is the ALL clause. Because the previous example can never produce duplicate rows, the ALL clause can be added to the UNION:

```
SELECT NUMBER,'MINIMUM:', MIN(SCORE)
FROM TEST_TAKEN
GROUP BY NUMBER
UNION ALL
SELECT NUMBER,'MAXIMUM:', MAX(SCORE)
FROM TEST_TAKEN
GROUP BY NUMBER
ORDER BY NUMBER,2
```

> **N O T E**   Always try to code a UNION ALL rather than a UNION.
> Code a UNION only when duplicates are possible and are not desired.
> The UNION ALL offers better performance, as a UNION will always
> invoke a sort to remove duplicates, and a UNION ALL will not.
> However, you can't always substitute a UNION with a UNION ALL.

> **N O T E**   A UNION (and UNION ALL) can be used between any
> combination of subselects and fullselects and in subqueries, views,
> and table expressions.

The ability to have a UNION within a view has provided an alternative for partitioned table designs that have grown beyond the DB2 physical limit of 128TB or for large partitioned table spaces that have become too much of an obstacle for 24/7 availability. A UNION ALL in a view would appear to applications using the view that it is a single table. This technique has many benefits, such as independence of the tables and no need for large NPIs.

However, some coding techniques have to be applied in order to best use this feature. Suppose that you have the following design: five independent tables (TC1–TC5), each holding data for different TEST_CENTERs. A view (TESTCTR_VIEW) could be developed to UNION all five tables together to appear as one larger table. The view definition follows:

```
CREATE TESTCTR_VIEW(TCID)
SELECT TCID FROM TC1 WHERE TCID = 1
UNION ALL
SELECT TCID FROM TC2 WHERE TCID = 2
UNION ALL
SELECT TCID FROM TC3 WHERE TCID = 3
UNION ALL
SELECT TCID FROM TC4 WHERE TCID = 4
UNION ALL
SELECT TCID FROM TC5 WHERE TCID = 5
```

Queries written against the TESTCTR_VIEW will need to repeat the predicate defined in the view in order for DB2 to use subquery pruning. Subquery pruning applies to UNION ALL queries and requires redundant predicates to be coded in view definition in order to compare distributed predicates with defined predicates in the view definition; then DB2 removes unnecessary query blocks at bind time or runtime. This limits the number of tables that are accessed to satisfy the query.

Using the preceding view definition, table TC1 contains values such that TCID = 1, table TC2 contains values such that TCID = 2, and so on. The predicate TCID BETWEEN 3 AND 4 will be distributed to each subselect in the view; therefore, only the necessary tables will be accessed. Figure 6-1 shows how the predicate in the select works with the tables in the view.

After the predicates are distributed, DB2 can then prune unnecessary query blocks. Unnecessary query blocks are those in which the distributed predicates, combined with the original view definition predicates, evaluate to `FALSE`. The original view definition must contain the predicates to allow pruning to occur, even if redundant.

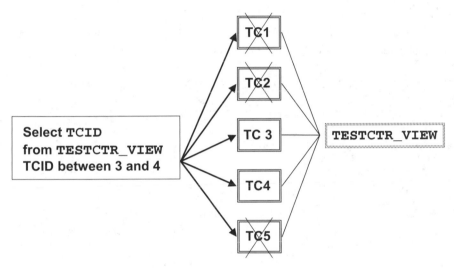

Figure 6-1   Predicates for subquery pruning

JOINS

The heart of SQL in a relational system is the ability to perform relational joins. Joins are specified by using more than one table name in the FROM clause of a query. A joined table specifies an intermediate-result table that is the result of either an inner join or an outer join.

> **N O T E**   Until version 8, the maximum number of tables that could be coded in a single FROM clause was 15, but up to 225 table references can be in an SQL statement. To increase the limit of 15, update the macro SPRMMXT to a value greater than 15. Also, the 15-tables limit does not apply to star join queries. Version 8 of DB2 fully supports 225 tables in a query, including subqueries.

Inner Joins

The join operation used most often is the one we have been using in the book exercises, which is known as an *inner join*. An inner join combines each row of the left table with each row of the right table, keeping only the rows where the join condition is TRUE. The result table may be missing rows from either or both of the joined tables. The following example shows an inner join without using the INNER JOIN syntax, which means that the inner join is implicitly defined. The tables in the FROM clause are separated by commas to indicate the join. This type of syntax is valid only for inner joins.

In the example following, we wish to find the scores of all DB2 tests taken by U.S. citizens in the small test centers year by year, in order of ascending year and descending score:

```
SELECT T.NAME, YEAR(TT.DATE_TAKEN) AS YEAR,
    TT.SCORE
FROM TEST T, TEST_TAKEN TT, TEST_CENTER TC,
    CANDIDATE C
WHERE C.CID = TT.CID AND
    TC.TCID = TT.TCID AND
    T.NUMBER = TT.NUMBER AND
    T.NAME LIKE 'DB2%' AND
    C.COUNTRY='USA' AND
    TC.NOSEATS < 10
    ORDER BY YEAR(TT.DATE_TAKEN), TT.SCORE DESC
```

If the inner join used the explicit syntax, it would appear as follows:

```
SELECT T.NAME, YEAR(TT.DATE_TAKEN) AS YEAR,
    TT.SCORE
FROM TEST T INNER JOIN TEST_TAKEN TT
ON T.NUMBER = TT.NUMBER
INNER JOIN TEST_CENTER TC
ON TC.TCID = TT.TCID
  INNER JOIN CANDIDATE C
ON C.CID = TT.CID
WHERE T.NAME LIKE 'DB2%'
  AND C.COUNTRY='USA'
  AND TC.NOSEATS < 10
ORDER BY YEAR(TT.DATE_TAKEN), TT.SCORE DESC
```

For the explicit join syntax, the keyword INNER is optional and, if omitted, implies an inner join. The ON clause determines the join predicates between the tables, and the WHERE clause applies the local or table access predicates. For an inner join, the result is not impacted if the local predicates appear in the WHERE or ON clause. It is recommended that, for consistency with outer joins, join predicates appear only in the ON clause; local predicates, in the WHERE clause. For outer joins, the placement of predicates in either the ON or WHERE clause can dramatically change the result. This is demonstrated in the section on outer joins.

Each join must be followed by its ON clause, which dictates the two tables that are being joined. The joined tables must appear in the FROM clause before they are referenced by join predicates in the ON clause. In the preceding example, the first join is between TEST and TEST_TAKEN. The second join is between TEST_CENTER and TEST_TAKEN as dictated by the ON clause. The third join is between CANDIDATE and TEST_TAKEN.

One exception to the rule that the ON clause must follow each join is when nesting joins within other joins. For simplicity, this syntax is not recommended and can easily be recoded to suit the rule just cited.

Deciding whether to code the explicit join syntax or to separate the joined tables with commas is purely a matter of preference and is not related to performance. However, the explicit join syntax has the benefits of compatibility with the outer join syntax; improved readability of large SQL statements, as each join is followed by its join predicate; and increased likelihood that all join predicates will be coded correctly.

Outer Joins

A different kind of join operation is the *outer join*. The result set of an inner join consists only of those matched rows that are present in both joined tables. What happens when we need to include those values that are present in one or another joined table but not in both of them? In this case, an OUTER JOIN operation is needed. Outer joins are designed to generate an answer set that includes those values that are present in joined tables and those that are not. This type of optional relationship between tables is very common. Figure 6-2 shows the best way to view outer joins, representing the data from each table that is included/excluded in each type of join.

Outer joins are of three types: left outer join, right outer join, and full outer join.

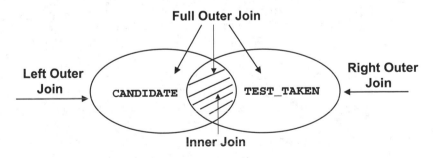

Figure 6-2 Outer joins

Left Outer Join

A LEFT OUTER JOIN operation, or left join, produces an answer set that includes the matching values of both joined tables—inner join rows—and those values present only in the left joined table—rows exclusive to the left table. The left joined table is the one used in the left part of the LEFT OUTER JOIN operator when coding the join operation in the FROM clause.

In a left outer join, the left table is referred to as the *preserved row table*. If a row is unmatched between the two joined tables, it is still returned, or preserved, from the left table. The opposite, or right, table is the null-supplying table. When a row is unmatched from the left to the right table in the join, the row is supplied with nulls from the right table.

> **N O T E**   With left and right outer joins, reversing the order of tables in the FROM clause may alter the result.

Suppose that we have been requested to generate a report that includes the first name, the phone number, and the highest score for all the candidates present in the CANDIDATE table. If an inner join is used, the report will include data for only those candidates present in the TEST_TAKEN table.

Without using the outer-join syntax, this request could be solved using some SQL statements already discussed; however, the construction would be complex. Instead, we will use the left outer join to satisfy the request, as the following example shows:

```
SELECT C.FNAME, C.WPHONE, MAX(TT.SCORE)
FROM CANDIDATE C
    LEFT OUTER JOIN TEST_TAKEN TT
ON C.CID=TT.CID
GROUP BY FNAME, WPHONE;
```

> **N O T E**   The keyword OUTER is optional. Provided that the JOIN is preceded by LEFT, RIGHT, or FULL, OUTER is implied.

Note the syntax used to indicate a left outer join. The LEFT OUTER JOIN operator is used to indicate the left outer join operation. In this example, the answer set includes those candidates not present in the TEST_TAKEN table. The MAX(TT.SCORE) column will show nulls for those candidates.

When coding outer joins, it is important to note the difference between WHERE and ON clause predicates. From the previous example, we may want to retrieve only those candidates with a CID of 111, 333, or 444:

```
SELECT C.CID, C.FNAME, C.WPHONE, MAX(TT.SCORE) AS MAX_SCORE
FROM CANDIDATE C
   LEFT OUTER JOIN TEST_TAKEN TT
ON C.CID=TT.CID
WHERE C.CID IN (111, 333, 444)
GROUP BY C.CID, C.FNAME, C.WPHONE


CID FNAME WPHONE       MAX_SCORE
--- ----- ---------- ---------
111 SUSAN  1115551234        92
333 DAN    4442314244        73
444 JOHN   5552143244         -
3 record(s) selected.
```

The WHERE clause predicate in this example is applied to the left, or preserved, row table. DB2 is able, therefore, to apply this predicate before the join to the CANDIDATE table and join only candidates 111, 333, and 444 to the TEST_TAKEN table. CID 444 in this example returns a MAX_SCORE of null because the candidate has not taken any tests and is therefore not found in the TEST_TAKEN table.

Consider the result if the query is written to also exclude those rows with a score less than 75, if found:

```
SELECT C.CID, C.FNAME, C.WPHONE, MAX(TT.SCORE) AS MAX_SCORE
FROM CANDIDATE C
   LEFT OUTER JOIN TEST_TAKEN TT
ON C.CID=TT.CID
WHERE C.CID IN (111, 333, 444)
AND    TT.SCORE >= 75
GROUP BY C.CID, C.FNAME, C.WPHONE

CID FNAME WPHONE       MAX_SCORE
--- ----- ---------- ---------
111 SUSAN 1115551234         92
1 record(s) selected.
```

Only one row qualifies from this query. The WHERE clause predicate on the preserved row table (WHERE C.CID IN (111, 333, 444)) can be applied before the join to limit the number of rows that must be joined. The additional WHERE clause predicate (AND TT.SCORE >= 75) is applied after the join because it is not known until after the join what the value of tt.score will be. This predicate is applied to each row, with the following result:

- Is Dan's score of 73 >= 75? FALSE
- Is Susan's score of 92 >= 75? TRUE
- Is John's score of NULL >= 75? UNKNOWN

Remember that for a row to be returned, the WHERE clause must evaluate to TRUE. Because the nulls introduced by the outer join are discarded by the WHERE clause applied to the null-supplying table, DB2 will rewrite the left join to an INNER JOIN, thus allowing the WHERE clause predicates to be applied to both tables before the joining of the rows occurs:

```
SELECT C.CID, C.FNAME, C.WPHONE, MAX(TT.SCORE) AS MAX_SCORE
FROM CANDIDATE C
    INNER JOIN TEST_TAKEN TT
ON C.CID=TT.CID
WHERE C.CID IN (111, 333, 444)
AND    TT.SCORE >= 75
GROUP BY C.CID, C.FNAME, C.WPHONE
```

> **N O T E** The outer join simplification will be recorded in the JOIN_TYPE column of the plan table. If a left, right, or full join has been simplified to an inner join, the JOIN_TYPE value will be blank.

If you wish to maintain the null-supplied rows, you must include an additional IS NULL predicate, such as:

```
SELECT C.CID, C.FNAME, C.WPHONE, MAX(TT.SCORE) AS MAX_SCORE
FROM CANDIDATE C
    LEFT OUTER JOIN TEST_TAKEN TT
ON C.CID=TT.CID
WHERE C.CID IN (111, 333, 444)
AND    (TT.SCORE >= 75 OR TT.SCORE IS NULL)
GROUP BY C.CID, C.FNAME, C.WPHONE

CID FNAME WPHONE      MAX_SCORE
--- ----- ---------- ---------
333 SUSAN 4442314244        92
444 JOHN  5552143244         -
2 record(s) selected.
```

In this case, DB2 will not simplify the left outer join to an inner join; because the null-supplied row is not discarded by the WHERE clause predicate. Thus, the row for Glen is included in the result set because it *is null*.

> **N O T E** WHERE clause predicates applied to the preserved row table can be applied before the join. Predicates applied to the null-supplying table will cause DB2 to simplify the join unless a predicate of the form OR COL IS NULL—or equivalent expression that retains nulls—is coded.

We've looked at WHERE clause predicates applied to either the preserved row or null-supplied tables. The next objective is to demonstrate the impact of coding local predicates in the ON clause. The following example displays the output if we specify the candidate predicate (111, 333, or 444) in the ON clause rather than in the WHERE clause:

```
SELECT C.CID, C.FNAME, C.WPHONE, MAX(TT.SCORE) AS MAX_SCORE
FROM CANDIDATE C
    LEFT OUTER JOIN TEST_TAKEN TT
ON C.CID=TT.CID
AND C.CID IN (111, 333, 444)
GROUP BY C.CID, C.FNAME, C.WPHONE
```

```
CID FNAME  WPHONE      MAX_SCORE
--- -----  ----------  ---------
111 BILL   1115551234         73
222 GEORGE 2226543455          -
333 SUSAN  4442314244         92
444 GLEN   5552143244          -
555 JIM    6662341234          -
666 KEVIN  7773142134          -
777 BERT   8886534534          -
888 PAUL   9992112212          -
8 record(s) selected.
```

Because no WHERE clause predicates restrict the result, this query returns all rows of the CAN-DIDATE table. Columns from the TEST_TAKEN table are supplied only when the ON clause is TRUE. Remember, WHERE clause predicates restrict the result, whereas ON clause predicates determine the criteria for the join. For the rows not matching the full ON clause (CID NOT IN 111, 333—note that 444 is not included, because it will not be found in the TEST_TAKEN table), DB2 will preserve the row from the left table and supply nulls from the right table. Rows matching the ON clause (CID IN 111, 333) will match and thus return columns from both tables.

> **N O T E**   If it can determine before joining the rows that the ON clause will fail, DB2 will automatically supply nulls for the null-supplied columns without attempting the join. This improves performance, as rows are not joined unnecessarily if the final result will not match.

Right Outer Join

A RIGHT OUTER JOIN operation, or right join, produces an answer set that includes the matching values of both joined tables and those values present only in the right joined table. The right joined table is the one used in the right part of the RIGHT OUTER JOIN operator when coding the join operation.

For a right join, the right table is the preserved row table, and the left table is the null-supplied table for unmatched rows. This is the opposite of a left join. An example using a right outer join follows:

```
SELECT NAME, COUNT(DISTINCT TT.CID)
FROM TEST_TAKEN TT
RIGHT OUTER JOIN TEST T
ON TT.NUMBER = T.NUMBER
```

This example requests all test names present in the TEST table and the number of candidates who scheduled or took each test. Note that there may be some tests for which no candidate was scheduled. You cannot report such tests using an inner join statement; however, you can do so using a right outer join.

> **N O T E**   The COUNT(DISTINCT TT.CID) will count unique occurrences of TT.CID after the exclusion of nulls. Thus, nulls introduced by the outer join will not be counted. This is intentional, as the addition of a null will falsely add 1 to the count. The right outer join is required, however, to also report those tests that have not been taken by any candidates.

As with a left join, the order of the tables in the FROM clause for a right join can impact the result. However, a right join can be converted to a left join by reversing the order of the tables in the FROM clause and by changing the RIGHT keyword to LEFT.

N O T E   DB2 converts all *right* joins to *left* joins at bind time. The
JOIN_TYPE column of the plan table will show an L for a right or a
left join unless the join has been simplified to an inner. For this
reason, you should avoid coding right joins, to minimize confusion
when evaluating the access path.

Full Outer Join

The FULL OUTER JOIN operation produces an answer set that includes the matching values of
both joined tables and those values not present in one or the other of the tables. Thus, it returns
the inclusive inner join rows plus the exclusive left and right outer rows.

To show a FULL OUTER JOIN operation, we will create two sample tables: CITY and COUNTRY.
They show the relationship between a city and a country (CITY table) and a country and a con-
tinent (COUNTRY table). The CITY table is designed to have countries that are not in the
COUNTRY table. The COUNTRY table is also designed to have countries that are not in the city
table. The contents of both tables are as follows:

```
TABLE:CITY
CITY_NAME              COUNTRY_NAME
---------------        ---------------
Sydney                 Australia
London                 England
Dublin                 Ireland
Firenze                Italy
Milano                 Italy
Mexico City            Mexico
Lima                   Peru
Toronto                Canada
Vienna                 Austria
Hannover               Germany
10 record(s) selected.

TABLE:COUNTRY
COUNTRY_NAME           CONTINENT
---------------        -------------------------
Australia              Australian Continent
England                European Continent
Ireland                European Continent
Italy                  European Continent
Mexico                 American Continent
Austria                European Continent
South Africa           African Continent
Spain                  European Continent
8 record(s) selected.
```

We want to show all the countries, cities, and continents that are in the tables. Therefore, we are using a full outer join, as the following example shows:

```
SELECT CTRY.CONTINENT, CTRY.COUNTRY_NAME,
CTY.COUNTRY_NAME, CTY.CITY_NAME
FROM COUNTRY CTRY
    FULL OUTER JOIN CITY CTY
ON CTY.COUNTRY_NAME=CTRY.COUNTRY_NAME
ORDER BY CTRY.CONTINENT,
    CTY.COUNTRY_NAME,
    CTY.CITY_NAME
```

CONTINENT	COUNTRY_NAME	COUNTRY_NAME	CITY_NAME
African Continent	South Africa	-	-
American Continent	Mexico	Mexico	Mexico City
Australian Continent	Australia	Australia	Sydney
European Continent	Austria	Austria	Vienna
European Continent	England	England	London
European Continent	Ireland	Ireland	Dublin
European Continent	Italy	Italy	Firenze
European Continent	Italy	Italy	Milano
European Continent	Spain	-	-
-	-	Canada	Toronto
-	-	Germany	Hannover
-	-	Peru	Lima

```
12 record(s) selected.
```

The rows that have a null value were added by the outer join operation. The COUNTRY_NAME column is shown twice to see those countries present in the COUNTRY table but not in the CITY table, and vice versa.

As shown by the full join example, both tables can preserve rows and also supply nulls for unmatched rows. Because WHERE clause predicates applied to null-supplied tables may cause DB2 to perform simplification of the outer join, predicates that are to be applied before the join to limit the result set must be coded within nested table expressions.

> **N O T E** DB2 can simplify a full join to either a left or an inner join if the WHERE clause predicates discard nulls from one or both tables, respectively. This is shown in the JOIN_TYPE column of the plan table as either an L for left, or blank, for an inner join rather than an F for a full join.

Consider the following example, which lists the information for only South Africa and Peru:

```
SELECT CTRY.CONTINENT, CTRY.COUNTRY_NAME,
CTY.COUNTRY_NAME, CTY.CITY_NAME
FROM (SELECT CONTINENT, COUNTRY_NAME
      FROM COUNTRY
      WHERE COUNTRY_NAME IN ('SOUTH AFRICA', 'PERU')) AS CTRY
   FULL OUTER JOIN
     (SELECT COUNTRY_NAME, CITY_NAME
      FROM CITY
      WHERE COUNTRY_NAME IN ('SOUTH AFRICA', 'PERU')) AS CTY
ON CTY.COUNTRY_NAME=CTRY.COUNTRY_NAME
ORDER BY CTRY.CONTINENT, CTY.COUNTRY_NAME,
   CTY.CITY_NAME
```

```
CONTINENT           COUNTRY_NAME    COUNTRY_NAME    CITY_NAME
----------------    ------------    ------------    ---------
African Continent   South Africa    -               -
-                   -               Peru            Lima
2 record(s) selected.
```

Because the country name can return null from either table, it is common to code the COALESCE or VALUE function to ensure that the value is always supplied and is not null. The select list for this example would be as follows:

```
SELECT CTRY.CONTINENT, COALESCE(CTRY.COUNTRY_NAME,CTY.COUNTRY_NAME)
   , CTY.CITY_NAME
```

N O T E COALESCE returns the first list element that is not null.

Combining Outer Joins

To this point, we have discussed each outer join operation separately. Now, we will show a more complex example: combining two outer joins in a single query. Let's display all the candidates and all the tests with their respective scores. To create this query, we need two outer joins. The first outer join will obtain all candidates and their scores, including candidates who did not schedule or take any tests. The second outer join will retrieve all the tests present in the TEST table, even if no candidate scheduled or took those tests:

```
SELECT C.CID, T.NAME, SCORE
FROM (CANDIDATE C
LEFT OUTER JOIN TEST_TAKEN TT
ON TT.CID=C.CID)
   FULL OUTER JOIN TEST T
   ON TT.NUMBER = T.NUMBER
ORDER BY C.CID
```

The first outer join is enclosed in parentheses, which are used for readability and to indicate that the left outer join will be resolved first. In reality, the join sequence is determined by the precedence of the join predicates. For example, because the full join in this example joins to a column from the null-supplied table of the previous left join, the left join must precede the full join.

> **N O T E**   When the join sequence is not dictated by the join predicates, DB2 will evaluate the most cost-effective join sequence.

The left outer join gathers all the candidate IDs. We need only a left outer join here. Because of referential integrity constraints, table TEST_TAKEN can have candidates present only in the CANDIDATE table.

The second part is a full outer join. With this outer join, we take all the tests taken by the candidates and the result of the left outer join, and we join them with all the tests in the TEST table. We need a full outer join this time, even though the TEST_TAKEN table can have only test numbers that are present in the TEST table; the left table of this outer join, which is the result of the first join, may include null values as a test number. The TEST table does not have null values, so we need to use a full outer join. Even if the TEST table did contain nulls, a null will never equal another null unless the predicates of the form IS NULL are included in the join criteria. The results are as follows:

```
CID NAME                             SCORE
--- -------------------------------- -----
111 DB2 Fundamentals                 65
111 DB2 Administration               73
111 DB2 Application Development       67
222 DB2 Fundamentals                 55
222 DB2 Application Development       53
222 DB2 Application Development       75
333 DB2 Fundamentals                 82
333 DB2 Administration               -
333 DB2 Application Development       92
444 -                                -
555 -                                -
666 -                                -
777 -                                -
888 -                                -
14 record(s) selected.
```

> **N O T E**   Care must be taken when joining the result of an outer join to subsequent tables. If the join predicate refers to columns from a null-supplied table, the join predicate must also cater for the occurrence of nulls. Where possible, code the join predicate from the preserved row table; if the preceding join was a full join, use the COALESCE function to ensure that the join predicate cannot be null.

Joins versus Denormalization

One issue that needs to be examined when discussing joins is that of denormalization, the process of pulling normalized tables back together into a single table to avoid joins. This is often done in an effort to minimize the joins and to improve performance. Because this is generally applied to tables in a one-to-many relationship, it results in multiple occurrences of the same data, introducing update anomalies, or a single piece of data occurring multiple times. When an attempt to update the data is made, all occurrences must be found, and there is no fixed way to determine the number or location of the multiple occurrences. Some denormalization in some environments, such as read-only data warehouses, may be legitimate, but each situation must be evaluated carefully. For additional information about normalization/denormalization and update anomalies, refer to Chapter 4.

NESTED AND COMMON TABLE EXPRESSIONS

A nested table expression, a special kind of subquery, is used in the FROM clause of an SQL statement. Nested table expressions create logical temporary tables that are known only in the SQL statement that defines them. They may or may not result in the creation of a physically materialized local table, as the SQL may be merged with the outer SQL statement.

These subqueries can be considered temporary views and are also sometimes referred to as inline views. You can use nested table expressions to select from a grouped table or to obtain the same results that you expect from a view.

Consider the problem of obtaining the maximum average score for the DB2 Certification program exams. To gather this result, you must first obtain the averages and then select the maximum value from that list. The following example uses a nested table expression to accomplish this request:

```
SELECT MAX(AVG_SCORE)
FROM (
    SELECT NUMBER,
    AVG(SCORE) AS AVG_SCORE
    FROM TEST_TAKEN
    GROUP BY NUMBER) AS AVERAGES
```

In this example, the nested subselect creates a temporary table that will be used by the outer SELECT to obtain the maximum average score. This temporary table is called AVERAGES.

Although included in the nested table expression, the number column is not required to be able to gather the average for each one of the exams, as it is not referenced in the outer query. After the subquery is completed, the outer SELECT will be able to obtain the maximum value of the averages calculated in the nested table expression with or without the number column present in the nested table expression.

An advantage of using nested table expressions rather than views is that nested table expressions exist only during the execution of the query, so you don't have to worry about their maintenance. Nested table expressions reduce contention over the system catalog tables. Because they are created at execution time, they can be defined using host variables. Nested table expressions also give the SQL programmer more information about the SQL statement. Views are hidden, so it is possible to introduce redundancy if the programmer is not aware of the full view description.

> **NOTE**   The TABLE clause can also be used to denote that the subquery following it is a nested table expression. This keyword is mandatory if the nested table expression contains a correlated reference to a prior FROM clause table. The TABLE keyword is also used to denote a user-defined TABLE function. Refer to Chapter 15 for more information on UDFs.

Version 8 of DB2 has support for common table expressions. These expressions can provide performance improvements by computing a value once, not multiple times, during the execution of a query. Common table expressions can be used in SELECT, CREATE VIEW, and INSERT statements and may also contain references to host variables. An example of a common table expression follows:

```
WITH DEPTOTAL (DEPT_NO, TOTSALARY) AS
SELECT WORKDEPT, SUM (SALARY+COMM)
    FROM EMP
    GROUP BY WORKDEPT
SELECT DEPT_NO FROM DEPTOTAL
WHERE TOTSALARY =
    (SELECT MAX(TOTSALARY)
          FROM DEPTOTAL)
```

In this example, the DEPTOTAL is established by calculating the sum, or the salary plus commissions, for each department. This data in the DEPTOTAL common table expression can then be used in the remainder of the query.

CASE EXPRESSIONS

You can add if-then-else logic to your SQL statements and output by using CASE expressions. Consider the generation of a list of those candidates who have passed the DB2 Fundamentals exam. In the report, you want to print the scores of the tests, but instead of printing the numeric scores, you want to print a message. If the score is below 65, you want to print Not Passed. If it is between 65 and 90, you want to print Passed, and if the score is above 90, you want to print Excellent. The following SQL statement using a CASE expression accomplishes this:

```
SELECT FNAME,LNAME,
    CASE
        WHEN SCORE < 65 THEN 'NOT PASSED'
        WHEN SCORE <= 90 THEN 'PASSED '
        ELSE
        'EXCELLENT'
    END AS TEST_RESULT
FROM CANDIDATE C, TEST_TAKEN TT
WHERE C.CID=TT.CID
AND TT.NUMBER='500';
```

This SQL statement provides string messages based on the conditions of the CASE expression. In this example, the score column features a numeric value, but we use it to produce a character string. The column derived from the CASE expression has been assigned the name TEST_RESULT.

The order of the conditions for the CASE expression is very important. DB2 will process the first condition first, then the second, and so on. If you do not pay attention to the order in which the conditions are processed, you might be retrieving the same result for every row in your table. For example, if you coded the <= 90 option before the < 65, all the data that is lower than 91, even 64 or 30, would display the message Passed.

CASE expressions can be used in places other than select lists, such as WHERE, ON, and HAVING clauses. CASE expressions can also be nested within other CASE expressions.

> **N O T E** You must use the END keyword to finish a CASE statement.

Using CASE Expressions in Functions

CASE expressions can be embedded as function parameters, allowing you to pass various parameters to the function in a single pass of the data. Suppose that the TEST_TAKEN table is very large and that the following need to be counted:

- The number of tests taken with a score higher than 90
- The number of tests taken with a score of 90
- The number of tests taken with a score lower than 70
- The number of DB2 Fundamentals exams taken

Without the use of CASE expressions, the count will require four queries that will potentially read the entire table. We want to do this in a single pass of the data, because the table is very large. To simulate the COUNT function, the query will use four SUM functions, each one evaluating different criteria, using a CASE expression:

```
SELECT SUM (CASE WHEN SCORE > 90 THEN 1
    ELSE NULL
    END) AS MOREGB90,
    SUM (CASE WHEN SCORE = 90 THEN 1
    ELSE NULL
    END) AS EQUALGB90,
    SUM (CASE WHEN SCORE < 70 THEN 1
    ELSE NULL
    END) AS MINORGB70,
    SUM (CASE WHEN NUMBER='500' THEN 1
    ELSE NULL
    END) AS EQUALGB500
FROM TEST_TAKEN
WHERE SCORE >= 90
    OR SCORE < 70
    OR NUMBER = '500';
```

This type of query may be useful for performing data inspection analysis. Note that the four requirements are solved in a single pass of the data. The query was created using a different SUM function for each one of the conditions presented as a requirement. The conditions are evaluated in the CASE expression inside each function. When the condition evaluates TRUE, it will return a value of 1, and the row will be summed. When the condition evaluates FALSE, the CASE expression will return a null value, and the row will not be summed.

> **N O T E**   It is important to remember to code the WHERE clause
> predicate. Although rows that do not qualify will not affect the result
> of the SUM functions, DB2 will still apply the CASE expression to
> these rows. If these rows are excluded by the WHERE clause,
> performance will be improved by avoiding unnecessary CASE
> expressions against these rows.

ROW EXPRESSIONS

Row expressions are an extension to predicates and allow more than one set of comparisons in a single predicate, using a subquery that returns more than one column and even more than one row. In the following example, the WHERE clause predicate will be TRUE when all three columns on the left equal the three values in any single row returned in the result set from the subquery. This will also allow the use of quantified predicates, such as = ANY, = SOME, or <> ALL, with row expressions:

```
SELECT * FROM TABLE
WHERE (COL1, COL2, COL3) IN
    (SELECT COLA, COLB, COLC
     FROM TABLE
     UNION ALL
     SELECT COLX, COLY, COLZ
     FROM ANOTHER_TABLE)
```

OLAP AND STAR JOINS

Databases normally hold large amounts of data that can be updated, deleted, queried, and inserted on a daily basis. Databases in which data is continually updated, deleted, and inserted are known as *online transaction processing (OLTP)* systems.

Databases that hold large amounts of data and do not have a heavy transaction workload but do have a large number of concurrent queries executing all the time are known as *decision-support systems (DSS)*. Certain decision-support systems have fewer queries, but each query can be very complex. These systems allow users to examine the data from various perspectives by performing *online analytical processing (OLAP)*.

The functionality of the database is required to provide multidimensional views of relational data without a significant performance effect. DB2 provides a star join access path to assist in the processing of the star schema and snowflake (star schema with further normalized dimensions) data models.

Star Schemas

The concept of a *star schema* is illustrated in Figure 6-3. A business view of a highly normalized database often requires a number of attributes associated with one primary object. Each of these attributes is contained in separate tables.

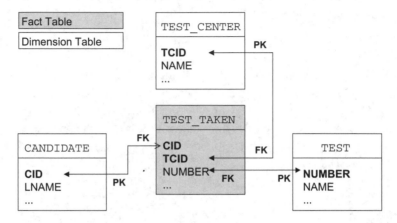

Figure 6-3 Star schema in the DB2CERT database

The following points are characteristic of a star schema design.

- A large centralized fact table is surrounded by normalized dimension tables. The fact table contains the fact or event. In Figure 6-3, TEST_TAKEN is the fact table. It contains detailed information on each test taken, including exactly which test was taken, in which center the test was taken, and who took the test.
- A number of small dimension tables typically hold descriptive information about an entity that has a relatively small number of rows. In Figure 6-3, the dimension tables are TEST, CANDIDATE, and TEST_CENTER.
- The primary keys of the dimension tables involved in the star schema supply foreign-key entries in the fact table. The concatenation of foreign keys from the dimension tables usually forms a small subset of the fact table. In Figure 6-3, the foreign keys are CID, TCID, and NUMBER.

This approach allows as few attributes as possible to be stored in the fact table. The benefit of this is that, because the fact table is usually very large, any data duplication in this table would be very costly in terms of storage and access times. If the DB2CERT database were used to store information on a university's entrance examinations, for example, the TEST_TAKEN table could grow enormously.

OLAP schemas, such as the star schema, are frequently used for large databases in data warehousing and decision-support systems. These schemas make it very important to access the data in these databases in the optimal manner. Otherwise, the joins involved in the schemas may result in poor performance, owing to the potentially large size and number of the rows and tables being joined.

OLAP Indexes

A typical star schema may include a large number of indexes because of the ad hoc nature of queries in an OLAP environment. Such an environment is typically not subjected to continual insert or update activity and therefore does not have to suffer from significant performance degradation as a result of index maintenance.

The prime considerations of indexes in an OLAP environment are to facilitate the filtering of the large result set as quickly as possible and the joining of the tables. This is particularly important for the fact table, where multiple indexes are defined, especially on combinations of foreign-key columns relating to the dimension tables. The benefit of multiple indexes in this environment is improved query performance against the fact table, as the query can focus on any combination of dimensions. Given that the fact table is the largest table, the application of restrictive join predicates and an efficient access path for the join to this table are significant. The indexes defined on the tables could be either single-column or multicolumn indexes. However, the exploitation of DB2's star join access path uses the most cost-effective multicolumn index on the fact table for access.

Some maintenance issues need to be considered when using multiple indexes in the OLAP environment. The first is that multiple indexes will require a certain amount of space, depending on the number of columns in each index and the size of the tables. The second is that there will be a significant one-time cost when building indexes, perhaps during a bulk load.

Star Joins

A typical query against databases designed with the star schema consists of multiple local predicates referencing values in the dimension tables and containing join predicates connecting the dimension tables to the fact table. These types of queries are called *star joins*, as shown in the following example:

```
SELECT NAME, YEAR_TAKEN,
   AVG(SCORE) AS AVGSC
FROM
(SELECT T.NAME, YEAR(TT.DATE_TAKEN), TT.SCORE
FROM TEST T, TEST_TAKEN TT, TEST_CENTER TC, CANDIDATE C
WHERE C.CID = TT.CID AND
   TC.TCID = TT.TCID AND
   T.NUMBER = TT.NUMBER AND
```

```
   T.NAME LIKE 'DB2%' AND
   C.COUNTRY='USA' AND
   TC.NOSEATS < 10) AS STAR_TABLE
GROUP BY NAME, YEAR(TT.DATE_TAKEN);
```

> **N O T E** Prior to version 8, a nested table expression would have
> been required in this example purely to overcome the limitation that
> the GROUP BY clause could contain only columns and not expressions.
> Now, since we have the ability to group by an expression, the
> YEAR(TT.DATE_TAKEN) expression can be explicitly used in
> the GROUP BY.

In this example, we wish to find the average score of DB2 tests taken by Canadian citizens in the small test centers year by year. A star join query can be difficult to execute efficiently. Even though the intersection of all dimensions with the fact table can produce a small result set, the predicates applied to a single dimension table are typically insufficient to reduce the enormous number of fact table rows.

If a join based on related tables—dimension to fact table—does not provide adequate performance, an alternative is to join unrelated tables. Joining unrelated tables results in a Cartesian product, whereby every row of the first table is joined with every row of the second table.

Performing a Cartesian join of all dimension tables before accessing the fact table may not be efficient. DB2 must decide how many dimension tables should be accessed first to provide the greatest level of filtering of fact table rows using available indexes. This can be a delicate balance, as further Cartesian products will produce a massive increase in the size of the intermediate-result sets. Alternatively, minimal prejoining of unrelated dimension tables may not provide adequate filtering for the join to the fact table.

PREDICATES AND FILTERING

The first part of this chapter discussed how to code predicates by using the WHERE, HAVING, and ON clauses. Predicates describe the attributes of the data. Usually based on the columns of a table, predicates either qualify rows, through an index, or reject rows, returned by a scan, when the table is accessed. The resulting qualified or rejected rows are independent of the access path chosen for that table.

Various classifications of predicates have been discussed previously in this chapter:

- **Compound.** A compound predicate is the result of two predicates, whether simple or compound, connected together by AND or OR Boolean operators.
- **Local.** Local predicates reference only one table. They are local to the table and restrict the number of rows returned for that table.

- **Join.** Join predicates involve more than one table or correlated reference. They determine the way rows are joined from two or more tables.
- **Boolean term.** Any predicate that is not contained by a compound OR predicate structure is a Boolean term. If a Boolean term is evaluated FALSE for a particular row, the whole WHERE clause is false.
- **Simple.** Predicates that are not compound, join, or Boolean term are called simple predicates.

Predicates are then further classified as indexable, stage 1, or stage 2. Indexable predicate types can match index entries. An example of an indexable predicate follows:

Assuming there is an index on LNAME, the following predicate is indexable:

```
SELECT FNAME, LNAME
FROM CANDIDATE
WHERE LNAME = 'LAWSON';
```

The following predicate is not a matching predicate and is not indexable:

```
SELECT FNAME, LNAME
FROM CANDIDATE
WHERE STATUS <> 'A';
```

To make your queries as efficient as possible, use indexable predicates in your queries, and create suitable indexes on your tables. Indexable predicates allow the possible use of a matching index scan, which is often a very efficient access path.

Rows retrieved for a query go through two stages of processing.

1. *Stage 1* predicates, sometimes called *sargable*, can be applied at the first stage.
2. *Stage 2* predicates, sometimes called *nonsargable,* or *residual*, cannot be applied until the second stage.

Following are some general rules about predicate evaluation.

- In terms of resource use, the earlier a predicate is evaluated, the better.
- Because they disqualify rows earlier and reduce the amount of processing needed at stage 2, stage 1 predicates are better than stage 2 predicates.
- When possible, try to write queries that evaluate the most restrictive predicates first. When predicates with a high filter factor are processed first, unnecessary rows are screened as early as possible, which can reduce processing cost at a later stage. However, a predicate's restrictiveness is effective only among predicates of the same type and the same evaluation stage.

When DB2 evaluates the predicates, two sets of rules are used to determine the order. The first set is as follows:

- Indexable predicates are applied first. All matching predicates on index-key columns are applied first and evaluated when the index is accessed. Next, stage 1 predicates that have not been picked as matching predicates but refer to index columns are applied to the index. This is called index screening.
- Other stage 1 predicates are applied next. After data page access, stage 1 predicates are applied to the data.
- Finally, the stage 2 predicates are applied on the returned data rows.

The second set of rules describes the order of predicate evaluation within each of the stages.

- All equal predicates—including the column IN list, where the list has only one element, or COL BETWEEN value1 AND value1—are evaluated.
- All range predicates and predicates of the form COL IS NOT NULL are evaluated.
- All other predicate types are evaluated. After both sets of rules are applied, predicates are evaluated in the order in which they appear in the query. Because you specify that order, you have some control over the order of evaluation. One exception here is the fact that, regardless of coding order, noncorrelated subqueries are evaluated before correlated subqueries, unless DB2 transforms the subquery into a join.

Table 6-1 shows whether predicates are indexable and whether they are processing at stage 1.

Table 6-1   Indexable and Stage 1 Predicates

Predicate Type	Indexable	Stage 1
COL = value	Y	Y
COL = noncol expr	Y	Y
COL IS NULL	Y	Y
COL op value	Y	Y
COL op noncol expr	Y	Y
COL BETWEEN value1 AND value2	Y	Y
COL BETWEEN noncol expr1 AND noncol expr2	Y	Y
value BETWEEN COL1 AND COL2	N	N
COL BETWEEN COL1 AND COL2	N	N
COL BETWEEN expression1 AND expression2	Y	Y
COL LIKE 'pattern'	Y	Y

Table 6-1 Indexable and Stage 1 Predicates (Continued)

Predicate Type	Indexable	Stage 1
`COL IN (list)`	Y	Y
`COL <> value`	N	Y
`COL <> noncol expr`	N	Y
`COL IS NOT NULL`	Y	Y
`COL NOT BETWEEN value1 AND value2`	N	Y
`COL NOT BETWEEN noncol expr1 AND noncol expr2`	N	Y
`value NOT BETWEEN COL1 AND COL2`	N	N
`COL NOT IN (list)`	N	Y
`COL NOT LIKE ' char'`	N	Y
`COL LIKE '%char'`	N	Y
`COL LIKE '_char'`	N	Y
`COL LIKE host variable`	Y	Y
`T1.COL = T2 col expr`	Y	Y
`T1.COL op T2 col expr`	Y	Y
`T1.COL <> T2 col expr`	N	Y
`T1.COL1 = T1.COL2`	N	N
`T1.COL1 op T1.COL2`	N	N
`T1.COL1 <> T1.COL2`	N	N
`COL=(noncor subq)`	Y	Y
`COL = ANY (noncor subq)`	N	N
`COL = ALL (noncor subq)`	N	N
`COL op (noncor subq)`	Y	Y
`COL op ANY (noncor subq)`	Y	Y
`COL op ALL (noncor subq)`	Y	Y
`COL <> (noncor subq)`	N	Y
`COL <> ANY (noncor subq)`	N	N
`COL <> ALL (noncor subq)`	N	N
`COL IN (noncor subq)`	Y	Y

continues

Table 6-1   Indexable and Stage 1 Predicates (Continued)

Predicate Type	Indexable	Stage 1
`(COL1,...COLn) IN` *(noncor subq)*	Y	Y
`COL NOT IN` *(noncor subq)*	N	N
`(COL1,...COLn) NOT IN` *(noncor subq)*	N	N
`COL =` *(cor subq)*	N	N
`COL = ANY` *(cor subq)*	N	N
`COL = ALL` *(cor subq)*	N	N
`COL op` *(cor subq)*	N	N
`COL op ANY` *(cor subq)*	N	N
`COL op ALL` *(cor subq)*	N	N
`COL <>` *(cor subq)*	N	N
`COL <> ANY` *(cor subq)*	N	N
`COL <> ALL` *(cor subq)*	N	N
`COL IN` *(cor subq)*	N	N
`(COL1,...COLn) IN` *(cor subq)*	N	N
`COL NOT IN` *(cor subq)*	N	N
`(COL1,...COLn) NOT IN` *(cor subq)*	N	N
`COL IS DISTINCT FROM` *value*	N	Y
`COL IS NOT DISTINCT FROM` *value*	Y	Y
`COL IS DISTINCT FROM` *noncol expr*	N	Y
`COL IS NOT DISTINCT FROM` *noncol expr*	Y	Y
`T1.COL1 IS DISTINCT FROM T2.COL2`	N	N
`T1.COL1 IS NOT DISTINCT FROM T2.COL2`	N	N
`T1.COL1 IS DISTINCT FROM T2` *col expr*	N	Y
`T1.COL1 IS NOT DISTINCT FROM T2` *col expr*	Y	Y
`COL IS DISTINCT FROM` *(noncor subq)*	N	Y
`COL IS NOT DISTINCT FROM` *(noncor subq)*	Y	Y
`COL IS DISTINCT FROM ANY` *(noncor subq)*	N	N
`COL IS NOT DISTINCT FROM ANY` *(noncor subq)*	N	N
`COL IS DISTINCT FROM ALL` *(noncor subq)*	N	N

Table 6-1   Indexable and Stage 1 Predicates (Continued)

Predicate Type	Indexable	Stage 1
COL IS NOT DISTINCT FROM ALL *(noncor subq)*	N	N
COL IS NOT DISTINCT FROM *(cor subq)*	N	N
COL IS DISTINCT FROM ANY *(cor subq)*	N	N
COL IS DISTINCT FROM ANY *(cor subq)*	N	N
COL IS NOT DISTINCT FROM ANY *(cor subq)*	N	N
COL IS DISTINCT FROM ALL *(cor subq)*	N	N
COL IS NOT DISTINCT FROM ALL *(cor subq)*	N	N
EXISTS *(subq)*	N	N
NOT EXISTS *(subq)*	N	N
expression = value	N	N
expression <> value	N	N
expression op value	N	N
expression op (subq)	N	N

SUMMARY

This chapter looked at some of the advanced features of SQL, including the various types of joins: inner, left outer, right outer, and full outer. Star joins, which are used in support of star schemas, were also examined.

SQL can become very useful for solving complex business problems by using such features as CASE expressions, nested table expressions, UNIONs, and subqueries. These features allow us to push a lot of business logic into the SQL statement.

This chapter also looked at the classification of predicates and how to most efficiently code them to minimize the amount of data returned.

ADDITIONAL RESOURCES

IBM DB2 UDB for z/OS Version 8 SQL Reference (SC18-7426-00)

IBM DB2 UDB for z/OS Version 8 Administration Guide (SC18-7413)

DB2 Universal Database V8 for Linux, UNIX, and Windows Database Administration Certification Guide, Fifth edition (Prentice Hall, 2003)

Database Administration

Maintaining Data

- Data movement: loading and unloading data
- Data maintenance
- Gathering statistics
- Statistics usage
- Resolving restricted and advisory states

This chapter examines the techniques for populating and extracting DB2 data by using the LOAD and UNLOAD utilities. The various options for using these utilities will be examined, along with some of the performance options.

We also take a close look at the REORG utility and its many options, and we look closely at the parallelism available for objects involved in the REORG process. Additional maintenance topics include gathering statistics via the RUNSTATS utility and examining the data and statistics of the database management system.

Some utilities help ensure that the data is always in a consistent state. These utilities, known as the CHECK utilities, are discussed. We also look at how to resolve restrictive and advisory states.

DATA MOVEMENT

Using DML INSERTs gets data into the DB2 tables, but it is not a feasible option for large amounts of data. The LOAD utility is needed for populating tables with large amounts of data.

For removing data from a DB2 table, we can use DML DELETEs, but doing so is not optimal for large amounts of data. For unloading data, better options are DSNTIAUL, UNLOAD, and REORG DISCARD or REORG UNLOAD EXTERNAL.

The LOAD utility is used to load one or more tables of a table space. This utility loads records into the tables and builds or extends any indexes defined on them. If the table space already contains data, you can either add the new data to the existing data or replace the existing data. The loaded data is processed by any edit or validation routine associated with the table and any field procedure associated with any column of the table. The LOAD utility will load data coming from a sequential data set into one or more tables in the same table space. Because data is coming in from a non-DB2 source, all integrity checking must be performed: entity integrity, referential integrity, and check integrity.

The output from LOAD DATA consists of a loaded table space or partition, a discard file of rejected records, and a summary report of errors encountered during processing. (This report is generated only if you specify ENFORCE CONSTRAINTS or if the LOAD involves unique indexes.)

The LOAD utility consists of several phases. In the first phase, UTILINIT, the LOAD performs initialization and start-up.

In the second phase, RELOAD loads the record types and writes temporary file records for indexes and foreign keys. Check constraints are checked for each row. One pass through the sequential input data set is made. Internal commits are taken to provide commit points at which to restart in case operation should halt in this phase. If you specified the COPYDDN or RECOVERYDDN keywords, inline copies are created. If SORTKEYS is used, a subtask is started at the beginning of the RELOAD phase to sort the keys. This subtask initializes and waits for the main RELOAD phase to pass its keys to SORT. The RELOAD phase loads the data, extracts the keys, and passes them in memory for sorting. At the end of the RELOAD phase, the last key is passed to SORT, and record sorting completes. PREFORMAT for table spaces occurs at the end of the RELOAD phase. Use SORT for sorting temporary file records before creating indexes or validating referential constraints, if indexes or foreign keys exist.

The SORT phase is skipped if all the following conditions apply for the data processed during the RELOAD phase.

- Each table has no more than one key
- All keys are the same type: index key, index foreign key, nonindexed foreign key.
- The data being loaded or reloaded is in key order, if a key exists.[1]

---

1. If the key is an index key only and the index is a data-partitioned secondary index, the data is considered to be in order if the data is grouped by partition and ordered within the partition by key value. If the key in question is an indexed foreign key and the index is a data-partitioned secondary index, the data is never considered to be ordered.

- The data being loaded or reloaded is grouped by table, and each input record is loaded into one table only. SORT passes the sorted keys in memory to the BUILD phase, which builds the indexes. As of version 8, SORTKEYS is the default, so the keyword is not needed.

In the third phase, BUILD creates indexes from temporary file records for all indexes defined on the loaded tables, detects any duplicate keys, and preformats index pages. If you specify a parallel index build, all activities that normally occur in both the SORT and BUILD phases occur in the SORTBLD phase instead.

Next, INDXVAL corrects unique-index violations from the information in SYSERR, if any exist. ENFORCE checks referential constraints, performs corrections of violations, and reports them to SYSERR. DISCARD copies the records causing errors from the input data set to the discard data set.

REPORT generates a summary report if you specified ENFORCE CONSTRAINT or if load index validation is performed. Finally, UTILTERM performs any necessary cleanup.

Loading Data

In order to load data into a DB2 table, we must supply an input data set and a target table. The input data set must match the target table. The following example loads data from the data set specified by the DB2LDS DD statement into the TEST_TAKEN table:

```
LOAD DATA INDDN DB2LDS
    INTO TABLE DB2USER1.TEST_TAKEN
```

Rules can be selectively added to the LOAD criteria to LOAD only rows that meet a specified criterion. An example follows:

```
LOAD DATA INDDN DB2LDS
    INTO TABLE DB2USER1.TEST_TAKEN
    WHEN (1:3)='300'
```

In order to map the position in the file to the columns in the table:

```
LOAD DATA RESUME YES
    INTO TABLE DB2USER1.TEST WHEN (1:1)='P'
    (NUMBER POSITION (1:6) CHAR,
    NAME POSITION (7:57) CHAR,
    TYPE POSITION (58:59) CHAR,
    CUTSCORE POSITION (60:68) DECIMAL EXTERNAL,
    LENGTH POSITION (69:74) SMALLINT,
    TOTALTKN POSITION (75:80) SMALLINT,
    TOTALPAS POSITION (81:86) SMALLINT)
```

This example shows how to identify the table that is to be loaded, the fields within the input record, and the format of the input record. The fields need to be mapped to the columns of the table that is being loaded; otherwise, errors will result.

Using REPLACE

The LOAD utility's REPLACE option can be used to replace data in a single-table table space or in a multiple-table table space. All the data can be replaced in the table space by using this option. If you want to preserve the records that are already in the table, use the LOAD RESUME option.

If an object is in REORG-pending status, you can perform a LOAD REPLACE of the entire table space, which resets REORG-pending status. In this situation, no other LOAD operations are allowed.

> **N O T E** LOAD REPLACE or LOAD PART REPLACE with LOG YES logs only the reset and not each deleted row. If you need to see what rows are being deleted, use the SQL DELETE statement.

The following example shows how to replace data in one table in a single-table table space:

```
LOAD DATA
   REPLACE
      INTO TABLE DSN861.DEPT
      (DEPTNO POSITION (1)CHAR(3),
       DEPTNAME POSITION (5)VARCHAR,
       )
   ENFORCE NO
```

When using LOAD REPLACE on a multiple-table table space, care must be taken because LOAD works on an entire table space at a time. In order to replace all rows in a LOAD multiple-table table space, you have to work with one table at a time, using the RESUME YES option on all but the first table. For example, if you have two tables in a table space, you first need to use LOAD REPLACE on the first table to empty out the table space and replace the data for the first table. Next, use LOAD with RESUME YES on the second table to add the records for the second table without destroying the data in the first table.

If only one table in a multiple-table table space needs to be replaced, all rows need to be deleted from the table. Use LOAD with RESUME YES.

If you need to add data to a table rather than replace, use LOAD with RESUME YES. The RESUME keyword specifies whether it is to be loaded into an empty or a nonempty table space. RESUME NO loads records into an empty table space. RESUME YES loads records into a non-empty table space.

If RESUME NO is specified and the target table space is not empty, no data is loaded. If RESUME YES is specified and the target table space is empty, data is loaded.

> **N O T E**   LOAD always adds rows to the end of the existing rows, but index entries are placed in key sequence.

> **N O T E**   You can run a LOAD REPLACE on a table space that has pages on the LPL (Logical Page List), and it will reset the status; however, you cannot run a LOAD RESUME on the object.

An efficient way of clearing a table space is to delete all the data in it, specifying LOAD REPLACE without loading any records. In order to do this, specify the input data set in the JCL as DD DUMMY.

The LOAD REPLACE method is efficient for the following reasons.

- LOAD REPLACE does not log any rows.
- LOAD REPLACE redefines the table space.
- LOAD REPLACE retains all views and privileges associated with a table space or table.
- LOG YES can be used to make the LOAD REPLACE recoverable.
- LOAD REPLACE will replace ALL TABLES in the table space.

Loading Ordered Rows

The LOAD utility loads records into a table space in the order in which they exist in the input stream. LOAD does not sort the input stream and does not insert records in sequence with existing records, even if there is a clustering index. To achieve clustering when loading an empty table or replacing data, sort the input stream.

> **N O T E**   When adding data to a clustered table, consider reorganizing the table afterward.

Loading Partitions

By using the PART clause of the INTO TABLE option, you load only the specified partitions of a partitioned table. If the PART keyword is omitted, the entire table will be loaded. The REPLACE and RESUME options can be specified separately by partition. The following example loads data into the first and second partitions of the employee table. Records with '0' in column 1 replace the contents of partition 1; records with '1' in column 1 are added to partition 2; all other records are ignored. (The example, simplified to illustrate the point, does not list field specifications for all columns of the table.)

```
LOAD DATA
INTO TABLE DB2USER1.CANDIDATE PART 1 REPLACE WHEN (1)= '0'
(CID POSITION (1:9) CHAR(9),
LNAME POSITION (10:40) VARCHAR(30),
...
)
INTO TABLE DB2USER1.CANDIDATE PART 2 RESUME YES WHEN (1)='1'
(CID POSITION (1:9) CHAR(9),
LNAME POSITION (10:40) VARCHAR(30),
...
)
```

> **N O T E** If you are not loading columns in the same order as in the
> `CREATE TABLE` statement, you must code field specifications for
> each `INTO TABLE` statement.

The next example assumes that the data is in separate input data sets. The data is already sorted by partition, so the WHEN clause of INTO TABLE is not necessary. The RESUME YES option placed before the PART option will not allow concurrent partition processing during the execution of the utility:

```
LOAD DATA INDDN CERTLD1 CONTINUEIF(72:72)='X'
RESUME YES
INTO TABLE DB2USER1.CANDIDATE REPLACE PART 1
LOAD DATA INDDN CERTLD2 CONTINUEIF(72:72)='X'
RESUME YES
INTO TABLE DB2USER1.CANDIDATE REPLACE PART 2
```

The following example allows partitioning independence when loading more than one partition concurrently:

```
LOAD DATA INDDN SYSREC LOG NO
INTO TABLE DB2USER1.CANDIDATE PART 2 REPLACE
```

> **N O T E** `LOAD INTO PART` x is not allowed if an identity
> column is part of the partitioning index.

Concurrent Access

If another table needs to access data during a LOAD utility, you can specify SHRLEVEL CHANGE on a LOAD RESUME with the LOG YES option. This option effectively combines the speed and performance of the LOAD utility with the availability and access offered by INSERT processing. This option operates similarly to an SQL INSERT program and uses claims instead of draining for best concurrent access.

The option is LOG YES only and will not require a COPY afterward. Locking problems are avoided through internal monitoring of the commit scope. You can also run it in parallel for partitioned table spaces.

Conversion

The LOAD utility converts data between compatible data types. Table 7-1 identifies the allowable data conversions and the defaults used when the input data type is not specified in a field specification of the INTO TABLE statement.

Table 7-1 Allowable Data Conversions

Input Data Type	Output Data Type			
Numeric Data Conversion				
	SMALLINT	**INTEGER**	**DECIMAL**	**FLOAT**
SMALLINT	Default	Allowed	Allowed	Allowed
INTEGER	Allowed	Default	Allowed	Allowed
DECIMAL	Allowed	Allowed	Default	Allowed
FLOAT	Allowed	Allowed	Allowed	Default
Character Data Conversion				
	BLOB/CLOB	**CHAR**	**VARCHAR**	**LONG VARCHAR**
CHAR	Allowed	Default	Allowed	Allowed
CHAR MIXED	Allowed			
VARCHAR	Allowed	Allowed	Default	Default
Time Data Conversion				
	DATE	**TIME**	**TIMESTAMP**	
DATE EXTERNAL	Default			
TIME EXTERNAL		Default		
TIMESTAMP EXTERNAL	Allowed	Allowed	Default	

continues

Table 7-1   Allowable Data Conversions (Continued)

Input Data Type	Output Data Type			
Graphic Data Conversion				
	DBCLOB	**GRAPHIC**	**VARGRAPHIC**	**LONG VARGRAPHIC**
GRAPHIC	Allowed	Default	Allowed	Allowed
VARGRAPHIC	Allowed	Allowed	Default	Default

Referential Integrity

The LOAD utility will not load a table with an incomplete definition. If the table has a primary key, the unique index on that key must exist. If any table named to be loaded has an incomplete definition, the LOAD job will terminate.

By default, LOAD enforces referential constraints (ENFORCE CONSTRAINTS). During this process, several errors could occur.

- The input file may have duplicate values of a primary key.
- The input file may have invalid foreign-key values—values not in the primary key of the corresponding parent table.
- The target table might lack primary-key values—values of foreign keys in dependent tables.

A primary index must be a unique index and must exist if the table definition is complete. Therefore, when a parent table is loaded, there must be at least a primary index.

> **N O T E**   An error data set, and probably also a map data set and a discard data set, will be needed for the LOAD utility for RI errors.

A dependent table has the constraint that the values of its foreign keys must be values of the primary keys of corresponding parent tables. By default, LOAD enforces that constraint in much the same way that it enforces the uniqueness of key values in a unique index. First, it loads all records to the table; subsequently, it checks their validity with respect to the constraints, identifies any invalid record by an error message, and deletes the record. The record can optionally be copied to a discard data set.

If a record fails to load because it violates a referential constraint, any of its dependent records in the same job also fail. For example, suppose that the sample project table and project activity tables belong to the same table space, that you load them both in the same job, and that an input record for the project table has an invalid department number. Then, that record fails to be loaded and does not appear in the loaded table; the summary report identifies it as causing a *primary* error.

But the project table has a primary key: the project number. In this case, the record rejected by LOAD defines a project number; in the project activity table, any record that refers to the rejected number is also rejected. The summary report identifies those as causing *secondary* errors. If you use a discard data set, both types of error records are copied to it.

The deletion of invalid records does not cascade to other dependent tables already in place. Suppose now that the project and project activity tables exist in separate table spaces and that they are both currently populated and possess referential integrity. Further, suppose that the data in the project table is now to be replaced, using LOAD REPLACE, and that the replacement data for a department was inadvertently not supplied in the input data. Records referencing that department number might already exist in the project activity table. LOAD therefore automatically places the table space containing the project activity table, and all table spaces containing dependent tables of any table being replaced, into CHECK-pending status.

The CHECK-pending status indicates that the referential integrity of the table space is in doubt; it might contain records that violate a referential constraint. The use of a table space in CHECK-pending status has severe restrictions; typically, you run the CHECK DATA utility to reset this status.

ENFORCE NO

If the ENFORCE NO option is used, the LOAD utility will not enforce referential constraints. But the result is that the loaded table space might violate the constraints. The following is an example of running without enforcing constraints:

```
LOAD DATA INDDN DB2LDS ENFORCE NO
INTO TABLE DB2USER1.TEST_TAKEN
```

> **N O T E**   LOAD places the loaded table space in CHECK-pending (CHKP) status. If you use REPLACE, all table spaces containing any dependent tables of the tables that were loaded are also placed in CHECK-pending status.

Correcting Violations

The referential integrity checking in LOAD can only delete incorrect dependent rows that were input to LOAD. But deletion is not always the best strategy for correcting referential integrity violations.

For example, the violations may occur because parent rows do not exist. In this case, it is better to correct the parent table, not to delete the dependent rows. Therefore, and in this case,

ENFORCE NO would be more appropriate than ENFORCE CONSTRAINTS. After the parent table is corrected, CHECK DATA can be used to reset the CHECK-pending status.

LOAD ENFORCE CONSTRAINTS is not equivalent to CHECK DATA. LOAD ENFORCE CONSTRAINTS deletes any rows causing referential constraint violations. CHECK DATA detects violations and optionally deletes such rows. CHECK DATA checks a complete referential structure, although LOAD checks only the rows being loaded. The CHECK DATA utility is discussed later in this chapter.

> **N O T E** When loading referential structures with ENFORCE CONSTRAINTS, you should load parent tables before dependent tables.

> **N O T E** Be aware that running the LOAD utility on a table space does not activate triggers defined on tables in the table space.

Loading ROWID Columns

Columns defined as ROWID can be designated as input fields, using the LOAD field specification syntax diagram. LOAD PART is not allowed if the ROWID column is part of the partitioning key. Columns defined as ROWID can be designated as GENERATED BY DEFAULT or GENERATED ALWAYS. With GENERATED ALWAYS, DB2 always generates a row ID.

Columns defined as ROWID GENERATED BY DEFAULT can be set by the LOAD utility from input data. The input field must be specified as ROWID. No conversions are allowed. The input data for a ROWID column must be a unique, valid value for a row ID. If the value of the row is not unique, a duplicate key violation will occur. If such an error occurs, the load will fail. In this case, the duplicate values will need to be discarded, and the load will need to be retried with a new unique value; alternatively, allow DB2 to generate the value of the row ID.

The DEFAULTIF attribute can be used with the ROWID keyword. If the condition is met, the column will be loaded with a value generated by DB2. The NULLIF attribute cannot be used with the ROWID keyword, because row ID columns cannot be null.

> **N O T E** A ROWID column defined as GENERATED ALWAYS cannot be included in the field specification list, because DB2 generates the ROWID value automatically.

Loading a LOB column

The LOAD utility treats LOB columns as varying-length data. The length value for a LOB column must be 4 bytes. When the input record is greater than 32KB, you might have to load the LOB data separately.

Free Space

When loading into a nonsegmented table space, LOAD leaves one free page after reaching the FREEPAGE limit, regardless of whether the records loaded belong to the same or different tables. When loading into a segmented table space, LOAD leaves free pages, and free space on each page, in accordance with the current values of the FREEPAGE and PCTFREE parameters. Those values can be set by the CREATE TABLESPACE, ALTER TABLESPACE, CREATE INDEX, or ALTER INDEX statements. LOAD leaves one free page after reaching the FREEPAGE limit for each table in the table space.

Inline Copies

The LOAD utility can also perform an inline copy, which is, for the most part, equivalent to a full image copy taken with SHRLEVEL REFERENCE. The only difference between an inline copy and a regular full image copy is that data pages and space map pages may be out of sequence or repeated; if a compression dictionary was built during the LOAD, the pages will be duplicated. These differences, however, should be negligible in terms of the amount of space required for the copy data set, and the copy is still valid for recovery.

The inline copy increases the availability of your data because, after the data has been loaded and the inline copy taken, the table space is not left in a copy-pending (COPY) status, even if you specify LOG NO, and the data is ready to be accessed. You can take multiple-image copies with this feature as well, with a maximum of two primary- and two secondary-image copies allowed.

Inline Statistics

Statistics can be collected during the LOAD utility, eliminating the need for executing the RUNSTATS utility after the LOAD. This is done by using the STATISTICS keyword to gather catalog statistics for the table space:

```
LOAD STATISTICS
INTO TABLE DB2USER1.TEST_TAKEN
```

More information on RUNSTATS is given later in this chapter.

Rebalancing Partitions

Changing the key ranges for the partitions can be done by using the REBALANCE keyword. DB2 automatically rebalances the keys over the specified partitions. The following example rebalances partitions 3 and 4:

```
REORG TABLESPACE DB2CERT.TSCERT PART(3:4) REBALANCE
```

SORTKEYS

Using the SORTKEYS option for the LOAD utility allows for elimination of the SYSUT1 and SORTOUT temporary data sets for sorting the key/RID pairs for foreign keys or for indexes, provided that they have been given a nonzero estimate for the key/RID pairs to be sorted. In this case, DFSORT exits are used to pass the unsorted key/RID pairs for the foreign keys or indexes to DFSORT and to accept the sorted key/RID pairs again rather than making the unsorted key/RID pairs available via the SYSUT1 data set and receiving the sorted key/RID pairs via the SORTOUT data set.

With the SORTKEYS option, the sorting of the key/RID pairs is done in parallel with the loading of the rows, the building of the indexes, and—if inline statistics are established—the collection of statistics. The parallelism is achieved by groups of z/OS subtasks. A task group can contain two or three tasks, depending on whether inline statistics are to be established. These subtasks are referred to as the SORT task, BUILD task, and STATISTICS task, respectively.

DB2 can allocate multiple task groups of two or three subtasks each to sort the key/RID pairs and to establish the indexes in parallel with one another. The degree of parallelism used depends on the specifications and the DD statements provided for sort-work data sets.

If the sort-work data sets are dynamically allocated by DFSORT—SORTDEVT has been specified—the degree of parallelism is determined by them. If manual allocation of the sort-work data sets and sort-message data sets is chosen, the degree of parallelism is determined by the data sets that have been allocated.

PREFORMAT

When DB2's preformatting delays impact the performance or execution time consistency of high-INSERT applications and the table size can be predicted for a business-processing cycle, LOAD PREFORMAT or REORG PREFORMAT might be a technique to consider. This technique will be of value only if DB2's preformatting causes a measurable delay with the INSERT processing or causes inconsistent elapsed times for INSERT applications. It is recommended that, to quantify its value in your environment, a performance assessment be conducted before and after LOAD or REORG PREFORMAT is used.

PREFORMAT is a technique used to eliminate DB2's having to preformat new pages in a table space during execution time. This might eliminate execution-time delays but adds the preformatting cost as set up prior to the application's execution. LOAD or REORG PREFORMAT primes a new table space and prepares it for INSERT processing. When the preformatted space is used and DB2 has to extend the table space, normal data set extending and preformatting occur.

Preformatting for INSERT processing may be desirable for high-INSERT tables that will receive a predictable amount of data, allowing all the required space to be preallocated prior to the application's execution. This would be the case for a table that acts as a repository for work items coming into a system subsequently used to feed a back-end task that processes the work items.

Preformatting of a table space containing a table used for query processing may cause a table space scan to read additional empty pages, extending the elapsed time for these queries. LOAD or REORG PREFORMAT is not recommended for tables that have a high ratio of reads to inserts if the reads result in table space scans.

> **N O T E** The PREFORMAT option can also be used on the REORG utility.

Parallel Index Builds

LOAD builds all the indexes defined for any table being loaded. At the same time, LOAD checks for duplicate values of any unique index key. If any duplicate values exist, one of the corresponding rows is loaded. Error messages identify the input records that produce duplicates; optionally, the records are copied to a discard data set. At the end of the job, a summary report lists all errors found. For unique indexes, any two null values are taken to be equal, unless the index was created with the UNIQUE WHERE NOT NULL clause. In that case, a single-key column can contain any number of null values, although its other values must be unique.

Neither the loaded table nor its indexes contain any of the records that might have produced an error. Using the error messages, you can identify faulty input records, correct them, and load them again. If you use a discard data set, you can correct the records there and add them to the table with LOAD RESUME.

Use parallel index builds to reduce the elapsed time for a LOAD job by sorting the index keys and rebuilding multiple indexes in parallel rather than sequentially. Optimally, a pair of subtasks process each index; one subtask sorts extracted keys, and the other subtask builds the index. LOAD begins building each index as soon as the corresponding sort emits its first sorted record. LOAD uses a parallel index build if all the following conditions are true: When more than one index is to be built, the LOAD utility specifies the SORTKEYS keyword, along with a nonzero estimate of the number of keys, in the utility statement. The utility can be allowed to either dynamically allocate the data sets needed by SORT or provide the necessary data sets in the job.

LOAD Parallelism for Partitioned Table Spaces

LOAD parallelism helps when dealing with short windows in which to load a lot of data. This allows us to load multiple partitions of a partitioned table space in parallel in the same job. Large loads have been a problem in the past when nonpartitioned indexes were involved, often causing the DBA to have to drop and recreate them in order to get large data loads done. Multiple tasks in a single job can be used to load the partitions in parallel, and a single job can be submitted with several input files to be loaded in parallel. The performance is fast, and the contention on the NPI is eliminated. The number of parallel load tasks will be determined by the number of CPUs and virtual storage available, as well as the number of threads available. In the following example of the necessary syntax, two partitions are being loaded in parallel, and part 1 is also being preformatted:

```
LOAD INTO TABLE tab1 PART 1 INDDN infile1 PREFORMAT
    INTO TABLE tab1 PART 2 INDDN infile2
```

> **N O T E**   If the data set definitions have been deferred—the DDL was run with DEFINE NO—a LOAD with an empty data file should be done on the first partition, and then the other partitions can be loaded in parallel in order to get LOAD parallelism on the initial load.

Cursors

The LOAD utility allows a cursor to be defined for the input data. This can be done with the EXEC SQL and INCURSOR parameters in the utility to invoke the family cross-loader function whereby data can be loaded from any DRDA remote server.

Some restrictions are that you cannot load into same table as a defined cursor, use SHRLEVEL CHANGE, or use field specifications or discard processing.

Following is an example of using a cursor in a LOAD utility:

```
EXEC SQL
   DECLARE C1 CURSOR
   FOR SELECT * FROM DB2CERT
ENDEXEC
LOAD DATA
INCURSOR(C1)
REPLACE
INTO DB2CERT2
```

Unloading Data

DSNTIAUL

You can use the DB2 sample unload program DSNTIAUL to unload data and to create control statements for use with the DB2 LOAD utility. The source code for this program can be found in the DSNSAMP folder.

Unload Utility

The UNLOAD utility unloads data from one or more source objects to one or more BSAM (Basic Sequential Access Method) sequential data sets in external formats. The source of the data can be

- DB2 table spaces.
- Full or incremental DB2 image-copy data sets. Image copies that were taken with the CONCURRENT keyword are not usable for the UNLOAD utility.
- Copies taken with DSN1COPY.

This utility allows an unload of rows from an entire table space, specific partitions, or individual tables. The utility can also unload specific columns of a table by using a field-specification list. If a table space is partitioned, all the selected partitions can be unloaded into a single data set, or you can unload each partition in parallel into physically distinct data sets. Multiple tables from the same table space can be unloaded in the same job; however, the unload cannot perform joins on tables. If the tables for the unload are not specified, all the tables in the table space are unloaded. The UNLOAD utility can also change data types of selected columns, change the order of the columns, use sampling to get a cross-section of data, specify conditions for row selection, and limit the number of rows to be unloaded.

The output records written by the UNLOAD utility are compatible as input to the LOAD utility. Thus, the original table or different tables can be reloaded with the data from UNLOAD.

Output from UNLOAD consists of an unloaded table space or partition and/or a discard file of rejected records.

The UNLOAD utility has three phases:

1. UTILINIT, for initialization and setup
2. UNLOAD, for unloading records to sequential data sets
3. UTILTERM, for cleanup

One pass through the input data set is made during the UNLOAD phase. If UNLOAD is processing a table space or a partition, DB2 takes internal commits to provide commit points at which to restart in case operation should halt in this phase.

Following is an example of using the UNLOAD utility:

```
UNLOAD TABLESPACE DB2CERT.CERTTS
FROM TABLE DB2USER1.TEST_TAKEN
WHEN (CID =300 AND SCORE > 90)
```

Delimited Load/Unload

Until version 8, the LOAD utility on DB2 for z/OS required input in positional format. This often required data from other platforms to be converted or to use INSERTs. With version 8, LOAD or UNLOAD now produces and accepts delimited files. A delimited file has row and column delimiters.

The FORMAT DELIMITED syntax on LOAD supports COLDEL, CHARDEL, and DECPT options to specify the column delimiter, character delimiter, and decimal-point character on the input file. The DELIMITED syntax on UNLOAD supports the same options—COLDEL, CHARDEL, and DECPT—to specify the column delimiter, character delimiter, and decimal-point character on the output file. The following example uses LOAD DATA with delimited input:

```
LOAD DATA RESUME YES FORMAT DELIMITED COLDEL ';'
```

Using Reorg to Remove Data

The REORG utility has an option for unloading or discarding data during the REORG utility execution. The UNLOAD EXTERNAL option unloads selected data and places it into a data set that can then be loaded into a table. The DISCARD option permits selected removal of rows during the REORG utility execution.

DATA MAINTENANCE

Establishing a data maintenance policy can help ensure that the data in your tables is stored as efficiently as possible. Otherwise, you may discover that your applications start to experience degradation in performance. This may be caused by the poor physical organization of the data.

The physical distribution of the data stored in tables has a significant effect on the performance of applications using those tables. The way the data is stored in a table is affected by the update, insert, and delete operations on the table. For example, a delete operation may leave empty pages of data that may not be reused later. Also, updates to variable-length columns may result in the new column value's not fitting in the same data page. This can cause the row to be moved to a different page and so produce internal gaps or unused space in the table. As a consequence, DB2 may have to read more physical pages to retrieve the information required by the application.

These scenarios are almost unavoidable. However, as the database administrator, you can use the DB2 data maintenance utilities to optimize the physical distribution of the data stored in your tables. Two related utilities can help you organize the data in your tables: REORG and RUN-STATS.

Certain SQL operations may produce internal gaps in tables. So how can you determine the physical organization of your tables or indexes? How can you know how much space is being used and how much is free? With the information collected from the system catalog tables, you can generally determine the state of any table space or index space.

Reorganizing Table Spaces

The following actions occur during reorganization of a table space.

- The data in the table space and the corresponding indexes defined in the table in the table space are reorganized.
- The space of dropped tables is reclaimed, if it was not reclaimed before.
- Free space is provided.
- New space allocation units become effective.
- Segments are realigned, and the rows of the tables are rearranged in clustering-index sequence, except for simple table spaces with multiple table
- Overflow pointers are eliminated.
- The corresponding indexes are rebuilt from scratch.
- The version number of each row is updated to the current version number.

The REORG utility is used to reorganize data in table spaces and in indexes. Following are some of the important phases in the REORG utility.

- UTILINIT, the initialization phase, performs the setup operations for the utility.
- UNLOAD unloads the rows of the table space and writes to the unload data set, specified in the UNLDDN parameter in the utility. SYSREC is the default DD name for the unload data set. The unload data set is also referred to as the SYSREC data set. The type of table space, the number of tables in the table space, and whether the tables have explicit clustering indexes will all affect the sequence in which the rows are unloaded.
- RELOAD reloads the rows from the unload data set into the table space. The sequence in which the rows were unloaded will be the sequence in which they are contained on the unload data set and subsequently the sequence in which they will be reloaded. All rows for a table were unloaded together for segmented table spaces and are then restored together, resulting in the contiguous segments for the table. Free space is reserved in the pages, and free pages are provided for future insertions during the reloading. This is provided as defined by the active PCTFREE and FREEPAGE values for the table space. As the rows are reloaded into the table space, the keys for the

indexes of the table of the table space are extracted and, together with the new RID for the rows, stored onto the first work data set specified via the WORKDDN parameter. The default DD name for the data set is SYSUT1, also referred to as the SYSUT1 data set. Because they are extracted as the rows are reloaded, the key/RID pairs for the indexes are in an arbitrary sequence with regard to the key values. Also, the key/RID pairs for the various indexes are intermixed.

• SORT sorts the key/RID pairs for the various indexes, using the DFSORT by index, key, and RID. At the end of this phase, the sorted key/RID pairs are contained on the second work data set, also referred to as the SORTOUT data set, specified in the WORKDDN parameter. The default name for this data set is SORTOUT.

> **N O T E** Although it is mentioned many times in reference to the REORG utility, DFSORT or an equivalent sort product can be used for the sorting, or equivalent utilities can be used.

• BUILD is the phase in which the output of the SORT phase—the sorted key/RID pairs for the various indexes—is used to build the indexes for the tables in the table space.
• UTILTERM, the final phase, performs the cleanup operations, such as releasing virtual storage.

The phases in the REORG utility are performed sequentially. But exploiting many of the other features of the REORG utility will cause many of the phases to be performed in parallel.

If the target table space is segmented, REORG unloads and reloads by table. If an explicit clustering index exists on a table in a segmented table space, that table is unloaded in clustering sequence. If no explicit clustering index exists, the table is unloaded in physical row and segment order.

For segmented table spaces, REORG does not normally have to reclaim space from dropped tables. Space freed by dropping tables in a segmented table space is immediately available if the table space can be accessed when DROP TABLE is executed. If the table space cannot be accessed when DROP TABLE is executed, REORG reclaims the space for dropped tables. After the execution of the REORG, the segments for each table are contiguous.

The entire table space does not need to be reorganized if it is partitioned. You may choose to simply reorganize one partition, if necessary. If you reorganize a single partition or a range of partitions, all indexes of the table space are affected. Depending on how disorganized the non-partitioning indexes are, they may need to be reorganized as well. The following example shows how to reorganize a partition of a table space:

```
REORG TABLESPACE DB2USER1.CANDIDATE
PART 3
```

```
SORTDATA
SORTDEVT SYSDA
```

Ranges of partitions can also be reorganized. The following syntax would reorganize parts 3, 4, 5, and 6:

```
REORG TABLESPACE DB2USER1.CANDIDATE
PART 3:6
```

Reorganizing a LOB table space is a separate task from reorganizing the base table space. A LOB table space that was defined with LOG YES or LOG NO will affect logging while reorganizing a LOB column. Specify LOG YES and SHRLEVEL NONE when you reorganize a LOB table space, to avoid leaving it in COPY-pending status after the REORG.

During the LOB reorganization, the LOB is not unloaded and space is not reclaimed. Embedded free space is removed, and attempts are made to make the LOB pages contiguous. As a result, prefetch should be more effective.

Reorg Options

The REORG utility has some important parameters that help achieve parallelism in the REORG phases.

SHRLEVEL. The SHRLEVEL parameter determines the level of access allowed during the REORG. The NONE option states that, during the UNLOAD phase, applications can read but not write to the affected area and that, during the RELOAD phase, applications have no access to the data. The REFERENCE option allows for read access during the unload and reload phases. SHRLEVEL CHANGE allows for reading and writing during both the UNLOAD and RELOAD phases.

 If you needed a more restrictive access—with no access by applications or to the end user—the table space should be started in utility mode (UT). These are all offline REORGS.

The next example shows the REORG utility that does not allow concurrent writes during RELOAD:

```
REORG TABLESPACE DB2USER1.CANDIDATE
SHRLEVEL REFERENCE
```

If an object is in REORG-pending status (REORP), a REORG SHRLEVEL NONE will need to be executed on the affected data.

SORTDATA. Several factors come into play when determining the sequence in which the rows of the table space to be reorganized are unloaded: the type of table space, the number of tables in the table space, and whether the tables have explicit clustering indexes.

- **Segmented table spaces.** Tables in segmented table spaces are unloaded one after the other. If a table has an explicit clustering index—a clustering index was defined with the CLUSTER keyword in the CREATE INDEX DDL—the clustering index is used to unload the rows of the table in the sequence of the clustering index that was defined. The table will then store the rows in the unload data set. If no explicit clustering index is defined, the data is unloaded and sorted in the physical sequence: segment by segment, page by page, and then row by row.
- **Partitioned table spaces.** For these table spaces, the rows of the table space, or the individual partitions, to be reorganized are unloaded and stored in the unload data set. This is done using the partitioning index in the sequence defined by the index.
- **Simple table space.** The unloading will depend on the number of tables in the table space. If multiple tables are in the table space, it is unloaded in physical sequence. The rows in the unload data set will have the same physical order as the table space, and the rows of the various tables are intermixed. If more than one table has an explicit clustering index, it will be used to unload the rows in the sequence defined by the index. If only one table is in the table space and does not have an explicit clustering index, the table will be unloaded in physical sequence.

When the SORTDATA option is used on the REORG utility control statement, DB2 always unloads the rows in physical sequence. Using SORTDATA will help with performance of the REORG utility. DFSORT or an equivalent sort utility is used to sort the rows in index sequence if the table space has at least one explicit clustering index and is not a simple table space with multiple tables. The index itself is not used for the sorting. SORTDATA operates differently for each type of table space.

- For *segmented table spaces*, if an explicit clustering index is on at least one of the tables of the segmented table space, the tables will be unloaded table by table in a physical sequence and the output passed to DFSORT for sorting. The rows are then sorted in the sequence of the explicit or implicit clustering index of the tables.

> **N O T E** The data will not be sorted if no indexes are on the tables.

> **N O T E** In the case of REORGs not using SORTDATA, the rows of tables are also sorted if the tables have an implicit clustering index but not an explicit one. But at least one of the tables in the segmented table space must have an explicit clustering index; otherwise, the tables are unloaded one by one in physical sequence and the rows are not sorted.

- For *partitioned table spaces*, the rows of the entire table space or the partitions to be reorganized are unloaded in physical sequence and passed to DFSORT to be sorted in the sequence defined by the clustering index. However, this index is not used for the sorting.
- For *simple table spaces*, if the table space contains multiple tables, the rows are unloaded in physical sequence and not sorted. If the table space contains a single table, the rows are unloaded in physical sequence and passed to DFSORT, provided that an explicit clustering index is defined. If not, the rows will not be sorted.

In most cases, physically unloading the rows and sorting them by means of DFSORT is faster than unloading the rows through a clustering index if the CLUSTERRATIO of the index is less that 95 percent, or if the percentage of nonclustered rows (100*FAROFFPOS/CARDF) is greater that 5 percent). The lower the CLUSTERRATIO, the higher the performance improvements when using SORTDATA. SORTDATA has no advantage if the table space does not have an explicit clustering index or a partitioning index or if it is a simple table space with several tables.

The following example uses the SORTDATA keyword on the REORG of a partitioned table space:

```
REORG TABLESPACE DB2USER1.CANDIDATE
PART 3
SORTDATA
SORTDEVT SYSDA
```

NOSYSREC. The intermediate storage of the rows in the unload data set—SYSREC, after the unloading and sorting of the rows by the UNLOAD phase—can be avoided by specifying the NOSYSREC option explicitly or implicitly for the REORG utility. NOSYSREC is assumed for read/write online reorganizations (SHRLEVEL CHANGE), covered later in this chapter.

> **N O T E**   Use of NOSYSREC requires that SORTDATA be used.

If the NOSYSREC parameter is used, the UNLOAD phase will not use the unload data set. Therefore, the UNLDDN parameter need not be specified or a SYSREC DD statement provided for the utility job.

Rows that must be sorted are passed to the RELOAD phase by the DFSORT exit after they have been sorted. If the rows do not need to be sorted, they are immediately passed to the RELOAD phase. DFSORT will need sort-work data sets if the number of rows to be sorted is large. If NOSYSREC is specified, either explicitly or implicitly, and dynamic allocation of the sort-work data set is not specified using SORTDEVT, you need to provide DD statements with the DD name DATAWK*nn:nn* = 01 for the first sort-work data set, 02 for the second, and so on.

When NOSYSREC is used, the DATAWKnn data set is used for the sorting of the rows, not the SORTWKnn-work data sets. DATAWKnn data sets need not be provided if you are not using NOSYSREC; they are not used if SORTDATA has been specified. In this case, the SORTWKnn data set is used if the sort-work data sets are not allocated dynamically.

Use of NOSYSREC will eliminate the I/O for the unload data set and will not cause additional I/O within DFSORT. The fact that different sort-work data sets are used does not change the I/O behavior of DFSORT. Therefore, use of NOSYSREC provides performance improvements.

> **N O T E**   The REORG utility cannot be restarted if NOSYSREC has been specified or is assumed.

SORTKEYS.   As of version 8, the SORTKEYS option is the default and no longer needs to be specified. The keyword is supported for compatibility only. The SYSUT1 and SORTOUT data sets can be eliminated from existing jobs to reduce any allocated and unused space. SORTKEYS allows for DFSORT exits to be used to pass the unsorted key/RID pairs for the indexes of the table space to DFSORT and to accept the sorted key/RID pairs again, rather than making the unsorted key/RID pairs available in the SYSUT1 data set and receiving the sorted key/RID pairs in the SORTOUT data set.

With SORTKEYS, the sorting of the key/RID pairs will be done in parallel with the reloading of the rows. Other activities can also be done in parallel, such as the building of the indexes and the inline statistics collection. The parallelism in the utility is accomplished by groups of z/OS subtasks. These task groups contain two or three subtasks—SORT, BUILD, and STATISTICS—depending on whether inline statistics are to be established.

DB2 can allocate multiple task groups, two or three subtasks each, in order to establish the indexes for the tables of the table space in parallel with one another. The degree of parallelism used will depend on the specifications and the DD statements provided for sort-work data sets. If they are dynamically allocated—SORTDEVT specified—the degree of parallelism will be determined by DFSORT. If you manually allocate the sort-work data set and sort-message data sets, the degree of parallelism will be determined by the data sets you have allocated.

The following example uses SORTKEYS to execute the REORG utility:

```
REORG TABLESPACE DB2CERT.CERTTS LOG NO SORTDATA SORTKEYS
```

Parallel Index Build.   Because SORTKEYS is specified by default, many of the operations are performed in parallel: multiple sort and index build operations or multiple SORT and BUILD phases performed in parallel by the subtasks of the allocated task groups. The SORTBLD phase refers to when these operations are done in parallel. This phase encompasses the sort and build activities for all indexes involved in the reorganization.

The `SORTBLD` phase, which is jointly performed by the allocated task groups, partly overlaps with the `RELOAD` phase. Every index is constructed by a predefined task group, which can process multiple indexes. The proper `SORT` tasks for the indexes pass the key/RID pairs to `DFSORT` for sorting as the keys for the indexes are extracted from the rows and the new RIDs for the rows are determined. This allows the sorting of the key/RID pairs to be performed in parallel with the `RELOAD` phase. If multiple tasks groups are used, the key/RID pairs for the various indexes are sorted in parallel.

When `DFSORT` emits the sorted key/RID pairs, the `BUILD` tasks of the index will begin constructing the index. The building of the indexes will be partially overlapped with the reloading of the table space and the sorting of the key/RID pairs, even those for the same index. The various indexes are constructed in parallel if multiple task groups are used.

The construction of an index finishes only after the table space has completely been reloaded, despite the fact that the building of the indexes is done in parallel with the reloading of the table space. The task groups have three subtasks if inline statistics have been requested. This third `STATISTICS` subtask collects the requested statistics as the rows are reloaded and the indexes are built.

> **N O T E** Each `SORT` task requires a sort-work data set and a message data set. The message data set can be common to all task groups it is assigned to the `SYSOUT`.

Logging. The `LOG` option specifies whether records are logged during the reload phase of `REORG`. If the records are not logged, the table space is recoverable only after an image copy has been taken. If you specify `COPYDDN`, `RECOVERYDDN`, `SHRLEVEL`, `REFERENCE`, or `SHRLEVEL CHANGE`, an image copy is taken during `REORG` execution.

With `LOG YES`, the logs record changes made during the `RELOAD` phase. The `LOG YES` option is not allowed for any table space in `DSNDB01` or `DSNDB06`, or if the `SHRLEVEL REFERENCE` or `CHANGE` options are used. If you specify `SHRLEVEL NONE`—explicitly or by default—the default is `LOG YES`. However, if you specify `LOG NO` with `SHRLEVEL NONE`, previous image copies may not be candidates for use during certain recoveries.

With `LOG NO`, DB2 does not log records. This puts the table space in COPY-pending status if either of these conditions is `TRUE`.

- `REORG` is executed at the local site, and `COPYDDN`, `SHRLEVEL REFERENCE`, or `SHRLEVEL CHANGE` is not specified.
- `REORG` is executed at the remote site, and `RECOVERYDDN` is not specified.

Online Reorganizations (OLR)

Most reorganizations limit or restrict access to the table space that is being reorganized, especially if SHRLEVEL NONE is used. During the UNLOAD phase, write access is prohibited; during the RELOAD phase, no type of access is allowed. With today's increasing demand for 24-hour service, it becomes less and less acceptable that access is blocked for long periods of time or at all. To deal with this issue, DB2 supports online reorganization, a reorganization whereby online processes can access the table space for most of the time. Online reorg comes in two flavors.

1. If you specify SHRELVEL REFERENCE, you will have read access to the table space and access via the associated indexes for most of the time. The SWITCH phase has only a small window during which no access is allowed. SHRLEVEL REFERENCE reorganizations are also referred to as read-only online reorgs.
2. If you specify SHRLEVEL CHANGE, you will have read/write access to the table space and access via the indexes associated with the table space for most of the time. For a short period at the end of the LOG phase, you will have only read access; for a short period within the SWITCH phase, no access is allowed. SHRLEVEL CHANGE reorgs are referred to as read/write online reorgs. The LOG and SWITCH phases exist only for online reorganizations.

Read-Only OLR.   Online reorg uses shadow data sets for the table space and the indexes being reorganized. Collectively, the shadow data sets for a table space are referred to as corresponding-shadow table space. Similarly, the shadow data sets for an index are referred to as corresponding-shadow index, or shadow index space. The shadow data sets never exist in the catalog.

Because the original table space does not change during a read-only online reorganization, four phases are sufficient. The rows of the space being reorganized are unloaded—UNLOAD phase—and then reloaded into the shadow table space—RELOAD phase. The reorganized indexes for the table space are not constructed in the original index spaces but in the shadow indexes spaces: in the SORTBLD phase or SORT/BUILD phases. During the SWITCH phase, the shadow data sets for the table/index spaces replace the original data sets, and all access is directed to them. As part of the switching process, the original data sets for the table/index spaces are renamed, and the shadow data sets receive their former names.

For DB2-managed table/index spaces, DB2 automatically creates the shadow data sets in the respective storage groups with the respective active space parameters and deletes the original data sets. For user-managed table/index spaces, you must use access method services (AMS) to define the data sets for the shadow tables/index space yourself. During the UTILTERM phase, the REORG utility completes the switch by renaming the original data sets again. They now receive the data set names the respective shadow data sets had before the reorganization. It is your responsibility to delete these data sets.

During all phases, excluding the SWITCH phase, the rows of the table space can be read, and the indexes of the table space can be used. However during the SWITCH phase, no access to the table space or through the indexes is allowed.

The FASTSWITCH keyword, the default, reduces the time that data is unavailable during the SWITCH phase. When this keyword is used, the online reorg no longer renames data sets, replacing the approximately 3-second outage associated with the renaming of original and shadow data set copies with a memory-speed switch of MVS catalog entries. In addition, FASTSWITCH does not have to invoke AMS to rename the data set.

- If the data sets are system managed storage controlled, may need to switch automatic class selection routines to new naming standard (J00001 I-J switch).
- The FASTSWITCH keyword cannot be used on catalog or directory objects.
- A point-in-time (PIT) recovery works in spite of the changed data set name, even when concurrent copies are used.

Read/Write OLR. Read/write online reorg (SHRELEVEL CHANGE) does not allow you to specify the parameters SORTDATA, NONSYSREC, or SYSKEYS but always operates as if these parameters were specified. Thus, read/write OLR uses DFSORT to sort the rows during the UNLOAD phase and does not use the unload data set. This sorts the key/RID pairs for the indexes in parallel with the RELOAD phase and with the building of the indexes in the shadow index spaces. If the sort-work data sets are dynamically allocated or explicitly allocated for multiple task groups, read/write OLR builds the indexes in parallel.

The algorithm for read/write online reorg is the same as for read-only online reorg. However, the fact that changes are allowed during the UNLOAD, RELOAD, and SORTBLD phases is reflected by an additional phase: the LOG phase. During SWITCH, the changes performed throughout these phases are applied to the shadow table/index spaces. Even during most of the LOG phase, the user has full read/write access. Only at the end of the LOG phase does the REORG utility restrict access to read-only to guarantee that the reorganization comes to an end.

During a read-only online reorg, no access is allowed during the SWITCH phase. Also, a read/write online reorg always creates an inline copy for the table space being reorganized. Therefore, a full-image copy does not need to be created after the reorganization of the table space.

During the LOG phase, changes for the original table space on the DB2 log are applied to the shadow table space and consequently to the shadow index. The RIDs for the DB2 records on the DB2 log point to the original table space. In order to map the changes to the shadow table space, the REORG utility uses a four-column mapping table—actually a unique index over the mapping table. This table and index must be created prior to REORG utility execution.

> **N O T E**   The mapping table must reside in a segmented table space that is not the table space being reorganized.

An example DDL of the four columns in the mapping table follows:

```
CREATE TABLE MAP_TABLE
   (TYPE CHAR(1) NOT NULL,
    SOURCE_RID CHAR(5) NOT NULL,
    TARGET_XRID CHAR(9) NOT NULL,
    LRSN CHAR(6) NOT NULL)
IN DB2CERT.MAPTS;

CREATE UNIQUE INDEX MAPINX1 ON MAP_TABLE
   (SOURCE_RID ASC,
    TYPE,
    TARGET_XRID,
    LRSN);
```

The SOURCE_RID contains the RIDs for the rows in the original table space, whereas the column and the TARGET_XRID contain the extended RIDs for the rows in the shadow table space. The key of the mapping table index has the same four columns as the mapping table but in a different sequence.

The name of the mapping table must be specified via the MAPPING TABLE parameter for the REORG utility and can be any name you choose. An example of using the mapping table follows:

```
      REORG TABLESPACE DB2CERT.CERTTS
SHRLEVEL CHANGE
…
MAPPING TABLE DB2USER1.MAP_TABLE
```

DELETE, INSERT, SELECT, and UPDATE authorization will be needed on the mapping table.

> **N O T E**   A mapping table is needed for each table space table being reorged in parallel, because exclusive locks are taken to prevent concurrent access to the mapping tables.

Only the index over the mapping table is filled; therefore, it is sufficient to allocate as little space as possible to the mapping table. For this index, you should assign at least 1.1 * Number of rows in TS * 27 bytes, assuming that the entire table space is being reorganized. For reorgs only of partitions of the table space, the number of rows in the partitions is to be used instead of the number of rows in the table space.

During read/write online reorganizations, application programs or end users may change the data in the original table space up to the end of the LOG phase. First, the LOG phase applies the changes made during the UNLOAD, RELOAD, and SORTBLD phases to the shadow table space and the shadow indexes. During most of the LOG phase, read/write access to the original table space is allowed. Because the data in the original table space may have changed during the first iteration, the second iteration must apply the changes made during the first iteration, a third iteration must apply the changes made during the second iteration, and so on. This could potentially cause the LOG phase to never end.

Ideally, fewer and fewer changes must be applied with each iteration. Conceivably, however, an endless number of iterations may be necessary. Therefore, the REORG utility must ultimately limit the access during the LOG phase to read, only to come to a final iteration. After this is done, REORG must apply only the changes accumulated during the previous iteration before it can enter the SWITCH phase.

Because the switch to read-only access impacts the operating environment, the REORG utility provides the ability to decide and specify how long a period this can be tolerated. This is done via the MAXRO parameter.

The REORG utility estimates how long the next iteration will take, based on the changes for the previous iteration. If its estimate is lower than or equal to the value specified via the MAXRO parameter, the REORG utility switches to read-only access or even to no access allowed, depending on what you have requested, and the last iteration takes place. The time of the last iteration may be larger than the estimate or the value you have specified. However, it should not be substantially larger.

If DRAIN WRITERS has been specified, either explicitly or by default, the REORG utility waits until all units of recovery accessing the table space have been committed and does not allow new units of recovery to begin. With DRAIN ALL, the REORG utility waits until all readers and writers are off the table space and does not allow any further read or write access. Readers may have locks (claims) not being released before they commit. Therefore, it is imperative that even long-running read-only programs commit from time to time to allow online reorganizations to succeed.

The default for MAXRO is 300 seconds. MAXRO DEFER causes log processing to continue indefinitely until you change MAXRO by means of the ALTER UTILITY command. The last iteration is forced by a different condition (Long-log) or the reorganization is terminated.

> **N O T E** Specifying a small value for MAXRO generally causes more iterations to take place and may increase the total elapsed time for the reorganization. A huge value for MAXRO will most likely lead to the second iteration's being the last one.

If a small value is specified for MAXRO, the log processing of the REORG utility may not catch up with the change activities performed for the table space. This is referred to as the long-log condition.

The REORG utility raises a long-log condition if the number of log records processed by the next iteration will not be sufficiently lower than the number of log records for the previous iteration and the next log iteration will take longer than the specified MAXRO values, that is, if the next iteration will not be the last one.

An option is available to specify what should happen in the case of long-log situations. After message DSNU3771 has been issued and the time specified through the DELAY parameter has passed, the action of the LONGLOG parameter is performed. The action can be CONTINUE, or continue log-processing iterations; TERM, or terminate the REORG; or DRAIN, or wait until all units of recovery involving the table space have been committed and prevent new units of recovery for the table space.

> **N O T E**   The time on the DELAY parameter and the actions specified in the LONGLOG parameter can be changed by using the ALTER command, if necessary.

The REORG utility also allows you to control when a reorg must complete. You can use the DEADLINE parameter to specify a deadline, at which time the reorg must finish. The deadline can be an absolute time—a time stamp—or a relative time—a labeled duration expression using CURRENT DATE or CURRENT TIMESTAMP. If it estimates that the SWITCH phase will not complete before the specified deadline, the REORG utility issues the message that the DISPLAY UTILITY command would issue and terminates the reorganization. The DEADLINE parameter can be changed by means of the ALTER UTILITY command if the reorganization appears that it will not finish before its deadline and you do not want the reorg to be terminated.

> **N O T E**   The deadline must be extended before it is reached.

Inline Statistics during REORG

After reorganization, the old statistics for the reorganized table space, index, or partitions are no longer valid; nor are the old statistics for the indexes associated with a table space being reorganized. New statistics must be established for these objects to ensure that the DB2 optimizer has the proper statistics for access-path determination. (For more information on access paths, refer to Chapter 18.)

Establishing the new statistics is done by executing the RUNSTATS utility after the reorganization or running the REORG utility for all the associated objects. These inline statistics can be requested by means of the STATISTICS clause. The DB2 catalog tables are updated accordingly and/or the statistics are reported in the output listing for the REORG utility. The following example requests inline statistics during a reorg:

```
REORG TABLESPCE DB2CERT.CERTTS
SORTDATA STATISTICS PART 5
```

By allowing REORG to perform inline statistics, the RUNSTATS utility does not need to be run after the reorg. It is faster to run the statistics inline, and they are done in parallel by subtasks during the reorg.

> **N O T E** Rebinds the plans and packages for application programs will still have to occur to make the statistics effective.

The keywords you can specify as a part of the STATISTICS clause are the same as you can specify for RUNSTATS, and the functions provided are the same. This includes statistics sampling, which will be discussed later in this chapter.

The REORG utility allows you to select the rows you want to remove, using the DISCARD clause, which may contain one or more FROM TABLE specifications identifying the tables from which rows should be removed.

In the FROM TABLE specification, you name a table of the table space from which rows should be removed and the selection condition for the removal of the rows (WHEN condition). In the WHEN condition, you can combine basic predicates by means of AND and OR to select the rows to be discarded. The predicates must refer to columns of the specified table.

> **N O T E** As the consequence of discarding rows, the check-pending (CHKP) conditions will be set for the table space containing dependent tables.

REORG also allows you to unload data by using the UNLOAD options: CONTINUE, PAUSE, ONLY, and EXTERNAL. CONTINUE tells REORG to continue processing after the data is unloaded; ONLY says to stop and terminate after the unload.

PAUSE tells REORG to stop after the UNLOAD phase. One common use for REORG UNLOAD PAUSE is to unload the data from the table space and then remove the extents from user-defined data sets by using access method services (AMS). The status of the REORG is recorded in SYSUTIL. The utility could then be restarted at the next phase (RESTART(PHASE)).

The UNLOAD EXTERNAL option allows you to unload data into a data set that will be in a format that the LOAD utility can use. The following examples show DISCARD and UNLOAD EXTERNAL:

```
REORG TABLESPACE DB2CERT.CERTTS
    UNLOAD EXTERNAL
    FROM TABLE DB2USER1.TEST_TAKEN
    WHEN (CID = 300)

REORG TABLESPACE DB2CERT.CERTTS
    DISCARD
    FROM TABLE DB2USER1.TEST_TAKEN
    WHEN (CID = 300)
```

Reorganizing Indexes

Reorganizing an index reclaims fragmented space and improves access performance. The REORG INDEX options are similar to those on REORG TABLESPACE, such as degree of access to the data during reorganization, collecting inline statistics using the STATISTICS keyword, preformatting pages, online reorg features, and the REPORTONLY feature. Sometimes, performance may be improved simply by reorganizing the index, not necessarily the table space.

The REORG INDEX statement will reorganize the entire index—all parts if partitioning. The REORG INDEX PART n reorganizes PART n of the partitioning index.

The execution phases of REORG INDEX are fairly similar to those of REORG TABLESPACE.

- UTILINIT performs initialization and setup.
- UNLOAD unloads index space and writes keys to a sequential data set.
- BUILD builds indexes and updates index statistics.
- LOG processes the log iteratively but is used only if you specify SHRLEVEL CHANGE.
- SWITCH changes access to a shadow copy of the index space or partition and is used only if you specify SHRLEVEL REFERENCE or CHANGE.
- UTILTERM performs any necessary cleanup.

Following is an example of the REORG INDEX utility with inline statistics:

```
REORG INDEX DB2USER1.CANDIDATE
SHRLEVEL REFERENCE STATISTICS
```

Triggering Reorganizations

Data that is organized well physically can improve the performance of access paths that rely on index or data scans. Well-organized data can also help reduce the amount of disk storage used by the index or table space. If the main reason for reorganizing is performance, the best way to determine when to reorganize is to watch your statistics for increased I/O, getpages, and processor consumption. When performance degrades to an unacceptable level, analyze the statistics described in the guidelines in this section to help you develop your own rules for when to reorganize in your particular environment. However, because running the REORG utility can be quite expensive and disruptive, it should be run only when a table space and indexes absolutely require it.

If the statistics are current in the DB2 catalog tables, REORG can determine whether it needs to perform the reorganization. The REORG utility allows for specification of criteria indicating when reorganization should be performed. This saves the DBA from having to do the analysis on the statistics and determining whether a reorg should be scheduled.

You can use some general guidelines to determine when to use the REORG utility. You query the catalog to manually determine to run REORG, or you can use the REORG utility to trigger reorgs, if necessary.

Catalog Queries

Catalog queries you can use to help you determine when to reorganize are included in DSNTESP in SDSNSAMP and can be used as input to SPUFI. The queries are as follows.

- List table spaces that are candidates for reorganization:

```
SELECT DBNAME, TSNAME
 FROM SYSIBM.SYSTABLEPART
  WHERE ((CARD > 0 AND (NEARINDREF + FARINDREF) * 100 / CARD > 10)
  OR PERCDROP  > 10);
```

> **N O T E**   Indirect references—growth in NEARINDREF and FARINDREF—can be caused by updates to columns defined as VARCHARs where the lengths of the rows change.

- List index spaces that are candidates for reorganization:

```
SELECT IXNAME, IXCREATOR
 FROM SYSIBM.SYSINDEXPART
  WHERE LEAFDIST > 200;
```

- List the number of varying-length rows that were relocated to other pages because of an update. (This query gives an indication of how well DASD (Direct Access Storage Device) space is being used.)

```
SELECT CARD, NEARINDREF, FARINDREF
 FROM SYSIBM.SYSTABLEPART
 WHERE DBNAME = 'xxx'
 AND TSNAME = 'yyy';
```

- List the percentage of unused space in a nonsegmented table space. (In nonsegmented table spaces, the space used by dropped tables is not reclaimed until you reorganize the table space.)

```
SELECT PERCDROP
 FROM SYSIBM.SYSTABLEPART
 WHERE DBNAME = 'xxx'
 AND TSNAME = 'yyy';
```

- Determine whether the rows of a table are stored in the same order as the entries of its clustering index. (A large value of FAROFFPOS indicates that clustering is degenerating. A large value of NEAROFFPOS might also indicate that the table space needs reorganizing, but the value of FAROFFPOS is a better indicator.)

```
SELECT NEAROFFPOS, FAROFFPOS
 FROM SYSIBM.SYSINDEXPART
 WHERE IXCREATOR = 'zzz'
 AND IXNAME = 'www';
```

- Return LEAFDIST, which is the average distance, multiplied by 100, between successive leaf pages during sequential access of an index. (If LEAFDIST increases over time, the index should be reorganized.)

```
SELECT LEAFDIST
 FROM SYSIBM.SYSINDEXPART
 WHERE IXCREATOR = 'zzz'
 AND IXNAME = 'www';
```

- List the LOB table spaces that should be reorganized. (A value of ORGRATIO greater than 2 generally indicates a LOB table space that needs reorganization.)

```
SELECT DBNAME, NAME, ORGRATIO
 FROM SYSIBM.SYSLOBSTATS
 WHERE ORGRATIO > 2;
```

REORG Triggers

The REORG utility embeds the function of catalog queries. If a query returns a certain result—you can use the default or supply your own—REORG will either reorganize or not. Optionally, you can have REORG run a report instead of doing the reorganization.

Following is an example of how to specify the OFFPOSLIMIT and INDREFLIMIT conditional reorg triggers:

```
REORG TABLESPACE DB2USER1.TEST_TAKEN
   SORTDATA NOSYSREC SORTKEYS
   COPYDDN SYSCOPY1
   OFFPOSLIMIT
   INDREFLIMIT
   STATISTICS TABLE(ALL)INDEX(ALL)
```

The REORG options OFFPOSLIMIT, INDREFLIMIT, and LEAFDISTLIMIT can also be equivalently described in the following SQL:

- OFFPOSLIMIT

```
SELECT CARDF
  , (NEAROFFPOSF + FAROFFPOSF) * 100 / CARDF
FROM SYSIBM.SYSINDEXPART
WHERE CARDF > 0
AND (NEAROFFPOSF + FAROFFPOSF) * 100
  / CARDF > :offposlimit
```

- INDREFLIMIT

```
SELECT CARD
  , (NEARINDREF + FARINDREF) * 100 / CARD
FROM SYSIBM.SYSTABLEPART
WHERE CARD > 0
AND (NEARINDREF + FARINDREF * 100
  / CARD > :indreflimit
```

- LEAFDISTLIMIT

```
SELECT LEAFDIST
FROM SYSIBM.SYSINDEXPART
WHERE LEAFDIST > :leafdistlimit
```

The REORG utility does not embed any function to help you determine when to reorganize LOB table spaces.

ALTER TABLE Statements

Another time to consider reorganizing data to improve performance is when ALTER TABLE statements have been used to add a column to the table or to change the data types or the lengths of existing columns. Such changes cause the table space to be placed in advisory REORG-pending (AREO*) status. In the case of changing the definition of an existing column, the table space is placed in AREO* status because the existing data is not immediately converted to its new definition.

Reorganizing the table space causes the rows to be reloaded, with the data converted to the new definition. Until the table space is reorganized, the changes must be tracked and applied as the data is accessed, possibly degrading performance. For example, depending on the number of changes, you may see decreased performance for dynamic SQL queries, updates, and deletes, as well as other ALTER statements, especially those that are run concurrently. In addition, multiple REORG and LOAD utilities running concurrently may perform slower or create timeouts. It may also take longer to unload a table that has had many changes prior to being reorganized.

Index Reorganizing

The LEAFNEAR and LEAFFAR columns of SYSIBM.SYSINDEXPART measure the disorganization of physical leaf pages by indicating the number of pages that are not in an optimal position. A REORG INDEX should be considered in the following cases.

- LEAFFAR/NLEAF is greater than 10 percent. (NLEAF is a column in SYSIBM.SYSINDEXES.)
- PSEUDO_DEL_ENTRIES/CARDF is greater than 10 percent. If you are reorganizing the index because of this value, consider using the REUSE option to improve performance.
- The data set has multiple extents. Keeping the number of extents to less than 50 is a general guideline. Many secondary extents can detract from the performance of index scans.
- The index is in advisory REORG-pending status (AREO*) or advisory-REBUILD-pending status (ARBDP) as the result of an ALTER statement.
- ((REORGINSERTS + REORGDELETES) X 100) / TOTALENTRIES is greater than RRIInsertDeletePct.
- (REORGAPPENDINSERT X 100) / TOTALENTRIES is greater than RRIInsertDeletePct.
- Mass delete occurred.

Table Space Reorganizing

SYSIBM.SYSTABLEPART contains the information about how the data in the table is physically stored. Consider running REORG TABLESPACE in the following situations.

- FAROFFPOSF/CARDF is greater than 10 percent. Or, if the index is a clustering index, the CLUSTERRATIOF column of SYSIBM.SYSINDEXES is less than 90 percent.
- (NEARINDREF + FARINDREF)/CARDF is greater than 10 percent.
- PERCDROP is greater than 10 percent for a simple table space. If you are reorganizing the table space because of this value, consider using the REUSE option to improve performance.
- The data set has multiple extents. Keeping the number of extents to less than 50 is a general guideline.
- The table space is in AREO* status as the result of an ALTER TABLE statement.

SYSIBM.SYSLOBSTATS contains information about how the data in the table space is physically stored. Consider running REORG on the LOB table space when the value in the ORGRATIO column is 2. Additionally, you can use real-time statistics to identify DB2 objects that should be reorganized, have their statistics updated, or be image copied.

> **N O T E** If you specify REPORTONLY on a reorg of a table space, partition, index, or index partition, the REORG does not take place independent of whether the limit is surpassed. You simply get a report of whether you needed a reorg.

DBA Analysis

The database administrator can choose not to use the REORG triggers and instead analyze the statistics manually to determine whether a reorg is necessary. For any table space, a reorg is needed if any of the following apply, using statistics from the clustering index.

- Any data set behind the table space has multiple extents.
- CLUSTERRATIO < 90 percent always. However, keep very small tables at 100 percent clustered; medium tables should be reorged below 98 percent; large tables should be reorged below 95 percent; and from 90 percent to 95 percent can cause very poor performance.
- (NEARINDREF + FARINDREF) / CARD > 10 percent.
- FAROFFPOS / CARD > 5 percent.
- NEAROFFPOS / CARD > 10 percent.
- DBD grows after successive drops/recreates in a table space.

To check whether your index space needs to be reorganized, review the LEAFDIST column in the SYSINDEXPART catalog table. Large numbers in the LEAFDIST column indicate that several pages are between successive leaf pages, and using the index will result in additional overhead. In this situation, DB2 may turn off prefetch use as well. Reorganizing the index space will solve these problems.

Reorganizing the Catalog and Directory

To determine when to reorganize the DB2 catalog table space and index spaces, you can also use the same techniques used for determining when to reorganize application table spaces and index spaces. First, you will want to ensure that statistics are kept current, by using RUNSTATS, based on the frequency of changes in the catalog, so that decisions for reorganizations are based on current numbers. A reorganization is also necessary if the objects are in extents or if unused space needs to be reclaimed.

> **NOTE** Every table space in the DSNDB06 database is eligible for reorganization, but DSNDB06.SYSPLAN cannot be reorganized with SHRLEVEL CHANGE.

DB2 directory reorganizations are also important because the directory contains critical information about internal DB2 control and structures. These elements are important to DB2 processing because they affect application plans and package execution, utility execution, and database access. If they become disorganized, transaction and utility performance can be affected.

The DB2 catalog and some of the DB2 directory tables have relationships. For instance, you would want to reorganize the directory table DBD01 when you reorganize catalog table SYSDBASE. Directory tables SCT02 and SPT01 would need to be reorganized with SYSPLAN and SYSPACKAGE, respectively.

Rebalancing Partitions

The limit keys for the partitions of a partitioned table space can be changed if the partitions become unbalanced. This is done via the ALTER TABLE SQL statement with the PARTITION BY parameter.

This changes only the definition in the DB2 catalog but does not move any rows in the partitioned table space or any index entries in the partitioned index. DB2 will also set the REORP status for those partitions because they may no longer contain the correct rows. The affected partitions—all partitions in the range affected by the ALTER—are no longer accessible.

> **NOTE** The index partitions will not be placed in REORP status, but they cannot be used for access to the partitions in REORP status. NPIs cannot be used for access to the affected data partitions, but if index-only access is needed, they can be used.

In order to redistribute the rows for the affected partitions, you must reorganize all these partitions at the same time by specifying a range in the PART n:m parameter of the REORG utility control statement. The following example shows REORG parts 5 through 10:

```
REORG TABLESPACE DB2CERT.CERTTS PART 5:10
```

> **N O T E** You cannot specify SHRLEVEL REFERENCE or
> SHRLEVEL CHANGE if partitions are in REORP. The REORG utility
> requires that you specify SHRLEVEL NONE—explicitly or by
> default—if at least one of the target partitions is in REORP.

If the limit key for the last partition in the key sequence for a large table space—created with LARGE or DSSIZE—is changed, there must be a discard data set if the key range had been reduced independent of whether some of its former rows no longer belong to the key range. The rows no longer belonging to any key range are then placed in the discard data set. This can be specified on the DD name for the discard data set via the DISCARDDN parameter, or use the default DD name of SYSDISC.

> **N O T E** The REORG utility always establishes an inline copy for at
> least one of the partitions being reorganized that is in REORP status.
> This is a single inline copy that includes all partitions of the specified
> range. The DD name for the local primary copy data set must be
> provided via the COPYDDN parameter, or provide a DD statement
> with the DD name SYSCOPY.

GATHERING STATISTICS

The system catalog tables contain information about columns, tables, and indexes: the number of rows in a table, the use of space by a table or index, and the number of values in a column. However, this information is not kept current but instead has to be generated by a utility called RUNSTATS. The statistics collected by the RUNSTATS utility can be used in two ways: to display the physical organization of the data and to provide information that the DB2 optimizer needs to select the best access path for executing SQL statements.

To have efficient access paths to data, current statistics must exist that reflect the state of your tables, columns, and indexes. Whenever a dynamic SQL statement is issued, the DB2 optimizer reads the system catalog tables to review the available indexes, the size of each table, the characteristics of a column, and other information to select the best access path for executing the query. If the statistics do not reflect the current state of the tables, the DB2 optimizer will not have the correct information to make the best choice in selecting an access path to execute your query.

This issue becomes more crucial as the complexity of the SQL statements increases. When only one table is accessed without indexes, fewer choices are available to the optimizer. However, when the SQL statement involves several tables, each with one or more indexes, the number of choices available to the optimizer increases dramatically.

Choosing the correct access path can reduce the response time considerably by reducing the amount of I/O needed to correctly retrieve that data. Depending on the size of the tables, the indexes available, and other considerations, the selected access path can affect the response time, which varies from minutes to hours. You may also want to consider the physical and logical design of your database.

The next step in improving performance involves the use of the RUNSTATS utility. It is recommended that you execute RUNSTATS on a frequent basis on tables that have a large number of updates, inserts, or deletes. For tables with a great deal of insert or delete activity, you may decide to run statistics after a fixed period of time or after the insert or delete activity.

DB2 allows you to reorganize and use the RUNSTATS utility on the system catalog tables. This important feature can improve the access plans generated when querying the system catalog tables. DB2 may access these tables when you issue an SQL statement, even though you are referencing only user tables. Therefore, it is very important to have current statistics on the system catalog tables.

> **N O T E** It is recommended that you use the RUNSTATS utility after REORG on a table.

RUNSTATS Utility

RUNSTATS is critical to a properly tuned DB2 environment. The utility gathers statistics about DB2 table spaces and indexes. It can also be embedded in other utilities, such as REORG and LOAD, enabling you to collect statistics during the execution of a given utility. The RUNSTATS utility can be executed on a table space and its indexes, for each object independently, or even for a specific column.

RUNSTATS should initially be executed on all columns after the data is loaded and reorganized. RUNSTATS execution should be done after

- A table space or an index has been reorganized and the statistics have changed significantly
- A new index has been added
- Any heavy update, insert, or delete processing has occurred

The statistics should be run before any binding/rebinding of packages or plans and before any performance tuning that would require monitoring the statistics in the catalog. Using SHRLEVEL

CHANGE with RUNSTATS will not lock or interfere with other processes. This access means that you can execute RUNSTATS as often as necessary.

Catalog Updates

An option allows RUNSTATS to report on the statistics gathered, using the REPORT NO|YES parameter. The following UPDATE options can control what and whether RUNSTATS updates the DB2 catalog.

- ALL will include both space and access-path statistics.
- NONE will not do any updating of the DB2 catalog.
- SPACE will update only statistics related to space management, that is, free space.
- ACCESSPATH will update only statistics used by the optimizer.

Following is an example of executing the RUNSTATS utility and updating the catalog with only the statistics that are collected for access-path selection. The REPORT option will route the collected statistics to the SYSPRINT output DD statement.

```
RUNSTATS TABLESPACE DB2CERT.CERTTS
REPORT YES
UPDATE ACCESSPATH
```

Sampling

The RUNSTATS sampling feature allows you to choose the percentage of nonindexed column statistics gathered and will help RUNSTATS to execute faster. The sampling technique can affect the optimizer's choice in access-path selection because the sampling must be representative of the data. In the absence of true representation, it would assume a linear distribution of data, which would affect the filter factor and costing done by the optimizer. Following is an example of using a sampling of 25 percent:

```
RUNSTATS TABLESPACE DB2CERT.CERTTS
    TABLE(ALL)SAMPLE 25
    INDEX(ALL)
    SHRLEVEL CHANGE
```

Key-Correlation Statistics

Key-correlation statistics enable DB2 to gather statistics about how one column's value is related to the value of another column. Without these statistics, only the FIRSTKEYCARD (number of distinct values in the first key column) and FULLKEYCARD (number of distinct values of the first key) columns are updated with limited information, and the correlation is on columns for FULLKEYCARD only. Without key-correlation statistics, no second- or third- key cardinality, and multikey cardinality is considered independently, often leading to inaccurate estimation of filter factors and inaccurate estimation of join size, join sequencing, and join methods, which can result in inefficient access-path selection.

Key-correlation statistics are collected by RUNSTATS with minimal additional overhead and can provide CPU and elapsed-time reductions through improved cost and resources estimations. These key-correlation statistics play a major role in access-path selection by providing the optimizer columns with information on multicolumn cardinalities and multicolumn frequent values.

This feature enables you to specify the number of columns (NUMCOLS) on which to collect statistics and to specify the number of values (COUNT). These keywords are used in the RUNSTATS utility. The KEYCARD parameter indicates that cardinalities for each column, concatenated with all previous key columns, are to be collected. This will provide more information for the optimizer when the related columns are used in a compound WHERE clause.

Using this RUNSTATS feature enables you to build the frequency values for critical concatenated key columns, such as the first and second columns, or maybe the first, second, and third columns.

The following example shows how to update statistics on frequently occurring values. For a given index, we can use the KEYCARD option to indicate that the utility is to collect cardinality statistics for the index. For a three-column index, the utility will collect cardinality statistics for the first column, the first and second, and the first, second, and third. By using NUMCOLS, the utility will also collect the 10 most frequently occurring values for the first group and then the 15 most frequently occurring values for the second group:

```
RUNSTATS INDEX (DBA1.CERTIX)
     KEYCARD
     FREQVAL NUMCOLS 1 COUNT 10
     FREQVAL NUMCOLS 2 COUNT 15
```

The next example shows how to update statistics for a group of columns. The COLGROUP keyword is used to group the columns; the distribution statistics for the group will be stored in SYSCOLDIST:

```
RUNSTATS TABLESPACE (DBA1.CERTTS)
     TABLE (DBA1.CANDIDATE)
     COLGROUP (CITY, STATE)
```

If the COLGROUP and FREQVAL options are used together, the frequency-distribution statistics for a specific group of nonindex columns can be collected. The COUNT keyword specifies the number of frequently occurring values to be collected from the specified column group:

```
RUNSTATS TABLESPACE (DBA1.CERTTS)
   TABLE (DBA1.CANDIDATE)
   COLGROUP (CITY, STATE) FREQVAL COUNT 10
```

> **NOTE** Collection of data-correlation information and skewed data distributions can help with better access-path selection and may help reduce RID list size.

These SYSCOLDIST and SYSCOLDISTSTATS values for frequency-distribution statistics are stored catalog table and columns as follows:

- TYPE - CHAR(1) NOT NULL DEFAULT 'F': type of statistic (cardinality or frequent value)
- CARDF - FLOAT NOT NULL DEFAULT -1: number of distinct values for column group
- COLGROUPCOLNO - VARCHAR(254) NOT NULL W/DEFAULT: the set of columns
- NUMCOLUMNS - SMALLINT NOT NULL DEFAULT 1: the number of columns in the group

> **NOTE** The COLCARDF column in SYSCOLUMNS contains the number of distinct values for a single column.

RUNSTATS on the DB2 Catalog

The RUNSTATS utility needs to be executed on the DB2 catalog, depending on the amount of DDL, DML, and other activities that will insert and delete rows in DB2 catalog tables. DB2 will not be able to appropriately optimize queries against the catalog without having current statistics on the table spaces and index spaces. The same principle applies here as with DB2 user-defined objects; a current view of all DB2 objects is also needed to determine the need for and frequency of reorganization of DB2 catalog table spaces and index spaces.

SQL Cache Invalidation

The only way to invalidate statements in the dynamic SQL cache is to execute the RUNSTATS utility on the objects that the queries are dependent on. If statistics are updated, affected dynamic SQL statements that are cached are invalidated so they can be reprepared. Cache invalidation is at table space and index space levels. This can be done using a RUNSTATS REPORT YES; however, this can also take a fair amount of time. Optionally, RUNSTATS can be run with REPORT NO and UPDATE NONE. This way, users can invalidate dynamic SQL cache statements without the overhead of collecting the stats, generating a report, or updating catalog tables.

```
RUNSTATS TABLESPACE DB1.CERTTS
        REPORT NO UPDATE NONE
```

Historical Statistics

DB2 provides the ability to keep a history of statistics for better proactive performance-analysis capabilities. This helps to better monitor objects in terms of growth over time, along with other information to determine whether objects need to change. The keyword HISTORY in the RUNSTATS, REORG, LOAD, and REBUILD utilities is used to specify that historical statistics are to be collected:

```
REORG INDEX.....HISTORY
    RUNSTATS TABLESPACE.....HISTORY
```

The historical statistics are kept in the following nine DB2 catalog tables:

- SYSIBM.SYSCOLDIST_HIST
- SYSIBM.SYSCOLUMNS_HIST
- SYSIBM.SYSINDEXPART_HIST
- SYSIBM.SYSINDEXES_HIST
- SYSIBM.SYSINDEXSTATS_HIST
- SYSIBM.SYSLOBSTATS_HIST
- SYSIBM.SYSTABLEPART_HIST
- SYSIBM.SYSTABLES_HIST
- SYSIBM.SYSTABSTATS_HIST

As the statistics age and are no longer needed, they can be deleted with the MODIFY STATISTICS utility.

Inline Statistics

In order to avoid having to run a separate RUNSTATS job, inline statistics can be collected when running REORG, LOAD, or REBUILD INDEX. Establishing inline statistics is faster than running RUNSTATS after REORG, LOAD, or REBUILD INDEX, because the inline statistics are established as a byproduct by separate subtasks of these utilities. An option to request a statistics report and/or update the DB2 catalog for the objects involved is available. For REORG, you can request the statistics for the table space being reorganized and/or the indexes associated with the tables of the table space or for the indexes being reorged.

> **NOTE** For the LOAD utility, you can request inline stats only for REPLACE or RESUME and for REBUILD INDEX only for indexes being built.

The inline statistics can be requested by using the STATISTICS clause in the REORG, LOAD, or REBUILD utilities. The same parameters as for the RUNSTATS utility can be used for inline statistics.

Inline statistics cannot be collected for the following:

- DB2 catalog or directory tables with links.
- Nonpartitioning indexes if a load or a reorganization is on individual partitions. DB2 would not know how to apply the partial values to the existing totals for the nonpartitioned indexes.
- If you restart the REORG utility using RESTART(CURRENT).
- If you restart the LOAD or REBUILD INDEX utility.

> **NOTE** Inline statistics established during LOAD may include the information about rows that have been discarded. If only a few rows have been discarded, this is not a concern, but if a large number of rows have been discarded, the inline stats may be very inaccurate, and it may be better to execute a separate RUNSTATS utility.

Real-Time Statistics

DB2 can collect statistics on table spaces and index spaces and then periodically write this information to two user-defined tables. The real-time statistics can be used by user-written queries/programs, a DB2-supplied stored procedure, or Control Center to make decisions about object maintenance.

Statistics Collections

DB2 is always collecting statistics for database objects. The statistics are kept in virtual storage and are calculated and updated asynchronously on externalization. In order to externalize them, the environment must be properly set up. A new set of DB2 objects must be created so that DB2 can write out the statistics. SDSNSAMP(DSNTESS) contains the information necessary to set up these objects.

Two tables, with appropriate indexes, must be created to hold the statistics:

- SYSIBM.TABLESPACESTATS
- SYSIBM.INDEXSPACESTATS

These tables are kept in a database named DSNRTSDB, which must be started in order to externalize the statistics that are being held in virtual storage. DB2 will then populate the tables with either one row per table space or index space or one row per partition. For tables in a data sharing environment, each member will write its own statistics to the real-time statistics (RTS) tables.

Some of the important statistics that are collected for table spaces are

- Total number of rows
- Number of active pages
- Time of last COPY, REORG, or RUNSTATS execution

Some statistics that may help determine when a reorg is needed are space allocated, extents, number of inserts/updates/deletes (singleton or mass) since the last REORG or LOAD REPLACE; number of unclustered inserts, number of disorganized LOBs, and number of overflow records created since the last REORG.

Other statistics help determine when RUNSTATS should be executed: number of inserts/updates/deletes (singleton and mass) since the last RUNSTATS execution. Statistics collected to help with COPY determination are distinct updated pages and changes since the last COPY execution and the RBA/LRSN of first update since last COPY.

Statistics are also gathered on indexes. Basic index statistics are total number of unique of duplicate entries, number of levels and active pages, space allocated, and extents. A statistic that helps to determine when a reorg is needed is the time when the last REBUILD, REORG, or LOAD REPLACE occurred. Statistics can be collected on the number of updates/deletes (real or pseudo, singleton or mass)/inserts (random and those that were after the highest key) since the last REORG or REBUILD execution. These statistics are, of course, very helpful for determining how the data physically looks after certain processes, such as batch inserts, have occurred, so we can take appropriate actions, if necessary.

Externalizing and Using Real-Time Statistics

Various events can trigger the externalization of the statistics. DSNZPARM STATSINST—default, 30 minutes—is used to control the externalization of the statistics at a subsystem level. Several processes will have an effect on the real-time statistics: SQL, utilities, and the dropping/creating of objects.

Once externalized, queries can then be written against the tables. For example, a query against the TABLESPACESTATS table can be written to identify when a table space needs to be copied because more than 30 percent of the pages have changed since the last image copy was taken:

```
SELECT NAME
  FROM SYSIBM.SYSTABLESPACESTATS
    WHERE DBNAME = 'DB1' and
    ((COPYUPDATEDPAGES*100)/NACTIVE)>30
```

This query compares the last RUNSTATS timestamp to that of the last REORG execution on the same object to determine when RUNSTATS is needed. If the date of the last REORG is more recent than the last RUNSTATS, it may be time to execute RUNSTATS:

```
SELECT NAME
FROM SYSIBM.SYSTABLESPACESTATS
WHERE DBNAME = 'DB1' and
    (JULIAN_DAY(REORGLASTTIME) >JULIAN_DAY(STATSLASTTIME))
```

The next example may be useful if you want to monitor the number of records that were inserted since the last REORG or LOAD REPLACE and that are not well clustered with respect to the clustering index. Ideally, *well clustered* means that the record was inserted into a page that was within 16 pages of the ideal candidate page, determined by the clustering index. The SYSTABLESPACESTATS table value REORGUNCLUSTINS can be used to determine whether you need to run REORG after a series of inserts:

```
SELECT NAME
FROM SYSIBM.SYSTABLESPACESTATS
WHERE DBNAME = 'DB1' and
    ((REORGUNCLUSTINS*100)/TOTALROWS) >10
```

A DB2-supplied stored procedure can help with this process and, possibly, even work toward automating the whole determination/utility execution process. This stored procedure, DSNACCOR, is a sample procedure that will query the RTS tables and determine which objects need to be reorganized, image copied, updated with current statistics, have taken too many extents, and those that may in a restricted status. DSNACCOR creates and uses its own declared temporary tables and must run in a WLM address space. The output of the stored procedure provides recommendations by using a predetermined set of criteria in formulas that use the RTS and user input for their calculations. DSNACCOR can make recommendations for everything (COPY, REORG, RUNSTATS, EXTENTS, RESTRICT) or for one or more of your choice and for specific object types (table spaces and/or indexes).

STOSPACE Utility

STOSPACE collects space information from the VSAM catalogs for storage groups and related table spaces and indexes. This utility then updates the DB2 catalog with information about the amount of space being used. This utility is executed against a storage group. (For more information about storage groups, refer to Chapter 4.)

An example of STOSPACE syntax follows:

```
STOSPACE STOGROUP CERTSTG
```

STATISTICS USAGE

Data maintenance should initially start with the RUNSTATS utility to collect the base statistics. After performing RUNSTATS, you can analyze the statistics to determine whether a REORG is necessary, or the REORG utility can review the statistics collected and, by using the REORG triggers, determine whether a REORG is needed.

If reorganization is needed, use the REORG utility on the selected objects, and then do RUNSTATS and REBIND. You must perform a REBIND on any packages affected by the preceding operations so that they can take advantage of the benefits of the new physical organization and updated statistics. After performing subsequent update, insert, and delete operations as part of the data maintenance process, repeat by first executing the RUNSTATS utility.

Establish a routine for RUNSTATS and the REBIND processes. Updated statistics will give you precise information about your database state.

A number of columns in the DB2 catalog can be updated in order for a DBA to model a production environment so that the access paths against production data can be determined even if the data does not physically exist. Refer to Chapter 2 for more information on the catalog tables, and refer to Chapter 17 for updating catalog columns to help predict access paths.

Rebinds

Packages should be rebound in order to have the access paths reevaluated when any of the following are true, based on current statistics from the catalog (for additional information on package binds, refer to Chapter 11).

- Changes > 20 percent (NLEAF, NPAGES, NACTIVE).
- Cluster ratio < 80 percent; NLEVELS > 2.
- HIGH2KEY and LOW2KEY ranges change > 10 percent.
- Cardinality and row count change > 20 percent.

For more information on packages and rebinds, refer to Chapter 11.

Other Data Maintenance Utilities

CHECK Utilities

Three utilities are used to check the integrity of data and indexes and are often required to remove restrictive statuses. The utilities are

- CHECK DATA
- CHECK INDEX
- CHECK LOB

CHECK DATA.   This online utility checks tables in table spaces for violations of referential and table-check constraints. It then reports information about any violations that are detected during its execution. The CHECK DATA utility will need to be executed after a conditional restart or a PIT recovery on all table spaces where parent and dependent tables might not be synchronized. (See Chapter 8 for more information on recovery.) The CHECK DATA utility can be executed against a base table space only, not a LOB table space.

Rows that violate referential or table-check constraints can be optionally deleted by the CHECK DATA utility. Any row that violates one or more constraints can also be copied, once, to an exception table. If any violation of constraints is found, CHECK DATA puts the table space being checked into the CHECK-pending status.

CHECK DATA has the following phases.

- UTILINIT is the initialization of the utility.
- SCANTAB extracts the foreign keys. If it exists, the foreign-key index will be used for this; otherwise, a table scan will be performed.
- SORT sorts the foreign keys if not already extracted from the foreign-key index.
- CHECKDAT looks in primary indexes for foreign-key parents and issue messages to report any errors detected. It will report the RID of the row, the table that contained the row, and the constraint name that was violated.
- REPORTCK copies the error rows into exception tables and then deletes these rows from the source table if the DELETE YES option was specified.
- UTILTERM performs any necessary cleanup operations.

An example of using the CHECK DATA utility to check for and delete all constraint violations in table space DB2CERT.CERTTS follows:

```
CHECK DATA TABLESPACE DB2CERT.CERTTS
    FOR EXCEPTION IN DB2USER1.TEST_TAKEN
    USE DB2USER1.EXCP_TT
    DELETE YES
```

After a successful execution, CHECK DATA will reset the CHECK-pending (CHKP) status.

CHECK INDEX.   This online utility tests whether indexes are consistent with the data on which the index is created. The utility then issues warning messages when an inconsistency is found. The CHECK INDEX utility should be executed after a conditional restart or a PIT recovery on all table spaces whose indexes may not be consistent with the data.

The CHECK INDEX utility should also be used before CHECK DATA to ensure that the indexes used by CHECK DATA are valid. This is especially important before using CHECK DATA with DELETE YES. When checking an auxiliary table index, CHECK INDEX verifies that each LOB is represented by an index entry and that an index entry exists for every LOB.

The CHECK INDEX utility generates several messages that show whether the indexes are consistent with the data. For unique indexes, any two null values are taken to be equal unless the index was created with the UNIQUE WHERE NOT NULL clause. In that case, if it is a single column, the key can contain any number of null values, and CHECK INDEX does not issue an error message. CHECK INDEX issues an error message if there are two or more null values and the unique index was not created with the UNIQUE WHERE NOT NULL clause.

The phases of execution of the CHECK INDEX utility are very simple. It starts with the initialization and setup; then it unloads the index entries, sorts them and performs a scan of data to validate index entries, and performs any necessary cleanup.

An example of using the CHECK INDEX utility for all indexes in table space CERTTS follows:

```
CHECK INDEX (ALL)TABLESPACE CERTTS
    SORTDEVT 3380
```

CHECK LOB. This online utility can be run against a LOB table space to identify any structural defects in the LOB table space and any invalid LOB values. Run the CHECK LOB online utility against a LOB table space that is marked CHECK-pending (CHKP) to identify structural defects. If none is found, the CHECK LOB utility turns off the CHKP status.

Run the CHECK LOB online utility against a LOB table space that is in auxiliary warning (AUXW) status to identify invalid LOBs. If none exists, the CHECK LOB utility turns AUXW status off. Run CHECK LOB after a conditional restart or a PIT recovery on all table spaces where LOB table spaces might not be synchronized.

The execution phases of the CHECK LOB utility are as follows.

- UTILINIT is the initialization of the utility.
- CHECKLOB scans all active pages of the LOB table space.
- SORT sorts four types of records from the CHECKLOB phase and reports four times the number of rows sorted.
- REPRTLOB examines records that are produced by the CHECKLOB phase and sorted by the SORT phase and then issues error messages.
- UTILTERM performs any necessary cleanup.

An example of executing the CHECK LOB utility against the CERTLBTS checks for structural defects or invalid LOBs:

```
CHECK LOB TABLESPACE DB2CERT.CERTLBTS
   EXCEPTIONS 3 WORKDDN SYSUT1,
   SORTOUT SORTDEVT SYSDA
   SORTNUM 4
```

After a successful execution of this utility, the CHECK-pending (CHKP) and auxiliary warning (AUXW) statuses will be reset.

MODIFY Utilities

Both MODIFY RECOVERY and MODIFY STATISTICS are considered maintenance utilities. Both are used to remove unwanted data from the catalog tables.

Modify Recovery.   The MODIFY online utility with the RECOVERY option deletes records from the SYSIBM.SYSCOPY catalog table, related log records from the SYSIBM.SYSLGRNX directory table, and entries from the DBD. Records can be removed if they were written before a specific date or if they are of a specific age. Records can be deleted for an entire table space, partition, or data set.

This MODIFY utility should be run regularly to clear outdated information from SYSIBM.SYSCOPY and SYSIBM.SYSLGRNX. These tables, particularly SYSIBM.SYSLGRNX, can become very large and take up considerable amounts of space. For processes that access data from these tables, performance can be improved by deleting outdated information.

The MODIFY RECOVERY utility automatically removes the SYSIBM.SYSCOPY and SYSIBM.SYSLGRNX recovery records that meet the age and date criteria for all indexes over the table space that were defined with the COPY YES attribute. MODIFY RECOVERY deletes image-copy rows from SYSIBM.SYSCOPY and SYSIBM.SYSLGRNX. For each full and incremental SYSCOPY record deleted from SYSCOPY, the utility returns a message giving the name of the copy data set.

> **N O T E**   If MODIFY RECOVERY deletes all the SYSCOPY records, causing the target table space or partition to not be recoverable, the target object is placed in COPY-pending status.

Three MODIFY RECOVERY phases are UTILINIT for initialization and setup, MODIFY for deleting records, and UTILTERM for performing cleanup. The following example of the MODIFY RECOVERY utility shows how to delete SYSCOPY records by date for a specific table space.

```
MODIFY RECOVERY TABLESPACE DB2CERT.CERTTS
DELETE DATE(20000414)
```

The MODIFY RECOVERY utility can also be used to reclaim space in the DBD after a drop of a user table has been performed. The following steps need to be performed to reclaim DBD space.

1. Commit the drop.
2. Run the REORG utility.
3. Run the COPY utility to make a full image copy of the table space.
4. Run MODIFY RECOVERY with the DELETE option to delete all previous image copies.

MODIFY RECOVERY can also be used to improve REORG performance after adding a column to a table. After you add a column to a table space, the next REORG of the table space materializes default values for the added column by decompressing all rows of the table space during the UNLOAD phase and then compressing them again during the RELOAD phase. Subsequently, each REORG job for the table space repeats this processing in the UNLOAD and RELOAD phases. The following procedure helps to avoid repeating the compression cycle with each REORG.

1. Run the REORG utility on the table space.
2. Run the COPY utility to make a full-image copy of the table space.
3. Run MODIFY RECOVERY with the DELETE option to delete all previous image copies.

Modify Statistics.   This online utility deletes unwanted statistics-history records from the corresponding catalog tables. Records written before a specific date can be removed, or records of a specific age can be removed. Records to be deleted can be specified for an entire table space, index space, or index.

The MODIFY STATISTICS utility should be run regularly to clear outdated information from the statistics-history catalog tables. Deleting outdated information from these tables can improve performance for processes that access data from these tables.

MODIFY STATISTICS deletes rows from the following catalog tables:

- SYSIBM.SYSCOLDIST_HIST
- SYSIBM.SYSCOLUMNS_HIST
- SYSIBM.SYSINDEXES_HIST
- SYSIBM.SYSINDEXPART_HIST
- SYSIBM.SYSINDEXSTATS_HIST
- SYSIBM.SYSLOBSTATS_HIST
- SYSIBM.SYSTABLEPART_HIST
- SYSIBM.SYSTABSTATS_HIST

These tables are used for collecting historical statistics from a RUNSTATS execution. For more information, refer to the RUNSTATS discussion earlier in this chapter.

> **N O T E** The DELETE ALL option must be specified to delete rows from the SYSIBM.SYSTABLES_HIST catalog table.

The phases for MODIFY STATISTICS are the same as for MODIFY RECOVERY: UTILINT, MODIFY, and UTILTERM.

An example of MODIFY STATISTICS follows. This example removes rows that are older than 90 days from the CERTTS table space:

```
MODIFY STATISTICS TABLESPACE DB2CERT.CERTTS
 DELETE ALL
 AGE 90
```

Repair Utility

The REPAIR online utility repairs data: either your own data or data you would not normally access, such as space map pages and index entries. REPAIR is intended as a means of replacing invalid data with valid data.

Be extremely careful using REPAIR. Improper use can damage the data even further. You can use the REPAIR utility to

- Test DBDs
- Repair DBDs
- Reset a pending status, such as COPY pending, on a table space or index
- Verify the contents of data areas in table spaces and indexes
- Replace the contents of data areas in table spaces and indexes
- Delete a single row from a table space
- Produce a hexadecimal dump of an area in a table space or index
- Reset the level ID
- Change the PSID (Page Set Identifier) in the header page
- Delete an entire LOB from a LOB table space
- Dump LOB pages
- Rebuild OBDs (object identifier) for a LOB table space

The potential output from the REPAIR utility consists of a modified page or pages in the specified DB2 table space or index, as well as a dump of the contents. Execution phases of REPAIR are simply initialize, perform the repair, and then terminate the utility. The REPAIR utility cannot be restarted or used at a tracker site. (For more information on tracker sites, refer to Chapter 8.)

N O T E   REPAIR should be used only by a knowledgeable person.
Be careful to grant REPAIR authorization only to appropriate
people.

Diagnose Utility

The DIAGNOSE utility generates information useful in diagnosing problems. The DIAGNOSE
utility can output the following types of information:

- OBD of the table space and/or index space
- Records from SYSIBM.SYSUTIL
- Module entry-point lists (MEPLs)
- Available utilities on the subsystem
- Database exception table (DBET)

In the following example, a DIAGNOSE utility views MEPLs that can be used to find the service
level, including most recent APAR (authorized program analysis report) and PTF (program temporary fix), and when they were installed, of a specific DB2 module:

```
DIAGNOSE DISPLAY MEPL
```

Standalone Utilities

A number of utilities can be executed outside of DB2. These utilities are often referred to as
standalone utilities, or offline utilities.

DSNJLOGF (Preformat Active Log).   When writing to an active log data set for the
first time, DB2 must preformat a VSAM control area before writing the log records. The
DSNJLOGF utility avoids this delay by preformatting the active log data sets before bringing
them online to DB2.

DSNJU003 (Change Log Inventory).   The DSNJU003 standalone utility changes the
bootstrap data sets (BSDSs). You can use the utility to

- Add or delete active or archive log data sets
- Add or delete checkpoint records
- Create a conditional restart control record to control the next start of the DB2
  subsystem
- Change the VSAM catalog name entry in the BSDS
- Modify the communication record in the BSDS
- Modify the value for the highest-written log RBA value (relative byte address within
  the log) or the highest-offloaded RBA value

DSNJU004 (Print Log Map). This utility lists the following information:

- Log data set name, log RBA association, and log LRSN (log record sequence number-for both copies of all active and archive log data sets
- Active log data sets that are available for new log data
- Status of all conditional restart control records in the bootstrap data set
- Contents of the queue of checkpoint records in the bootstrap data set
- The communication record of the BSDS, if one exists
- Contents of the quiesce history record
- System and utility timestamps
- Contents of the checkpoint queue

In a data sharing environment, the DSNJU004 utility can list information from any or all BSDSs of a data sharing group.

DSN1CHKR. The DSN1CHKR utility verifies the integrity of DB2 directory and catalog table spaces and DSN1CHKR scans the specified table space for broken links, broken hash chains, and records that are not part of any link or chain. Use DSN1CHKR on a regular basis to promptly detect any damage to the catalog and directory.

DSN1COMP. This utility estimates space savings to be achieved by DB2 data compression in table spaces. For more information on compression, refer to Chapter 4.

This utility can be run on the following types of data sets containing uncompressed data:

- DB2 full-image-copy data sets
- VSAM data sets that contain DB2 table spaces
- Sequential data sets that contain DB2 table spaces, such as DSN1COPY output

DSN1COMP does not estimate savings for data sets that contain LOB table spaces or index spaces.

Following is an example of the type of output from a DSN1COMP utility:

```
DSN194 I DSN1COMP COMPRESSION REPORT
301 KB WITHOUT COMPRESSION
224 KB WITH COMPRESSION
25 PERCENT OF THE BYTES WOULD BE SAVED
1,975 ROWS SCANNED TO BUILD DICTIONARY
4,665 ROWS SCANNED TO PROVIDE COMPRESSION ESTIMATE
4,096 DICTIONARY ENTRIES
81 BYTES FOR AVERAGE UNCOMPRESSED ROW LENGTH
52 BYTES FOR AVERAGE COMPRESSED ROW LENGTH
16 DICTIONARY PAGES REQUIRED
```

```
110 PAGES REQUIRED WITHOUT COMPRESSION
99 PAGES REQUIRED WITH COMPRESSION
10 PERCENT OF THE DB2 DATA PAGES WOULD BE SAVED
```

DSN1COPY.   The DSN1COPY standalone utility lets you copy

- DB2 VSAM data sets to sequential data sets
- DSN1COPY sequential data sets to DB2 VSAM data sets
- DB2 image-copy data sets to DB2 VSAM data sets
- DB2 VSAM data sets to other DB2 VSAM data sets
- DSN1COPY sequential data sets to other sequential data sets

These copies can then be used to restore data. The restore can occur on the same DB2 or another DB2 subsystem. This is one way to be able to move data between subsystems.

DSN1COPY also provides the ability to

- Print hexadecimal dumps of DB2 data sets and databases
- Check the validity of data or index pages, including dictionary pages for compressed data
- Translate database object identifiers (OBIDs) to enable moving data sets between different systems and resetting to 0 the log RBA that is recorded in each index page or data page

DSN1COPY is compatible with LOB table spaces, when you specify the LOB keyword and omit the SEGMENT and INLCOPY keywords.

DSN1LOGP.   The DSN1LOGP utility formats the contents of the recovery log for display. The formats can be either a *detail report* of individual log records or a *summary report*. The detail report helps IBM Support Center personnel analyze the log in detail. (This book does not include a full description of the detail report.) The summary report helps you perform a conditional restart, resolve in-doubt threads with a remote site, and detect problems with data propagation.

You can specify the range of the log to process and select criteria within the range to limit the records in the detail report. For example, you can specify one or more units of recovery identified by URID (unit of recovery ID) or a single database.

By specifying a URID and a database, you can display recovery-log records that correspond to the use of one database by a single unit of recovery.

DSN1PRNT.   With the DSN1PRNT standalone utility, you can print

- DB2 VSAM data sets that contain table spaces or index spaces, including dictionary pages for compressed data
- Image copy data sets
- Sequential data sets that contain DB2 table spaces or index spaces

Using DSN1PRNT, you can print hexadecimal dumps of DB2 data sets and databases. If you specify the FORMAT option, DSN1PRNT formats the data and indexes for any page that does not contain an error that would prevent formatting. If it detects such an error, DSN1PRNT prints an error message just before the page and dumps the page without formatting. Formatting resumes with the next page. Compressed records are printed in compressed format.

DSN1PRNT is especially useful when you want to identify the contents of a table space or an index. You can run DSN1PRNT on image copy data sets, as well as on table spaces and indexes. DSN1PRNT accepts an index image copy as input when you specify the FULLCOPY option.

DSN1PRNT is compatible with LOB table spaces, when you specify the LOB keyword and omit the INLCOPY keyword.

DSN1SDMP.   Under the direction of the IBM Support Center, use the IFC Selective Dump (DSN1SDMP) utility to force dumps when selected DB2 trace events occur and to write DB2 trace records to a user-defined MVS data set.

RESOLVING RESTRICTIVE AND ADVISORY STATES

DB2 sets a restrictive or advisory status on an object to control access and help ensure data integrity. The following list outlines the restrictive and nonrestrictive object states that affect utilities and the steps required to correct each status for a particular object.

Use the -DISPLAY DATABASE command to display the current status for an object. Following is an example of this command to display those objects that are in a restrictive state:

```
-DISPLAY DATABASE(DBASE1) SPACE(*) RESTRICT
```

Output for objects in a restrictive state is shown next:

```
DSNT360I   +DSN8 **********************************
DSNT361I   +DSN8 *   DISPLAY DATABASE SUMMARY
                 *      RESTRICTED
DSNT360I   +DSN8 **********************************
DSNT362I   +DSN8       DATABASE = DBASE1   STATUS = RW
                       DBD LENGTH = 4028
```

```
DSNT397I  +DSN8
NAME      TYPE PART  STATUS              PHYERRLO PHYERRHI CATALOG  PIECE
--------  ---- ----- ----------------    -------- -------- -------- -----
TS001     TS         RW,RESTP
****** DISPLAY OF DATABASE DBASE1  ENDED   ********************
DSN9022I  +DSN8 DSNTDDIS 'DISPLAY DATABASE' NORMAL COMPLETION
```

The -DISPLAY DATABASE command can also be used to display objects in an advisory state:

```
-DISPLAY DATABASE(DBASE1) SPACE(*) ADVISORY
```

Output for objects in an advisory state is as follows:

```
DSNT360I  +DSN8 **********************************
DSNT361I  +DSN8 *  DISPLAY DATABASE SUMMARY
                *     ADVISORY
DSNT360I  +DSN8 **********************************
DSNT362I  +DSN8     DATABASE = DBASE1  STATUS = RW
                    DBD LENGTH = 4028
DSNT397I  +DSN8
NAME      TYPE PART  STATUS              PHYERRLO PHYERRHI CATALOG  PIECE
--------  ---- ----- ----------------    -------- -------- -------- -----
TS002     TS         RW,ICOPY
****** DISPLAY OF DATABASE DBASE1  ENDED ********************
DSN9022I  +DSN8 DSNTDDIS 'DISPLAY DATABASE' NORMAL COMPLETION
```

Some options find objects that are in a particular status. The following output shows objects in LPL status:

```
DSNT360I  +DSN8 **********************************
DSNT361I  +DSN8 *  DISPLAY DATABASE SUMMARY
                *    GLOBAL LPL
DSNT360I  +DSN8 **********************************
DSNT362I  +DSN8     DATABASE = DBASE1  STATUS = RW
                    DBD LENGTH = 4028
DSNT397I  +DSN8
NAME      TYPE PART  STATUS              LPL PAGES
--------  ---- ----- ----------------    ------------------
TS002     TS         RW                  000039-00003C
****** DISPLAY OF DATABASE DBASE1  ENDED   ********************
DSN9022I  +DSN8 DSNTDDIS 'DISPLAY DATABASE' NORMAL COMPLETION
```

Table 7-2 shows all the restrictive and advisory states, the objects affected, and what corrective actions need to be taken.

Table 7-2   Restrictive and Advisory States

Status Code	Status Name	Objects Affected	Corrective Action(s)
ACHKP	Auxiliary CHECK Pending	Base table space, LOB table spaces	1. Update or delete invalid LOB, using SQL. 2. Run the `CHECK DATA` utility to verify the validity of LOBs.
AUXW	Auxiliary Warning	Base table space	1. Update or delete invalid LOBs, using SQL. 2. Run the `CHECK DATA` utility to verify the validity of LOBs.
		LOB table space	1. Update or delete invalid LOBs, using SQL. 2. Run the `CHECK LOB` utility to verify the validity of the LOB.
CHKP	CHECK Pending	Table space, base table space	Check and correct RI constraints, using the `CHECK DATA` utility.
		Partitioned index, nonpartitioned index, index on auxiliary table	1. Run `CHECK INDEX` on index. 2. If errors, run `REBUILD INDEX` utility.
		LOB table space	Use the `CHECK LOB` utility. If errors: 1. Correct defects found in LOB table space with the `REPAIR` utility. 2. Run `CHECK LOB` again.
COPY	Copy Pending	Table space, table space partition	Take an image copy (best action), or use `-START DATABASE (db) SPACENAM(ts) ACCESS FORCE`, or run `REPAIR` and reset `COPY` flag.
GRECP	GBP Recover Pending	Table space, index space	`RECOVER` the object, or use `START DATABASE` command
ICOPY	Informational COPY Pending	Partitioned index, nonpartitioned index, index on auxiliary table	Copy the affected index.
LPL	Logical Page List	Table spaces, index space	• `START DATABASE ACCESS R/W` or `R/O`. • Run `RECOVER` or `REBUILD INDEX` utility. • Run `LOAD REPLACE`. • `DROP` the object.

continues

Table 7-2   Restrictive and Advisory States (Continued)

Status Code	Status Name	Objects Affected	Corrective Action(s)
RBDP	REBUILD Pending	Physical or logical index partition	Run the REBUILD or RECOVER utility on the affected index partition.
RBDP*		Logical partitions of nonpartitioned secondary indexes	Run REBUILD INDEX PART or RECOVER utility on the affected logical partitions.
PSRBD		Nonpartitioned secondary index, index on the auxiliary table	Run REBUILD INDEX ALL, the RECOVER utility, or run REBUILD INDEX.
			The following actions also reset the REBUILD status: • LOAD REPLACE with table space or partition. • REPAIR SET INDEX with NORBDPEND on index part; however, does not correct inconsistencies. • Start database ACCESS FORCE; however, does not correct inconsistencies. • Run REORG INDEX SORTDATA on index.
RECP	RECOVER Pending	Table space	Run the RECOVER utility on the affected object.
		Table space partition	Recover the logical partition.
		Index on the auxiliary table	Run REBUILD INDEX, RECOVER INDEX, or REORG SORTDATA.
		Index space	Run one of the following utilities on the affected index space: • REBUILD INDEX • RECOVER INDEX • REORG INDEX SORTDATA
		Any	The following actions also reset the RECOVER status: • LOAD REPLACE with table space or partition. • REPAIR SET TABLESPACE or INDEX with NORCVRPEND on index part; however, does not correct inconsistencies. • Start database ACCESS FORCE; however, does not correct inconsistencies.

Table 7-2 Restrictive and Advisory States (Continued)

Status Code	Status Name	Objects Affected	Corrective Action(s)
REFP	Refresh pending	Table space or index space	• Run a LOAD REPLACE. • Object will also be in RECP or RBDP status and will need appropriate action taken.
REORP	REORG Pending	Table space	Perform one of the following: • LOAD REPLACE entire table space • REORG TABLESPACE SHRLEVEL NONE • REORG TABLESPACE PART n:m SHRLEVEL NONE
		Partitioned table space	Rows <= 32KB 1. Run REORG TABLESPACE SHRLEVEL NONE SORTDATA Rows > 32KB 2. Run REORG TABLESPACE UNLOAD ONLY 3. Run LOAD TABLESPACE FORMAT UNLOAD
AREO*	Advisory REORG	Table space	Run one of the following utilities: • REORG TABLESPACE • LOAD REPLACE • REPAIR TABLESPACE
		Index space	Run one of the following utilities: • REORG TABLESPACE • LOAD REPLACE • REORG INDEX • REPAIR INDEX
RESTP	Restart Pending	Table space, partitions, index spaces, physical index partitions	Objects are unavailable until back-out work is complete or until restart is canceled and a conditional restart or cold start is performed.
WEPR	Write Error Page Range	Page range in error	Run a RECOVER utility on affected data.

SUMMARY

This chapter has dealt with the issues of data movement, organization, and placement in your database. Various DB2 Universal Database utilities that load data into database tables and unload data from tables have been reviewed: LOAD, UNLOAD, and DSNTIAUL. We looked at various options for the LOAD.

Having data in your tables is only the first step. The DB2 utilities that allow you to perform data maintenance on your environment were also reviewed. This included analysis of data in tables and indexes by executing REORG with specific conditions. This would physically change the organization of your table and index data by then using REORG if the conditions were met. We also looked at how to update the statistics of table and index data by using the RUNSTATS utility.

An important component of data maintenance is ensuring that your applications are aware of the updated statistics in your environment.

Many of the utilities, or particular circumstances, can put your data into a restrictive or advisory state. We looked at each of these and how to resolve them.

ADDITIONAL RESOURCES

IBM DB2 z/OS Version 8 Administration Guide (SC18-7413)

IBM DB2 z/OS Version 8 Utility Guide (SC18-7427)

IBM DB2 z/OS Version 8 Command Reference (SC18-7416)

Recovery and Restart

- Database recovery concepts
- Logging
- Image copies
- Data recoveries
- Disaster recoveries
- System-level backup/recovery
- DB2 restart

DATABASE RECOVERY CONCEPTS

DB2 has several methods for recovering data in the event of failures or when errors occur or disaster strikes. DB2 allows you to recover data to the current state or to an earlier state.

Many of the objects in DB2 can be recovered using various methods. You can recover

- Table spaces
- Index spaces
- Indexes
- Partitions of a table space
- Individual data sets
- Pages within an error range
- Individual pages

In order to ensure consistent operation and integrity of data, a DBA must develop a strategy for several recovery scenarios. These scenarios can include but are not limited to recovery from

- Application failures
- Hardware failures
- z/OS failures
- Space failures

It is possible to recover the DB2 catalog and directory, data, and objects to a point of consistency. This point of consistency can be the situation that is most current—called "to current" or to the end of the log—or to a prior point in time when the data was still consistent.

With current technology, hardware failures hardly ever happen anymore. Most likely, you have to perform a recovery because errors in program logic deleted too much or because update runs were run twice.

You can recover from failures only if you have taken the proper backups: image copies and log records. DB2 has its own copy utility that allows you to save the data by producing an image copy. Saving all data is called a full copy; saving only the changes since the last copy is called an incremental copy. DB2 for z/OS does its backup and recovery on a table space level or on an index space level. This means that if you perform a recovery to a table space and go back in time, *all* tables in this table space go back in time. It is not possible to perform a backup and recovery at a more granular object, or table, level, but you can recover at a more granular level, down to an individual page.

> **NOTE** DB2 will save only data, not the layout of your structures. Also, if you drop your structures, all recovery information is lost, and recovery cannot be performed. When you change your application, you often have to drop the structures and recreate them. In this case, you have to develop special scenarios whereby you have to unload and reload the tables.

A *unit of work*—also referred to as a unit of recovery, or a commit scope—is a series of recoverable changes within an application sequence. An application can have several units of work within it. If an error occurs, you can perform a rollback—back out of changes—of all the changes within the unit of work.

DB2 can perform a rollback only on a unit of work. Once a unit of work is committed, it cannot be rolled back in time. An example of a unit of work that can't be rolled back is a mass delete, which will update only the segment table, which is the only thing logged for a mass delete. After the mass delete is committed, the data no longer exists, and changes cannot be rolled back. The only information the log contains is the single update to the segment table.

LOGGING

When changes are made to the data in tables, subsequently changing the table space and index spaces, DB2 writes one or more records to its log so that a backout of the changes can be performed if the unit of work fails. DB2 can also use this information to reapply changes that may have been lost when recovering to a previous point in time. The primary purpose of the active log is to record all changes—inserts, updates, and deletes—made to DB2 objects.

The DML statements are recorded in the log as follows:

- INSERT: Entire after-image of the record is logged; called a redo record
- DELETE: The before-image is recorded; called an undo record
- UPDATE: Both the before and after images—undo and redo record—are recorded

Each log record has its own unique identifier. In a parallel sysplex DB2 data sharing environment, it is known as the LRSN (log record sequence number). When you are operating in a non-data sharing environment, this number is known as the log RBA, or the offset of the record in the log from the beginning of the log. In a data sharing environment, the LRSN helps to track the sequence of events that happen over multiple members in the data sharing group. Each member has its own log; if multiple members are making updates to the same data, the logs must be merged during a recovery. Because the LRSN is unique across the sysplex, this type of merging is possible.

Log Data Sets

DB2 physically records changes in log data sets. Every DB2 subsystem will have a predefined set of active logs on disk. The log records are then written to these active log data sets. When the active log data sets become full, DB2 automatically switches to the next-available log data set. After all the active log data sets have been used, DB2 will wrap around to the first active log. However, we do not want to lose log records, because we may want to use them for recovery or backout, so the active log data sets will be offloaded when they become full. Offloaded active logs are called archive log data sets and can be stored on disk or on cartridge tapes. As with the active log, you can have multiple copies of your archive data sets to protect yourself against failure. In the DSNZPARMs, you can specify the medium for archive storage, disk or cartridge, and how many archive copies you want to create.

> **N O T E** Recovery from disk archive data sets is much faster, and you can take advantage of DB2's ability to process the logs in parallel.

DB2 allows many archive log data sets, and you will want to keep them if a recovery is necessary. The retention period of the archive log data sets depends on your image-copy frequency and how far you want to go back in time during a point-in-time recovery.

DB2 also provides a dual logging capability to ensure that there are two copies of the active log data sets; if one is lost, the other can be used for recovery. During a recovery, DB2 applies from the active log the changes that are required to recover to the specified point in time. If the records needed to recover are no longer on the active log, DB2 will call for the appropriate archive log(s).

> **N O T E**   All production systems should be using dual logs to ensure that data can be recovered successfully.

Bootstrap Data Set

The BSDS is a VSAM data set that contains information about the DB2 logs and the records contained in those logs, as well as other information. The DB2 system will record all the current active log data sets in the BSDS. During offload processing, DB2 will dynamically allocate a new data set with a unique name. After the offload completes successfully, this data set is recorded in the BSDS, and a copy of the BSDS is created; if the archive log is placed on a cartridge, this copy of the BSDS is also placed on the same cartridge as the archive log. During a recovery, DB2 will use the BSDS to find all the available archive logs. The number of records that the BSDS can contain is determined by the MAXARCH parameter in the DSNZPARMs.

The BSDS should be large enough to record all archive logs. You should have the MAXARCH parameter set high enough for your environment and retain your archive log data sets long enough so that in the event of a recovery and you have to go back through older archive logs, the archive log data sets will still exist. If the data set is not recorded in the BSDS anymore but is still physically available, it is possible to place its entry in the BSDS by using the change-log inventory utility (DSNJU003). However, this can be done only when the DB2 subsystem is stopped and therefore will cause an outage. The proper setting for the MAXARCH parameter will depend on how large your archive logs are and the oldest point in time an application is allowed to recover to.

DB2 should always be operating with dual BSDSs. If for some reason one is lost, it will need to be restored, using the following general steps.

1. Rename the damaged BSDS.
2. Define a new BSDS.
3. Use RERPO to copy from the nondamaged BSDS to the new one.
4. Run DSNJU004 to list contents of replacement BSDS.

These steps must be performed to restore dual BSDS operation. If DB2 has to be stopped, it cannot be restarted until it is reestablished.

SYSIBM.SYSLGRNX

In the DB2 directory is a catalog table, known as SYSIBM.SYSLGRNX, used to determine the log records for a table space and recoverable indexes by recording the periods of updates for these objects. A row exists for the time period that a table space or index spaces had update activity occurring. Recorded in this row are the following:

- DBID (database identifier) and OBID (object identifier) of the object
- LRSN and local log RBA of the first update after open
- LRSN and local log RBA when a pseudoclose occurred, that is, no more update activity
- If data sharing, the member that performed the updates

This information will help DB2 determine what log data sets or parts of the log will be needed in the event of a recovery and speeds up the recovery process because logs that contain no updates for the object being recovered are skipped. The MODIFY utility can be used to delete outdated information from the tables that store image copy information.

The utility should be executed often and on a scheduled basis, depending on system activity. This will help improve performance for several processes that access the SYSIBM.SYSCOPY and SYSIBM.SYSLGRNX catalog tables. Owing to the nature of the data in these tables, they can grow considerably in size and require a good deal of space. It is recommended that, if the SYSCOPY and SYSLGRNX tables are very large, outdated information be deleted by using the MODIFY utility to delete entries by age. For example, it might be best to have one run of the utility remove rows older than 20 months. If you want to keep information longer, it is recommended that you unload the tables and also keep the DDL to recreate these tables. This will allow you to recreate very old data, possibly under a different name. The DB2 recovery information is not intended for these scenarios.

IMAGE COPIES

In order to be able to recover data when a problem occurs, you must have a solid recovery plan and a strategy for each of the many situations. This plan will include performing image copies on a regular basis. You create image copies of your table spaces and selected index spaces.

Frequency of Image Copies

The frequency with which image copies should be taken depends on the allowable down time for the primary user of the application. You should determine the clock time needed if you have to recover your data. If an application cannot be unavailable for more than 2 hours, you will need to take image copies more frequently than if your application can be unavailable for a complete day. Depending on the currency of data required in the recovery, you will have to determine when image copies can be taken and what types of image copies need to be taken. You may need to have incremental image copies taken throughout the day, or you may have to do only one full copy at the end of the day's processing. In some situations, an image copy is taken at the beginning of a batch window, especially if there are long-running batch processes. This allows for a restore in case something goes wrong during the batch cycle.

A number of technical considerations are involved in image copy frequency. The bare minimum you should allow is half the retention period of the archive log, less 1 day ([retention period / 2] – 1 day). This will guarantee that, at any moment, there are two valid image copies of the table spaces. You always want two valid copies because of possible media failure or to reduce the risk of inconsistent data on the image copy. After a drop and recreate of an object, all system-retained recovery information is gone. After you run utilities that will recreate the data (REORG, LOAD REPLACE without the LOG YES option), you have to run an image copy to establish a new base for recovery.

Dual Image Copies

DB2 provides for the ability to create dual image copies. If the primary image copy has an error and no secondary copy of your data exists, a recovery will fail. Even when it is possible to fall back to a previous image copy, substantial time is needed to perform the log apply from the previous image to where the failed image copy was taken. A previous image copy should be regarded as a safety net, in case the pages have errors. By uncataloging the most current image copy, it is possible to force a fallback. This works only if the image copies are cataloged.

In addition to using dual copies, you can make two sets of copies so that two copies are on site (local) and two copies are off site (remote). Using just the second copy of a dual-copy image for off-site backup is not the best choice, because if an on-site copy is bad, obtaining the off-site copy after a failure may be inconvenient, depending on where the off-site disaster recovery is located. Keeping two copies on the primary site will ensure that an immediate backup is available to use if a copy is bad; the same concept applies when recovering from image copies at the disaster-recovery site, where two copies should be maintained also. In order to do this, you could do the following in the COPY utility:

```
COPY TABLESPACE DB2CERT.CERTS COPYDDN(DD1, DD2) RECOVERYDDN(DD3,DD4)…
```

This would ensure that you took two copies for the primary site and two for the recovery site.

COPYTOCOPY

The COPYTOCOPY utility permits additional image copies to be made from the primary image copy. The copies are registered in the DB2 catalog with the following information:

- Original values from source copy: ICDATE, ICTIME, and START_RBA
- Additional values for COPYTOCOPY: DSNAME, GROUP_MEMBER, JOBNAME, and AUTHID

The target object is left in read/write access mode (UTRW), which will allow SQL statements and some utilities to run concurrently with the same target objects. A maximum of three copies can be taken at once. This is a total of four: local primary, local backup, remote-site primary, and recovery-site backup.

COPYTOCOPY has about a 5 percent performance benefit over the COPY utility and helps minimize the time needed for copying critical options in order to create additional remote-site copies.

The following is an example of the syntax:

```
COPYTOCOPY TABLESPACE DB2CERT.CERTTS
FROM LASTFULLCOPY RECOVERY DDN(rempri)
```

Tape versus Disk Image Copies

The fastest recoveries occur when the input data sets reside on disk. This applies to both image copy recoveries and archive logs. However, because disk space is more expensive than cartridges, there is a tradeoff between the cost of an unavailable application and the cost of disk space. Mounting, remounting, and winding cartridges can take a very long time. If you use the cartridge method and stack the files, you should use the proper JCL options during image copy and recovery so that the cartridge stays mounted and positioned. The handling of stacked files on cartridge can be automated by using TEMPLATE statements in the utility parameters.

Full and Incremental Image Copies

Two types of backups are available: full copies or incremental copies. A full image copy copies all the pages in the table space, whether or not it has changed (FULL YES is the utility default). Incremental image copies copy only the pages that have changed since the last image copy.

You can view the type of copy in the ICTYPE column in the SYSCOPY catalog table, along with the database name, the table space name, time of the copy, the start RBA/LRSN, data set name, and volume serial number, if the image copy is not cataloged. A full image copy will have an ICTYPE of F, and an incremental will have an ICTYPE of I.

Incremental copies of data can be useful. But because the procedures involved in taking incremental copies are more complex than those for full image copies—for example, how often to take incremental copies, and when to run the MERGE COPY utility—many database administrators choose to take only full image copies.

Data may be lost or the recovery time may be extended when using incremental image copies. Incremental copies are a substitute for the log. DB2 will try to mount the incremental-image copies to skip large parts of the log during the log-apply phase. But if this fails, DB2 notes the RBA, or LOGPOINT, of the last successful incremental and uses the archive log from that point on. If the archive log does not exist anymore from this point on, the recovery will fail.

Some administrators use the incremental copy utility for its speed and then run the MERGECOPY utility to merge the last full copy and latest incremental into a new full copy. This procedure combines the best of both worlds: ease of recovery and the speed of incremental image copies.

> **N O T E** You might want to reconsider the use of incremental copies if the data is very volatile and has more than 5 percent of the pages updated between copies, because the runtime of the incremental image copy will be longer than that of a full copy. If runtime is not an issue and the size of the image copy data set is, an incremental copy might be the best solution.

> **N O T E** If the feature for tracking space map changes is turned off (TRACKMOD NO) in the table space definition, incremental copies are required to perform a table space scan in order to find the individual pages that have changed and need to be copied. Only full image copies can be used in this case; therefore, if incremental copies are needed, avoid using TRACKMOD NO.

The image-copy utility has parameters to determine whether an incremental or a full image copy should be made. You can use user-defined thresholds in the image copy utility to control subsequent steps, depending on whether an incremental copy or a full copy was done.

Both full and incremental copies are important for creating backups in a 24/7 environment that must always be operational and that must be able to meet an acceptable recovery window. Full copies should be taken when

- A table is newly loaded using LOAD LOG NO **
- A table is loaded with LOAD RESUME LOG NO **
- A table is reorganized with REORG LOG NO **
- Table data has been modified extensively

> **N O T E** In many cases, marked by **, DB2 will enforce an image copy by setting the image copy pending (ICP) condition for the object. It is unwise to ignore this status—by, for example, using the REPAIR utility—unless you never intend to update the data again and keep the original input of the utility, such as a load in a data warehouse environment.

Incremental copies should be taken when changes have been made to the table since the last full image copy and processing the log would take too much time during the recovery. During the recovery, DB2 requires access to all incremental copies at the same time. If they reside on cartridge, this could be a problem because of the number of available units. If DB2 cannot mount all incremental image copies, it will ignore them and start processing the log again. You can prevent this situation by running the MERGECOPY utility to merge incremental image copies into a single set.

Copying Partitions and Data Sets

For both table spaces and index spaces, individual partitions can be backed up by the image-copy utility by specifying the partition number in the DSNUM keyword on the control statement of the COPY utility. Logical partitions of nonpartitioning indexes cannot be image copied; if PIECESIZE has been used, the pieces of an index cannot be individually image copied. This DSNUM will be recorded in the SYSCOPY table for each partition or data set that was copied.

If you image copy by partition, you also have to recover by partition. If you image copy the entire partitioned table space—no use of the DSNUM—you can recover the entire table space or one or more partitions.

Copy Data Sets

It is advisable to have multiple copies for an image copy in the event that one image copy becomes damaged. This can be easily accomplished via the COPYDDN parameter on the COPY utility control card. Here, you can specify a primary copy and a secondary, or backup, copy by specifying the DD names for the two copy data sets. This backup copy is intended to be a local backup copy so that during a recovery, it can be used if the primary copy is not usable. In many installations, this local backup copy is in addition to having a copy for remote-site recovery.

Follow these recommendations for making image-copy data sets.

- Consider using GDG (generation data groups) for backups to generate unique data set names for the image copy.
- Use DISP=(MOD, CATLG) for the ability to restart the COPY utility.

> **NOTE** Remember that GDG's are cataloged at the end of a job (not job step). If a job fails, the dataset name is already recorded in SYSIBM.SYSCOPY, but not the z/OS catalog. The next run will result in duplicate names being rejected by the COPY utility.

You can specify multiple objects in a single COPY utility, allowing you to take image copies of multiple objects—table space, partitions, and so on—in one job and to use parallelism. This is performed by repeating the object clause as many times as needed:

```
COPY TABLESPACE DB2CERT.CERTTS COPY DDN dsname1
 TABLESPACE DB2CERT.CERTTSPT COPY DDN dsname2
 INDEX DB2USER1.TESTIX COPY DDN dsname3
PARALLEL (3)
```

This example provides the ability to copy multiple objects using three parallel streams (PARALLEL (3)). DB2 will attempt three streams, but storage constraints may cause this to be lessened or ignored. DB2 supports parallelism for image copies on disk or tape devices. You can control the number of tape devices to allocate for copy function by using TAPEUNITS with the PARALLEL keyword.

CHANGELIMIT

You can use the CHANGELIMIT feature of the COPY utility to tell DB2 to look for a specified percentage of changed pages in a table space or partition before taking a full or incremental image copy. You can specify value(s) in the CHANGELIMIT parameter to allow for an incremental image copy or full image copies to be taken only when those values are reached.

Another COPY feature that can be used to observe changes is REPORTONLY, which would allow you to see whether an image copy is recommended because the CHANGELIMIT values were met. This feature could help to report whether any changes occurred against an object, possibly for auditing purposes. The following example shows the use of the CHANGELIMIT and REPORTONLY features:

```
COPY TABLESPACE DB2CERT.CERTTS CHANGELIMIT (5,30) REPORTONLY
```

This example gives a recommendation for a full image copy if the number of changed pages is greater than 30 percent. It recommends an incremental image copy to be taken if the number of changed pages is greater than 5 percent and less than 30 percent. An image copy will not actually be taken, only recommended, because we are using the REPORTONLY feature.

Possibly, an image copy will not be taken when CHANGELIMIT is used, thus creating an empty-copy data set. This situation is not very desirable, especially with GDGs, because you could lose previous image copies. Using the REPORTONLY option will set the condition code for this job step. The condition code will depend on the advice given and can be used in conjunction with conditional JCL; for example, full copies go to cartridge and incremental copies go to disk. This option can also be used to prevent an empty-copy data set.

Access during Image Copying

During the taking of an image copy you can choose whether to allow concurrent access. Two methods are available. The first method is to simply start the object in utility mode, issuing the -START DATABASE command and using the ACCESS(UT) option. Utility mode can be used for both table spaces and index spaces. Choosing this option will allow utilities to be executed only against the objects. Any other concurrent processes that try to access those objects will be rejected.

The second method to control concurrent access is to use the SHRLEVEL parameter on the COPY utility. The options are CHANGE and REFERENCE.

- SHRLEVEL REFERENCE forces the COPY utility process to wait until all writers are not using the table space or index space. They must commit their changes before the utility can continue. The benefit of this option is that readers are allowed against the objects being copied during the utility execution. However, no updating is allowed. This option also guarantees that the copies are created in a single COPY utility and do not have any incomplete units of work.
- SHRLEVEL CHANGE allows other applications to update the objects during the image copy. This means that some of the changes that were made during the copy may be on the log but not necessarily in the copy itself. An image copy created by this method is often called a *fuzzy copy*.

Regardless of the SHRLEVEL option that is chosen, DB2 will associate a log RBA or LRSN to the image copy and record this in SYSIBM.SYSCOPY. This is the point in the DB2 log from which DB2 will then need to apply log records during a recovery process.

Inline Copies

After using a LOAD REPLACE or reorganizing a table space, you must establish a full image copy so that you can avoid long log-apply phases in case recovery is necessary or if you are resolving a COPY-pending status. Taking a copy inline during the utility execution is much faster than executing the COPY utility afterward and avoids the setting of the COPY-pending status, allowing for increased availability of the table space.

This copy can easily be taken inline during the execution of the LOAD REPLACE or REORG utility. These inline copies are equivalent to a full image copy taken with SHRLEVEL REFERENCE, with a few minor differences, such as out-of-order pages or multiple versions. This would possibly cause the inline copy to be slightly larger than a normal full copy. But regardless, the inline copy is fine for recoveries, can be processed by all DB2 utilities, and can be the basis for future incremental image copies.

Inline copies can be requested on the COPYDDN keyword in the LOAD utility:

```
LOAD....REPLACE
    COPYDDN (local-primary,(local-backup))
    (RECOVERYDDN (remote-primary,(remote-backup))
```

They can also be requested on the COPYDDN keyword of the REORG UTILITY:

```
REORG
    COPYDDN (local-primary,(local-backup))
    (RECOVERYDDN (remote-primary,(remote-backup))
```

DFSMS Concurrent Copy

A DFSMS (data facility storage management system) concurrent copy can copy a data set concurrently with other processes. A concurrent copy can be used in two ways.

1. If the COPY utility with the CONCURRENT keyword is used, DB2 records the copy in SYSIBM.SYSCOPY. The RECOVER utility can use these copies and the logs for recovery.
2. A concurrent copy can be used to make copies outside DB2. In order to recover, the data sets will need to be restored before the logs can be applied.

> **N O T E**   CONCURRENT cannot be used if page size is > 4K or if the DSCVI DSNZPARM is set to allow the control-interval size to match the page size.

MERGECOPY Utility

The MERGECOPY utility merges existing incremental image copies into a single copy to help lessen recovery time. This utility should be executed based on the amount of exposure perceived and the amount of down time allowed in a recovery. For recover-"to-current" to be effective, running MERGECOPY frequently would be beneficial. If point-in-time recoveries are more likely, MERGECOPY will not be beneficial.

MERGECOPY improves performance for "to-current" recoveries because the full copy and possibly only one incremental copy would be needed to recover, instead of having to read through multiple incremental copies. However, for a point-in-time recovery (TORBA or TOCOPY), MERGECOPY may not have any benefit.

> **N O T E**   The MERGECOPY utility cannot merge image copies that are from different share levels (SHRLEVEL), and like the RECOVER utility will allocate all copies at the same time. So, if you create more incremental image copies than you have tape drives, you will have a problem.

Consider the timeline in Figure 8-1. If you want to recover to May 20 and the MERGECOPY on June 5 has not yet been done, the incremental from May 20 will still be in SYSCOPY and can be used to recover to. After the MERGECOPY, the copy for May 20 will no longer be in SYSCOPY, and DB2 must then go back to the full image copy on May 1 and do a forward log apply to May 20, making the time for recovery longer because more of the log will have to be applied.

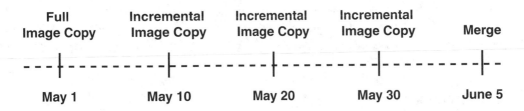

Figure 8-1 Sample recovery timeline

You can specify whether you want a new full copy or a merge of all the incremental into one new incremental copy. This is done with the NEWCOPY keyword: MERGECOPY...NEWCOPY YES or MERGECOPY...NEWCOPY NO.

When you perform a MERGECOPY and create a new incremental copy, all the rows in SYSIBM.SYSCOPY for the merged copies are deleted.

> **N O T E** Another important reason to merge copy frequently is that if DB2 cannot mount all incremental copies during a recovery— for example, if the incremental copies are on cartridge and there are not enough units—DB2 will choose to apply changes from the log. This increases the amount of time needed for a recovery and could possibly cause the recovery to fail because this log is unavailable.

You can obtain a report that identifies all referential relationships to a given table by using the REPORT utility with the option TABLESPACESET. You can then determine what table spaces need to be quiesced and image copied together. Keep in mind that this report covers only the relationships defined in DB2; other, application-defined relationships between tables may have to be included in the same recovery scope. The TABLESPACESET option is available for all utilities in combination with TEMPLATES. This will automate utilities if you use DB2-enforced RI.

Index Copy

It is not necessary to have an image copy of the index in order to recover it. An index can be rebuilt from the data in the tables by using the REBUILD utility. You can also recover the index from an image copy. In some cases, it may be faster to recover from an image copy of an index rather than rebuild it, especially if the index has little or no change activity. Index recovery can also be done in parallel with the table space recovery when you recover an index from an image copy. Once you enable an index for image copies by using COPY YES on the CREATE/ALTER INDEX DDL, DB2 records recovery information in both SYSIBM.SYSCOPY and

SYSIBM.SYSLGRNX. There are no changes to the log, because indexes are always logged to be able to roll back a unit of work. Copies of indexes can be only full image copies because the indexes do not have a space map to determine the updated pages. Incremental image copies do not apply to indexes.

DATA RECOVERIES

In order to ensure that it is possible to recover to a point in time when everything is consistent and in sync, a point of consistency, or a common quiesce point, must be established. This point of consistency is to establish a recovery set so that related objects will be recovered to a consistent point in time.

A point of consistency is established by executing the QUIESCE utility, which "quiets" the system and writes to the log the time during which there was no activity and everything was in sync. The utility does this by waiting for current units of work to complete and prevents any new ones from beginning. When the last unit of work has completed, a quiesce point is established. This point is recorded for each table space and index space in a recovery set by recording the START_RBA of the quiesce point in SYSIBM.SYSCOPY. This row will also have an ICTYPE of Q. These objects have a common point to which they can recover.

You determine which objects will be together in establishing this common point by using the TABLESPACESET keyword on the QUIESCE utility. You can also specify particular partitions of a partitioned table space:

```
QUIESCE TABLESPACESET
        TABLESPACE dbname1.tsname1
        TABLESPACE dbname2.tsname2
```

> **NOTE** By specifying WRITE YES, the default, you can ensure that all changed pages of the table spaces are written to disk.

> **NOTE** QUIESCE will drain the table spaces one by one. In a system that is heavily updated and long-running units of recovery can be in the way, the QUIESCE utility can cause a serious outage because it will keep the table spaces that it was able to drain locked, causing SQL to fail.

Another way to establish a consistent point for your data is to establish a copy set. If you perform a single copy of multiple objects using the COPY utility with SHRLEVEL REFERENCE, the objects will have the same START_RBA value, which will create a recovery copy set.

Planning for Recovery

Report Recovery Utility
This utility provides information that can help plan for recovery:

- Recovery history from SYSIBM.SYSCOPY
- Log ranges from SYSIBM.SYSLGRNX
- VOL-SER numbers of archive logs and BSDS
- VOL-SER numbers of image copy data sets

The information from the REPORT RECOVERY utility helps you identify what image copies, active logs and archive logs are needed to recover a table space.

Fast Log Apply
The RECOVER utility can use either a standard log-apply process during recoveries or a fast log apply (FLA). Normal use is the standard log-apply process, but the FLA process can be used if it has been enabled.

The FLA process is enabled if a nonzero value for the size of the log-apply storage resides in the DBM1 address space. This is the DSNZPARM LOGAPSTG set on the DSNTIPL installation panel.

The FLA process will use two buffers, known as FLA buffers. One buffer is for reading the log records, and the other is used for applying the log records to the table space or index space. When the read buffer fills, the pages are sorted and then applied, making this now the write buffer, and the older write buffer becomes the new read buffer and begins to fill. These two buffers continue this flipping process until all the records have been read and applied.

FLA also takes advantage of parallelism. It uses one task per object being recovered for applying the logs and an additional task for reading the next set of log records at the same time.

Check Data Utility
This utility will check the table space for violations of table-check constraints or referential constraints and report this information. Check constraints would be violated only if they were added after the recovery, so only referential constraints should show up as violated. You can execute the CHECK DATA utility on the entire table space or on individual partitions. The utility will provide options for handling various violations.

Violations will be reported only in the utility output listing unless the FOR EXCEPTION clause on the utility is specified. If the DELETE NO clause is specified, the utility will report the violations and copy the violators to an exception (shadow) table provided. When DELETE YES is specified, the violators are removed after they are moved to the exception tables. The rows will have to be moved back to the original tables after they are corrected, but telling DB2 to delete the violators will reset the check-pending flag.

> **N O T E**   Because it uses the primary index and, if available, the index on the foreign key, it is necessary to rebuild indexes before running the CHECK DATA utility.

Exception tables will have to be created for the CHECK DATA utility prior to its execution. These tables must have the same columns, in the same order, with the same data type, as the original table, although the column names can be different. The easiest way to do this is via the CREATE TABLE LIKE statement, creating an exception table exactly like the original. Two additional columns can be added to this table: a five-character column that gives you the RID or the original row and a timestamp column that gives you the starting data and time for the CHECK DATA utility.

> **N O T E**   If a timestamp column is desired, a RID column must already exist. But you can have the RID column even without the TIMESTAMP column.

Catalog and Directory Recovery

You start a DB2 systemwide recovery by first recovering the catalog and directory; no other recoveries are possible before this process is completed. Therefore, the catalog and directory need to be image copied often, so that the recovery process for these objects is as fast as possible.

> **N O T E**   If you lose your catalog and/or directory, you will not have an operational DB2 subsystem.

The time required for recovery of the catalog and the directory is crucial and needs to be kept to a minimum. Because DB2 performs the log apply for the catalog and the directory, it does not matter when you take the image copy of the catalog. However, it helps if you take a SHRLEVEL REFERENCE image copy just before you cut your last archive and take both this image and the archive logs to the vault or off site. This way, you make sure that the DB2 catalog contains all updates and that it is also valuable without the archive logs.

It is also important that the ICF (Integrated Catalog Facility) catalog be kept in sync with your DB2 catalog. For example, if the ICF catalog has yesterday's image in a disaster-recovery scenario, your DB2 catalog will reference data sets, such as image copies and/or table spaces, that do not exist, according to the ICF catalog. To avoid this problem, make sure that the recovery procedures of the ICF catalog match those of the DB2 catalog.

Because they also comprise table spaces and index spaces, the DB2 catalog and directory can fall subject to failures, such as a media failure, and these objects may need to be recovered. Recovering catalog data sets must be done in a specific order, owing to relationships and dependencies in the catalog. This order is as follows:

1. DSNDB01.SYSUTILX
2. SYSUTILX indexes
3. DSNDB01.DBD01
4. DSNDB06.SYSCOPY
5. SYSCOPY (3) indexes (IBM only)
6. DSNDB01.SYSLGRNX
7. SYSLGRNX indexes
8. DSNDB06.SYSDBAUT
9. SYSDBAUT (3) indexes (IBM only)
10. DSNDB06.SYSUSER
11. DSNDB06.SYSDBASE
12. SYSDBASE indexes (IBM only)
13. SYSUSER (3) indexes (IBM only)
14. All other catalog and directory table spaces and indexes
15. Catalog indexes (user defined)
16. System utility table spaces, such as QMF
17. Communications database
18. Object and application registration tables
19. Resource-limit specification tables

The objects in steps 1–11 need to be recovered serially; the objects in steps 12–19 can be recovered in parallel.

> **N O T E**   Never recover the catalog and directory to a point in time unless all user data is also recovered to the same point in time. Otherwise, the inconsistency introduced will corrupt data and can cause systemwide DB2 failure.

Table Space Recovery

The RECOVER utility is used to recover a table space. The utility's two major phases are RESTORE and LOGAPPLY.

To determine which full image copy is needed, the RECOVER utility looks at the rows in the SYSIBM.SYSCOPY catalog table. This full image copy is taken and merged with any incremental copies that are found in the SYSCOPY table, replacing any updated pages in the full copy and providing the basis for the restoration of the table space.

It is possible to use backups not created by DB2. However, restoring any object is then your own responsibility, and you must specify that the RECOVER utility has to perform a LOGAPPLY only.

After the full image copy is brought up to current from the merging of the incremental image copies, the next phase is the LOGAPPLY. This phase applies any changes that are on the DB2 log that were made after the image copies were taken. The utility reads the logs and applies these changes to the restored table space. The utility uses the SYSLGRNX table to identify the DB2 log range that pertains to the table space being recovered. LOGAPPLY also uses the START_RBA in SYSCOPY to identify the latest image copy that was used during the RESTORE phase and to know from what point records in the log must be applied. The LOGAPPLY phase is very efficient because it can sort the log on page number and then on RBA/LRSN.

> **N O T E** The START_RBA will depend on whether the image copy was SHRLEVEL REFERENCE or SHRLEVEL CHANGE.

Index Space Recovery

You can also recover indexes if they were enabled for image copies in the DDL definition. Using image copies, an index is recovered rather than being rebuilt from the table by using the REBUILD utility. Only full image copies can be taken on indexes. The LOGAPPLY phase works the same way and applies necessary changes from the log since the time of the last image copy. Even if an index was marked to be recoverable, it can still be rebuilt by using the REBUILD utility. This utility will extract the index keys from the data, sort them, and build the index again, ignoring all recovery information available.

Object Recovery

Partial object recovery is possible against a partition, a data set of an NPI, a partition of a DPSI, a single page, and an error page range.

> **N O T E** A single table cannot be independently recovered.

Just as it is possible to back up multiple objects in the same job execution, it is possible to recover multiple objects at the same time. In a single RECOVER statement, you can recover multiple table spaces, index spaces, partitions, or data sets. You simply repeat the `TABLESPACE`, `INDEXSPACE`, or `INDEX` clause:

```
RECOVER TABLESPACE dbname1.tsname1
        TABLESPACE dbname2.tsname2
        INDEXSPACE creator1.ixname1
        (PARALLEL (2))
```

The `RESTORE` phase is performed in parallel by using the `PARALLEL` option. In the preceding example, two streams of parallelism are attempted. The `RESTORE` phases for the objects are started and executed in parallel: One of the tasks reading the pages from the image copy, and the other tasks writing the pages that have been read.

The log is read only once during the `LOGAPPLY` phase. This phase is common for all the objects being recovered and does not use parallelism but can sort the log to improve performance.

> **N O T E** DB2 will lessen the parallel degree or even serialize the recoveries if storage is insufficient to support multiple streams.

Prior to version 8, parallel recovery was possible only if the image copies were on disk; if the copies were stacked on cartridge, the recovery processes were serialized. As of version 8, the stacked copies on tape can be recovered in parallel, improving usability and performance by implicitly retaining mounted volumes for input data sets used by `RECOVER` and `COPYTOCOPY`. Version 8 also allows dynamic allocation access for data sets stacked onto a tape volume. There is no unnecessary unloading and remounting of tapes between access

> **N O T E** This can also be applied via APARs (authorized program analysis report) for version 7.

Fallback Recovery

Sometimes, things can go wrong in recoveries, as when an image copy is not available, is defective, or is deleted. In these cases, DB2 has a few choices:

- **Use of local copies.** If the local primary copy cannot be used, DB2 will try to use the local backup copy. DB2 will not try to use the remote copies, assuming that they are being keep off site.
- **Use of incremental copies.** If an incremental copy cannot be used, DB2 will merge all prior incremental copies with the full copy, ignoring the defective incremental and all subsequent incremental image copies. DB2 will then start the `LOGAPPLY` phase at the `START_RBA` of the last incremental that was merged.

- **Invalid full copies.** If the full copy cannot be used, DB2 will fall back to a previous full image copy and then merge it with the incremental image copies, if available. If no good full copy exists, the table space is recovered from the log or a DSNU510I error message is issued, and the utility terminates in error.
- **Index space invalid copies.** If no valid index space copies exist, the same message as the previous point is issued, and the utility is terminated. It would then be necessary to perform a rebuild of the index from the table, using the REBUILD utility.

> **NOTE** If a REORG LOG NO or LOAD LOG NO was performed and no image copy was created, fallback processing will fail.

Point-in-Time Recovery

You can use the TOLOGPOINT parameter in your RECOVERY job in order to recover to any previous point in time. This parameter is specified to provide the log RBA or LRSN of the point in time for the recovery. This should be a quiesce point that was established for the copy recovery set. This information is obtained from the SYSIBM.SYSCOPY table or by using the REPORT RECOVERY utility.

After a point-in-time recovery has been performed, a row will be inserted into the SYSIBM.SYSCOPY table, with an ICTYPE of P for each object that was recovered, in order to allow future recoveries to skip those associated log ranges.

> **NOTE** In a non-data sharing environment, the TORBA keyword can be used, but it is recommended that TOLOGPOINT be used. In a distributed environment, TOLOGPOINT can also be used to recover two table spaces in two separate subsystems to the same point in time.

In order to avoid any pending conditions when you recover a table space set to a prior point in time, you will need to ensure that all the table spaces are in the same RECOVER control statement. You can use the TABLESPACESET keyword in the table space statement.

When a point-in-time recovery is performed for multiple objects in a single RECOVER utility control statement with TOCOPY, there is no LOGAPPLY phase but rather only a RESTORE phase to the last image copy. Therefore, multiple control statements must be used to prevent a CHKP status being set on the objects having RI relations. This will also cause an RBDP or CHKP on the indexes. It is wiser to specify a common START_RBA for a recovery copy set via the TOLOGPOINT parameter.

A point-in-time recovery can result in a variety of pending conditions.

- RBDP (rebuild-pending) results for indexes that existed on tables that were part of a table space that was recovered. This status is for indexes that were not copy enabled. A copy-enabled index will get this status only if it was not included in the recovery set. Recovering only certain partitions can result in RDBP*, a nonpartitioning index rendering it inaccessible.
- CHKP (check-pending) results from recovery of a table space that has tables with RI relationships with tables that were not recovered. This status also results when indexes are recovered for table spaces that were not also recovered.

In order to resolve these statuses, certain actions need to be taken. For an RBDP condition, the index will need to be rebuilt via the `REBUILD INDEX` utility. You will need to rebuild the index if a logical partition of a nonpartitioning index has RBDP* status.

For a CHKP, the `CHECK DATA` utility has to be performed. It will find any violations of referential integrity constraints and can optionally resolve them by removing the offending rows and any directly or indirectly dependent rows. CHKP conditions on an index may indicate that the index is inconsistent with the data in the table. The `CHECK INDEX` utility can help to resolve these inconsistencies by determining whether there are any; if so, you can run the `REBUILD INDEX` utility to rebuild the index and get it back in sync with the data.

> **N O T E**   `CHECK INDEX` will reset the CHKP flag if no inconsistencies are detected. If inconsistencies between the index and the data exist, you may want to immediately run `REBUILD INDEX` to resolve problems in a timely manner.

> **N O T E**   If any unexpected pending conditions, especially recovery pending (RECP), are encountered, carefully review the utility output. Utilities set and resolve pending conditions while they are processing. If, by the end of the utility, pending conditions still exist, perhaps something was wrong.

LOB Recovery

Special recovery considerations for LOB are needed because of the way large objects are stored and maintained.

Logging

An option allows you to decide whether to log changes to LOB columns. This option is specified on the creation of the LOB table space by using the LOG option; LOG YES is the default. LOBs larger than 1GB cannot be logged. If you have a LOB defined as LOG NO and then decide to alter it to be LOG YES, the LOB will be placed in copy-pending status. For LOBs that are defined as LOG NO, the force-at-commit protocol will ensure that the LOB values persist once committed. Even with LOG NO, the changes to the system pages and the auxiliary indexes are logged.

Point-in-Time Recovery

Even though there are no referential constraints between the LOB table space and its associated base table, the LOB table space belongs to the same table space set as the associated base table. A point-in-time recovery will need to recover both the base table and the LOB table space to a common point of consistency. Thus, a point of consistency will need to be established by quiescing the table space set or by using the COPY utility to generate a set of SHRLEVEL REFERENCE image copies for the table space set. The table space set will then need to be recovered to the RBA, the quiesce point, or the image copy set. A QUIESCE WRITE YES will record the point for the index on the auxiliary table if the index was defined with COPY YES.

AUXW Status

The LOG NO option—to not log the LOBs—means any log-apply processing required during a recovery will invalidate the LOB values that were recorded after the last restored image copy of the table space, because DB2 records when the LOB values were changed but not the update itself. This will place the LOB table space in AUXW status (auxiliary warning), and the invalid LOB values will not be able to be read by SQL.

The table space that was defined with LOG NO will need to be recovered to current by running the CHECK LOB utility on the LOB table space to identify which rows are invalid. The rows are identified by their ROWID. Then SQL is used on the base table to update the invalid LOB values or delete the row that contains the invalid LOB value. A second run of the CHECK LOB utility will be needed to verify the LOB value, and then it will reset the AUXW status. Even if the LOB table space is in AUXW status, DML statements can be used on the base table but will fail with an SQLCODE of −904 when they try to read an invalid LOB.

Recover Pending

A recovery-pending (RECP) state can be set on table spaces and index spaces to prevent access to the affected objects. This state can be set on indexes after executing a recovery utility to TOCOPY and TORBA on a table space or from utility abends or terminations of RECOVER, LOAD, or REORG. The condition can be reset by executing a RECOVER, LOAD REPLACE, or REPAIR utility.

DISASTER RECOVERIES

Another type of recovery requiring preparation is disaster recovery. The possibility always exists of losing an entire data center and having to recover at another site, usually known as the disaster, or recovery site. This type of recovery can be successful only with careful planning and practice.

In order to ensure success for a disaster recovery, regular backups of the data and log must be available at the disaster site. The more current the backups are, the better, in order to minimize data loss and update processing. The goal is to be restored and running as soon as possible.

Preparation

Many steps are involved in preparing for disaster recovery at a recovery site. This site needs to have copies of the data, including the catalog and directory, and the archive log data sets.

In order to prepare a recovery site to be able to recover to a fixed point in time, a weekly copy of the data, possibly with a DFSMS logical volume dump, must be available. This then needs to be sent to the recovery site, where it can be restored.

In order to do a recovery through the last archive copy, all the following objects need to be sent to the recovery site in a timely manner:

- Image copies of all user data
- Image copies of the catalog and directory
- Archive logs
- ICF EXPORT and list
- BSDS lists

A disaster site can also be made ready by using the log-capture exit in order to capture real-time log data and then having that data sent periodically to the recovery site. However, this is not often a viable option, owing to the overhead of use of the log capture in high-volume environments.

> **N O T E** It is possible that you are using special facilities that you have become dependent on, such as DFSMS/HSM. In this case, these facilities should be in working order again at the recovery site and completely up to date. If these facilities go back in time, you might be forced to go back in time also. If you use these facilities, include them in your recovery scenarios.

Image Copies

Image copies of the application data will be required. In the event of a disaster recovery, it is assumed that a copy of the local copies is available at the disaster site. An option exists in the COPY utility to make copies to be sent regularly to the remote recovery site. A remote primary and a remote backup copy can be made like the local primary and backup by specifying the data set names in the DD statements for the RECOVERYDDN parameter in the COPY utility control cards. Those copies can be used for recovery on a subsystem that has the RECOVERYSITE DSNZPARM enabled or if you run a RECOVER using the RECOVERYSITE parameter.

You will also need image copies of the catalog and directory and a listing of the contents of SYSCOPY, which can be obtained via an SQL SELECT.

> **N O T E**   If the image copies need to be tracked, you will want to catalog them. It is wise to have a single ICF catalog for a DB2 system so that all information about a system is in sync.

> **N O T E**   It is not necessary to keep index copies at the disaster site; they can be rebuilt, if necessary.

Archive Logs

Copies of the archive logs need to be made and taken to the disaster recovery site. These copies can be made by issuing the ARCHIVE LOG command to archive the current active DB2 log. A BSDS report needs to be created by using the print log map utility to have a listing of the archive logs, as DB2 will use the BSDS to find all the available archive logs during a recovery.

ICF Catalog

It is also necessary to back up the ICF catalog via the VSAM EXPORT command. A list of DB2 entries needs be recorded daily via the VSAM LISTCAT command and sent to the recovery site.

> **N O T E**   Often, the ICF catalog is the responsibility of a different department. Make sure that the ICF is always in sync with DB2. Create a single ICF catalog per DB2 system; perform EXPORT on the ICF after the DB2 catalog and directory have been image copied.

DB2 Libraries

The DB2 libraries need to be backed up to tape if they are changed. These libraries are as follows:

- SMP/E, load, distribution, target libraries, DBRMs (database request modules), and user applications

- The DSNTIJUZ job, which builds the DSNZPARM module and the DECP module
- Data set allocations for the BSDS, logs, catalog, and directory

> **NOTE** It is good practice to record when all these items arrive at the recovery site and to have backups of all documentation.

Minimizing Data Loss

One disaster recovery scenario is to perform volume dumps and restores. But significant data loss can occur. In order to minimize the data loss, you should perform a dump of all the table spaces, logs, and BSDS while DB2 is up, after issuing an -ARCHIVE LOG MODE(QUIESCE) command.

The ARCHIVE LOG command is useful when you are performing a DB2 backup in preparation for a remote-site recovery. The command allows the DB2 subsystem to quiesce all users after a commit point and to capture the resulting point of consistency in the current active log *before* the archive is taken. Therefore, when the archive log is used with the most current image copy, during an off-site recovery, the number of data inconsistencies will be minimized.

> **NOTE** If a -STOP DB2 MODE (FORCE) operation is in progress, the ARCHIVE command will not be allowed.

Taking the Table Spaces Offline

During a disaster recovery, the table space can be taken offline, or made unavailable, until the recovery is done. To do so, set the DSNZPARM DEFER to ALL, on install panel DSNTIPB, to allow the necessary log process to continue.

Tracker-Site Recovery

The TRACKER SITE option allows for the creation of a separate DB2 subsystem or data sharing group that exists only for keeping shadow copies of the primary site's data. The primary full image copies need to be sent to the site after they have undergone a point-in-time recovery to ensure that they are up to date. A tracker site is supported by transferring the BSDS and archive logs from the primary site to the tracker site, which periodically runs LOGONLY recoveries to keep shadow data current. If a disaster occurs at the primary site, the tracker site will become the takeover site (Figure 8-2).

Because the tracker-site shadows activity on the primary site, image copies do not have to continually be shipped. This allows the tracker site to take control more quickly.

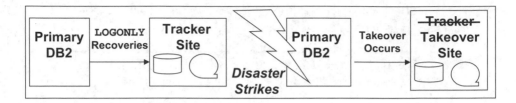

Figure 8-2   Tracker-site recovery

The two main reasons for choosing a tracker site are to minimize

1. The data lost during a disaster
2. The amount of time to get access to data during a disaster

You should to use a tracker site if it is important to recover data quickly at a disaster-recovery site with minimal data loss. This requires a DSNZPARM to be set in order to support the tracker-site option. Install panel DSNTIPO has a field called TRACKER SITE (DSNZPARM TRKRSITE), with 0 as the default setting. After installing the tracker-site subsystem, TRACKERSITE is set to YES in order to enable tracker-site support.

In order to start tracker-site support, both sites must be brought in sync by shutting down the primary DB2 subsystem and taking a disk dump of everything. This dump is restored on the tracker site. After the tracker site is started, the primary site can be started. If both sites keep connected, they keep in sync, but if the connection is lost, the primary site cannot queue the log data, and you have to bring both sites in sync again, using manual intervention.

It is important to make sure that both sites never lose their connection if this option is chosen. A situation to watch for when using this option is the fact that table spaces get out of sync because of utilities with the LOG NO option.

The nature of the tracker site means that some operations are not allowed:

- Some SQL statements: GRANT, REVOKE, DROP, ALTER, CREATE, UPDATE, INSERT, and DELETE
- Read-only SELECTs are allowed but not recommended
- Binds
- Many utilities, including COPY, RUNSTATS, and REPAIR

System-Level Backup and Recovery

DB2 version 8 provides more usability, flexibility, and faster recovery by allowing for system-level backup and recovery. This technology may be useful for disaster recovery and subsystem cloning.

The feature is implemented with two new utilities, BACKUP SYSTEM and RESTORE SYSTEM. The utilities perform the backups and restores of volumes defined to a COPYPOOL in hierarchical storage manager (HSM) and SMS. The COPYPOOL is a set of SMS groups that can be backed up and restored in a single command. This capability was introduced in z/OS 1.5 and invokes new HSM services to back up and restore subsystems.

Every subsystem will define two COPYPOOLs: one for data and one for logs. HSM and SMS will determine which volumes belong to the COPYPOOL and are needed for backup/restore.

The database COPYPOOL should contain volumes of associated databases and ICF catalogs. The log COPYPOOL should contain volumes with BSDS, active logs, and ICF catalogs.

Two methods are used for performing the copies and restores.

1. A FULL copy will copy the database and log COPYPOOLs; then these copies can be used to recover the entire system, using normal restart recovery or with the RESTORE SYSTEM utility.
2. A DATA ONLY copy will copy on the database COPYPOOL. These copies can be used with the RESTORE SYSTEM utility to recover the system to a point in time.

> **N O T E** The RESTORE SYSTEM utility can be executed from any member in a data sharing group.

After the RESTORE SYSTEM is complete, objects that are in recovery-pending (RECP) or rebuild-pending (RDBP) status will need to be recovered. These objects may include ones affected by a REORG or LOAD with LOG NO after the last copy was taken.

Two options can be used to back up the entire subsystem. One is the BACKUP SYSTEM FULL option, which copies both log and database SMS storage groups. Restoration can then be done, using normal DB2 restart recovery.

> **N O T E** DB2 logs and their ICF catalogs should be in the same SMS storage group.

The other option, BACKUP SYSTEM DATA ONLY, copies only database storage groups. The RESTORE SYSTEM utility may be used to recover the system to an arbitrary point between system copies.

> **N O T E** ICF catalogs for databases should be separate and reside with the data.

DSNJU003 (change log inventory) can be used to create a conditional restart control record to truncate the logs at the desired point in time:

```
CRESTART CREATE SYSPITR=log-point
```

The same PIT can be used for each member of the data sharing group. When restarting DB2, DB2 will enter System Recover Pending mode, and every DB2 member of a data sharing group must be restarted. At this point, you must run the SYSTEM RESTORE utility and then stop DB2 to reset the System Recover Pending mode. For data sharing, all members must be stopped. Then a start DB2 can be performed.

DB2 RESTART

DB2 can be stopped normally, or it may experience an abnormal termination for a variety of reasons. In order to bring the DB2 subsystem back up, the restart process must be performed.

DB2 can be stopped normally by using operator command −STOP DB2. If DB2 stops for other reasons, it is considered an abnormal termination. A STOP DB2 command has two modes: FORCE and QUIESCE. The FORCE option will roll back all active threads and not allow any new connections or work. QUIESCE will allow new threads to be allocated for an application that is currently running and will allow existing threads to complete but will not allow new connections. Following is an example of stopping DB2 with the QUIESCE mode:

```
-STOP DB2 MODE (QUIESCE)
```

DB2 uses its recovery log and the bootstrap data set (BSDS) to determine what to recover when restarting. The BSDS identifies the active and archive log data sets, the location of the most recent DB2 checkpoint on the log, and the high-level qualifier of the Integrated Catalog Facility catalog name. Many controls in DB2 help minimize the time necessary to restart DB2. We discuss some of those here.

- The −SET LOG SUSPEND/RESUME command can be used to temporarily freeze all DB2 activity. This command provides for a fast copy of an entire DB2 subsystem. A fast copy can be accomplished via ESS "Shark" FlashCopy or RVA Snapshot. These copies can be used for remote-site recovery or point-in-time recovery. When a −SET LOG SUSPEND command is executed, a single DB2 subsystem checkpoint is taken, log buffers are flushed, a log-write latch is obtained, the BSDS is updated with the highest written RBA, and a message will be issued to the console that DB2 update activity has been suspended. A −SET LOG RESUME command will release the log-write latch, delete the suspended message, and issue a log-resumed message.

- The checkpoint interval is important for DB2 recovery processing. The longer the time between checkpoint intervals, the more your DB2 applications are exposed to a longer restart time in case of a system failure. The checkpoint interval, set with the CHKFREQ parameter in the DSNZPARMs, can be changed dynamically with the -SET LOG command. This parameter is based on the number of log records (LOGLOAD) written between checkpoints or a given number of minutes (CHKFREQ). The following example sets the checkpoint time to 20 minutes:

```
- SET LOG CHKTIME (20)
```

In order to immediately force a system checkpoint you can issue the following statement.

```
- SET LOG LOGLOAD(0)
```

- An option in DB2 issues a warning message when a unit of work has written more log records than a defined threshold without a commit. This will let you identify those applications that would require a long backout and/or recovery in case of system or application failure. This option is set through the URCHKTH DSNZPARM. In order to minimize the amount of time it takes to recover from a system failure, we need to ensure that our applications are taking frequent commits.

Viewing Threads Affected by a Failure

If DB2 experiences an abnormal termination while transactions are running, you may need to determine which transactions were affected. This is important because these threads may be holding resources; they may have been making database changes when DB2 came down. The status of these units of recovery during the termination will be based on the point in time of the failure. The four states are in-doubt, in-commit, in-abort, and postponed-abort. To view the status of a thread, use the DISPLAY THREAD command. The following example shows the use of the command to find in-doubt threads after a termination that were not resolved during start-up:

```
-DISPLAY THREAD(*) TYPE(INDOUBT)
```

SUMMARY

We have looked at what it takes to back up and recover objects in DB2. Many scenarios need to be accounted for, and a successful recovery can come only from careful planning. Setting up and practicing these steps for recovery is key to knowing whether you can achieve your availability requirements.

ADDITIONAL RESOURCES

DB2 Universal Database Version 8 for z/OS Administration Guide (SC26-9003-00)

DB2 UDB Version 8 for z/OS and Continuous Availability (SG24-5486-00)

DB2 UDB Version 8 for z/OS Utility and Reference Guide (SG18-7427-00)

DB2 UDB Version 8 for z/OS Command Reference (SG18-7416-00)

Using RVA and SnapShot for BI with OS/390 and DB2 (SG24-5333-00)

DB2 on MVS Platform: Data Sharing Recovery (SG24-2218-00)

Developing Applications with DB2

Data Sharing

- Data sharing components
- Maintaining data integrity
- Performance and processing costs
- Movement to data sharing
- Distributed processing
- Recovery considerations

Data sharing, available in DB2 since version 4, allows an application to run on one or more DB2 subsystems in a parallel sysplex environment. The applications can read and write to the same data concurrently. Prior to data sharing, DDF was used to access data on other subsystems, or other, more creative means were used, such as replication between subsystems.

The subsystems that can share data must belong to a data sharing group. The subsystems in the group are known as members. Up to 32 members are allowed in a data sharing group. Only members in the group can share data, and a member can belong to only one group.

DB2 data sharing operates in a parallel sysplex environment, which is a cluster of z/OS systems that can communicate with one another. Some important components allow for this communication to occur and ensure the consistency and coherency of the data being shared. All members in a group share the same DB2 catalog, directory, and user data, as shown in Figure 9-1.

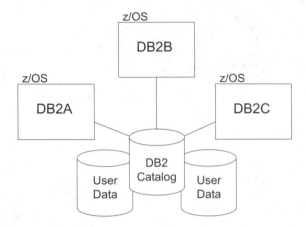

Figure 9-1   Data sharing

DB2 data sharing has many benefits:

- Improved price/performance by using S/390 microprocessor technology.
- Increased capacity with more power and a higher degree of intertransaction parallelism available.
- Continuous availability through the ability to hide unplanned outages and to plan outages and the ability to keep running even if a member is lost.
- Incremental, or horizontal, growth by adding processors without any disruption.
- Configuration flexibility, with the ability to start/stop members as required and separate subsystems by function, such as batch, ad hoc, and OLTP.
- Ability to split large queries across all CPCs (Central Processor Complexes) with sysplex query parallelism.
- Flexibility for scheduling existing workloads by cloning a CICS region on another MVS and removing the restriction of a CICS application that can run on only one MVS system.
- Increased throughput because applications can run concurrently on several subsystems.
- Reduced need for distributed processing, because applications will not have to use DRDA to communicate in order to share data, eliminating the overhead of DRDA for this purpose.
- Ability to have affinity and nonaffinity workloads in the same group, run workloads on different processors, or run a workload on a particular processor.
- Shared Data Architecture (SDA), based on coupling technology, which allows the use of high-speed coupling facility channels and reduced system-to-system communication, supplying multiple paths to the data for higher availability; dynamic workload routing; and is based on capacity, not location. Data partitioning is not needed for growth, and SDA does not rely on node-to-node communication for resources.

DATA SHARING COMPONENTS

Most of the hardware components in a data sharing environment are simply those in the parallel sysplex, but they are vital to the operation and success of data sharing. DB2 database administrators must learn about these components, how they are configured, and how they are used. Many performance and availability issues stem from these components.

Coupling Facility

The coupling facility is one of the most important components of a data sharing environment. This specialized piece of hardware with dedicated high-speed links is connected to each DB2 in the data sharing group. The coupling facility is the center for communication and data sharing among the subsystems.

At least two coupling facilities are needed for each data sharing group: One is required, and the other is mainly for availability and capacity. Also, for reasons of both availability and performance, at least one of these coupling facilities should be a dedicated processor that runs only the coupling facility control code.

An S/390 9674 or z900 Model-100 is a dedicated microprocessor that is used as an external coupling facility. The microprocessor is a CPC that runs only as a coupling facility in a logical partition with dedicated processor resources. This is the more optimal configuration because a failure of a coupling facility and a connected MVS image, which is more likely when on the same CPC, can lead to extended recovery times. You also get better performance by using dedicated hardware, as well as better connectivity to the coupling facility.

Internal Coupling Facilities (ICFs) are a relatively new option for coupling facility configurations. An IBM 9672 or z/900 machine can be configured with an internal coupling facility and can use one or more engines, depending on the generation of the machine. Such an ICF is a more attractive alternative to the dedicated 9674 or z/900 Model 100, mainly for economic reasons. You will still want to have at least one external coupling facility for high availability.

The coupling facility, usually one of the most important items in this environment, is usually significantly undersized in terms of storage. To start, you should have at least 1GB on each coupling facility. Attempting to support a data sharing group with anything less can be very difficult, if not impossible.

You will need enough storage to hold all the necessary structures and enough empty room to hold the structures from the other coupling facility in the group, in order to be able to rebuild, or support duplexed structures, all the necessary structures from a failing coupling facility, or a coupling facility that has been taken offline for maintenance.

The coupling facility consists of three structures important for DB2 data sharing: the shared communication area (SCA), lock, and group buffer pool (GBP). When a coupling facility is configured, it is often recommended practice to have the lock and SCA structures in one coupling facility and the GBPs in the other, as shown in Figure 9-2.

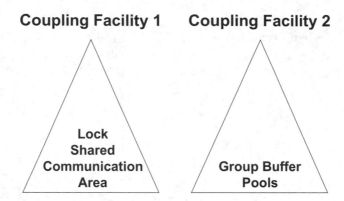

Figure 9-2   Structure placement in coupling facilities

Shared Communication Area

The SCA structure, also known as the list structure, holds all database status information, system information, and any critical information for any recovery situation. The SCA contains an array of lists that includes some of the following:

- Database exception table (DBET)
- BSDS information
- Stopped page sets
- LPL entries
- GRECP entries (Group Buffer Pool Recover Pending)
- GCLSN (Global Commit Log Sequence Number)
- EDM pool invalidations

Lock Structure

The lock structure controls intersystem locking and serialization on records, pages, table spaces, and so on. It also holds all the global locks. The lock structure comprises two parts. The first part, the lock list, contains

- Names of modified resources
- Lock status of the resource
- Modify and retained locks

The second part, the lock hash table, is used for quick intersystem lock-contention detection and contains

- Owning members of modified resources
- Lock-status information

The lock structure is connected by the IRLM during the DB2 member start-up. Sizing of the lock structure is not too difficult; normally, you can start with 32MB or more; for above-average workloads—high-volume DML—you could start with 64MB. If the lock structure is too small, you can have increased lock contention because there are only so many entries in the hash table for locks to be held.

Group Buffer Pools

The group buffer pools, known as the cache structures, provide high-performance access to shared data, data coherency, and serialization of updates to data on DASD. The group buffer pools are shared by all the DB2 subsystems that have a corresponding local buffer pool defined; if objects are defined in local BP1 and a GBP1 exists, these objects can be shared. This is done by providing a corresponding group buffer pool in the coupling facility.

Up to 80 virtual, or local, buffer pools are possible, so up to 80 group buffer pools are allowed. Of course, this number is limited by the size of the coupling facility; the group buffer pools will take up space in the coupling facility. Sizing group buffer pools is more of an art than a science, requiring knowledge of how the data in each buffer pool is accessed and a good breakout of objects into individual pools.

The GBP is allocated the first time it is used, and all the pages in it can be shared. The GBP registers data pages and also handles the invalidation of data pages cross-system. More information on group buffer pools is provided later in this chapter.

Structures and Policies

The structures mentioned so far are defined to the coupling facility via policies. Various policies are used for various definitions in the parallel sysplex environment. Policies, or couple data sets, store information about the systems in the sysplex, Cross-System Facility (XCF) groups and members' definitions, and general status information. Policies are formatted using the MVS IXCL1DSU utility in SYS1.MIGLIB and must be accessible by all members residing in shared DASD. Following are a few policies that are key to the operation of a data sharing environment.

Coupling Facility Resource Management. The CFRM policy defines the structures to the coupling facility, which is where you define the SCA, lock, and GBP structures. When defining the policies to the coupling facilities, it is important to leave room for growth of the structures. Also, you will want to plan carefully what the size should be, according to the space available in your coupling facility, and account for failover conditions.

An example of a CFRM policy follows:

```
/*--------------------------------------------------------*/
/* DB2 DATA SHARING GROUP: DSNDSGA / LIST STRUCTURE     */
/*--------------------------------------------------------*/
          STRUCTURE NAME(DSNDSGA_SCA)
                 INITSIZE(4000)
                 SIZE(10000)
                 PREFLIST(CF01,CF02)
                 REBUILDPERCENT(5)
 /*--------------------------------------------------------*/
 /* DB2 DATA SHARING GROUP: DSNDSGA / CACHE STRUCTURE(S)*/
 /*--------------------------------------------------------*/
          STRUCTURE NAME(DSNDSGA_GBP0)
                 INITSIZE(8000)
                 SIZE(16000)
                 PREFLIST(CF02,CF01)
                 REBUILDPERCENT(5)

          STRUCTURE NAME(DSNDSGA_GBP1)
                 INITSIZE(8000)
                 SIZE(16000)
                 PREFLIST(CF02,CF01)
                 REBUILDPERCENT(5)
```

Sysplex Failure Management.   The SFM policy holds information about the importance of each subsystem in the sysplex. During a coupling-facility failure and subsequent structure rebuilds, the REBUILDPERCENT contained in the CFRM is compared to the WEIGHT in the SFM policy to determine whether to rebuild a structure. An example of a SFM policy follows:

```
DATA TYPE(SFM)
DEFINE POLICY NAME(POLICY1) CONNFAIL(NO) REPLACE(YES)
   SYSTEM NAME(*)
   ISOLATETIME(0)
DEFINE POLICY NAME(POLICY2) CONNFAIL(YES) REPLACE(YES)
   SYSTEM NAME(*)
   ISOLATETIME(0)
   WEIGHT(5)
   SYSTEMNAME(SYS1)
   PROMPT
   WEIGHT(25)
```

Automatic Restart Manager.   The ARM policy is optional, but is highly recommended. The ARM keeps specific work running in the event of a failure. ARM will restart a DB2 member subsystem on the same or on a different system as defined in the policy. The more quickly you can get DB2 restarted in the event of a hardware failure or abend, the better. It is important for availability that all retained locks, discussed later in this chapter, are resolved quickly. The only way to do this is to restart the failing member, and this is where ARM is critical.

Links

High-speed links are used to connect coupling facilities to processors running the operating systems (z/OS and OS/390). There are several types:

- Multimode fiber (50/125 micron), supporting distances up to 1km.
- Single-mode fiber (9/125, or 10/125 micron), supports distances up to 3km whose characteristics are the same as those used by ESCON XDF.
- Internal coupling channels, supporting connections between LPARs and in a CPC.

One link between the coupling facility and the processor will suffice, but at least two are recommended for performance and, of course, availability. These links are not the same as XCF links, which may use channel to channel (CTC) and are used for inter-MVS communications. Rather, coupling-facility links are used for high-speed communication between MVS systems and the coupling facility (CF) via XES (Cross-System Extended Services).

Sysplex Timer

The sysplex timer is a required component of the parallel sysplex environment. You must have at least one—two are highly recommended. This timer keeps timestamps of the S/390 and zSeries processors. Synchronized timestamps are used by the DB2 members in the data sharing group. The timer is used to determine the order of events, regardless of which processor in the sysplex performed them. For example, the LRSNs can be guaranteed to order events for recovery because they are based on the TOD (time of day) clock generated by the timer.

> **N O T E**   The sysplex time should be on a separate power source or UPS. If all timers fail, all MVS systems in the sysplex are placed in nonrestartable wait states.

Cross System Coupling Facility

XCF is a component of z/OS. All DB2 members join an XCF group when they join the data sharing group. Each IRLM will join another XCF group. XCF is used for communication between IRLM and XES and to notify other members to retrieve database or system status and to control information changes made to SCA. DB2 also uses XCF for some intersystem communication and for processing DB2 commands and utilities within the group. Figure 9-3 shows two XCF groups.

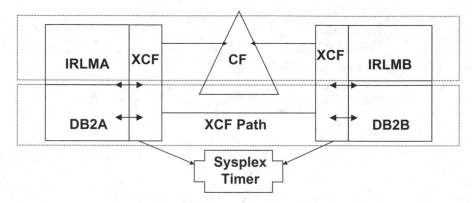

Figure 9-3 XCF groups

XCF services are of three types:

1. **Group services** provide means for requesting information about other members in the same XCF group via DISPLAY XCF commands.
2. **Signaling services** provide means for intragroup communication.
3. **Status-monitoring services** enable members to check their own status and to relay this information to others in the group. These services also allow for monitoring other members in the sysplex.

Shared Data

In a data sharing environment, many items are shared by all the members in the group. In order to have these available for each member in the group, the items must reside on shared DASD. The following items need to be on shared DASD:

- MVS catalog
- DB2 catalog
- DB2 directory
- Couple data sets
- Shared databases
- ICF user catalog for shared databases
- LOG data sets for read access, although separate log exists for each member
- BSDS data sets for read access, although separate BSDS data sets exist for each member
- Work files: required for queries using sysplex query parallelism, keeps DB2 connected to its work files regardless of where the DB2 has to be restarted; no longer DSNDB07

However, not all the data must be shared. Some data can be isolated for use on one member subsystem. These nonshared objects, defined unique to one member, can reside/remain on nonshared DASD, if you wish. Figure 9-4 shows how DB2 can exist in a data sharing group but not share data. To leave objects isolated to one member subsystem, you simply put the object in a virtual buffer pool that is not backed by a group buffer pool in the coupling facility. Any attempt to access an isolated object from the wrong member will result in an unavailable resource error.

> **N O T E**   Not sharing data may be a consideration if the application is not suited for data sharing or the data is not required to be shared among several DB2s.

MAINTAINING DATA INTEGRITY

Data defined as "sharable" can be accessed by any DB2 system in the group. Several subsystems can read and write simultaneously against the same data. This sharing is controlled via inter-DB2 read/write interest. Changed data, or data with inter-DB2 R/W interest, is always cached in the group buffer pool; this data becomes group buffer pool dependent. DB2 uses the coupling facility to control the invalidations of changed pages in each member's local buffer pools.

Consistency of data among the DB2 members in the data sharing group is protected through both concurrency controls and coherency controls. In order to provide concurrency controls among the DB2 members in the data sharing group, a new locking mechanism is used. Tuning locking is extremely critical to performance in a data sharing environment.

Locking

Locking in a data sharing environment works differently from the locking we have been accustomed to. Data sharing introduces explicit hierarchical locking (EHL). (Prior to data sharing,

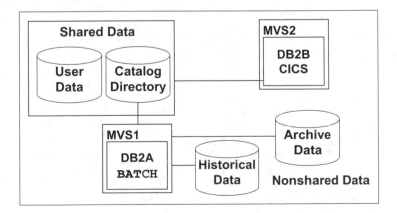

Figure 9-4   Sharing data

you were using implicit hierarchical locking.) The only difference is that with EHL a token is kept that identifies parent/child relationships. A parent lock is a table space/partition lock, and a child lock is a page/row lock (Figure 9-5). The benefit of using EHL is that only the most restrictive lock moves to the coupling facility, reducing the number of calls to the coupling facility to control concurrency, which can create a great deal of overhead. Lock avoidance still works with EHL, and type 2 indexes work best. This does not lessen the fact that the use of uncommitted read (UR) should still be considered wherever possible.

With EHL, only the most restrictive parent lock is propagated until it is necessary for the child lock to be propagated—recorded in the coupling facility—thus lessening the amount of lock activity. For example, if the parent lock on a table space is intent exclusive (IX), a child lock in share (S) mode on a page would not have to be propagated to the coupling facility lock structure, because the lock on the parent is more restrictive. In short, we lock only what is necessary and negotiate locks in CF if there is conflict. Child locks are propagated only if the parent locks are in conflict.

Local locks are the same in both non-data sharing and data sharing environments. These locks are requested on the local subsystem and provide only intra-DB2 concurrency control.

Global locks are the locks that a DB2 subsystem needs to make known to the group through the coupling facility. These locks are propagated to the coupling facility and provide intra-DB2 and inter-DB2 concurrency control. In a data sharing environment, almost all locks are global.

Whether a lock becomes global depends on whether the lock request is for an L-lock (logical) or P-lock (physical). Physical locks are owned by a DB2 member and are negotiable. Unlike normal transaction locks, P-locks are not used for concurrency but rather for coherency. Physical locks are of two types: page set and page.

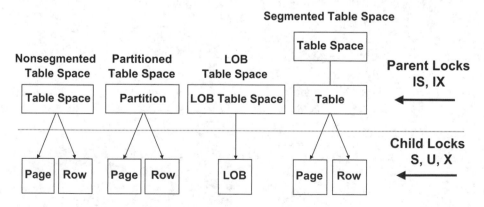

Figure 9-5 Parent/child locks

Page set P-locks are used to track intersystem interest between DB2 members and to determine when a page set becomes GBP dependent. These locks have different modes, depending on the level of read/write interest on the page set among the DB2 members. A P-lock cannot be negotiated if it is retained (kept due to a subsystem failure). It is released when the page set or partitioned data set is closed. Few P-locks are taken; they are usually held for long periods of time.

Page P-locks are used to ensure physical consistency of a page when it is being modified; these locks work at the subpage level and are used in the same manner as latches in a non-data sharing environment. Page locks are also used when changes are being made to a GBP-dependent space map page.

Page set P-lock negotiation takes place when P-locks are noted as being incompatible. The two members with the incompatible locks will negotiate the lock mode so that both can still use the object. Because the P-lock is used for coherency, not concurrency, this negotiation does not sacrifice any data integrity.

The reason for P-lock negotiation is to lessen the number of locks propagated to the coupling facility. The most restrictive P-lock is taken first and then, if necessary, negotiated so that another process can have access to the page set. Page set P-locks are used to track interest in a page set and to know when it is necessary to begin propagation of child locks, because of the level of interest in the DB2 members for the page set.

P-locks and negotiation can be thought of as "I need to know what you are doing; here is what I am doing; let's find a way to work together, or do we have to take turns?" It can also be thought of as an activity indicator.

L-locks occur in both data sharing and non-data sharing subsystems. L-locks can be local or global. Logical locks, transaction or program owned, are non-negotiable locks and work like the normal locks in a single-subsystem environment to serialize access to objects. L-locks are controlled by IRLM of members and are held from update to commit.

Logical locks are of two types. Parent L-locks are at table space or partition level—page set—and are almost always propagated to determine whether a conflict exists with another member. Child L-locks can be on a table, data page, or row. They are based on parent L-lock conflict. If no conflict exists, the child L-locks are not propagated to the coupling facility.

Two more types of locks introduced in data sharing are modified locks and retained locks. *Modified locks* are used to identify a lock on a resource that is being shared (updated). This includes any active X type (X, IX, SIX) P-lock or L-lock. A modified lock is kept in the modified resource list in the lock structure of the coupling facility and is kept regardless of group buffer pool dependency of the object. Modified locks are used to create retained locks if the DB2 member holding the modify lock fails.

Retained locks are modified locks that are converted to retained locks if a member of the group fails. Retained locks are necessary to preserve the data integrity in the event of a failure. This type of lock will be held when a DB2 subsystem fails and the locks belongs to the failing member and must be resolved before access to the locked object will be allowed by other members.

A performance/availability bottleneck may occur if proper procedures are not in place for recovering a failed DB2 member. Retained locks are held at the global lock manager (GLM) level and are owned by the local lock manager (LLM), not a transaction. Thus, only the DB2 member that had the lock can resolve it, so the failed subsystem *must* come up to resolve the lock. So, regardless of whether a transaction resumes activity in another subsystem, the locks are still retained, and the data is still not accessible by any process: Readers using uncommitted read can still view the data. The failed DB2 can be restarted on the same system or another system in the same group; it does not matter, as long as it comes up.

> **NOTE** Each local IRLM also keeps a local copy of retained locks for fast reference, so retained locks can survive a coupling facility failure.

It is critically important that retained locks be resolved immediately. The `RESTART LIGHT(YES)` command can be used to help perform this. The restart light option brings the DB2 subsystem up just enough to resolve the retained locks before shutting it back down. During a restart light, DB2 does not accept connections. To set up restart light in the ARM policy, the following syntax would be used:

```
RESTART_METHOD(SYSTEM, STC, 'cmdprfx STA DB2, LIGHT(YES)')
```

To manually start DB2 with restart light the following command would be used:

```
START DB2 LIGHT(YES)
```

Lock Contention

Three types of lock contention can occur in a data sharing environment.

1. Global lock contention (IRLM/real) occurs when there is real contention against two resources.
2. False lock contention occurs when two locks hash to the same entry in the lock table, but the locks are not in contention.
3. XES contention occurs because XES interprets locks only as X or S; therefore, some locks that appear to be in contention are compatible because they are intent locks.

> **N O T E**   All forms of lock contention need to be monitored and
> minimized because the process of contention resolution in a data
> sharing environment can get expensive and can be detrimental to
> performance.

Group Buffer Pools

Group buffer pools are structures in a data sharing environment coupling facility. They are used to allow for the sharing of data among multiple subsystems. When it is read by a member, a page is read into that member's virtual buffer pool and registered in the group buffer pool. If the page is updated, a force-at-commit will cache that changed page in the group buffer pool and invalidate the page in any other member's virtual buffer pool. This process, known as cross-invalidation, ensures that everyone is working with the most current page. Figure 9-6 shows how the registration of pages works.

Page directory entries are used to check the existence of a page copy in the group buffer pool and to determine which members will need to be sent cross-invalidation messages. Only one directory entry is needed for a page, regardless of how many virtual buffer pools the page is cached in.

Interest for a page is registered in the page directory when a member reads a page into the local buffer pool from disk or into the group buffer pool for a group buffer pool–dependent page set. If using coupling facilities at `CFLEVEL=2` or higher, DB2 prefetch can register up to 32 pages with a single CF interaction; otherwise, it is done on a page-by-page basis. When a page set or

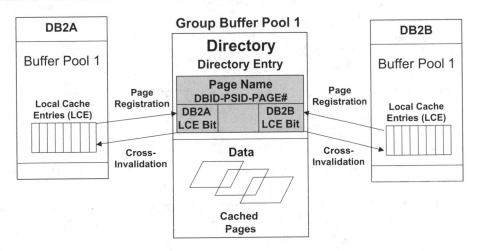

Figure 9-6   Group buffer pool page registration

partition becomes GBP dependent, all changed pages in the local buffer pool are moved synchronously into the GBP. All these pages, clean and changed, are registered in the directory in the GBP.

Each group buffer pool has a ratio setting as well as a size setting. The *ratio* is a GBP setting that establishes the number of directory entries to the number of data entries in the GBP. Without enough directory entries—entry for each page read on any DB2 member; only one page is registered, regardless of the number of members with interest—when a new page needs to be registered it will claim a directory slot and deregister the existing page in order to be registered. The process requiring the page that was deregistered will have to go to disk to reread and register the page. Depending on the number of time this occurs, significant overhead can develop. Use the -DISPLAY GROUPBUFFERPOOL command to determine how many times this occurs.

In order to change the ratio, you can issue the -ALTER GROUPBUFFERPOOL command. In the following example, the ratio is changed to be 20:1, or 20 directory entries for every data entry:

```
-ALTER GROUPBUFFERPOOL(GBP3) RATIO(20)
```

A few situations can cause the deregistration of a page. If buffers are stolen from the local buffer pool of a GBP-dependent page set, the pages are deregistered. This occurrence indicates a possible problem with the size and/or threshold in the virtual buffer pool because the pages are falling off the LRU (least recently used) queue. This would not be a problem if the page was not referenced, but if it is needed and has to be read back into the virtual buffer pool, it must also be reregistered.

If an existing directory entry must be reclaimed for new work, the page is marked invalid and deregistered and so must then be reread in from disk. This can happen if the group buffer pool is too small or the ratio is incorrect.

Sizing Group Buffer Pools

Sizing group buffer pools is not like sizing normal, virtual buffer pools. Group buffer pools are defined as structures in the coupling facility. They are given an initial size when they are defined in the CFRM policy and for performance and availability reasons should be created in a coupling facility separate from the one that holds the Lock and SCA structures.

Some standard rules of thumb exist for sizing, but most are generic at best. For the best sizing of your group buffer pools, you will need a good understanding of the amount of sharing that will be occurring against the objects that are in the group buffer pool. In other words, you will need to worry about object separation in virtual buffer pools even more so when implementing group buffer pools; otherwise, your initial sizing estimates will be rather difficult.

Castout

Because no connection exists between the coupling facility and disk, DB2 must have a way to move changed pages out to disk. The *castout* process, performed by castout engines, moves the changed pages from the group buffer pool through a private area in the DBM1 address space— not a virtual buffer pool—and from there they are written to disk.

The castout process (Figure 9-7) is triggered when the number of changed pages exceeds the CLASST (number of changed pages in the class queue) or the GBPOOLT (number of changed pages in the GBP) threshold or a psuedo/physical close performed on a data set by the last updating member. The CLASST threshold is similar to the VDWQT threshold on local buffer pools, and the GBPOOLT is similar to the DWQT threshold. Castout can also be triggered if the GBPCHKPT (number of minutes between GBP checkpoints) threshold is reached and a group buffer pool checkpoint is taken.

PERFORMANCE AND PROCESSING COSTS

Data sharing has thrown a whole new spin on DB2 performance and tuning. From application selection to postimplementation troubleshooting, problems can arise in several new places. Old performance problems that were acceptable or tolerable in the past are magnified in the data sharing environment. You need new skills in diverse areas to monitor and tune for overall performance.

New hardware and new rules operate in a data sharing environment. Contrary to popular belief, data sharing is not simply an install option! The introduction of the coupling facility in the parallel sysplex data sharing architecture accounts for a whole new set of factors to be concerned with

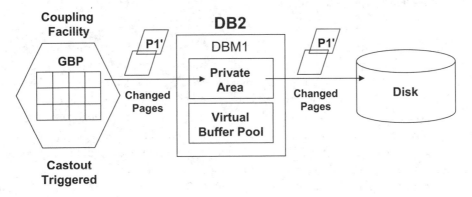

Figure 9-7 Castout process

in terms of performance. The coupling facility, unique to DB2 data sharing, provides many performance benefits over other sharing architectures used by other products, but it must also be cared for. You need to be concerned with activity involving the coupling facility owing to the number of accesses DB2 will have to issue to the coupling facility in terms of LOCK/UNLOCK requests, physical directory reads, cache updates, and reads of buffer-invalidated data, in order to maintain the consistency and coherency of the shared data.

In an ideal world with more processors in the complex, the transaction rate achieved by a single DB2 would be that multiplied by the number of available processors. Not necessarily. Because of the requirement of additional buffer management and global locking capability, DB2 and IRLM processing costs are increased, which can decrease the overall transaction rate attainable. Typical overhead seen for data sharing has been around 5 percent to 15 percent after the second member was enabled in the data sharing group. As each member is added, overhead is generally low but is very dependent on the amount of sharing among the members.

It is key for estimating data sharing performance to understand the overhead involved and to gain an appreciation of the tuning efforts required to minimize the impact of this overhead. First, you must set realistic goals, define performance objects, and, most importantly, tune your current environment. Keep in mind that bad performers will become worse and that new problems will surface. The key to a successful implementation is education of those involved in the migration and support of the data sharing environment. This will make the monitoring, tuning, and troubleshooting much less painful.

> **N O T E**   The majority of all DB2 performance problems in a data sharing environment will be concentrated in two areas: locking and buffer pools. However, many times these performance problems are still related to poor application design.

Processing costs for data sharing will vary, owing to the degree of data sharing, locking factors, workload characteristics, hardware/software configurations, application design, physical design, and various application options. The processing costs can be controlled to some degree by application and system tuning. Data sharing costs are a function of the processing required, in addition to the normal processing in order to have concurrency control for inter-DB2 interest and data coherency. Hardware/software costs can include speed of the processors and level of the coupling facility control code (CFCC), coupling facility structure sizes, and link configurations, level of hardware, software maintenance, and number of members in the data sharing group. Workload characteristics can include real, false, and XES contention and disk contention; workload dynamics; thread reuse; and application use of lock avoidance.

MOVEMENT TO DATA SHARING

The movement to a DB2 data sharing environment can be done in two ways. A new install of DB2 can be done, giving you the opportunity to start with a clean subsystem to move applications into. This also makes the monitoring of initial data sharing performance easier, and new naming standards could be implemented at this time. So, although a new install is less painful, it is not often practical.

The other option, of course, is to migrate existing subsystems together by enabling a DB2 subsystem as a data sharing subsystem and then adding members to the group. This is much easier for the movement of very large applications and has less impact on distributed processing. It is also the more common scenario for moving to a data sharing environment.

The complications come with the catalog merge process and the measure of application performance as the migration occurs. Whether you decide to do a new install or enable/migrate of existing subsystems, there will be issues of you can effectively measure the performance of data sharing and the impact it is having on your system. Keep in mind that not all applications belong in a data sharing environment. Some applications will still benefit from isolation.

Application Analysis

Application analysis, or selection, is the process of evaluating which applications will benefit from data sharing and so belong in a data sharing environment. You will need to determine the application objectives for data sharing in order to set performance objectives. Ask such questions as the following.

- What is the overall goal to accomplish with the implementation of data sharing?
- Are we looking to offload CPU cycles?
- Will we benefit from transaction-routing capabilities?
- Is 24/7 availability the driving requirement?

These are just a few of the questions that should be addressed in order to implement data sharing with maximum performance-benefit achievement in mind.

Current Environment Evaluation

Evaluate your current DB2 environment in terms of both system and applications before moving to data sharing. Even a movement to one-way data sharing can expose missed performance problems, although few because interaction with the coupling facility is minimal, and two-way data sharing can further magnify them. The time to fix known application/system performance issues is prior to any movement into the data sharing environment. Of course, these same items will still need to be investigated as workload and other factors change in the new data sharing environment. Such items to evaluate are locking activity, application commit frequency, bind parameters, use of standard rule-of-thumb recommendations, DSNZPARMs, software maintenance schedule/hiper application, buffer pools, and recovery/restart procedures.

Migration Issues

Despite the many issues when migrating to a data sharing environment, careful planning and testing the process will help things go smoothly.

Catalog Merging

Merging existing subsystems is most common and has various pros and cons. The advantages include easier movement of large applications and less distributed processing implications. However, the disadvantages include complications with the catalog merge process, owing to the fact that no automated tool is available to help with this process. Depending on the number of objects and methods, this process can be laborious and error prone. You will also have to deal with naming convention issues.

You do not want to merge subsystems that do not need shared data; nor do you want to merge test and production subsystems. Rather, you would want to merge subsystems if they are split out only because of capacity constraints, if they need common data, or if they rely on distributed connections or replication to satisfy needs that could be resolved by moving to a data sharing environment. When merging subsystems be sure to evaluate the security schemes for both subsystems and ensure that the same level of security will be in place when they are merged.

Migration of the catalog is not too bad, compared to migration of the data. You first decide which catalog to migrate all other objects to, taking into consideration the preceding items. Query the catalog to determine which databases, table spaces, and indexes must be defined in the target system. Then use DDL to define the objects in the target catalog. Depending on the number of objects, the creation of DDL for this could become a cumbersome process, especially if your DDL is not current, or you do not have a product or process to re-engineer the DDL from the DB2 catalog.

Naming Conventions

The establishment of a flexible naming convention is the most important planning event in the process of migrating to a data sharing environment. When done properly, it will reduce operational and administration errors by reducing confusion and will allow easy extension to the sysplex. You will want to plan names carefully because some cannot be changed at all, and any changes are difficult and often error prone.

The names need to be unique within the sysplex, and several categories of names need to be decided on: group-level names, DB2 member level names, IRLM group and member names, subsystem data sets (DB2), and ICF catalog names. Many may have to change from current naming convention. Of course, this will depend on migration options, especially if you are starting a data sharing group from scratch or migrating existing systems into the group. For a complete list of items to be named, refer to the *DB2 UDB for z/OS Version 8 Data Sharing Planning and Administration Guide*.

Workload Management and Affinity Processing

One of the biggest advantages of the data sharing environment is the ability to balance your workload across the members in the group. The DB2 subsystems work very closely with the workload manager (WLM) component of z/OS, which allows users to optimally balance incoming work across the subsystems in the group. WLM will manage workloads on the basis of predefined parameters, according to the characteristics and priorities of the work.

This allows you to give more priority and resources to OLTP transactions over long-running batch queries. WLM balances these workloads by ensuring that the long-running batch queries do not consume the resources needed by the online transactions, allowing the OLTP transaction to achieve the desired response times.

Deciding how to distribute the workload across the data sharing group will affect the sizing of coupling facility structures and affect certain aspects of hardware configurations. With data sharing, you can move parts of a DB2 application workload across processors in the sysplex. All the processors in the sysplex will have efficient and direct access to the same DB2 data. It is up to you to decide how that workload is going to use its resources.

Data sharing allows you to move processing away from processors with capacity constraints. This is probably one of the best and quickest benefits that can be realized by an organization that is constrained and having problems completing its workload because it has simply outgrown its processor capacity.

You can have all members concurrently processing the same data by allowing a transaction to run on any member in the group or only one member accessing data. This decision will directly affect the amount of data sharing overhead you will experience, owing to the control of inter-DB2 read/write interest among the members to maintain coherency and concurrency. By using affinity processing, you can force an application to run on only one DB2 subsystem; perhaps you could run OLTP on one subsystem, batch on another, and ad hoc on a third.

Distributed Processing

The DB2 data sharing group configuration can be transparent to SQL users and programs; they are not aware that a DB2 sysplex exists and that the system can select which DB2 member processes the SQL request. The group-generic, member-specific, and hard-coded methods support this.

- By using VTAM generic resources (group generic method), the client requester connects to a generic logical-unit (LU) name representing all members. Then VTAM controls which DB2-member LU is selected, and the workload is balanced at the client level.
- The member-specific method is the DDF sysplex support for distributed workload distribution, whereby a client requester can connect to one or more DB2 LU names, and then the MVS workload manager tells the client which DB2 LU names should be used. The workload at the thread level and can be stopped/started on an individual member basis.
- With hard-coded support, the client connects to a single DB2 member LU name. This way, the client controls which DB2 member is selected, and the workload is balanced at the client level.

Sysplex Query Parallelism

With sysplex query parallelism, a single query can be split over several members, providing a scalable solution for complex queries for decision support. Sysplex query parallelism works in much the same multitasking way as CPU parallelism but also enables you to take a complex query and run across multiple members in a data sharing group, as shown in Figure 9-8.

Good candidate queries for sysplex query parallelism are long-running read-only queries; static and dynamic, local and remote, private and DRDA protocols; table space and index scans; joins—nested loop, merge scan, hybrid without sort on new table—and sorts. Sysplex query parallelism is best used with isolation level uncommitted read to avoid excess lock propagation to the coupling facility.

A query is issued by a coordinator, who then sends the query to the assistant members in the group. The data is then processed and returned to the coordinator either by a work file, whereby the coordinator reads each of the assistant's work files, or by XCF links, if a work file was not necessary.

> **N O T E** Sysplex query parallelism uses resources in the subsystems in which it runs: buffer pools and work files. If these resources are unavailable or not sufficient, the degree—number of members used to process the query—may be decreased for the query.

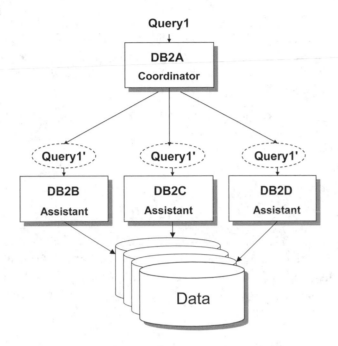

Figure 9-8 Sysplex query parallelism

RECOVERY CONSIDERATIONS

In a data sharing environment, each DB2 member writes to its own recovery logs and BSDS data sets, achieving a sort of striping effect. Each DB2 member must be able to read the logs and BSDS data sets of every other member in the group, so they must be on shared DASD with appropriate access granted. The reason it must be accessible is that the logs may be required from multiple DB2 members to do media recovery. A group restart will require access to all logs.

The SCA contains information about all members' logs and BSDS data sets; during the backward log-recovery phase of DB2 start-up, each member updates the SCA with new log information, which is then read by all DB2 members during a recovery. The BSDS data sets back up the contents of the SCA. Every member's BSDSs contains the same information that is held in the SCA, because the SCA can fail, as it is a cache in the coupling facility.

Logs and Recovery

The logs from several DB2 members may need to be merged for object recovery. The log record sequence number (LRSN) provides common log-record sequencing across members and is used to control REDO/UNDO records for data sharing. The LRSN is based on a 6-byte value derived from the sysplex timer timestamp and is store-clock-instruction based. The RBA is used for non-data sharing data.

Archive logs on tape should be avoided, as recovery will increase by the number of members whose archive logs must be processed. Depending on where archive logs are kept, this can become a lengthy process. Keep archive logs needed to a minimum by having large active logs, incremental copies, and frequent commits. Archiving to DASD is best; if using tape, never archive logs for more than one DB2 in the data sharing group to the same tape.

During a recovery, DB2 accesses the logs of all DB2 subsystems in the group and merges the log records in sequence by the LRSNs. DB2 then compares the LRSN in the log record to that on the data page; if larger, the change is applied. See Figure 9-9.

Recovery Scenarios

DASD Failure

When recovering from a DASD failure, you execute the RECOVER utility to restore to the most recent image copy and then apply log records; in LRSN sequence, to the end of the logs. This will require merging logs from all updating members, and the logs must be on DASD. If tape archives must be read, enough drives must be available for all RECOVERs, and there must be no deallocation delay, to avoid tape not being accessible to other members.

DB2 Failure

When a DB2 member subsystem fails, the locks are retained, and the other members remain active—one of the biggest benefits of a data sharing environment. When DB2 is restarted, forward recovery processing begins from the unit of recovery of the oldest in-doubt UR and the oldest pending write from the virtual pool to GBP. This is not as bad as non-data sharing because

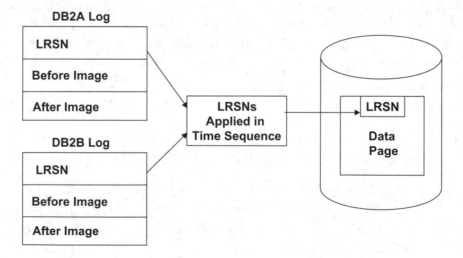

Figure 9-9   LRSNs and recovery

only checkpoint forces data to DASD, and data sharing has updated pages forced-at-commit to GBP. Retained locks are freed at the end of the subsequent restart. A DB2 subsystem can be restarted on the same or a different MVS subsystem. The RESTART LIGHT option on the START DATABASE command is used here to bring the DB2 subsystem up quickly just to release the retained locks.

Coupling Facility Failure

If a coupling facility fails or connectivity to it is lost, a dynamic rebuild of Lock or SCA structure is triggered. This rebuild will be triggered only if thresholds of the system that was lost exceeds the rebuild threshold in CFRM; alternatively, this can be done via an operator command.

When rebuild is caused by storage failure and rebuild fails, a group restart is necessary. In this case, all DB2 members come down, and then a coordinated group restart of all members is performed to rebuild SCA/lock from the logs.

Some pages may be marked GRECP (group buffer pool recover pending) and require page set recovery. These pages were in the GBP when the CF failed. This recovery requires a LOGONLY recovery; no image copy is needed. A -START DATABASE command will start the recovery. The GBP checkpoint determines how far back in the log to process.

Structure Failures

In these cases, you can lose a structure in the coupling facility. Each case has different recovery needs.

- A *lock structure* failure is detected by all active members at the time of failure; all members initiate rebuild, but only one rebuild occurs. The lock structure will be rebuilt into the backup coupling facility. The rebuild will use the active member's rebuild locks from local information. If connectivity to CF is lost, the weights from the SFM will determine whether the structure is rebuilt.
- An *SCA structure* failure is detected by all members, and attempts are made to rebuild into the backup coupling facility. During the rebuild, the remaining active members rebuild SCA from local information. If connectivity to a coupling facility is lost, the weights from the SFM will determine whether the structure is rebuilt.
- For a *group buffer pool* failure, the GBP will be rebuilt in the backup CF; any pages that were in the GBP will be marked GRECP. To recover page sets marked GRECP, you can issue a -START DATABASE() SPACENAM() ACCESS(RO) or ACCESS(RW). DB2 merges logs from the oldest modified page LRSN or the oldest pending write to DASD from the GBP to the end of the logs. Alternatively, you could run a RECOVER utility, LOAD REPLACE utility, or DROP TABLE statement to remove GRECP status. If connectivity is lost, DB2 will quiesce GBP-dependent page sets, and the result will be an SQLCODE -904 to a requesting application. Writes will then go on the LPL list, and GBP-dependent page sets will be marked GRECP.

NOTE   If the structures are duplexed—the primary exists in one CF and an active secondary exists in the other—during a failure, the activity is switched from the primary to the secondary, without the rebuild process.

SUMMARY

Data sharing provides many benefits and is being used in many shops throughout the world, supporting some of the most high-volume transaction systems to date. Migration to a data sharing environment is relatively easy and can be done with few or no application changes. Data sharing entails some new components, as well as some new tuning opportunities.

ADDITIONAL RESOURCES

OS/390 Parallel Sysplex Configuration, Volume 1: Overview (SG24-5637-00)

OS/390 Parallel Sysplex Configuration, Volume 2: Cookbook (SG24-5638-00)

OS/390 Parallel Sysplex Configuration, Volume 3: Connectivity (SG24-5639-00)

Parallel Sysplex Performance Health Case Study (SG24-5373-00)

Parallel Sysplex Continuous Availability—Case Studies (SG24-5346-00)

Batch Processing in a Parallel Sysplex (SG24-5329-00)

DB2 on MVS Platform: Data Sharing Recovery (SG24-2218-00)

DB2 for MVS/ESA Version 4 Data Sharing Implementation (SG24-4791-00)

DB2 for MVS/ESA V4 Data Sharing Performance Topics (SG24-4611-00)

DB2 UDB for z/OS Version 8 Data Sharing: Planning and Administration (SG26-9007-00)

Using SQL in an Application Program

- Table and view definitions
- Host variables and structures
- SQL execution validation
- Cursors
- Dynamic SQL

Suppose that you are writing an application program to access data in a DB2 database. When it executes an SQL statement, your program needs to communicate with DB2. When DB2 finishes processing an SQL statement, DB2 sends back a return code, which your program should test to examine the results of the operation.

To communicate with DB2, you need to choose one of these methods:

- Static SQL
- Dynamic SQL
- Open Database Connectivity (ODBC)
- Java Database Connectivity (JDBC) application support

Static and dynamic SQL statements can be embedded in application source programs. During the compilation process, these statements are extracted from the source program by the DB2 precompiler. The extracted statements are placed in a database request module (DBRM) that is the input to the DB2 bind process to create a package or plan that will be used when the program is executed.

ODBC lets you access data through ODBC function calls in your application. You execute SQL statements by passing them to DB2 through an ODBC function call. ODBC eliminates the need for precompiling and binding your application and increases the portability of your application by using the industry-standard ODBC interface, but the ODBC processor does issue dynamic SQL.

If you are writing your applications in Java, you can use the industry-standard JDBC application support to access DB2. JDBC is similar to ODBC but is designed specifically for use with Java and is therefore a better choice than ODBC for making DB2 calls from Java applications. Java applications can also use embedded SQL statements by following the SQLJ standard.

DELIMITING SQL IN A PROGRAM

Delimiters are used to distinguish SQL calls from the rest of the program. Delimiters and methods differ considerably by language. For all languages using the standard precompiler, however, the methods are very similar. For example, use `EXEC SQL` and `END-EXEC` to delimit an SQL statement in a COBOL program:

```
EXEC SQL
    A SQL statement
END-EXEC.
```

> **N O T E**   For REXX, precede the statement with `EXEC SQL`.
> If it is in a literal string, enclose the statement in single or double
> quotation marks.

TABLE AND VIEW DEFINITIONS

Before your program issues SQL statements that retrieve, update, delete, or insert data, you should declare the tables and views your program accesses. To do this, include an SQL `DECLARE` statement in your program.

You do not have to declare tables or views, but there are advantages if you do. One advantage is documentation. For example, the `DECLARE` statement specifies the structure of the table or view you are working with and the data type of each column. You can refer to the `DECLARE` statement for the column names and data types in the table or view. Another advantage is that the DB2 precompiler uses your declarations to make sure that you have used correct column names and data types in your SQL statements. The DB2 precompiler issues a warning message when the column names and data types do not correspond to the SQL `DECLARE` statements in your program. If the `DECLARE` statements are omitted, the precompiler will also generate a warning.

One way to declare a table or a view is to code a `DECLARE` statement in the *working-storage section*, or *linkage section*, within the *data division* of your COBOL program. Specify the name of the table, and list each column and its data type. When you declare a table or a view, you specify the table name in the DECLARE TABLE statement, regardless of whether the table name refers to a table or a view. For example, the DECLARE TABLE statement for the DB2USER1.TEST table looks like this:

```
EXEC SQL
DECLARE DB2USER1.TEST_TABLE
     (NUMBER          CHAR(6)          NOT NULL,
      NAME            VARCHAR(50)      NOT NULL,
      TYPE            CHAR(1)          NOT NULL,
      CUT_SCORE       DECIMAL(6,2),
      LENGTH          SMALLINT         NOT NULL,
      TOTALTAKEN      SMALLINT         NOT NULL)
END-EXEC.
```

> **N O T E**   An alternative to coding the DECLARE statement manually is to use DCLGEN, the declarations generator supplied with DB2. DCLGEN is covered later in this chapter.

> **N O T E**   When a table or a view that contains a column with a distinct type is declared, it is best to declare that column with the source type of the distinct type rather than with the distinct type itself. When the column is declared with the source type, DB2 can check embedded SQL statements that reference that column at precompile time.

HOST VARIABLES AND STRUCTURES

A *host variable* is a data item declared in the host language for use within an SQL statement. Using host variables, you can

- Retrieve data into the host variable for your application program's use
- Place data into the host variable to insert into a table or to change the contents of a row
- Use the data in the host variable when evaluating a WHERE or HAVING clause
- Assign the value in the host variable to a special register, such as CURRENT SQLID and CURRENT DEGREE
- Insert null values in columns, using a host indicator variable that contains a negative value
- Use the data in the host variable in statements that process dynamic SQL, such as EXECUTE, PREPARE, and OPEN

A *host structure* is a group of host variables that an SQL statement can refer to using a single name. You can use host structures in all languages except REXX. Use the host language statements to define the host structures.

In some languages, such as C, the program variables that are used as host variables must be defined in a section of the program that is delimited by BEGIN DECLARE SECTION and END DECLARE SECTION statements, as follows:

```
EXEC SQL BEGIN DECLARE SECTION;
DECLARE DB2USER1.TEST_TABLE
   CHAR NUMBER[7];
   CHAR NAME[51];
   SHORT LENGTH;
EXEC SQL END DECLARE SECTION;
```

Using Host Variables

Any valid host variable name can be used in an SQL statement. Host variables must be declared to the host program before they can be used. Host variables are used by DB2 to

- Retrieve data and put it into the host variables for use by the application program
- Insert data into a table or update it from the data in the host variable
- Evaluate a WHERE or HAVING clause using the data in the host variable

However, host variables cannot be used to represent a table, a column, or a view.

To optimize performance, make sure that the host language declaration maps as closely as possible to the data type of the associated data in the database. Table, view, or column names can be specified at runtime when using dynamic SQL. We discuss dynamic SQL later in this chapter.

Host variables follow the naming conventions of the host language. A colon (:) must precede host variables used in SQL to tell DB2 that the variable is not a column name. A colon must *not* precede host variables outside of SQL statements.

In the following example, :CANPHONE and :CIDNO are host variables; the values will be supplied at runtime.

```
EXEC SQL
   UPDATE CANDIDATE
      SET PHONE = :CANPHONE
      WHERE CID = :CIDNO
END-EXEC.
```

The host variables can be used to specify a program data area to contain the column values of a retrieved row or rows.

Using Host Structures

A host structure can be used in place of one or more host variables. In the following example, assume that a COBOL program includes the following SQL statement:

```
EXEC SQL
    SELECT CID, LNAME, FNAME
    INTO :CIDHV,:LNAMEHV,:FNAMEHV
    FROM DB2USER1.CANDIDATE
    WHERE CID =:CIDHV
END-EXEC.
```

If you want to avoid listing host variables, you can substitute the name of a structure, say, :CANDHS, that contains :CIDHV, :LNAMEHV, and :FNAMEHV. The example then reads

```
EXEC SQL
    SELECT CID, LNAME, FNAME
    INTO :CANDHS
    FROM DB2USER1.CANDIDATE
    WHERE CID =:CIDHV
END-EXEC.
```

Host structures can be declared manually, or DCLGEN can be used to generate a COBOL record description, PL/I structure declaration, or C structure declaration that corresponds to the columns of a table. DCLGEN, the declarations generator supplied with DB2, produces a DECLARE statement for use in a C, COBOL, or PL/I program so that the declares for the tables do not need to be manually coded. DCLGEN generates a table declaration and puts it into a member of a partitioned data set that you can include in your program. When you use DCLGEN to generate a table's declaration, DB2 gets the relevant information from the DB2 catalog, which contains information about the table's definition and the definition of each column within the table. DCLGEN uses this information to produce a complete SQL DECLARE statement for the table or view and a matching PL/I or C structure declaration or COBOL record description.

> **NOTE**   DCLGEN can be used only on existing tables.

Before the program is precompiled, DCLGEN must be used, and the DCLGEN name of the table or view must be supplied. In order to use the declarations generated by DCLGEN in the program, the SQL INCLUDE statement is used. The following example shows this INCLUDE statement for the CAND source member generated by DCLGEN:

```
EXEC SQL
    INCLUDE CAND
END-EXEC
```

DB2 must be active before DCLGEN can be used. DCLGEN can be started in several ways:

- **From ISPF through DB2I.** Select the DCLGEN option on the DB2I Primary Option Menu panel. Fill in the DCLGEN panel with the information it needs to build the declarations. Then press Enter.
- **Directly from TSO.** Sign on to TSO, issue the TSO command DSN, and then issue the subcommand DCLGEN.
- **From a CLIST.** In TSO foreground or background, run a CLIST that issues DSN, and then run DCLGEN.
- **With JCL.** Supply the required information, using JCL, and run DCLGEN in batch.

Following is an example of DCLGEN output:

```
****************************************************************
      DCLGEN TABLE(DB2USER1.TEST)
          LIBRARY(DB2U01.DCLGEN.LIB(TEST))
          LANGUAGE(COBOL)
          APOST
****************************************************************
   EXEC SQL DECLARE DB2USER1.TEST TABLE
      (NUMBER           CHAR(6)           NOT NULL,
       NAME             VARCHAR(50)       NOT NULL,
       TYPE             CHAR(1)           NOT NULL,
       CUT_SCORE        DECIMAL(6,2),
       LENGTH           SMALLINT          NOT NULL,
       TOTALTAKEN       SMALLINT          NOT NULL)
        END-EXEC.
****************************************************************
* COBOL DECLARATION FOR TABLE DB2USER1.TEST
****************************************************************
   01   DCLTEST.
        10 NUMBER               PIC X(63).
        10 NAME.
           49 NAME-LEN          PIC S9(4) COMP-4.
           49 NAME-TEXT         PIC X(50).
        10 TYPE                 PIC X(1).
        10 CUTSCRE              PIC S(4)V9(2) COMP-3.
        10 LENGTH               PIC 9(5) COMP.
        10 TOTALTKN             PIC 9(5) COMP.
****************************************************************
*    THE NUMBER OF COLUMNS DESCRIBED BY THIS DECLARATION IS 6
****************************************************************
```

Retrieving a Single Row of Data

The INTO clause of the SELECT statement names one or more host variables to contain the column values returned. The named variables correspond one to one with the list of column names in the SELECT list. The following example retrieves CID, LNAME, and FNAME from the CANDIDATE table and populates the host variables. Note that a colon precedes each host variable. You can define a data area in your program to hold each column and then name the data areas with an INTO clause, as in the following example:

```
EXEC SQL
    SELECT CID, LNAME, FNAME
    INTO :CIDHV,:LNAMEHV,:FNAMEHV
    FROM DB2USER1.CANDIDATE
    WHERE CID =:CIDHV
END-EXEC.
```

In the DATA DIVISION of the program, the host variables CIDHV, LNAMEHV, and FNAMEHV must be declared and need to be compatible with the data types in the columns CID, LNAME, and FNAME of the DB2USER1.CANDIDATE table.

> **NOTE** If the SELECT statement returns more than one row, a -811 error code will result, and any data returned is undefined and unpredictable.

Retrieving Multiple Rows of Data

If the number of rows returned by DB2 is unknown or if you expect more than one row to return, you must use an alternative to the SELECT...INTO statement. A *cursor* enables an application to process a set of rows and retrieve one row at a time from the result table. We will take a look at cursors later in this chapter.

Inserting and Updating Data

You can set or change a value in a DB2 table to the value of a host variable. To do this, you use the host variable name in the SET clause of UPDATE or the VALUES clause of INSERT. This example changes a candidate's home phone number:

```
EXEC SQL
    UPDATE DB2USER1.CANDIDATE
        SET PHONENO =:HPHONEHV
        WHERE CID =:CIDHV
END-EXEC.
```

Searching Data

You can use a host variable to specify a value in the predicate of a search condition or to replace a constant in an expression. For example, if you have defined a field called `CIDHV` that contains a candidate number, you can retrieve the name of the candidate whose number is `'012345678'` with

```
MOVE '012345678' TO CIDHV.
EXEC SQL
    SELECT LNAME
    INTO :LNAMEHV
    FROM DB2USER1.CANDIDATE
    WHERE CID =:CIDHV
END-EXEC.
```

SQL EXECUTION VALIDATION

A program that includes SQL statements needs to have an area set apart for communication with DB2—an *SQL communication area* (SQLCA). When it processes an SQL statement in a program, DB2 places return codes in the `SQLCODE` and `SQLSTATE` host variables or corresponding fields of the SQLCA.

The return codes indicate whether the executed statement succeeded or failed. Because the SQLCA is a valuable problem-diagnosis tool, it is a good idea to include instructions to display some of the information contained in the SQLCA in your application programs. For example, the contents of `SQLERRD(3)`, which indicates the number of rows that DB2 updates, inserts, or deletes, could be useful. If `SQLWARN0` contains `W`, DB2 has set at least one of the SQL warning flags (`SQLWARN1` through `SQLWARNA`). A description of the SQLCA is shown in Table 10-1.

Table 10-1   SQLCA Codes

Name	Data Type	Purpose
SQLCAID	CHAR(8)	An "eye catcher" for storage dumps containing the text `'SQLCA'`.
SQLCABC	INTEGER	Contains the length of the SQLCA: 136.
SQLCODE	INTEGER	Contains the SQL return code: 0 (successful execution, although there might have been warning messages); positive (successful execution, with an exception condition); negative (error condition).
SQLERRML	SMALLINT	Length indicator for SQLERRMC, in the range 0 through 70: 0 means that the value of SQLERRMC is not pertinent.

Table 10-1 SQLCA Codes (Continued)

Name	Data Type	Purpose
SQLERRMC	VARCHAR(70)	Contains one or more tokens, separated by X'FF', that are substituted for variables in the descriptions of error conditions.
SQLERRP	CHAR(8)	Provides a product signature and, in the case of an error, diagnostic information, such as the name of the module that detected the error. In all cases, the first three characters are DSN for DB2 for z/OS.
SQLERRD(1)	INTEGER	Contains an internal error code.
SQLERRD(2)	INTEGER	Contains an internal error code.
SQLERRD(3)	INTEGER	Contains the number of rows affected after INSERT, UPDATE, and DELETE but not rows deleted as a result of CASCADE delete. Set to 0 if the SQL statement fails, indicating that all changes made in executing the statement were canceled. Set to –1 for a mass delete from a table in a segmented table space. SQLERRD(3) can also contain the reason code of a timeout or deadlock for SQLCODES –911 and –913.
SQLERRD(4)	INTEGER	Generally contains a timer-on, a short floating-point value that indicates a rough relative estimate of resources required. It does not reflect an estimate of the time required. When preparing a dynamically defined SQL statement, you can use this field as an indicator of the relative cost of the prepared SQL statement. For a particular statement, this number can vary with changes to the statistics in the catalog. It is also subject to change between releases of DB2 for z/OS.
SQLERRD(5)	INTEGER	Contains the position or column of a syntax error for a PREPARE or EXECUTE IMMEDIATE statement.
SQLERRD(6)	INTEGER	Contains an internal error code.
SQLWARN0	CHAR(1)	Contains a W if at least one other indicator also contains a W; otherwise, contains a blank.
SQLWARN1	CHAR(1)	Contains a W if the value of a string column was truncated when assigned to a host variable.
SQLWARN2	CHAR(1)	Contains a W if null values were eliminated from the argument of a column function; not necessarily set to W for the MIN function, because its results are not dependent on the elimination of null values.

continues

Table 10-1   SQLCA Codes (Continued)

Name	Data Type	Purpose
SQLWARN3	CHAR(1)	Contains a W if the number of result columns is larger than the number of host variables. Contains a Z if fewer locators were provided in the ASSOCIATE LOCATORS statement than the stored procedure returned.
SQLWARN4	CHAR(1)	Contains a W if a prepared UPDATE or DELETE statement does not include a WHERE clause.
SQLWARN5	CHAR(1)	Contains a W if the SQL statement was not executed because it is not a valid SQL statement in DB2 for z/OS.
SQLWARN6	CHAR(1)	Contains a W if the addition of a month or year duration to a DATE or TIMESTAMP value results in an invalid day, such as June 31. Indicates that the value of the day was changed to the last day of the month to make the result valid.
SQLWARN7	CHAR(1)	Contains a W if one or more nonzero digits were eliminated from the fractional part of a number used as the operand of a decimal multiply or divide operation.
SQLWARN8	CHAR(1)	Contains a W if a character that could not be converted was replaced with a substitute character.
SQLWARN9	CHAR(1)	Contains a W if arithmetic exceptions were ignored during COUNT DISTINCT processing. Contains a Z if the stored procedure returned multiple result sets.
SQLWARNA	CHAR(1)	Contains a W if at least one character field of the SQLCA or the SQLDA names or labels is invalid because of a character-conversion error.
SQLSTATE	CHAR(5)	Contains a return code for the outcome of the most recent execution of an SQL statement.

SQLCODE and SQLSTATE Fields

Whenever an SQL statement executes, the SQLCODE and SQLSTATE fields of the SQLCA receive a return code. Although both fields indicate whether the statement executed successfully, they have some differences.

DB2 returns the following codes in SQLCODE:

- If SQLCODE = 0, execution was successful.
- If SQLCODE > 0, execution was successful with a warning.
- If SQLCODE < 0, execution was not successful.
- If SQLCODE = 100, no data was found.

The meaning of SQLCODEs other than 0 and 100 varies with the particular product implementing SQL.

SQLSTATE allows an application program to check for errors in the same way for different IBM database management systems. An advantage to using the SQLCODE field is that it can provide more specific information than can SQLSTATE. Many of the SQLCODEs have associated tokens in the SQLCA that indicate, for example, which object incurred an SQL error. The advantage of SQLSTATE is its cross-vendor usability.

To conform to the SQL standard, the SQLCODE and SQLSTATE fields (SQLCOD and SQLSTA in FORTRAN) can be declared as standalone host variables. If the STDSQL(YES) precompiler option is specified, these host variables receive the return codes, and the SQLCA does not need to be included in the program.

GET DIAGNOSTICS Statement

The GET DIAGNOSTICS statement can be used to return diagnostic information about the last SQL statement that was executed. Requests can be made for all diagnostic items or individual items of diagnostic information from the following categories:

- Statement items, which contain information about the SQL statement as a whole
- Condition items, which contain information about each error or warning that occurred during the execution of the SQL statement
- Connection items, which contain information about the SQL statement if it was a CONNECT statement

The GET DIAGNOSTICS statement can be used to handle multiple SQL errors that might result from the execution of a single SQL statement. First, check SQLSTATE or SQLCODE to determine whether diagnostic information should be retrieved by using GET DIAGNOSTICS. This method is especially useful for diagnosing problems that result from a multiple-row INSERT that is specified as NOT ATOMIC CONTINUE ON SQLEXCEPTION.

Even if the GET DIAGNOSTICS statement is used in the application program to check for conditions, instructions must be included to use the SQLCA, or SQLSTATE or SQLCODE must be declared separately in the program.

When the GET DIAGNOSTICS statement is used, the requested diagnostic information is assigned to host variables. Declare each target host variable with a data type that is compatible with the data type of the requested item. Then, in order to retrieve condition information, the number of condition items must first be retrieved.

Table 10-2 shows the data types for the GET DIAGNOSTICS items that return statement information. The various GET DIAGNOSTIC statements can provide useful and informative information for application communication. The following example shows how to use the GET

DIAGNOSTIC statement to get the count of the number of rows that a particular statement updated:

```
EXEC SQL
   GET DIAGNOSTICS :rcount = ROW_COUNT;
```

Table 10-2   Data Types for **GET DIAGNOSTICS** Items Returning Statement Information

Item	Description	Data Type
DB2_GET_DIAGNOSTICS _DIAGNOSTICS	After a GET DIAGNOSTICS statement, if any error or warning occurred, contains all the diagnostics as a single string	VARCHAR (32672)
DB2_LAST_ROW	After a multiple-row FETCH statement, contains a value of +100 if the last row in the table is in the row set that was returned.	INTEGER
DB2_NUMBER_PARAMETER _MARKERS	After a PREPARE statement, contains the number of parameter markers in the prepared statement.	INTEGER
DB2_NUMBER_RESULT_SETS	After a CALL statement that invokes a stored procedure, contains the number of result sets that are returned by the procedure.	INTEGER
DB2_NUMBER_ROWS	After an OPEN or FETCH statement for which the size of the result table is known, contains the number of rows in the result table. After a PREPARE statement, this item contains the estimated number of rows in the result table for the prepared statement. For SENSITIVE DYNAMIC cursors, this item contains the approximate number of rows.	DECIMAL (31,0)
DB2_RETURN_STATUS	After a CALL statement that invokes an SQL procedure, contains the return status if the procedure contains a RETURN statement.	INTEGER
DB2_SQL_ATTR _CURSOR_HOLD	After an ALLOCATE or OPEN statement, indicates whether the cursor can be held CHAR(1) open across multiple units of work (Y or N).	CHAR(1)
DB2_SQL_ATTR _CURSOR_ROWSET	After an ALLOCATE or OPEN statement, indicates whether the cursor can use row set positioning (Y or N).	CHAR(1)
DB2_SQL_ATTR _CURSOR_SCROLLABLE	After an ALLOCATE or OPEN statement, indicates whether the cursor is scrollable (Y or N).	CHAR(1)

Table 10-2   Data Types for **GET DIAGNOSTICS** Items Returning Statement Information (Continued)

Item	Description	Data Type
DB2_SQL_ATTR _CURSOR_SENSITIVITY	After an ALLOCATE or OPEN statement, indicates whether the cursor shows updates made by other processes (sensitivity A, I, or S).	CHAR(1)
DB2_SQL_ATTR _CURSOR_TYPE	After an ALLOCATE or OPEN statement, indicates whether the cursor is declared static (S for INSENSITIVE or SENSITIVE STATIC) or dynamic (D for SENSITIVE DYNAMIC).	CHAR(1)
MORE	After any SQL statement, indicates whether some condition items were discarded because of insufficient storage (Y or N).	CHAR(1)
NUMBER	After any SQL statement, contains the number of condition items. If no warning or error occurred or if no previous SQL statement has been executed, the number 1 is returned.	INTEGER
ROW_COUNT	After DELETE, INSERT, UPDATE, or FETCH, contains the number of rows deleted, inserted, updated, or fetched. After PREPARE, contains the estimated number of result rows in the prepared statement.	DECIMAL (31,0)

Table 10-3 shows the data types for GET DIAGNOSTICS items that return condition information.

Table 10-3   Data Types for **GET DIAGNOSTICS** Items Returning Condition Information

Item	Description	Data Type
CATALOG_NAME	Contains the server name of the table that owns a constraint that caused an error or that caused an access rule or check violation.	VARCHAR(128)
CONDITION_NUMBER	Contains the number of the condition.	INTEGER
CURSOR_NAME	Contains the name of a cursor in an invalid cursor state.	VARCHAR(128)
DB2_ERROR_CODE1	Contains an internal error code.	INTEGER
DB2_ERROR_CODE2	Contains an internal error code.	INTEGER

continues

Table 10-3   Data Types for **GET DIAGNOSTICS** Items Returning Condition Information (Continued)

Item	Description	Data Type
DB2_ERROR_CODE3	Contains an internal error code.	INTEGER
DB2_ERROR_CODE4	Contains an internal error code.	INTEGER
DB2_INTERNAL_ERROR _POINTER	For some errors, contains a negative value that is an internal error pointer.	INTEGER
DB2_MESSAGE_ID	Contains the message ID that corresponds to the message contained in the CHAR(10)MESSAGE_TEXT diagnostic item.	INTEGER
DB2_MODULE_DETECTING _ERROR	After any SQL statement, indicates which module detected the error.	CHAR(8)
DB2_ORDINAL_TOKEN_n	After any SQL statement, contains the nth token, where n is a value from 1 to 100.	VARCHAR(515)
DB2_REASON_CODE	After any SQL statement, contains the reason code for errors that have a reason-code token in the message text.	INTEGER
DB2_RETURNED_SQLCODE	After any SQL statement, contains the SQLCODE for the condition.	INTEGER
DB2_ROW_NUMBER	After any SQL statement that involves multiple rows, contains the row number on which DB2 detected the condition.	DECIMAL (31,0)
DB2_TOKEN_COUNT	After any SQL statement, contains the number of tokens available for the condition.	INTEGER
MESSAGE_TEXT	After any SQL statement, contains the message text associated with the SQLCODE.	VARCHAR (32672)
RETURNED_SQLSTATE	After any SQL statement, contains the SQLSTATE for the condition.	CHAR(5)
SERVER_NAME	After a CONNECT, DISCONNECT, or SET CONNECTION statement, contains the name of the server specified in the statement.	VARCHAR(128)

Table 10-4 shows the data types for GET DIAGNOSTICS items that return connection information.

Table 10-4   Data Types for **GET DIAGNOSTICS** Items Returning Connection Information

Item	Description	Data type
DB2_AUTHENTICATION _TYPE	Contains the authentication type (S, C, D, E, or blank).	CHAR(1)
DB2_AUTHORIZATION_ID	Contains the authorization ID used by the connected server.	VARCHAR(128)
DB2_CONNECTION_STATE	This item indicates whether the connection is unconnected (-1), local (0), or remote (1).	INTEGER
DB2_CONNECTION_STATUS	This item indicates whether updates can be committed for the current unit of work (1 for yes or 2 for no).	INTEGER
DB2_ENCRYPTION_TYPE	Contains A or D, indicating the level of encryption for the connection: (A = only the authentication tokens (authid and password) are encrypted; D = all the data for the connection is encrypted).	CHAR(1)
DB2_SERVER_CLASS_NAME	After a CONNECT or SET CONNECTION statement, contains the DB2 server class name.	VARCHAR(128)
DB2_PRODUCT_ID	Contains the DB2 product signature.	VARCHAR(8)

CURSORS

Use a *cursor* in an application program to retrieve multiple rows from a table or from a result set returned by a stored procedure. This section looks at how an application program can use a cursor to retrieve rows from a table.

Row Retrieval

When the SELECT statement associated with the cursor is executed, a set of rows is retrieved. The set of rows returned is referred to as the *result table,* or *result set.* An application program must be able to retrieve one row at a time from the result set into host variables. A cursor performs that function. A program can have several cursors, all open at the same time. A cursor can also be used to retrieve multiple rows at a time. This is covered in Chapter 12.

DECLARE CURSOR Statement

To define and identify a set of rows to be accessed with a cursor, issue a DECLARE CURSOR statement. This statement names a cursor and specifies a SELECT statement. The SELECT statement defines the criteria for the rows that will make up the result table. The simplest form of the DECLARE CURSOR statement is as follows:

```
EXEC SQL
   DECLARE CERTCUR CURSOR FOR
      SELECT TCID, NAME, CODE
      FROM DB2USER1.TEST_CENTER
      WHERE TCID = :TCIDHV
END-EXEC.
```

If any of the columns are to be updated in the rows of the identified table, include the FOR UPDATE clause. This clause has two forms: one form for when the columns to be updated are known and another for when the columns are not known. Use the following form when the columns intended for update are known:

```
EXEC SQL
   DECLARE CERTCUR CURSOR FOR
      SELECT TCID, NAME, CODE
      FROM DB2USER1.TEST_CENTER
      WHERE TCID = :TCIDHV
      FOR UPDATE OF CODE
END-EXEC.
```

If a cursor might be used to update any of the columns of the table, use the following form of the FOR UPDATE clause, which allows for updates to any columns of the table that can be updated:

```
EXEC SQL
   DECLARE CERTCUR CURSOR FOR
      SELECT TCID, NAME, CODE
      FROM DB2USER1.TEST_CENTER
      WHERE TCID = :TCIDHV
      FOR UPDATE
END-EXEC.
```

> **N O T E** DB2 must do more processing when you use the FOR UPDATE clause without a column list than when you use the FOR UPDATE OF clause with a column list. Therefore, if only a few columns of a table are going to be updated, the program can run more efficiently if a column list is included.

A column of the identified table can be updated even though it is not part of the result table. In this case, you do not need to name the column in the SELECT statement. When the cursor retrieves a row, using FETCH, that contains a column value you want to update, you can use the UPDATE...WHERE CURRENT OF statement to update the row.

> **N O T E** Some result tables—for example, the result of joining two or more tables—cannot be updated.

OPEN Statement

To tell DB2 that you are ready to process the first row of the result table or result set, you must issue an OPEN statement. DB2 then uses the SELECT statement within DECLARE CURSOR to identify a set of rows. If host variables are used in that SELECT statement, DB2 uses the *current value* of the variables to select the rows. The result table that satisfies the search conditions can contain zero, one, or many rows. The OPEN statement looks like this:

```
EXEC SQL
   OPEN CERTCUR
END-EXEC.
```

> **N O T E** DB2 cannot determine the number of rows that qualified during the OPEN. An empty result table or result set is identified by an SQLCODE of +100 on the subsequent FETCH, UPDATE, or DELETE statement.

When used with cursors, DB2 evaluates CURRENT DATE, CURRENT TIME, and CURRENT TIMESTAMP special registers once when the OPEN statement executes. (More information on special registers is provided later in this chapter.) DB2 uses the values returned in the registers on all subsequent FETCH statements.

Two factors that influence the amount of time that DB2 requires to process the OPEN statement are

- Whether DB2 must perform any sorts before it can retrieve rows from the result table
- Whether DB2 uses parallelism to process the SELECT statement associated with the cursor

Once a cursor is opened, one of the following SQL statements is executed, using the cursor:

- FETCH
- Positioned UPDATE
- Positioned DELETE

FETCH Statements.   Execute a FETCH statement for one of the following purposes:

- To copy data from a row of the result table into one or more host variables
- To position the cursor before a positioned UPDATE or positioned DELETE operation is performed

The simplest form of the FETCH statement looks like this:

```
EXEC SQL
    FETCH CERTCUR
    INTO :TCIDHV,:NAMEHV, ...
END-EXEC.
```

The SELECT statement within the DECLARE CURSOR statement identifies the result table from which to fetch rows, but DB2 does not retrieve any data until the application program executes a FETCH statement.

When the program executes the FETCH statement, DB2 uses the cursor to point to a row in the result table. That row is called the *current row*. DB2 then copies the contents of the current row into the program host variables that you specified in the INTO clause of FETCH. This sequence repeats for each subsequent FETCH until you have processed all the rows in the result table.

The row that DB2 points to when a FETCH statement is executed depends on whether the cursor is declared as scrollable or nonscrollable (covered later in this chapter). When querying a remote subsystem with FETCH, consider using BLOCK FETCH for better performance. BLOCK FETCH processes rows ahead of the current row.

> **N O T E**   BLOCK FETCH cannot be used when a positioned UPDATE or DELETE is performed.

Positioned UPDATE.   After the program has executed a FETCH statement to retrieve the current row, a positioned UPDATE statement can be used to modify the data in that row. An example of positioned UPDATE is as follows:

```
EXEC SQL
    UPDATE DB2USER1.TEST_CENTER
        SET CODE = 123456
        WHERE CURRENT OF CERTCUR
END-EXEC.
```

A positioned UPDATE statement updates the row that *cursor name* (CERTCUR) points to. A positioned UPDATE statement must meet these conditions.

- The row cannot be updated if the update violates any unique, check, or referential constraints.
- An UPDATE statement cannot be used to modify the rows of a created global temporary table but can be used to modify the rows of a declared global temporary table (covered later in this chapter).
- If the right side of the SET clause in the UPDATE statement contains a subselect, that subselect cannot include a correlated name for a table that is being updated.

Positioned DELETE. After the program has executed a FETCH statement to retrieve the current row, a positioned DELETE statement can be used to delete that row. An example of a positioned DELETE statement follows:

```
EXEC SQL
    DELETE FROM DB2USER1.TEST_CENTER
    WHERE CURRENT OF CERTCUR
END-EXEC.
```

A positioned DELETE statement deletes the row that CERTCUR points to. A positioned DELETE statement must meet these conditions.

- A DELETE statement cannot be used with a cursor to delete rows from a created global temporary table but can be used to delete rows from a declared global temporary table.
- After a row has been deleted, you cannot update or delete another row using that cursor until you execute a FETCH statement to position the cursor on another row.
- A row cannot be deleted if the delete violates any referential constraints.

CLOSE Statement

When the program is finished processing the rows of the result table, issue a CLOSE statement to close the cursor:

```
EXEC SQL
    CLOSE CERTCUR
END-EXEC.
```

This statement will destroy the result set that was created during the OPEN cursor.

Cursor WITH HOLD

A held cursor, which is declared WITH HOLD, does not close after a COMMIT operation. A cursor that is not declared WITH HOLD is automatically closed after a COMMIT operation. When a cursor is declared, the inclusion or exclusion of the WITH HOLD clause tells DB2 whether the cursor is to be held. After a COMMIT operation, a held cursor is positioned after the last row retrieved and before the next logical row of the result table to be returned.

A held cursor will close when

- A CLOSE cursor or ROLLBACK statement is issued
- A Call Attach Facility (CAF) CLOSE function call or an RRSAF TERMINATE THREAD function call is issued
- The connection from a remote client application is released
- The application program terminates

If the program abnormally terminates, the cursor position is lost. To prepare for restart, your program must reposition the cursor. The following restrictions apply to cursors that are declared WITH HOLD.

- Do not use DECLARE CURSOR WITH HOLD with the new user sign-on from a DB2 attachment facility, because all open cursors are closed.
- Do not declare a WITH HOLD cursor in a thread that could become inactive. If you do, its locks are held indefinitely.

Some restrictions apply when using CURSOR WITH HOLD with IMS or CICS programs. (Refer to *IBM DB2 Application Programming Guide and SQL Guide* for more details.)

> **N O T E**   The use of CURSOR WITH HOLD also will prevent some options in DB2 that are used for performance, such as parallelism and drains needed for an online REORG.

A simple example of declaring a held cursor follows:

```
EXEC SQL
    DECLARE CERTCUR CURSOR WITH HOLD FOR
        SELECT TCID, NAME, CODE
        FROM DB2USER1.TEST_CENTER
        WHERE TCID = :TCIDHV
END-EXEC.
```

Types of Cursors

Cursors can be scrollable or not scrollable, as well as held or not held. Table 10-5 characterizes the types of cursors.

When you declare a cursor, you tell DB2 whether you want the cursor to be scrollable or non-scrollable, by including or omitting the SCROLL clause. This clause determines whether the cursor moves sequentially forward through the data set or has random access to the data set.

> **N O T E** If it references more than one table or contains a GROUP BY or similar clause, the SELECT statement becomes read-only.

Nonscrollable Cursor

The simplest type of cursor is a nonscrollable cursor, which always moves sequentially forward in the result table. When a cursor is opened, it is positioned before the first row in the result table. When the first FETCH is executed, the cursor is positioned on the first row. The next FETCH statement moves the cursor one row ahead for each FETCH.

After each FETCH statement, the cursor is positioned on the row that was fetched. After an execution of a positioned UPDATE or positioned DELETE operation, the cursor stays at the current row of the result table. Rows cannot be retrieved backward or moved to a specific position in a result table with a nonscrollable cursor.

Table 10-5 Types of Cursors

Cursor Type	Result Table	Visibility of Own Cursor's Changes	Visibility of Other Cursors' Changes	Updatability
Nonscrollable (join, sort, and so on)	Fixed, work file	No	No	No
Nonscrollable	No work file, base table access	Yes	Yes	Yes
Insensitive scroll	Fixed, declared temporary table	No	No	No
Sensitive static scroll	Fixed, declared temporary table	Yes (inserts not allowed)	Yes (not inserts)	Yes
Sensitive dynamic scroll	No declared temporary table, base table access	Yes	Yes	Yes

Scrollable Cursor

Scrollable cursors allow for movement to any row in the result table. DB2 uses declared temporary tables for processing scrollable cursors. The declaration for a scrollable cursor has the following form:

```
EXEC SQL
   DECLARE CERTCUR sensitivity STATIC SCROLL CURSOR FOR
      SELECT TCID, NAME, CODE
      FROM DB2USER1.TEST_CENTER
      WHERE TCID = :TCIDHV
END-EXEC.
```

STATIC SCROLL indicates that the cursor is scrollable and follows the static model.

The sensitivity in the DECLARE statement indicates whether changes that are made to the underlying table after the cursor is opened are visible to the result table. *Sensitivity* can be INSENSITIVE or SENSITIVE. INSENSITIVE means that no changes to the underlying table after the cursor is opened are visible to the result table. SENSITIVE means that some or all changes that are made to the underlying table after the cursor is opened are visible to the result table.

The sensitivity clause of the FETCH statement determines which changes to the underlying table are visible to the result table. When the cursor is opened, the cursor is positioned before the first row. A clause is included in each FETCH statement to tell DB2 where to position the cursor in the result table. The FETCH clause for a scrollable cursor has the following form:

```
EXEC SQL
   FETCH sensitivity cursor-position cursor-name
   INTO :host-variable1, :host-variable2 ...
END-EXEC.
```

Sensitivity in the FETCH statement indicates whether changes that are made to the underlying table by means other than the cursor are visible to the result table. Sensitivity can be INSENSITIVE or SENSITIVE. INSENSITIVE means that the only time changes to the underlying table are visible to the result table is when a positioned UPDATE or positioned DELETE using CERTCUR makes those changes. SENSITIVE means that the result table is updated when the underlying table changes. The sensitivity options can be summarized as follows:

- DECLARE C1 INSENSITIVE SCROLL/FETCH INSENSITIVE: read-only cursor; not aware of updates or deletes in base table
- DECLARE C1 SENSITIVE STATIC SCROLL/FETCH INSENSITIVE: updatable cursor; aware of own updates or deletes within cursor; other changes to base table not visible to cursor; all inserts not recognized

- DECLARE C1 SENSITIVE STATIC SCROLL/FETCH SENSITIVE: Updatable cursor; aware of own updates and deletes within cursor; sees all committed updates and deletes; all inserts not recognized

Scrollable Cursor Fetching. Several options are available when fetching with a scrollable cursor. Cursor positioning becomes very flexible, as you can fetch forward and backward and do relative and absolute positioning. The following example shows several fetching options:

```
FETCH
FETCH LAST (or FIRST)
FETCH ABSOLUTE +7
FETCH INSENSITIVE RELATIVE -3
FETCH CURRENT (or BEFORE or AFTER)
FETCH RELATIVE 2
FETCH PRIOR (or NEXT)
```

> **N O T E** In a distributed environment, you can use scrollable cursors only if you use DRDA access.

Dynamic Scrollable Cursors. As of DB2 version 8, dynamic scrollable cursors can be implemented in applications, with better performance and more usability than static scrollable cursors. Dynamic scrollable cursors allow for base table access instead of having to use a declared global temporary table and do not materialize at any time. Each FETCH shows the most current activity and is sensitive to all INSERTs, UPDATEs, and DELETEs: no more delete holes and missing updates.

These cursors default to single-row fetch but also support multirow fetch, as well as positioned updates/deletes with multirow fetch. Order is always maintained with these cursors.

Following is an example of the syntax for defining a dynamic scrollable cursor:

```
DECLARE CERTCUR SENSITIVE DYNAMIC CURSOR
FOR SELECT TCID, NAME, FROM TEST_CENTER
```

Some SQL statements require that result sets be placed in work files for joins. These statements are considered read-only and cannot support dynamic scrolling. A new option, ASENSITIVE, allows DB2 to decide whether the cursor is SENSITIVE DYNAMIC or INSENSITIVE based on the complexity of the SQL statement. If ASENSITIVE and read-only, the statement will be INSENSITIVE. If ASENSITIVE and not read-only, the statement will be SENSITIVE DYNAMIC.

The dynamic scrollable cursors will take advantage of backward index scans and backward sequential detection. They will support both index scan access and table scan access paths.

Dynamic SQL

Before deciding to use dynamic SQL, you should consider whether using static SQL or dynamic SQL is the better technique for the application. For most DB2 users, *static SQL*—embedded in a host language program and bound before the program runs—provides a straightforward, efficient path to DB2 data. Static SQL should be used when the SQL statements the application needs to execute are known before runtime.

Dynamic SQL prepares and executes the SQL statements within a program while the program is running. Dynamic SQL is of four types:

- **Embedded dynamic SQL.** The application puts the SQL source in host variables and includes PREPARE and EXECUTE statements that tell DB2 to prepare and run the contents of those host variables at runtime. The programs that include embedded dynamic SQL must go through the precompile and bind steps.
- **Interactive SQL.** A user enters SQL statements through SPUFI, QMF, or another facility. DB2 prepares and executes these statements as dynamic SQL statements. The programs that implement this functionality use embedded dynamic SQL statements.
- **Deferred embedded SQL.** Deferred embedded SQL statements are neither fully static nor fully dynamic. Like static statements, deferred embedded SQL statements are embedded within applications but like dynamic statements are prepared at runtime. DB2 processes deferred embedded SQL statements with bind-time rules. For example, DB2 uses the authorization ID and qualifiers determined at bind time as the plan or package owner.
- **Dynamic SQL executed through ODBC functions.** The application contains ODBC function calls that pass dynamic SQL statements as arguments. Programs that use ODBC function calls do need to be precompiled and bound.
- **Dynamic SQL executed through JDBC methods.** Java applications that contain JDBC class objects can use their methods to pass dynamic SQL statements as arguments. There is no need to precompile and bind programs that use JDBC methods.

Applications using dynamic SQL use three types of SQL statements:

- **Dynamic SQL for non-SELECT statements.** Those statements include DELETE, INSERT, and UPDATE. For execution, use either of the following SQL statements: EXECUTE IMMEDIATE or PREPARE and then EXECUTE.
- **Dynamic SQL for fixed-list SELECT statements.** A SELECT statement is *fixed-list* if you know in advance the number and type of data items in each row of the result. For execution, use the following SQL statements: PREPARE (an SQL cursor definition), OPEN the cursor, FETCH from the cursor, and CLOSE the cursor.

- **Dynamic SQL for varying-list SELECT statements.** A SELECT statement is *varying-list* if you cannot know in advance how many data items to allow for or what their data types are: DECLARE CURSOR for the statement, PREPARE the statement, DESCRIBE the statement, OPEN the cursor, FETCH using DESCRIPTOR, and CLOSE the cursor.

Using dynamic SQL has many other variations. Host variables can also be used, and the literal data can be put into the dynamic SQL statement. When parameter markers are used in the dynamic SQL statement, to be replaced by the host variables later, the bind feature REOPT(ONCE or ALWAYS) can also be used to assist the optimizer in picking the right access path, based on the host variable data, at execution time.

The use of parameter markers instead of literals is encouraged to allow the reuse of prepared dynamic SQL statements. DB2 caches dynamic SQL statements and their access paths in a memory area called the dynamic statement cache. Reuse of an access path from the dynamic statement cache can save 90 percent of the resources to prepare the same statement twice.

SUMMARY

A DB2 application program has various components. This chapter looked at how to construct a program and have it communicate with DB2. DB2 can use data in an application program by means of host variables and host structures. You can move through result sets of your data by means of cursors. These cursors must be declared and opened before rows of data can be fetched. Scrollable and nonscrollable cursors are the two types of cursors that can be used with various options.

ADDITIONAL RESOURCES

DB2 for z/OS Version 8 Application Programming and SQL Guide (SC26-9933)

DB2 for z/OS Version 8 SQL Reference (SC26-9944)

Binding an Application Program

- Precompiling
- Binding
- Plan or package ownership

DB2 application programs often include embedded SQL statements. In order to compile these programs, the SQL statements must be converted into a language recognized by the compiler or the assembler. The DB2 precompiler or a host-language compiler needs to be used to

- Replace the SQL statements in the source programs with compilable code
- Create a database request module (DBRM), which communicates the SQL requests to DB2 during the bind process

After the source program has been precompiled, a load module is created and, possibly, one or more packages and an application plan created. Creating a load module involves compiling and link-editing the modified source code that is produced by the precompiler. Creating a package or an application plan, a process unique to DB2, involves binding one or more DBRMs. See Figure 11-1.

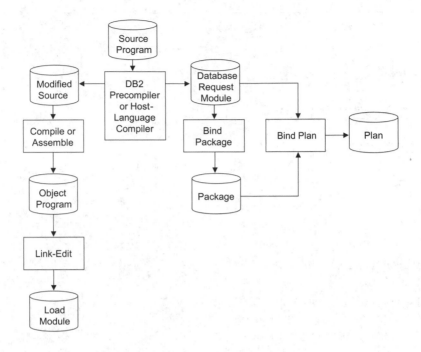

Figure 11-1   Program preparation

PRECOMPILING

The precompiler "prepares" the source program for compilation by replacing each EXEC SQL statement with a language-specific CALL statement and placing the SQL text in comment. (DB2 is not accessed during this process.) The precompiler can be invoked in DB2I or in batch and

- Includes the DCLGEN member as specified and the SQLCA
- Looks for SQL statements and for host-variable definitions
- Verifies the SQL syntax
- Matches each column and table name in the SQL to the DECLARE TABLE statements
- Prepares the SQL for compilation or assembly in the host language
- Produces a DBRM and stores it in a partitioned data set (PDS)

The DBRM that is created contains extracted, somewhat modified, parsed SQL source code that can be stored as a member in a PDS. One DBRM is created for each precompiled source program, and it will then become the input to the BIND process.

The SQL statements are replaced during the precompile process with a call to the DSNHLI module. This call will contain the necessary parameters—DBRM name, timestamp, statement number, address of host variables, and address of SQLCA—in order to locate the access path needed to execute the SQL statement associated with the call when the DBRM and modified source are used together at execution time.

BINDING

The bind process establishes a relationship between an application program and its relational data. This step is necessary before a program can be executed. DB2 allows two basic ways of binding a program: to a package or directly to an application plan.

> **N O T E**   If the application uses DRDA access to distribute data, you must use packages.

When a program is preprocessed for DB2, the two outputs are a modified source program to be passed to a compiler where the original SQL statements have been replaced by statements to invoke the appropriate DB2 interface functions, as well as information on how those SQL statements will be used by DB2. This second output, a DBRM, must be bound so that all the DB2 functions used in the program can be checked for validity and authorization and so that a proper access path can be determined. The bind process performs the following:

- Checks SQL syntax
- Checks security
- Compares column and table names against the DB2 catalog
- Builds an access path strategy for each SQL statement

These processes are discussed in more detail later in this chapter.

Packages and Plans

A DBRM can be bound in a package or directly into a plan. In addition, packages can be bound into logical groups called collections, which can then be bound into a plan. A package can be bound for only a single SQL statement, for a subset of the program, or for an entire program. The package will contain information representing optimized SQL, which may simply be an access path for the SQL to use to process the data required, or it could be information representing an SQL statement that was first rewritten by the optimizer.

A plan can contain multiple packages, collections, and/or DBRMs. Each package can be bound independently of a plan. If a list of DBRMs is bound into a plan and then the plan is rebound, all DBRMs are rebound as well. The output will contain the access path information for each SQL statement.

It is extremely difficult to justify the use of one plan containing all the packages for an installation or even for only all CICS transactions or batch jobs. Plans need to be granular. Large, cumbersome plans can cause performance degradation, buffer pool problems, and EDM pool problems. The number of packages put into a single plan needs to be based on functionality, such as all the packages supporting a particular function of an online application.

When determining the maximum size of a plan, you must consider several physical limitations, including the time required to bind the plan, the size of the environmental descriptor manager (EDM) pool, and fragmentation. Any number of DBRMs can be included in a plan. However, packages provide a more flexible method for handling large numbers of DBRMs within a plan.

Packages are database objects that contain executable forms of SQL statements. These packages contain statements that are contained in a DB2 application. A package corresponds to a program source module. Packages and their descriptions are stored in the DB2 catalog and directory tables. The packages contain the DB2 access plan that was selected by DB2 during the BIND or PREPARE process. This type of BIND is known as *static binding*, as it is performed prior to the execution of the SQL statement. Packages cannot be directly referenced in an SQL data manipulation statement.

Most applications that access a DB2 database will have a package or group of packages stored, or bound, in the system catalog and directory tables. Packages are input to the plan bind, using the PKLIST options. To be usable, a package must be bound into a plan. An example of a plan bind follows:

```
BIND PLAN (certpln) PKLIST (col1.*)
```

Packages need to be used based on the application design and objectives. Using packages provides a number of advantages:

- **Ease of maintenance.** With packages, the entire plan does not need to be bound again when a change is made to one SQL statement. Only the package associated with the changed SQL statement needs to be bound.
- **Incremental development of a program.** Binding packages into package collections, discussed later, allows adding packages to an existing application plan without having to bind the entire plan again.
- **Versioning.** As discussed later, several versions of a plan can be maintained without using packages requiring a separate plan for each version and therefore separate plan names and RUN commands.
- **Flexibility in using bind options.** The options of BIND PLAN apply to all DBRMs bound directly to the plan. The options of BIND PACKAGE apply only to the single DBRM bound to that package. The package options need not all be the same as the plan options and need not be the same as the options for other packages used by the same plan.

- **Flexibility in using name qualifiers.** The bind option QUALIFIER can be used to name a qualifier for the unqualified object names in SQL statements in a plan or package. Using packages allows different qualifiers for SQL statements in different parts of an application. For example, in order to redirect SQL statements from a test table to a production table, all that is required is a rebind.
- **CICS flexibility.** With packages, no dynamic plan selection and the associated exit routine are needed. A package listed within a plan is not accessed until it is executed. However, dynamic plan selection and packages can be used together. Doing so can reduce the number of plans in an application and hence require less effort to maintain the dynamic plan exit routine.

Collections

A *collection* is a group of associated packages. If a collection name is included in the package list when a plan is bound, any package in the collection becomes available to the plan. The collection can even be empty when the plan is first bound. Later, packages can be added to the collection, and existing packages can be dropped or replaced, without binding the plan again.

A collection is implicitly created at the first package bind that references a named collection. The name of the package is `collection.packagename.`

> **N O T E**   Collections are used in order to group packages by application or function.

The CURRENT PACKAGESET special register allows package searches on specific collections and disregards any other DBRMs. The following example uses the special register to search only the certcol collection:

```
EXEC SQL SET CURRENT PACKAGESET = 'certcol'
```

Without the use of CURRENT PACKAGESET, all the DBRMs would be searched, and then collections would be searched.

> **N O T E**   It is also possible to have two different copies of a program by binding them into two different collections.

The CURRENT PACKAGE PATH special register allows a list of collections to be specified as search locations when attempting to execute a package. The CURRENT PACKAGE PATH takes priority over the CURRENT PACKAGESET. Following is an example of using the special register to search the certcol and certcol2 collections:

```
EXEC SQL SET CURRENT PACKAGE PATH='"certcol","certcol2"'
```

Versioning

Maintaining several versions of a plan without using packages requires a separate plan for each version and therefore separate plan names and RUN commands. Isolating separate versions of a program into packages requires only one plan and helps to simplify program migration and fallback. At precompile time, the user can assign versions to the program, allowing multiple copies of the same package in the DB2 system. For example, separate development, test, and production levels of a program can be maintained by binding each level of the program as a separate version of a package, all within a single plan. The precompiler can also be set to automatically generate a version for the package that is based on a timestamp; using the VERSION(AUTO) option.

Binding and Rebinding

The BIND PACKAGE subcommand allows you to bind DBRMs individually. It provides the ability to test different versions of an application without extensive rebinding.

> **NOTE** Package binding is also the only method for binding applications at remote sites.

Even when DBRMs are bound into packages, all programs must be designated in an application plan for execution by local jobs. BIND PLAN establishes the relationship between DB2 and all DBRMs or packages in that plan. Plans can specify explicitly named DBRMs, packages, collections of packages, or a combination of these elements. The plan contains information about the designated DBRMs or packages and about the data the application program intends to use. The plan is stored in the DB2 catalog.

In addition to building packages and plans, the bind process

- Validates the SQL statements, using the DB2 catalog. During the bind process, DB2 checks the SQL statements for valid table, view, and column names. Because the bind process occurs as a separate step before program execution, errors are detected and can be corrected before the program is executed.

- Verifies that the process binding the program is authorized to perform the data-accessing operations requested by your program's SQL statements. When the BIND command is issued, an authorization ID can be specified as the owner of the plan or package. The owner can be any one of the authorization IDs of the process performing the bind. The bind process determines whether the owner of the plan or package is authorized to access the data the program requests.
- Selects the access paths needed to access the DB2 data that the program wants to process. In selecting an access path, DB2 considers indexes, table sizes, and other factors. DB2 considers all indexes available to access the data and decides which ones, if any, to use when selecting a path to the data. BIND PLAN and BIND PACKAGE can be accomplished using DB2I panels, the DSNH CLIST, or the DSN subcommands BIND PLAN and BIND PACKAGE.

Depending on how the DB2 application was designed, all DBRMs could be bound in one operation, creating only a single application plan. Or, you might bind some or all of your DBRMs into separate packages in separate operations. After that, the entire application must still be bound as a single plan, listing the included packages or collections and binding any DBRMs not already bound into packages.

> **N O T E**   Regardless of what the plan contains, it must be bound before the application can run on z/OS.

Binding or Rebinding a Package or Plan in Use

Packages and plans are locked during binding and execution. Packages that run under a plan are not locked until the plan uses them. If you execute a plan and some packages in the package list are never executed, those packages are never locked.

A package or a plan cannot be bound or rebound while it is running. However, a different version of a package that is running can be bound.

Options

A few methods are used for binding and rebinding packages and plans.

- The BIND(ADD) option can be used for creating a new plan or package.
- BIND(REPLACE) is used when the program has been changed.
- REBIND is used when a program has not changed but perhaps an index has been added or RUNSTATS has been executed, and any access path changes need to be accounted for.

Several of the options of BIND PACKAGE and BIND PLAN can affect your program design. For example, a bind option can be used to ensure that a package or plan can run only from a particular CICS connection or a particular IMS region; this cannot be enforced in your code. An example follows:

```
BIND PLAN(CICSONLY)-
   MEMBER(CERTDBRM)-
   ACTION(ADD)-
   ISOLATION(CS)-
   OWNER(DB2USER1)-
   QUALIFIER(DB2USER1)-
   CACHESIZE(0)-
   ENABLE(CICS)CICS(CON1)
```

Later chapters discuss several other options at length, particularly the ones that affect the program's use of locks, such as the option ISOLATION. Table 11-1 lists options for BIND/ REBIND and what is valid for plans, packages, and trigger packages (REBIND only; trigger packages are discussed in Chapter 15). The options chosen are recorded in the SYSPLAN and SYSPACKAGE catalog tables.

Table 11-1 BIND/REBIND Options

Option	Function	Valid Values	Plan	Package	Trigger
ACQUIRE	Determines whether to acquire resources specified in the DBRM at first access or allocation	**USE**, ALLOCATE	X	X	
ACTION	Determines whether the object (plan or package) replaces an existing object with same name or is new	**REPLACE**, ADD	X, BO	X, BO	
		REPLACE(RPLVER)		X, BO	
		REPLACE(RETAIN)	X, BO		
CACHESIZE	Determines the size, in bytes, of the authorization cache acquired in the EDM pool for the plan	Value of PLAN AUTH CACHE; decimal value	X		
COPY	Determines that you are copying an existing package and names the package	*Collection-id*, *package-id*, COPYVER		X, BO	

Table 11-1 **BIND/REBIND** Options (Continued)

Option	Function	Valid Values	Plan	Package	Trigger
CURRENTDATA	Determines whether to require data currency for RO (read-only) and ambiguous cursors when isolation level is CS (cursor stability)	**YES**, NO	X	X	X
CURRENTSERVER	Determines the location to connect to before running the plan	Location-name	X		
DBPROTOCOL	Specifies which protocol to use when connecting to a remote site identified by a three-part name	**DRDA**, PRIVATE	X	X	
DEFER	Whether to defer preparation of dynamic SQL that refers to remote objects or to prepare them immediately	DEFER(PREPARE), **NODEFER** (PREPARE)	X	X	
DEGREE	Determines whether to attempt to run a query using parallel processing to maximize performance	**1**, ANY	X	X	
DISCONNECT	Determines which remote connections to destroy during commit operations	**EXPLICIT**, AUTOMATIC, CONDITIONAL	X		
DYNAMICRULES	Determines what values apply at runtime for dynamic SQL attributes	**RUN**, BIND	X	X	
		DEFINEBIND, DEFINERUN, INVOKEBIND, INVOKERUN		X	

continues

Table 11-1 `BIND/REBIND` Options (Continued)

Option	Function	Valid Values	Plan	Package	Trigger
ENABLE/ DISABLE	Determines which connections can use the plan or package	BATCH, CICS, DB2CALL, DLIBATCH, IMS, IMSBMP, IMSMPP, RRSAF , *	X	X	
		REMOTE		X	
ENCODING	Specifies the application encoding for all static statements in the plan or package (defaults to installed selection)	ASCII, EBCIDIC, UNICODE, ccsid	X	X	
EXPLAIN	Determines whether to populate the PLAN_TABLE with information about the SQL statements	**NO**, YES	X	X	X
FLAG	Determines what messages to display	**I**, W, E, C	X	X	X
IMMEDIATE	Determines whether immediate writes will be done for updates made to GBP-dependent page sets/partitions	**NO**, PH1, YES	X	X	X
ISOLATION	Determines how far to isolate an application from the effects of other running applications	**RR**, RS, CS, UR, NC	X	X	X
KEEPDYNAMIC	Determines whether DB2 keeps dynamic SQL statements after commit points	**NO**, YES	X	X	
LIBRARY	Determines what PDS to search for DBRMs listed in the member option	*dbrm-pds-name* (can be multiple for PLAN)	X, BO	X, BO	

Table 11-1 `BIND/REBIND` Options (Continued)

Option	Function	Valid Values	Plan	Package	Trigger
MEMBER	Determines what DBRMs to include in the plan or package	*dbrm-member-name* (can be multiple for PLAN)	X, BO	X, BO	
OPTHINT	Controls whether query optimization hints are used for static SQL	*Hint-id*	X	X	
OPTIONS	Specifies which bind options to use for the new package	**COMPOSITE**, COMMAND		X, BC	
OWNER	Determines the authorization ID or the owner of the object (plan or package)	*Authorization-id*	X	X	
PACKAGE	Determines what package or packages to bind or rebind	*Location-name. collection-id. package-id (version-id)*		X	
		REBIND ONLY		X, RO	
PATH	Determines the SQL path that DB2 uses to resolve unqualified UDTs, functions, and stored procedure name	*Schema-name*, USER, (*schema-name*, (USER)...)	X	X	
PKLIST or NOPKLIST	Determines what package to include for the package list in the plan	(*Location-name. collection-id. package-id*...), PKLIST only	X		
PLAN	Determines what plan or plans to bind or rebind	*Plan-name*	X		
		*	X, RO		
QUALIFIER	Determines the implicit qualifier for unqualified names of objects in the plan or package	*Qualifier-name*	X	X	

continues

Table 11-1 `BIND/REBIND` Options (Continued)

Option	Function	Valid Values	Plan	Package	Trigger
RELEASE	Determines when to release resources that the program uses: either at commit or at termination	**COMMIT**, DEALLOCATE	X	X	X
REOPT	Determines whether access path should be determined at runtime with host variables, parameter markers, and special registers	ONCE, ALWAYS, **NONE**	X	X	
SQLERROR	Determines whether to create a package if there is an SQL error in it	**NOPACKAGE**, CONTINUE		X	
SQLRULES	Determines whether a type 2 connection can be made according to DB2 rules for an existing connection	**DB2**, STD	X		
VALIDATE	Determines whether to recheck at runtime "not found" and "not authorized" errors found at bind time	**RUN**, BIND	X	X	

*   **Bold**=default; BO=BIND only; BC=BIND COPY; RO=REBIND only

> **N O T E**   If the values in the BIND/REBIND PACKAGE are different from those in the BIND/REBIND PLAN, the values for the BIND/REBIND PACKAGE will prevail, unless the plan is more restrictive.

Preliminary Steps

Before performing a bind, consider the following.

- Determine how the DBRMs should be bound: into packages, directly into plans, or a combination of both methods.
- Develop a naming convention and strategy for the most effective and efficient use of the plans and packages.
- Determine when the application should acquire locks on the objects it uses: on all objects when the plan is first allocated or on each object in turn when that object is first used. For more details on locking, refer to Chapter 16.

Invalidations

If an object that a package depends on is dropped, the following occur.

- If the package is not appended to any running plan, the package becomes invalid.
- If the package is appended to a running plan and the drop occurs outside of that plan, the object is not dropped, and the package does not become invalid.
- If the package is appended to a running plan and the drop occurs within that plan, the package becomes invalid.

In all cases, the plan does not become invalid unless it has a DBRM referencing the dropped object. If the package or plan becomes invalid, automatic rebind occurs the next time the package or plan is allocated. If automatic rebind fails, the package or plan may be marked as inoperative and execution fails.

Rebinding a Package

The way in which the collection ID (coll-id), package ID (pkg-id), and version ID (ver-id) on the REBIND PACKAGE subcommand are specified determines which packages are bound. REBIND PACKAGE does not apply to packages for which you do not have the BIND privilege.

An asterisk (*) used as an identifier for collections, packages, or versions does not apply to packages at remote sites. The asterisk can be used on the REBIND subcommand for local packages but not for packages at remote sites. Any of the following commands rebinds all versions of all packages in all collections at the local DB2 system for which you have the BIND privilege:

```
REBIND PACKAGE (*)
REBIND PACKAGE (*.*)
REBIND PACKAGE (*.*.(*))
```

Either of the following commands rebinds all versions of all packages in the local collection REGS for which you have the BIND privilege:

```
REBIND PACKAGE (REGS.*)
REBIND PACKAGE (REGS.*.(*))
```

Either of the following commands rebinds the empty string version of the package TESTPK in all collections at the local DB2 system for which you have the BIND privilege:

```
REBIND PACKAGE (*.TESTPK)
REBIND PACKAGE (*.TESTPK.())
```

Package Lists

Using the PKLIST keyword during rebind replaces any previously specified package list. Omitting the PKLIST keyword allows the use of the previous package list for rebinding. Using the NOPKLIST keyword deletes any package list specified when the plan was previously bound. The following example rebinds PLANTK and changes the package list:

```
REBIND PLAN(PLANTK) PKLIST(GROUP1.*) MEMBER(TEST)
```

The following example rebinds the plan and drops the entire package list:

```
REBIND PLAN(PLANTK) NOPKLIST
```

A list of REBIND subcommands can be generated for a set of plans or packages that cannot be described by using asterisks, using information in the DB2 catalog. You can then issue the list of subcommands through DSN.

One situation in which the technique is particularly useful is in completing a rebind operation that has terminated for lack of resources. A rebind for many objects—say, REBIND PACKAGE (*) for an ID with SYSADM authority—terminates if a needed resource becomes unavailable. As a result, some objects are successfully rebound and others are not. If you repeat the subcommand, DB2 attempts to rebind all the objects again. But if you generate a REBIND subcommand for each object that was not rebound and issue those, DB2 does not repeat any work already done and is not likely to run out of resources.

Automatic Rebinding

Automatic rebind might occur if an authorized user invokes a plan or package when the attributes of the data on which the plan or package depends have changed or if the environment in which the package executes changes. Whether the automatic rebind occurs depends on the value of the field AUTO BIND on installation panel DSNTIPO. The options used for an automatic rebind are those used during the most recent bind process.

In most cases, DB2 marks as invalid a plan or package that needs to be automatically rebound. Following are a few common situations in which DB2 marks a plan or package as invalid:

- When a table, index, or view on which the plan or package depends is dropped
- When the authorization of the owner to access any of those objects is revoked
- When the authorization to execute a stored procedure is revoked from a plan or package owner, and the plan or package uses the CALL *literal* form to call the stored procedure
- When a table on which the plan or package depends is altered to add a TIME, TIMESTAMP, or DATE column
- When a created temporary table on which the plan or package depends is altered to add a column
- When a user-defined function on which the plan or package depends is altered
- Whether a plan or package is valid is recorded in column VALID of catalog tables SYSPLAN and SYSPACKAGE
- When an index, table, or column definition changes via an ALTER

In the following cases, DB2 might automatically rebind a plan or package that has not been marked as invalid.

- A plan or package is bound in a different release of DB2 from the release in which it was first used.
- A plan or package has a location dependency and runs at a location other than the one at which it was bound. This can happen when members of a data sharing group are defined with location names, and a package runs on a different member from the one on which it was bound.

DB2 marks a plan or package as *inoperative* if an automatic rebind fails. Whether a plan or package is operative is recorded in column OPERATIVE of the SYSPLAN and SYSPACKAGE catalog tables.

Whether EXPLAIN runs during automatic rebind depends on the value of the field EXPLAIN PROCESSING on installation panel DSNTIPO and on whether you specified EXPLAIN(YES). Automatic rebind fails for all EXPLAIN errors except "PLAN_TABLE not found."

> **N O T E**   The SQLCA is not available during automatic rebind; therefore, some error messages may not be available.

Removing a Plan or Package

One way to remove a plan or a package is to use the FREE command. The FREE command removes the object from the catalog tables, and it will no longer be available for use. The following example frees all the packages in the CERTCL collection:

```
FREE PACKAGE (CERTCL.*)
```

A package can also be dropped using the DROP PACKAGE SQL statement. The following is an example of dropping the DB2CERT package:

```
DROP PACKAGE DB2USER.DB2CERT
```

PLAN OR PACKAGE OWNERSHIP

All the actions an application plan or a package takes on tables require one or more privileges. The owner of the plan or package must hold every required privilege. Another ID can execute the plan or package, requiring only the EXECUTE privilege. In that way, another ID can exercise all the privileges that are used in validating the plan or package but only within the restrictions imposed by the SQL statements in the original program.

The executing ID can use some of the owner's privileges, within limits. If the privileges are revoked from the owner, the plan or the package is invalidated. It must be rebound, and the new owner must have the required privileges.

The BIND and REBIND subcommands create or change an application plan or a package. On either subcommand, use the OWNER option to name the owner of the resulting plan or package. Keep the following points in mind when naming an owner if the OWNER option is used.

- Any user can name the primary or any secondary ID.
- An ID with the BINDAGENT privilege can name the grantor of that privilege.
- An ID with SYSCTRL or SYSADM authority can name any authorization ID on a BIND command but not on a REBIND command.

The following apply if the OWNER option is omitted.

- BIND: The primary ID becomes the owner.
- REBIND: The previous owner retains ownership.

Unqualified Objects

A plan or a package can contain SQL statements that use unqualified table and view names. For static SQL, the default qualifier for those names is the owner of the plan or package. However, you can use the QUALIFIER option of the BIND command to specify a different qualifier.

For plans or packages that contain static SQL, using the BINDAGENT privilege and the OWNER and QUALIFIER options gives you considerable flexibility in performing bind operations. For plans or packages that contain dynamic SQL, the DYNAMICRULES behavior determines how DB2 qualifies unqualified object names.

For unqualified distinct types, user-defined functions, stored procedures, and trigger names in dynamic SQL statements, DB2 finds the schema name to use as the qualifier by searching schema names in the CURRENT PATH special register. For static statements, the PATH bind option determines the path that DB2 searches to resolve unqualified distinct types, user-defined functions, stored procedures, and trigger names.

However, an exception exists for ALTER, CREATE, DROP, COMMENT ON, GRANT, and REVOKE statements. For static SQL, specify the qualifier for these statements in the QUALIFIER bind option. For dynamic SQL, the qualifier for these statements is the authorization ID of the CURRENT SQLID special register.

Plan Execution Authorization

The plan or package owner must have authorization to execute all static SQL statements that are embedded in the plan or package. These authorizations do not need to be in place when the plan or package is bound, nor do the objects that are referred to need to exist at that time.

A bind operation always checks whether a local object exists and whether the owner has the required privileges on it. Any failure results in a message. To choose whether the failure prevents the bind operation from completing, use the VALIDATE option of BIND PLAN and BIND PACKAGE and also the SQLERROR option of BIND PACKAGE. If you let the operation complete, the checks are made again at runtime. The corresponding checks for remote objects are always made at runtime. Authorization to execute dynamic SQL statements is also checked at runtime.

SUMMARY

This chapter looked at what it takes to compile and bind an application program to DB2 and to be able to execute that program. This process must be completed in order to have a program access and manipulate DB2 data. Packages and DBRMs are used to store the bound program; the plan is the executable object. We also looked at the special authorities needed to execute the plan.

ADDITIONAL RESOURCES

DB2 UDB Version 8 Application Programming and SQL Guide (SC26-9933)

DB2 UDB Version 8 Command Reference (SC26-9934)

Application Program Features

- Commit, rollback, and savepoint operations
- Global transactions
- Fetching for limited rows
- Identity columns
- Sequence objects

All SQL programs execute as part of an *application process*, which involves the execution of one or more programs and is the unit to which DB2 allocates resources and locks. Different application processes might involve the execution of different programs or different executions of the same program. The means of initiating and terminating an application process are dependent on the environment.

COMMIT, ROLLBACK, AND SAVEPOINT OPERATIONS

More than one application process might request access to the same data at the same time. Locking is used to maintain data integrity under such conditions, preventing, for example, two application processes from updating the same row of data simultaneously. For more information, refer to Chapter 16.

DB2 implicitly acquires locks to prevent uncommitted changes made by one application process from being perceived by any other. DB2 implicitly releases all locks it has acquired on behalf of an application process when that process ends, but an application process can also explicitly request that locks be released sooner.

Commit and Rollback Operations

A *commit* operation releases locks acquired by the application process and commits database changes made by the same process. Two good reasons to commit are to improve concurrency and to prevent massive, long-running rollbacks when abnormal terminations occur. Even programs that have no concurrency problems should do a commit at least every 10 minutes, as a general rule.

If you design a good batch program, commit processing is part of it. If you do commit processing, you have to identify the unit of work (UOW) in your program and also design the batch program to be restartable.

When concurrency is an issue, you probably want a commit frequency between 2 seconds and 20 seconds. A good practice is to make sure that the commit frequency can be influenced from the outside. In your program, identify a logical UOW and execute it *x* number of times before doing a commit. The magic number *x* could come from a control card to your program or from a heuristic control table. This way, programs that cause concurrency problems can be tuned, and you can also have separate settings depending on the time of day. It is a good idea to have the same design in all your programs. Software solutions from independent software vendors (ISVs) take care of all commit and restart problems.

It is not good practice to do intermittent committing in online transactions rather than commit at the end of the transaction. When you have a long-running, or background, transaction—printing, for example—you should design your transaction such that it will reschedule itself and then terminate, doing an implicit commit. This way, all resources are released, and the transaction server can shut down in an orderly way when needed.

DB2 also provides a way to *back out* uncommitted changes made by an application process. This might be necessary if an application process fails or is in a *deadlock* situation. An application process, however, can explicitly request that its database changes be backed out. This operation is called *rollback*. DB2 creates undo log records for rollbacks and redo log records for recovery for every row that is changed. DB2 also logs these records for changes to all affected indexes.

The interface an SQL program uses to explicitly specify these commit and rollback operations depends on the environment. If the environment can include recoverable resources other than DB2 databases, the SQL COMMIT and ROLLBACK statements cannot be used. Thus, these statements cannot be used in IMS, CICS, or WebSphere environments.

Unit of Work

A *UOW*, sometimes called a *logical UOW*, is a recoverable sequence of operations within an application process. At any time, an application process has a single UOW, but the life of an application process can involve many UOWs as a result of commit or full-rollback operations.

A UOW is initiated when an application process is initiated. A UOW is also initiated when the previous UOW is ended by something other than the end of the application process. A UOW is ended by a commit operation, a full-rollback operation—either explicitly initiated by the application process or implicitly initiated by DB2—or the end of an application process. A commit or rollback operation affects only the changes made to recoverable resources within the UOW.

While changes to data—via insert, update, or delete—remain uncommitted, other application processes are unable to perceive them unless they are running with an isolation level of uncommitted read. The changes can still be backed out by a rollback. Once committed, these database changes are accessible by other application processes and can no longer be backed out by a rollback. Locks acquired by DB2 on behalf of an application process to protect uncommitted data are held at least until the end of a UOW.

The initiation and termination of a UOW define *points of consistency* within an application process. A point of consistency is a claim by the application that the data is consistent. For example, a banking transaction might involve the transfer of funds from one account to another. Such a transaction would require that these funds be subtracted from the first account and added to the second. Following the subtraction step, the data is inconsistent. Consistency is reestablished only after the funds have been added to the second account. When both steps are complete, the commit operation can be used to end the UOW, thereby making the changes available to other application processes.

Unit of Recovery

A *DB2 unit of recovery* (UR) is a recoverable sequence of operations executed by DB2 for an application process. If a UOW involves changes to other recoverable resources, such as VSAM or MQSeries, the UOW will be supported by those URs. If relational databases are the only recoverable resources used by the application process, the scope of the UOW and the UR is the same, and either term can be used.

Rolling back Work

DB2 can back out all changes or only selected changes made in a UR. Only backing out all changes results in a point of consistency.

Without the TO SAVEPOINT clause, the SQL ROLLBACK statement causes a full-rollback operation. If such a rollback operation is successfully executed, DB2 backs out uncommitted changes to restore the data consistency that it assumes existed when the UOW was initiated. That is, DB2 *undoes* the work.

Savepoints

A savepoint enables milestones within a transaction or UR to be bookmarked. An external savepoint represents the state of the data and schema at a particular time. After the savepoint is set, changes made to data and schemas by the transaction can be rolled back to the savepoint, as application logic requires, without affecting the overall outcome of the transaction:

```
EXEC SQL
SAVEPOINT name (other options)
END-EXEC.

EXEC SQL
ROLLBACK TO SAVEPOINT name
END-EXEC.
```

ROLLBACK can be used to restore to a savepoint. This is useful when a point has been reached during a unit of work and there is a need to back out without undoing the entire unit of work. Individual savepoints can be named, and then ROLLBACK can be used to roll back work to whichever point is required, based on the application-processing requirements, skipping over individual savepoints, if necessary.

If there are outstanding savepoints, access to a remote database management system—via DRDA or private protocol, using aliases or three-part names—is not permitted, because the scope of a savepoint is within the database management system on which it was set. DRDA access using a CONNECT statement is allowed; however, the savepoints are local to their site. DB2 does not restrict the use of aliases and three-part names to connect to a remote site when there are outstanding savepoints at the remote site. But this is not recommended. There is no limit to the number of savepoints that can be set.

Establishing a Savepoint

In order to set a savepoint, you use the SAVEPOINT statement. You must choose the name for the savepoint, so the name can be meaningful, if you wish. Application logic will determine whether the savepoint name needs to be reused as the application progresses or needs to denote a unique milestone. You can specify the UNIQUE option on the SAVEPOINT statement if you do not intend for the name to be reused. This will prevent an invoked procedure from unintentionally reusing the name. If a savepoint is coded in a loop, however, there is no choice; do not use UNIQUE.

If the name of the savepoint identifies a savepoint that already exists within the UR and the savepoint was not created with the UNIQUE option, the existing savepoint is destroyed and a new one created. Destroying a savepoint by reusing its name for another savepoint is not the same as releasing the savepoint. Reusing a savepoint name destroys only the one savepoint. Releasing a savepoint releases the named savepoint and all savepoints that were subsequently set. (Releasing savepoints is described later.)

The following statement shows an example of setting a unique savepoint named START_AGAIN. After executing this statement, the application program needs to check the SQL return code to verify that the savepoint was set:

```
EXEC SQL
SAVEPOINT START_AGAIN UNIQUE ON ROLLBACK RETAIN CURSORS
END-EXEC.
```

The SAVEPOINT statement sets a savepoint within a UR. This statement, as well as the ROLLBACK and RELEASE statements, can be embedded in application programs, external user-defined functions, stored procedures—that are defined as MODIFIES SQL DATA—or issued interactively. It cannot be issued from the body of a trigger. It is an executable statement that can be dynamically prepared only if DYNAMICRULES (RUN) behavior is implicitly or explicitly in effect. The syntax is as follows:

```
EXEC SQL
SAVEPOINT svptname
UNIQUE
   ON ROLLBACK RETAIN CURSORS
   ON ROLLBACK RETAIN LOCKS
END-EXEC.
```

Table 12-1 provides a brief description of each part of the SAVEPOINT syntax.

Table 12-1 Savepoint Syntax

Syntax	Description
svptname	Identifier that names the savepoint.
UNIQUE	Specifies that the application program cannot reuse this savepoint name within the UR. An error occurs if a savepoint with the same name as svptname already exists within the UR. If you do not use UNIQUE, the application can reuse this savepoint name within the UR.
ON ROLLBACK RETAIN CURSORS	Specifies that any cursors opened after the savepoint is set are not tracked and thus are not closed on rollback to the savepoint. Even though these cursors do remain open after rollback to the savepoint, they may not be usable.
ON ROLLBACK RETAIN LOCKS	Specifies that any locks that are acquired after the savepoint is set are not tracked and therefore are not released on rollback to the savepoint.

Restoring to a Savepoint

In order to restore to a savepoint, the ROLLBACK statement is used with the TO SAVEPOINT clause. The next example shows pseudocode for an application that sets and restores to a savepoint. This IBM-supplied example application makes airline reservations on a preferred date and then makes hotel reservations. If the hotel is unavailable, the application rolls back the airline reservations and repeats the process for a next-best date. Up to three dates are tried:

```
EXEC SQL SAVEPOINT START_AGAIN UNIQUE
            ON ROLLBACK RETAIN CURSORS;
   Check SQL code;
   Do i = 1 to 3 UNTIL got_reservation;
      Book_Air (dates(i),ok);
      If ok then
         Book_Hotel(dates(i),ok);
      If ok then
         got_reservations
      Else
         EXEC SQL ROLLBACK TO START_AGAIN;
      End loop;
EXEC SQL RELEASE SAVEPOINT START_AGAIN;
```

The ROLLBACK statement with the new TO SAVEPOINT option backs out data and schema changes that were made after a savepoint. This can be embedded. The skeleton syntax is as follows:

```
EXEC SQL
ROLLBACK WORK
TO SAVEPOINT svptname
END-EXEC.
```

In the skeleton syntax, ROLLBACK WORK rolls back the entire UR. All savepoints that were set within the UR are released. TO SAVEPOINT specifies that the rollback of the UR occurs only to the specified savepoint. If no savepoint name is specified, rollback is to the last active savepoint; svptname is the name of the savepoint to roll back to.

In the following example, the ROLLBACK TO SAVEPOINT statement will cause the rollback to savepoint two, which will cause the second and third sets of application code to be rolled back:

```
EXEC SQL
SAVEPOINT ONE ON ROLLBACK RETAIN CURSORS;
END-EXEC
```

First application code set ..

```
EXEC SQL
SAVEPOINT TWO ON ROLLBACK RETAIN CURSORS;
END-EXEC.
```

Second application code set..

```
EXEC SQL
SAVEPOINT THREE ON ROLLBACK RETAIN CURSORS;
END-EXEC.
```

Third application code set..

```
EXEC SQL
RELEASE SAVEPOINT THREE;
END-EXEC.
```

```
EXEC SQL
ROLLBACK TO SAVEPOINT;
END-EXEC.
```

If the named savepoint does not exist, an error will occur. Data and schema changes made after the savepoint was set are backed out. Because changes made to global temporary tables are not logged, they are not backed out, but a warning is issued. A warning is also issued if the global temporary table is changed and there is an active savepoint. None of the following items are backed out:

- Opening or closing of cursors
- Changes in cursor positioning
- Acquisition and release of locks
- Caching of the rolled-back statements

Savepoints that are set after the one to which rollback is performed are released. The savepoint to which rollback is performed is not released. For example, in the following scenario, the ROLLBACK TO SAVEPOINT TWO statement causes savepoint three to be released but not savepoint two:

```
EXEC SQL
SAVEPOINT ONE ON ROLLBACK RETAIN CURSORS;
END-EXEC.
```

First application code set ..

```
EXEC SQL
SAVEPOINT TWO ON ROLLBACK RETAIN CURSORS;
END-EXEC.
```

Second application code set..

```
EXEC SQL
SAVEPOINT THREE ON ROLLBACK RETAIN CURSORS;
END-EXEC.
```

Third application code set..

```
EXEC SQL
ROLLBACK TO SAVEPOINT TWO;
END-EXEC.
```

Releasing a Savepoint

Releasing a savepoint involves the use of the RELEASE SAVEPOINT statement. You cannot roll back to a savepoint after it is released. Only a small amount of overhead is needed to maintain savepoints, but it is more important to release them, because any outstanding savepoints will block any system-directed connections to remote locations. After an application no longer needs to roll back to that savepoint, you should release it. The following example releases a savepoint named START_AGAIN and all the savepoints that were subsequently set by the transaction:

```
EXEC SQL
RELEASE SAVEPOINT START_AGAIN;
END-EXEC.
```

The RELEASE SAVEPOINT statement releases the named savepoint and any subsequently established savepoints. Once a savepoint has been released, it is no longer maintained, and roll-back to the savepoint is no longer possible. The syntax is as follows:

```
EXEC SQL
RELEASE
        TO
SAVEPOINT svptname
END-EXEC.
```

The svptname is the savepoint identifier that identifies the savepoint to be released. If there is no named savepoint, an error will occur. The named savepoint and all the savepoints that were subsequently established by the transaction are released.

Savepoints in a Distributed Environment

In a distributed environment, you can set savepoints only if you use DRDA access with explicit CONNECT statements. If you set a savepoint and then execute an SQL statement with a three-part name, an SQL error occurs.

The site at which a savepoint is recognized depends on whether the CONNECT statement is executed before or after the savepoint is set. For example, if an application executes the statement SET SAVEPOINT C1 at the local site before executing a CONNECT TO S1 statement, savepoint C1 is known only at the local site. If the application executes CONNECT TO S1 before SET SAVEPOINT C1, the savepoint is known only at site S1. For more information on the CONNECT statement, refer to Chapter 10.

GLOBAL TRANSACTIONS

Global transactions allow an application to modify data managed by different resource managers within a single unit of work. The Recoverable Resource Manager Services (RRS) component of z/OS manages the unit of work for the application and coordinates the activities of the participating resource managers. DB2 participates as a resource manager in global transactions, as do MQ Series, IMS, and other products. When using a global transaction, an application needs to use interfaces defined by RRS to commit or roll back work. These transactions will be identified via a token—global transaction ID, or XID.

Within DB2, global transactions allow several processes to share locks if they are all participants in a unit of work. The larger unit of work is referred to as a global transaction. This provides a way to avoid deadlocks between separate threads that are part of the same work unit.

The sharing of locks is limited to normal transaction locks and an explicit LOCK TABLE statement, or partition-key updates could still cause deadlocks or timeouts. Many design issues need to be considered prior to the use of global transactions, and there are also additional risks and exposures.

GLOBAL TEMPORARY TABLES

Sometimes, a table does not need to exist for a long period of time. For example, a table may be needed to act as a staging area for data for use by a program. Temporary tables can be used to accommodate this. Temporary tables are either created or declared.

Created Temporary Tables

Created temporary tables (CTTs) can help improve performance in many ways. Whenever repetitive SQL is being used to return a result set, producing exactly the same result each time, a CTT might provide benefit. A subquery that is used more than once is a prime example. It would be better to issue the subquery once, storing the result-set rows in the CTT, and use the CTT in subsequent subqueries. The biggest advantage of CTTs is that no logging is done, as no recovery is possible. However, no indexing is done either, so a table space scan will always be used as the access path. Also, an SQL UPDATE or DELETE can not make modifications to the data in the CTT. Only INSERTs are allowed. The CTT will exist for the duration of the unit of work and will be automatically deleted when a commit is issued unless the table is used in a cursor definition using CURSOR WITH HOLD.

CTTs are very useful for stored procedures. For example, global temporary tables can be used as a holding area for nonrelational or non-DB2 data, such as data extracted from VSAM files. The data will be held for the duration of the unit of work and can be referenced in SQL statements. This is particularly valuable when a left or full outer join is required, using one DB2 table and one non-DB2 table—for example, extracted VSAM data. An INSERT statement can load the temporary table with the VSAM data, and then the following SQL statement can perform the outer join:

```
EXEC SQL
SELECT * FROM T1 LEFT JOIN global-temp-name ON join predicates END-EXEC.
```

This technique logically fits in a stored procedure so that any other process that needs the result can simply execute it. A table function may be even better, as it would allow the retrieval of this data using standard SQL statements. The benefit is that the DB2 join algorithms, instead of a homegrown program, are used to perform the outer join.

CCTs have another major benefit. They can be used when a materialized set is present for a result set, a view, or a table expression and the materialized set needs to be used more than once.

Sometimes, it is necessary to use a workaround in SQL, owing to the 15-table limits on an SQL statement. CTTs can be used to hold the results of some of the tables prior to a later statement, which would join the global temporary table with the remaining tables.

The only access path available against a CTT is a table space scan, so keep the size of the scan in mind when doing performance analysis. When a CTT is used in a join, the access path will generally be a merge-scan join that might require sorting the CTT.

A CTT can be held longer than a unit of work when it is used inside a cursor definition that is defined WITH HOLD.

Creating a Temporary Table

A created temporary table is created in the same manner as a normal table, through DDL, except that it is not physically created in a table space. These tables cannot be created with default values and cannot have unique, referential, or check constraints defined for them. The following example shows the creation of a created temporary table that will hold rows containing an amount and a date:

```
CREATE GLOBAL TEMPORARY TABLE SUMMARY
AMOUNT_SOLD DECIMAL(5,2) NOT NULL,
SOLD_DATE DATE NOT NULL)
```

An empty instance of the table is created when the first implicit or explicit reference is made to it in an SQL statement. In normal use, an `INSERT` would be the first statement issued. The temporary table exists only until the originating application commits, does a rollback, or terminates, unless the table is used in a cursor using the `WITH HOLD` option.

Determining How Often CTTs Are Materialized

CTTs are materialized in DSNDB07. If multiple global temporary tables are being continually materialized, you could run into a problem with the performance of all processes, such as sorting using DSNDB07 work files. In order to keep control over DSNDB07, you can monitor this materialization through DB2 traces.

Performance trace, class 8, IFCID 311 contains information about CTT materialization and cursor processing. Field QW0311CI shows whether an instance of a temporary table was created in a work file. You can also see whether a cursor was opened or closed. This will give you an idea of the amount of work occurring against the work file table space for temporary tables. If you find that a lot of activity is occurring and feel that it may be causing problems, you can also use the trace fields to determine what queries or programs are causing the materialization:

```
0017 QW0017TT   'TT'=TEMPORARY TABLE SCAN.
```

Declared Temporary Tables

Declared temporary tables (DTTs) enable you to declare a temporary table for use in a program. The `DECLARE GLOBAL TEMPORARY TABLE` statement defines a temporary table for the current session, not only for a UOW. The table description does not appear in the DB2 catalog, is not persistent, and cannot be shared, unlike a CTT.

This statement can be embedded in an application program or issued through the use of dynamic SQL statements. The statement is executable and can also be dynamically prepared. Each session that defines a declared global temporary table of the same name has its own unique instantiation of the temporary table. When the session terminates, the temporary table is dropped. With DTTs, some of the locking, DB2 catalog updates, and DB2 restart forward and backward log recoveries that are associated with persistent tables are avoided. No authority is required to issue the `DECLARE GLOBAL TEMPORARY TABLE` statement, but authority will be required to use the new user temporary table space where the table will be materialized.

DTTs can be useful for applications that need to extract data from various sources and use it in SQL joins or for data that needs to be used repetitively or kept separate from other online transaction processing processes. DTTs can also be used as staging areas for data that comes from various sources so that the data can be manipulated before it is stored permanently in regular tables.

Following are a couple of examples of the syntax for DTTs:

```
EXEC SQL
DECLARE GLOBAL TEMPORARY TABLE SESSION.CERTTEST
   LIKE DB2USER1.TEST
INSERT INTO SESSION.CERTEST
   SELECT * FROM DB2USER1.TEST
END-EXEC.

EXEC SQL
DECLARE GLOBAL TEMPORARY TABLE SESSION.CERTEST
   AS
   (SELECT * FROM DB2USER1.TEST)
DEFINITION ONLY
END-EXEC.
```

Usage Considerations

DTTs could be used as a way to temporarily hold or sort data within a program. DTTs are useful for relational online analytical processing (ROLAP) and multidimensional online analytical processing (MOLAP) queries for warehouse tools and as a staging area for IMS or VSAM data so it is SQL and ODBC accessible. The word SESSION must be the qualifier for a DTT and can be named explicitly in the table name or can be in the QUALIFIER BIND option on the plan or package.

Only undo records are logged, and the full range of DML—INSERT, UPDATE, SELECT, DELETE—can be performed on them. DTTs are supported by rollback to savepoint or last commit point. The table exists until thread termination; if thread reuse is being used, it will exist until it is implicitly dropped, which may or may not be desirable, depending on the application.

No locks are taken (PAGE, ROW, or TABLE) on DTTs; however, locks are taken on table space and DBD in share mode. DDTs also do not require a declared cursor to hold rows across commits.

Static SQL referencing a DTT will be incrementally bound at runtime. The cost associated with a DTT is equivalent to the cost of executing a dynamic SQL statement. High-volume transaction applications need careful evaluation when you are planning to use DTTs.

> **N O T E** Any dynamic SQL statements that reference DTTs will not be able to use the dynamic statement cache.

Some restrictions apply when using DTTs. They do not support the following:

- LOBs or ROWIDs
- Referential integrity

- Use in a `CREATE TABLE LIKE` statement
- Sysplex query parallelism
- Dynamic statement caching
- ODBC/JDBC functions that rely on the catalog definitions
- Thread reuse for DDF pool threads
- Use within triggers

TEMP Database

DTTs are not materialized in DSNDB07 but rather in a segmented `TEMP` table space. A `TEMP` database must be created prior to the creation of the DTTs. This database is not sharable across data sharing members; each member must have its own. Several segmented table spaces will need to be created. DB2 will decide where tables are created. `PUBLIC` will automatically have authority to create DTTs in these table spaces.

The DTTs cannot span table spaces. This fact enables you to have small table spaces and to be able to control the size of any DTT that is created. Different table spaces for 4K, 8K, 16K, and 32K pages may be needed. DB2 will choose the appropriate one; if one does not exist, the `DECLARE` fails.

> **N O T E** It is recommended that you use the same-sized pages for each table space and spread the data sets across several volumes.

> **N O T E** It is important to size this database accordingly to accommodate growth and concurrent transactions—those transactions that are all using DTTs at a given point in time

Commit Options for Declared DTTs

Prior to version 8, declared temporary tables persisted until the end of the application. This made for a requirement to discard prior to this point. Version 8 has some options on the `DECLARE GLOBAL TEMPORARY TABLE` statement to provide alternatives. Those options are as follows.

- `ON COMMIT DELETE ROWS` will delete rows if no open cursor `WITH HOLD`.
- `ON COMMIT PRESERVE ROWS` will preserve rows, but thread reuse cannot be used.
- `ON COMMIT DROP TABLE` drops the table if no open cursor `WITH HOLD`.

These options are useful for self-contained stored procedures with several DTTs and the cursors defined on them. The invokers, or creators, of the DTTs can access results, then commit and drop the DTT. The user will not need to specify the name of the DDT in this process. These features will also improve DDF threads (`CMSTAT=INACTIVE`) because DTTs will no longer stop a thread from becoming inactive.

FETCH FOR LIMITED ROWS

Limited-Row FETCH

During cursor processing, the ability to tell DB2 to fetch only the first, or top, n rows is a requirement in many applications. SQL and the application program can do this but not efficiently. For example, a query could be written as follows:

```
EXEC SQL
SELECT *
  FROM EMPLOYEE A
  WHERE 5 >= (SELECT COUNT(*)
    FROM EMPLOYEE B
    WHERE B.EMPNO <= A.EMPNO)
END-EXEC.
```

However, the result is terrible performance because DB2 will have to read rows proportional to the square of the numbers of table rows.

With the FETCH FIRST clause of a fullselect, DB2 has this functionality with improved performance, as the clause sets a maximum number of rows that can be retrieved through a cursor. The application specifies that it does not want to retrieve more than a fixed number of rows, regardless of how many rows qualified for the result set.

The OPTIMIZE FOR n ROWS clause, which provides additional information to the optimizer about the intent, is different from the FETCH FIRST clause. The OPTIMIZE FOR clause can allow the entire answer set to be retrieved. In contrast, the FETCH FIRST n ROWS ONLY stops processing after the specified number of rows. Thus, the application programmer has direct control over the size of the result table. For example, an implementation limit on the number of rows displayed for an online screen can now be enforced. The following example shows the use of the FETCH FIRST n ROWS ONLY clause with the OPTIMIZE FOR n ROWS:

```
EXEC SQL
DECLARE FIRST_FIVE CURSOR FOR
  SELECT EMPNO
  FROM EMPLOYEE
  ORDER BY EMPNO
  FETCH FIRST 5 ROWS ONLY
  OPTIMIZE FOR 5 ROWS
END-EXEC.
```

The FETCH FIRST clause is valid for singleton SELECTs, whereas the OPTIMIZE clause is not. The FETCH FIRST clause is thus a perfect solution for optimal existence checking. It will perform a maximum of only one fetch to determine existence, and there is no internal second fetch for the -811 return code required. The clause automatically implies OPTIMIZE FOR 1 ROW and therefore discourages sequential prefetch, multi-index access, and list prefetch. This technique requires minimal coding to support singleton select, and no cursor logic is required. The clause can also be coded within an application program or dynamically: Query Management Facility, DSNTEP2, and so on. The following is an example of FETCH FIRST for existence checking:

```
EXEC SQL
  SELECT 1 INTO :hv-check
  FROM TABLE
  WHERE COL1 = :hv1
  FETCH FIRST 1 ROW ONLY
END-EXEC.
```

Multirow FETCH and Multirow INSERT

Multirow FETCH and INSERT take advantage of arrays in which each element in the array contains a value for the same column. These host-variable arrays are allowed in COBOL, C++, PL/1, and, in some cases, assembler.

The ability to perform a multirow INSERT or FETCH can greatly improve the performance of distributed applications. It allows for multiple rows to be inserted or fetched in a single API call. Multirow FETCH and INSERT are supported by static, dynamic, nonscrollable, and scrollable cursors.

The multirow FETCH capability is done by declaring a cursor to be able to retrieve a row set with a single FETCH statement. Then the FETCH will specify the group of rows to be returned by fetching the row set. The FETCH controls how many rows are returned. Up to 32,767 rows can make up a single row set.

Following is an example of multirow FETCH:

```
DECLARE CUR1 CURSOR
WITH ROWSET POSITIONING
FOR SELECT COL1, COL2 FROM TABLE1;

OPEN CUR1;

FETCH NEXT ROWSET FOR 3 ROWS FROM CUR1
FOR :hv ROWS INTO :values1, :values2;
```

The multirow FETCH is useful for queries that perform large table space scans.

There is also support for positioned UPDATEs and DELETEs for cursors using multirow FETCH. Following is an example of a positioned UPDATE with a cursor defined with a row set:

```
UPDATE TABLE1
    SET COL1 = :newvalue
    FOR CURSOR CUR1
    FOR ROW :rownum OF ROWSET
```

With multirow inserts, multiple rows can be inserted into a table or view using values that were supplied in the host variable array. Each array represents multiple rows for a single column. Up to 32,767 values can be specified.

An example of a multirow INSERT follows:

```
INSERT INTO TABLE1
VALUES (:values1, values2) FOR 20 ROWS ATOMIC
```

IDENTITY COLUMNS

Identity columns provide a way to have DB2 automatically generate unique, sequential, and recoverable values for each row in a table. The identity column is defined with the AS IDENTITY attribute provided in its column definition. Each table can have only one identity column defined to it. Identity columns are ideally suited for the task of generating unique primary-key values, such as employee number, order number, item number, or account number. Identity columns can also be used to alleviate concurrency problems caused by application-generated sequence numbers.

An identity column value can always be generated by DB2 or by default. DB2 always generates the column value and guarantees its uniqueness for identity columns defined as GENERATED ALWAYS. Applications cannot provide an explicit value for a column defined this way. If an identity column is defined as GENERATED BY DEFAULT, an application can provide an explicit value for the column; if it is absent, DB2 will generate a value. But DB2 will guarantee the uniqueness of the value only if it is always generated by DB2. The use of GENERATED BY DEFAULT is intended for data propagation, or copying the contents of an existing table or unloading and reloading a table.

Identity column counters are increased or decreased independently of the transaction. There may be gaps between two numbers that are generated, because several transactions may concurrently increment the same identity counter by inserting rows into the same table. Exclusive locks should be taken on the tables that contain identity columns if an application must have a consecutive range of numbers. Gaps in the generated identity column numbers can also appear if a transaction that generated a value for the identity column gets rolled back or a DB2 subsystem that has a range of identity values cached terminates abnormally. As a general rule, gaps in identity values should not cause a great deal of concern unless you are still using preprinted forms. Additional properties of identity column values are as follows.

- Values must have a numeric data type.
- Types must be SMALLINT, INTEGER, DECIMAL with a scale of zero, or a distinct type based on one of these types.
- The identity column can specify the difference between consecutive values.
- The counter value for the identity column is recoverable from the DB2 log.
- Identity column values are incremented across multiple members in a data sharing group.
- Identity column values can be cached for better performance.

The CREATE TABLE, ALTER TABLE, INSERT, and UPDATE have all been enhanced to support the identity columns. For information on the creation and the identity column options, refer to Chapter 4.

INSERT and UPDATE

The DEFAULT keyword can be used in the VALUES clause for identity columns. This allows DB2 to generate the value to be inserted into the column:

```
EXEC SQL
  INSERT INTO ACCOUNT_TRANS (ACCOUNT_NO, TYPE, LAST_NAME)
  VALUES (DEFAULT, :type, :lname)
END-EXEC.
```

DB2 always generates the identity column value defined as GENERATED ALWAYS. Even if you specify a value to insert, DB2 will either ignore it or issue an error. DB2 will ignore the value and generate a value for insertion if the OVERRIDING USER VALUE clause is used. Because the value is not used in the following statement, it will produce an error:

```
EXEC SQL
  INSERT INTO ACCOUNT_TRANS (ACCOUNT_NO, TYPE, LAST_NAME)
   VALUES (:account, :type, :lname)
END-EXEC.
```

DB2 will use a specified value if the identity column is defined as GENERATED BY DEFAULT. But DB2 will not verify the uniqueness of the value, and it might be a duplicate of another value in the column, if you do not have a unique index defined on the column.

The rules for an insert with a subselect are similar to those for an insert with a VALUES clause. If you want the value implicitly specified in the column list to be inserted into a table's identity column, the column of the table that the data is being selected from must be defined as GENERATED BY DEFAULT. If you want to have DB2 ignore the value and insert a generated value into the identity column of the table being inserted into, the identity column of the table being selected from must be defined as GENERATED ALWAYS, and the INSERT statement must include the OVERRIDING USER VALUE clause. The following is an example of this clause:

```
EXEC SQL
  INSERT INTO ACCOUNT_TRANS OVERRIDING USER VALUE
  SELECT * FROM ACCOUNT_UPDT;
END-EXEC.
```

Updates are allowed on a value in an identity column only if it is defined as GENERATED BY DEFAULT. DB2 does not verify the value to guarantee uniqueness during the update. You cannot make updates to identity columns defined with GENERATED ALWAYS.

You can find the last column number generated by using the following:

```
EXEC SQL
SET :HV = IDENTITY_VAL_LOCAL()
EXEC SQL.
```

The result will be returned as DECIMAL(31,0). If a commit or rollback occurred since the insert, a null will be returned. It is recommended that you store the value after the insert and check the return code.

Updatable Identity Column Values in Version 8

Version 8 gave some relief to such identity column issues as the ability to obtain the identity column value before the insert with the new INSERT within a SELECT feature. The following example shows how to use this feature to obtain the identity column values during the insert. (Assume that the table was created with an identity column on ACCT_ID GENERATED ALWAYS.)

```
SELECT ACCT_ID
FROM FINAL TABLE (INSERT INTO UID1.ACCOUNT (NAME, TYPE, BALANCE)
        VALUES ('Master Card', 'Credit', 50000) )
```

Several other values can be altered in version 8:

- CACHE/NO CACHE
- CYCLE/NO CYCLE
- MINVALUE
- MAXVALUE
- INCREMENT BY
- RESTART WITH
- GENERATE ALWAYS/DEFAULT

The ability to perform these ALTERs, especially the RESTART WITH, gives greater flexibility in the use of identity columns. However, they are still somewhat restricted because of being defined on a single table and still a bit limited in terms of how applications can take advantage of them. Also, these ALTERs will cause the table space to be put into REORG-pending status, thus causing an outage to the availability of the table.

SEQUENCE OBJECTS

A sequence object is a user-defined object that generates a sequence of numeric values according to the specifications in which it was created. It provides an incremental counter generated by DB2 and is similar to an identity column. An identity column can be thought of as a special kind of sequence object; however, a sequence column is separate from the table.

Sequence object values can be used in applications for a variety of reasons and have several benefits:

- No waits for incrementing values
- Standalone sequential-number-generating object not tied to a table
- Ascending or descending number generation
- Useful for application porting from the other database management systems
- Helpful in generating keys that can be used to coordinate keys across multiple tables (RI or application related)

The sequence name is made up of two parts: the 128-byte schema name and the 128-byte identifier. A sequence object is created by using a new CREATE SEQUENCE statement; all attributes are completely user defined or defaults. The values in the sequence object can be of any exact numeric data type. The starting value is defined with a START WITH value and advances with INCREMENT BY (ascending or descending). The values can be cached and are generated in the order of request. Figure 12-1 shows the creation and simple use of a sequence object.

```
CREATE SEQUENCE  ACCOUNT_SEQ

        AS INTEGER

        START WITH 10

        INCREMEMENT BY 10

        CYCLE

        CACHE 20
```

ACCOUNT_SEQ

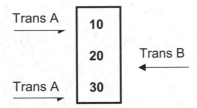

Figure 12-1   Sequence object creation and use

The sequence object, relatively similar to the workaround many people were using for identity columns, is much more efficient and has some nice usage benefits, such as the ability to do NEXT VALUE FOR and PREVIOUS VALUE FOR. NEXTVAL FOR generates and returns the next value for the sequence object; PREVVAL FOR generates and returns the previous value for the sequence object. These statements can be used with the following:

- SELECT and SELECT INTO
- An INSERT statement within the SELECT clause of fullselect
- An UPDATE statement within the SET clause (searched or positioned)
- SET host variable
- VALUES or VALUES INTO
- CREATE PROCEDURE, FUNCTION, TRIGGER

Following are examples of usage for these statements (assume that ACCT_SEQ is START WITH 10 INCREMENT BY 10):

```
SELECT NEXTVAL FOR ACCT_SEQ            → Returns 10
SELECT NEXTVAL FOR ACCT_SEQ            → Returns 20
COMMIT
SELECT PREVVAL FOR ACCT_SEQ            → Returns 20
***
UPDATE ACCOUNTS
SET ACCT_NO = NEXTVAL  FOR ACCT_SEQ    → Returns 30
***
INSERT INTO ACCOUNTS (ACCT_NO)
VALUES( SELECT NEXTVAL FROM ACCT_SEQ)  → Returns 40
```

As you can see, using sequence objects instead of identity columns has many benefits. Table 12-2 compares the two.

Table 12-2   Sequence Objects versus Identity Columns*

Sequence Object	Identity Columns with Version 8 Features
Standalone sequence objects created at user request	Internal sequence objects generated/maintained and populated by DB2
Can supply values for one or more table columns	Can have only one per table
Used for whatever purpose users choose	Associated with a particular table
CYCLEing will wrap around and repeat with no uniqueness consideration	CYCLEing may have a problem if a unique index is on the identity column and duplicates are created
When used to populate a table, can later be updated	Cannot be updated if GENERATED ALWAYS
Supports NEXT VALUE FOR expression and PREVIOUS VALUE FOR expression	Must use ID_VAL_LOCAL and returns only most recent values in that user's commit scope
ALTER, DROP, COMMENT, GRANT/REVOKE	ALTER TABLE only; if adding an identity column to a populated table, it will be put in REORG-pending status; cannot remove from a table

*   If future designs would benefit more from sequence objects than from identity columns, careful consideration should be made when choosing to use identity columns. If they are defined on populated tables and you want to remove them, the table must be dropped and recreated. This could be a big problem for large tables in a high-availability environment.

SUMMARY

This chapter looked at the various features that can be used in a DB2 application program. We looked at how a unit of work is defined and how to use commits, rollbacks, and savepoints to protect the integrity of the data being manipulated by the program. Other features, such as temporary tables and identity columns, were considered in terms of how to make use of them in a program. Some coding techniques were also examined—such as FETCH FIRST *n* ROWS—and various usages of this feature were also discussed. Many of these features can be used in an application program for enhanced functionality and optimal performance.

ADDITIONAL RESOURCES

IBM DB2 UDB for z/OS Version 8 Administration Guide (SC26-9931)

IBM DB2 UDB for z/OS Version 8 Application Programming and SQL Guide (SC26-9933)

IBM DB2 UDB for z/OS Version 8 SQL Reference (SC26-9944)

Advanced Functions and Performance

Stored Procedures

- Benefits of using stored procedures
- Writing stored procedures
- Defining stored procedures
- Execution environments
- SQL Procedure Language
- Developing SQL stored procedures
- DB2 Development Center

A stored procedure is a program that is stored and executed within the control of the DBMS. Some DBMS products limit stored procedures to a subset of SQL functionality. DB2 implements stored procedures as externally compiled programs that run within specialized DB2 address spaces.

All DB2 stored procedures are compiled programs stored in a load library available at the DB2 server. The DB2 server can be either the local DB2 subsystem or a remote DB2 subsystem. These programs can execute SQL statements, connect to other DB2 servers, and retrieve data from nondatabase sources. A stored procedure typically contains two or more SQL statements and some manipulative or logical processing in a host language. A client application program uses the SQL CALL statement to invoke a stored procedure:

```
EXEC SQL
CALL MYSP (:parm1, :parm2, :parm3)
END-EXEC.
```

BENEFITS OF USING STORED PROCEDURES

Using DB2 stored procedures has many benefits. The major advantage to stored procedures comes when they are implemented in a client/server application that must issue several remote SQL statements. The network overhead involved in sending multiple SQL commands and receiving result sets is quite significant. Therefore, proper use of stored procedures to accept a request, process it with encapsulated SQL statements and business logic, and return a result will lessen the traffic across the network and reduce the application overhead, as shown in Figure 13-1.

Stored procedures can also provide access to host-server data that is required to be secure. By using a stored procedure, the client will need to have authority to execute only the stored procedures and will not need authority to the DB2 tables that are accessed from the stored procedures. They can also help simplify development and maintenance and improve availability. By removing client dependency on database design at the server, the client code can continue to run while changes are made to the underlying databases. Business logic can be incorporated into the stored procedures, minimizing changes to client code, and changes to stored procedures can be implemented while the client code is still executing.

Encapsulation of core business functions is also a great way to implement stored procedures. This allows functions to be programmed once and executed by any and all processes required for a business process. Keep in mind that simple SQL statements should not be used in a stored procedure to act as an I/O module. This should never be done, as the performance overhead is enormous.

Another nice feature about using stored procedures is that they provide access to non-DB2 data for use in DB2 applications. Stored procedures can be used to retrieve data from a VSAM or IMS data store to be used by a DB2 client. One way to do this is by retrieving the data into a

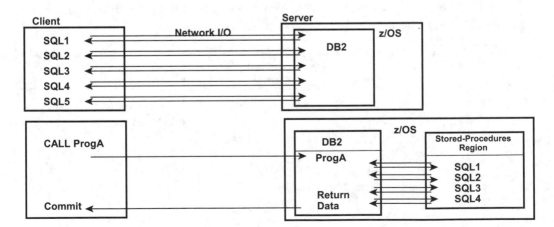

Figure 13-1   Stored-procedure network improvements

global or declared temporary table in the stored procedure and returning that to the caller as a result set. Applications can then use SQL and result-set logic for row retrieval of this data. Stored procedures can also execute a CICS transaction on behalf of a client.

In summary, stored procedures have the following benefits:

- Reduce network traffic
- Simplify development and maintenance
- Remove client dependency on database design at the server
- Allow for the ability to dynamically change application programs
- Changed and refreshed code at the server
- No need to change client code
- Can continue to run client code while changes are made
- Allow most of an application to exist at the server, not the client
- Need less code to be globally changed at all client locations
- Reusable code
- Improve security
- Eliminate the need for end user table authority
- Move processing away from end users
- Provide the ability to access and update data that is not stored in DB2, such as VSAM IMS data

WRITING STORED PROCEDURES

The programs that implement stored procedures can be written in several languages: C/C++, COBOL/OO COBOL, PL/1, assembler, REXX, Java, and SQL Procedure Language. The calling program and the stored-procedure program can be implemented in different languages. For example, the client code could be COBOL, and the stored procedure could be C. The connection is through the DB2 thread, so individual coding does not matter. With the exception of REXX, the stored-procedure code is compiled and stored at the server and can contain static SQL and dynamic SQL, as well as IFI calls, and can issue DB2 commands. The stored-procedure program can also access external resources, such as VSAM files, and can even call CICS transactions.

Language Environment

The Language Environment product libraries are used to load and execute the stored procedures in one of the stored-procedure address spaces. When you create a stored procedure, you may pass runtime options for Language Environment to use when the stored procedure is executed. Language Environment is used because it establishes a common runtime environment for the many languages used for building stored procedures, providing a consistent set of interfaces for essential runtime services. When using Language Environment, you do not have to specify language-specific libraries in the JCL procedure of the stored-procedure address space.

Language Environment performs several functions for DB2: hiding the differences among programming languages, providing the ability to make a stored procedure resident in the stored-procedures address space, and supporting a large number of runtime options. Language Environment, along with the language compiler, provides the ability to debug your program using the IBM Debug Tool, also known as CODE/370. Stored-procedure programs can be debugged in batch mode or interactively, using the VisualAge Remote Debugger or IBM Distributed Debugger, or under z/OS using the VTAM MFI (Main Frame Interface) and a 3270 terminal emulator.

Stored-procedure programs should be written and compiled to be reentrant and reusable. This allows Language Environment to share a single copy of the program in memory. You can also use the STAY RESIDENT YES option, which will keep the program in memory for the next stored-procedure call to avoid having to retrieve the module from disk again.

Parameters

Stored procedures usually have parameters that are passed in and, possibly, out. From the caller, the parameters are passed in the same manner as the commonly available CALL syntax:

```
EXEC SQL
   CALL SP1(:parm1, :parm2, :parm3);
END-EXEC.
```

Here, the parameters are host variables. Each parameter can be defined as input to the stored procedure, output from the stored procedure, or both input and output. The calling program must define appropriate storage areas for each parameter. Null values are passed by using indicator variables, as in

```
EXEC SQL
   CALL SP1(:parm1 :ind1, :parm2 :ind2, :parm3 :ind3);
END-EXEC.
```

The parameters used by the stored-procedure program must match those defined on the CREATE PROCEDURE statement. DB2 cannot verify that the stored-procedure program handles the correct number and type of parameters, so the programmer must make sure they do this correctly. DB2 will validate that the calling program specified the correct parameters as compared to the CREATE PROCEDURE statement and will set up the parameter list accordingly.

PARAMETER STYLE Option

The PARAMETER STYLE option of the CREATE PROCEDURE statement controls the number and method of passing parameters into the stored-procedure program. To illustrate the differences in parameter passing, we'll use a stored-procedure program written in C and defined as follows:

```
CREATE PROCEDURE YLA.TWOTOONE
                ( IN   PARM1 CHAR(8)
                , IN   PARM2 CHAR(5)
                , OUT PARM3 CHAR(80)
                )
                EXTERNAL NAME SP1
                LANGUAGE C
                PROGRAM TYPE SUB
                PARAMETER STYLE xxxxxxx
                COLLID TEST
                STAY RESIDENT YES
                WLM ENVIRONMENT WLMENV1;
```

PARAMETER STYLE GENERAL conforms to the way DB2 passed parameters to stored procedures prior to version 6. In this style, the parameters passed to the program are essentially the same parameters that are defined in the CREATE PROCEDURE statement. The function declaration would look like this:

```
void sp1(char   parm1[9],      /* Input parm1 */
         char   parm2[6],      /* Input parm2 */
         char   parm3[81],     /* Output parm3 */
         )
```

Generally, C programs use a null-terminated character array to hold character string fields. DB2 handles the conversion from fixed-length character fields to null-terminated strings automatically for the stored-procedure program. This is why the parameter fields in our example are one byte longer than the parameters specified on the CREATE PROCEDURE statement.

PARAMETER STYLE GENERAL WITH NULLS extends the GENERAL style to pass null indicators back and forth. The null indicators are input/output variables passed in an array, as in

```
void sp1(char   parm1[9],      /* Input parm1 */
         char   parm2[6],      /* Input parm2 */
         char   parm3[81],     /* Output parm3 */
         short* p_indparm[3]   /* Indicators for parms */
         )
```

The newest way of passing parameters, PARAMETER STYLE DB2SQL, is the recommended style for new stored procedures. It is the default for all external languages except JAVA and is invalid for REXX. With the DB2SQL specification, the parameters passed to the stored-procedure program look like this:

```
void sp1(char    parm1[9],       /* Input parm1 */
         char    parm2[6],       /* Input parm2 */
         char    parm3[81],      /* Output parm3 */
         short*  p_indparm1,     /* Indicator for parm1 */
         short*  p_indparm2,     /* Indicator for parm2 */
         short*  p_indparm3,     /* Indicator for parm3 */
         char    p_sqlstate[6],  /* sqlstate to return */
         char    p_proc[28],     /* stored procedure name */
         char    p_spec[19],     /* specific name */
         char    p_diag[71],     /* message to return */
         )
```

As you can see, DB2SQL passes null indicators as separate variables and includes several additional parameters. The most significant of these are the p_sqlstate and p_diag parameters, which allow the stored-procedure program to pass error information back to the caller without using additional output parameters. This simplifies error checking in the client programs. As of version 8, there are no restrictions on the allowable SQLSTATE values other than that they be valid. Prior to version 8, the actual values allowed for the returned SQLSTATE are as follows:

- 00000 returns SQLCODE 0
- 01Hxx returns SQLCODE +462
- 02000 returns SQLCODE +100
- 38001 returns SQLCODE -487
- 38002 returns SQLCODE -577
- 38003 returns SQLCODE -751
- 38004 returns SQLCODE -579
- 38yxx returns SQLCODE -443

The p_diag message area is limited to 70 bytes, but the caller may not receive the entire string. DB2 takes the message text from this field and appends it to the SQLERRMC field in the SQLCA. DB2 includes other information at the beginning of the SQLERRMC field, so your message may be truncated.

The last available style is PARAMETER STYLE JAVA and is used only for Java stored procedures.

DBINFO Clause
If desired, the stored-procedure program can get an additional block of information from DB2 when called. This is requested by adding the DBINFO clause to the CREATE or ALTER

PROCEDURE statement. When this clause is specified, DB2 passes the DBINFO block as the last parameter to the stored-procedure program. This block contains

- The length of the location name.
- The current location name.
- The length of the authorization ID.
- The authorization ID of the application.
- A structure that provides information about the CCSIDs and encoding scheme of the subsystem.
- The length of the table qualifier.
- The qualifier of the table that is specified in the table name.
- The length of the table name.
- The name of the table for a user-defined function.
- The length of the column name.
- The name of the column for a UDF.
- Information that identifies the product on which the program executes. This field has the form DSNvvrrm, where vv is a two-digit version identifier, rr is a two-digit release identifier, and m is a one-digit modification-level identifier.
- The operating system on which the program that invokes the UDF runs.
- A reserved area of 24 bytes.
- A pointer to a string that uniquely identifies the application's connection to DB2.
- A reserved area of 20 bytes.

Note that this block does not contain the number of entries in the table function column list or the table function column list pointer; this information is not used for stored procedures.

Result Sets

In addition to returning parameters, a stored procedure can return one or more result sets. A result set is a relational table implemented as a cursor from which the client program can fetch rows. This way, an ODBC client can retrieve data from DB2 without the end user's requiring privileges to the underlying tables. The user requires only execute privileges for the stored procedure.

Result sets from DB2 or nonrelational sources can be returned from either base tables or temporary tables to clients on any platform. In order for a stored procedure to return result sets to clients, the procedure needs to be defined for returning result sets, cursors must be opened using the WITH RETURN clause, and a DRDA client needs to support level 3 result sets.

Client programs on platforms other than z/OS must use the ODBC/CLI interfaces. DB2 for z/OS implements enhancements that allow embedded SQL programs to also retrieve result sets. The following is a skeleton example of coding to receive a stored-procedure result set when the application program is running on the same z/OS server running the stored procedure:

```
EXEC SQL BEGIN DECLARE SECTION;
SQL TYPE IS RESULT_SET_LOCATOR VARYING * locater1;
EXEC SQL END DECLARE SECTION;
EXEC SQL CALL SP1(:parm1, :parm2, …);
EXEC SQL ASSOCIATE LOCATOR (:locater1) WITH PROCEDURE SP1;
EXEC SQL ALLOCATE CSR1 CURSOR FOR RESULT SET :locater1;
EXEC SQL FETCH CSR1 INTO :acctno, :billingno;
```

To allow result sets to be returned from the stored procedure on the server, the WITH RETURN clause must be used in the cursor definition in the stored procedure, and the cursors may not be closed before the program ends. DB2 will return the rows in the result set from the opened cursors to the application program when the stored procedure ends. The following example shows the stored-procedure code necessary to return the result set to the application code shown in the previous example:

```
EXEC SQL DECLARE SP_CSR1 CURSOR
                 WITH RETURN FOR
                 SELECT ACCT_NO, BILLING_NO
                 FROM ORDER_TABLE
                 WHERE ITEM = :parm1;
EXEC SQL OPEN SP_CSR1;
RETURN;
```

When returning a result set from a stored procedure, the cursor must not be unintentionally closed. The cursor that the stored procedure opens will be closed if the unit of work is terminated by a commit. This includes the commit generated internally by DB2 if the COMMIT ON RETURN option is specified during the creation of the stored procedure.

From a design standpoint, most of the result sets will be of the previous variety. But a very powerful way of building totally dynamic stored procedures can be used and still be able to interface with client processes. This process can be significant with the move toward Web-enabled applications that provide dynamic pages to a client.

The DESCRIBE PROCEDURE statement can be used to retrieve all the information about a procedure's result set. This statement is not required if result sets are predefined, and it cannot be dynamically prepared. It returns information that a "dynamic" client needs to use the result sets. The SQLDA (SQL Descriptor Area) contains the number of result sets, with one SQLVAR entry for each result set in the stored procedure. The SQLDATA(x) contains the result-set locator value, and the SQLNAME(x) contains the server application's cursor name. This is invoked by using either of the following:

```
EXEC SQL DESCRIBE PROCEDURE SP1 INTO :sqlda
EXEC SQL DESCRIBE PROCEDURE :hv INTO :sqlda
```

The DESCRIBE CURSOR statement can be used to retrieve information about a cursor that was left open inside a stored procedure and returned as a result set. This works for any allocated cursor but is not needed for predefined result sets. This statement cannot be dynamically prepared. This feature returns information needed by dynamic clients, such as the name, length, and type for columns contained in a result set. The output SQLDA is very similar to that produced from the DESCRIBE of a PREPARE statement. This is invoked by using either of the following:

```
DESCRIBE CURSOR SPC1 INTO sqlda
DESCRIBE CURSOR :hv INTO sqlda
```

Unit of Work

Stored procedures execute by using the same logical unit of work as the client program that executes the SQL CALL statement. Starting with version 7, stored-procedure programs can issue COMMIT statements. This commit will impact the entire unit of work, including any uncommitted changes made by the caller prior to invoking the stored procedure.

COMMIT ON RETURN

In addition to issuing a commit within a stored-procedure program, the stored procedure can be defined to commit on successful completion. This is done using the COMMIT ON RETURN clause on the CREATE or ALTER PROCEDURE statement.

The COMMIT ON RETURN option for stored procedures reduces network traffic and allows locking in a stored procedure to be performed on a predictable basis. Without COMMIT ON RETURN, the locks would be held until the client application issued the commit. The client commit could be some time later, and additional network messages would be required. With the COMMIT ON RETURN option, the locks are freed as soon as the stored procedure ends.

There are always tradeoffs. COMMIT ON RETURN cannot be used in nested stored procedures. The design of nested stored procedures requires some delicate planning.

Issuing COMMITs

Starting with version 7, DB2 can have commits issued in a stored procedure. In the first instantiation of stored procedures, there was no commit at all. Then came COMMIT ON RETURN, to reduce the network traffic. In version 7, the ability to commit or roll back in stored procedure was added. This has implications only on new stored procedures or on careful enhancements to existing stored procedures and will not be needed in the majority of existing stored procedures, as they were written with the knowledge that a stored procedure was simply a continuation of an existing thread. But with more movement to object-oriented programming, using stored procedures as one way of introducing classes and methods, this feature will have more use.

Nesting

Stored procedures and UDFs can be nested. This means that a stored-procedure program can itself issue an SQL CALL statement or include a UDF within another SQL statement. Triggers can also call UDFs or stored procedures. With nesting, careful planning is required to avoid looping. DB2 has a limit of 16 nesting levels for triggers, UDFs, and stored procedures.

Nesting has obvious impacts on resource consumption and the scope of special registers. When nesting stored procedures, the following DB2 special registers are saved when pushing deeper and are restored when popping back up:

- CURRENT DATE
- CURRENT DEGREE
- CURRENT PACKAGESET
- CURRENT PATH
- CURRENT RULES
- CURRENT SERVER
- CURRENT SQLID
- CURRENT TIME
- CURRENT TIMESTAMP
- CURRENT TIMEZONE
- CURRENT USER

Some important limitations apply when nesting stored procedures.

- Nesting between DB2-managed and workload manager–managed address spaces is not allowed, which is another reason to move away from DB2-managed address spaces.
- No COMMIT ON RETURN is executed when nested.
- Query result sets are returned onto the previous nesting level.

Careful communication among the application programmers, database procedural programmers, system programmers, and database administrators is needed in order to balance needs and make sure that unnecessary levels, trigger cascading, and looping cannot occur.

DEFINING STORED PROCEDURES

The following statement shows an example of creating a stored procedure. Many options are available when creating stored procedures, but some of the main ones include a parameter list, the language, and its external program name. The definition is stored in the SYSIBM.SYSROUTINES catalog table, and the parameter definitions are stored in SYSIBM.SYSPARMS. The CREATE PROCEDURE statement creates a stored procedure:

```
CREATE PROCEDURE SYSPROC.MYSP1
        ( IN     PARM1   SMALLINT,
          INOUT PARM2   CHAR(10),
          OUT   CODE    INTEGER )
        EXTERNAL NAME 'CERTSP1'      -- Load module name
        LANGUAGE COBOL               -- language
        PARAMETER STYLE GENERAL      -- type of parameter list
        COLLID DB2SPS                -- collection ID
        ASUTIME LIMIT 2000           -- maximum amount of SUs allowed
        STAY RESIDENT YES            -- make memory resident
        DYNAMIC RESULT SETS 3        -- 3 result sets returned
        NOT DETERMINISTIC            -- different results with each call
        MODIFIES SQL DATA            -- Issues SQL
        WLM ENVIRONMENT MYAPPS       -- WLM environment
        PROGRAM TYPE MAIN            -- main, not subprogram
        RUN OPTIONS('TRAP(ON)')      -- specifies the LE run options
        STOP AFTER 2 FAILURES        -- stops after 2 failures
        COMMIT ON RETURN NO          -- do not commit on exit
```

The ALTER PROCEDURE statement can be used to modify the options of a stored procedure:

```
ALTER PROCEDURE SYSPROC.MYSP1 STAY RESIDENT NO
```

The ALTER PROCEDURE command will take effect immediately if the stored procedure is not already active in the system. If the stored procedure is active, it will have to be stopped and restarted. If the stored procedure is running in a WLM environment, that environment should also be refreshed.

Removing Stored Procedures

Procedures are removed from the system by using the DROP PROCEDURE command, as in

```
DROP PROCEDURE MYSPAP RESTRICT
```

This will drop the stored procedure unless the rules identified by the required keyword RESTRICT hold true. RESTRICT prevents the procedure from being dropped if a trigger definition contains a CALL statement with the name of the procedure.

When a procedure is directly or indirectly dropped, all privileges on the procedure are also dropped. In addition, any plans or packages that are dependent on the procedure are made inoperative.

Schema Qualification

Stored-procedure names are implicitly or explicitly qualified by a schema name. If no schema name is used to qualify the name, it is qualified by the following rules.

- If the CREATE PROCEDURE statement is embedded in a program, the schema name is the authorization ID specified in the QUALIFIER bind option when the plan or package was created or last rebound. If QUALIFIER was not specified, the schema name is the owner of the plan or package.
- If the CREATE PROCEDURE statement is dynamically prepared, the schema name is the SQL authorization ID in the CURRENT SQLID special register.

When calling a stored procedure, the CURRENT PATH special register is used to identify unqualified procedure names. If no path is specified, the default path is used:

1. SYSIBM
2. SYSFUN
3. SYSPROC
4. Value of CURRENT SQLID

> **N O T E**   SYSFUN is a schema used for additional functions shipped from other servers in the DB2 product family. Although DB2 for z/OS does not have the SYSFUN schema, it can be useful to have SYSFUN in the path when doing distributed processing that involves a server that uses the SYSFUN schema.

EXECUTION ENVIRONMENTS

Stored procedures on z/OS execute under the control of DB2. Stored procedures have two execution environments: DB2 Stored Procedure Address Space (DSNSPAS) and WLM-managed environments.

Administration of stored procedures for either environment includes the use of the following commands:

- START PROCEDURE and STOP PROCEDURE, which allow queuing options for callers to dynamically start and stop the ability to use or execute the stored procedure. It is possible to start or stop procedures with the SCOPE(GROUP) option for data sharing.
- DISPLAY PROCEDURE provides the ability to display the status of a stored procedure.

The START and STOP can be issued for individual stored procedures or can include wildcards to affect multiple procedures.

The DISPLAY PROCEDURE command will yield information about the status of any stored procedure currently started or executing but does not display any information on the individual threads using the stored procedure. For that, the DISPLAY THREAD command must be used. Following is an example of the DISPLAY PROCEDURE command:

```
-DISPLAY PROCEDURE
DSNX940I -DSNX9DIS DISPLAY PROCEDURE REPORT FOLLOWS -
PROCEDURE STATUS ACTIVE QUEUED MAXQUE TIMEOUT FAIL  WLM_ENV
APPL1     STARTED 1      0      0      0       1     TESTENV
APPL2     STARTED 1      0      0      0       0     TESTENV
APPL2     STARTED 0      1      2      0       0     TESTENV
APPL5     STOPREJ 0      0      0      0       0     TESTENV
APPL6     STOPABN 0      0      0      0       0     TESTENV
PROC1     STOPQUE 0      0      0      0       0     TESTENV
DSNX9DIS DISPLAY PROCEDURE REPORT COMPLETE
```

DB2-Established Stored-Procedure Address Space

DSNSPAS is a single address space that is started by DB2 when it initializes. The address space is stopped by DB2 if a STOP PROCEDURE(*.*) command is issued, and it is restarted with a START PROCEDURE(*.*) command. All stored procedures associated with the DB2-established address space in that one address space. If one procedure fails, it can affect the others that are also executing in that address space.

Stored procedures in the SPAS environment execute at the priority of the address space. There is no support for two-phase commit when updating nonrelational data.

Stored procedures that execute in the SPAS environment use the Call Attach Facility implicitly. The DSNALI interface module must be linked into the application load module, but the program must not make any DSNALI calls.

In order to minimize the amount of storage used in a stored-procedure address space, the NUMTCB parameter can be altered to allow only a certain number of address spaces to be started.

Workload Manager

Although stored procedures can run in a DB2-established SPAS, it is highly recommended that they execute in a WLM goal-mode application environment, because WLM can support multiple address spaces. Each DB2 subsystem can have many WLM-managed environments, each with its own JCL. This means that the stored-procedure programs for different applications can execute in different environments. You can also create separate test and quality assurance (Q/A) environments for the same application within the same subsystem, using different load libraries to allow for different levels of application code.

Stored procedures that execute in WLM-managed environments use the performance character-istics of the calling application. This provides a much more granular level of performance man-agement than DB2-managed SPAS do.

The impact of program failures is limited to the execution address space, reducing the likelihood of impacting other critical stored procedures. Stored procedures that execute in WLM-managed environments use the Recoverable Resource Manager Services Attachment Facility (RRSAF) implicitly. The DSNRLI interface module must be linked into the application load module, but the program must not make any DSNRLI calls. Two-phase commit is supported for any access to nonrelational data updates if the data is managed by RRSAF.

Benefits of WLM

Workload Manager is an OS/390 component that provides a tool for performing workload bal-ancing and distribution. This is done based on user definitions that are established ahead of time. DB2 has been designed to work cooperatively with WLM. The enclaves enable the workload management and allow a transaction to span multiple TCBs and/or SRBs. Transactions can also span multiple address spaces. Without enclaves, workload can be managed only by address space. This benefit gives great flexibility to setting application and stored-procedure priorities. The priorities can be set at the level of caller or of stored-procedure address space. Priorities can also be established for specific applications, users, or stored procedures.

WLM has two modes of operation: compatibility and goal. Goal mode requires definitions to be established for such things as priority settings and ability to refresh stored-procedure environ-ments. Goal mode also uses rule-based guidelines to adjust task priorities. When running in goal mode, WLM automatically starts and stops application environments, based on the definition for each environment. WLM will start a new address space if a stored procedure is executed and an existing environment is not already available or the running environments are busy executing other stored procedures. Goal-mode execution is highly recommended for z/OS and OS/390 sys-tems that will run DB2 stored procedures.

> **NOTE** As of version 8, all new stored procedures are required to be WLM managed in goal mode.

Compatibility mode uses the older, non-WLM system-performance definitions to control task priorities. In compatibility mode, the executing of WLM environments must be controlled man-ually, and the number of environments is limited. Many shops often run in compatibility mode, as it does not require the complex setup that goal mode does; however, they need to begin to work with goal mode, as it is the future direction.

Stored Procedures and WLM

WLM-established address spaces provide multiple isolated environments for stored procedures, which means that failures need not affect other stored procedures as they can in a DB2-managed SPAS. WLM-established address spaces also reduce demand for storage below the 16MB line, thus removing the limitation on the number of stored procedures that can run concurrently within an address space. With WLM, the stored procedures also inherit the dispatching priority of the DB2 thread that issues the CALL statement. This allows high-priority work to have its stored procedures execute ahead of lower-priority work and its stored procedures. In a DB2-established address space, prioritization of stored procedures is not possible, and you are limited by storage in the address space. There is also no separation of the work by dispatching priorities, so high-priority work could potentially be penalized. WLM-managed stored procedures can also run as subprograms with certain runtime options for better performance.

Stored procedures using WLM can have static priority assignment and dynamic workload balancing. High-priority stored procedures in WLM achieve very consistent response times, and WLM provides dynamic workload balancing and distribution. WLM routes incoming requests to the stored-procedure address space that is the least busy or starts a new address spaces, if required. Then, the actions are fully automatic, without requiring monitoring, tuning, or operator intervention.

Another benefit that WLM-managed address spaces can provide is better options for stopping runaway stored procedures. If a procedure is looping outside of DB2's control, various options can be used for regaining control. If you are using DB2-managed SPAS, you have to cancel the address space, which is not a good option as everything running in that address space is affected.

With a runaway stored procedure in a WLM-managed application environment in goal mode, one option is to refresh the environment, which will quiesce all address spaces running under that environment, start a new address space, and route all new requests to the new address space. Once assured that all normal work in the address space containing the runaway stored procedure has finished, you can cancel that address space. This completely isolates all other stored procedures from failure. With compatibility mode, you can only cancel the address space and restart the address space later.

The stored procedure has an option that can help with runaway stored procedures. You can use the ASUTIME parameter to protect against runaways. Stored procedures are normally designed or high-volume online transactions, and using this parameter limits the resources used by stored procedures. The value for ASUTIME is stored in the ASUTIME column in the SYSIBM.SYSROUTINES catalog table.

Setting ASUTIME allows DB2 to cancel stored procedures that are in a loop. This feature was designed to be used for runaway stored procedures. DB2 checks for overages on ASUTIME every 20 seconds of clock time. Therefore, this is not a strict control on how much CPU time a stored procedure can use. This is where WLM is also beneficial. WLM allows you to establish priorities and service goals, providing an additional mechanism for tight control of system resource use. By using both ASUTIME and WLM priorities and goals, you can have total control of the stored procedures in this environment.

Program Type.   Programs that run in WLM environments can be defined to execute as subprograms or as main programs. Subprograms execute more efficiently but must take care to clean up resources and close files. Specify PROGRAM TYPE SUB on the CREATE PROCEDURE statement, and make sure that the program is properly coded to execute as a subprogram. Programs that run as subprograms must be dynamically fetchable. For COBOL, a main program and a subprogram have no real difference. PL/I subprograms may not perform I/O. C programs must be defined as fetchable, as in the following:

```
#include <sqludf.h>
#pragma linkage(sprslt,fetchable)
void sprslt (const char    parmCreator[9]
            ,short       * pIndCreator
            ,char         p_sqlstate[6]
            ,char         p_proc[28]
            ,char         p_spec[19]
            ,char         p_diag[71]
            )
```

Managing WLM Environments.   When being used in a WLM-managed address space, administration of stored procedures is under the control of WLM. The START and STOP PROCEDURE commands are the same but work a little differently. They stop and start the procedure but do not cause the load module to be reloaded by DB2. To refresh a stored-procedure load module, you must use the following command from the console:

```
VARY WLM,APPLENV=wlmenv,REFRESH
```

The WLM REFRESH command recycles all WLM address spaces that run within that environment. New environment address spaces are started, and any new work is routed to the new address spaces. Threads executing in the existing address spaces are allowed to complete in the old environment before it is brought down.

The WLM environment as a whole can be stopped and restarted by using the following commands:

```
VARY WLM,APPLENV=wlmenv,QUIESCE
VARY WLM,APPLENV=wlmenv,RESUME
```

Obtaining Diagnostic Information. The start-up procedure for a WLM-managed stored-procedure address space contains a DD statement for CEEDUMP. The Language Environment writes a small diagnostic dump to CEEDUMP when a stored procedure terminates abnormally. The output for this dump waits to print until the stored-procedures address space terminates. The dump is obtained by stopping the stored-procedures address space running the stored procedure.

SQL PROCEDURE LANGUAGE

The SQL Procedure Language was designed only for writing stored procedures and is available across the entire DB2 family, including the iSeries systems. This procedural language is based on the ANSI/ISO standard language SQL/PSM. Its major benefit is that users can create stored procedures very quickly, using a simple, easily understood language, without the headaches of precompilers, compilers, link editors, binding, and special authorizations. Stored procedures written using SQL Procedure Language will be managed mostly by DB2; this automates the process and allows programmers and users to simply write the logic and pass if off to DB2.

SQL procedures support multiple parameters for input, output, and returning output results sets to clients. SQL procedures are defined in the DB2 catalog, and the source can be stored there also. The following shows an SQL procedure that was created from a client workstation, using the DB2 Development Center. It accepts one input parameter and returns a result set to the client:

```
CREATE PROCEDURE DW.SQLProc1 ( IN gender char(6) )
    SPECIFIC DW.Genders        RESULT SETS 1
    LANGUAGE SQL
P1: BEGIN
    DECLARE gender_value CHAR(1);
    DECLARE bad_gender CONDITION FOR SQLSTATE '99001';
    CASE gender
       WHEN 'MALE' THEN
           SET gender_value = 'M';
       WHEN 'FEMALE' THEN
           SET gender_value = 'F';
       ELSE SIGNAL bad_gender;
    END CASE;
```

```
-- Declare cursor
DECLARE cursor1 CURSOR WITH RETURN FOR
    SELECT E.EMPNO, E.LASTNAME, E.HIREDATE, D.DEPTNO,
           D.DEPTNAME
    FROM DW.DEPARTMENT D, DW.EMPLOYEE E
    WHERE E.WORKDEPT = D.DEPTNO
      AND E.SEX = :gender_value
    ORDER BY E.WORKDEPT;
-- Cursor left open for client application
OPEN cursor1;
END P1
```

The language itself is primarily SQL (DML and DDL), with local variables, cursors, assignment statements, flow control, and signal/resignal conditions. The real difference with the SQL Procedure Language is how it becomes a stored procedure; all the programmer does is write a CREATE PROCEDURE...LANGUAGE SQL...name: BEGIN...END name DDL statement. All the code is in the body of the create statement. The procedure body includes compound, declaration, assignment, and conditional statements; iterative control structures—LOOP, REPEAT, WHILE—exception handling; and calling another stored procedure.

The primary language statements that show the strength of this approach are

```
IF, CASE, and LEAVE
LOOP, REPEAT, and WHILE
FOR, CALL, and RETURN
GET DIAGNOSTICS
SIGNAL and RESIGNAL
```

DEVELOPING SQL STORED PROCEDURES

DB2 implements SQL stored procedures as external C programs. The DB2 precompiler can take an SQL procedure as input and write out a C source module. An SQL procedure is created by using one of the following three methods: DB2 Development Center stored procedure, directly invoking DSNTPSMP, or using JCL or CLIST to prepare.

When an SQL procedure is built using the DB2 Development Center, all the "code" is developed on the client workstation, and the completed procedure is passed to the DSNTPSMP stored procedure. DSNTPSMP is the z/OS SQL Procedure Processor, a REXX-stored procedure, and it is also fully customizable. This processor invokes the following steps:

1. SQL precompile
2. C precompile
3. C compile
4. Prelink
5. Link

6. Procedure definition

7. Bind

Once the procedure is built in this fashion, it is immediately executable. When using the other two methods for developing an SQL procedure, they bypass the DB2 Development Center and either directly invoke DSNTPSMP or execute these steps under manual control.

DB2 Development Center

The DB2 Development Center (DB2 DC) is the successor to the DB2 version 7 Stored Procedure Builder (DB2 SPB). This tool builds on the DB2 Stored Procedure Builder, with many new features and functions.

DB2 DC provides a rapid iterative development environment for building stored procedures, user-defined functions, structured data types, and much more. Developers can build DB2 business logic anywhere, and all DB2 platforms are supported. Support is provided for developing SQL and Java stored procedures, SQL scalar and table user-defined functions, MQSeries, OLE DB, and XML table functions, and structured data types for Enterprise JavaBeans methods and properties.

The tool lets you view live database tables, views, triggers, stored procedures, and UDFs. A quick-start launch pad guides new users through the initial set of development tasks. Some features for enhanced z/OS support are specialized SQL IDs—package owner, build owner, and secondary SQL ID—and advanced build options

DB2 DC provides an excellent facility for testing and debugging stored procedures and UDFs written in any language. Using the Development Center, you can

- Create new stored procedures
- Build stored procedures on local and remote DB2 servers
- Modify and rebuild existing stored procedures
- Run stored procedures to test the execution of installed stored procedures

Summary

Stored procedures provide a powerful mechanism for storing application code on the database server. They improve performance, enhance the security of the application, and can support legacy data sources to DB2-based programs running on the mainframe and on other platforms. Workload Manager provides many benefits for stored procedures and as of version 8 is required.

The new DB2 Development Center also offers many new options for developing and deploying stored procedures.

ADDITIONAL RESOURCES

www.ibm.com/software/data/db2

www.ibm.com/software/data/db2/os390/sqlproc

www.ibm.com/software/data/db2/udb/ide

Developing Crossplatform DB2 Stored Procedures: SQL Procedures and the DB2 Stored Procedure Builder (SG24-5485)

DB2 for z/OS Version 8 Application Programming and SQL Guide (SC26-9933)

Accessing Distributed Data

- Distributed data
- Coding methods for distributed data
- Programming considerations
- Remote query performance

The DB2 Distributed Data Facility (DDF) allows access to data held by other data management systems or makes your DB2 data accessible to other systems. A DB2 application program can use SQL to access data controlled by non-DB2 database management systems at which the application's plan is bound. This DB2 is known as the *local DB*2 or application requester (AR). Any DBMS that supports remote connectivity is called an *application server* (AS). Any application server other than the local DB2 is considered a *remote server* (RS), and access to its data is a distributed operation. DB2 provides two methods of accessing data at remote application servers: DRDA and DB2 private-protocol access. For application servers that support the two-phase commit process, both methods allow for updating data at several remote locations within the same unit of work.

The location name of the DB2 subsystem is defined during DB2 installation as stored in the BSDS. The communications database (CDB) records the location name and the network address of a remote DBMS. The tables in the CDB are part of the DB2 catalog.

DISTRIBUTED DATA

Distributed Relational Database Architecture

Communicating between platforms introduces several issues, ranging from character conversion to definition of the actions that you want executed on the other platform. Several years ago, with DB2 for MVS/ESA, Version 2, Release 3, IBM introduced a set of protocols known as Distributed Relational Database Architecture (DRDA). An open standard that can be licensed by other companies, DRDA provides for communication between a client, or application requester, and an application server. DRDA was developed to maximize functionality and reduce the overhead when communicating between like platforms.

The overhead for like platforms and the maximization of functionality are achieved by putting the work on the platform that receives the message. For example, the request to fetch from a cursor will be processed by the application server, and the rows that are returned will be translated by the application requester. The support of ASCII tables in DB2 for z/OS allows you to have both the application server and the application requester on the same data representation model (code page), thereby effectively eliminating any data conversion. The original specifications identified four levels of support:

1. **Remote request**, a single request to one remote DBMS, consisting of one SQL statement. This level does not allow you to define a unit of work. Every SQL statement is an independent unit of work.
2. **Remote unit of work (RUW)**, a unit of work requesting services to a single remote DBMS. RUW provides integrity within a single DBMS. Several statements can be grouped together in a single unit of work, but these statements cannot span more than one DBMS. Programs that take advantage of RUW can only connect to a single database at a time, but can switch between databases at the end of a unit of work.
3. **Distributed unit of work (DUW)**, a unit of work requesting services to two or more DBMSs. DUW provides integrity across multiple DBMSs. However, access is to only a single DBMS in an SQL statement. The changes at all DBMSs are backed out if the execution of one SQL statement is not successful. Two-phase commit protocols are used to maintain consistency.
4. **Distributed request**, a request to two or more remote DBMSs residing on the same or different locations. Distributed request provides integrity across multiple locations and access to more than one location in an SQL statement. This level of distributed processing is not directly supported in the DRDA specification.

No immediate plans exist to extend the DRDA architecture and include the distributed-request functionality. The implementation of a standard technique to solve the distributed-request problem is much more complicated, as it would require the addition of optimization-related concepts, such as network performance and estimation of the cost of the remote SQL component. With DB2, however, you can find a solution for the distributed request, which is based on logic that is not part of the DRDA architecture but that is part of DB2's unique design.

You need to differentiate the two potential target data locations of the distributed request. If you want to combine DB2 data—on any platform—your solution will be different if you want non-DB2 data. The first question—how to perform a distributed request—is answered by any DB2 for UNIX, Windows, or Linux manual that is at least version 7. The section on nicknames explains the steps required to make this work. What you need to remember is that you have full read/write access to any DB2 DRDA-enabled data source. Furthermore, that version of DB2 will also, as will any DRDA server, provide the full flavor of SQL syntax available on that platform, including recursion, rollup, cube, and many other SQL functions that do not exist on the z/OS platform.

The second question—how to incorporate non-DB2 data sources—requires a two-part answer. The full support for distributed-request functionality is available only when using DataJoiner, which uses a private solution to solve this problem and does not use the DRDA extensions. DB2 LUW version 7 implements this solution partially, by integrating the read-only (R/O) part of the DataJoiner code. Non-DB2 R/O access to Oracle is provided by the Relational Connect option, of which several versions are available, including Oracle, Sybase, SQL Server, Informix, and Life Sciences. The current DataJoiner/DB2 LUW version 7 solution has a performance model of the target database and uses a copy of the remote object statistics to help the optimizer decide on the optimal placement of the SQL parts. The information required to determine this best-access plan is based on information added by the system administrator, such as relative network speed and processor capacity, and information obtained by extracting the catalog of the remote system.

With DRDA, the recommended method, the application connects to a server at another location and executes packages that have been previously bound at that server. The application uses a CONNECT statement, a three-part name, or, if bound with DBPROTOCOL (DRDA), an alias to access the server. For more information on bind options, refer to Chapter 11.

Queries can originate from any system or application that issues SQL statements as an *application requester* in the formats required by DRDA. DRDA access supports the execution of dynamic SQL statements and SQL statements that satisfy all the following conditions.

- The static statements appear in a package bound to an accessible server.
- The statements are executed using that package.
- The objects involved in the execution of the statements are at the server where the package is bound. If the server is a DB2 subsystem, three-part names and aliases can be used to refer to another DB2 server.

DRDA communication conventions are invisible to DB2 applications and allow DB2 to bind and rebind packages at other servers and to execute the statements in those packages. For two-phase commit using SNA connections, DB2 supports both presumed-abort and presumed-nothing protocols that are defined by DRDA. If you are using TCP/IP, DB2 uses the sync-point manager defined in the documentation for DRDA level 3.

> **N O T E** DRDA protocols are documented by the Open Group Technical Standard in *DRDA Volume 1: Distributed Relational Database Architecture (DRDA)*.

DB2 Private Protocol

An application program running under DB2 can refer to a table or view at another DB2. This is done with private protocol. With private protocol, the application must use an alias or three-part name to direct the SQL statement to a given location. Private protocol works only between application requesters and application servers that are both DB2 for z/OS subsystems.

A statement is executed using DB2 private-protocol access if it refers to objects that are not at the current server and is implicitly or explicitly bound with DBPROTOCOL(PRIVATE).The *current server* is the DBMS to which an application is actively connected. DB2 private-protocol access uses *DB2 private connections*. The statements that can be executed are SQL INSERT, UPDATE, DELETE, and SELECT statements with their associated SQL OPEN, FETCH, and CLOSE statements.

The location name identifies the other DB2 to the DB2 application server. A three-part name consists of a location, an authorization ID, and an object name. For example, the name NYSERVER.DB2USER1.TEST refers to a table named DB2USER1.TEST at the server with location name NYSERVER. Alias names have the same allowable forms as table or view names. The name can refer to a table or a view at the current server or to a table or a view elsewhere.

> **N O T E** Private protocol does not support many distributed functions, such as TCP/IP or stored procedures. The newer data types, such as LOB or user-defined types, are also not supported by private protocol. It is not the recommended method to use and is no longer being enhanced.

Communications Protocols

The DDF uses TCP/IP or SNA to communicate with other systems. *SNA* is the description of the logical structure, formats, protocols, and operational sequences for transmitting information through and controlling the configuration and operation of the networks. It is one of the two main network architectures used for network communications to the enterprise servers. On z/OS, SNA communication is implemented by VTAM.

Transmission Control Protocol/Internet Protocol (TCP/IP) is a standard communication protocol for network communications. Current levels of DB2 suppport full DRDA functionality over TCP/IP.

The security aspects of TCP/IP are different from those of SNA. With SNA, it is possible to tighten security; with TCP/IP, it is much easier to modify the address you are coming from. As a result, not all features available with the SNA protocol have been implemented for TCP/IP. DDF can be configured in such a way that it does inbound user ID translation. If a specific user ID enters the system, replace it with a new value.

Several systems use this to map a user ID to a functional user ID, which is very often the owner of the objects used in the application. IBM has decided not to implement inbound user ID translation for TCP/IP clients. If you need this functionality and are sure that your network is sufficiently secured so that you don't have any issues, you have to use the DB2 exits to perform the inbound user ID translation. You have to make sure that you modify the proper exit, as TCP/IP clients do not use the sign-on exit. The module that should be adapted is the DSN3@ATH exit.

DB2 can use virtual terminal access method (VTAM) for communicating with remote databases. This is done by assigning two names for the local DB2 subsystem: a location name and a logical unit name. A *location name* distinguishes a specific DBMS in a network, so applications use this name to direct requests to the local DB2 subsystem. Other systems use different terms for a location name. For example, DB2 Connect calls this the *target database name*. DB2 uses the DRDA term *RDBNAM* to refer to non-DB2 relational database names.

Communications Database

The DB2 catalog includes the communications database (CDB), which contains several tables that hold information about connections with remote systems. These tables are

- SYSIBM.LOCATIONS
- SYSIBM.LUNAMES
- SYSIBM.IPNAMES
- SYSIBM.IPLIST
- SYSIBM.MODESELECT
- SYSIBM.USERNAMES
- SYSIBM.LULIST
- SYSIBM.LUMODES

Some of these tables must be populated before data can be requested from remote systems. If this DB2 system services only data requests, the CDB does not have to be populated; the default values can be used.

When sending a request, DB2 uses the `LINKNAME` column of the `SYSIBM.LOCATIONS` catalog table to determine which protocol to use.

- To receive VTAM requests, an LU name must be selected in installation panel DSNTIPR.
- To receive TCP/IP requests, a DRDA port and a resynchronization port must be selected in installation panel DSNTIP5. TCP/IP uses the server's port number to pass network requests to the correct DB2 subsystem. If the value in the `LINKNAME` column is found in the `SYSIBM.IPNAMES` table, TCP/IP is used for DRDA connections. If the value is found in the `SYSIBM.LUNAMES` table, SNA is used.
- If the same name is in both `SYSIBM.LUNAMES` and `SYSIBM.IPNAMES`, then TCP/IP is used to connect to the location.

> **NOTE** A requester cannot connect to a given location name using both SNA and TCP/IP. For example, if `SYSIBM.LOCATIONS` specifies a `LINKNAME` of LU1, and if LU1 is defined in both the `SYSIBM.IPNAMES` and `SYSIBM.LUNAMES` tables, TCP/IP is the only protocol used to connect to LU1 from this requester for DRDA connections. For private-protocol connections, the SNA protocols are used. If private-protocol connections are being used, the `SYSIBM.LUNAMES` table must be defined for the remote location's LU name.

Gathering Configuration Information

How do you obtain the information to fill in the CDB and set up the connection with the remote system? DB2 UDB for Linux, UNIX, and Windows has a piece of software called the *Client Configuration Assistant*, which communicates with a server component called the DB2 Database Administration Server (DAS), which provides the client with all the information required to define the target database. Today, DB2 for z/OS version 8 provides this DAS in the optional DB2 Management Client Package for z/OS component. Alternatively, the user can find the required information manually. The DB2 command `-DIS DDF` lists all the information required to set up the connection to the DB2:

```
DSNL080I  -DBT5 DSNLTDDF DISPLAY DDF REPORT FOLLOWS:
DSNL081I STATUS=STARTD
DSNL082I LOCATION            LUNAME              GENERICLU
```

```
DSNL083I DBT5                    TU0.BSYSDBT5        -NONE
DSNL084I IPADDR          TCPPORT RESPORT
DSNL085I 10.35.4.16      2590    2591
DSNL086I SQL    DOMAIN=t390.rpc.com
DSNL086I RESYNC DOMAIN=t390.rpc.com
DSNL090I DT=A  CONDBAT=      64 MDBAT=     64
DSNL092I ADBAT=      0 QUEDBAT=       0 IN1DBAT=       0 CONQUED=       0
DSNL093I DSCDBAT=       0 IN2CONS=       0
             DSNL099I DSNLTDDF DISPLAY DDF REPORT COMPLETE
```

Without this command, you would have to print the content of the bootstrap data set (BSDS), which contains other sensitive information you may not want exposed.

When setting up clients that will access DB2 for z/OS using TCP/IP, it is a good idea to use a host name that corresponds to the DB2 subsystem rather than the host name of the z/OS system where DB2 is currently running. This will make it easier to move the DB2 subsystem to a different z/OS system without having to reconfigure all of the client systems.

Communicating with a Data Sharing Group

All the members of the DB2 data sharing group have the same location name, but each individual member has its own specific communication parameters. Each member can also be designated with one or more alias location names. The mapping to the group or an individual member should be defined at the level of the configuration of the client. On z/OS, that would be the definitions in the CDB; with DB2 Connect, the target is defined in the node directory.

In fact, one of the purposes of the data sharing implementation is to make the entire group virtually one in order to increase the availability of the overall data sharing group. Every new release of DB2 Connect makes the routing to the data sharing members more transparent and efficient.

At the networking level, solutions allow you to "virtualize" the DB2 server. These solutions include the use of SNA-APPC (Advanced Program-to-Program Communication) generic resources and such techniques as TCP/IP VIPA (Virtual IP Address). Both require a considerable investment in configuration on the networking side. Another alternative is the definition of dynamic APPC application definitions, using the concept of a model. The application used by DB2 is no longer defined in a static fashion but refers to a model that is active on all systems in the data sharing group.

CODING METHODS FOR DISTRIBUTED DATA

Distributed data is accessed in various ways, and various considerations must be made for preparing and binding programs that will be executing statements against this data. This section looks at connect options, program preparation, and bind options, as well as additional considerations for coordinating updates.

Three-Part Names

You can use three-part table names to access data at a remote location through DRDA access or DB2 private-protocol access. When you use three-part table names, the way you code your application is the same, regardless of the access method you choose. You determine the access method when you bind the SQL statements into a package or a plan. If you use DRDA access, you must bind the DBRMs for the SQL statements to be executed at the server into packages that reside at that server. Because platforms other than DB2 for z/OS might not support the three-part name syntax, you should not code applications with three-part names if you plan to port those applications to other platforms.

In a three-part table name, the first part denotes the location. The local DB2 makes and breaks an implicit connection to a remote server as needed. An application uses a location name to construct a three-part table name in an SQL statement and then prepares the statement and executes it dynamically. If it is an INSERT, the values to be inserted are transmitted to the remote location and substituted for the parameter markers in the INSERT statement. The following overview shows how the application uses three-part names:

```
Read input values
Do for all locations
Read location name
Set up statement to prepare
Prepare statement
Execute statement
End loop
Commit
```

After it obtains a location name—for example, SAN_JOSE—the application creates the following character string:

```
INSERT INTO SAN_JOSE.DSN8710.PROJ VA UES (?,?,?,?,?,?,?,?)
```

The application assigns the character string to the variable INSERTX and then executes these statements:

```
EXEC SQL
PREPARE STMT1 FROM :INSERTX;
EXEC SQL
EXECUTE STMT1 USING :PROJNO, :PROJNAME, :DEPTNO, :RESPEMP,
:PRSTAFF, :PRSTDATE, :PRENDATE, :MAJPROJ;
```

To keep the data consistent at all locations, the application commits the work only when the loop has executed for all locations. Either every location has committed the INSERT or, if a failure has prevented any location from inserting, all locations have rolled back the INSERT. (If a failure occurs during the commit process, the entire unit of work can be in doubt.)

N O T E   Instead of using full three-part names, it might be more convenient to use aliases when creating character strings that become prepared statements.

Three-Part Names and Multiple Servers

If you use a three-part name or an alias that resolves to one in a statement executed at a remote server by DRDA access, and if the location name is not that of the server, the method by which the remote server accesses data at the named location depends on the value of DBPROTOCOL. If the package at the first remote server is bound with DBPROTOCOL(PRIVATE), DB2 uses DB2 private-protocol access to access the second remote server. If the package at the first remote server is bound with DBPROTOCOL(DRDA), DB2 uses DRDA access to access the second remote server. To ensure that access to the second remote server is by DRDA access, we recommend that you (1) rebind the package at the first remote server with DBPROTOCOL(DRDA), and then (2) bind the package that contains the three-part name at the second server.

Accessing Declared Temporary Tables

You can access a remote declared temporary table by using a three-part name only if you use DRDA access. However, if you combine explicit CONNECT statements and three-part names in your application, a reference to a remote declared temporary table must be a forward reference. For example, you can perform the following series of actions, which include a forward reference to a declared temporary table:

```
EXEC SQL CONNECT TO CHICAGO; /* Connect to the remote site */
EXEC SQL
DECLARE GLOBAL TEMPORARY TABLE TEMPPROD /*Define the temporary table*/
  (CHARCO CHAR(6) NOT NULL); /* at the remote site */
EXEC SQL CONNECT RESET; /* Connect back to local site */
EXEC SQL INSERT INTO CHICAGO.SESSION.T1
(VALUES 'ABCDEF'); /* Access the temporary table*/
/* at the remote site (forward reference) */
```

However, you cannot perform the following series of actions, which include a backward reference to the declared temporary table:

```
EXEC SQL
DECLARE GLOBAL TEMPORARY TABLE TEMPPROD /*Define the temporary table*/
(CHARCO CHAR(6) NOT NULL ); /* at the local site (ATLANTA)*/
EXEC SQL CONNECT TO CHICAGO; /* Connect to the remote site */
EXEC SQL INSERT INTO ATLANTA.SESSION.T1
(VALUES 'ABCDEF'); /* Cannot access temp table */
/* from the remote site (backward reference)*/
```

CONNECT Statements

With this method, the application program explicitly connects to each new server. You must bind the DBRMs for the SQL statements to be executed at the server into packages that reside at that server. An application executes a CONNECT statement for each server; in turn, it can execute statements, such as INSERTs, at each server. In this case, the tables to be updated each have the same name, although each is defined at a different server. The application executes the statements in a loop, with one iteration for each server.

The application connects to each new server by means of a host variable in the CONNECT statement. CONNECT changes the special register CURRENT SERVER to show the location of the new server. The values to insert in the table are transmitted to a location as input host variables. When looping through locations to which the application is already connected, the SET CONNECTION statement is used. The following overview shows how the application uses explicit CONNECTs:

```
Do for all locations (connect loop)
   Connect to location
End connect loop
Do for all input (read loop)
   Read input values
   Do for all locations (insert loop)
      Set Connection to location
      Execute insert statement
   End insert loop
   Commit
End read loop
Release all connections
Commit
```

In connecting to each location, the application places the location name into the variable LOCATION_NAME and executes the following statement:

```
EXEC SQL
CONNECT TO :LOCATION_NAME;
EXEC SQL
```

For each insert to be done, the application inserts a new location name into the variable LOCATION_NAME and executes the following statements:

```
EXEC SQL
SET CONNECTION TO : LOCATION_NAME;
EXEC SQL
INSERT INTO DSN8710.PROJ VALUES
(:PROJNO, :PROJNAME, :DEPTNO,:RESPEMP,
:PRSTAFF, :PRSTDATE, :PRENDATE, :MAJPROJ);
```

To keep the data consistent at all locations, the application commits the work only when the loop has executed for all locations. Either every location has committed the INSERT or, if a failure has prevented any location from inserting, all other locations have rolled back the INSERT. (If a failure occurs during the commit process, the entire unit of work can be in doubt.)

Releasing Connections

When you connect to remote locations explicitly, you must also break those connections explicitly. You have considerable flexibility in determining how long connections remain open, so the RELEASE statement differs significantly from CONNECT in the following ways.

- CONNECT makes an immediate connection to exactly one remote system.
- CONNECT (type 2) does not release any current connection.
- RELEASE *does not* immediately break a connection. *The RELEASE statement labels connections for release at the next commit point.* A connection so labeled is in the *release-pending state* and can still be used before the next commit point.
- RELEASE can specify a single connection or a set of connections for release at the next commit point.

Preparing Programs for DRDA Access

For the most part, binding a package to run at a remote location is like binding a package to run at your local DB2. Binding a plan to run the package is like binding any other plan.

Precompiler Options

The following precompiler options are relevant to preparing a package to be run using DRDA access.

- Use CONNECT (2) explicitly or by default. CONNECT (1) causes your CONNECT statements to allow only the restricted function known as remote unit of work. Be particularly careful to avoid CONNECT (1) if your application updates more than one DBMS in a single unit of work.
- Use SQL (ALL) explicitly for a package that runs on a server that *is not* DB2 for z/OS. The precompiler then accepts any statement that obeys DRDA rules. Use SQL (DB2) explicitly or by default if the server is DB2 for z/OS only. The precompiler then rejects any statement that does not obey the rules of DB2 for z/OS.

BIND PACKAGE Options

The following options of BIND PACKAGE are relevant to binding a package to be run using DRDA access.

- Use location-name to name the location of the server at which the package runs. The privileges needed to run the package must be granted to the owner of the package at the server. If you are not the owner, you must also have SYSCTRL authority or the BINDAGENT privilege granted locally.

- Use SQLERROR(CONTINUE) if you used SQL(ALL) when precompiling. That creates a package even if the bind process finds SQL errors, such as statements that are valid on the remote server but that the precompiler did not recognize. Otherwise, use SQLERROR(NOPACKAGE) explicitly or by default.

- Use CURRENTDATA(NO) to force block fetch for ambiguous cursors.

- Use OPTIONS when you make a remote copy of a package using BIND PACKAGE with the COPY option; use this option to control the default bind options that DB2 uses. Specify COMPOSITE to cause DB2 to use any options you specify in the BIND PACKAGE command. For all other options, DB2 uses the options of the copied package. This is the default command to cause DB2 to use the options you specify in the BIND PACKAGE command. For all other options, DB2 uses the defaults for the server on which the package is bound. This helps ensure that the server supports the options with which the package is bound.

- Use DBPROTOCOL(PRIVATE) if you want DB2 to use DB2 private-protocol access for accessing remote data that is specified with three-part names. Use DBPROTOCOL(DRDA) if you want DB2 to use DRDA access to access remote data that is specified with three-part names. You must bind a package at all locations whose names are specified in three-part names. These values override the value of DATABASE PROTOCOL on installation panel DSNTIP5. Therefore, if the setting of DATABASE PROTOCOL at the requester site specifies the type of remote access you want to use for three-part names, you do not need to specify the DBPROTOCOL bind option.

BIND PLAN Options

The following options of BIND PLAN are particularly relevant to binding a plan that uses DRDA access.

- For the most flexibility, use DISCONNECT(EXPLICIT) explicitly or by default. This requires you to use RELEASE statements in your program to explicitly end connections. But the other values of the option are also useful. DISCONNECT(AUTOMATIC) ends all remote connections during a commit operation without the need for RELEASE statements in your program. DISCONNECT(CONDITIONAL) ends remote connections during a commit operation except when an open cursor defined as WITH HOLD is associated with the connection.

- Use SQLRULES (DB2) explicitly or by default. SQLRULES (STD) applies the rules of the SQL standard to your CONNECT statements, so that CONNECT TO x is an error if you are already connected to x. Use STD only if you want that statement to return an error code. If your program selects LOB data from a remote location and you bind the plan for the program with SQLRULES (DB2), the format in which you retrieve the LOB data with a cursor is restricted. After you open the cursor to retrieve the LOB data, you must retrieve all the data by using a LOB variable or a LOB locator variable. If the value of SQLRULES is STD, this restriction does not exist. If you intend to switch between LOB variables and LOB locators to retrieve data from a cursor, execute the SET SQLRULES=STD statement before you connect to the remote location.
- Use CURRENTDATA (NO) to force block fetch for ambiguous cursors.
- Use DBPROTOCOL (PRIVATE) if you want DB2 to use DB2 private-protocol access for accessing remote data that is specified with three-part names. Use DBPROTOCOL (DRDA) if you want DB2 to use DRDA access to access remote data that is specified with three-part names. You must bind a package at all locations whose names are specified in three-part names. The package value for the DBPROTOCOL option overrides the plan option. For example, if you specify DBPROTOCOL (DRDA) for a remote package and DBPROTOCOL (PRIVATE) for the plan, DB2 uses DRDA access when it accesses data at that location using a three-part name. If you do not specify any value for DBPROTOCOL, DB2 uses the value of DATABASE PROTOCOL on installation panel DSNTIP5.

Coordinating Updates

Two or more updates are *coordinated* if they must all commit or all roll back in the same unit of work. Updates to two or more DBMSs can be coordinated automatically if both systems implement a method called *two-phase commit*.

DB2 and IMS or DB2 and CICS jointly implement a two-phase commit process. You can update an IMS database and a DB2 table in the same unit of work. If a system or communication failure occurs between committing the work on IMS and on DB2, the two programs restore the two systems to a consistent point when activity resumes.

You cannot have coordinated updates with a DBMS that does not implement two-phase commit. In the description that follows, we call such a DBMS a *restricted system*. DB2 prevents you from updating both a restricted system and any other system in the same unit of work. In this context, *update* includes the statements INSERT, DELETE, UPDATE, CREATE, ALTER, DROP, GRANT, REVOKE, and RENAME.

To achieve the effect of coordinated updates with a restricted system, you must first update one system and commit that work, and then update the second system and commit its work. If a failure occurs after the first update is committed and before the second is committed, no automatic provision brings the two systems back to a consistent point. Your program must assume that task.

For CICS and IMS, you cannot update at servers that do not support two-phase commit. For TSO and batch, you can update if and only if no other connections exist or if all existing connections are to servers that are restricted to read-only operations. If these conditions are not met, you are restricted to read-only operations.

If the first connection in a logical unit of work is to a server that supports two-phase commit and no connections or only read-only connections exist, that server and all servers that support two-phase commit can update. However, if the first connection is to a server that does not support two-phase commit, only that server is allowed to update.

> **NOTE** Rely on DB2 to prevent updates to two systems in the same unit of work if either of them is a restricted system.

If you are accessing a mixture of systems, some of which might be restricted, you can

- Read from any of the systems at any time.
- Update any one system many times in one unit of work.
- Update many systems, including CICS or IMS, in one unit of work, provided that none of them is a restricted system. If the first system you update in a unit of work is not restricted, any attempt to update a restricted system in that unit of work returns an error.
- Update one restricted system in a unit of work, provided that you do not try to update any other system in the same unit of work. If the first system you update in a unit of work is restricted, any attempt to update any other system in that unit of work returns an error.

PROGRAMMING CONSIDERATIONS

When working with more than one location, you need to find a way to identify which DB2 holds the data you want to process. With application-directed data distribution, before executing the SQL, you identify to DB2 the location to which the SQL statement should be directed. This can be done either explicitly, by coding a CONNECT statement in the application, or by relying on the CURRENT SERVER register. The value of the CURRENT SERVER register is initially determined by the BIND option CURRENT SERVER. If this was not specified, CURRENT SERVER is set to blanks until you issue a CONNECT TO statement.

When a package is bound with DBPROTOCOL(DRDA) and you use a three-part name, DB2 will issue the CONNECT statement under the covers. The SQLRULES bind option will also determine how DB2 will handle connection management. When using SQLRULES(DB2), you can connect to a database location even though you were already connected. The previous CONNECT will simply be put in the current state. However, with SQLRULES(STD), the control is more strict. When you are already connected to a location, the SET CONNECTION must be used to switch between connections.

It is possible that your bind will get errors if your program contains SQL statements that use more than one DB2. Some of the tables may not be defined at all locations or could have different definitions. It is important to bind your package with `SQLERROR(CONTINUE)` to allow the bind to ignore these errors. The errors are not causing any problem as long as you execute the SQL against the proper DB2. The same comment applies to the precompiler option: `SQL(ALL)` will make the precompiler flag the statements, but it will not prevent the creation of the DBRM.

When DRDA is used, the SQL statement will be processed by the remote location and will adhere to the syntax rules of the target database. When using a non-z/OS target, you may find some differences. This can work to your advantage, as you can exploit the full capabilities of your target database.

The DRDA protocol allows an application to perform any SQL statement as if the database were local to the application. Figure 14-1 is an example of a program connecting to a remote database and issuing several SQL statements. We note that the application requester already performs some optimization, as not all fetches seem to access the remote database. The second fetch finds the data on the client without having to access the server. This concept is called *block fetch*. Block fetch sends a number of rows in one transmission when the context allows this to happen without creating data-consistency problems.

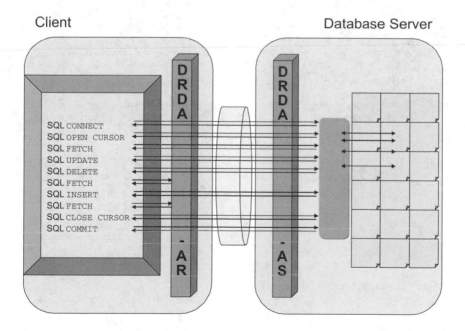

Figure 14-1 Accessing a remote database

Let's assume that the client program doesn't need any interaction between the start and the end. What keeps us from running the entire program on the server and not only the SQL statements? We just invented the concept of a stored procedure. The program logic and SQL statements are ported to the database server, and the client program simply needs to connect to the database server and start the stored procedure (see Figure 14-2).

In the stored-procedure programming model, the application logic is moved from the client program to the database server. The database server has the responsibility of invoking the stored-procedure program and handling the parameters flowing to and from the stored procedure. The implementation of the environment in which the program runs depends on the platform of deployment. On z/OS, you can either configure a stored-procedure address space or use address spaces that are controlled by the workload manager. The second option is by far the better technique, as you have much more control over the resources that are used and not all procedures that are running will share the same address space. On UNIX, Windows, or Linux, you do not need to define a separate runtime environment.

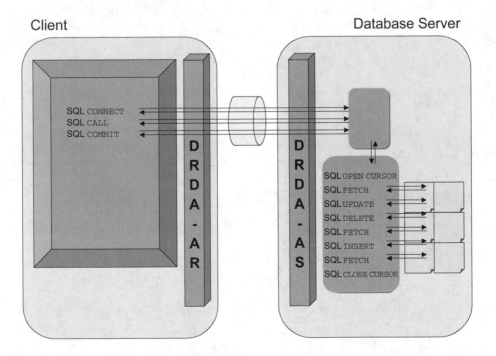

Figure 14-2   Stored-procedure flow

The DB2 Development Center provides a cross-platform development environment, allowing you to code programs either in Java or as SQL Procedure Language. The SQL Procedure Language is defined in the SQL99 standard and is very similar to BASIC. The SQL Procedure code is translated by DB2 into a C program, resulting in much better performance and the ability to run static SQL.

If you don't need the portability of the stored procedure but need to exploit non-DB2 resources, such as DL/I databases, sequential files, CICS transactions, or any other resource on z/OS, it is better to develop the stored procedure outside the scope of the DB2 Development Center and use your existing application-development environment. (See Figure 14-3.) IBM already has delivered integration with the MQSeries, thereby enriching the capabilities of the stored-procedures programming environment. Have a look at the MQ UDF wizard, in the DB2 Development Center.

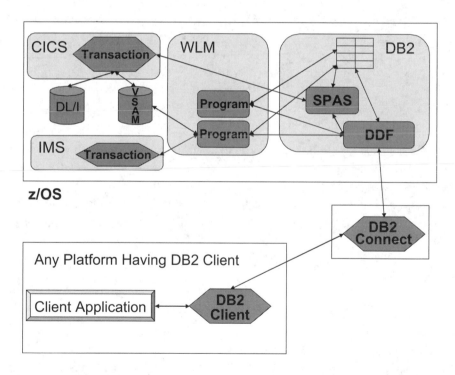

Figure 14-3 Non-DB2 resources

REMOTE QUERY PERFORMANCE

The performance of remote queries can be improved in many ways.

OPTIMIZE FOR *n* ROWS

Use the OPTIMIZE FOR *n* ROWS for distributed applications to limit the number of rows returned in a DRDA client query block so that only a portion of the answer set is fetched. This option can also optimize cases when a large number of rows are fetched, allowing a client to request multiple query blocks from a DRDA requester in a single network transmission. This allows you to specify the number of query blocks to retrieve.

OPTIMIZE FOR *n* ROWS is supported for result sets returned by a SELECT statement or by a stored procedure. DRDA level 3 is implemented to enable the client to specify the number of extra query blocks it wants to receive—instead of the default of one at a time. Any value *n* will allow the DRDA server to send multiple query blocks in a single transmission.

DB2 will send *n* number of rows of the result set in each network transmission if the result set fits in a query block. If the rows do not fit in a query block, extra query blocks will be sent in the same transmission up to either the query-block limit set for the server (DSNZPARM EXTRASRV) or the query-block limit set by the client (DSNZPARM EXTRAREQ, which is also the value in DDM MAXBLKEXT on the DRDA requester). You want to be careful with these parameters, as the default is 100 query blocks per transmission, and this default can negatively affect the performance of your applications, depending on your workload mix.

You want to take advantage of this clause when the value *n* is less than the total number of rows that will fit in a DRDA query block and the application is going to process only the same *n* number of rows. You can also significantly reduce elapsed time for large query result sets by using OPTIMIZE FOR *n* ROWS if *n* is greater than the number of rows that can fit in one DRDA query block, because this will allow the requester to get multiple query blocks with each network transmission.

If your DRDA application meets the following criteria, you may want to use OPTIMIZE FOR *n* ROWS:

- Read-only queries fetching a large number of rows
- SQL cursors rarely being closed before fetching the entire result set
- When cursor is open, no statements other than FETCH used
- Multiple cursors defined with OPTIMIZE FOR *n* ROWS not issuing a FETCH

You do not want to set a large number of query blocks for cursors defined WITH HOLD, because if the requester application commits while several blocks are in the network, DB2 will buffer the blocks in memory. A WITH HOLD cursor will also prevent a thread from going inactive.

Inactive Threads

Access threads that do not hold any cursors are known as inactive threads. Two types of inactive threads are supported: type 1 and type 2. Type 2 threads are available only for DRDA connections; use a pool of database threads, which can be switched as needed among connections; and use less storage than type 1. You want to use type 2 inactive threads when possible.

Displaying Distributed Threads

Distributed threads can be displayed to find out information about their status by using the -DISPLAY THREAD command, using the LOCATION option. An example of this command follows:

```
DISPLAY THREAD(*) LOCATION(*) DETAIL
```

Distributed Application Tuning Guidelines

- Use stored procedures to reduce network traffic.
- Use COMMIT ON RETURN YES to issue an implicit commit for a stored procedure when there is a return from the CALL statement.
- Commit frequently.
- Limit the number of SQL statements; the fewer, the better.
- Use the SQL RELEASE statement to release the remote connection at commit time, and also use the DISCONNECT(EXPLICIT).
- Use the CURRENT RULES of DB2, not STD, special register so that DB2 can send multiple blocks of data back to the program when requesting LOB data.
- Use DRDA-type connections instead of the DB2 private protocol.

SUMMARY

Access to DB2 from remote locations is a necessary part of most application environments. DB2 provides that capability through various means. Using the Distributed Data Facility (DDF) of DB2 allows for access to data held by other DBMSs or makes your DB2 data accessible to other systems. A DB2 application program can use SQL to access data at DBMSs other than the DB2 at which the application's plan is bound.

We saw that DB2 provides two methods for accessing data at remote application servers: DRDA and DB2 private-protocol access. We also looked at the use of three-part names and the DB2 CONNECT statement. Last, we covered some of the ways to improve performance of remote queries.

ADDITIONAL RESOURCES

IBM DB2 Version 8 UDB for z/OS Installation Guide (GC26-9936)

IBM DB2 Version 8 UDB for z/OS Administration Guide (SC26-9931)

IBM DB2 Version 8 UDB for z/OS SQL Guide and Reference (SC26-9944)

Open Group Technical Standard in DRDA Volume 1: Distributed Relational Database Architecture (DRDA) (C911)

DRDA information: www.opengroup.com

SNA LU 6.2 Peer Protocols Reference (SC31-6808)

CHAPTER 15

Object-Relational Functionality

- Triggers
- Object-relational extensions
- Large objects

This chapter covers some of the more powerful features of DB2's SQL. The extended programming features, user-defined functions, and table functions are discussed, along with triggers and distinct types. The object-relational extensions used to support these features are also covered, as are implementing and using large objects (LOBs) and DB2 extenders.

TRIGGERS

An active trigger is a set of actions that will be executed when a defined event occurs. Such an event can be any of the the following SQL statements:

- INSERT
- UPDATE
- DELETE

A trigger is defined for a specific table. Once defined, a trigger is automatically active. A table can have multiple triggers defined for it; if multiple triggers are defined for a given table, the order of trigger activation is based on the trigger-creation timestamp, or the order in which the triggers were created.

469

Trigger definitions are stored in the DB2 catalog tables. The SYSIBM.SYSTRIGGERS table has one row for each trigger, and the TEXT column contains the full text of CREATE TRIGGER. The SYSIBM.SYSPACKAGE table has one row for each trigger package, and the TYPE column is set to T to indicate a trigger package.

Trigger Use

A trigger can be used for

- **Data validation** to ensure that a new data value is within the proper range. This use is similar to table-check constraints but is a more flexible data-validation mechanism.
- **Data conditioning**, or using triggers that fire before data-record modification. This allows the new data value to be modified or conditioned to a predefined value.
- **Data integrity** to ensure that cross-table dependencies are maintained. Useful when a child table can have multiple parent tables.
- **Data propagation**, with which audit, history, and summary tables can be updated based on the values placed in base tables.

The triggered action could involve updating data records in related tables. This is similar to referential integrity but is a more flexible alternative.

Triggers can also be used to enforce business rules, create new column values, edit column values, validate all input data, or maintain summary tables or cross-reference tables. Triggers provide for enhanced enterprise and business functionality, faster application development, and global enforcement of business rules.

In short, a trigger is a way of getting control to perform an action whenever a table's data is modified. A single trigger invoked by an update on a financial table could invoke a UDF and/or call a stored procedure to invoke another external action, triggering an e-mail to a pager to notify the DBA of a serious condition. Farfetched? No, it is already being done.

Triggers can cause other triggers to be invoked and, through the SQL, can call stored procedures, which could issue SQL updates that invoke other triggers. This allows great flexibility.

The cascading of triggers, stored procedures, and UDFs has an execution-time nesting depth of 16 to prevent endless cascading. The *big* performance concern is that, if the seventeenth level is reached, an SQLCODE of -724 is set, but all 16 levels are backed out. That could be a significant problem and not something you want to see. The real issue here is processes that are executed outside the control of DB2, as they would not be backed out, and it might be very difficult to determine what was changed. There are limitations in the calling sequences; for example, stored procedures managed by the WLM cannot call stored procedures managed by DB2.

Trigger Activation

A trigger can be defined to fire—be activated—in one of two ways.

1. A *before trigger* will fire for each row in the set of affected rows before the triggering SQL statement executes. Therefore, the trigger body is seeing the new data values prior to its being inserted or updated into the table.

2. An *after trigger* will fire for each row in the set of affected rows or after the statement has successfully completed, depending on the defined granularity. Therefore, the trigger body is seeing the table as being in a consistent state, namely, that all transactions have been completed.

Triggers can fire other triggers—or the same trigger—or other constraints. These are known as *cascading trigger*s. Only an after trigger can update other data causing this cascade.

During the execution of a trigger, the new and old data values can be accessible to the trigger, depending on the nature of the trigger: before or after. By using triggers, you can

- Reduce the amount of application development and make development faster. Because triggers are stored in DB2 and are processed by DB2, you do not need to code the triggers or their actions into your applications.
- Provide a global environment for your business rules. The triggers have to be defined only once and then are stored in the database, so they are available to all applications executing against the database.
- Reduce the maintenance of your applications. As the trigger is handled by DB2 and is stored in the database itself, any changes to the trigger owing to changes in your environment have to occur in only one, not multiple, applications.

Triggers can contain only SQL, but through SQL, stored procedures and UDFs can be invoked. Because stored procedures and UDFs are user-written code, almost any activity can be performed from a triggered event. The action causing the trigger may need a message sent to a special place via e-mail. The trigger might be a before trigger written to handle complex referential integrity checks, which could involve checking whether data exists in another non-DB2 storage container. Through the use of stored procedures and UDFs, the power of a trigger is almost unlimited.

Creating Triggers

Triggers are defined using the CREATE TRIGGER statement, which contains many options. The primary options are whether it is a before trigger or an after trigger, whether it is a row trigger or a statement trigger, and the language of the trigger, which is only SQL, but that will probably change in the future. The phrase MODE DB2SQL is the execution mode of the trigger. This phrase is required for each trigger to ensure that an existing application will not be negatively impacted if alternative execution modes for triggers are added to DB2 in the future. You can have up to 12 types of triggers on a single table. See Figure 15-1.

> **N O T E**   Triggers are invoked in the order they were *created*.
> A timestamp is recorded when the trigger is created and recreated.
> A DROP and (re)CREATE of a trigger can completely mess up your
> process by changing the order in which triggers are executed. Be
> careful!

When triggers are added, the rows that are in violation of a newly added trigger will not be rejected. When a trigger is added to a table that has existing rows, triggered actions will not be activated. If the trigger is designed to enforce some type of integrity constraint on the data rows in the table, those constraints may not be enforced by rules defined in the trigger, or held true, for the rows that existed in the table before the trigger was added.

If an update trigger without an explicit column list is created, packages with an update usage on the target table are invalidated. If an update trigger with a column list is created, packages with update usage on the target table are invalidated only if the package also has an update usage on at least one column in the column-name list of the CREATE TRIGGER statement. If an insert

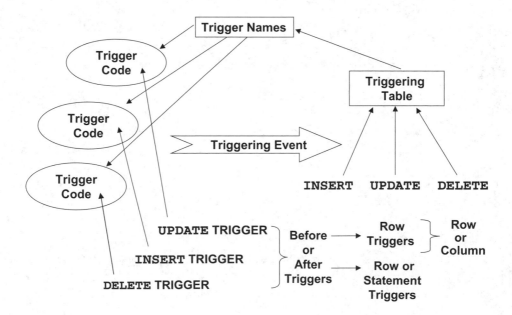

Figure 15-1   Trigger types

trigger is created, packages that have an insert usage on the target table are invalidated. If a delete trigger is created, packages that have a delete usage on the target table are invalidated.

A lot of functionality can be used within a trigger. For example, a CASE expression can be used in a trigger but needs to be nested inside a VALUES statement, as shown here:

```
BEGIN ATOMIC
   VALUES CASE
      WHEN condition
         THEN something
      WHEN other condition
         THEN something else    END
END;
```

The best way to understand the use of triggers is to see some in action. The DB2CERT database contains many relationships that can be maintained using triggers.

After Trigger

In the following example, a trigger is defined to set the value of the PASS_FAIL column for each of the tests taken by a candidate. (Note that we add this column for this scenario.) The trigger has been given the name PassFail, which has no relationship with the column called PASS_FAIL. Once the trigger has been created, it is active.

The PassFail trigger is an AFTER, INSERT, and FOR EACH ROW trigger. Every time a row is inserted into the test_taken table, this trigger will fire. The trigger-body section will perform an UPDATE statement to set the value of the PASS_FAIL column for the newly inserted row. The column is populated with either the value P, representing a passing grade, or the value F, representing a failing grade.

> **N O T E**   Remember that an after trigger defined against one table can modify other tables in the trigger body.

```
CREATE TRIGGER PASSFAIL
  AFTER INSERT ON DB2CERT.TEST_TAKEN
  REFERENCING NEW AS N
  FOR EACH ROW MODE DB2SQL
UPDATE DB2CERT.TEST_TAKEN
  SET PASS_FAIL =
    CASE
      WHEN N.SCORE >=
        (SELECT CUT_SCORE FROM DB2CERT.TEST
        WHERE NUMBER = N.NUMBER)
      THEN'P'
      WHEN N.SCORE <
```

```
              (SELECT CUT_SCORE FROM DB2CERT.TEST
               WHERE NUMBER = N.NUMBER)
               THEN'F'
               END
      WHERE N.CID = CID
        AND N.TCID = TCID
        AND N.NUMBER = NUMBER
        AND N.DATE_TAKEN = DATE_TAKEN
```

Before Trigger

A before trigger will be activated before the trigger operation has completed. The triggering operation can be on an INSERT, UPDATE, or DELETE statement. This type of trigger is very useful for three purposes:

1. To condition data
2. To provide default values
3. To enforce data-value constraints dynamically

The three before-trigger examples shown are used in the DB2 Certification application. All three of these triggers have been implemented to avoid seat conflicts for test candidates. The triggers will fire during an insert of each new candidate for a test.

```
** Example 1 **
CREATE TRIGGER pre9 NO CASCADE BEFORE
    INSERT ON DB2CERT.TEST_TAKEN
    REFERENCING NEW AS n
    FOR EACH ROW MODE DB2SQL
WHEN (N.START_TIME <'09:00:00')
    SIGNAL SQLSTATE 70003'
    ('Cannot assign seat before 09:00:00!')
** Example 2 **
CREATE TRIGGER AFT5 NO CASCADE BEFORE
    INSERT ON DB2CERT.TEST_TAKEN
    REFERENCING NEW AS N
    FOR EACH ROW MODE DB2SQL
WHEN (N.START_TIME +
    (SELECT SMALLINT(LENGTH) FROM DB2CERT.TEST
    WHERE NUMBER = N.NUMBER) MINUTES
      >'17:00:00')
    SIGNAL SQLSTATE'70004'
    ('Cannot assign seat after 17:00:00!')
** Example 3 **
CREATE TRIGGER START NO CASCADE BEFORE
    INSERT ON DB2CERT.TEST_TAKEN
    REFERENCING NEW AS N
```

```
        FOR EACH ROW MODE DB2SQL
WHEN (
        EXISTS (SELECT CID FROM DB2CERT.TEST_TAKEN
        WHERE SEAT_NO = N.SEAT_NO
        AND TCID = N.TCID
        AND DATE_TAKEN = N.DATE_TAKEN
        AND N.START_TIME BETWEEN
            START_TIME AND FINISH_TIME))
        SIGNAL SQLSTATE '70001' ('Start Time Conflict!')
```

If the conditions are encountered, an SQL error will be flagged, using the SQL function called SIGNAL. A different SQLSTATE value will be provided when the triggered conditions are encountered.

The pre9 trigger is used to ensure that a test candidate is not scheduled to take a test before 9:00 A.M. The aft5 trigger is used to ensure that a test candidate is not scheduled to take a test after 5:00 P.M. The start trigger is used to avoid conflicts during a testing day.

Row and Statement Triggers

In order to understand the concept of trigger granularity, you need to understand the rows affected by the triggering operations. The set of affected rows contains all rows that are deleted, inserted, or updated by the triggering operations. The keyword FOR EACH ROW is used to activate the trigger as many times as the number of rows in the set of affected rows. The previous example shows a row trigger. The keyword FOR EACH STATEMENT is used to activate the trigger once for the triggering operation.

Transition Variables and Tables

Transition Variables. Transition variables allow row triggers to access columns of affected row data in order to see the row data as it existed both before and after the triggering operation. These variables are implemented by a REFERENCING clause in the definition:

```
REFERENCING OLD AS OLD_ACCOUNTS
            NEW AS NEW_ACCOUNTS
```

The following example uses transition variables to prevent an update from occurring:

```
CREATE TRIGGER TR1 NO CASCADE BEFORE
    UPDATE ON EMP
    REFERENCING NEW AS T1
    FOR EACH ROW MODE DB2SQL
WHEN (
    EXISTS (SELECT 1
    FROM DEPT B, EMP C
```

```
      WHERE B.DEPTNO=T1.WORKDEPT
      AND B.MGRNO=C.EMPNO
      AND C.SALARY <= T1.SALARY)
SIGNAL SQLSTATE '70001' ('Salary too big!')
```

Here, whenever an update is made to the EMP table, the new value of the salary of the employee, referenced in the before-trigger transition variable T1.SALARY, is checked against the salary of that employee's manager. This is done by joining the employee table to the department table, using the transition variable T1.WORKDEPT to get the department information for the employee being updated. The EMP table is then joined, using the manager's employee number in order to get the salary of the manager.

Transition Tables.   Transition tables allow after triggers to access a set of affected rows and see how they were before the triggering operation and then see all rows after the triggering operation. Transition tables are also implemented using the REFERENCING clause in the trigger definition:

```
REFERENCING OLD_TABLE AS OLD_ACCT_TABL
NEW_TABLE AS NEW_ACCT_TABLE
```

> **N O T E**   Transition tables are materialized in DSNDB07.

Transition tables allow an SQL statement embedded in the trigger body to access the entire set of affected data in the state it was in before or after the change. In the following example, a fullselect reads the entire set of changed rows to pass qualifying data to a user-defined function:

```
CREATE TRIGGER EMPMRGR
AFTER UPDATE ON EMP
REFERENCING NEW_TABLE AS NTABLE
FOR EACH STATEMENT MODE DB2SQL
BEGIN ATOMIC
   SELECT SALARYALERT(EMPNO, SALARY)
   FROM NTABLE
   WHERE SALARY > 150000;
END;
```

Transition tables can also be passed to stored procedures and UDFs that are invoked within the body of the trigger. The table is not passed as a parameter; instead, a table locator is passed, which can then be used to establish a cursor within the stored procedure or UDF. The following example demonstrates the passing of a transition table to a UDF:

```
CREATE TRIGGER EMPMRGR
AFTER UPDATE ON EMP
```

```
REFERENCING NEW_TABLE AS NTABLE
FOR EACH STATEMENT MODE DB2SQL
BEGIN ATOMIC
    VALUES (SALARYALERT(TABLE NTABLE));
END;
```

The corresponding function definition would look something like this:

```
CREATE FUNCTION SALARYALERT (TABLE LIKE EMP AS LOCATOR)
    RETURNS INTEGER
    EXTERNAL NAME SALERT
    PARAMETER STYLE DB2SQL
    LANGUAGE C;
```

The C program would declare a cursor against the transition table by referencing the locator variable that was passed as a parameter in place of a table reference:

```
DECLARE C1 CURSOR FOR
    SELECT EMPNO, SALARY
    FROM TABLE(:LOC1 LIKE EMP)
    WHERE SALARY > 150000;
```

Once the input locator parameter is accepted into the :LOC1 variable, the cursor can be opened and processed.

Allowable Combinations

Although different combinations of trigger options are available, not all are compatible. Table 15-1 shows the valid combinations for trigger options.

Table 15-1   Trigger-Option Combinations

Granularity	Activation Time	Trigger Operation	Transition Variables Allowed	Transition Tables Allowed
Row	Before	INSERT	New	None
		UPDATE	Old, new	
		DELETE	Old	
	After	INSERT	New	NEW_TABLE
		UPDATE	Old, new	OLD_TABLE, NEW_TABLE
		DELETE	Old	OLD_TABLE

continues

Table 15-1 Trigger-Option Combinations (Continued)

Granularity	Activation Time	Trigger Operation	Transition Variables Allowed	Transition Tables Allowed
Statement	Before	Invalid	None	Invalid
	After	INSERT		NEW_TABLE
		UPDATE		OLD_TABLE, NEW_TABLE
		DELETE		OLD_TABLE

Trigger Packages

When a trigger is created, DB2 creates a trigger package, which is different from a package created for an application program. (For more information on packages, refer to Chapter 11.) Trigger packages can be rebound locally, but you cannot bind them; binding is done automatically during creation. The package can be rebound only with the REBIND TRIGGER PACKAGE command, and this will allow you to change subsets of default bind options (CURRENTDATA, EXPLAIN, FLAG, ISOLATION, RELEASE). For more information on the bind options, refer to Chapter 11.

Trigger packages cannot be copied, freed, or dropped. In order to delete a trigger package, the DROP TRIGGER SQL statement must be issued.

> **N O T E**   Rebinding trigger packages after creation is also useful for picking up new access paths.

The qualifier of the trigger name determines package collection. For static SQL, the authorization ID of the QUALIFIER bind option will be the qualifier; for dynamic SQL, whatever the CURRENT SQLID is will be the qualifier if not specified explicitly in the statement.

Trigger Invalidations

Invalid updates can be detected and stopped by triggers in a couple of ways. You can use the SIGNAL SQLSTATE statement or the RAISE_ERROR function.

SIGNAL SQLSTATE is a new SQL statement used to cause an error to be returned to the application with a specified SQLSTATE code and a specific message to stop processing. This statement can be used only as a triggered SQL statement within a trigger and can be controlled with a WHEN clause. The following example shows the use of the SIGNAL statement:

```
WHEN NEW_ACCT.AMOUNT < (OLD_ACCT.AMOUNT)
   SIGNAL SQLSTATE '99001' ('Bad amount field')
```

If you use the SIGNAL statement to raise an error condition, a rollback will also be performed to back out the changes made by an SQL statement, as well as any changes caused by the trigger, such as cascading effects resulting from a referential relationship. SIGNAL can be used in either before or after triggers. Other statements in the program can be either committed or rolled back.

RAISE_ERROR is not a statement but a built-in function that causes the statement that includes it to return an error with a specific SQLSTATE, SQLCODE −438, and a message. This function does basically the same thing as the SIGNAL statement and can be used wherever an expression can be used. The RAISE_ERROR function always returns null with an undefined data type and is most useful in CASE expressions, especially when they are used in a stored procedure. The following example shows a CASE expression with the RAISE_ERROR function:

```
VALUES (CASE
   WHEN NEW_ACCT.AMOUNT < OLD_ACCT.AMOUNT
   THEN RAISE_ERROR('99001', 'Bad amount field'))
```

Performance Issues

Recursive triggers are updates applied by a trigger, causing it to fire again. Recursive triggers can easily lead to loops and can be very complex statements. However, this may be required by some applications for related rows. You will need code to stop the trigger.

The ordering of multiple triggers can be an issue because the same type of triggers on the same table are activated in the order created, identified in the creation timestamp. The interaction among triggers and referential constraints can also be an issue, because the order of processing can be significant on results produced.

Invoking stored procedures and UDFs from triggers raises performance and manageability concerns. Triggers can include only SQL but can call stored procedures and UDFs, which are user-written and therefore have many implications for integrity and performance. Transition tables can be passed to stored procedures and UDFs also.

Trigger cascading occurs when a trigger could modify the triggering table or another table. Triggers can be activated at the same level or different levels; when activated at different levels, cascading occurs. Cascading can occur only for after triggers. Cascading can occur for UDFs, stored procedures, and triggers for up to 16 levels.

Monitoring Triggers

The actions of triggers can be monitored in various ways. The DB2 Performance Expert statistics and accounting reports show the number of times a trigger has been activated, a row trigger was activated, and an SQL error occurred during the execution of a triggered action.

Other details can be found in the traces. For example, IFCID 16 has information about the materialization of a work file in support of a transition table, where TR is the transition table for triggers. Other information in IFCID 16 includes the depth level of the trigger (0–16), where 0 indicates that there are no triggers. You can also find the type of SQL that invoked the trigger:

- I = INSERT
- U = INSERT into a transition table because of an update
- D = INSERT into a transition table because of a delete

The type of referential integrity (RI) that caused an insert into a transition table for a trigger is also indicated with an S for SET NULL—can occur when the type is Update—or C for CASCADE DELETE—can occur when the type is Delete).

If a transition table needs to be scanned for a trigger, you can find this occurrence in IFCID 17: TR for transition table scan for a trigger.

Catalog Information

The SYSIBM.SYSTRIGGERS catalog table contains information about the triggers defined in your databases. To find all the triggers defined on a particular table and the characteristics of each trigger and to determine the order in which the triggers are executed, you can issue the following query:

```
SELECT DISTINCT SCHEMA, NAME, TRIGTIME, TRIGEVENT,
       GRANULARITY, CREATEDTS
FROM SYSIBM.SYSTRIGGERS
WHERE TBNAME = table-name
  AND TBOWNER = table-owner
ORDER BY CREATEDTS
```

You can get the text of the trigger with the following statement:

```
SELECT TEXT, SEQNO
FROM SYSIBM.SYSTRIGGERS
WHERE SCHEMA = schema_name
  AND NAME = trigger_name
ORDER BY SEQNO
```

Triggers versus Table-Check Constraints

If a trigger and a table-check constraint can enforce the same rule, it is better to use a table-check constraint to enforce business rules. You would want to explore the use of triggers only when a constraint is not flexible enough to enforce a business rule. Constraints and declarative RI are more useful when you have only one state to enforce in a business rule. Although triggers are more powerful than table-check constraints and can be more extensive in terms of rule enforcement, constraints can be better optimized by DB2.

Table-check constraints are enforced for all existing data at the time of creation and are enforced for all statements affecting the data. A table-check constraint is defined on a populated table, using the ALTER TABLE statement, and the value of the CURRENT RULES special register is DB2. Constraints offer a few other advantages over triggers: Constraints are written in a less procedural way than triggers and are better optimized. Constraints protect data against being placed into an invalid state by any kind of statement, whereas a trigger applies only to a specific kind of statement, such as an update or a delete.

Because they can enforce several rules that constraints cannot, triggers are more powerful than check constraints. You can use triggers to apply rules that involve different states of data, perhaps where you need to know the state of the data before and after a calculation.

Triggers and Declarative RI

Trigger operations may result from changes made to enforce DB2-enforced referential constraints. For example, if you are deleting an EMPLOYEE table row that causes cascaded deletes to the PAYROLL table through referential constraints, the delete triggers that are defined on the PAYROLL table are subsequently executed. The delete triggers are activated as a result of the referential constraint defined on the EMPLOYEE table. This may or may not be the desired result, so you need to be aware of cascading effects when using triggers. When triggers cascade in this manner, they are considered to be at the same nesting level so the 16-level limit will not interfere with long chains of cascading deletes.

Triggers and UDFs

You can use a UDF in a trigger, and these types of functions can help to centralize rules to ensure that they are enforced in the same manner in current and future applications. To invoke a UDF in a trigger, the VALUES clause has to be used. Figure 15-2 is an example of how to invoke a UDF in a trigger.

In the following example, PAGE_DBA is a user-written program, perhaps in C or Java, that formulates a message and triggers a process that sends a message to a pager:

```
BEGIN ATOMIC
    VALUES(PAGE_DBA('Table spaces:' CONCAT TS.NAME,
        'needs to be reorged NOW!'));
END
```

Using these kinds of UDFs in triggers enables them to perform any kind of task and not be limited to SQL.

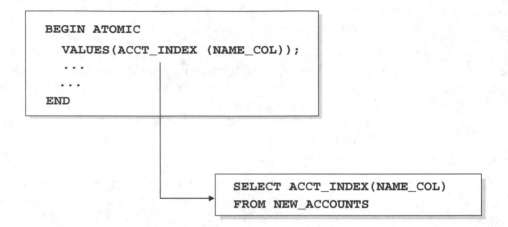

Figure 15-2   Invoking a UDF from a trigger

Dropping Triggers

Triggers can be dropped by using the `DROP TRIGGER` statement. If the table on which the trigger is defined is dropped, so is the trigger. Regardless of what caused the trigger to be dropped, the information about the trigger is removed from `SYSIBM.SYSTRIGGERS` and `SYSIBM.SYSPACKAGE`. It is a good idea to keep a copy of the trigger code so it can be recreated if dropped.

OBJECT-RELATIONAL EXTENSIONS

With the object extensions of DB2, you can incorporate object-oriented concepts and methodologies into your relational database by extending DB2 with richer sets of data types and functions. With those extensions, you can store instances of object-oriented data types in columns of tables and operate on them using functions in SQL statements. In addition, you can control the types of operations that users can perform on those data types. The object extensions that DB2 provides are large objects (LOBs), distinct types, and UDFs.

Schemas are qualifiers used to qualify user-defined distinct types, UDFs, stored procedures, triggers, sequences, and jars. All the objects qualified by the same schema name can be thought of as a group of related objects. A schema name has a maximum length of 8 bytes. The schema name `SYSIBM` is used for built-in data types and built-in functions, and `SYSPROC` is used for some stored procedures delivered by IBM in support of the Control Center and Visual Explain. Stored procedures that were created prior to DB2 version 6 may also use the `SYSPROC` schema name.

The schema name can be specified explicitly when the object is referenced in the CREATE, ALTER, DROP, or COMMENT ON statement. If the object is unqualified and the statement is dynamically prepared, the SQL authorization ID contained in the CURRENT SQLID special register is used for the schema name of the objects.

Certain authorities are associated with schemas. Schema privileges include CREATIN, ALTERIN, and DROPIN. This allows you to create, alter, or drop objects in the identified schema. If the schema name is the same as an authorization ID, it has those privileges implicitly.

The PATH bind option is applicable to BIND PLAN, BIND PACKAGE, REBIND PLAN, and REBIND PACKAGE. The list of schemas specified is used to resolve unqualified references to user-defined distinct types and UDFs in static SQL statements. This list is also used to resolve unqualified stored procedure names when the SQL CALL statement specifies a literal for the procedure name. The list specifies an ordered list of schemas to be searched to resolve these unqualified references.

The PATH has a corresponding special register. The SET CURRENT PATH statement changes the value of the PATH special register. This PATH special register is used in the same way as the PATH bind option—to resolve unqualified references in dynamic SQL—and can also be used to resolve unqualified stored-procedure names in CALL host-variable statements. The PATH bind option is used to set the initial value for this special register. SYSIBM and SYSPROC do not need to be specified as part of the PATH; they are implicitly assumed as the first schema.

Distinct Types

A distinct type is the DB2 implementation of a user-defined data type. By using distinct types, you can avoid some excess code in order to support data typing that is not included in the DB2 product. You enable DB2 to do strong-typing: Only functions and operations defined on the distinct type can be applied to instances of the distinct type. This is beneficial for applications so that you do not have to code for comparison errors.

Once the distinct type is defined, column definitions can reference that type during the issuing of the CREATE or ALTER statements, just as they would any DB2 built-in data type. If a distinct type is specified without a schema name, the distinct type is resolved by searching the schemas in the current path.

Distinct types allow you to use DB2 built-in data types in special ways. Distinct types are built off of the DB2 built-in types. Distinct types allow you to extend these types and declare specialized usage on them. DB2 then enforces these rules by performing only the kinds of computations and comparisons that you have defined for the data type.

Defining

In order to use a distinct type, you must first create it. Distinct types are created by using one of the DB2 built-in types as a base. You create them by using the CREATE DISTINCT TYPE statement:

```
CREATE DISTINCT TYPE distinct-type-name
   AS source-data-type
   WITH COMPARISONS
```

The name of the distinct type is a two-part name, which must be unique within the DB2 subsystem. The qualifier is a schema name. The distinct type shares a common internal representation with its source data type. However, the distinct type is considered to be an independent data type that is different from the others.

> **N O T E**   LONG VARHCAR and LONG VARGRAPHIC cannot be used as source types.

An instance of a distinct type can be compared only with another instance of the same distinct type. For compatibility with DB2 on other platforms, you can also specify the WITH COMPARISONS clause at the end of the CREATE statement. DB2 z/OS allows comparisons only between items of the same distinct type. This clause is not allowed if the source data type is not a LOB type, such as BLOB, CLOB, or DBCLOB. Comparisons for these types are not allowed.

Operations on Distinct Types

Two operations are allowed on distinct types: comparisons and casting. You can compare the values of distinct types (non-LOB), or you can cast between the distinct type and the source type.

> **N O T E**   Character and arithmetic operators that are used in built-in functions that are used on a source type are *not* automatically inherited by the distinct type. These operators and functions need to be created explicitly.

The following comparison operators are allowed on distinct types.

=	>=	¬>	IN
<>	<=	BETWEEN	NOT IN
>	¬=	NOT BETWEEN	IS NOT NULL
<	¬<	IS NULL	

Note that LIKE and NOT LIKE are not supported.

Casting functions are used to convert instances of source data types into instances of a different data types. These functions have the name of the target data type and will have a single parameter, which is the source data type. They will return the target data type. Two cast functions are generated by DB2 when the CREATE DISTINCT TYPE is issued. These functions, used to convert between the distinct type and its source type, will be created in the same schema as the distinct type. The following shows an example of creating a distinct type and then using it both with and without casting:

```
CREATE DISTINCT TYPE EURO AS DECIMAL (9,2) WITH COMPARISONS
    EURO(DECIMAL)
    -- where EURO is the target and DECIMAL is the source
    DECIMAL (EURO)
    -- where DECIMAL is the target and EURO is the source

Without casting - using the function name
    SELECT ITEM
    FROM INVENTORY
    WHERE COST > EURO (1000.00)

With casting - using cast function
    SELECT ITEM
    FROM INVENTORY
    WHERE COST > CAST (1000.00 AS EURO)
```

> **NOTE** Constants are always considered to be source-type values.

If you want to find all items that have a cost greater than 1,000.00 euros, you will have to cast, because you cannot compare the data of type EURO with data of the source data type of the EURO, which is DECIMAL. You will need to use the cast function to cast data from DECIMAL to EURO. You can also use the cast function DECIMAL to cast from EURO to DECIMAL and cast the column COST to type DECIMAL. Depending on the way you choose to cast—from or to the distinct type—you can use the function-name notation data-type(argument) or the cast notation CAST(argument AS data-type).

Built-in Functions
The built-in data types come with a collection of built-in functions that operate on them. Some of these functions implement operators, such as the arithmetic operators on numeric data types and substring operators on character data types. Other functions, such as scalar and column functions, are discussed in Chapter 6.

When you create a distinct type, you can also set it up to inherit some or all of the functions that operate on the corresponding source type. This is done by creating new functions, called *sourced functions*, that operate on the distinct type and duplicate the semantics of the built-in functions that work on the source type. Built-in functions without sourced functions for a distinct type will not be available for use against that distinct type. The following example shows how to create a sourced function:

```
CREATE FUNCTION '+' (EURO, EURO) RETURNS EURO
   SOURCE SYSIBM.'+' (DECIMAL(9,2), DECIMAL(9,2))
```

You can also give distinct types distinct semantics of their own by creating external functions that you write in a host language that will operate on your distinct types.

Privileges

You need to have privileges granted in order to use distinct types. The GRANT USAGE ON DISTINCT TYPE is used in order to grant privileges to use the distinct type as a column data type in a CREATE or ALTER statement or to use the distinct type as a parameter in a stored procedure or UDF. The GRANT EXECUTE ON enables users to cast functions on a distinct type.

Catalog Information

Information about the distinct types is stored in the DB2 catalog. The following tables contain information about distinct types:

* SYSIBM.SYSDATATYPES: Row for each distinct type
* SYSIBM.SYSROUTINES: Row for each cast function
* SYSIBM.SYSROUTINEAUTH: Authorizations for EXECUTE privilege on functions
* SYSIBM.SYSRESAUTH: Authorizations for USAGE privilege on distinct types

User-Defined Functions

UDFs form the basis of object-relational extensions to SQL, along with distinct types and LOBs. Fundamentally, a database function is a relationship between a set of input data values and a result value. DB2 Universal Database comes with many built-in functions; however, it is possible to create your own column, scalar, and table functions.

There are three types of functions in DB2: column, scalar, and table. Column, or aggregate, functions can only be created as sourced functions as described in the section on distinct types. Scalar functions receive parameters and return a single result value. Table functions return an entire table, making them completely different from our common concept of a "function."

In DB2, you can create your own scalar or table functions. A UDF can be written in a high-level programming language such as COBOL, C, C++, or Java, or you can use a single SQL statement.

> **N O T E**   The built-in column and scalar functions are covered in
> Chapter 5.

Types of UDFs

UDFs are of four types:

1. **Sourced**, based on another scalar UDF or on a built-in scalar or column function. This concept is similar to *overloading* classes in object-oriented programming.
2. **SQL scalar**, based on a single SQL expression. The source code for an SQL UDF is contained entirely within the UDF definition.
3. **External scalar**, written in a supported language, it returns a single value.
4. **External table**, written in a supported language and used in the FROM clause of a SELECT statement. Table functions return a set of rows to DB2 for processing in the query statement.

External UDFs

An external UDF is similar to any other program written for the z/OS platform. External UDFs may contain SQL statements, IFI (Instrumentation Facility Interface), or DB2 commands and may be written in assembler, COBOL, C, C++, PL/I, or Java. External UDFs, once written and generated as dynamically loadable libraries or classes, must be registered with the database. An external function is defined to DB2 with a reference to an z/OS load module that DB2 should load when the function is invoked. The z/OS load module contains the object code for the application program that contains the logic of the external function. If the program contains SQL statements, an associated package contains the access path for the embedded SQL statement. External functions cannot be column functions. The following congrat function is an external scalar UDF and is registered using the CREATE FUNCTION statement:

```
CREATE FUNCTION congrat(VARCHAR(30),VARCHAR(40))
    RETURNS VARCHAR(30)
    EXTERNAL NAME 'CONGRAT'
    LANGUAGE C
    PARAMETER STYLE DB2SQL
    DETERMINISTIC
    FENCED
    READS SQL DATA
    COLLID TEST
    WLM ENVIRONMENT WLMENV1
    NO EXTERNAL ACTION
    DISALLOW PARALLEL;
```

DB2 passes parameters to external UDFs in a standard manner, as parameters are passed to stored procedures. DB2 uses the following structure:

Address of Parameter 1
Address of Parameter 2
Address of Parameter 3
…
Address of Result 1
Address of Result 2
Address of Result 3
…
Address of Parameter 1 Null Indicator
Address of Parameter 2 Null Indicator
Address of Parameter 3 Null Indicator
…
Address of Result 1 Null Indicator
Address of Result 2 Null Indicator
Address of Result 3 Null Indicator
…
Address of SQLSTATE
Address of Procedure Name
Address of Specific Name
Address of Message Text
Address of the Scratchpad (if SCRATCHPAD specified in DDL)
Address Call Type Indicator (if FINAL CALL specified in DDL)
Address of DBINFO (if DBINFO specified in DDL)

> **N O T E**   A scalar function can return only a single result parameter, whereas table functions return multiple result parameters, each representing a column in a row of the table being returned.

The SQLSTATE can be returned from the external UDF to DB2 to indicate a condition that DB2 can then act on. It is highly recommended that the UDF return a SQLSTATE to the caller.

If the UDF returns a SQLSTATE that is not allowed, DB2 replaces the SQLSTATE with 39001 and returns a SQLCODE of -463. The *IBM DB2 Messages and Codes* manual documents the valid SQLSTATE values.

Sourced UDFs. Sourced UDFs are registered simply by specifying the DB2 built-in source function. Sourced functions can be scalar functions or column functions but cannot be table functions. Sourced functions are often helpful when use of a built-in function on a distinct type is needed.

This example allows you to create an AVG function for the SCORE data type:

```
CREATE FUNCTION AVG (SCORE)
   RETURNS SCORE
   SOURCE SYSIBM.AVG(DECIMAL);
```

These CREATE FUNCTION statements place an entry for each UDF in the SYSIBM.SYSROUTINES catalog table, and the parameters are recorded in SYSIBM.SYSPARMS. These catalog tables can be queried for information about the UDFs.

SQL Scalar UDFs. An SQL scalar function is a UDF whose entire functionality is a single SQL expression and is coded into the CREATE FUNCTION statement. The function is identified as an SQL scalar function by coding the LANGUAGE SQL option of the CREATE FUNCTION statement. This enables you to code an expression used commonly within more than one statement and to modularize that expression by storing it separately as a UDF. Any SQL statement can then reference the UDF in the same manner in which any scalar function can be invoked. This enables common expressions to be coded only once and stored separately in the DB2 catalog, centralizing the coding and administration of these types of functions.

The SQL expression is specified in the RETURN clause of the CREATE FUNCTION statement and can contain references to the function input parameters, as in the following example, which computes the total number of months between two dates:

```
CREATE FUNCTION TOTMON (STARTX DATE, ENDY DATE)
RETURNS INTEGER
LANGUAGE SQL
CONTAINS SQL
NO EXTERNAL ACTION
DETERMINISTIC
RETURN ABS( (YEAR(STARTX - ENDY)*12) + MONTH(STARTX - ENDY) );
```

The expressions contained in the SQL scalar UDF cannot contain references to columns names or host variables. However, an SQL scalar UDF can invoke other UDFs, which may be external UDFs that can be an SQL program.

The source code for an SQL scalar function is stored in the SYSIBM.SYSVIEWS DB2 catalog table. When an SQL statement referencing an SQL scalar function is compiled, the function source from the SYSIBM.SYSVIEWS catalog table is merged into the statement. Package and plan dependencies on the SQL scalar functions, as with all UDFs, are maintained in the SYSIBM.SYSPACKDEP and SYSIBM.SYSPLANDEP tables, respectively.

Table Functions.   With DB2, you can also create another type of UDF: a table function, which returns a table to the SQL statement that calls it. This means that a table function can be referenced only in the FROM clause of a SELECT statement. The table function provides a means of including external data or complex processes in SQL queries. Table functions can read non-DB2 data—for instance, a file on the operating system or over the World Wide Web—tabularize it, and return the data to DB2 as a relational table that can subsequently be treated like any other relational table. For example, the APPFORM table function in the next example takes in a candidate application form, processes it, and returns the data—except for the candidate ID, which is generated—in an appropriate format to be inserted in the CANDIDATE table:

```
CREATE FUNCTION APPFORM(VARCHAR(30))
RETURNS TABLE
   (LNAME VARCHAR(30),
    FNAME VARCHAR(30),
    INITIAL CHAR(1),
    HPHONE PHONE,
    WPHONE PHONE,
    STREETNO VARCHAR(8),
    STREETNAME VARCHAR(20),
    CITY VARCHAR(20),
    PROV_STATE VARCHAR(30),
    CODE CHAR(6),
    COUNTRY VARCHAR(20))
EXTERNAL NAME APPFORM
LANGUAGE C
WLM ENVIRONMENT WLMENV1
PARAMETER STYLE DB2SQL
NO SQL
DETERMINISTIC
NO EXTERNAL ACTION
FINAL CALL
DISALLOW PARALLEL
CARDINALITY 20;
```

If we wanted to insert into the CANDIDATE table a new candidate, based on his or her application form, we could use the following SELECT statement:

```
INSERT INTO CANDIDATE
   SELECT CID,
      LNAME, FNAME, INITIAL,
      HPHONE, WPHONE,
```

```
        STREETNO, STREETNAME, CITY,
        PROV_STATE, CODE, COUNTRY
FROM TABLE(APPFORM(' \DOCS\NEWFORM.TXT')) AS AP
```

Invoking UDFs

Scalar UDFs are invoked in much the same way as any built-in DB2 scalar function. A function name identifies the function, and one or more parameters pass information from the invoking SQL statement to the UDF. The parameters passed can be table columns, constants, or expressions. If an expression is passed to an external UDF, DB2 resolves the expression and then passes the result to the UDF. The result of the UDF execution replaces the function invocation at execution time. In the following example, the SQL scalar function TOTMON is used to calculate the number of months between two dates:

```
SELECT   HIREDATE, BIRTHDATE,
         TOTMON(HIREDATE, BIRTHDATE) as total_months,
FROM     DSN8710.EMP;
```

Here, the HIREDATE and BIRTHDATE columns are selected from the EMP table, and the TOTMON function, previously defined in this chapter, determines the total number of months between the two dates, which were fed to the function as parameters. In this case, the TOTMON function, being an SQL scalar function, is merged with the statement during statement compilation as if the expression itself were coded within the SQL statement.

A UDF can be defined as *deterministic* or *not deterministic*. A deterministic function will return the same result from one invocation to the next if the input parameter values have not changed. Although DB2 does not have a mechanism to "store" the results of a deterministic function, the designation can impact the invoking query execution path relative to materialization. If a table expression has been nested within an SQL statement, a nondeterministic function may force the materialization of the inner query. For example:

```
SELECT   WORKDEPT, SUM(TOTAL_MONTHS), AVG(TOTAL_MONTHS)
FROM
(SELECT  WORKDEPT,
         TOTMON(HIREDATE, BIRTHDATE) as total_months,
 FROM    DSN8710.EMP) AS TAB1

GROUP BY WORKDEPT;
```

Here, if an index is on the WORKDEPT column of the EMP table, the inner table expression called TAB1 may not be materialized but rather be merged with the outer select statement. This is possible because the TOTMON function is deterministic. If the TOTMON function were not deterministic, DB2 would have to materialize the TAB1 table expression, possibly storing it in the DSNDB07 temporary table spaces and sorting to perform the desired aggregation. However, it is not clear whether having TOTMON be deterministic is a good thing. If the TOTMON function is CPU intensive, it may be better to materialize the result of the inner table expression because the merged TOTMON function, if it is deterministic, will be executed twice in the outer query: once per reference—for the SUM and AVG functions, in this case.

A table function can be referenced in an SQL statement anywhere that a table can normally be referenced. The table function, or a nested table expression, is identified in the query by the use of the TABLE keyword, as in the following example:

```
SELECT TAB1.EMPNO, TAB2.TEMPURATURE, TAB2.FORECAST
FROM   EMP, TABLE(WEATHERFUNC(CURRENT DATE)) AS TAB2
```

In this query, the TABLE keyword identifies a nested table expression called TAB2 that was an invocation of the table UDF called WEATHERFUNC. The query returns the employee number and some weather information in some of the columns that are returned from the WEATHERFUNC table function. This is a fairly simple invocation of a table function.

More important, you can embed correlated references within a nested table expression. Although the weather may not be useful information to return with employee data, perhaps retrieving the resume and credit information from an external source is. In this case, you can pass the employee number as a correlated reference into the table expression identified by the TABLE keyword and ultimately pass it into the table UDF:

```
SELECT TAB1.EMPNO, TAB2.RESUME, TAB2.CREDITINFO
FROM   EMP AS TAB1, TABLE(EMPRPT(TAB1.EMPNO)) AS TAB2
```

The TABLE keyword tells DB2 to look to the left of the keyword when attempting to resolve any otherwise unresolvable correlated references within the table expression. If the join was coded in reverse—that is, the invocation of the EMPRPT table UDF appears in the statement before the EMP table—the correlated reference to the TAB1.EMPNO column would not have been resolved, and the statement would not have compiled successfully.

The use of the TABLE keyword can be expanded beyond that of correlated references as input into table UDFs. The same keyword can be used with a nested table expression that may benefit from a correlated reference. This can be especially useful when the nested expression is performing an aggregation and needs to work on only a subset of the data in the table it is accessing. The following example lists the employee number and salary of each employee, along with the average salary and head count of all employees in their associated departments. This is traditionally coded as a left outer join of two table expressions, the first getting the employee numbers and salaries and the second calculating the head count and average salary for all departments. If there is filtering against the employee table, the entire table might be unnecessarily read to perform the aggregations:

```
SELECT    TAB1.EMPNO, TAB1.SALARY,
          TAB2.AVGSAL,TAB2.HDCOUNT
FROM
    (SELECT EMPNO, SALARY, WORKDEPT
    FROM    DSN8610.EMP
    WHERE   JOB='SALESREP') AS TAB1
LEFT OUTER JOIN
    (SELECT AVG(SALARY) AS AVGSAL,
            COUNT(*)AS HDCOUNT,
            WORKDEPT
    FROM    DSN8610.EMP
    GROUP   BY WORKDEPT) AS TAB2
ON TAB1.WORKDEPT = TAB2.WORKDEPT;
```

Here, the entire EMP table has to be read in the TAB2 nested table expression in order to calculate the average salary and headcount for all departments. This is unfortunate, because we need only the departments that employ sales reps. We can use the TABLE keyword and a correlated reference to TAB1 within the TAB2 expression to perform filtering before the aggregation:

```
SELECT    TAB1.EMPNO, TAB1.SALARY,
          TAB2.AVGSAL,TAB2.HDCOUNT
FROM      DSN8610.EMP TAB1
,TABLE(SELECT AVG(SALARY) AS AVGSAL,
            COUNT(*) AS HDCOUNT
      FROM    DSN8610.EMP
      WHERE   WORKDEPT = TAB1.WORKDEPT) AS TAB2

WHERE TAB1.JOB = 'SALESREP';
```

Polymorphism and UDFs.   DB2 UDFs subscribe to the object-oriented concept of polymorphism. Ad hoc polymorphism, better described as overloading, allows an SQL statement to issue the same function against varying parameter lists and/or data types. This overloading requires you to create a unique definition for each variation of a particular function in data types or number of parameters. Polymorphism means "many changes"; for DB2 functions, many functions can have the same name.

These functions are identified by their *signature,* comprising the schema name, the function name, the number of parameters, and the data types of the parameters. This enables you to create UDFs for your distinct types. These sourced UDFs can assume the same name as the UDFs of built-in functions they are sourced from but are unique in the system, owing to the data type of their parameter(s). Signatures also allow you to define SQL or external UDFs to accommodate any variation in data type or number of parameters. For example, if you need a variation of the TOTMON function that accommodates timestamps, you can create the following function:

```
CREATE FUNCTION TOTMON (STARTX TIMESTAMP, ENDY TIMESTAMP)
RETURNS INTEGER
LANGUAGE SQL
CONTAINS SQL
NO EXTERNAL ACTION
NOT DETERMINISTIC
RETURN ABS( (YEAR(STARTX - ENDY)*12) + MONTH(STARTX - ENDY) );
```

The only difference between this TOTMON and the original TOTMON is that the input parameters here are TIMESTAMPs instead of DATEs. From the application programming point of view, this enables an SQL statement to issue a TOTMON function, regardless of whether it is using a pair of dates or timestamps as input. However, the people responsible for deploying the UDFs must do so with consistency of functionality for like-named functions.

External UDF Execution.   The external scalar and table UDF programs execute in a z/OS WLM environment, in much the same way as stored procedures. The WLM environment is supported by one or more WLM address spaces. The WLM keywords that name the WLM environment in which to execute should be specified when creating the function; otherwise, the program defaults to the WLM environment specified at installation time. This default environment can be seen in the SYSIBM.SYSROUTINES catalog table. UDFs execute under the same thread as the invoking program and will run at the same priority, using the WLM enclave processing.

Monitoring and Controlling UDFs

You can invoke UDFs in an SQL statement wherever you can use expressions or built-in functions. UDFs, like stored procedures, run in WLM-established address spaces. DB2 UDFs are controlled by the following commands.

- START FUNCTION SPECIFIC activates an external function that has been stopped. You cannot start built-in functions or UDFs that are sourced on another function. You can use the START FUNCTION SPECIFIC command to activate all or a specific set of stopped external functions. To activate an external function that is stopped, you would issue the following command:

  ```
  START FUNCTION SPECIFIC (specific-function-name)
  ```

  The SCOPE (GROUP) option can also be used on the START FUNCTION command to allow you to start a UDF on all subsystems in a data sharing group.

- `DISPLAY FUNCTION SPECIFIC` displays statistics about external UDFs that are accessed by DB2 applications. This command displays an output line for each function that a DB2 application has accessed. The information returned by this command reflects a dynamic status for a point in time and may change before another `DISPLAY` is issued. This command does not display information about built-in functions or UDFs that are sourced on another function. To display statistics about an external UDF accessed by DB2 applications, issue the following command:

  `- DISPLAY FUNCTION SPECIFIC` *(specific-function-name)*

- `STOP FUNCTION SPECIFIC` prevents DB2 from accepting SQL statements with invocations of the specified functions. This command will not prevent SQL statements with invocations of the functions from running if they have already been queued or scheduled by DB2. Built-in functions or UDFs that are sourced on another function cannot be explicitly stopped. While the `STOP FUNCTION SPECIFIC` command is in effect, any attempt to execute the stopped functions are queued. You can use the `STOP FUNCTION SPECIFIC` command to stop access to all or a specific set of external functions.

`STOP FUNCTION SPECIFIC` stops an external function. Use the `START FUNCTION SPECIFIC` command to activate all or a specific set of stopped external functions.

To prevent DB2 from accepting SQL statements with invocations of the specified functions, issue the following statement:

`STOP FUNCTION SPECIFIC` *(specific-function-name)*

UDF Statistics. The optimizer will use statistics, if available, for estimating the costs for access paths where UDFs are used. The statistics that the optimizer needs can be updated by using the `SYSSTAT.FUNCTIONS` catalog view. The statistics report contains a field that allows you to view the maximum level of indirect SQL cascading, including cascading stemming from triggers, UDFs, or stored procedures (see Figure 15-3).

Cost Information. User-defined table functions add access cost to the execution of an SQL statement. In order for DB2 to determine the cost factor for the use of user-defined table functions in the selection of the best access path for an SQL statement, the total cost of the user-defined table function must be determined. This cost has three components:

1. Initialization cost that results from the first call processing
2. Cost associated with acquiring a single row
3. Final-call cost, which performs the cleanup processing

To determine the elapsed and CPU time spent for UDF operations, you can view an accounting report (see Figure 15-3).

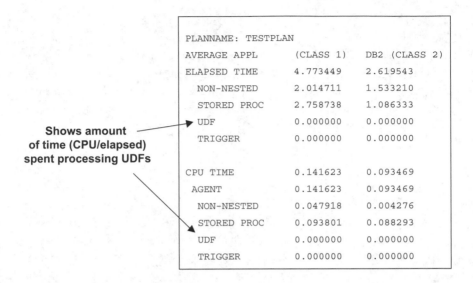

Figure 15-3   Accounting report information for UDF operations

Catalog Information.   The `SYSIBM.SYSROUTINES` catalog table describes UDFs. To retrieve information about UDFs, you can use the following query:

```
SELECT SCHEME, NAME, FUNCTION_TYPE, PARM_COUNT
FROM SYSIBM.SYSROUTINES
WHERE ROUTINETYPE='F'
```

LARGE OBJECTS

Three DB2 data types support LOBs:

1. A BLOB (binary large object) has binary strings, not associated with a CCSID, and is good for storing image, voice, and sound data.
2. A CLOB (character large object) has strings made of single-byte characters or single-/ double-byte characters with an associated CCSID and is used if data is larger than `VARCHAR` allows.
3. A DBCLOB (double-byte character large object) has strings made of double-byte characters with an associated CCSID and is good for storing documents.

Each of these data types can contain up to 2GB of data, although in most cases, the amount of storage for individual columns will be considerably less, depending on the type of data stored.

Today, the 32KB-long VARCHAR column, which has limitations in both size and functionality, is widely used. Most of this use will probably be replaced by using LOBs in the future, especially for new applications and functions.

LOBs are implemented with structures that are different from normal tables and table spaces. A LOB table space must be created for each column—or each column of each partition—of the base table. This table space contains the auxiliary table, which must have an auxiliary index associated with it. The LOB table space has a different recovery scheme, optional logging, and different locking options. For information on LOB locking, refer to Chapter 16.

If a table contains a LOB column and the plan or package is bound with SQLRULES(STD), DB2 will implicitly create the LOB table space, the auxiliary table, and the auxiliary index. DB2 will choose the name and characteristics for these implicitly created objects.

> **NOTE** It is better to develop naming standards beforehand for these objects and to control placement of them. This is critical for both management and performance.

Inserting and Loading LOBs

LOB loading and insertion is also different from processes for non-LOB data. The methods are also entirely different, depending on whether extenders are used. Without extenders, some limitations need to be addressed when inserting LOB data, primarily the 32KB limit and logging impacts. If the total length of the LOB column and the base table row is less than 32KB, the LOAD utility can insert the LOB column. When the limits of LOAD are exceeded, SQL INSERT or UPDATE statements need to be used. But the SQL INSERT has its own limitations in that enough memory needs to be available to hold the entire value of the LOB. The limitations are the amount of memory available to the application and the amount of memory that can be addressed by the language used. If the LOBs are all small, it is not as much of an issue, as memory and language constructs will be available.

When dealing the very large LOBs, the differences can be seen easily when comparing the C language construct with COBOL. For example, following is the C language for a LOB host variable:

```
SQL TYPE IS CLOB(20000K) my_clob;
```

This is generated by DB2 as

```
struct { unsigned long length;
        Char data[20960000];
      } my_clob;
```

The COBOL language for a LOB host variable is

```
01 MY-CLOB      USAGE IS SQL TYPE IS CLOB(20000K).
```

This is generated by DB2 as

```
01  MY-CLOB.
    02  MY-CLOB-LENGTH     PIC 9(9) COMP.
    02 MY-CLOB-DATA.
        49  FILLER     PIC  X(32767).
        49  FILLER     PIC  X(32767).
        49  FILLER     PIC  X(32767).
--Repeated 622 times
```

Extenders can assist in solving the problem. When a table and a column are enabled for an extender, the whole process changes. An INSERT statement can be used in the program with extender functions (UDFs) that allow the image to be loaded into the database directly from an external file. With the image extender, for example, the image content is inserted into an administrative support table, and another record is then inserted into another administrative table describing the attributes of the image, such as number of colors, thumbnail-sized version, and format characteristics (JPEG, TIFF, and so on). The extenders require WLM to be installed in support of the extender UDFs and stored procedures, and the use of WLM in goal mode, for performance reasons.

Even though the LOB data is stored in an auxiliary table, the INSERT statement specifies the base table. You can read the LOB data from a file in your DB2 program and place the data into the declared DB2 LOB variable. The insert statement then simply references the LOB variable. For example, if you wanted to insert employee resumes into the EMP_RESUME table, which includes a 2MB CLOB data type to hold resumes, you would declare the resume variable in your program:

```
SQL TYPE IS CLOB(2000K) resume;
```

Then you would populate the resume variable with the CLOB data and perform the insert:

```
EXEC SQL INSERT INTO EMP_RESUME VALUES (:EMPNO, :RESUME);
```

DB2 uses contiguous storage in data spaces to store LOBs that your program is manipulating. Because LOBs can be quite large, DB2 avoids materializing them until completely necessary. The amount of storage required depends on the size of the LOBs and the number of LOBs referenced within a statement. The amount of storage required by your program and DB2 can become quite large. For this reason, you can use LOB locators to manipulate LOB data without retrieving that data from the DB2 table. A LOB locator is declared in the application program:

```
SQL TYPE IS CLOB_LOCATOR resume_loc;
```

An SQL statement can reference the locator, and the LOB is not materialized in DB2 until absolutely necessary, and it is never moved into the application memory:

```
SELECT  RESUME
INTO    :resume_loc
FROM    EMP_RESUME
WHERE   EMPNO=:empno;
```

Further SQL statements can reference the locator variable, allowing the LOB to be manipulated in various ways. One way would be by using SQL SET commands. DB2 will manipulate the LOB data within the table and materialize the LOB only as needed.

LOBs and Distinct Types

Being able to store LOBs and to manipulate them through extenders is only part of the story. New distinct data types can be defined based on the needs of particular applications. A distinct type provides a way to differentiate one LOB from another LOB, even of the same base type, such as BLOB or CLOB. A distinct type is not limited to objects and can be created for standard data types, as well as LOBs.

Even though stored as binary or character LOBs, image, video, spatial, XML, and audio objects are treated as types distinct from BLOBs and CLOBs and distinct from one another. For example, suppose that an application that processes spatial data features needs a polygon data type. You can create a distinct type named polygon for polygon objects, as follows:

```
CREATE DISTINCT TYPE polygon AS BLOB (512K)
```

The polygon-type object is treated as a distinct type of object, even though, internally, it is represented as a 512KB binary object (BLOB). Distinct types are used like SQL built-in types to describe the data stored in columns of tables. The extenders create distinct data types for the type of object they process, such as image, audio, and video, which makes it easier for applications to incorporate these types of objects:

```
CREATE TABLE DB2_MAG_DEMO
    (GEO_ID CHAR(6),
    EURO_ANNUAL      EURO_DOLLAR,
    OZ_ANNUAL        AUSTRALIAN_DOLLAR,
    US_ANNUAL        US_DOLLAR,
    DEMO_GRAPHIC     POLYGON)
```

Casting functions allow operations between different data types—for example, comparing a slide from a video distinct type to an expression. You must cast the expression to a distinct type—video, in this example—in order for the comparison to work. Some casting functions are supplied with DB2—`CHAR`, `INTEGER`, and so on—and others are created automatically whenever a distinct type is created with the `CREATE DISTINCT TYPE` statement.

LOBs and Extenders

Extenders for DB2 help in the use of LOBs, the base storage for the object-relational environment. Extenders are complete packages that define distinct data types and special functions for many types of LOBs, including image, audio, video, text, XML, and spatial objects. Thus, you do not have to worry about defining these data types and functions in applications. You can use SQL and functions to manipulate these data types. LOBs can range in size from relatively small to extremely large and can be cumbersome to deal with.

The DB2 extenders installation package includes a Software Developers Kit (SDK) and a client and server runtime environment. DB2 extender applications can be executed in a server machine that has the extender client runtime code—automatically installed when the server runtime code is installed—and server runtime code. Extender applications can also be run on a client machine with the client runtime code, and you must ensure that a connection can be made to the server.

When storing image, audio, video, or text objects, you do not store the object in the user table but instead use extender-created character strings, referred to as handles, that represent the objects; the handle will be stored in the user tables. The object is stored in an administrative support table, or file identifier if the content is a file. The attributes and handles are also stored in these administrative tables. The extender then links the handle in the user table to the object and its attributes in the administrative tables.

When an extender for a particular LOB type is used, additional options allow the data to be stored in its native format in separate files, such as a picture that is a single JPEG file. In this example, the hierarchical path name would be stored in support tables that would allow the extender to use this indirect reference to process the data. The extenders also require administrative support tables that vary based on the extender used. The content of these metadata tables enables the extenders to appropriately handle user requests, such as inserting audio, displaying images, and so on. These tables identify base tables and columns that are enabled for the extender and reference other support tables used to hold attribute information about LOB columns. Triggers supplied by the extenders are used to update many of these support tables when underlying LOB data is inserted, updated, or deleted. Six extenders are available in the DB2 family: image, audio, video, text, XML, and spatial. Many others are planned, and vendors also supply extender packages.

Applications generally use SQL to retrieve pointers to the data, and UDFs are used to assist with more complex and unique operations. Extender APIs will be more commonly used, as all the coding is supplied for dealing with the LOBs. The extender for image data comes with 18 UDFs; audio has 27 UDFs, video has 18 UDFs, and the QBIC (Query by Image Content) API has 24 UDFs.

For applications, the advantages of "not-having-to-program-it" and easing the pain of the learning curve are considerable. For example, several formats are supported for dealing with the image extenders. The common ones—BMP, EPS, GIF, JPG, TIF—are provided, of course, along with more than 15 others. Thus, each LOB picture could be of a different format, but the program would not have to be aware of this because it would be taken care of by the extender. The same is true of the text extender. A user could browse through a series of text documents, one in Microsoft Word format, another in WordPerfect, and so on.

The greatest power of the LOB extenders is their searching ability. For example, with the text extender, searching can be done by soundex, synonym, thesaurus, proximity, linguistic, and several other criteria. With images, the QBIC API is supplied to allow searching by image content, and this is a very extensive and powerful API.

Application programming for objects generally requires the use of the extenders. Without their use, little can be done without extensive user programming. The power of objects comes with the UDFs and API libraries that are packaged with the extenders, allowing an application to easily store, access, and manipulate any of the supported object types. Although only six extenders are available now, many others are in development and will be released in the future as they are completed.

The application programmer will be able to use UDFs in the SQL to position to the necessary LOB and then use an API to manipulate it in order to display a picture on the screen, for example. Thus, two completely different libraries can be strategized from. As a simple example, without forcing it to match any particular programming language, the following represents first storing a picture in a LOB and then displaying it on the screen. First, insert the data into the LOB by using the DB2IMAGE extender:

```
EXEC SQL BEGIN DECLARE SECTION;
   storage_type;
EXEC SQL END DECLARE SECTION;

SET storage_type = MMDB_STORAGE_TYPE_INTERNAL

EXEC SQL INSERT INTO MY_PERSONAL_DIGITAL_PICTURES
    VALUES ('OZ TRIP 2',
        'Sydney Opera House',
        DB2IMAGE (
            CURRENT SERVER,
            'c:/My Pictures/1999/Australia/OpraHse.jpg',
            'ASIS',
            :storage_type));
```

Second, retrieve and display the data on the screen, using API DBiBROWSE:

```
EXEC SQL BEGIN DECLARE SECTION;
   image_handler;
EXEC SQL END DECLARE SECTION;

EXEC SQL SELECT PICTURE INTO :image_handler
   WHERE NAME = 'Sydney Opera House';
Set return_code to DBiBROWSE("ib %s,
   MMDB_PLAY_HANDLE,
   image_handler,
   MMDB_PLAY_BI_WAIT);
```

From the pseudocode, it is easy to see that the extenders offer significant power and enable applications to be written quickly. In addition, most of the work is going on at the server, and the client is simply the recipient of all that power. When implementing extenders, keep in mind that the program will need to have enough memory available to support the use of LOBs on GUI clients.

Text Extenders

Text extenders bring full-text retrieval to SQL queries for searching large text documents intelligently. With the use of text extenders, you can search several thousand large text documents very quickly. You can also search on the basis of word variations and synonyms. These documents can be stored directly in the database or in a separate file.

Text extenders allow applications to

- Search documents of several languages and formats
- Perform wildcard searches using masks
- Perform a search for words that sound like the search input
- Perform fuzzy searches for like words (various spellings)
- Perform searches for specific text, synonyms, phrases, and proximity
- Perform free-text searches with natural-language input

Native word-processing documents can be searched by keywords, wildcards, phrases, and proximity. IBM has built into these text extenders a high-performance linguistic search technology, giving you multiple options for searching and retrieving documents. These text searches can be integrated with your normal SQL queries, enabling you to integrate into your SELECT statements the ability to perform attribute and full-text searches very easily.

The following example shows how to perform this integration. This example performs a SELECT from a table that also performs a search on a specified document, using a text extender called DB2TX.CONTAINS. A legal cases document is being searched to see whether the words *malpractice* and *won* appear in the same paragraph for cases occurring after 1990-01-01. LEGCSE_HANDLE refers to the column LEGCSE that contains the text document:

```
SELECT DOC_NUM, DOC_DATE
FROM LEGAL_CLAIMS
WHERE DOC_DATE > '1990-01-01'
AND DB2TX.CONTAINS
   (LEGCSE_HANDLE,
   "malpractice"
   IN SAME PARAGRAPH AS "won") = 1
```

Indexing Text Extenders. Scans are just as undesirable in text documents as they are within DB2 tables. Indexes need to be created so that sequential scans of documents are not necessary. By using a text index, you can speed up the searches performed on these documents.

A text index contains important words and a list of words known as *stop words,* such as *and* and *the*, which will not be in a text index. This list can be modified, but you would want to do it only once, at installation time. When a request is made, the index is searched for the important terms to determine which documents contain those specified terms.

To set up a text index, you first record the text documents that need to be indexed in a log table. This process occurs when a DB2 trigger is fired off during an insert, update, or delete of a column of a text document. Then, when the terms are inserted or updated in the text document, they are added to the index. They are also deleted from the index if they are deleted from the text document.

Text indexes are of four types, and the type must be established before you implement columns that will be using text extenders. Not all search options are available by all index types, so you want to make sure that the index will suit your criteria for searching.

1. *Linguistic* indexes perform linguistic processing during the analysis for the text when creating an index. Before being inserted into the index, a word is reduced to its base form. Queries also use linguistic processing when searching against this index. This index requires the least amount of space, but searches may be longer than those done against a precise index.
2. *Precise* indexes use search terms that are exactly as they are in the text document and are case-sensitive. The same processing is used for the query search terms, so they must match exactly. The search can be broadened by using masks. This index provides a more precise search, and the retrieval and indexing are fast, but more space is required for its storage.
3. *Dual* indexes are combinations of linguistic and precise indexes. This allows the user to decide which type of search to use. This type of index requires the most amount of disk space. It is slower for searching and indexing than the linguistic indexes and is not recommended for a large number of text documents.
4. *Ngram* indexes are used primarily for indexing DBCS documents; they analyze text by parsing sets of characters. This index type also supports fuzzy searches.

When creating tables that will support the ability to search text using extenders, you must consider a few design options. You can create one text index for all text columns in the table, or you can have several different text indexes, one for each text column. Using separate indexes for each text column offers the most flexibility in terms of support for your searches. It also gives you other options, such as how frequently the index is updated and where it is stored. One common index is easier to maintain but is less flexible. If your indexes are large, consider storing them on separate disks, especially if you expect to have concurrent access to the indexes.

You can also have multiple indexes on a single text column. You may want to do this if you need to allow different types of searches on a text column. And just like other DB2 indexes, these indexes will need to be reorganized. If you have a text column that is continually updated, you will need to reorganize it. However, when using these indexes, the text extender automatically reorganizes them in the background. Despite this feature, you still may have to reorganize an index manually every so often, depending on its volatility. This is done with the REORGANIZE INDEX command. Issue the GET INDEX STATUS command to see whether an index needs reorganization.

Frequency of Index Updates.   When text documents are added, deleted, or changed, their content must be synchronized with the index. This information is automatically stored by triggers in a log table, and the documents will be indexed the next time an index update is executed.

The indexes can be immediately updated via the UPDATE INDEX command, but it is easier to have this performed automatically on a periodic basis. This time-based information is kept in an environment variable called DB2TXUPDATEFREQ, which provides default settings that can be changed with the ENABLE TEXT COLUMN or ENABLE TEXT TABLE command. For an existing index, you can use the CHANGE INDEX SETTINGS command to change the variable settings.

The variable for determining when indexing should occur is based on the minimum number of queued text documents in the log table; when this minimum is reached, the index is updated. Because updating indexes is a very resource-intensive and time-consuming task, this frequency should be set carefully.

Catalog View for Text Extenders.   A catalog view is created for each subsystem when you run the ENABLE SERVER. This view, DB2TX.TEXTINDEXES, has information about the tables and the columns that have been enabled for the text extender. The entries are made during table, column, or external file enablement. If they are disabled, the row is removed. You can view the entries in the catalog view via SQL. In this view, you can see such information as how often the indexes are scheduled for updates, whether you have a multiple-index table, and the type of index.

Image, Audio, and Video Extenders

The DB2 video extender can store as many as three representative frames per shot. Displaying the frames gives you a quick yet effective view of a video's content. The DB2 video extender provides sample programs that demonstrate how to build and display a video storyboard.

Video storyboards allow you to preview videos before you download and view them, which can save you time and reduce video traffic on the network. When image data is placed into a table using the DB2IMAGE UDFs, many processes are performed for the application automatically. The following code demonstrates using this function:

```
EXEC SQL INSERT INTO CONSULTANTS VALUES(
    :cons_id,
    :cons_name,
    DB2IMAGE(
        CURRENT SERVER,
        '/RYC/images/current.bmp'
        'ASIS',
        MMDB_STORAGE_TYPE_INTERNAL,
        :cons_picture_tag);
```

In this particular example, the DB2IMAGE reads all the attributes about the image—height, width, colors, layers, pixels, and more—from the source image file header: in this case, the current.bmp. All the input is of a standard supported format, and all graphic files contain header information about the structure of the content. The function then creates a unique handle for the image and records all the information in the support table for administrative control of the image. This table contains

- The handle for the image
- A timestamp
- The image size, in bytes
- The comment contained in :cons_picture_tag
- The content of the image

The content of the image source file is inserted into the LOB table as a BLOB. No conversion is done, and the image is stored in its native format. A record in the administrative table contains all the image-specific attributes, such as the number of colors in the image, as well as a thumbnail-sized version of the image.

This example uses the storage type constants; MMDB_STORAGE_TYPE_INTERNAL was used to store the image into a database table as a BLOB. By using the extenders, we could have stored it elsewhere. If you want to store the object and have its content remain in the original file on the server, you can specify the constant MMDB_STORAGE_TYPE_EXTERNAL. Your use of LOBs does not mean that they have to be in DB2-managed tables. The administrative support table for image extenders tells where the LOB is stored. This does require UNIX System Services support on z/OS. A performance perspective requires many considerations as to where the LOB is stored, how it is used, where it is materialized, and so on.

XML Extender

XML has been added to the list of available extenders. For the next generation of business-to-business (B2B) e-commerce solutions, XML is the standard for data interchange. With the XML extender for DB2, you will be able to leverage your critical business information in DB2 databases in order to engage in B2B solutions using XML-based interchange formats.

In terms of Web publishing, you can use XML documents stored in DB2 in a single column or as a collection of data items in multiple columns and tables. The text extender in DB2 supports structured documents, such as XML. The powerful search functions provided can now be applied to a section or a list of sections within a set of XML documents, significantly improving the effectiveness of the search. Additionally, specific XML elements or attributes can be automatically extracted into traditional SQL data types to leverage DB2's sophisticated indexing and SQL query capabilities. The DB2 XML extender also supplies a visual administration tool for easy definitions for mapping elements and attributes from an XML document into columns and tables.

SUMMARY

This chapter discussed powerful DB2 and SQL features, such as UDFs and triggers. These features can reduce the amount of application development time and maintenance. You can use these features to encapsulate your code into one place for use by many applications.

DB2 has implemented some object-relational functions, such as LOB support, distinct types, and UDFs. These features also provide great application flexibility and power. LOBs, of course, enable you to store large amounts and different types of data, such as multimedia, giving you the ability to develop sophisticated applications.

ADDITIONAL RESOURCES

IBM DB2 V8 for z/OS Application Programming and SQL Guide (SC18-7415)

IBM DB2 V8 for z/OS SQL Reference (SC18-7426)

IBM DB2 V8 Administration Guide (SC18-7413)

IBM DB2 V8 for z/OS Image, Audio, and Video Extenders Administration and Programming (SES1-2199-0)

IBM DB2 V8 for z/OS XML Extender Administration and Programming (SES1-2201-00)

IBM DB2 V8 for z/OS Text Extender Administration and Programming (SES1-2200-00)

Locking and Concurrency

- Locking data
- Avoiding locks
- Claims and drains
- Locking issues and problems
- Designing for concurrency

I t would be easy to have one process simply lock all the data while using it, but that, of course, would lead to other applications' being unable to access the data during this time. Concurrency, the ability for multiple applications to access the same data at the same time, needs to be allowed but also controlled in order to prevent lost updates, access to uncommitted data, and data changing between reads.

A balance must be achieved for maximum concurrency of all processes. Many controls in DB2 allow you to achieve maximum concurrency while maintaining data integrity. These controls range from the parameters for binding our programs with to options of the DDL for the creation of objects, to subsystem-level parameters.

DB2 uses locks to control concurrency within a database, that is, to manage simultaneous access to a resource by more than one user, or serialization. Locks also prevent access to uncommitted data, which prevents updates from becoming lost and allows a user to see the same data, without the data ever changing, within a period of processing called a *commit scope*. From a performance standpoint, everything done in DB2 has a tradeoff. In locking, the tradeoff is between concurrency and performance: More concurrency comes at a higher cost of CPU use, owing to lock management. In some cases, DB2 will override the locking strategy designed because processes hold locked resources exceeding the site-established thresholds. However, only certain combinations of parameters cause this to occur.

LOCKING DATA

DB2 uses transaction locking, via the IRLM, latches, and other non-IRLM mechanisms to control concurrency and access of SQL statements and utilities. These mechanisms associate a resource with a process so that other processes cannot access the same resource when it would cause lost updates and access to uncommitted data. Generally, a process will hold a lock on manipulated data until completing its work so as to ensure that other processes do not get hold of data that has been changed but not committed. Another use is for repeatable read, that is, when an application needs to reread data that must still be in the same state as it was when it was initially read. In addition, user options are available to avoid locking and to allow for access to uncommitted data, as well as system settings and mechanisms to provide for lock avoidance when it would not cause a data-integrity problem.

The following objects can be locked: user tables, catalog tables, and directory tables. Not all objects need to have locks acquired on them to establish concurrency, however. Indexes are not locked, as serialization is controlled by latches, and concurrency is controlled by data locking. Drains and claims can be used to control utilities and DB2 commands. Draining allows utilities and commands to acquire partial or full control of a needed object, with minimal interruption to concurrent access.

DB2 often needs to access data in the catalog, and the data being read or updated must be locked. The following locks can be used during binding: SKCT (skeleton cursor table) for a plan and SKPT (skeleton package table) for a package. During DDL activity, DBD (database descriptor) can be used.

Lock Attributes

Locks should be viewed as having size (how much data is locked), mode (whether others are allowed to read and/or update the locked object), and duration (how long the lock is held). Each attribute plays a role in the acquisition and release of a lock, and understanding these attributes can help you use them wisely and avoid contention.

More than one type of lock can exist for a specific user for a particular table space. This depends on the mode of the lock. For example, locks might be held on the table space, table, page, and row simultaneously for a particular user. Each lock has its own mode.

Lock Sizes

Locks can be taken on various objects in DB2. The size of the lock determines how much of the total object will be locked. For non-LOB data, locks can be taken on a

- Table space
- Table in a segmented table space
- Partition
- Page
- Row

For LOB data, LOB locks can be taken.

Table Space and Table Locks.   These locks are the most encompassing and allow the least amount of concurrency. A table space lock locks the entire table space and may prevent access to all pages of all tables contained in that table space. Table locks in a simple table space may lock data in other tables, as the rows can be intermingled on different pages. In a segmented table space, the pages with rows from a single table will be locked and will not affect other tables in the table space. For more information on simple and segmented table spaces, refer to Chapter 4.

Partition Locking.   DB2 can choose to lock only a partition of a partitioned table space, known as selective partition locking (SPL). Prior to version 8, you could get only SPL if the tablespace defined with LOCKPART(YES). Now, SPL will be used regardless of the LOCKPART setting. SPL can also tell DB2 not to escalate locks to the table space level but rather to the partition level. This allows for less propagation of locks to the coupling facility in a data sharing environment and better concurrency for applications accessing data in various partitions. This feature can be especially useful if usage against the partitions is spread over multiple members using affinity routing.

However, SPL will help in a non-data sharing environment only if an agent escalates. Without SPL, the parent intent lock is taken on the last partition, regardless of which ones you access. These locks are almost always intent locks and therefore almost never cause a problem. With SPL, the parent intent lock is taken on whichever partition you access. Escalation with SPL occurs only for the partition(s) on which excessive locks occurred. Without SPL, the parent lock is only on the last one, so the lock size is escalated to the entire page set, and access to all partitions is denied.

SPL cannot be used in the following situations:

- Plan/package bound ACQUIRE(ALLOCATE)
- Table space defined LOCKSIZE TABLESPACE
- LOCK TABLE statement used without PART option

Page Locks.   Page locking, usually the lock size of choice for best concurrency and performance, allows DB2 to lock only a single page of data, whether it is 4K, 8K, 16K, or 32K. Page locks for a table in a simple table may lock rows of more than one table, as the rows can be intermingled on the page. Page locks for tables in a segmented table space will lock only rows of a single table.

Row Locks.   DB2 supports row-level locking; if applications are experiencing a lot of concurrency problems, row locks might be considered. However, row locks should not be used as a fix for what could be a physical-design issue or an application-design issue. They should be used when a page of data is needed simultaneously by multiple applications, and each user's interest is on different rows. If the interest is on the same row, row-level locking buys you nothing. Use row-level locking only if the increase of the cost—concurrency and wait-time overhead—of locking is tolerable and you can definitely justify the benefit.

> **N O T E**   In the hierarchy of locks, row locks and page locks occur at the same level. If either a page lock or a row lock is escalated, it moves to the same higher level, and a row lock can never escalate to a page lock.

LOB Locking.   LOBs have a different lock mode: a *LOB lock*. LOB locks have different characteristics from regular locks. A LOB has no concept of row or page locking. LOB locking is not at all like the traditional transaction-level locking. Because LOBs are in an associated object, concurrency between the base table and the LOB must be maintained at all times, even if the base table is using uncommitted read. A LOB lock still needs to be held on the LOB to provide consistency and, most importantly, to maintain space in the LOB table space. LOB locks avoid conflicts between readers and deletes and updates. A SELECT or a DELETE will acquire a share-mode LOB lock. The lock doesn't prevent the DELETE but will prevent the reuse of the deallocated pages until all the LOB locks are released. A shadow copy of the LOB will exist until the LOB locks are released. INSERTs will acquire exclusive LOB locks on new LOBs; an UPDATE is basically a DELETE followed by an INSERT. The LOCK TABLE statement, which acquires a lock on the entire object, can still be used and will not require individual LOB locks.

The ACQUIRE option of BIND has no effect on when the table space lock on the LOB table space is taken. Locks on LOB table spaces are acquired when they are needed. The table space lock is released according to the value specified on the RELEASE option of BIND, with a couple of exceptions: when a cursor is defined WITH HOLD or a LOB locator is held. When a cursor is defined WITH HOLD, LOB locks are held through commit operations. When a LOB value is assigned to a LOB locator, the lock acquired will remain until the application commits. If the application uses HOLD LOCATOR, the locator and the LOB lock must be held and cannot be freed until certain conditions exist. The locks would be held until the first commit operation after a FREE LOCATOR statement is issued or until the thread is deallocated. Using LOB columns generally requires an increase in the number of locks held by a process. As a starting point for preventing unforeseen problems, LOCKMAX should be nonzero on the LOB table spaces. An even better strategy is to use the gross locks during heavy inserting processes to prevent most of the locking difficulties.

LOCK TABLE Statement. Some situations may call for the ability to exclusively lock a table or a partition. A single SQL statement can override locking at any time: LOCK TABLE. You can prevent all other access with LOCK TABLE IN EXCLUSIVE MODE. A typical reason to override locking is if you want to take a snapshot of data and be able to access a table without any other concurrent processes changing data. You can allow other processes read-only access to the table by using the LOCK TABLE IN SHARE MODE statement. This is different from the repeatable read (RR) isolation, because RR prevents changes only from rows or pages that you have already accessed. You can prevent all other access with LOCK TABLE IN EXCLUSIVE MODE.

The LOCK TABLE/TABLESPACE statement can be used only to get a lock, in either share (S) mode or exclusive (X) mode. The lock is acquired when the SQL statement is executed. Its release is dependent on the previous settings of the ACQUIRE and RELEASE parameters. The table or table space lock is released at thread deallocation if RELEASE(DEALLOCATE) was specified in the options when the program was bound. The lock also can be released at either COMMIT or ROLLBACK time if the RELEASE(COMMIT) option was specified at bind time. Despite the type of locking held when the SQL LOCK TABLE statement was issued, when the COMMIT or ROLLBACK is issued, the system falls back to page-level locking unless another SQL LOCK TABLE statement is issued. A user or an application must continually reissue the SQL LOCK TABLE statement after the COMMIT or ROLLBACK when RELEASE(COMMIT) has been specified if locking is still needed at the table or table space level.

The LOCK TABLE IN EXCLUSIVE MODE statement can also be used to avoid additional overhead if you are updating a large portion of a table. This can be more efficient; by preventing concurrent accesses to the data, DB2 avoids the overhead to lock and unlock each page during updates.

Timeouts can be prevented by using either the LOCK TABLE IN EXCLUSIVE or IN SHARE MODE statement. This allows you to process the data quickly, without the possibility of having to contend for locks with other applications.

If further granularity is needed, you can choose to lock only the partition, as seen in the following example:

```
LOCK TABLE CERTTB PART 1 IN EXCLUSIVE MODE
```

This example would take an X lock on Part 1, regardless of any other locks held on other partitions in the table space.

N O T E   As of version 8, the LOCKPART keyword on the
CREATE TABLESPACE statement is ignored, so the PART option
on the LOCK TABLE statement can be used whether or not
LOCKPART(YES) was specified.

Lock Modes

DB2 has the following lock modes:

- IS (intent share)
- S (share)
- IX (intent exclusive)
- U (update)
- SIX (share with intent exclusive)
- X (exclusive)

Modes are easy to understand with a simple formula. If the table or table space lock has an
I (*intent*) in it, row or page locks are in use on the individual pages. In all other cases, the table or
table space lock will be the only lock used. The intent locks act as an indicator to DB2 to identify what is occurring within the table or table space. Some locking is beyond the control of the
programmer and designer; other locks can be controlled to a degree. Table 16-1 lists the compatibility of the various lock modes for table spaces, tables, and partitions. Table 16-2 lists the com-
patibilities for pages and rows.

Table 16-1   Table Spaces, Tables, and Partitions

Lock Mode	IS	IX	S	U	SIX	X
IS	Yes	Yes	Yes	Yes	Yes	No
IX	Yes	Yes	No	No	No	No
S	Yes	No	Yes	Yes	No	No
U	Yes	No	Yes	No	No	No
SIX	Yes	No	No	No	No	No
X	No	No	No	No	No	No

Table 16-2   Pages and Rows

Lock Mode	S	U	X
S	Yes	Yes	No
U	Yes	No	No
X	No	No	No

Table or Table Space Locks. When using page or row locks, the table or table space lock will be IS/IX/SIX:

IS

- Lock owner wants to read only (may lock pages/rows)
- Allow read of lock owner's pages/rows and read/update of all other pages/rows
- Lock owner has share locks on the pages
- Allows other users to read and update

IX

- Lock owner wants to update (may lock pages/rows)
- Allow read/update of all other pages/rows
- Lock owner can have share, update, or exclusive locks on the pages
- Other users still able to read and update

SIX

- Lock owner wants to read (will not lock pages/rows)
- Lock owner wants to update (may lock pages/rows)
- Allow read of all other pages/rows
- Lock owner can have share, update, or exclusive locks on the pages
- Other users still able to read, but no other user can update

> **N O T E** SIX is not a common lock. This mode usually occurs when an IX lock already exists and a share has to be acquired.

When not using row or page locks, the table/table space lock will be S/U/X:

S

- Lock owner wants to read only
- Others are allowed read only
- No one can update

U

- Lock owner wants to read with possibility of update
- Others allowed read only
- No other user can update

X

- Lock owner wants to update
- Other access not allowed
- User needs exclusive use of the table or table space
- No other user allowed

Page or Row Locks.   Page locks can be one of three types:

S

- Restricts other users to read-only use of this page
- S or U locks can be acquired by other users
- Using SELECT or FETCH without update intent will acquire this lock

U

- Allows the user to go to the update step, if required
- Other applications can get S locks but nothing else

X

- User has updated the data on the page; no other user can get any page lock on the page

The lock mode is determined by the DML statement according to the following:

```
SELECT...                       S

SELECT...FOR UPDATE OF...        U

UPDATE/DELETE/INSERT             X
```

DB2 does not allow update (UPDATE/INSERT/DELETE) of uncommitted changes by other users. Reading of uncommitted data is allowed only if an isolation level of UR is specified in the SQL WITH clause or as a BIND option.

Lock Durations

The duration of a lock is the length of time the lock is held. It can vary depending on the type of lock, the mode of the lock, and when the process chooses to release it.

Table, Partition, and Table Space Lock Durations. Lock duration for table spaces and table locks is determined by the BIND ACQUIRE and RELEASE parameters. ACQUIRE determines when table, table space, or partition locks are taken:

- ALLOCATE, the maximum required lock, is taken on all the objects in the plan or package when the first SQL statement is issued.
- USE, the required lock, is taken on the involved objects when an SQL statement is issued.

RELEASE determines when table, table space, or partition locks are released:

- DEALLOCATE: at the end of the program
- COMMIT: at COMMIT

An exception applies when a cursor has been defined using the WITH HOLD option. The locks needed to maintain the position of the cursor are then held until the next commit after the cursor is closed (RELEASE COMMIT) or until the application deallocates its resources (RELEASE DEALLOCATE).

Page or Row Lock Durations. Lock duration for pages and rows defines the length of time that the lock will be held: the period between acquiring and releasing the lock. You can control how long locks are held by means of commit scopes, program bind parameters, and system parameters. To maximize concurrency, locks should not be held longer than necessary, using a large lock for the duration of the process; nor should excessive memory and CPU overhead be consumed by taking an excessive number of smaller locks, such as taking several row locks over a period of time for the same process.

Isolation levels are set when a program is bound or when used in an individual SQL statement using the WITH clause. The isolation levels directly affect the duration that locks are held. The isolation levels that can be used either at bind time or with an individual SQL statement are

- UR (uncommitted read)
- CS (cursor stability)
- RS (read stability)
- RR (repeatable read)

Of these, cursor stability, read stability, and repeatable read have to do with lock durations; uncommitted read has to do with overriding locks.

Cursor stability holds a lock on the row or page, depending on the lock size defined, only if the cursor is positioned on that row or page. The lock will be released when the cursor moves to a new row or page, but the lock will be held until a commit is issued if changes are being made to the data. This option allows for the maximum concurrency for applications that are accessing the same data but cannot allow uncommitted reads.

Read stability holds locks on all rows or pages qualified by stage 1 predicates for the application until the commit is issued. Nonqualified rows or pages, even though touched, are not locked. Uncommitted changes of other applications cannot be read, but if an application issues the same query again, any data changed or inserted by other applications will be read, as RS allows other applications to insert new rows or update rows that could fall within the range of the query. This option is less restrictive but similar in function to repeatable read.

Repeatable read holds a lock on all rows or pages touched by an application program since the last commit was issued, whether or not all those rows or pages satisfied the query. Repeatable read holds these locks until the next commit point, which ensures that if the application needs to read the data again, the values will be the same—no other process could update the locked data. This option is the most restrictive in terms of concurrency of applications and is the default.

Uncommitted read tells DB2 not to take any locks and to ignore other locks and allow read access to the locked data. This option allows an application to run concurrently with other processes, except mass deletes and utilities that drain all claim classes.

Table 16-3 compares various isolation levels.

Table 16-3   Comparison of Isolation Levels

Access by Other Applications	UR	CS	RS	RR
Can the application see uncommitted changes made by other application processes?	Yes	No	No	No
Can the application update uncommitted changes made by other application processes?	No	No	No	No
Can the reexecution of a statement be affected by other application processes?	Yes	Yes	Yes	No
Can updated rows be updated by other application processes?	No	No	No	No
Can updated rows be read by other application processes that are running at an isolation level other than UR?	No	No	No	No
Can updated rows be read by other application processes that are running at the UR isolation level?	Yes	Yes	Yes	Yes
Can accessed rows be updated by other application processes?	Yes	No	No	No
Can accessed rows be read by other application processes?	Yes	Yes	Yes	Yes

The mode of the lock will also factor into the duration of the lock.

Share Lock Duration (S).   Using SELECT or FETCH without update intent will acquire this lock. It is released for plans bound with cursor stability (CS) when

- A process issues an SQL COMMIT or ROLLBACK
- An IMS process issues the next SYNCH or ROLB
- A CICS synch point call occurs
- A noncursor SELECT statement completes without update
- The cursor position moves to a new row/page without update
- The cursor is closed

Using the cursor WITH HOLD option will hold the locks over COMMIT or ROLLBACK processes in TSO and CAF. If no COMMIT is used in the program, the locks will be held until the cursor is closed. It is important to understand that the lock will be held on the previous row/page until DB2 gets the lock on the new one.

Update Lock Duration (U).   A FETCH on a cursor that specifies FOR   UPDATE   OF acquires this lock. UPDATE and DELETE statements without a cursor also acquire this lock. UPDATE and DELETE statements cause an implicit SELECT to occur first, matching the conditions in the WHERE clause. During this SELECT, DB2 places a U lock on the page accessed, before completing the UPDATE or DELETE. DB2 releases the lock for plans bound with CS when

- A process issues an SQL COMMIT or ROLLBACK
- An IMS process issues the next SYNCH or ROLB
- The next synch point call occurs in CICS
- A noncursor SQL statement has completed without update
- The cursor position moves to a new page without update
- The cursor is closed without an update having occurred

Using the cursor WITH HOLD option in TSO will hold the lock over COMMIT and ROLLBACK. However, the COMMIT will demote the U lock back to an S lock. If an update is to occur, the lock will be promoted to an X lock before changing the data page.

Exclusive Lock Duration (X).   Exclusive locks are released when

- A process issues an SQL COMMIT or ROLLBACK
- An IMS process issues the next SYNCH or ROLB
- The next synch point call occurs in CICS

The lock will be held over `COMMIT` and `ROLLBACK` in TSO and CAF when using the cursor `WITH HOLD` option. However, the `COMMIT` will demote the X lock back to an S lock.

System Parameters

Table 16-4 lists some system parameters that are used to control various aspects of locking.

Table 16-4   System Parameters for Locking

Parameter	Description
RECURHL	The use of `RECURHL = YES` can help with concurrency, allowing DB2 to release the locks that are held by a cursor defined `WITH HOLD`.
IRLMRWT	The number of seconds that a transaction will wait for a lock before a timeout is detected. The IRLM uses this parameter for timeout and deadlock detection. Most shops take the default of 60 seconds; if detection must occur sooner so that the applications are not incurring excessive lock wait times, it is set lower. If timeouts or deadlocks are hit often, the application is reviewed and tuned.
XLKUPDLT	New with version 6, allows you to specify the locking method to use when a searched `UPDATE` or `DELETE` is performed. The default is `NO`, best for concurrency, which says that DB2 will use an S or U lock when scanning qualifying rows and then upgrade to an X lock when a qualifying row is found. The value of `YES` is useful in a data sharing environment when the searches involve an index, because it takes an X lock on qualifying rows or pages.
NUMLKTS	The maximum number of locks on an object. If you are turning off lock escalation (`LOCKMAX 0`), you will need to increase this number. If you are using `LOCKMAX SYSTEM`, the value here will be the value for `SYSTEM`.
NUMLKUS	The maximum number of page or row locks that a single application can have held concurrently on all table spaces: data pages, index pages, subpages, and rows. If you specify 0, there is no limit on the number of locks. You want to be careful with 0, because if you turn off lock escalation and do not commit frequently enough, you could run into storage problems. (DB2 uses 250 bytes for each lock.)
URCHKTH	Finds long-running units of work that are not committing; specifies the number of checkpoints that should occur before a message is issued identifying a long-running unit of work.
LRDRTHLD	Can be used to proactively identify reader threads that have exceeded the user-specified time limit threshold without `COMMIT`. When this value is nonzero, DB2 records time a task holds a read claim. When passed a specified number of minutes, an IFCID 313 record is written.

AVOIDING LOCKS

Page and row locking can be avoided at execution time by letting the system use lock-avoidance mechanisms. DB2 can test whether a row or a page has committed data on it. If it does, no lock is required on the data. Lock avoidance is valid only for read-only or ambiguous cursors and requires a combination of events and settings to occur. First, the statement must be a read-only or an ambiguous cursor, along with the proper isolation level and the appropriate CURRENTDATA setting. The best setting for maximum lock avoidance is using an isolation level of CS, either as a bind parameter or on the individual SQL statement, and CURRENTDATA set to NO as a bind option.

Lock avoidance is normally the default for most use, as it removes a lot of locking overhead. DB2 executes a small instruction set to determine whether an IRLM lock is truly needed for read-only cursors or ambiguous cursors.

Page and row locking may also be overridden at bind time or execution time. Locking can be overridden for read-only, not ambiguous, cursors by using the UR isolation level at bind time or on the individual statement level, as follows:

```
EXEC SQL SELECT ... WITH UR
```

An SQL SELECT statement is considered to be read-only when it uses any of the following:

- JOIN
- SELECT DISTINCT
- GROUP BY
- ORDER BY
- UNION
- UNION ALL
- SELECT of a column function
- FOR FETCH ONLY (FOR READ ONLY)
- SELECT FROM nonupdatable catalog table

If the SELECT statement does not incorporate any of the preceding, it is said to be ambiguous, meaning that DB2 does not know for sure whether modifying DML will be issued against the cursor. The CURRENTDATA setting of NO states to DB2 that the ambiguous cursor is read-only. If the statement is targeted by updating SQL, you will get an error. Table 16-5 shows when locking is avoided or overridden.

> **NOTE** If your program is bound with ISOLATION(UR), mass deletes cannot run concurrently with your program.

Table 16-5 Lock-Avoidance Determination

Isolation Level	CURRENTDATA	Cursor Type	Avoid Locks on Returned Data	Avoid Locks on Rejected Data
UR	—	Read-only	—	—
CS	Yes	Read-only	No	Yes
		Updatable		
		Ambiguous		
	No	Read-only	Yes	
		Updatable	No	
		Ambiguous	Yes	
RS	—	Read-only	No	Yes
		Updatable		
		Ambiguous		
RR	—	Read-only	No	No
		Updatable		
		Ambiguous		

In order to determine whether your application is getting lock avoidance, you can run a performance trace class 6, IFCID 214, to obtain information about whether lock avoidance was used for a particular page set in a unit of work. Field QW0218PC will have a Y or N indicating its use. IFCID 223 in trace class 7 includes more detailed information about the use of lock avoidance on a particular resource.

```
DSNI031I - csect - LOCK ESCALATION HAS OCCURRED FOR
RESOURCE NAME = name
LOCK STATE = state
PLAN NAME : PACKAGE NAME = id1 : id2
STATEMENT NUMBER = id3
CORRELATION-ID  = id4
CONNECTION-ID   = id5
LUW-ID  = id6
THREAD-INFO = id7 : id8 : id9 : id1
```

CLAIMS AND DRAINS

Claims and drain locks are used to control currency between SQL processes and utilities, with partition independence being a major focus. Utilities and SQL can concurrently access and update different partitions, including different logical partitions of nonpartitioned indexes.

A logical partition refers to the set of index entries that point to rows in a particular data partition. Logical partitions exist only in nonpartitioned indexes of partitioned tables. An index entry belongs to one and only one logical partition.

Claims

When it first accesses an object within a unit of work, an application makes a claim on the object and releases the claim at the next commit point. Unlike a transaction lock, the claim cannot persist past the commit point. To access the object in the next unit of work, the application must make a new claim. Claims can be acquired on

- Simple table space
- Segmented table space
- Index space
- Data partition
- Index partition

The three claim classes are write, repeatable read, and cursor stability and are described in Table 16-6. Claims are released at COMMIT except for utilities and cursors defined WITH HOLD that are still positioned on an object. All SQL processes are claimers, but only occasionally is a utility a claimer, such as an online load resume.

> **N O T E**   DB2 has no limit on the number of concurrent claimers.

Drains

Drain locks are used to serialize access to partitions and page sets among utilities, commands, and SQL applications. The drain is initiated at any time, but the takeover of an object occurs only when all access to the object has been quiesced. The drain process acquires a lock to prevent subsequent access from occurring until the lock is released.

To drain a resource, a utility or a command first acquires a drain lock and then waits until all claimers of a particular class on the resource are released. Only then is the resource considered

Table 16-6   Claim Classes

Claim Class	Isolation Level	Allows Reading	Allows Updating	Allows Inserting	Allows Deleting
Write	Any	Yes	Yes	Yes	Yes
Repeatable read	RR	Yes	No	No	No
Cursor stability	CS	Yes	No	No	No

drained. A utility trying to take over can time out if a long-running SQL process does not release the claim quickly enough.

A utility that needs only read-only access will drain on the write class, which will prevent any new updating claimers. A utility that needs to change data will drain all claim classes.

LOCKING ISSUES AND PROBLEMS

At times, too much locking can be a problem, resulting in suspensions, timeouts, or even deadlocks.

Timeouts and Deadlocks

While waiting for a lock, a process can exceed an allowable amount of wait time that has been established. A systemwide option determines the maximum time a process can wait before it gets a resource-unavailable error. This value is called the RESOURCE TIMEOUT value and is calculated as follows.

1. Divide RESOURCE TIMEOUT by DEADLOCK TIME.
2. Round the result up to the next larger integer.
3. Multiply this integer by the DEADLOCK TIME.
4. Multiply the result by the appropriate factor.

Table 16-7 shows the resource timeout factors.

The result is the timeout value, which is always greater than or equal to the RESOURCE TIMEOUT. When the timeout value has been reached, the requesting task is informed of the unavailable resource. Several conditions can cause a timeout value to be exceeded by a process, and each returns a different message to a different location.

The deadlock time is determined by system parameter DEADLOCK TIME (default is 5 seconds). This is the time interval between two successive scans for a deadlock. For every deadlock interval, the IRLM will verify whether there are deadlock situations. In those cases, DB2 will inform

Table 16-7 Timeout Factors

Component	Factor	Notes
Transaction and queries	× 1	
BIND	× 3	
IMS BMP	× 4	
IMS fast path	× 6	Nonmessage processing
Utility	× Utility timeout	Defaults to 6

the task—usually the one that made the smaller number of changes—that a deadlock has occurred. The other tasks will continue without any problems. The main causes of a timeout are that a program holding a lock has not freed it soon enough and that a deadlock has occurred between DB2 and a non-DB2 resource.

The main causes for deadlocks are the following:

- Two hot pages
- Lock escalation
- One hot page, promotion from S to X lock, and FOR UPDATE OF missing on the cursor

When a timeout or a deadlock has occurred, the following error codes and messages are sent to the application program.

- −911 = "THE CURRENT UNIT OF WORK HAS BEEN ROLLED BACK DUE TO DEADLOCK OR TIMEOUT, REASON [reason-code], TYPE OF RESOURCE [resource-type], AND RESOURCE NAME [resource-name]." The reason code indicates whether a timeout or a deadlock has occurred. The application is rolled back to the previous commit. On receipt of the −911 return code, the application should terminate or retry.
- −913 = "UNSUCCESSFUL EXECUTION CAUSED BY DEADLOCK OR TIMEOUT, REASON [reason-code], TYPE OF RESOURCE [resource-type], AND RESOURCE NAME [resource-name]." The reason code indicates whether a time-out or a deadlock has occurred. The current unit of work *has not been rolled back*. The application should either commit or roll back. Then the application should terminate or retry.
- The following messages are sent to the console: DSNT376I and DSNT500I.

A −911 SQL return code means that a deadlock or a timeout occurred and that DB2 has issued a successful ROLLBACK to the last commit point. If the ROLLBACK was not successful, the application will receive a −913 SQL return code signifying that a ROLLBACK was not per-formed. A−912 SQL return code occurs when the maximum number of lock requests has been reached for the database because insufficient memory was allocated to the lock list. With a −912 or a −913 return code, the application needs to issue a COMMIT or ROLLBACK before proceeding with any other SQL.

When a −911 occurs, the choice of whether to use retry logic depends on the individual applica-tion. If a large amount of work has been rolled back and if other non-DB2 files are present, it may be difficult to reposition everything and retry the unit of work. With most −911 situations, a restart process—vendor supplied or user written—is generally easier than a programmatic reposition and retry. If a small amount of work was lost, a simple retry could be performed up to a fixed number of times. It is important not to retry with a breakpoint, as the source of the prob-lem that caused the negative codes might still exist.

With the -913 SQL return code, the single statement could be retried; if successful, the program could simply continue on. However, if repeated attempts at retry logic fail, the application probably needs to be rolled back.

Lock Escalation and Promotion

Lock Escalation

Lock escalation can occur when the value for LOCKMAX is reached. At this time, DB2 will release all the locks held and take a more comprehensive lock—release several page or row locks to escalate to a table lock. DB2 tries to balance the number of locks on objects, based on the amount of concurrent access. The LOCKMAX option will then further determine when/ whether escalation occurs.

> **N O T E** Lock escalation can occur for objects defined with LOCKSIZE ANY, PAGE, or ROW. ANY simply allows DB2 the choice of lock to take initially.

The value of LOCKMAX is set on the CREATE TABLESPACE statement to define how many locks can be held simultaneously on an object. Locks will be escalated when this number is reached. You can specifically set this value to a number or leave it at the default of SYSTEM, and it will use the number set by NUMLKTS.

> **N O T E** If you specify LOCKSIZE ANY, the default for LOCKMAX is SYSTEM. If you specify LOCKSIZE ROW, PAGE, TABLE, or TABLESPACE, the default for LOCKMAX is 0 (no escalation).

You can turn off lock escalation by using the LOCKMAX = 0 parameter on the CREATE TABLESPACE statement. If you choose to turn off lock escalation, be sure that applications accessing those objects are committing frequently and that you have adjusted NUMLKTS to allow for more locks to be taken; otherwise, you run the risk of hitting negative SQL codes when you reach the maximum number of locks. (Without escalation, you could hold more, smaller locks.) Lock escalation exists to protect you from taking excessive system resources, so if you turn it off, you will need to control it. If you are CPU-bound, it may not be a good idea to turn off lock escalation, because it will take DB2 longer to traverse long chains of locks, and it will take more CPU for IRLM latch activity.

Details about lock-escalation activity can be found in the DB2 logs identified by the DSNI031I message. This message will contain the resource that experienced the escalation and the details about the new state of the lock. Figure 16-1 shows the output of the DSNI031I message.

```
DSNI031I - csect - LOCK ESCALATION HAS OCCURRED FOR
RESOURCE NAME                     = name
LOCK STATE                        = state
PLAN NAME : PACKAGE NAME          = id1 : id2
STATEMENT NUMBER                  = id3
CORRELATION-ID                    = id4
CONNECTION-ID                     = id5
LUW-ID                            = id6
THREAD-INFO                       = id7 : id8 : id9 : id1
```

Figure 16-1   Lock escalation

Lock Promotion

A lock mode that will be used for any table, table space, or table space partition for an SQL statement is reflected in the PLAN_TABLE populated by EXPLAIN in the column TSLOCKMODE if the isolation can be determined at bind time. This is the lock mode that the SQL statement would use for the table or table space lock if and only if it had not been raised by a preceding SQL statement. For example, an SQL SELECT statement might have a TSLOCKMODE of IS, yet during execution, it could have been promoted to IX, and that is what the SELECT statement would use. Such lock promotion is generally not a concern but simply a fact.

DESIGNING FOR CONCURRENCY

Database Design

Following are some recommendations for creating a database for maximum concurrency. Most of the recommendations must be considered during design, before the tables and table spaces are physically implemented, because changing after the data is in use would be difficult.

- Use segmented, not simple, table spaces. Doing so will keep rows of different tables on different pages, so the page locks will lock rows for only a single table.
- Use LOCKSIZE parameters appropriately. Keep the amount of data locked at a minimum unless the application requires exclusive access.
- Consider spacing out rows for small tables with heavy concurrent access by using MAXROWS =1. Row-level lock could also be used to help with this, but the overhead is greater, especially in a data sharing environment.
- Use partitioning where possible. Doing so can reduce contention and increase parallel activity for batch processes and can reduce overhead in data sharing by allowing for the use of affinity routing to different partitions. Locks can be taken on individual partitions.
- Use Data Partitioned Secondary Indexes (DPSI), which promotes partition independence and reduces contention for utilities.

- Consider using `LOCKMAX 0` to turn off lock escalation. In some high-volume environments, this may be necessary. `NUMLKTS` may need to be increased, and the applications must commit frequently.
- Use volatile tables (discussed in Chapter 4). Doing so reduces contention because an index will also be used to access the data by applications that always access the data in the same order.
- Have an adequate number of databases. Reduce DBD locking if DDL, DCL, and utility execution are high for objects in the same database.
- Use sequence objects to provide for better number generation, without the overhead of using a single control table.

Application Design

Following are some recommendations for lessening the number of locks taken by the application and for best concurrency.

- Access tables in the same order to prevent applications from deadlocking.
- Have commits in the applications. With a proper commit strategy, you can reduce contention, achieve lock avoidance, reduce rollback time for an application, reduce elapsed time for system restart, and allow other processes, such as online reorgs, to interrupt.
- Code retry logic for deadlocks.
- Bind with appropriate parameters. Use `CURRENTDATA(NO)` and `ISOLATION(CS)` to allow DB2 to attempt lock avoidance, which will also allow for releasing locks as soon as possible. Use `ACQUIRE(USE)`, which takes locks only when necessary.
- Use uncommitted read where appropriate, especially at the statement level.
- Close all cursors as soon as possible, allowing for locks and resources to be freed. `WITH HOLD` will release locks at commit if `RECURHL` is set to `YES`.

Lock Monitoring

A few tools are available for monitoring lock activity in DB2:

- Explain
- Accounting and statistics reports
- `DISPLAY` command

Explain

When using Explain to see what access path DB2 will choose, you can also view what object locks are planned for the query. (For information on how to run Explain, see Chapter 17.) The `PLAN_TABLE` has a column named `TSLOCKMODE`, which shows the initial lock mode for the table. This mode will apply to the table or table space, depending on the value of `LOCKSIZE` and whether the table space is simple or segmented.

Accounting and Statistics Reports

A DB2 monitoring tool produces accounting and statistics reports for reviewing the locking activity.

> **N O T E**   In order to ensure that the correct information is available for the reports, it is advised to always have statistics classes 1, 3, and 4 and accounting classes 1 and 3 active.

In these reports, you can view counters for timeouts, deadlocks, suspensions, escalation, lock/unlock requests, and claim/drain requests. The following example shows the accounting-trace output for an application.

```
LOCKING                     TOTAL
------------------          --------
TIMEOUTS                    1
DEADLOCKS                   0
ESCAL. (SHAR)               0
ESCAL. (EXCL)               0
MAX PG/ROW LCK HELD         5
LOCK REQUEST                0
UNLOCK REQST                0
QUERY REQST                 0
CHANGE REQST                0
OTHER REQST                 0
LOCK SUSPENS                2
IRLM LATCH SUSPENS          0
OTHER SUSPENS               0
TOTAL SUSPENS               2

DRAIN/CLAIM                 TOTAL
------------------          --------
DRAIN REQST                 0
DRAIN FAILED                0
CLAIM REQST                 5
CLAIM FAILED                0
```

The statistics report would show very similar counts, by subsystem, as well as information about events per second/thread/commit.

Displaying Locks

To help solve application concurrency problems, you can display the locks that are being held. By using the -DISPLAY DATABASE (*dbname*) *LOCKS* command, you can see many properties about a given lock, as shown in Figure 16-2.

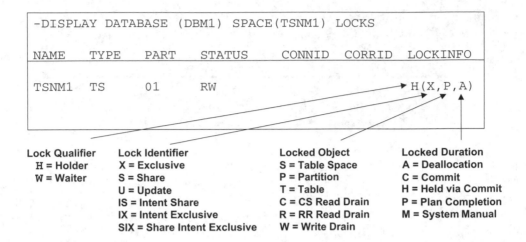

Figure 16-2 DISPLAY DATABASE LOCKS

SUMMARY

This chapter discussed how concurrency, or serialization, is controlled. To protect the data as it is being modified, rules are established and the changes are grouped into units of work. The updated data is made permanent by the COMMIT statement or removed by the ROLLBACK statement. The rules of concurrency are determined by the isolation level, the lock size, and the rules of lock duration.

DB2 implements the isolation-level semantics of data access by implicitly acquiring locks on behalf of applications. Applications can decide to lock a resource for exclusive or share modes. The resources that can be locked are the row, page, table, table space, and partition.

If a requested lock is more restrictive and if another application already has the resource locked, a wait on the release of the lock will occur. The amount of time an application will wait is determined by systemwide parameters for both resource timeout and deadlocks.

If multiple applications require access to data that is held by other applications, a deadlock scenario can occur. DB2 will detect the occurrence of any deadlocks and force one of the transactions to roll back. Every lock requested requires memory in the IRLM, and the amount of lock storage is configurable by using IRLM parameters.

Many opportunities exist for avoiding excessive locks and lock problems. These opportunities come through proper database and application designs.

ADDITIONAL RESOURCES

IBM DB2 z/OS Version 8 Administration Guide (SC18-7413-00)

IBM DB2 z/OS Version 8 Application Programming Guide (SC18-4518-00)

SQL Optimization and Performance

- Access paths and optimization
- Designing indexes and SQL for performance

Tuning DB2 queries is critical to performance. You need to understand how the DB2 optimizer works and how to create the best possible indexes for your queries. You also need to know how to determine whether DB2 is using that index and whether it is performing joins and other operations effectively by using the various tools available.

ACCESS PATHS AND OPTIMIZATION

If you want to know how DB2 will execute a query, you must analyze its access path, which is the method for retrieving data from a specific table or set of tables. Oftentimes, unexpected decreases in performance, such as excessive GETPAGEs, can be attributed to a change in the access path. The *Explain facility* provides information about how DB2 accesses the data to resolve the SQL statements.

You should have a high-level understanding of how SQL statements are processed by the DB2 database engine: DB2 analyses each SQL statement and then determines how to process it during a static bind or when executed dynamically. The method used to retrieve data from tables is called the *access plan*.

The DB2 component that determines the access plan to be used is known as the *optimizer*. During the static preparation of an SQL statement, the SQL compiler is called on to generate an access plan. The access plan contains the data-access strategy, including index usage, sort methods, locking semantics, and join methods.

The executable form of the SQL statement is stored in the system tables when a `BIND` command is executed. When DB2 processes a program that contains embedded SQL statements, those statements are extracted and placed in a member of a partitioned data set (PDS). This member, called a DBRM (database request module), is the primary input to the `BIND` command, which can then be bound into a package. For more on packages, refer to Chapter 11.

Sometimes, the complete statement is not known during application development. In this case, the compiler is invoked during program execution to generate a query access plan that can be used by the database manager to access the data. Such an SQL statement is called a dynamic SQL statement. The access plans for a dynamic SQL statement are not stored in the system catalogs but can be cached in memory in the dynamic SQL cache and will not be reprepared if the access plans for the dynamic SQL statements already exist in the dynamic SQL cache.

Explain

Explain is a monitoring tool that produces information about the following:

- A plan, package, or SQL statement when it is bound. The output appears in a table you create, called `PLAN_TABLE`, which is also called a *plan table*. Experienced users can use `PLAN_TABLE` to give optimization hints to DB2. Access-path hints are provided later in this chapter.
- An estimated cost of executing an SQL `SELECT`, `INSERT`, `UPDATE`, or `DELETE` statement. The output appears in a table you create, called `DSN_STATEMNT_TABLE`, which is also called the *statement table*.
- User-defined functions referred to in the statement, including the specific name and schema. The output appears in a table you create, called `DSN_FUNCTION_TABLE`, which is also called a *function table*.

Gathering Explain Data

Populating the `PLAN_TABLE` can be done in three ways.

1. Execute the SQL statement `EXPLAIN`. You can populate the `PLAN_TABLE` by executing the SQL statement `EXPLAIN`. In the statement, specify a single explainable SQL statement in the `FOR` clause. You can execute `EXPLAIN` either statically from an application program or dynamically, using QMF or SPUFI.
2. Bind with the option `EXPLAIN(YES)`. You can populate `PLAN_TABLE` by executing the SQL statement in a package bound with `EXPLAIN(YES)`.
3. Executing an `EXPLAIN STMTCACHE STMTID` or `EXPLAIN STMTCACHE STMTTOKEN` will populate the `PLAN_TABLE` with the access path of a statement that is in the dynamic statement cache.

Before you can use EXPLAIN, you must create the PLAN_TABLE to hold the results of EXPLAIN. A copy of the statements needed to create the table is in the DB2 sample library under the member name DSNTESC. (Unless you need the information the statements provide, it is not necessary to create a function table or a statement table to use EXPLAIN.)

> **N O T E** DB2 does not automatically delete rows from the PLAN_TABLE. To clear the table of obsolete rows, use DELETE, just as you would for deleting rows from any table.

PLAN_TABLE

Explain will populate this table; from there, you must interpret the data and act accordingly. Table 17-1 shows the columns in PLAN_TABLE.

Table 17-1 **PLAN_TABLE** Columns

Column Name	Description
QUERYNO	A number identifying the statement being explained. For a row produced by an EXPLAIN statement, specify the number in the QUERYNO clause. For a row produced by non-EXPLAIN statements, specify the number using the QUERYNO clause, which is an optional part of the SELECT, INSERT, UPDATE, and DELETE statement syntax. Otherwise, DB2 assigns a number based on the line number of the SQL statement in the source program.
	FETCH statements do not have individual QUERYNOs assigned to them. Instead, DB2 uses the QUERYNO of the DECLARE CURSOR statement for all corresponding FETCH statements for that cursor.
	When the values of QUERYNO are based on the statement number in the source program, values greater than 32,767 are reported as 0. Hence, in a very long program, the value is not guaranteed to be unique. If QUERYNO is not unique, the value of TIMESTAMP is unique.
QBLOCKNO	A number that identifies each query block within a query. The values of the numbers are not in any particular order; nor are they necessarily consecutive.
APPLNAME	The name of the application plan for the row. Applies only to embedded EXPLAIN statements executed from a plan or to statements explained when binding a plan. Blank if not applicable.
PROGNAME	The name of the program or package containing the statement being explained. For statements explained dynamically, such as QMF or SPUFI, the associated plan/package is listed. Blank if not applicable.
PLANNO	The number of the step in which the query indicated in QBLOCKNO was processed. This column indicates the order in which the steps were executed.

continues

Table 17-1 `PLAN_TABLE` Columns (Continued)

Column Name	Description
METHOD	A number (0, 1, 2, 3, or 4) that indicates the join method used for the step: 0 First table accessed, continuation of previous table accessed, or not used. 1 Nested loop join. For each row of the present composite table, matching rows of a new table are found and joined. 2 Merge-scan join. The present composite table and the new tables are scanned in the order of the join columns, and matching rows are joined. 3 Sorts needed by ORDER BY, GROUP BY, SELECT DISTINCT, UNION, a quantified predicate, or an IN predicate. This step does not access a new table. 4 Hybrid join. The current composite table is scanned in the order of the join-column rows of the new table. The new table is accessed using list prefetch.
CREATOR	The creator of the new table accessed in this step; blank if METHOD is 3.
TNAME	The name of a table, materialized query table, created or declared temporary table, materialized view, or materialized table expression. The value is blank if METHOD is 3. The column can also contain the name of a table in the form DSNWFQB(qblockno). DSNWFQB(qblockno) is used to represent the intermediate result of a UNION ALL or an outer join that is materialized. If a view is merged, the name of the view does not appear.
TABNO	Values are for IBM use only.
ACCESSTYPE	The method of accessing the new table: I By an index, identified in ACCESSCREATOR and ACCESSNAME I1 By a one-fetch index scan M By a multiple-index scan, followed by MX, MI, or MU MX By an index scan on the index named in ACCESSNAME MI By an intersection of multiple indexes MU By a union of multiple indexes N By an index scan when the matching predicate contains the IN keyword R By a table space scan RW By a work file scan of the result of a materialized user-defined table function T By a spare index (star join work files) V By buffers for an INSERT statement within a SELECT blank Not applicable to the current row
MATCHCOLS	For ACCESSTYPE I, I1, N, or MX, the number of index keys used in an index scan; otherwise, 0.

Table 17-1 `PLAN_TABLE` Columns (Continued)

Column Name	Description
ACCESSCREATOR	For `ACCESSTYPE` I, I1, N, or MX, the creator of the index; otherwise, blank.
ACCESSNAME	For `ACCESSTYPE` I, I1, N, or MX, the name of the index; otherwise, blank.
INDEXONLY	Whether access to an index alone is enough to carry out the step or whether data too must be accessed. `Y` = yes; `N` = no. For `UPDATE`/`DELETE`, this indicates whether an index alone is enough to determine the row(s) to be updated or deleted.
SORTN_UNIQ	Whether the new table is sorted to remove duplicate rows. `Y` = yes; `N` = no.
SORTN_JOIN	Whether the new table is sorted for join method 2 or 4. `Y` = yes; `N` = no.
SORTN_ORDERBY	Whether the new table is sorted for `ORDER BY`. `Y` = yes; `N` = no.
SORTN_GROUPBY	Whether the new table is sorted for `GROUP BY`. `Y` = yes; `N` = no.
SORTC_UNIQ	Whether the composite table is sorted to remove duplicate rows. `Y` = yes; `N` = no.
SORTC_JOIN	Whether the composite table is sorted for join method 1, 2, or 4. `Y` = yes; `N` = no.
SORTC_ORDERBY	Whether the composite table is sorted for an `ORDER BY` clause or a quantified predicate. `Y` = yes; `N` = no.
SORTC_GROUPBY	Whether the composite table is sorted for a `GROUP BY` clause. `Y` = yes; `N` = no.
TSLOCKMODE	An indication of the mode of lock to be acquired on the new table or its table space or table space partitions. If the isolation can be determined at bind time, the values are IS Intent share lock IX Intent exclusive lock S Share lock U Update lock X Exclusive lock SIX Share with intent exclusive lock N UR isolation; no lock If the isolation cannot be determined at bind time, the lock mode determined by the isolation at runtime is shown by the following values: NS For UR isolation, no lock; for CS, RS, or RR, an S lock NIS For UR isolation, no lock; for CS, RS, or RR, an IS lock NSS For UR isolation, no lock; for CS or RS, an IS lock; for RR, an S lock SS For UR, CS, or RS isolation, an IS lock; for RR, an S lock The data in this column is right-justified. For example, IX appears as a blank followed by I followed by X. If the column contains a blank, no lock is acquired.

continues

Table 17-1 `PLAN_TABLE` Columns (Continued)

Column Name	Description
TIMESTAMP	Usually, the time at which the row is processed, to the last 0.01 second. If necessary, DB2 adds 0.01 second to the value to ensure that rows for two successive queries have different values.
REMARKS	A field into which you can insert any character string of 254 or fewer characters.
PREFETCH	Whether data pages are to be read in advance by prefetch. S = pure sequential prefetch; L = prefetch through a page list; D = optimizer expects dynamic prefetch; blank = unknown at bind time or no prefetch.
COLUMN_FN_EVAL	When an SQL column function is evaluated. R = while the data is being read from the table or index; S = while performing a sort to satisfy a GROUP BY clause; blank = after data retrieval, after any sorts, or not applicable.
MIXOPSEQ	The sequence number of a step in a multiple-index operation. 1, 2, ... *n* For the steps of the multiple-index procedure (ACCESSTYPE is MX, MI, or MU). 0 For any other rows (ACCESSTYPE is I, I1, M, N, R, or blank)
VERSION	The version identifier for the package. Applies only to an embedded EXPLAIN statement executed from a package or to a statement that is explained when binding a package. Blank if not applicable.
COLLID	The collection ID for the package. Applies only to an embedded EXPLAIN statement executed from a package or to a statement that is explained when binding a package. Blank if not applicable. The value DSNDYNAMICSQLCACHE indicates that the row is for a cached statement.
ACCESS_DEGREE	The number of parallel tasks or operations activated by a query. This value is determined at bind time; the number of parallel operations used at execution time could be different. This column contains 0 if there is a host variable.
ACCESS_PGROUP_ID	The identifier of the parallel group for accessing the new table. A parallel group is a set of consecutive operations, executed in parallel, that have the same number of parallel tasks. This value is determined at bind time; it could change at execution time.
JOIN_DEGREE	The number of parallel operations or tasks used in joining the composite table with the new table. This value is determined at bind time and can be 0 if there is a host variable. The number of parallel operations or tasks used at execution time could be different.
JOIN_PGROUP_ID	The identifier of the parallel group for joining the composite table with the new table. This value is determined at bind time; it could change at execution time.

Table 17-1 **PLAN_TABLE** Columns (Continued)

Column Name	Description
SORTC_PGROUP_ID	The parallel group identifier for the parallel sort of the composite table.
SORTN_PGROUP_ID	The parallel group identifier for the parallel sort of the new table.
PARALLELISM_MODE	The kind of parallelism, if any, that is used at bind time: I Query I/O parallelism C Query CP parallelism X Sysplex query parallelism
MERGE_JOIN_COLS	The number of columns that are joined during a merge-scan join (METHOD = 2).
CORRELATION_NAME	The correlation name of a table or a view that is specified in the statement. If there is no correlation name, the column is blank.
PAGE_RANGE	Whether the table qualifies for page-range screening, so that plans scan only the partitions that are needed. Y = yes; blank = no.
JOIN_TYPE	The type of an outer join: F FULL OUTER JOIN L LEFT OUTER JOIN S STAR JOIN blank INNER JOIN or no join RIGHT OUTER JOIN converts to LEFT OUTER JOIN when you use it, so that JOIN_TYPE contains L.
GROUP_MEMBER	The DB2 member name that executed EXPLAIN. The column is blank if the DB2 subsystem was not in a data sharing environment when EXPLAIN was executed.
IBM_SERVICE_DATA	Values are for IBM use only.
WHEN_OPTIMIZE	When the access path was determined: blank At bind time, using a default filter factor for any host variables, parameter markers, or special registers. B At bind time, using a default filter factor for any host variables, parameter markers, or special registers; however, the statement is reoptimized at runtime, using input variable values for input host variables, parameter markers, or special registers. The bind option REOPT (ALWAYS) or REOPT (ONCE) must be specified for reoptimization to occur. R At runtime, using input variables for any host variables, parameter markers, or special registers. The bind option REOPT (ALWAYS) or REOPT (ONCE) must be specified for this to occur.

continues

Table 17-1   `PLAN_TABLE` Columns (Continued)

Column Name	Description
QBLOCK_TYPE	For each query block, the type of SQL operation performed. For the outermost query, it identifies the statement type. Possible values: SELECT SELECT INSERT INSERT UPDATE UPDATE DELETE DELETE SELUPD SELECT with FOR UPDATE OF DELCUR DELETE WHERE CURRENT OF CURSOR UPDCUR UPDATE WHERE CURRENT OF CURSOR CORSUB Correlated subquery NCOSUB Noncorrelated subquery TABLEX Table expression TRIGGR WHEN clause on CREATE TRIGGER UNION UNION UNIONA UNION ALL
BIND_TIME	The time at which the plan or the package for this statement or query block was bound. For static SQL statements, this value is a full-precision timestamp. For dynamic SQL statements, this value is contained in the TIMESTAMP column of PLAN_TABLE, appended by four zeroes.
OPTHINT	A string that you use to identify this row as an optimization hint for DB2. DB2 uses this row as input when choosing an access path.
HINT_USED	If it used one of your optimization hints, DB2 puts the identifier for that hint (the value in OPTHINT) in this column.
PRIMARY_ACCESSTYPE	Indicates whether direct row access will be attempted first: D DB2 will try to use direct row access. If it cannot use direct row access at runtime, DB2 uses the access path described in the ACCESSTYPE column of PLAN_TABLE. blank DB2 will not try to use direct row access.
PARENT_QBLOCK	Number that indicates the QBLOCKNO of the parent query.

Table 17-1 `PLAN_TABLE` Columns (Continued)

Column Name	Description
TABLE_TYPE	The type of new table: B Buffers for an `INSERT` statement within a `SELECT` C Common table expression F Table function M Materialized query table Q Temporary intermediate result table (not materialized). The name of the view or nested table expression; a value of Q indicates that the materialization was virtual, not actual. Materialization can be virtual when the view or nested table expression definition contains a `UNION ALL` that is not distributed. RB Recursive common table expression T Table W Work file (materialized)
TABLE_ENCODE	The encoding scheme of the table. If the table has a single CCSID set, possible values are A ASCII E EBCDIC U Unicode M is the value of the column when the table contains multiple CCSID set, the value of the column is M.
TABLE_SCCSID	The SBCS CCSID value of the table. If column TABLE_ENCODE is M, the value is 0.
TABLE_MCCSID	The mixed CCSID value of the table. If column TABLE_ENCODE is M, the value is 0.
TABLE_DCCSID	The DBCS CCSID value of the table. If column TABLE_ENCODE is M, the value is 0.
ROUTINE_ID	Values for IBM use only.
CTREF	If the referenced table is a common table expression, the value is the top-level query block number.
STMTTOKEN	User-specified statement token.

Access-Path Evaluation.   This section explains how to examine some of the most useful data in the PLAN_TABLE and determine what the DB2 optimizer is using to access the data.

Index Access   The following describes the various types of index access and how they are represented in the PLAN_TABLE.

Index Access (ACCESSTYPE is I, I1, N, or M).   If the column ACCESSTYPE in the plan table has a value I, I1, N, or M, DB2 uses an index to access the table named in column TNAME. The columns ACCESSCREATOR and ACCESSNAME identify the index.

Multiple-Index Access (ACCESSTYPE = M).   This value indicates that DB2 uses a set of indexes to access a single table. A set of rows in the plan table contain information about the multiple-index access. The rows are numbered in column MIXOPSEQ in the order of execution of steps in the multiple-index access. (If you retrieve the rows in order by MIXOPSEQ, the result is similar to postfix arithmetic notation.) Additional ACCESSTYPE values for the set of rows describing the multiple-index access further define the type of access: MI for the intersection of multiple indexes, MU for the union of multiple indexes, and MX for an index scan of a named index (in the ACCESSNAME column).

Number of Matching Index Columns (MATCHCOLS = n).   If MATCHCOLS is 0, the access method is called a nonmatching index scan. All the index keys and their row identifiers are read. If MATCHCOLS is greater than 0, the access method is called a matching-index scan: The query uses predicates that match the index columns.

In general, the matching predicates on the leading index columns are equal or IN predicates. The predicate that matches the final index column can be an equal, IN, or range predicate (<, <=, >, >=, LIKE, or BETWEEN). The following example illustrates matching predicates:

```
SELECT *
FROM EMP
WHERE JOBCODE = '5'
AND LOCATION ='CA'
AND SALARY > 60000
AND AGE > 21;

INDEX XEMP5 on (JOBCODE,LOCATION,SALARY,AGE)
```

The index XEMP5 is the chosen access path for this query, with MATCHCOLS = 3. Two equal predicates are on the first two columns, and a range predicate is on the third column. Although the index has four columns, only three of them can be considered matching columns.

At most, one IN predicate can be a matching predicate; the exception, however, is a noncorrelated IN subquery. IN-list predicates cannot be matching predicates for MX access or list prefetch.

Increasing the number of matching columns can help query performance; however, if the column that is added is highly correlated to the existing columns, it may not provide much of a benefit in terms of filtering.

> **N O T E** Only Boolean predicates can use matching-index access
> on a single index.

Index-Only Access (INDEXONLY = Y).   In this case, the method is called index-only access. For a SELECT operation, all the columns needed for the query can be found in the index, and DB2 does not access the table. For an UPDATE or DELETE operation, only the index is required to read the selected row.

Index-only access is not possible when returning varying-length data in the result set or when a VARCHAR column has a LIKE predicate, unless the VARCHAR FROM INDEX field of installation panel DSNTIP4 is set to YES, and plan or packages have been rebound to pick up the change. Also, as of version 8, if the index (with a VARCHAR) is created or altered with the NOT PADDED keyword, it can also be used for index-only access.

If access is by more than one index, INDEXONLY is Y for a step with access type MX. The data pages are not accessed until all the steps for intersection (MI) or union (MU) take place.

When an SQL application uses index-only access for a ROWID column, the application claims the table space or table space partition. As a result, contention may occur between the SQL application and a utility that drains the table space or partition. Index-only access to a table for a ROWID column is not possible if the associated table space or partition is in an incompatible restrictive state. For example, an SQL application can make a read claim on the table space only if the restrictive state allows readers.

Table Access.   The following information describes the various types of table accesses and how they are represented in the PLAN_TABLE.

Table Space Scans (ACCESSTYPE=R, PREFETCH = S)   Table space scan (R = relational scan) is most often used for one of the following reasons.

- Access is through a created temporary table. (Index access is not possible for a created temporary table.)
- A matching-index scan is not possible, because an index is not available or no predicates match the index columns.
- A high percentage of the rows in the table are returned. In this case, an index is not very useful, because most rows need to be read anyway.
- The indexes that have matching predicates have low cluster ratios and are therefore efficient for only small amounts of data.

Assume that table DB2USER1.CANDIDATE has no index on the column identifier (CID). The following is an example that uses a table space scan:

```
SELECT * FROM DB2USER1.CANDIDATE WHERE CID = :CIDHV;
```

In this case, at least every row in the CANDIDATE table must be examined to determine whether the value of CID matches the given value.

Prefetching (PREFETCH = L, S, D, or blank)   Prefetching is a method of determining in advance that a set of data pages is about to be used and then reading the entire set into a buffer with a single asynchronous I/O operation. If the value of PREFETCH is S, the method is called *sequential prefetch*. The data pages that are read in advance are sequential. A table space scan always uses sequential prefetch. An index scan might not use it.

If the value of PREFETCH is L, the method is called *list prefetch*. One or more indexes are used to select the RIDs for a list of data pages to be read in advance; the pages need not be sequential. Usually, the RIDs are sorted. The exception is the case of a hybrid join (METHOD = 4) when the value of column SORTN_JOIN is N.

If the value of PREFETCH is D, the optimizer expects dynamic prefetch.

If the value of PREFETCH is blank, prefetching is not chosen as an access method. However, depending on the pattern of the page access, data can be prefetched at execution time through a process called *sequential detection*, also know as dynamic prefetch.

> **N O T E**   DB2 always attempts to use sequential prefetch for a table space scan. For a segmented table space, if DB2 determines that fewer than four pages will be read at runtime, sequential prefetch is disabled. The OPTIMIZE FOR 1 ROW also potentially disables sequential and list prefetch at bind time.

Limited Partition Scanning (PAGE_RANGE=Y)   DB2 can limit the number of partitions scanned for data access. The query must provide the leading column of the partitioning key. The following example would limit the search for the name of the candidate by providing the high and low numbers of the candidates' CID, therefore limiting the number of partitions to be scanned, assuming that the limit key for the partitions is on CID:

```
SELECT NAME
FROM CANDIDATE
WHERE CID BETWEEN :low AND :high
```

SORT (SORTN_ and SORTC_)   The plan table shows the reasons a sort was invoked. Those reasons could include a sort of data rows or a sort of RIDs in a RID list. SORTN_JOIN indicates that the new table of a join is sorted before the join. (For a hybrid join, this is a sort of the RID list.) When SORTN_JOIN and SORTC_JOIN are both Y, two sorts are performed for the join. The sorts for joins are indicated on the same row as the new table access.

> **N O T E** A sort of the composite table for a join (SORTC_JOIN) is beneficial in avoiding death by random I/O. Providing a cluster ratio for an index and keycard statistics for multicolumn cardinalities gives DB2 the information to determine whether a query will suffer from excessive synchronous I/O. In this case, sorting the composite for a nested loop or sorting both, if required, for a sort merge or a hybrid join can provide sequential access to the data.

SORTC_UNIQ indicates a sort to remove duplicates, as might be needed by a SELECT statement with DISTINCT or UNION. SORTC_ORDERBY usually indicates a sort for an ORDER BY clause. But SORTC_UNIQ and SORTC_ORDERBY also indicate when the results of a non-correlated subquery are sorted, both to remove duplicates and to order the results. A SORTC_GROUPBY would indicate a sort for processing a GROUP BY clause.

> **N O T E** If more than one SORTC indicator is set to Y on the same Explain output line, DB2 is performing one sort to accomplish two tasks, such as sorting for uniqueness and ordering. This does not apply to SORTN_JOIN and SORTC_JOIN, as one sort is for the composite and one is for the new table.

To perform list prefetch, DB2 sorts RIDs into ascending page number order. A RID sort is usually not indicated in the PLAN_TABLE, but a RID sort normally is performed whenever list prefetch is used. The only exception to this rule is when a hybrid join is performed and a single, highly clustered index is used on the inner table. In this case, SORTN_JOIN is N, indicating that the RID list for the inner table was not sorted.

> **N O T E** SORTN_GROUPBY, SORTN_ORDERBY, and SORTN_UNIQ are not used by DB2.

Nested Loop Join (METHOD = 1) For a nested loop join, DB2 scans the composite, or outer, table. For each table row that qualifies, by satisfying the predicates on that table, DB2 searches for matching rows of the new, or inner, table, concatenating any it finds with the current row of the composite table. If no rows match the current row:

- For an inner join, DB2 discards the current row.
- For an outer join, DB2 concatenates a row of null values.

Stage 1 and stage 2 predicates can eliminate unqualified rows before the physical joining of rows occurs. Nested loop join is often used if

- The outer table is small.
- Predicates with small filter factors reduce the number of qualifying rows in the outer table.
- An efficient, highly clustered index exists on the join columns of the inner table.
- The number of data pages accessed in the inner table is small.

> **N O T E** The nested-loop join repetitively scans the inner table. That is, DB2 scans the outer table once and scans the inner table as many times as the number of qualifying rows in the outer table. Hence, the nested loop join is usually the most efficient join method when the values of the join column passed to the inner table are in sequence and the index on the join column of the inner table is clustered, or the number of rows retrieved in the inner table through the index is small. If the tables are not clustered in the same sequence, DB2 can sort the composite to match the sequence of the inner table. Accesses to the inner table can then use sequential or dynamic prefetch.

Merge-Scan Join (METHOD = 2)   The merge-scan join is also known as a merge join, or sort-merge join. This method must have one or more predicates of the form TABLE1.COL1 = TABLE2.COL2, where the two columns have the same data type, length, and null attributes. If the null attributes do not match, the maximum number of merge-join columns is 1. The exception is a full outer join, which permits mismatching null attributes.

> **N O T E** Join columns cannot be matching columns for a merge-scan join. Instead, these columns are listed as MERGE_JOIN_COLS in the plan table. Local predicates can be matching predicates and will be applied before the join.

DB2 scans both tables in the order of the join columns. If no efficient indexes on the join columns provide the order, DB2 might sort the outer table, the inner table, or both. The inner table is put into a work file; the outer table is put into a work file only if it must be sorted. When a row of the outer table matches a row of the inner table, DB2 returns the combined rows.

A merge-scan join is often used if

- The qualifying rows of the inner and outer tables are large, and the join predicate does not provide much filtering, that is, in a many-to-many join.

- The tables are large and have no indexes with matching columns.
- Few columns are selected on inner tables. This is the case when a DB2 sort is used. The fewer the columns to be sorted, the more efficient the sort is.

> **N O T E** A merge-scan join is always chosen for a full outer join.

Hybrid Join (METHOD = 4)   The method applies only to an inner join and requires an index on the join column of the inner table. The method requires obtaining RIDs in the order needed to use list prefetch. In the successive steps, DB2

1. Scans the outer table (OUTER).
2. Joins the outer tables with RIDs from the index on the inner table. The result is the phase 1 intermediate table. The index of the inner table is scanned for every row of the outer table.
3. Sorts the data in the outer table and the RIDs, creating a sorted RID list and the phase 2 intermediate table. The sort is indicated by a value of Y in column SORTN_JOIN of the plan table. If the index on the inner table is highly clustered, DB2 can skip this sort; the value in SORTN_JOIN is then N.
4. Retrieves the data from the inner table, using list prefetch.
5. Concatenates the data from the inner table and the phase 2 intermediate table to create the final composite table.

A hybrid join is often used if

- A nonclustered index or indexes are used on the join columns of the inner table.
- The outer table has duplicate qualifying rows.

> **N O T E** DB2 may also choose to sort the composite for a hybrid join.

Star Join (METHOD = 0, 1; JOIN TYPE = S)   Star join is the access path used in processing a star schema, a logical database design that is included in many data warehouse and decision-support applications. A star schema is composed of a fact table and a number of dimension tables that are connected to it. A dimension table contains several values that are given an ID, which is used in the fact table instead of all the values. You can think of the fact table, which is much larger than the dimension tables, as being in the center, surrounded by dimension tables; the result resembles a star formation.

To access the data in a star schema, you write SELECT statements that include join operations between the fact table and the dimension tables; no join operations exist between dimension tables. A query must satisfy a number of conditions before it qualifies for the star join access path. The first requirement is detection of the fact table. Given that the access-path objective is efficient access to the fact table, it is important that the fact table be correctly identified.

The first fact-table detection algorithm is known as the unique-index check. Beginning outside-in, the optimizer will evaluate each set of join predicates. For each set of join predicates between two tables, the table with a unique index on the join predicates is considered to be the parent in a parent/child relationship. As DB2 continues outside-in, the table without any further children—and that therefore has only parents—is considered to be the fact table.

The second fact-table detection algorithm is based on the values of the STARJOIN DSNZPARM, which are

- ENABLE: Star join is enabled and the fact table is 25 times larger than the largest dimension table.
- DISABLE: Star join is disabled (default).
- 1: The fact table will be the largest in the star join query.
- 2-32,768: This is the fact table and the largest dimension table ratio. The fact table must be *n* times larger than the largest dimension table.

The third fact-table detection algorithm is the topology check. The fact table is considered to be the table with the most number of join predicates in the query.

Once a fact table is identified by using any of the three fact-table detection algorithms, the following conditions must be met for DB2 to use the star join technique:

- The number of tables in the query block must be at least ten (altered via DSNZPARM SJTABLES).
- All join predicates are between the fact table and the dimension tables or within tables of the same dimension (snowflake).
- All join predicates between the fact and dimension tables must be equal-join predicates.
- All join predicates between the fact and dimension tables must be Boolean term predicates; fact-to-dimension join predicates cannot be ORed.
- A local predicate on a dimension table cannot be ORed with a local predicate of another dimension table.
- A single fact-table column cannot be joined to columns of different dimension tables in join predicates. For example, fact table column F1 cannot be joined to column D1 of dimension table T1 and also joined to column D2 of dimension table T2.
- No correlated subqueries exist across dimensions.
- The data type and length of both sides of a join predicate are the same between the fact and dimension tables.

- Dimensions cannot be a table function.
- After DB2 simplifies join operations, no outer join operations can exist between the fact and dimension tables.

A successful match on all of the star schema detection rules will immediately qualify the query for star join optimization. A failure on any of those rules for a fact table will result in the next fact-table detection algorithm to be evaluated. A failure of these rules for all the fact-table detection rules will result in the query's being optimized, using standard dynamic programming—exhaustive search—techniques or algorithms.

> **N O T E** When a star join is performed, it is identified by an S in the JOIN_TYPE column of the PLAN_TABLE for dimension tables that are accessed before the fact table.

For a star schema, even though the intersection of all dimensions with the fact table can produce a small result set, the predicates applied to one single dimension table are typically insufficient to reduce the enormous number of fact-table rows.

If a join based on related tables—dimension table to fact table—does not provide adequate performance, an alternative is to join unrelated tables. Joining unrelated tables results in a Cartesian product, whereby every row of the first table is joined with every row of the second table.

Performing a Cartesian join of all dimension tables before accessing the fact table may not be efficient. DB2 must decide how many dimension tables should be accessed first to provide the greatest level of filtering of fact-table rows, using available indexes. This can be a delicate balance, as further Cartesian products will produce a massive increase in the size of the intermediate result sets. Alternatively, minimal prejoining of unrelated dimension tables may not provide adequate filtering for the join to the fact table. For an efficient Cartesian process, DB2 uses a logical rather than a physical Cartesian of the dimension tables. Each dimension or snowflake—further normalized dimension—covered by the chosen fact-table index is accessed independently before the fact table. Each qualifying dimension and snowflake has all local predicates applied, with the result sorted into join-column order and, finally, materialized into its own separate work file. If many of the dimensions involve snowflakes, this preprocessing and materialization significantly reduce the number of overall tables joined, as the snowflake is resolved into a single dimension.

Rather than requiring the physical work file storage involved in a physical Cartesian, DB2 simulates a Cartesian by repositioning itself within each work file to potentially join all possible combinations to the central fact table. The sequence of this simulated Cartesian join respects the column order of the selected fact-table index.

The sparseness of data within the fact table implies that a significant number of values generated by the Cartesian process are not to be found by a join to the fact table. To minimize the CPU overhead of joining unnecessarily derived rows to the fact table, DB2 introduces an index-key feedback loop to return the next-highest key value whenever a not-found condition is encountered.

A hit on the fact-table index will return the matching fact-table row. A miss will return the next valid fact-table index key so that the data manager can reposition itself within the dimension work files, thus skipping composite rows with no possibility of obtaining a fact-table match.

To further improve the performance of the join to the fact table, the entire join has been pushed down to data manager (stage 1), but this applies only for star join access from the composite (dimensions) to the fact table. This ensures a reduced path length, as rows no longer need to be returned to RDS (stage 2) for the join to occur. The join method used by this process is a nested loop join.

To help the performance of star join queries the following can be considered: promoting the use of the dynamic SQL cache, increasing the size of the work file pool for star joins via the SJMXPOOL DSNZPARM, increasing the number of parallel degrees with CURRENT DEGREE, or considering the use of access-path hints.

Parallelism Usage (PARALLELISM_MODE = I, C, or X)   Parallel processing applies only to read-only queries. The values are

      I   Parallel I/O operations
      C Parallel CP operations
      X Sysplex query parallelism

Non-null values in columns ACCESS_DEGREE and JOIN_DEGREE indicate to what degree—number of concurrent processes—DB2 plans to use parallel operations. However, this can change at runtime.

DSN_STATEMNT_TABLE

If it exists, this table is populated when EXPLAIN is run. Some of the columns are similar to those in the PLAN_TABLE, and some are new and related only to the statement cost. The columns that are unique to the DSN_STATEMNT_TABLE are

- STMT_TYPE: type of SQL statement
- COST_CATEGORY: how much information was available
- PROCMS: estimated processor cost in milliseconds
- PROCSU: estimated processor cost in service units
- REASON: reasons that COST_CATEGORY may be inaccurate

The COST_CATEGORY determination is affected by such things as the number of tables, the number of rows in the tables, column cardinality, cluster ratio, first key cardinality, full key cardinality, the number leaf pages, the number of index levels, host variables, special registers, triggers, UDFs, RI, LOBs, and expressions. Table 17-2 describes the contents of the DSN_STATEMNT_TABLE, and Table 17-3 describes the contents of the DSN_FUNCTION_TABLE.

Table 17-2   DSN_STATEMNT_TABLE

Column Name	Description
QUERYNO	A number identifying the statement being explained. If QUERYNO is not unique, the value of EXPLAIN_TIME is unique.
APPLNAME	The name of the application plan for the row, or blank.
PROGNAME	The name of the program or package containing the statement being explained, or blank.
COLLID	The collection ID for the package. Applies only to an embedded EXPLAIN statement executed from a package or to a statement that is being explained when binding a package. Blank is not applicable. The value DSNDYNAMICSQLCACHE indicates that the row is for a cached statement.
GROUP_MEMBER	The DB2 member name that executed EXPLAIN, or blank.
EXPLAIN_TIME	The time at which the statement is processed. This time is the same as the BIND_TIME column in PLAN_TABLE.
STMT_TYPE	The type of statement being explained. Possible values: SELECT SELECT INSERT INSERT UPDATE UPDATE DELETE DELETE SELUPD SELECT with FOR UPDATE OF DELCUR DELETE WHERE CURRENT OF CURSOR UPDCUR UPDATE WHERE CURRENT OF CURSOR
COST_CATEGORY	Indicates whether DB2 was forced to use default values when making its estimates. Possible values: A DB2 had enough information to make a cost estimate without using default values. B A condition exists for which DB2 was forced to use default values. See the values in REASON to determine why DB2 was unable to put this estimate in cost category A.
PROCMS	The estimated processor cost in milliseconds for the SQL statement. The estimate is rounded up to the next integer value. The maximum value for this cost is 2,147,483,647 milliseconds, which is equivalent to approximately 24.8 days. If the estimated value exceeds this maximum, the maximum value is reported.

continues

Table 17-2 DSN_STATEMNT_TABLE

Column Name	Description
PROCSU	The estimated processor cost in service units for the SQL statement. The estimate is rounded up to the next integer value. The maximum value for this cost is 2,147,483,647 service units. If the estimated value exceeds this maximum, the maximum value is reported.
REASON	A string indicating the reasons for putting an estimate into cost category B. HAVING clause: A subselect in the SQL statement contains a HAVING clause. HOST VARIABLES: The statement uses host variables, parameter markers, or special registers. REFERENTIAL CONSTRAINTS: Referential constraints of the type CASCADE or SET NULL exist on the target table of a DELETE statement. TABLE CARDINALITY: The cardinality statistics are missing for one or more of the tables used in the statement. Or the statement required the materialization of views or nested table expression. UDF: The statement uses user-defined functions. TRIGGERS: Triggers are defined on the target table of an INSERT, UPDATE, or DELETE statement.
STMT_ENCODE	The encoding scheme of the statement. If it represents a single CCSID set, possible values are A ASCII E EBCDIC U Unicode If the statement has multiple CCSID sets, the value is M.

Table 17-3 DSN_FUNCTION_TABLE

Column Name	Description
QUERYNO	A number identifying the statement being explained. If QUERYNO is not unique, the value of EXPLAIN_TIME is unique.
APPLNAME	The name of the application plan for the row, or blank.
PROGNAME	The name of the program or package containing the statement being explained, or blank.
COLLID	The collection ID for the package, or blank.
GROUP_MEMBER	The DB2 member name that executed EXPLAIN, or blank.
EXPLAIN_TIME	The time at which the statement is processed. This time is the same as the BIND_TIME column in PLAN_TABLE.

Table 17-3 `DSN_FUNCTION_TABLE` (Continued)

Column Name	Description
SCHEMA_NAME	The schema name of the function invoked in the explained statement.
FUNCTION_NAME	The name of the function invoked in the explained statement.
SPEC_FUNC_ID	The specific name of the function invoked in the explained statement.
FUNCTION_TYPE	The type of function invoked in the explained statement. Possible values: SU Scalar function TU Table function
VIEW_CREATOR	If the function specified in the FUNCTION_NAME column is referenced in a view definition, the creator of the view; otherwise, blank.
VIEW_NAME	If the function specified in the FUNCTION_NAME column is referenced in a view definition, the name of the view; otherwise, blank.
PATH	The value of the SQL path that was used to resolve the schema name of the function.
FUNCTION_TEXT	The text of the function reference: more than the function name and parameters. If the function reference is more than 1,500 bytes, this column contains the first 1,500 bytes. For functions specified in fixed notation, FUNCTION_TEXT contains only the function name. For example, for a function named /, which overloads the SQL divide operator, if the function reference is A/B, FUNCTION_TEXT contains only /, not A/B.

Access Path Hints

DB2 provides a facility for telling it how to process a query. This is done by giving DB2 *hints*. The process of giving hints to DB2 is relatively simple, but determining what those hints should be is not. Giving optimization hints to DB2 is useful in the following situations:

- To ensure consistency of response times across rebinds and across release migrations or maintenance releases
- To temporarily bypass the access path chosen by DB2

The facility for implementing access-path hints requires many tasks to be performed, as well as making sure that the subsystem has been enabled for hints. Some of the items that will be affected by using hints are

- Modifying the SQL to use the hint
- Updating a PLAN_TABLE with the correct access-path information or using an existing one
- Changing the bind options for those affected

Even after a hint has been established, it is not always possible for the optimizer to use it. As part of the normal bind process, the optimizer will have to evaluate the hint and determine whether it is valid. Processes will have to be in place to make sure that rebinds do not change the process. For this reason, hints should not be used unless all else fails in establishing an acceptable access path.

Using Statistics to Model a Production Environment

The optimizer uses statistics in the catalog in calculating the costs of SQL to determine the best access path to pick. In building a test environment, it is often helpful to copy statistics from a production environment or to update the statistics to an approximation of what production might be like. Table 17-4 lists the catalog statistics that can be updated and are used by the optimizer in access-path selection.

Table 17-4 Catalog Statistics

Table	Statistics
SYSIBM.SYSCOLDIST	CARDF COLGROUPCOLNO COLVALUE FREQUENCYF NUMCOLUMNS TYPE
SYSIBM.SYSCOLUMNS	COLCARDF HIGH2KEY LOW2KEY
SYSIBM.SYSINDEXES	CLUSTERRATIOF FIRSTKEYCARDF FULLKEYCARDF NLEAF NLEVELS
SYSIBM.SYSROUTINES	CARDINALITY INITIAL_INSTS INITIAL_IOS INSTS_PER_INVOC IOS_PER_INVOC
SYSIBM.SYSTABLES	CARDF NPAGES NPAGESF PCTROWCOMP

Table 17-4   Catalog Statistics (Continued)

Table	Statistics
SYSIBM.SYSTABLESPACE	NACTIVE
SYSIBM.SYSTABSTATS	CARDF NPAGES

Guidelines for Using Explain Output

Analyzing the Explain data can help you to tune your queries and environment in a number of ways. For example, *are indexes being used?* Creating appropriate indexes can have a significant positive impact on performance. You can use the Explain output to determine whether the indexes you have created to help a specific set of queries are being used. In the Explain output, you should look for index usage in the following areas:

- Join predicates
- Local predicates
- GROUP BY clauses
- ORDER BY clauses
- The select list

You can also use Explain to evaluate whether a different index can be used instead of an existing index or no index at all. After creating a new index, collect statistics for that index, using the RUNSTATS utility, and rebind the query.

> **N O T E**   Collecting additional statistics, including statistics on non-key columns, can enhance the optimizer's access-path selection for queries involving joins.

Over time, you may notice, through the Explain data, that instead of an index scan, a table scan is now being used. This can result from a change in the clustering of the table data. If the index that was previously being used now has a low cluster ratio, you want to do the following.

- Reorganize your table to cluster the data according to that index.
- Use the RUNSTATS utility to update the catalog statistics.
- Rebind the query.
- Reexamine the Explain output to determine whether reorganizing the table has affected the access plan.

> **N O T E**   The more indexes that are created, the more importance
> is placed on accurate and detailed statistics. DB2 uses these statistics
> to differentiate among the indexes for access-path selection.
> Increasing the number of indexes increases the potential access paths
> that DB2 must evaluate. This may lead to a less efficient access path
> being selected if statistics do not adequately distinguish each index
> for DB2.

Is the type of access appropriate for the application? You can analyze the Explain output and look for types of data access that, as a rule, are not optimal for the type of application being executed. For example, OLTP applications are prime candidates to use matching-index scans with range-delimiting predicates; these applications tend to return only a few rows in their queries, using an equality predicate against a key column. If your OLTP queries are using a table scan, nonmatching-index scan, or filtering on too few columns, you may want to analyze the Explain data and index statistics to determine why a matching-index scan was not used.

Similarly, the search criteria for a *read-only* query may be vague, causing a large number of rows to qualify. A user who usually looks at only a few screens of the output data may want to try to ensure that the entire answer set need not be computed before some results are returned. In this case, the goals of the user are different from the basic operating principle of the optimizer, which attempts to minimize resource consumption for the entire query, not just the first few screens of data.

For example, if the Explain output shows that both merge-scan join and sort operators were used in the access plan, the entire answer set will be materialized in a temporary table before any rows are returned to the application. In this case, you can attempt to change the access plan by using the `OPTIMIZE FOR` clause on the `SELECT` statement. The value specified for the `OPTIMIZE` clause should represent the number of rows to be processed by the application. In this way, the optimizer can attempt to choose an access plan that does not produce the entire answer set in a temporary table before returning the first rows to the application.

Visual Explain is a GUI utility that enables the database administrator or application developer to examine the access plan determined by the optimizer. The utility provides

- An easy-to-understand display of a selected access path
- Suggestions for changing an SQL statement
- An ability to invoke `EXPLAIN` for dynamic SQL statements
- An ability to provide DB2 catalog statistics for referenced objects of an access path
- A subsystem parameter browser with keyword find capabilities
- Single predicate filter factor estimates

- Whether a predicate is sargable (stage 1 or stage 2)
- Estimated number of rows at different stages in the query
- Time of predicate application
- Index filter factor estimates
- Parallelism details
- Sort key and sort data length

Visual Explain can be used to analyze previously generated Explains or to gather Explain data and Explain dynamic SQL statements. It will also allow you to generate reports and have the analysis output saved as an XML document.

DESIGNING INDEXES AND SQL FOR PERFORMANCE

Indexes provide various access paths. You need to ensure that indexes are in place to provide the best access path possible for all critical queries.

Indexes for Efficient Access

DB2 uses the following index access paths:

- Matching-index scan (`MATCHCOLS > 0`)
- Index screening
- Nonmatching-index scan (`ACCESSTYPE = I` and `MATCHCOLS = 0`)
- `IN`-list index scan (`ACCESSTYPE = N`)
- Multiple-index access (`ACCESSTYPE` is M, MX, MI, or MU)
- One-fetch access (`ACCESSTYPE = I1`)
- Index-only access (`INDEXONLY = Y`)
- Equal unique index (`MATCHCOLS = ` number of index columns)

Matching-index scan (MATCHCOLS > 0)

In a *matching-index scan,* predicates are specified on either the leading index-key columns or all of them. These predicates provide *filtering*; only specific index pages and data pages need to be accessed. If the degree of filtering, or cardinality, is high, the matching-index scan is efficient.

Index-matching predicates are applied in the sequence of the index columns. Therefore, coding sequence is not important for index-matching predicates. DB2 evaluates WHERE clause predicates, based on the following sequence:

1. Indexed predicates: (a) matching predicates and (b) index-screening predicates
2. Stage 1 predicates
3. Stage 2 predicates

Excluding index-matching predicates, within each stage—screening, stage 1, or stage 2—predicates are generally applied in the following sequence:

1. All equal predicates (and IS NULL)
2. All range predicates (and IS NOT NULL)
3. All other predicates

The final rule for predicate evaluation dictates that within each of the preceding guidelines, predicates are evaluated in the sequence they are coded. This gives some control: therefore, the programmer should code the most restrictive predicates first.

For more information on stage 1 and stage 2 predicates, refer to Chapter 4.

Index Screening

In *index screening*, predicates are specified on index-key columns but are not part of the matching columns. Those predicates improve subsequent data page access by reducing the number of rows that qualify while searching the index. For example, with an index on T (C1, C2, C3, C4) in the following SQL statement, C3 > 0 and C4 = 2 are index-screening predicates, whereas C1 = 1 is a matching-index predicate:

```
SELECT *FROM T
WHERE C1 =1
AND C3 >0 AND C4 =2
AND C5 =8;
```

Nonmatching-Index Scan (ACCESSTYPE = I and MATCHCOLS = 0)

In a *nonmatching-index scan,* no matching columns are in the index. Hence, all the index keys must be examined. Because a nonmatching-index scan usually does not provide strong filtering, only a few cases provide an efficient access path if subsequent data pages must also be accessed. If the access path is index-only, a nonmatching-index scan may prove beneficial, especially if the index is smaller than the table space.

> **N O T E** An index-only nonmatching-index scan may not always be more efficient than a table space scan. A table space may be smaller than an index if the number of index keys is large or the table space is compressed. Also, assuming that both are of similar size, an index scan may be less efficient because the scan must follow the leaf page pointer chain, which may not be sequential, owing to index page splits.

IN-list index scan (ACCESSTYPE = N)

An *IN-list index scan* is a special case of the matching-index scan; a single indexable IN predicate is used as a matching-equal predicate. You can regard the IN-list index scan as a series of matching-index scans with the values in the IN predicate being used for each matching-index scan. The following example has an index on (C1, C2, C3, C4) and might use an IN-list index scan:

```
SELECT *FROM T
WHERE C1=1 AND C2 IN (1,2,3)
AND C3>0 AND C4<100;
```

This example could result in an ACCESSTYPE = N and MATCHCOLS = 3 (C1, C2, C3). C4 would be an index-screening predicate.

> **NOTE** At most, one IN predicate can be a matching predicate; the exception, however, is a noncorrelated IN subquery. IN-list predicates cannot be matching predicates for MX access or list prefetch.

Multiple-index access (ACCESSTYPE is M, MX, MI, or MU)

Multiple-index access uses more than one index to access a table. It is a good access path when no single index provides efficient access and/or a combination of index accesses does provide efficient access.

RID lists are constructed for each of the indexes involved. The unions (OR conditions) or intersections (AND conditions) of the RID lists produce a final list of qualified RIDs; this list is used to retrieve the result rows, using list prefetch. You can consider multiple-index access as an extension to list prefetch, with more complex RID-retrieval operations in its first phase. The complex operators are union and intersection. DB2 may choose multiple-index access for the following query:

```
SELECT * FROM EMP
WHERE (AGE=34) OR
(JOB='MANAGER');
```

For this query:

- EMP is a table with columns EMPNO, EMPNAME, DEPT, JOB, AGE, and SAL.
- EMPX1 is an index on EMP with key column AGE.
- EMPX2 is an index on EMP with key column JOB.

One-fetch access (ACCESSTYPE = II)

One-fetch index access requires retrieving only one row. It is the best possible access path and is chosen whenever it is available. It applies to a statement with a MIN or MAX column function: The order of the index allows a single row to give the result of the function. Either an ascending or a descending index can be used to satisfy a MIN or MAX function using one-fetch index access.

Index-only access (INDEXONLY = Y)

With *index-only access,* the access path does not require any data pages, because the access information is available in the index. Conversely, when an SQL statement requests a column that is not in the index, updates any column in the table, or deletes a row, DB2 has to access the associated data pages. Because the index is generally smaller than the table itself, an index-only access path usually processes the data efficiently.

> **N O T E**   The number of levels of the index can determine whether index-only access will be chosen instead of index and data access via a different index. Assume that IX1 has four levels and provides an index-only access path and that IX2 has three levels and is not index-only. DB2 may choose IX2 and access the data pages, as both access paths result in four I/Os.

Equal Unique Index (MATCHCOLS = Number of Index Columns)

An index that is fully matched and unique and in which all matching predicates are equal predicates is called an *equal unique index* case. This case guarantees that only one row is retrieved. If no one-fetch index access is available, this is considered the most efficient access over all other indexes that are not equal unique. (The uniqueness of an index is determined by whether it was defined as unique.) Sometimes, DB2 can determine that an index that is not fully matching is an equal unique index case. This is based on the existence of another unique index with a subset of the key columns.

Indexes to Help Avoid Sorts

As well as providing selective access to data, indexes can order data, sometimes eliminating the need for sorting. Some sorts can be avoided if index keys are in the order needed by ORDER BY, GROUP BY, a join operation, or DISTINCT in a column function. A DISTINCT sort can also be avoided if a unique index exists on the selected columns and/or WHERE clause columns. In other cases, as when list prefetch is used, the index does not provide useful ordering, and the selected data might have to be sorted.

When it is absolutely necessary to prevent a sort, consider creating an index on the column or columns necessary to provide that ordering. Consider also using the clause OPTIMIZE FOR 1 ROW to discourage DB2 from choosing a sort for the access path. Consider the following query:

```
SELECT C1,C2,C3 FROM T
WHERE C1 >1
ORDER BY C1 OPTIMIZE FOR 1 ROW;
```

An ascending index on C1 or an index on (C1, C2, C3) could eliminate a sort.

> **N O T E**   The OPTIMIZE FOR 1 ROW has implications other than
> avoiding a sort and therefore should be used only when necessary.
> Consider specifying a value that represents the number of rows that
> are required to be processed by the application.

Not all sorts are inefficient. For example, if the index that provides ordering is not an efficient one and many rows qualify, using another access path to retrieve and then sort the data might be more efficient than the inefficient, ordering index.

As of version 8, DB2 can backward scan an index and avoid a sort on queries that can use this. This backward scan will work if the index is the exact opposite of the queries. DB2 will be able to avoid a sort in both of the following examples:

```
Index: COL1 ASC, COL2 DESC

SELECT COL1, COL2
FROM T
ORDER BY COL1 ASC, COL2 DESC

SELECT COL1, COL2
FROM T
ORDER BY COL1 DESC, COL2 ASC
```

Dynamic SQL

Dynamic SQL performance is critical for many applications but a bit more difficult to guarantee and tune. A few items can help you get the best performance for dynamic SQL:

- Reorganize the DB2 catalog
- Reorganize the application table space and indexes
- Use dynamic statement caching
- SET CURRENT DEGREE = 'ANY' to attempt parallelism

The dynamic SQL cache is important to the performance of dynamic SQL so that the statements do not have to be reprepared. For more information on monitoring and tuning the dynamic SQL cache, refer to Chapter 18. In order to pick up new statistics for objects used in the dynamic SQL, the dynamic SQL cache needs to be refreshed. This is done by executing RUNSTATS on the objects on which the query is dependent. This can also be done by using RUNSTATS NONE REPORT NO if you wish not to update catalog statistics or report on changes.

Query Parallelism

In order to reduce elapsed time for a query, DB2 can provide a query with parallel resources, such as several I/O paths or processors. By taking advantage of these resources, queries can run in a shorter period of time, allowing more work to be pushed through the system. Parallelism can help improve the performance of I/O and CPU-bound read-only queries and can help queries that are reading large amounts of data, regardless of the filtration.

Some overhead is associated with the use of parallelism in terms of CPU. DB2 scales processor-intensive work across all available processors. Parallelism can average less than 1 percent additional CPU overhead for long-running queries and less than 10 percent for short-running queries.

I/O and CPU Parallelism (PARALLELISM_MODE = I or O)

DB2 can use two methods for achieving query parallelism: I/O or CPU. With I/O parallelism, the goal is to move elapsed time toward CPU time by splitting data access into equal, sequential prefetch streams to bring I/O time down to estimated CPU time. If CPU is estimated at 1 second, and I/O at 3 seconds, the three I/O parallel streams of approximately equal size will be started. Each I/O stream should cost about 1 second. This is implemented with a round-robin type of GET paging. With current releases of DB2, I/O parallelism is infrequently chosen; the preferred method is CPU parallelism.

DB2 splits queries into equal multiple smaller queries and processing those queries in multiple execution units, or parallel tasks. At execution time, DB2 will take into consideration the number of CPUs available; if not enough CPUs are available to support the degree of parallelism initially chosen by the optimizer, the degree will be degraded.

DB2 parallelism is decided at both bind time and runtime. If parallelism is not chosen at bind time, it cannot be chosen at runtime. Even if it is chosen at bind time, parallelism may not be used at runtime, owing to several factors. If not enough space is in the virtual buffer pool to support the requested degree of parallelism, the degree can be reduced from that chosen at bind time, or parallelism can be turned of altogether. If host variables are used in the SQL query, DB2 may be prevented from determining which partitions will qualify in a query; therefore, the degree chosen for parallelism will be decided at runtime. If DB2 determines that an ambiguous cursor can be updated, parallelism will be disabled. If parallelism is disabled, the query does not fail; DB2 simply uses a sequential plan for access to the data.

During BIND or PREPARE, DB2 chooses the access path best suited for the query and then does a postoptimization step to identify the sections of the access path that will benefit most from parallelism. DB2 then identifies the part of the query that can be executed in parallel and determines the degree of parallelism to be used.

Queries Best Suited for Parallelism

Queries with the following characteristics will be able to take advantage of parallelism:

- Long-running, read-only queries, both static and dynamic SQL, from both local and remote sites, and when using either private or DRDA protocols
- Table space scans and index scans
- Joins
- Nested loops
- Merge scans
- Hybrid, without sort on new tables
- Sorts
- Aggregate functions

Parallelism will not be considered in only a few places:

- Queries that materialize views
- Queries that perform materialization because of nested table expressions
- Queries performing a merge-scan join of more than one column
- Queries using direct row access

The following will cause only sysplex parallelism not to be considered:

- Queries with list prefetch and multiple index access
- Queries accessing LOB data

Parallelism should not be used if a system is already CPU constrained, because parallelism would only add to the problem in most situations. CPU parallelism cannot be used when a cursor is defined WITH HOLD, as this cursor's use is potentially interrupted by a commit, which causes a stoppage in processing.

Short-running queries are usually not going to see a great benefit from parallelism. (Generally, a short-running query is one that is subsecond.) But how often are long-running queries separated from short-running queries? If you are trying to get the benefits from parallelism without placing unnecessary overhead where it does not belong, you will need to consider this type of granularity of processing.

You have two potential options: You could separate the long-running queries into a separate package and bind it DEGREE(ANY) in a different collection and then use the SET CURRENT-PACKAGESET statement to switch between it and a program bound with DEGREE(1) for shorter queries that are better to let run sequentially. Or you could set the macro SPRMPTH to disable parallelism for short-running queries. The default for this value is 120; thus, any query with an estimated cost of less than 120 milliseconds will have parallelism disabled. Parallelism is enabled for any query above this threshold.

Sysplex Query Parallelism (PARALLELISM_MODE = X)

Sysplex query parallelism works in much the same multitasking way as CPU parallelism and also enables you to take a complex query and run across multiple members in a data sharing group. Sysplex query parallelism is best used with isolation-level UR (uncommitted read) to avoid excess lock propagation.

A query is issued by a coordinator, who sends the query to the assistant members in the group. The data is then processed and returned to the coordinator either by a work file—the coordinator will read each assistant's work files—or by Cross-System Coupling Facility (XCF) links when a work file is not necessary.

SUMMARY

Understanding the DB2 database environment is an important part of any database administrator's job. Various facilities can be used to gain this understanding. Database activity can be analyzed in several ways. Graphical monitoring tools, such as DB2PM and Visual Explain, can be used with DB2 Universal Database.

The DB2 optimizer is one of the most advanced in the relational database industry. The optimizer generates an access plan during query compilation. Access paths are stored in the system catalog tables for static SQL applications. Access paths for dynamic SQL statements are generated at query execution time and are stored in memory.

To gain an understanding of the access path, or strategy, chosen by the DB2 optimizer, the Explain utility can be used. Explain populates a PLAN_TABLE and optional DSN tables with detailed information for the SQL statements. These tables can then be queried to determine the plan information about index use and other database resources. This graphical version of the access path can be examined by using Visual Explain. The ability to determine whether an SQL access path is appropriate is critical to the best performance for DB2 queries.

ADDITIONAL RESOURCES

IBM DB2 Version 8 UDB for z/OS Command Reference Guide (SC26-9934)

IBM DB2 Version 8 UDB for z/OS Administration Guide (SC26-9931)

IBM DB2 Version 8 UDB for z/OS Application and SQL Guide (SC26-9933)

IBM DB2 PM Version 8 for z/OS General Information (GC26-9172)

IBM DB2 Version 8 UDB for z/OS Utility Guide and Reference (SC18-7427)

IBM DB2 for z/OS and OS/390: Squeezing the Most out of Dynamic SQL (SG24-6418)

CHAPTER **18**

DB2 Monitoring and Tuning

- Overview of performance and tuning
- Database monitoring
- Memory tuning
- Problem determination

Understanding the performance of the DB2 database management system, its databases, and active applications in a dynamic environment requires monitoring. This means that a database administrator should gather information about the use of the database. An application programmer may also require information about SQL statement execution. This chapter discusses gathering database information by using DB2's monitoring facilities and information about SQL statement processing.

The various DB2 facilities for monitoring and gathering information that is input into the tuning process are reviewed, along with the Explain process, trace, commands, and other tools used to monitor DB2 database objects and SQL statements. These tools may be used to perform the following tasks:

- Understand user and application activity within DB2
- Better understand how an SQL statement is processed
- Determine the sources and causes of problems
- Tune buffer pool and system parameters
- Improve database and application performance

OVERVIEW OF PERFORMANCE AND TUNING

Performance is the way a computer system behaves given a particular workload. Performance is measured through the system's response time, throughput, and availability and is affected by the resources available and how well the resources are used.

Performance tuning should be undertaken when you want to improve the cost-benefit ratio of your system. Specific situations include the following.

- You want to process a larger, more demanding workload without increasing processing costs that may include having to acquire additional hardware.
- You want to obtain faster system response time or higher throughput without increasing processing costs.
- You want to reduce processing costs without negatively affecting service to the client(s).

Translating performance from technical terms to economic terms is difficult. Performance tuning costs money through labor and machine resources, so the cost of tuning must be weighed against the benefits tuning may or may not deliver. Some of these benefits, including less resource use and the ability to add more users to the system, are tangible; other benefits, such as increased customer satisfaction, are less tangible from a monetary perspective.

Tuning Guidelines

The following guidelines should be considered in developing an overall approach to performance tuning.

- **Remember the law of diminishing returns.** Your greatest performance benefits usually come from your initial efforts. Further changes generally produce smaller and smaller benefits and require greater effort.
- **Do not tune just for the sake of tuning.** Tune to relieve identified constraints. Tuning resources that are not the primary cause of performance problems can have little or no effect on response time until you have relieved the major constraints, and it can make subsequent tuning work more difficult. Any significant improvement potential lies in improving the performance of the resources that are major factors in the response time.
- **Consider the whole system.** You can never tune one parameter or system in isolation. Before you make any adjustments, consider how it will affect the system as a whole.
- **Change one parameter at a time.** Do not change more than one performance-tuning parameter at a time. Even if you are sure that all the changes will be beneficial, you will have no way of evaluating how much each change has contributed. You also cannot effectively judge the tradeoff you have made by changing more than one parameter at a time. Every time you adjust a parameter to improve one area, you almost always affect at least one other area that may not have been considered.

- **Measure and reconfigure by levels.** For the same reasons that you should change only one parameter at a time, tune one level of your system at a time: hardware, operating system, application server and requester, database, SQL statements, and application programs.
- **Check for hardware and software problems.** Some performance problems may be corrected by applying service to your hardware, your software, or both. Do not spend excessive time monitoring and tuning your system if simply applying service may be the solution to the problem.
- **Understand the problem before upgrading hardware.** Even if it seems that an additional storage or processor resource could immediately improve performance, take the time to understand where the bottlenecks are. You may spend money on additional disk storage only to find that you do not have the processor resources to exploit it.
- **Put fallback procedures in place before you start tuning.** Because changes are being made to an existing system, you must be prepared to back out those changes if they do not have the desired effect or have a negative effect on the system.

> **NOTE** It is important to take into consideration the cost of detailed performance analysis—running traces—and the time needed to perform the analysis, because the process of detailed performance analysis can be costly.

Performance-Improvement Process

Monitoring and tuning a database and its applications should be performed using the following basic process.

1. Establish performance indicators.
2. Define performance objectives.
3. Develop a performance-monitoring plan.
4. Implement the plan.
5. Analyze the measurements. Determine whether the objectives have been met. If so, consider reducing the number of measurements to keep to a minimum the amount of resources consumed for monitoring.
6. Determine the major constraints in the system.
7. Decide where you can afford to make tradeoffs and which resources can bear an additional load. Most tuning activities involve tradeoffs among system resources and various elements of performance.
8. Adjust the configuration of the system. If you think that it is feasible to change more than one tuning option, implement one at a time.
9. Based on the results, start another iteration of the monitoring cycle.

You may want to follow this process for periodic monitoring or when significant changes occur to the system, to the workload taken on by the system, or to both.

Scope of System Tuning

There are limits to how much you can improve the efficiency of a system. Consider how much time and money you should spend on improving system performance and how much the spending of additional time and money will help the users of the system.

Your system may perform adequately without any tuning at all, but it probably will not perform to its potential. Each database is unique. As soon as you develop your own database and applications for it, investigate the tuning parameters available and learn how you can customize their settings to reflect your situation. In some circumstances, tuning a system will yield only a small benefit. In most circumstances, however, the benefit may be significant.

If your system encounters performance bottlenecks, tuning will probably be effective. If you are close to the performance limits and you increase the number of users on the system by about 10 percent, the response time may rise by much more than 10 percent. In this situation, you will need to determine how to counterbalance this degradation in performance by tuning your system. However, there is a point beyond which tuning cannot help. At that point, you should consider revising your goals and expectations within that environment. Or you should change your system environment by considering more disk storage, faster or additional processors, additional memory, or faster networking solutions.

If you do not have enough time to set performance objectives and to monitor and tune in a comprehensive manner, you can address performance by listening to your users. Find out whether they are having performance-related problems. You can usually locate the problem or determine where to start looking for the problem by asking a few simple questions.

- What do you mean by slow response? Is it 10 *percent* slower or 10 *times* slower than you expect it to be?
- When did you notice the problem? Is it recent, or has it always been there?
- Do you know of other users who are complaining of the same problem? Are one or two individuals or a whole group complaining?
- Are the problems you are experiencing related to a specific transaction or application program?
- Do your problems appear during regular periods, such as at lunch hour, or are they continuous?

DATABASE MONITORING

Database monitoring should be an ongoing, proactive process. Specialized monitoring software and traces can be used to monitor DB2.

DB2 Performance Monitor and Omegamon

IBM's DB2 Performance Monitor (PM) and Omegamon for DB2 are both analysis tools for the subsystem and applications. Their primary objective is to report DB2 instrumentation data in a form that is easy to understand and analyze. Both products present this instrumentation data in the following ways.

- The batch reports present the data you select in comprehensive reports or graphs containing systemwide and application-related information for both single DB2 subsystems and DB2 members of a data sharing group. You can combine instrumentation data from several DB2 locations into one report. Batch reports can be used to examine performance problems and trends over a period of time.
- The online monitor gives a current snapshot view of a running DB2 subsystem, including applications that are running. Its history function displays information about subsystem and application activity in the recent past.
- The statistics reports provide an excellent source of information, such as buffer pools, EDM pools, RID processing, and logging, all at a subsystem level.
- The accounting reports provide information about applications for specific time periods. Those are the most popular, most useful reports for ongoing analysis, trend analysis, and predictive monitoring.

More detailed reports, such as the lock detail analysis report for monitoring locking problems, require additional traces to be turned on and should be used only for problem analysis, not run on a continual basis. Both accounting and statistics reports have long and short versions. Which is used depends on the amount of detail needed for analysis. PM also includes user-tailored reports (UTRs) that allow you to tailor reports for more precise analysis.

> **N O T E**   The DB2 PM product and Omegamon for DB2 will soon be merged into one product solution.

Resource Limit Facility

DB2's resource limit facility, or governor, lets you perform the following activities:

- Set warning and error thresholds by which the governor can inform users, via your application programs, that a certain processing limit might be exceeded for a particular dynamic SELECT, INSERT, UPDATE, or DELETE statement. This is called *predictive governing*.
- Stop a currently executing dynamic SQL statement (SELECT, INSERT, UPDATE, or DELETE) that exceeds the processor limit that you have specified for that statement. This is sometimes called *reactive governing* to differentiate its function from that of predictive governing, a function that also is handled by the resource limit facility. The resource limit facility does not control static SQL statements, whether or not they are executed locally or remotely.
- Restrict bind and rebind activities to avoid performance impacts on production data.
- Restrict particular parallelism modes for *dynamic* queries.

USING TRACES TO SOLVE PROBLEMS IN DB2

DB2 Traces

DB2 traces allow you to trace and record subsystem data and events and determine problems:

- DB2 trace
- IMS attachment facility trace
- CICS trace
- Three TSO attachment facility traces
- CAF trace stream
- z/OS RRS trace stream
- MVS component trace used for IRLM

Five different types of traces exist, and DB2 traces can record six types of data: statistics, accounting, performance, audit, monitor, and global. The tables later in this chapter indicate which Instrumentation Facility IDs (IFCIDs) are activated for the various types of traces, the classes within those trace types, and the information each IFCID returns. The trace records are written using Generalized Trace Facility (GTF) or System Management Facility (SMF) records. We now take a look at the types of data DB2 collects for each trace class.

Trace Classes

Statistics. The data collected in the statistics trace allows you to conduct DB2 capacity planning and to tune the entire set of DB2 programs. The statistics trace reports information about how much the DB2 system services and database services are used. This systemwide trace should not be used for charge-back accounting. Use the information the statistics trace provides to plan DB2 capacity or to tune the entire set of active DB2 programs.

Statistics trace classes 1, 3, 4, and 5 are the default classes for the statistics trace if YES is specified in panel DSNTIPN. If the statistics trace is started using the START TRACE command, class 1 is the default class.

- Class 1 provides information about system services and database statistics. It also includes the system parameters that were in effect when the trace was started.
- Class 3 provides information about deadlocks and timeouts.
- Class 4 provides information about exceptional conditions.
- Class 5 provides information about data sharing.

If you specified YES in the SMF STATISTICS field on the tracing panel (DSNTIPN), the statistics trace starts automatically when you start DB2, sending class 1, 3, 4, and 5 statistics data to SMF. SMF records statistics data in both SMF type 100 and type 102 records. IFCIDs 0001, 0002, 0202, and 0230 are of SMF type 100. All other IFCIDs in statistics trace classes are of SMF type 102. From panel DSNTIPN, you can also control the statistics collection interval (STATISTICS TIME field). The statistics trace is written on an interval basis, and you can control the exact time that statistics traces are taken.

Accounting. The accounting trace provides data that allows you to assign DB2 costs to individual authorization IDs and to tune individual programs. The DB2 accounting trace provides information related to application programs, including such things as

- Start and stop times
- Number of commits and aborts
- Number of times certain SQL statements are issued
- Number of buffer pool requests
- Counts of certain locking events
- Processor resources consumed
- Thread wait times for various events
- RID pool processing
- Distributed processing
- Resource limit facility statistics

Accounting times are usually the prime indicator of performance problems, and most often should be the starting point for analysis. DB2 times are classified as follows.

- Class 1 shows the time the application spent since connecting to DB2, including time spent outside DB2.
- Class 2 shows the elapsed time spent in DB2. This time is divided into CPU time and waiting time.
- Class 3, elapsed time, is divided into various waits, such as the duration of suspensions owing to waits for locks and latches or waits for I/O.

DB2 trace begins collecting this data at successful thread allocations to DB2 and writes a completed record when the thread terminates or when the authorization ID changes. Accounting data for class 1, the default, is accumulated by several DB2 components during normal execution. This data, collected at the end of the accounting period, does not involve as much overhead as individual event tracing.

On the other hand, when you start class 2, 3, 7, or 8, many additional trace points are activated. Every occurrence of these events is traced internally by DB2 trace, but these traces are not written to any external destination. Rather, the accounting facility uses these traces to compute the additional total statistics that appear in the accounting record, IFCID 003, when class 2 or class 3 is activated. Accounting class 1 must be active to externalize the information.

To turn on accounting for packages and DBRMs, accounting trace classes 1 and 7 must be active. Although you can turn on class 7 while a plan is being executed, accounting trace information is gathered only for packages or DBRMs executed after class 7 is activated. Activate accounting trace class 8 with class 1 to collect information about the amount of time an agent was suspended in DB2 for each executed package. If accounting trace classes 2 and 3 are activated, additional performance cost for activating accounting trace classes 7 and 8 is minimal.

If you want information from either accounting class 2 or 3 or both, be sure to activate classes 2 and/or 3 before your application starts. If these classes are activated during the application, the times gathered by DB2 trace are only from the time the class was activated.

Accounting trace class 5 provides information on the amount of elapsed time and task control block (TCB) time that an agent spent in DB2 processing Instrumentation Facility Interface requests. If an agent did not issue any IFI requests, these fields are not included in the accounting record.

If you specified YES for SMF ACCOUNTING on the tracing panel, the accounting trace starts automatically when you start DB2 and sends IFCIDs that are of SMF type 100 to SMF. The accounting record IFCID 0003 is of SMF type 101.

Performance.   The performance trace provides information about a variety of DB2 events, including events related to distributed data processing. You can use this information to further identify a suspected problem or to tune DB2 programs and resources for individual users or for DB2 as a whole. To trace performance data, you must use the –START TRACE(PERFM) command. Performance traces cannot be automatically started.

Audit.   This trace provides data that can be used to monitor DB2 security and access to data to ensure that data access is allowed only for authorized purposes. On the CREATE TABLE or ALTER TABLE statement, you can specify whether a table is to be audited and in what manner; you can also audit security information, such as any access denials, grants, or revokes for the table. The default causes no auditing to take place. If you specified yes for AUDIT TRACE on the tracing panel, audit trace class 1 starts automatically when you start DB2. By default, DB2 sends audit data to SMF.

Monitor.   The monitor trace records data for online monitoring with user-written programs. This trace type has several predefined classes; the following are used explicitly for monitoring.

- Class 1, the default, allows any application program to issue an IFI READS request to the IFI facility. If monitor class 1 is inactive, a READS request is denied. Activating class 1 has a minimal impact on performance.
- Class 2 collects processor and elapsed-time information. The information can be obtained by issuing a READS request for IFCID 0147 or 0148. In addition, monitor trace class 2 information is available in the accounting record, IFCID 0003. Monitor class 2 is equivalent to accounting class 2 and results in equivalent overhead. Monitor class 2 times appear in IFCIDs 0147, 0148, and 0003 if either monitor trace class 2 or accounting class 2 is active.
- Class 3 activates DB2 wait timing and saves information about the resource causing the wait. The information can be obtained by issuing a READS request for IFCID 0147 or 0148. In addition, monitor trace class 3 information is available in the accounting record, IFCID 0003. As with monitor class 2, monitor class 3 overhead is equivalent to accounting class 3 overhead. When monitor trace class 3 is active, DB2 can calculate the duration of a class 3 event, such as when an agent is suspended because of an unavailable lock. Monitor class 3 times appear in IFCIDs 0147, 0148, and 0003 if either monitor class 3 or accounting class 3 is active.
- Class 5 traces the amount of time spent processing IFI requests.
- Class 7 traces the amount of time an agent spent in DB2 to process each package. If monitor trace class 2 is active, activating class 7 has minimal performance impact.
- Class 8 traces the amount of time an agent was suspended in DB2 for each package executed. If monitor trace class 3 is active, activating class 8 has minimal impact.

Invoking Traces

Traces can be started automatically via the DB2 install panels or can be stopped and started dynamically by using the TRACE commands, as follows.

- START TRACE invokes one or more types of trace.
- DISPLAY TRACE displays the trace options that are in effect.
- STOP TRACE stops any trace that was started by either the START TRACE command or the parameters specified when installing or migrating.
- MODIFY TRACE changes the trace events (IFCIDs) being traced for a specified active trace. Several parameters can be specified to further qualify the scope of a trace. Specific events within a trace type, as well as events within specific DB2 plans, authorization IDs, resource manager IDs, and locations, can be traced. The destination to which trace data is sent can also be controlled.

Trace Classes.   It is important to have the appropriate classes always gathering information about your DB2 subsystem and its activity. It is a general recommendation that you have SMF accounting classes 1, 2, and 3 and SMF statistics classes 1, 3, and 4—1 and 3 at a minimum—selected during normal execution. Any other trace classes should not be run constantly, because they cause excessive overhead if run for long periods of time.

When executing performance traces, it is wise to limit the trace to only the IFCIDs necessary for the appropriate performance analysis or problem diagnosis. These traces also should be run for only short periods of time. Following is an example of limiting a trace.

```
-START TRACE(PERFM) CLASS(8) IFCID(0221) PLANNAME(CERTPLA)
```

This example limits a performance trace to class 8 with IFCID 221, which is used to view the degree of parallelism at runtime.

IFCIDs.   Tables 18-1 through 18-5 show the various IFCIDs that are started for each type of class within a trace.

Table 18-1   Accounting Trace

Class	IFCID	Description
1	3	All accounting
	106	System parameters in effect
	239	Package accounting
2	200	UDF entry/exit signal
	232	DB2 thread entry/exit signal

Table 18-1   Accounting Trace (Continued)

Class	IFCID	Description
3	6	Beginning of a read I/O operation
	7	CC after read I/O operation
	8	Beginning of synchronous write I/O
	9	CC of synchronous or asynchronous write I/O
	32	Beginning of wait for log manager
	33	End of wait for log manager
	44	Lock suspend or identify call IRLM
	45	Lock resume
	51	Shared latch resume; serviceability
	52	Shared latch wait; serviceability
	56	Exclusive latch wait; serviceability
	57	Exclusive latch resume; serviceability
	117	Begin thread wait time for log I/O
	118	End thread wait time for log I/O
	127	Agent ready to suspend page wait
	128	Page requester resumed by I/O initialization
	170	Suspend for synchronous `EXEC.N` unit switch
	171	Resume agent waiting DB2 service task
	174	Begin archive log mode (`QUIESCE`)
	175	End archive log mode (`QUIESCE`)
	213	Beginning of wait for claim request
	214	End of wait for claim request
	215	Beginning of wait for drain request
	216	End of wait for drain request
	226	Beginning of suspend for page latch
	227	End of suspend for page latch
	242	Begin wait for scheduled stored procedure
	243	End wait for scheduled stored procedure
	313	Messages for long-running URs

continues

Table 18-1 Accounting Trace (Continued)

Class	IFCID	Description
4	151	User-defined accounting trace
5	187	Entry to and exit from IFI
7	232	DB2 thread entry/exit signal
	232	For package-level or DBRM-level accounting
	240	Event signal for package accounting
8	6	Beginning of a read I/O operation
	7	CC after read I/O operation
	8	Beginning of synchronous write I/O
	9	CC of sync or async write I/O
	32	Beginning of wait for log manager
	33	End of wait for log manager
	44	Lock suspend or identify call IRLM
	45	Lock resume
	51	Shared latch resume; serviceability
	52	Shared latch wait; serviceability
	56	Exclusive latch wait; serviceability
	57	Exclusive latch resume; serviceability
	117	Begin thread wait time for log I/O
	118	End thread wait time for log I/O
	127	Agent ready to suspend page wait
	128	Page requester resumed by I/O initialization
	170	Suspend for synchronous EXEC.N unit switch
	171	Resume agent waiting DB2 service task
	174	Begin archive log mode (QUIESCE)
	175	End archive log mode (QUIESCE)
	213	Beginning of wait for claim request
	214	End of wait for claim request
	215	Beginning of wait for drain request

Table 18-1   Accounting Trace (Continued)

Class	IFCID	Description
8	216	End of wait for drain request
	226	Beginning of suspend for page latch
	227	End of suspend for page latch
	241	Begin/end suspension of package or DBRM
	242	Begin wait for scheduled stored procedure
	243	End wait for scheduled stored procedure
	329	Asynchronous GBP requests

Table 18-2   Audit Trace

Class	IFCID	Description
1	140	Authorization failures
2	141	Explicit grants and revokes
3	142	Creates, alters, drops audit
4	143	First attempted write-audited object
5	144	First attempted read-audited object
6	145	Audit log record of some SQL statements
7	55	Issuance of SET CURRENT SQLID
	83	End identify request
	87	Ending of sign-on request
	169	Distributed authorization ID translation
	312	Distributed Computing Environment Security
	319	Audit trail for security processing
8	23	Utility start information
	24	Utility object or phase change
	25	Utility end information
	219	Listdef data set information
	220	Utility-output data set information
9	146	User-defined audit trace

Table 18-3   Monitor Trace

Class	IFCID	Description
1	1	System services
	2	Database services
	106	System parameters in effect
	124	Current SQL statement
	129	VSAM CIs—DB2 recover log
	147	Summary-thread status record
	148	Detailed thread status record
	149	Lock information for a resource
	150	Lock information for an agent IFCID
	202	System parameters
	230	Data sharing global statistics
	254	Group buffer pool usage
	306	Log record retrieval
	316	Prepared-statement cache statistics
	317	Prepared-statement cache statement text
2	232	DB2 thread-entry exit signal
3	6	Beginning of a read I/O operation
	7	CC after read I/O operation
	8	Beginning of synchronous write I/O
	9	CC of synchronous or asynchronous write I/O
	32	Beginning of wait for log manager
	33	End of wait for log manager
	44	Lock suspend or identify call IRLM
	45	Lock resume
	51	Shared latch resume; serviceability
	52	Shared latch wait; serviceability
	56	Exclusive latch wait; serviceability
	57	Exclusive latch resume; serviceability
	117	Begin thread wait time for log I/O

Table 18-3　Monitor Trace (Continued)

Class	IFCID	Description
3	118	End thread wait time for log I/O
	127	Agent ready to suspend page wait
	128	Page requester resumed by I/O initialization
	170	Suspend for synchronous EXEC unit switch
	171	Resume agent waiting DB2 service task
	174	Begin archive log mode (QUIESCE)
	175	End archive log mode (QUIESCE)
	213	Beginning of wait for claim request
	214	End of wait for claim request
	215	Beginning of wait for drain request
	216	End of wait for drain request
	226	Beginning of suspend for page latch
	227	End of suspend for page latch
	242	Begin wait for scheduled stored procedure
	243	End wait for scheduled stored procedure
	329	Asynchronous GBP requests
4	155	User-defined monitor trace
5	187	Entry or exit to IFI
6	185	Data-capture information
7	232	DB2 thread entry/exit signal
	232	For package-level or DBRM-level accounting
	240	Event signal for package accounting
8	6	Beginning of a read I/O operation
	7	CC after read I/O operation
	8	Beginning of synchronous write I/O
	9	CC of sync or async write I/O
	32	Begin of wait for log manager
	33	End of wait for log manager
	44	Lock suspend or identify call IRLM

continues

Table 18-3   Monitor Trace (Continued)

Class	IFCID	Description
8	45	Lock resume
	51	Shared latch resume; serviceability
	52	Shared latch wait; serviceability
	56	Exclusive latch wait; serviceability
	57	Exclusive latch resume; serviceability
	117	Begin thread wait time for log I/O
	118	End thread wait time for log I/O
	127	Agent ready to suspend page wait
	128	Page requester resumed by I/O initialization
	170	Suspend for synchronous EXEC unit switch
	171	Resume agent waiting DB2 service task
	174	Begin archive log mode (QUIESCE)
	175	End archive log mode (QUIESCE)
	213	Beginning of wait for claim request
	214	End of wait for claim request
	215	Beginning of wait for drain request
	216	End of wait for drain request
	226	Beginning of suspend for page latch
	227	End of suspend for page latch
	241	Begin/end suspension of package/DBRM
	242	Begin wait for scheduled stored procedure
	243	End wait for scheduled stored procedure

Table 18-4   Performance Trace

Class	IFCID	Description
1	1	System services
	2	Database services
	31	EDM pool-full condition
	42	A checkpoint started

Table 18-4 Performance Trace (Continued)

Class	IFCID	Description
1	43	A checkpoint ended
	76	Beginning of an end-memory request
	77	End of an end-memory request
	78	Beginning of an end-task request
	79	End of an end-task request
	102	Detection of short on storage
	103	Setting off of short on storage
	105	Internal DBID OBID to DB/TS
	106	System parameters in effect
	107	Data set open/close information
	153	User-defined except-condition trace
2	3	All accounting
	68	Beginning of a rollback request
	69	End of a rollback request
	70	Begin commit phase 2 request
	71	End commit phase 2 request
	72	Beginning of create-thread request
	73	End of a create-thread request
	74	Beginning of terminate-thread request
	75	End of a terminate-thread request
	80	Beginning of an establish-exit request
	81	End of an establish exit request
	82	Begin identify request
	83	End identify request
	84	Begin phase 1 commit request
	85	End phase 1 commit request
	86	Beginning of sign-on request
	87	End of sign-on request
	88	Beginning of synchronous request

continues

Table 18-4 Performance Trace (Continued)

Class	IFCID	Description
2	89	Ending of synchronous request
	106	System parameters in effect
	174	Begin archive log mode (QUIESCE)
	175	End archive log mode (QUIESCE)
3	22	Miniplans generated
	53	End of descr, commit, rollback, or error
	55	Issuance of set current SQLID
	58	End of SQL statement execution
	59	Start of FETCH SQL statement execution
	60	Start of SELECT SQL statement execution
	61	Start of INSERT, UPDATE, DELETE SQL
	62	Start of DDL statement execution
	63	SQL statement to be parsed
	64	Start PREPARE SQL statement execution
	65	Start open cursor static or dynamic SQL
	66	Start close cursor static or dynamic SQL
	92	Start access method services
	95	Sort started
	96	Sort ended
	97	Access method services cmd compl
	106	System parameters in effect
	112	Attributes plan after thread allocation
	177	Successful package allocation
	233	Start/end call to user routine
	237	Set current degree information
	272	Associate locators information
	273	Allocate cursor information
	324	Function resolution information

Table 18-4 Performance Trace (Continued)

Class	IFCID	Description
3	325	Start/end trigger activation
	350	Complete SQL statement
4	6	Beginning of a read I/O operation
	7	Completion code after read I/O
	8	Beginning of synchronous write I/O
	9	CC of synchronous or asynchronous write I/O
	10	Beginning of asynchronous write I/O
	29	Start EDM I/O request; load DBD or CT
	30	End of EDM I/O request
	105	Internal DBID OBID to DB/TS
	106	System parameters in effect
	107	Data set open/close information
	127	Agent ready to suspend page wait
	128	Page requester resumed by I/O initialization
	226	Begin of suspend for page latch
	227	End of suspend for page latch
5	32	Begin of wait for log manager
	33	End of wait for log manager
	34	Log manager wait for read I/O begin
	35	Log manager wait for read I/O end
	36	Log manager wait for non-I/O begin
	37	Log manager wait for non-I/O end
	38	Log manager wait active log write begin
	39	Log manager wait active log write I/O end
	40	Log manager archive write I/O begin
	41	Log manager archive write I/O end
	104	Log data set mapping
	106	System parameters in effect

continues

Table 18-4   Performance Trace (Continued)

Class	IFCID	Description
5	114	Start archive read I/O wait
	115	End read archive I/O wait on DASD
	116	End read archive I/O wait on tape
	117	Begin archive read
	118	End archive read
	119	BSDS write I/O beginning
	120	BSDS write I/O end
	228	Start archive allocation wait
	229	End archive allocation wait
6	20	Locking summary
	44	Lock suspend or an ID; call to IRLM
	45	Lock resume
	105	Internal DBID OBID to DB/TS
	106	System parameters in effect
	107	Data set open/close information
	172	Units of work involved in deadlock
	196	Lock timeout details
	213	Beginning of wait for drain lock
	214	End of wait for drain lock
	218	Summary of lock-avoidance technique
	337	Lock escalation occurred
7	21	Detail lock request on return from IRLM
	105	Internal DBID OBID to DB/TS
	106	System parameters in effect
	107	Data set open/close information
	199	Buffer pool data set statistics
	223	Detail of lock-avoidance technique

Table 18-4   Performance Trace (Continued)

Class	IFCID	Description
8	13	Input to hash scan
	14	End of hash scan
	15	Input matching- or nonmatching-index scan
	16	Input to the first insert
	17	Input to sequential scan
	18	End index scan, insert, sequential scan
	105	Internal DBID OBID to DB/TS
	106	System parameters in effect
	107	Data set open/close information
	125	RID list processing usage
	221	Parallel degree for parallel group
	222	Parallel group elapsed time
	231	Parallel group completion
	305	Table-check constraints
	311	Temporary tables
9	26	Work file obtained for sort
	27	Number of ordered records sort run
	28	Detailed sort information
	95	Sort started
	96	Sort ended
	106	System parameters in effect
10	23	Utility start information
	24	Utility object or phase change
	25	Utility end information
	90	Command text of entered DB2 command
	91	Completion status of a DB2 command
	105	Internal DBID OBID to DB/TS

continues

Table 18-4   Performance Trace (Continued)

Class	IFCID	Description
10	106	System parameters in effect
	107	Data set open/close information
	108	Beginning of bind/rebind
	109	End of bind/rebind
	110	Beginning of free plan
	111	End of free plan
	201	Status before/after alter buffer pool
	219	Listdef data set information
	220	Utility-output data set information
	256	Attributes before/after alter buffer pool
11	46	Agent begin execution unit switch
	47	New service request block execution unit started
	48	New service request block execution unit completed
	49	Begin new TCB
	50	End new TCB
	51	Shared-latch resume
	52	Shared-latch wait
	56	Exclusive latch wait
	57	Exclusive latch resume
	93	Suspend was called
	94	Event resumed
	106	System parameters in effect
	113	Attributes plan after agent allocation
12	98	Begin `getmain`/`freemain` (nonpool)
	99	End `getmain`/`freemain` (nonpool)
	100	Begin `getmain`/`freemain` (pool)
	101	End `getmain`/`freemain` (pool)
	106	System parameters in effect
13	11	Results of a validation exit call

Table 18-4   Performance Trace (Continued)

Class	IFCID	Description
13	12	Results edit exit call encode record
	19	Results edit exit call decode a row
	105	Internal DBID OBID to DB/TS
	106	System parameters in effect
	107	Data set open/close information
14	67	Start of accounting collection
	106	System parameters in effect
	121	Entry allocating DB2 connection
	122	Exit allocating DB2 connection
15	154	User-defined routine cond perf
16	157	DRDS interface with RDS RDI call types
	158	DRDS interface with conversation manager
	159	DRDS requesting location data
	160	Requesting agent data
	161	Serving agent data
	162	Distributed transaction manager request agent data
	163	Distributed transaction manager response agent data
	167	Conversation allocation request queued
	183	DRDS RDS/SCC interface data
17	211	Information about claims
	212	Information about drains
	213	Beginning of wait for drain lock
	214	End of wait for drain lock
	215	Beginning of wait of claim count to 0
	216	End of claim count to go to 0
20	249	EDM pool DBD invalidation
	250	Group buffer pool continued/discontinued
	251	P-lock operations
	256	Alter buffer pool command

continues

Table 18-4   Performance Trace (Continued)

Class	IFCID	Description
20	257	Details of IRLM notify request
	261	Group buffer pool checkpoint
	262	Group buffer pool cast-out threshold processing
	267	Begin CF structure rebuild/expand/contract
	268	End CF structure rebuild/expand/contract
	329	Asynchronous GBP request
21	255	Buffer refresh due to XI
	259	P-lock request/negotiation request
	263	Page set and partition cast-out data
	314	Authorization exit parameters
	327	Language environment runtime information

Table 18-5   Statistics Trace

Class	IFCID	Description
1	1	System services
	2	Database services
	105	Internal DBID OBID to DB/TS
	106	System parameters in effect
	202	Buffer pool attributes
2	152	User-defined statistics trace
3	172	Units of work involved in deadlock
	196	Lock timeout details
	250	Connect/disconnect from GBP
	258	Data set extend information
	330	Active log shortage
	335	Stalled system event notification
	337	Lock escalation occurred
4	191	Data capture for DDIS errors
	192	DDM-level 6a header errors

Table 18-5   Statistics Trace (Continued)

Class	IFCID	Description
4	193	UOW disposition/SQLCODE mismatch
	194	Invalid SNA FMH5 received
	195	First failure data capture for DRDS
	203	Heuristic decision occurred
	204	Partner cold start detected
	205	Incorrect log name/synchronous parameters
	206	SNA compare-states protocol error
	207	Heuristic damage occurred
	208	SNA synchronous point protocol error
	209	Synchronous point communication failure
	210	Log name changed on warm start
	235	Conditional restart data loss
	236	Exchange log names protocol error
	238	DB2 restart error
	267	Start of CF structure rebuild
	268	End of CF structure rebuild
5	230	Data sharing global statistics
7	326	Workload manager delay monitor support

Using DISPLAY Commands

A lot of the information you can get via the accounting and statistics reports can also be obtained using the DISPLAY command. The DISPLAY command can show details about current activity in the subsystem. Following are the various types of DISPLAY commands:

- DISPLAY ARCHIVE
- DISPLAY BUFFERPOOL
- DISPLAY DATABASE
- DISPLAY DDF
- DISPLAY FUNCTION SPECIFIC
- DISPLAY GROUP
- DISPLAY GROUPBUFFERPOOL
- DISPLAY LOCATION

- DISPLAY LOG
- DISPLAY PROCEDURE
- DISPLAY RLIMIT
- DISPLAY THREAD
- DISPLAY TRACE
- DISPLAY UTILITY

> **N O T E**   This type of information can also be viewed in the DB2
> Control Center.

For more information on all the options on the DISPLAY command, refer to the *IBM DB2 UDB Version 8 for z/OS Command Reference*. Examples of the DISPLAY command can also be seen in Chapters 2 and 7.

MEMORY TUNING

Buffer Pools and Buffer Pool Queue Management

Buffer pools are areas of virtual storage that temporarily store pages of table spaces or indexes. When a program accesses a row of a table, DB2 places the page containing that row in a buffer. When a program changes a row of a table, DB2 must write the data in the buffer back to disk, eventually, normally at either a checkpoint or a write threshold. The write thresholds are either a vertical threshold at the page-set level or a horizontal threshold at the buffer pool level.

The way buffer pools work is fairly simple by design, but it is tuning these simple operations that can make all the difference in the world to the performance of your applications. The data manager issues GETPAGE requests to the buffer manager to satisfy the request from the buffer pool instead of having to retrieve the page from disk. CPU is often traded for I/O in order to manage buffer pools efficiently. Buffer pools are maintained by the subsystem, but individual buffer pool design and use should be by object granularity and, in some cases, also by application.

DB2 buffer pool management by design allows the ability to alter and display buffer pool information dynamically, without requiring a bounce of the DB2 subsystem. This improves availability by allowing you to dynamically create new buffer pools when necessary and to dynamically modify or delete them. You may need to do ALTERs of buffer pools a couple times during the day because of varying workload characteristics.

Initial buffer pool definitions are set at installation/migration but are often difficult to configure properly at this time because the application process against the objects is usually not detailed at installation. But regardless of what is set at installation, you can use ALTER after the install to add/delete new buffer pools, resize them, or change any of the thresholds. The buffer pool definitions are stored in BSDS, and you can move objects between buffer pools via an ALTER INDEX/TABLESPACE and a subsequent START/STOP command of the object.

Virtual pools have three types of pages:

- **Available pages:** pages on an available queue (LRU, FIFO, MRU) for stealing.
- **In-use pages:** pages updated or currently in use by a process but not available for stealing. In-use counts do not indicate how to size the buffer pool, but this count can help determine residency for initial sizing.
- **Updated pages:** pages not in-use and not available for stealing; considered dirty pages in the buffer pool, waiting to be externalized.

Pages are of four sizes:

BP0–BP49	4K pages
BP8K0–BP8K9	8K pages
BP16K0–BP16K9	16K pages
BP32K–BP32K9	32K pages

The 8K and 16K page sizes are logical constructs of physical 4K control intervals (CI), the same as the 32K pages size. Index page sizes are 4K. Work file table spaces are 4K or 32K. A version 8 DSNZPARM called DSVCI allows the control interval to match the actual page size.

Asynchronous page writes per I/O will change with each page size accordingly:

4K pages	32 pages per write I/O
8K pages	16 pages per write I/O
16K pages	8 pages per write I/O
32K pages	4 pages per write I/O

With the larger page sizes, you can achieve better hit ratios and have less I/O because you can fit more rows on a page. For instance, if you had a 2,200-byte row—perhaps for a data warehouse—a 4K page would be able to hold only one row, but if an 8K page were used, three rows could fit on a page, one more than if 4K pages were used, and one less lock is required. However, the larger page sizes should not be used as a bandaid for what may be a poor design. You may want to consider decreasing the row size, based on usage, to get more rows per page.

We can have up to 80 virtual buffer pools. This allows for up to 50 4K-page buffer pools (BP0–BP49), up to 10 32K-page buffer pools (BP32K, BP32K1–BP32K9), up to 10 8K-page buffer pools, and up to 10 16K-page buffer pools.

Pages used in the buffer pools are processed in two categories: random—pages read one at a time—or sequential—pages read via prefetch. These pages are queued separately: LRU (random least recently used) queue or SLRU (sequential least recently used) queue. (Prefetch will steal only from the SLRU queue).

The percentage of each queue in a buffer pool is controlled via the VPSEQT parameter (sequential steal threshold). This threshold becomes difficult to adjust and often requires two settings: for example, one setting for batch processing and another setting for online processing. Processing of batch and online data often differs. Batch is usually more sequentially processed, whereas online is processed more randomly.

DB2 breaks up these queues into multiple LRU chains, producing less overhead for queue management because the latch that is taken at the head of the queue—on the hash control block, which keeps the order of the pages on the queue—will be latched less because the queues are smaller. Multiple subpools are created for a large virtual buffer pool and the threshold is controlled by DB2 not to exceed 4,000 buffers in each subpool. The LRU queue is managed within each of the subpools in order to reduce the buffer pool latch contention when the degree of concurrency is high. Stealing of these buffers occurs in a round-robin fashion through the subpools.

FIFO (first-in, first-out) can be used instead of the default of LRU. With this method, the oldest pages are moved out, regardless. This decreases the cost of doing a GETPAGE operation and reduces internal latch contention for high concurrency. FIFO would be used only where there is little or no I/O and where table space or index is resident in the buffer pool. Buffer pools with LRU and FIFO objects will be separate, and this can be set via the ALTER BUFFERPOOL command with a PGSTEAL option of FIFO. LRU is the PGSTEAL option default.

I/O Requests and Externalization

Synchronous reads are physical 4K pages that are read in one page per I/O. Synchronous writes are pages written one page per I/O. Synchronous reads and writes should be kept to only what is truly necessary, meaning small in occurrence and number. If not, the result may be buffer pool stress: perhaps too many checkpoints. DB2 will begin to use synchronous writes if the IWTH threshold (immediate write) is reached or if two checkpoints pass without a page being written that has been updated and not yet committed.

Asynchronous reads are several pages read per I/O for prefetch operations such as sequential prefetch, dynamic prefetch, or list prefetch. Asynchronous writes are several pages per I/O for such operations as deferred writes.

Pages are externalized to disk when the following occur:

- DWQT threshold reached
- VDWQT threshold reached

- Data set is physically closed or switched from R/W to R/O
- DB2 takes a checkpoint (LOGLOAD or CHKFREQ is reached)
- QUIESCE (WRITE YES) utility is executed
- Page is at the top of LRU chain and another update is required of the same page by another process

Controlling page externalization via DWQT and VDWQT thresholds is best for performance and avoids surges in I/O. If page externalization were controlled by DB2 system checkpoints, too many pages would be written to disk at one time, causing I/O queuing delays, increased response time, and I/O spikes. During a checkpoint, all updated pages in the buffer pools are externalized to disk, and the checkpoint is recorded in the log, except for the work files (DSNDB07).

Checkpoints and Page Externalization

DB2 checkpoints are controlled through the DSNZPARM LOGLOAD or CHKFREQ. The LOGLOAD parameter is the number of log records written between DB2 checkpoints; the default was changed from the older 10,000 to 500,000 in a recent version, which can be too low for some production subsystems. The CHKFREQ is the number of minutes between checkpoints. Often, different settings for this parameter may be needed, depending on workload. For example, you may want it higher during batch processing. Recognizing the importance of the ability to change this parameter is based on workloads. The SET LOG LOGLOAD and SET LOG CHKFREQ commands allow you to dynamically set the LOGLOAD or CHKFREQ parameter.

Other options have been added to the -SET LOG command to be able to suspend and resume logging for a DB2 subsystem. SUSPEND causes a system checkpoint to be taken in a non-data sharing environment. By obtaining the log-write latch, any further log records are prevented from being created, and any unwritten log buffers will be written to disk. Also, the BSDS will be updated with the high-written RBA. All further database updates are prevented until update activity is resumed by issuing a -SET LOG command to resume logging or until a -STOP DB2 command is issued. These single-subsystem-only commands will have to be entered for each member when running in a data sharing environment.

In very general terms,DB2 should checkpoint about every 15 to 20 minutes during an online processing, or some other value based on investigative analysis of the impact on restart time after a failure. The frequency of taking checkpoints raises two concerns: the cost and disruption of the checkpoints and the restart time for the subsystem after a crash.

Hundreds of checkpoints per hour is definitely too many, but the general guideline—three to six checkpoints per hour—is likely to cause problems in restart time, especially if it is used for batch-update timing. After a normal quiesce stop, there is no work to do. The real concern for checkpointing is for DB2 abend situations or when a MODIFY IRLM,ABEND command is issued, which will also cause DB2 to have to be restarted.

Many times, the costs and disruption of DB2 checkpoints are overstated. A DB2 checkpoint is a tiny hiccup, but it does not prevent processing from proceeding. Having a LOGLOAD setting that is too high, along with large buffer pools and high thresholds, such as the defaults, can cause enough I/O to make the checkpoint disruptive. In trying to control checkpoints, some clients increase the LOGLOAD value and make the checkpoints less frequent, but that makes them much more disruptive.

The situation is corrected by reducing the amount written and increasing the checkpoint frequency, which yields much better performance and availability. It is not only possible, but does occur at some installations, that a checkpoint every minute does not impact performance or availability. The write efficiency at DB2 checkpoints is the key factor to be observed to see whether LOGLOAD can be reduced. If the write thresholds (DWQT/VDQWT) are doing their jobs, there is less work to perform at each checkpoint. Also, using the write thresholds to cause I/O to be performed in a level, nondisruptive fashion is helpful for the nonvolatile storage in storage controllers.

However, even if the write thresholds (DWQT/VDQWT) are set properly, as well as the checkpoints, an unwanted write problem could nonetheless exist if the log data sets are not properly sized. If the active log data sets are too small, active log switches will occur often. When an active log switch takes place, a checkpoint is taken automatically. Therefore, the logs could be driving excessive checkpoint processing, resulting in continual writes, preventing a high ratio of pages written per I/O from being achieved, because the deferred write queue is not allowed to fill as it should.

Sizing

Buffer pool sizes are determined by the VPSIZE parameter, which determines the number of pages to be used for the virtual pool. In order to size buffer pools, it is helpful to know the residency rate of the pages for the object(s) in the buffer pool. DB2 can handle large buffer pools efficiently, as long as enough real memory is available. If insufficient real storage exists to back the buffer pool storage requested, paging can occur. Paging occurs when the buffer pool size exceeds the real memory on the z/OS image. DB2 limits the total amount of storage allocated for buffer pools to approximately twice the amount of real storage, but less is recommended. A maximum of 1TB is allowed for all buffer pools, provided that real storage is available. However, none of the current machines available have this much memory (for example, a z990 has a maximum of 256GB). Therefore, proper sizing is very important. There is also a feature called PGFIX that will allow you to fix pages in real storage to help avoid processing time that DB2 needs to fix and free pages during an I/O.

Sequential versus Random Processing

The VPSEQT (virtual pool sequential steal threshold) is the percentage of the virtual buffer pool that can be used for sequentially accessed pages. This is to prevent sequential data from using all the buffer pool and to keep some space available for random processing. The value is 0 to

100 percent, with a default of 80 percent, indicating that 80 percent of the buffer pool is to be set aside for sequential processing; 20 percent, for random processing. This percentage needs to be set according to how your objects in that buffer pool are processed.

One tuning option often used is altering the VPSEQT to 0 to set the pool up for only random use. When the VPSEQT is altered to 0, the SLRU will no longer be valid, making the buffer pool totally random. Because only the LRU will be used, all pages on the SLRU have to be freed, which will also disable prefetch operations in this buffer pool. This is beneficial for certain strategies: It will turn off the CPU for each GETPAGE—up to 10 percent GETPAGE overhead reduction. However, this strategy has problems for certain buffer pools.

Writes

The DWQT, also known as the horizontal deferred write threshold, is the percentage threshold that determines when DB2 starts turning on write engines to begin deferred writes (32 pages/asynchronous I/O). The value can be from 0 to 90 percent, with a default of 50 percent. When the threshold is reached, up to 600 write engines begin writing pages out to disk. Running out of write engines can occur if the write thresholds are not set to keep a constant flow of updated pages being written to disk. This can occur and is okay if it is uncommon, but daily occurrence is a tuning opportunity.

DB2 turns on these write engines one vertical page set, queue, at a time, until a 10 percent reverse threshold is met. When DB2 runs out of write engines, it can be detected in the statistics reports in the WRITE ENGINES NOT AVAILABLE indicator on statistics reports.

When you set the DWQT threshold, a high value is useful to help improve the hit ratio for updated pages but will increase I/O time when deferred write engines begin. You use a low value to reduce I/O length for deferred write engines, but this will increase the number of deferred writes. This threshold should be set based on the referencing of the data by the applications. If the DWQT is set to zero so that all objects defined to the buffer pool are scheduled to be written immediately to disk, DB2 uses its own internal calculations for exactly how many changed pages can exist in the buffer pool before it is written to disk. Thirty-two pages are still written per I/O, but it will take 40 dirty, or updated, pages to trigger the threshold so that the highly rereferenced updated pages, such as space map pages, remain in the buffer pool.

When implementing LOBs, a separate buffer pool should be used and should not be shared—backed by a group buffer pool in a data sharing environment. The DWQT should be set to 0 so that, for LOBs with LOG NO, force-at-commit processing occurs, and the updates continually flow to disk instead of surges of writes. For LOBs defined with LOG YES, DB2 could use deferred writes and avoid massive surges at checkpoint.

The DWQT threshold works at a buffer pool level for controlling writes of pages to the buffer pools, but for a more efficient write process, you will want to control writes at the page set/partition level. This can be controlled via the VDWQT. The percentage threshold determines when DB2 starts turning on write engines and begins the deferred writes for a given data set. This helps to keep a particular page set/partition from monopolizing the entire buffer pool with its updated pages. The value is 0 to 90 percent, with a default of 10 percent. The VDWQT should always be less than the DWQT.

A good rule of thumb for setting the VDWQT is that if fewer than ten pages are written per I/O, set it to 0. You may also want to set it to 0 to trickle-write the data out to disk. It is normally best to keep this value low in order to prevent heavily updated page sets from dominating the section of the deferred write area. As of version 6, both a percentage and a number of pages from 0 to 9,999 can specify the VDWQT. You must set the percentage to 0 to use the number specified. Set it to 0,0, and the system uses MIN(32,1%), which is good for trickle I/O.

If you set the VDWQT to 0, 32 pages are still written per I/O, but it will take 40 dirty pages to trigger the threshold so that the highly rereferenced updated pages, such as space map pages, remain in the buffer pool. It is a good idea to set the VDWQT using a number rather than a percentage. If someone increases the buffer pool, that means more pages for a particular page set can occupy the buffer pool, and this may not always be optimal or what you want.

When looking at any performance report showing the amount of activity for the VDWQT and the DWQT, you would want to see the VDWQT being triggered most of the time (VERTIC.DEFER.WRITE THRESHOLD) and the DWQT much less (HORIZ.DEFER.WRITE THRESHOLD). No general ratios are possible, as that would depend on both the activity and the number of objects in the buffer pools. The bottom line is that you want to control I/O by the VDWQT, with the DWQT watching for and controlling activity across the entire pool and in general writing out rapidly queuing-up pages. This will also assist in limiting the amount of I/O that checkpoint would have to perform.

Parallelism

The VPPSEQT (virtual pool parallel sequential threshold) is the percentage of VPSEQT setting that can be used for parallel operations. The value is 0 to 100 percent, with a default of 50 percent. If the value is set to 0, parallelism is disabled for objects in that particular buffer pool. Doing so can be useful in buffer pools that cannot support parallel operations. The VPXPSEQT (virtual pool sysplex parallel sequential threshold) is a percentage of the VPPSEQT to use for inbound queries. It too defaults to 50 percent. If it is set to 0, sysplex query parallelism is disabled. In affinity data sharing environments, this is normally set to 0 to prevent inbound resource consumption of DSNDB07 and work files.

Stealing Method

The VPSTEAL threshold allows you to choose a queuing method for the buffer pools. The default is LRU, but FIFO is also an option. This option turns off the overhead for maintaining the queue and may be useful for objects that can completely fit in the buffer pool or if the hit ratio is less than 1 percent.

Internal Thresholds

The following thresholds are a percentage of unavailable pages to total pages, where unavailable means either updated or in use by a process.

- The SPTH (sequential prefetch threshold) is checked before a prefetch operation is scheduled and during buffer allocation for a previously scheduled prefetch. If the SPTH is exceeded, prefetch either will not be scheduled or will be canceled. PREFETCH DISABLED - NO BUFFER (indicator on statistics report) will be incremented every time a virtual buffer pool reaches 90 percent of active stealable buffers, disabling sequential prefetch. This value should always be 0. If this value is not 0, it is a clear indication that you are probably experiencing degradation in performance because all prefetch is disabled. To eliminate this, you may want to increase the size of the buffer pool (VPSIZE). Another option may be to have more frequent commits in the application programs to free pages in the buffer pool, as this will put the pages on the write queues.

- The DMTH (data manager threshold), also referred to as the buffer critical threshold, occurs when 95 percent of all buffer pages are in use, and therefore unavailable. This can also be seen as unaccounted-for I/Os in a user's TCB. The buffer manager will request all threads to release any possible pages immediately. This occurs by performing GETPAGE/RELPAGE processing by row instead of by page. After a GETPAGE, a single row is processed and then a RELPAGE is issued, causing the CPU to become high for objects in that buffer pool, and I/O-sensitive transactions can suffer. This can occur if the buffer pool is too small. You can observe when this occurs by seeing a non-zero value in the DM THRESHOLD REACHED indicator on statistics reports. This is checked every time a page is read or updated. If this threshold is not reached, DB2 will access the page in the virtual pool once for each page, no matter how many rows are used. If this threshold has been reached, DB2 will access the page in the virtual pool once for every row that is retrieved or updated on the page. This can lead to serious performance degradation.

- The IWTH (immediate write threshold) is reached when 97.5 percent of buffers are in use. If this threshold is reached, synchronous writes begin, presenting a performance problem. For example, if a page has 100 rows and if there are 100 updates, 100 synchronous writes will occur, one by one for each row. Synchronous writes are serial, not concurrent, with SQL, so the application will be waiting while the write occurs, including 100 log writes, which must occur first. This causes large increases in I/O time. It is not recorded explicitly in a statistic report, but DB2 will appear to be hung, and you will see synchronous writes begin to occur when this threshold is reached. Be careful with some monitors that send exception messages to the console when synchronous writes occur and refer to it as IWTH reached; not all synchronous writes are caused by this threshold being reached. This is simply being reported incorrectly.

NOTE   Be aware that the IWTH counter can also be incremented when dirty pages on the write queue have been referenced, which causes a synchronous I/O before the page can be used by the new process. This threshold counter can also be incremented if more than two checkpoints occur before an updated page is written, as this will cause a synchronous I/O to write out the page.

Virtual Pool Design Strategies

Separate buffer pools should be used, based on their type of usage by the applications, such as buffer pools for objects that are randomly accessed versus those that are sequentially accessed. Each of these buffer pools will have its own unique settings, and the type of processing may even differ between the batch cycle and the online day. These are very generic breakouts just for this example. Actual definitions would be much finer-tuned and less generic. The following list provides a more detailed example of buffer pool object breakouts:

BP0, PB8K0, BP16KQ, BP32K	Catalog and directory: DB2-only use
BP1	DSNDB07: cursor tables, work files, sorts
BP2	Code and reference tables: heavily accessed
BP3	Small tables, heavily updated: transition tables, work tables
BP4	Basic tables
BP5	Basic indexes
BP6	Special for large, clustered, range-scanned table
BP7	Special for master table full index (Random-searched table)
BP8	Special for an entire database for a special application
BP9	Derived tables and "saved" tables for ad hoc queries
BP10	Staging tables (edit tables for short-lived data)
BP11	Staging indexes (edit tables for short-lived data)

Tuning with the -DISPLAY BUFFERPOOL Command

In several cases, the buffer pools can be tuned effectively by using the DISPLAY BUFFERPOOL command. When a tool is not available for tuning, the following steps can be used to help tune buffer pools.

1. Use command and view statistics.
2. Make changes such as thresholds, size, object placement.
3. Use the command again during processing and view statistics.
4. Measure statistics.

The output contains valuable information, such as prefetch information (sequential, list, dynamic requests), pages read, prefetch I/O, and disablement (no buffer, no engine). The incremental detail display shifts the time frame every time a new display is performed.

RID Pool

The row identifier pool is used for storing and sorting RIDs for such operations as

- List prefetch
- Multiple-index access
- Hybrid joins
- Enforcing unique keys while updating multiple rows

The optimizer looks at the RID pool for prefetch and RID use. The full use of the RID pool is possible for any single user at runtime. Runtime can result in a table space scan if not enough space is available in the RID. For example, if you want to retrieve 10,000 rows from a 100,000,000-row table and no RID pool is available, a scan of 100,000,000 rows will occur, at any time and without external notification. The optimizer assumes that physical I/O will be less with a large pool.

Sizing

The default size of the RID pool is 8MB, with a maximum size of 10,000MB. The RID pool is created at start-up time, but no space is allocated until RID storage is needed. It is then allocated in 32KB blocks as needed, until the maximum size you specified on the installation panel DSNTIPC is reached. When setting the RID pool size, you should have as large a RID pool as required, as it is a benefit for processing and can lead to performance degradation if it is too small. A good guideline for sizing the RID pool is as follows:

Number of concurrent RID processing activities × Average number of RIDs × 2 × 5 bytes per RID

Statistics to Monitor

You should monitor three statistics for RID pool problems: RIDs over the Relational Data System limit, RIDs over the Data Manager limit, and insufficient pool size.

RIDs over the RDS Limit. This statistic is the number of times list prefetch is turned off because the RID list built for a single set of index entries is greater that 25 percent of the number of rows in the table. In this case, DB2 determines that, instead of using list prefetch to satisfy a query, it will be more efficient to perform a table space scan, which may or may not be good, depending on the size of the table accessed. Increasing the size of the RID pool will *not* help in this case. This is an application issue for access paths and needs to be evaluated for queries using list prefetch.

There is one very critical issue with this type of failure. The 25 percent threshold is stored in the package/plan at bind time; therefore, it may no longer match the real 25 percent value and in fact could be far less. It is important to know what packages/plans are using list prefetch and on what tables. If the underlying tables are growing, the packages/plans that are dependent on it should be rebound after the RUNSTATS utility has updated the statistics. Key correlation statistics and better information about skewed distribution of data can also help to gather better statistics for access-path selection and may help avoid this problem (see Chapter 7 for more information about data correlation statistics.

RIDS over the DM Limit. This occurs when more than 16 million RIDS are required to satisfy a query. DB2 has a 16 million RID limit. The consequences of hitting this limit can be fallback to a table space scan. In order to control this, you can do the following.

- Fix the index.
- Add an index better suited for filtering.
- Force list prefetch off and use another index.
- Rewrite the query.
- Perform a table space scan.

Insufficient Pool Size. This indicates that the RID pool needs to be enlarged.

The SORT Pool

Sorts are performed in two phases: initialization and merge. During the first phase, DB2 builds ordered sets of runs from the given input; in the second phase, DB2 merges the runs.

At start-up, DB2 allocates a sort pool in the private area of the DBM1 address space. DB2 uses a special sorting technique called a tournament sort. During the sorting processes, this algorithm commonly produces logical work files called runs, which are intermediate sets of ordered data. If the sort pool is large enough, the sort completes in that area. More often than not, the sort cannot complete in the sort pool, and the runs are moved into DSNDB07. These runs are later merged to complete the sort. When DSNDB07 is used for holding the pages that make up the sort runs, you can experience performance degradation if the pages get externalized to the physical work files, as they will have to be read back in later in order to complete the sort.

The sort pool size defaults to 2MB unless specified but can range in size from 240KB to 128MB. The size is set with an installation DSNZPARM. The larger the sort pool (sort work area) is, the fewer sort runs are produced. If the sort pool is large enough, the buffer pools and DSNDB07 will not be used. If buffer pools and DSNDB07 are not used, better performance will result from less I/O. You should size the sort pool and DSNDB07 large because you do not want sorts to have pages being written to disk.

The Environmental Descriptor Manager Pool

The EDM pool is made up of three components, each of which is in its own separate storage; each contains many items, including the following:

- EDM pool: skeleton cursor tables, copies of the SKCTs, skeleton package tables, copies of the SKPTs, and an authorization cache block for each plan except those with CACHESIZE set to 0
- EDM DBD cache: database descriptors
- EDM statement cache: skeletons of dynamic SQL for CACHE DYNAMIC SQL

Sizing.   The EDM storage pools cannot be undersized, as this can cause performance degradation. If the EDM DBD cache is too small, you will see increased I/O activity in the DSNDB01.DBD01 table space in the DB2 directory. If the EDM pool storage is too small, then you will see increased I/O activity in the DSNDB01.SPT01 and DSNDB01.SCT02 DB2 table spaces, which also support the DB2 directory. If the EDM statement cache is too small, the cache hit ratio on the dynamic statement cache will drop.

Your main goal for the EDM pool is to limit the I/O against the directory and the catalog. If the pool is too small, you will also see increased response times, owing to the loading of the SKCTs, SKPTs, and DBDs, and repreparing the dynamic SQL statements because they could not remained cached. By correctly sizing the EDM pool, you can avoid unnecessary I/Os from accumulating for a transaction. Reloading an SKCT, SKPT, or DBD into the EDM pool creates additional I/O. This can happen if the pool pages are stolen because the EDM pool is too small. Pages in the pool are maintained on an LRU queue, and the least recently used pages get stolen, if required.

If a new application is migrating to the environment, it may be helpful to look in SYSIBM.SYSPACKAGES to give you an idea of the number of packages that may have to exist in the EDM pool, and this can help determine the size.

Efficiency.   You can measure the following ratios to help determine whether your EDM pool is efficient. Think of these as EDM pool hit ratios:

- CT requests versus CTs not in EDM pool
- PT requests versus PTs not in EDM pool
- DBD requests versus DBDs not in EDM DBD pool

Your goal is a value of 5 for each of the preceding (1 out of 5). An 80 percent hit ratio is what you are aiming for.

Dynamic SQL Caching

If you are going to use dynamic SQL caching, you have to pay attention to your EDM statement cache pool size. If it is too small, you can affect the performance of your static SQL also. Cached statements are not backed by disk; if its pages are stolen and the statement is reused, it will have to be prepared again. Static minibinds can be flushed from EDM by LRU but are backed by disk and can be retrieved when used again. Statistics help to monitor cache use, and trace fields show the effectiveness of the cache and can be seen on the statistics long report.

SUMMARY

This chapter discussed performance topics such as how to use DB2 traces and IFCIDs to help diagnose problems in DB2 and how to monitor statistics. Various areas of memory, such as buffer pools, RID pool, EDM pool, sort pool, and dynamic SQL caching, were also discussed.

ADDITIONAL RESOURCES

IBM DB2 UDB Version 8 for z/OS Command Reference Guide (SC26-9934)

IBM DB2 UDB Version 8 for z/OS Administration Guide (SC26-9931)

IBM DB2 PM Version 8 for z/OS General Information (GC26-9172)

DDL for the DB2CERT Database

The following DDL represents the statements needed to create DB2 objects for the DB2CERT database: stogroup, database, segmented table space, partitioned table space, LOB table space, tables, indexes, auxiliary table, auxiliary index, and user-defined types:

```
-- CREATE STOGROUP
CREATE STOGROUP CERTSTG
VOLUME(*) VCAT DB2USER1;

-- CREATE DATABASE
CREATE DATABASE DB2CERT
STOGROUP CERTSTG
BUFFERPOOL BP7
INDEXBP BP8;

-- CREATE SEGMENTED TABLESPACE
CREATE TABLESPACE CERTTS
IN DB2CERT
USING STOGROUP CERTSTG
   PRIQTY 52
   SECQTY 20
   ERASE NO
 LOCKSIZE PAGE
 BUFFERPOOL BP6
 CLOSE YES
 SEGSIZE 32;
```

```
-- CREATE PARTITIONED TABLESPACE WITH 2 PARTITIONS
CREATE TABLESPACE CERTTSPT
IN DB2CERT
USING STOGROUP CERTSTG
    PRIQTY 100
    SECQTY 120
    ERASE NO
NUMPARTS 2
(PART 1
 COMPRESS YES,
 PART 2
 FREEPAGE 20)
ERASE NO
LOCKSIZE PAGE
CLOSE NO;

-- CREATE LOB TABLESPACE
CREATE LOB TABLESPACE CERTPIC
  IN DB2CERT
  USING STOGROUP CERTSTG
      PRIQTY 3200
      SECQTY 1600
  LOCKSIZE LOB
  BUFFERPOOL BP16K1
  GBPCACHE SYSTEM
  LOG NO
  CLOSE NO;

-- CREATE DISTINCT DATA TYPES
CREATE DISTINCT TYPE PHONE AS CHAR(10) WITH COMPARISONS;
CREATE DISTINCT TYPE BITMAP AS BLOB(1M);
CREATE DISTINCT TYPE MINUTES AS SMALLINT WITH COMPARISONS;

-- CREATE PARENT TABLE
CREATE TABLE DB2USER1.CANDIDATE
 (CID            CHAR(9)          NOT NULL,
  LNAME          VARCHAR(30)      NOT NULL,
  FNAME          VARCHAR(30)      NOT NULL,
  INITIAL        CHAR(1),
  HPHONE         PHONE,
  WPHONE         PHONE,
  STREETNO       VARCHAR(8),
  STREETNAME     VARCHAR(20)      NOT NULL,
  CITY           VARCHAR(30)      NOT NULL,
  STATE          VARCHAR(30)      NOT NULL,
  CODE           CHAR(6)          NOT NULL,
  COUNTRY        VARCHAR(20)      NOT NULL,
```

```
   CERT_DBA        CHAR(1) NOT NULL WITH DEFAULT,
   CERT_APP        CHAR(1) NOT NULL WITH DEFAULT,
   PHOTO           BITMAP,
   PRIMARY KEY (CID)
   IN DB2CERT.CERTTS
 );

-- CREATE PARENT TABLE WITH CHECK CONSTRAINT
CREATE TABLE DB2USER1.TEST
(NUMBER          CHAR(6)          NOT NULL,
 NAME            VARCHAR(50)      NOT NULL,
 TYPE            CHAR(1)          NOT NULL,
 CUT_SCORE       DECIMAL(6,2)     NOT NULL,
 LENGTH          MINUTES          NOT NULL,
 TOTALTAKEN      SMALLINT         NOT NULL WITH DEFAULT,
 TOTALPASSED     SMALLINT         NOT NULL WITH DEFAULT,
CONSTRAINT UNIQUE_TEST PRIMARY KEY (NUMBER),
CONSTRAINT UNIQUE_TEST_NAME UNIQUE (NAME),
CONSTRAINT TEST_TYPE CHECK (TYPE IN ('P','B'))
 IN DB2CERT.CERTTS
 );

-- CREATE UNIQUE CLUSTERING INDEX
CREATE UNIQUE INDEX DB2USER1.TESTIX
  ON DB2USER1.TEST
   (NUMBER ASC)
  USING STOGROUP CERTSTG
  PRIQTY 512
  SECQTY 64
  ERASE NO
  CLUSTER


-- CREATE TABLE WITH PARITIONING
CREATE TABLE DB2USER1.TEST_CENTER
  (TCID          CHAR(6)          NOT NULL,
   NAME          VARCHAR(40)      NOT NULL,
   STREETNO      VARCHAR(8)       NOT NULL,
   STREETNAME    VARCHAR(20)      NOT NULL,
   CITY          VARCHAR(30)      NOT NULL,
   PROV_STATE    VARCHAR(30)      NOT NULL,
   COUNTRY       VARCHAR(20)      NOT NULL,
   CODE          CHAR(6)          NOT NULL,
   TYPE          CHAR(1)          NOT NULL,
   PHONE         PHONE            NOT NULL,
   NOSEATS       SMALLINT         NOT NULL,
   PRIMARY KEY (TCID)
   IN DB2CERT.CERTTSPT
```

```
        PARTITION BY (TCID)
              (PARTITION 1 ENDING AT ('300'),
               PARTITION 2 ENDING AT ('500'));


-- CREATE UNIQUE INDEX
CREATE UNIQUE INDEX DB2USER1.TESTCNTX
  ON DB2USER1.TEST_CENTER
   (TCID ASC)
  USING STOGROUP CERTSTG
  PRIQTY 512
  SECQTY 64
  ERASE NO
  CLUSTER
  BUFFERPOOL BP3
  CLOSE YES;

-- CREATE NON-PARTITIONING INDEX WITH PIECES
CREATE UNIQUE INDEX DB2USER1.TESTCN2X
  ON DB2USER1.TEST_CENTER
   (CODE ASC)
  USING STOGROUP CERTSTG
  PIECESIZE 512K;

-- CREATE DEPENDENT TABLE
CREATE TABLE DB2USER1.TEST_TAKEN
( CID           CHAR(6)          NOT NULL,
  TCID          CHAR(6)          NOT NULL,
  NUMBER        CHAR(6)          NOT NULL,
  DATE_TAKEN    DATE             NOT NULL WITH DEFAULT,
  START_TIME    TIME             WITH DEFAULT,
  FINISH_TIME   TIME             WITH DEFAULT,
  SCORE         DECIMAL(6,2),
  PASS_FAIL     CHAR(1),
  SEAT_NO       CHAR(2)          NOT NULL,
  PRIMARY KEY (TCID,CID,DATE_TAKEN),
  FOREIGN KEY (CID)
       REFERENCES CANDIDATE ON DELETE CASCADE,
  FOREIGN KEY (TCID)
       REFERENCES TEST_CENTER ON DELETE CASCADE,
  FOREIGN KEY (NUMBER)
       REFERENCES TEST ON DELETE RESTRICT
  IN DB2CERT.CERTTS
);

-- CREATE AUXILARY TABLE
CREATE AUX TABLE CAND_PHOTO
  IN DB2CERT.CERTPIC
```

```
STORES DB2USER1.CANDIDATE
COLUMN PHOTO;

-- CREATE AUXILARY INDEX
CREATE UNIQUE INDEX DB2CERT.PHOTOIX
   ON DB2USER1.CAND_PHOTO
   USING VCAT DB2USER1
   COPY YES;
```

IBM Certified Database Administrator for DB2 UDB Version 8 for z/OS

A n IBM Certified Database Administrator (DBA) for the DB2 UDB version 8 product for the z/OS operating system is an individual with significant experience as a DBA and extensive knowledge of the DB2 Universal Database, including the features and functionality related to version 8. This person is capable of performing the intermediate to advanced tasks related to database design and implementation, operation and recovery, security and auditing, performance, and installation and migration specific to the z/OS operating system.

In order to attain the IBM Certified Database Administrator DB2 Universal Database V8 for z/OS certification, candidates must pass two tests:

1. Test 700, IBM DB2 UDB Version 8 Family Fundamentals
2. Test 702, IBM DB2 UDB Version 8 for z/OS Database Administration

It is recommended that this individual have at least two years of experience as a database administrator on DB2 UDB version 8 for z/OS. Some knowledge and experience in both the application DBA and system programming DBA areas will be necessary, as well as knowledge of major programming languages, such as COBOL, Java, and C++. The ability to work independently and effectively in complex environments will also be necessary.

The DB2 UDB V8 Family Fundamentals 700 exam covers the DB2 family. The exam has 54 questions and requires a 61 percent pass rate. The DB2 UDB V8 for z/OS Database Administration 702 exam has approximately 61 questions and requires a pass rate of 55 percent.

DB2 UDB V8 Family Fundamentals: 700 Exam

The 700 exam—DB2 UDB V8 Family Fundamentals—is divided into six sections.

Section 1: Planning (15 Percent)

- Knowledge of DB2 UDB products: client, server, and so on
- Knowledge of the features in DB2 tools, such as DB2 Extenders, Configuration Assistant, Visual Explain, Command Center, Control Center, Relational Connect, Replication Center, Development Center, and Health Center
- Knowledge of data warehouse and OLAP concepts
- Knowledge of nonrelational data concepts, such as Extenders

Section 2: Security (9 Percent)

- Knowledge of restricting data access
- Knowledge of various privileges

Section 3: Accessing DB2 UDB Data (15 Percent)

- Ability to identify and locate DB2 UDB servers
- Ability to access and manipulate DB2 UDB objects
- Ability to create basic DB2 UDB objects

Section 4: Working with DB2 UDB Data (31 Percent)

- Knowledge of transactions
- Given a DDL SQL statement, knowledge to identify results
- Given a DML SQL statement, knowledge to identify results
- Given a DCL SQL statement, knowledge to identify results
- Ability to use SQL to select data from tables
- Ability to use SQL to sort or group data
- Ability to use SQL to update, delete, or insert data
- Ability to call a procedure

Section 5: Working with DB2 UDB Objects (19 Percent)

- Ability to demonstrate use of DB2 UDB data types
- Given a situation, ability to create table
- Knowledge to identify when referential integrity should be used
- Knowledge to identify methods of data constraint
- Knowledge to identify characteristics of a table, view, or index

Section 6: Data Concurrency (11 Percent)

- Knowledge to identify factors that influence locking
- Ability to list objects on which locks can be obtained
- Knowledge to identify characteristics of DB2 UDB locks
- Given a situation, knowledge to identify the isolation levels that should be used

DB2 UDB V8 FOR Z/OS DATABASE ADMINISTRATION: 702 EXAM

The 702 exam—DB2 UDB V8 for z/OS Database Administration—is divided into five sections.

Section 1: Database Design and Implementation (26 Percent)

- Design tables and views: columns, data type considerations for large objects, column sequences, user-defined data types, temp tables, MQTs, and so on.
- Explain the various performance implications of identity column, ROWID, and sequence objects definitions (applications, utilities).
- Design indexes: key structures, type of index, index page structure, index column order, index space, clustering.
- Create and alter database objects, design table spaces—choose a DB2 page size, clustering—and determine space attributes—automatic space.
- Perform table and index partitioning.
- Normalize data—Entity-Relationship model, process model—and translate data model into physical model, or denormalize tables.
- Implement user-defined integrity rules: referential integrity, user-defined functions, check constraints, triggers.

Section 2: Operation and Recovery (28 Percent)

- Issue database-oriented commands for normal operational conditions: START, STOP, DISPLAY.
- Issue database-oriented commands and utility control statements for use in abnormal conditions: RECOVER, RESTART.
- Identify and perform actions needed to protect databases from planned and unplanned outages—BACKUP, RESTORE, monitoring—and ensure that timely image copies are taken periodically.
- Load data into the created tables.
- Reorganize objects when necessary.
- Monitor the object by collecting statistics.
- Monitor threads: utilities, distributed, local, in-doubt, new special registers.
- Identify and respond to restrictive statuses on objects.

- Establish timely checkpoints: checkpoint frequencies, system quiesce points.
- Perform problem determination: run traces (DB2, DRDA, ODBC, JDBC), SQL queries, dumps, `GET DIAGNOSTICS`.
- Perform health checks: maintenance, check utilities, offline utilities, queries.
- Develop backup scenarios—tables spaces; indexes; full pack; hardware; Flash copies; full, incremental, reference update; copy-to-copy, nondata objects; catalog—and recovery scenarios—table spaces, indexes, roll forward, roll back, current point in time, prior point in time, system point-in-time copy and restore, catalog, and directory.
- Describe the special considerations for recovery in a data sharing environment.
- Implement disaster recovery.
- Plan for disaster recovery.
- Perform offsite and local disaster recovery.

Section 3: Security and Auditing (10 Percent)

- Protect DB2 objects.
- Establish a security profile: define authorization roles.
- Identify the appropriate DB2 privileges required for access to DB2 resources.
- Define and implement authorization and privileges on user and system database objects: revokes, grants.
- Protect connection to DB2; describe access to the DB2 subsystem—local request, remote request; coordinate the effort between DB2 and RACF team—groupings, secondary authorization identifiers, stored procedures; identify conditions when external security mechanisms, such as RACF, should be used in place of DB2 internal security mechanisms.
- Audit DB2 activity and resources and identify primary audit techniques.
- Identify and respond appropriately to symptoms from trace output or error messages that signify security problems.

Section 4: Performance (31 Percent)

- Plan for performance monitoring by setting up and running monitoring procedures: continuous, detailed, periodic, exception.
- Analyze the `CREATE` and `ALTER` process for DB2 objects: table, index, table space definition.
- Analyze performance: manage and tune CPU requirements, memory, I/O, locks, response time.
- Analyze and respond to `RUNSTATS` statistics analysis: real time, batch, catalog queries, reports.
- Determine when and how to run the `REORG` utility.

- Design and alter index structures: DPSI, VARCHAR column index implications, backward index scan, sparse indexes.
- Analyze cache—buffer pool tuning, pool sizes, threshold, page set positioning, sort pool, RID pool, EDM pool—and recommend buffer pool changes.
- Calculate cache requirements for new applications: DBD sizes, plan and package, average and maximum sizes, number of data sets.
- Evaluate and set appropriately the performance parameters for various utilities.
- Describe the performance concerns for the distributed environment: DDF, DBAT threads, pool threads, connection pooling.
- Describe DB2 interaction with WLM: distributed, stored procedures, user-defined functions.
- Interpret traces—statistics, accounting, performance—and explain the performance impact of various DB2 traces.
- Identify and respond to critical performance thresholds: excessive I/O wait times, lock-latch waits, and CPU waits; deadlocks, timeouts.
- Review and tune SQL.
- Interpret EXPLAIN output.
- Analyze access paths: query parallelism; indexable, stage 1, and stage 2 predicate types; join methods; block fetching.
- Explain the performance impact of multirow functionality in version 8: multirow insert scenario, multirow fetch.

Section 5: Installation and Migration (5 Percent)

- Identify and explain the application of runtime considerations and parameters.
- Run catalog health checks, using queries and utilities.
- Identify the critical ZPARMs: database, object, and application oriented.
- Identify modes of version 8 migration.

702 Sample Exam

The following 61 questions are similar to those on the 702 DB2 UDB V8 for z/OS Database Administration exam. That test can be taken online, and your results will be scored by category. For information on how to take the test online refer to http://www1.ibm.com/certify/tests/obj702.shtml.

This appendix includes the answers, which have references to the chapters in which more information about the topic can be found.

Questions

1. A DBA is coordinating a DB2 disaster recovery and wants DB2 to

— Consider the table spaces unavailable until the disaster recovery is complete
— Do the necessary log processing

Which of the following should the DBA use to accomplish this?

  a. Issue -START DB2 ACCESS(FORCE).
  b. Issue -START DB2 ACCESS(MAINT).
  c. Set DSNZPARM parameter DEFER ALL, and then issue -START DB2.
  d. Set DSNZPARM parameter RESTART ALL, and then issue -START DB2.

2. The audit trace *cannot* capture information for which of the following actions?

  a. Access to catalog tables
  b. Denied-access attempts
  c. Explicit GRANTs and REVOKEs
  d. Start of a utility job

3. A database administrator needs the ability to create an object in a buffer pool (BP1). Which GRANT statement would provide the necessary privilege to perform this action?

    a. `GRANT BUFFERPOOL1 USAGE TO authorization-id`
    b. `GRANT EXECUTE ON BUFFERPOOL TO authorization-id`
    c. `GRANT USE OF BUFFERPOOL BP1 TO authorization-id`
    d. `GRANT CREATIN BUFFERPOOL BP1 TO authorization-id`

4. Which of the following statements about the INCURSOR option of the LOAD utility is *false*?

    a. The INCURSOR option can be specified with the SHRLEVEL CHANGE option.
    b. The cursor must be defined before it is used by the LOAD utility.
    c. The specified cursor can be used with the DB2 UDB cross-loader function.
    d. Data cannot be loaded into the same table on which the cursor is defined.

5. To verify the integrity of DB2 directory and catalog table spaces and to scan for broken links, which of the following should be run?

    a. DSNJU004
    b. DSN1CHKR
    c. DSN1LOGP
    d. CHECK INDEX

6. If materialization has occurred for an SQL statement, which of the following will the PLAN_TABLE show?

    a. The view or nested table expression name and TABLE_TYPE of 'W'
    b. Only query blocks with the base table names and TABLE_TYPE of 'M'
    c. The base table name and TABLE_TYPE of 'W'
    d. An entry with TABLE_TYPE of 'M'

7. To allow the image copy of an index to be used by the RECOVER utility, which of the following procedures should *not* be performed?

    a. Prepare and test incremental image copy jobs.
    b. Prepare and test full image copy jobs.
    c. Prepare and test recovery jobs.
    d. Create or alter the index with the COPY YES option.

8. The statement CREATE LOB TABLESPACE ts1 creates a table space in which database?

    a. DSNLOB
    b. DSNDB01
    c. DSNDB04
    d. DSNDB06

9. The results of the command -DISPLAY UTILITY(*) will provide all the following information *except*

a. Type of utilities running
b. Status of the utility jobs
c. Estimated elapsed time of completion for the utility jobs
d. Estimate of how much processing has completed for the utility jobs

10. Compression dictionary memory is allocated within which of the following?

a. BP0
b. EDM pool
c. MSTR address space
d. DBM1 address space

11. DB2 automatically converts to table-controlled partitioning in all the following conditions except

a. Altering the table to add a new partition
b. Altering the table space to specify NUMPARTS option
c. Altering the table to rotate a partition from first to last
d. Dropping the table space index that is defined with PART VALUES

12. When the command DISPLAY DATABASE ADVISORY is used without the RESTRICT option, which of the following *cannot* be determined?

a. A table space of a base table is in CHECK-pending (CHKP) status.
b. A LOB table space is in auxiliary warning (AUXW) status.
c. An index space is in the REBUILD-pending (ARBDP) status.
d. An index space is in the informational COPY-pending (ICOPY) status.

13. Which of the following applies to an identity column but not to a sequence object?

a. Can be restarted
b. Can be a decimal or an integer
c. Is associated with a user table
d. Is used to generate sequence values

14. Which of the following is a main performance advantage of multirow INSERT of non-LOB data in a client/server environment?

a. There is only one network flow from the client to the server.
b. The data is inserted onto only one data page, so only one I/O needs to occur.
c. Only one log record is cut, because multiple data rows are inserted as a single block.
d. The data is inserted directly from the communication buffer to the data page in one move.

15. If the following SQL EXEC SQL UPDATE T1 SET C1 = C1 +1; is executed, which of the following GET DIAGNOSTICS statements could be used to determine how many rows were updated?

    a. EXEC SQL GET DIAGNOSTICS :rcount = ROW_COUNT;
    b. EXEC SQL GET DIAGNOSTICS :rcount = SQLERRD;
    c. EXEC SQL GET DIAGNOSTICS :rcount = NUMBER;
    d. EXEC SQL GET DIAGNOSTICS :rcount = DB2_ROW_COUNT;

16. Which of the following is true regarding the recovery of the DB2 catalog and directory?

    a. All objects that are related to SYSUTILX can be recovered in parallel.
    b. All catalog and directory objects can be recovered in parallel.
    c. All catalog and directory objects can be recovered in a single job step.
    d. The catalog and directory objects after SYSDBASE can be recovered in parallel.

17. A materialized query table (MQT) is defined with the MAINTAINED BY SYSTEM option. Which of the following can be used to populate the MQT?

    a. INSERT
    b. LOAD RESUME
    c. REPLACE TABLE
    d. REFRESH TABLE

18. When trying to determine whether a reorganization of an index is necessary, which of the following would *not* be of use to you?

    a. SYSIBM.SYSINDEXPART column LEAFDIST
    b. SYSIBM.SYSINDEXES column CLUSTERING
    c. SYSIBM.SYSINDEXES column CLUSTERRATIOF
    d. SYSIBM.SYSINDEXPART columns LEAFNEAR and LEAFFAR

19. Which of the following REORG parameters will greatly reduce the elapsed time of the utility phase that alternates application usage from the original data sets to the shadow data sets of a 12-partition table space?

    a. LOG NO
    b. SORTKEYS 12
    c. KEEPDICTIONARY
    d. FASTSWITCH YES

20. Data in a DB2 table is stored in VSAM data sets. How can sensitive DB2 data in these VSAM data sets be protected from unauthorized user access outside of DB2?

    a. Encode the data in the DB2 tables, using compression.
    b. Encrypt the data by using DB2 edit procedures or field procedures.

    c. Use RACF profiles and permits, or their equivalents, for the data sets.

    d. Use DB2 GRANT and REVOKE statements to allow certain DB2 users access to the data.

21. The table columns CITY and STATE are used in a compound SQL WHERE clause. The optimizer might incorrectly estimate the number of qualifying rows in the table if

    a. Correlation statistics are not collected

    b. The columns are defined as variable character

    c. These columns form a composite partitioning key

    d. A single index, which contains both columns, is created

22. After altering a check constraint on a table, which of the following utilities should you run before the table can be used?

    a. CHECK LOB

    b. CHECK DATA

    c. CHECK INDEX

    d. CHECK CONSTRAINT

23. In the plan table, METHOD = 2 signifies

    a. Star join

    b. Hybrid join

    c. Merge-scan join

    d. Nested-oop join

24. Which of the following is the most important factor to consider when choosing the clustering index?

    a. Random data access

    b. Sequential data access

    c. How the data is partitioned

    d. How many partitions are defined for the table space

25. Which of the following REORG utility options can be used to determine whether a table space needs to be reorganized?

    a. REBALANCE

    b. REPORTONLY

    c. RUNSTATSONLY

    d. STATISTICS

26. The command `-DIS DB(DBTST1A) SPACE(*) RESTRICT LIMIT(*)` is issued; the output shows that index space IX1 has the following status: RW,RBDP. Based on the status information, which of the following is *not* true about the scope of unavailability for dynamic SQL?

    a. Deletes are allowed for the table rows.

    b. Queries are allowed for the table, but DB2 does not choose an index in RBDP for an access path.

    c. Updates and inserts are allowed for table rows, even if their corresponding non-unique indexes are in RBDP status.

    d. Updates and inserts are allowed for table rows, causing DB2 to insert keys into a unique index that is in RBDP status.

27. At a conceptual level, an "entity" on a logical model will often map to which DB2 object?

    a. Index

    b. Table

    c. Column

    d. Database

28. Which of the following does the `PAGE_RANGE` column of the `PLAN_TABLE` indicate?

    a. Access that is limited to a subset of the table or index partitions

    b. The start and stop range for a matching index scan

    c. Index screening that has occurred for the query

    d. The range of pages for each parallelism group

29. The `PAYROLL` table is defined with `AUDIT ALL`. A TSO user has user ID DBA007, with primary authorization ID `JONES` and secondary authorization ID `PAYGROUP`. This user updates a row in the `PAYROLL TABLE` after issuing a `SET CURRENT SQLID = 'DBA007'`. In this situation, what authorization ID is used in a DB2 audit trace record?

    a. `JONES`

    b. `DBA007`

    c. `PAYGROUP`

    d. `DISTSERV`

30. When you are defining a primary key and before the table is usable, which of the following must be created?

    a. A unique index, using the primary-key columns

    b. A duplicate index, using the primary-key columns

    c. A clustering index, using the primary-key columns

    d. A partitioning index, using the primary-key columns

31. Which of the following is *not* considered an essential disaster-recovery element?

    a. Archive logs

    b. DB2 load and exit libraries

    c. Recent image copies of all database objects

    d. REPORT RECOVERY utility output for all objects

32. Which of the following is true when you are preparing to do a system-level point-in-time recovery to an arbitrary point in time?

    a. The SET LOG SUSPEND command is required prior to executing a BACKUP SYSTEM FULL.

    b. To restore the DB2 system to an arbitrary point in time, a BACKUP SYSTEM FULL utility is required.

    c. To restore the DB2 system to the point in time of a prior system-level backup, a cold start is required.

    d. To restore the DB2 system to an arbitrary point in time, running a BACKUP SYSTEM DATA ONLY is sufficient.

33. Which of the following single-table predicates is considered stage 1?

    a. CASE expressions

    b. COL NOT EQUAL value

    c. COL NOT IN (correlated subquery)

    d. COL NOT EQUAL (correlated subquery)

34. Which of the following ALTER statements could necessitate an application program modification?

    a. ALTER TABLE PROD.EMPLOYEE PRIMARY KEY(LAST_NAME)

    b. ALTER TABLE PROD.EMPLOYEE ALTER COLUMN LAST_NAME CHAR(45)

    c. ALTER TABLE PROD.EMPLOYEE ADD PART 15 VALUES("2004-01-19")

    d. ALTER TABLE PROD.EMPLOYEE ADD MATERIALIZED QUERY (fullselect)

35. What type of cursor can take advantage of block fetching in a distributed environment to reduce the number of messages sent across the network?

    a. Cursors that update data

    b. Cursors that delete data

    c. Cursors that are defined FOR UPDATE OF

    d. Cursors that do not update or delete data

36. A subsystem has been successfully converted to version 8. Which of the following would result if the -DISPLAY GROUP DETAIL command were run and it reported a mode of E?

   a. The system is in enable new-function mode.

   b. The catalog and directory are in Unicode and can accept long names.

   c. The catalog and directory are in Unicode and can accept long names; new V8 functions are available.

   d. The catalog and directory are in Unicode and can accept long names; data has been converted to Unicode.

37. Which *two* of the following are design considerations for the version 8 Data Partitioned Secondary Indexes (DPSI)?

   a. The DPSI indexes are defined as nonunique.

   b. The DPSI index requires its own storage group.

   c. The DPSI index can be defined for a single partition.

   d. The DPSI index helps eliminate BUILD2 phase utility processing.

   e. The DPSI index cannot be used with a partitioning or type 2 index in an access path.

38. Which of the following statements is false when the command STOP DB2 MODE(QUIESCE) is entered?

   a. There are no pending writes.

   b. There are no outstanding units of recovery.

   c. DB2 does not need to access the data sets on restart through the log.

   d. DB2 does not allow currently executing programs to complete processing.

39. Which of the following keywords would be used to collect frequency distribution statistics on nonindexed columns?

   a. KEYCARD only

   b. FREQVAL only

   c. KEYCARD and FREQVAL

   d. COLGROUP and FREQVAL

40. Which of the following data types allows for direct row access (PRIMARY_ACCESSTYPE=D)?

   a. ROWID

   b. INTEGER

   c. SMALLINT

   d. IDENTITY

41. The design requirement for the TRANS table is to divide the data into 13 partitions, each of which contains one month of data that is partitioned on the transaction date. The user normally accesses the transaction table through the customer account column. The design needs to support a critical requirement for availability on the TRANS table and to allow the DBA to run a SHRLEVEL NONE REORG job at the partition level, with minimal disruption to data availability. To facilitate reorganization, which of the following would best satisfy the design requirements?

   a. Create a partitioning index on the transaction date and a secondary index on the customer account.

   b. Create a single partitioning, clustering index on the combined transaction date and customer account columns.

   c. Create a table-controlled partitioned table that partitions on the transaction date. Also, create a partitioned clustering index on the customer account.

   d. Create a table-controlled partitioned table that partitions on the transaction date. Also, create a partitioning index on the combined columns transaction date and customer account.

42. If a secondary authorization ID has been established for the DBA group DBAGRP, how can it be used to qualify unqualified objects in an SQL statement?

   a. SET CURRENT PATH = 'DBAGRP'
   b. SET CURRENT SQLID = 'DBAGRP'
   c. SET CURRENT AUTHID = 'DBAGRP'
   d. SET CURRENT USERID = 'DBAGRP'

43. A DB2 data sharing group consists of two members: DSN1 and DSN2 on z/OS logical partitions zOS1 and zOS2, respectively. zOS1 has an unplanned outage, causing member DSN1 to fail. Now applications running on DSN2 cannot access some of the DB2 data, owing to retained locks that are held by member DSN1. Which of the following will get these retained locks resolved as quickly as possible to allow access to all the application data?

   a. Restart DB2 for member DSN1 on zOS1.

   b. Restart DB2 for member DSN1 on zOS2, using the ACCESS MAINT mode.

   c. Restart DB2 for member DSN1 on zOS2, using the restart-light mode.

   d. Recycle DSN2 and perform a group restart on zOS2 for both members DSN1 and DSN2.

44. Which of the following statements about the RESTORE SYSTEM utility is *true*?

    a. Terminate the RESTORE SYSTEM utility by using the TERM UTILITY command.

    b. The RESTORE SYSTEM utility can be run from any member in a data sharing group.

    c. The RESTORE SYSTEM utility restores the logs from the log copy pool and the data from the database copy pool.

    d. If specified, a particular backup version can be used by the RESTORE SYSTEM utility.

45. Which of the following statistics trace classes provides information about deadlocks and timeouts?

    a. Class 1

    b. Class 3

    c. Class 4

    d. Class 5

46. Which of the following DB2 traces could be used by the DBA to assign DB2 costs to individual authorization IDs?

    a. Lock trace

    b. Audit trace

    c. Statistics trace

    d. Accounting trace

47. If overall system performance is slow, analysis should begin with which of the following?

    a. Monitoring buffer pool hit ratios

    b. Identifying poorly performing SQL statements

    c. Locating problems at the z/OS level, using RMF

    d. Collecting trace data, using DB2 accounting classes 1, 2, 3, 7, and 8

48. Which SQL clause provides the necessary privilege to create an object using the volumes VOL1 and VOL2 that are defined to storage group STOGRP1?

    a. USE OF STOGROUP STOGRP1

    b. USE OF VOLUMES (VOL1, VOL2)

    c. CREATE IN STOGROUP STOGRP1

    d. CREATE USING VOLUMES (VOL1, VOL2)

49. When a CREATE INDEX statement specifies the NOT PADDED clause, which of the following statements is *false*?

   a. DB2 can use index-only access for the varying-length columns within the index key.

   b. DB2 does not pad any varying-length columns in the index key to their maximum lengths.

   c. Index-key comparisons are faster because DB2 compares pairs of corresponding varying-length columns as the entire key.

   d. Storage requirements for the index key can be reduced because DB2 stores only a 2-byte-length field along with the data.

50. In a WHERE clause, why are Boolean term predicates often preferred over non-Boolean term predicates?

   a. Non-Boolean term predicates are stage 2 predicates.

   b. The optimizer does not use default filter factors for Boolean term predicates.

   c. Non-Boolean term predicates can be coded only in a query containing inner joins.

   d. Only Boolean term predicates can use matching index access on a single index.

51. Which of the following parameter settings would allow the buffer pool to contain 20 percent random pages?

   a. VPSEQT = 80

   b. VPSIZE = 20

   c. VPRAND = 20

   d. VPSTEAL = FIFO

52. Which of the following statements is *true* when adding a check constraint to a table that is not empty?

   a. The constraint is enforced immediately when it is defined.

   b. The constraint is added to the table description, but its enforcement is deferred until the next bind.

   c. The constraint is enforced or deferred, depending on the contents of the CURRENT PATH special register.

   d. The constraint is enforced or deferred, depending on the contents of the CURRENT RULES special register.

53. Which of the following will happen when a primary key is dropped by using the DROP PRIMARY KEY clause of the ALTER TABLE?

   a. The dependent tables no longer have foreign keys.

   b. The dependent tables are placed in a CHECK-pending restricted status.

   c. The table is placed in a CHECK-pending restricted status.

   d. The table's primary index is no longer a unique index.

54. Which of the following is *true* if the ALTER INDEX CLUSTER statement is used to change an index to be the clustering index for a table?

   a. A table can have multiple clustering indexes.
   b. New data inserted into the table is not placed in clustering order.
   c. Preexisting data rows are immediately put into the new clustering order.
   d. A table must be reorganized to put existing data rows into clustering order.

55. Which of the following is an invalid WLM command to perform an operation against the application environment?

   a. VARY WLM,APPLENV=name,RESUME
   b. VARY WLM,APPLENV=name,RESTART
   c. VARY WLM,APPLENV=name,QUIESCE
   d. VARY WLM,APPLENV=name,REFRESH

56. A DBA wants to check the health of the DB2 catalog or directory. Which of the following utilities should the DBA *not* use?

   a. REPAIR
   b. REPORT
   c. DSN1COPY
   d. DSN1CHKR

57. Which of the following statements about declared temporary tables is *false*?

   a. Can have an index
   b. Qualified by SESSION
   c. Materialized in DSNDB07
   d. Not recorded in the catalog

58. Table space DB1.TS1 has pages in the LPL. Which of the following can be used to start the recovery of the object?

   a. -STA DB(DB1)
   b. -STA FUNCTION SPECIFIC
   c. -STA DB(DB1) SPACENAM(TS1) ACCESS(RW)
   d. -STA DB(DB1) SPACENAM(TS1) ACCESS(FORCE)

59. Which of the following utilities can be used to help reduce DB2 I/O?

   a. REPORT
   b. RECOVER
   c. RUNSTATS
   d. STOSPACE

60. Which of the following most accurately describes the default buffer pool for a user-defined `INDEX`?

    a. `BPO`
    b. `DSNDB04`
    c. `TBSBPOOL`
    d. `IDXBPOOL`

61. In referencing a 4,096-partition table space, when would a DBA create an NPSI instead of a DPSI?

    a. If there is a lot of contention when running utilities
    b. When the ability to rotate partitions is needed
    c. When predicates do not exist to allow page range screening
    d. When partitioned data is accessed randomly the majority of the time

ANSWERS AND CHAPTER REFERENCES

Table C-1 shows the answers for the questions on the sample test. For more information about a particular topic, refer to the chapter cited.

Table C-1 Question Answers and Chapter References

Question	Answer	Chapter
1	c	Chapter 8
2	a	Chapter 3
3	c	Chapter 3
4	a	Chapter 7
5	b	Chapter 2
6	a	Chapter 17
7	a	Chapter 4; Chapter 8
8	c	Chapter 4
9	c	Chapter 2
10	d	Chapter 2
11	b	Chapter 4
12	a	Chapter 7
13	c	Chapter 4
14	a	Chapter 12

continues

Table C-1 Question Answers and Chapter References (Continued)

Question	Answer	Chapter
15	a	Chapter 10
16	d	Chapter 8
17	d	Chapter 4
18	b	Chapter 7
19	d	Chapter 7
20	c	Chapter 3
21	a	Chapter 7
22	b	Chapter 7
23	c	Chapter 17
24	b	Chapter 4
25	b	Chapter 7
26	d	Chapter 7
27	b	Chapter 4
28	a	Chapter 17
29	b	Chapter 3
30	a	Chapter 4
31	d	Chapter 8
32	d	Chapter 8
33	b	Chapter 6
34	b	Chapter 4
35	d	Chapter 14
36	b	Chapter 2
37	a, d	Chapter 4
38	d	Chapter 8
39	d	Chapter 7
40	a	Chapter 17
41	c	Chapter 4
42	b	Chapter 3

Table C-1 Question Answers and Chapter References (Continued)

Question	Answer	Chapter
43	c	Chapter 9
44	b	Chapter 8
45	b	Chapter 18
46	d	Chapter 18
47	c	Chapter 18
48	a	Chapter 3
49	c	Chapter 4
50	d	Chapter 17
51	a	Chapter 18
52	d	Chapter 4
53	a	Chapter 4
54	d	Chapter 4
55	d	Chapter 13
56	b	Chapter 2
57	c	Chapter 12
58	c	Chapter 7
59	c	Chapter 7
60	d	Chapter 2
61	c	Chapter 4

BIBLIOGRAPHY

IBM DB2 for z/OS Version 8 SQL Reference (SC18-7426-00) March 2004.

IBM DB2 for z/OS Version 8 Utility Guide & Reference (SC18-7427-00) March 2004.

IBM z/OS Managed System Infrastructure for Setup DB2 Customization Center User's Guide (SC33-7985-03) March 2004.

IBM DB2 for z/OS Version 8 Command Reference (SC18-7416-00) March 2004.

IBM DB2 for z/OS Version 8 Data Sharing: Planning and Administration (SC18-7417-00) March 2004.

IBM DB2 for z/OS Version 8 Installation Guide (GC18-7418-00) March 2004.

IBM DB2 for z/OS Version 8 Administration Guide (SC18-7413-00) March 2004.

IBM DB2 for z/OS Version 8 Application Programming and SQL Guide (SC18-7415-00) March 2004.

IBM DB2 for z/OS Version 8 Application Programming and Reference for Java™ (SC18-7414-00) March 2004.

IBM DB2 for z/OS Version 8 Utility Guide and Reference (SC18-7427-00) March 2004.

DB2 Universal Database v8 for UNIX, Linux, and Windows Database Administration Certification Guide, 5th ed. George Baklarz, Bill Wong, and Jonathan Cook (Prentice Hall, 2003). ISBN 0-13-046361-2

IBM z/OS Managed System Infrastructure for Setup User Guide (SC33-7985-03) March 2004.

IBM Planning for Multilevel Security (GA22-7509) March 2004.

IBM DB2 for z/OS Version 8 RACF Access Control Module Guide Reference (SA22-7983)
March 2004.

IBM DB2 for z/OS Technical Preview (SG24-6871-00) November 2003

IBM DB2 for z/OS Version 8 and Continuous Availability (SG24-5486-00) March 2004

IBM Using RVA and SnapShot for BI with OS/390 and DB2 (SG24-5333-00) November 2002

IBM DB2 on MVS Platform: Data Sharing and Recovery (SG24-2218-00) September 1997

IBM DB2 PM Version 8 for z/OS General Information (GC26-9172) November 2003

IBM DB2 V8 for z/OS Image, Audio, and Video Extenders Administration and Programming
(SES1-2199-0) March 2003

IBM DB2 V8 for z/OS XML Extender Administration and Programming (SES1-2201-00)
March 2004

IBM DB2 V8 for z/OS Text Extender Administration and Programming (SES1-2200-00)
March 2004

*IBM Redbook—Developing Crossplatform DB2 Stored Procedures: SQL Procedures and the
DB2 Stored Procedure Builder* (SG24-5485) May 2001

IBM OS/390 Parallel Sysplex Configuration, Volume 1: Overview (SG24-5637-00)
September 2001

IBM OS/390 Parallel Sysplex Configuration, Volume 2: Cookbook (SG24-5638-00)
September 2001

IBM OS/390 Parallel Sysplex Configuration, Volume 3: Connectivity (SG24-5639-00)
September 2001

IBM Parallel Sysplex Performance Health Case Study (SG24-5373-00) July 1999

IBM Parallel Sysplex Continuous Availability—Case Studies (SG24-5346-00) June 1999

IBM DB2 on MVS Platform: Data Sharing Recovery (SG24-2218-00) August 1997

IBM DB2 for MVS/ESA Version 4 Data Sharing Implementation (SG24-4791-00)
December 1996

IBM DB2 for MVS/ESA V4 Data Sharing Performance Topics (SG24-4611-00) December 1995

IBM DB2 UDB for z/OS Version 8 Data Sharing: Planning and Administration (SG26-9007-00)
March 2004

IBM DB2 for z/OS and OS/390: Squeezing the Most out of Dynamic SQL (SG24-6418-00)
May 2002

INDEX

A

Access and security, 73
    auditing in, 95–98
    data set protection, 76
    multilevel security, 94–95
    to objects, 77
        administrative authorities for, 83–88
        authorization identifiers for, 77–78
        catalog table information for, 93
        explicit privileges for, 77–83
        ownership with, 88–93
        plan execution authorization for, 93
        views for, 94
    subsystem, 74–76
ACCESS_DEGREE column, 534
Access paths, 529
    in bind process, 393
    DSN_FUNCTION_TABLE for, 548–549
    DSN_STATMNT_TABLE for, 546–548
    Explain for, 529–531, 551–553
    hints for, 549–550
    PLAN_TABLE for, 530
        columns in, 531–537
        index access in, 537–539
        table access in, 539–546
    production environment models for, 550–551
ACCESS_PGROUP_ID column, 534
Access plans, 529
ACCESS (UT) option, 314
ACCESSCREATOR column, 533
ACCESSNAME column, 533
ACCESSTYPE column, 532, 538–539, 554–556
Accounting
    for lock monitoring, 527
    traces for, 567–568, 570–573
ACHKP state, 301
ACQUIRE option, 394
ACTION option, 394
Activating triggers, 471
Active triggers, 469
ADD CHECK clause, 128
ADD option for binding, 393
Address spaces, 24–27
    priority of, 28
    Workload Manager for, 443
ADMF (Advanced Database Management Facility) address space, 26
Administration Client, 10, 17
Administration Tool, 19
Administration tools, 16–19

Administrative authorities, 83–88
Advanced Database Management Facility
        (ADMF) address space, 26
Advisory states, 299–303
Affinity processing, 355
After triggers, 471, 473–474
Aliases, 65–66, 105–106
ALL clause, 215–216
Allied address spaces, 27
ALTER command
    for auditing, 98
    purpose of, 109–110
ALTER BUFFERPOOL command, 68–69, 588
ALTER DATABASE command, 159
ALTER GROUPBUFFERPOOL command, 350
ALTER INDEX command, 158
    for buffer pools, 587
    for clustering, 154
    for rebalancing partitions, 280
ALTER PROCEDURE command, 439
ALTER STOGROUP command, 160
ALTER TABLE command, 133
    with check constraints, 128–129
    for partitioned table spaces, 139–140
    for reorganizations, 278
ALTER TABLESPACE command
    for buffer pools, 587
    modifications by, 147
Analytics, 15–16
Anomalies, 165–166
Application Client, 13
Application development, 12–16
Application Development Client, 10
Application requesters (ARs), 65, 449, 451
Application servers (ASs), 63, 449
Applications
    commit and rollback operations in,
            405–407
    concurrency design for, 526
    data sharing analysis for, 353
    global transactions in, 413–417
    identity columns in, 420–423
    savepoints in, 407–408
        in distributed environments, 413
        establishing, 408–409
        releasing, 412

    restoring to, 410–412
    sequence objects in, 423–425
    SQL in. See SQL
APPLNAME column
    in DSN_FUNCTION_TABLE, 548
    in DSN_STATMNT_TABLE, 547
    in PLAN_TABLE, 531
Archival partitioned table spaces, 140
Archive Log Accelerator, 19
ARCHIVE LOG command, 329
Archive logs for disaster recovery, 328
AREO* state, 303
ARM (Automatic Restart Manager) policy, 343
ARs (application requesters), 65, 449, 451
AS clause
    for correlation names, 188
    for derived columns, 191
AS SECURITY LABEL clause, 94
ASs (application servers), 63, 449
Asterisks (*)
    with COUNT, 195–196
    with SELECT, 178–179
ASUTIME parameter, 443–444
Asynchronous reads, 588
Atomic keys for indexes, 155
Attachments, 28–32
Attributes
    characteristics of, 162
    for locks, 508
    mapping, 169
Audio extenders, 14, 505–506
Auditing, 95–96
    IDs, 97
    tables, 98
    traces for, 96–97, 569, 573
Authentication, 75–76
Authorization identifiers, 77–78
Autocommit option, 35
Automatic rebinding, 400–401
Automatic Restart Manager (ARM) policy, 343
Automatic summary tables, 106, 150–151
Automation Tool, 20
Auxiliary tables
    creating, 602–603
    for LOB data, 131–132

AUXW state
    characteristics of, 301
    in LOB recovery, 326
Available pages in buffer pools, 587
AVG function, 193

B

Backing out of changes, 306, 405–407
BACKUP SYSTEM utility, 331
Backups
    for recovery, 306
    system-level, 330–332
Before triggers, 471, 474–475
BETWEEN predicate, 197
Binary large objects (BLOBs), 110–111
    characteristics of, 114
    conversions with, 251
    support for, 496
BIND ACQUIRE parameter, 515
BIND command, 92
Bind Manager, 20
BIND PACKAGE command
    for DBRM, 392–393
    for DRDA access, 460
    options for, 394
    privileges for, 93
BIND PLAN command
    for DBRM, 392–393
    for DRDA access, 460
    options for, 394
    privileges for, 93
BIND_TIME column, 536
BINDAGENT privilege, 92
Binding, 387–388
    invalidations in, 399
    options for, 393–398
    package lists in, 400
    packages and plans, 389–392
        execution authorization in, 403
        ownership in, 402
        rebinding, 399–400
        removing, 402
    precompiling in, 388–389
    preliminary steps in, 399

    for privileges, 93
    process, 389
    rebinding, 392–393
        automatic, 400–401
        packages, 399–400
    unqualified objects in, 402–403
BLOBs (binary large objects), 110–111
    characteristics of, 114
    conversions with, 251
    support for, 496
Boolean terms
    in filtering, 237
    for matching-index access, 539
    for row restrictions, 182
Bootstrap data set logging, 308
Bottom-up data model design approach, 161
Browse output option, 35
Buffer Pool Analyzer, 19
Buffer pools, 68–69
    for coupling facility, 341
    default, 159
    group. *See* Group buffer pools
    managing, 586–588
    size, 590, 596
    virtual, 68, 587
BUFFERPOOL parameter, 159
BUILD phase
    in LOAD, 247
    in REORG, 262
    in REORG INDEX, 274
Built-in functions, 192, 485–486
Business challenges, 4–5
Business rules
    check constraints for, 129
    triggers for, 470–471, 480

C

CACHE keyword, 119
Caches
    for coupling facility, 341
    dynamic SQL, 557, 598
    invalidating, 285–287
CACHESIZE option, 394
Calculations in derived columns, 190–191

Call Attach Facility (CAF), 29
CALL command
    in precompiling, 388
    for stored procedures, 429, 432
CANDIDATE table, 168
Cartesian joins, 545–546
Cartesian products, 183–185
CASCADE clause, 127
Cascade revokes, 83
Cascading triggers, 471, 479
CASE expressions
    in functions, 232–233
    working with, 231
Casting
    on distinct types, 182, 484–485
    for LOBs, 500
Castout process, 351
Catalog and catalog information, 57–62
    consistent queries with, 63
    for distinct types, 486
    integrity of, 297
    merging in, 354
    for object access, 93
    for production environment models, 550–
        551
    recovering, 319–321
    reorganizing, 280
    statistics for, 63, 281–283, 285
    for triggers, 275–276, 480
    for UDFs, 496
Catalog view, 504
CDBs (communications databases)
    for catalog information, 58, 64
    for distributed data, 449, 453–454
    tables in, 67
CEEDUMP for Workload Manager, 445
CFCC (coupling facility control code), 352
CFRM (Coupling Facility Resource Manage-
        ment) policy, 341
Change Accumulation Tool, 19
Change defaults option, 35
CHANGE INDEX SETTINGS command, 504
Change Log Inventory (DSNJU003) utility, 296
Change Log Map (DSNJU004) utility, 297
CHANGELIMIT feature, 314

Character data
    characteristics of, 113
    conversions with, 251
Character large objects (CLOBs)
    characteristics of, 113
    conversions with, 251
Check constraints, 128–129
CHECK DATA utility, 128, 291, 319
CHECK INDEX utility, 291–292, 325
CHECK LOB utility, 292–293, 326
CHECKDAT phase, 291
CHECKLOB phase, 292
CHECKP state, 301
Checkpending (CHKP) status
    with LOAD, 253
    in recovery, 325
    removing, 128
    with REORG, 273
Checkpoints, 589–592
CHKFREQ for checkpoints, 589
CICS (Customer Information Control System),
        29
    flexibility in packages for, 391
    security for, 75
Claims locks, 520–521
Classes
    for audit and events, 96–97
    overloading, 487
    for traces, 567–570
CLASST threshold, 351
Client Configuration Assistant, 454
Client mode, 9
Clients, 10, 13, 17
CLIST command, 54
CLIST (command list), 37
CLOBs (character large objects)
    characteristics of, 113
    conversions with, 251
CLOSE command for cursors, 379
CLUSTER option, 153
Clustering indexes, 153–154
CLUSTERRATIO keyword, 265
CM (compatibility mode) migration
    in migration, 38–39
    in Workload Manager, 442
COALESCE function, 227, 229

COBOL programs
    definitions in, 362–363
    delimiting in, 362
    for host structures, 365
    subprograms in, 444
COLGROUP keyword, 284
Collections
    of packages, 391–392
    privileges for, 79
COLLID column
    in DSN_FUNCTION_TABLE, 548
    in DSN_STATMNT_TABLE, 547
    in PLAN_TABLE, 534
COLUMN_FN_EVAL column, 534
Columns
    defining, 171–172
    derived, 190–191
    functions for, 192–193, 486
    identity, 118–121, 420–421
        INSERT and UPDATE with, 421–422
        vs. sequence objects, 135–136, 425
        updatable values, 422–423
    inserting data into, 201–202
    maximum, 129–130
    ordering, 180–181
    projecting, 180
    selecting from multiple tables, 182–188
    in sorting, 189–190
Combining outer joins, 227–229
Command list (CLIST), 37
Commands, 50–53
COMMIT ON RETURN clause, 437
Commit operations, 405–407
    for declared temporary tables, 417
    savepoints in. See Savepoints
    two-phase, 461
Commit scope, 507
COMMITs, issuing, 437
Common table expressions, 230
Communications databases (CDBs)
    for catalog information, 58, 64
    for distributed data, 449, 453–454
    tables in, 67
Communications protocols
    DDF, 66
    for distributed data, 452–453

Comparisons
    on distinct types, 484
    operators for, 181
Compatibility mode (CM)
    in migration, 38–39
    in Workload Manager, 442
Composite keys, 155
Compound predicates, 236
COMPRESS clause, 146–147
Compression
    vs. encryption, 76
    space savings from, 297–298
    table spaces, 146–147
Concurrency, 507–508
    application design for, 526
    commit frequency for, 406
    database design for, 525–526
    with LOAD, 250–251
CONCURRENT keyword, 316
Conditional reorg triggers, 277
Conditioning, triggers for, 470
Conditions in data retrieval, 181–182
Configuration information for distributed data,
        454–455
CONNECT command
    for declared temporary tables, 457
    for distributed data, 458–459
    for DRDA, 64–65
    with savepoints, 413
Connect location option, 35
Connect product, 9–11
Connectivity, 9–12
Consistency queries, 63
Constraints, 125
    check, 128–129
    foreign-key, 174
    referential, 126–128
    vs. triggers, 480–481
    unique, 125–126
Contention in locking, 348–349
Control
    in migration, 38
    for UDFs, 494–495
Control Center, 55
Conversions, data type, 251–252
Coordinated updates, 461–462

COPY option for binding, 394
COPY state, 301
COPY utility, 313–314
COPYDDN parameter, 313
Copying
    DSN1COPY for, 298
    image. *See* Image copies
    table definitions, 132
COPYPOOL groups, 331
COPYTOCOPY utility, 310–311
Correlated references, 212
CORRELATION_NAME column, 535
Correlation names, 188
COST_CATEGORY column, 547
Costs
    in data sharing, 351–352
    Explain for, 530
    for UDFs, 495–496
COUNT function, 195–196
Coupling facility, 339–342, 359
Coupling facility control code (CFCC), 352
Coupling Facility Resource Management
    (CFRM) policy, 341
CPU parallelism, 558
CREATE command
    for auditing, 98
    for ownership, 88–90
    uses for, 108
CREATE AUX TABLE command, 602
CREATE DATABASE command, 171, 599
CREATE DISTINCT TYPE command, 484,
    499, 600
CREATE FUNCTION command, 486–491
CREATE INDEX command, 152–155
CREATE LOB TABLESPACE command, 600
CREATE PROCEDURE command, 432–434,
    438–439
CREATE SEQUENCE command, 134, 423–
    424
CREATE STOGROUP command, 160, 599
CREATE TABLE command, 129–131
    for auxiliary tables, 131–132
    for DB2CERT database, 600–602
    for distinct types, 171
    for MQTs, 150
CREATE TABLE LIKE command, 132

CREATE TABLESPACE command, 143–145,
    599–600
CREATE TRIGGER command, 471–473
CREATE UNIQUE INDEX command, 601–603
CREATE VIEW command, 148–149
Created temporary tables (CTTs), 413–415
CREATOR column, 532
Cross invalidation, 349
Cross System Coupling Facility (XCF), 343–
    344
CS (cursor stability) isolation level
    lock avoiding in, 520
    purpose of, 515–516
CTREF column, 537
CTTs (created temporary tables), 413–415
Cube Views, 12, 14–15
Current-environment evaluation for data shar-
    ing, 353–354
CURRENT PACKAGE PATH special register,
    391–392
CURRENT PACKAGESET special register,
    391–392
Current rows in cursors, 378
CURRENT SERVER special register, 458, 462
Current servers, 65, 452
Current SQLIDs, 78
Current values in cursors, 377
CURRENTDATA option
    for BIND PACKAGE, 460
    for BIND PLAN, 461
    for binding, 395
CURRENTSERVER option, 395
Cursor stability (CS) isolation level
    lock avoiding in, 520
    purpose of, 515–516
Cursors, 203
    closing, 379
    held, 380
    with LOAD, 258
    nonscrollable, 381
    in row retrieval, 375–379
    scrollable, 382–383
    types of, 381
Customer Information Control System (CICS),
    29
    flexibility in packages for, 391

security for, 75
Customization Center, 16–17, 37

D

DAS (Database Administration Server), 454
DASD (Direct Access Storage Device)
    failures in, 358
    shared, 344–345
    storage groups for, 160
Data anomalies, 165–166
Data Archive Expert, 20
Data Control Language (DCL), 58, 103
Data definition (DD) cards, 56
Data Definition Language (DDL), 57, 103
    for database objects, 108–110
    for DB2CERT database, 599–603
Data division for definitions, 362
Data Facility Storage Management Subsystem
        (DFSMS), 33
Data in ranges, searching for, 197
DATA INITIALLY DEFERRED option, 151
Data integrity, 345
    CHECK utilities for, 290–293
    group buffer pools in, 349–351
    locking in, 345–349
    triggers for, 470
Data maintenance, 260–261
    CHECK utilities, 290–293
    DIAGNOSE utility, 296
    MODIFY utilities, 293–295
    movement, 245–247
        loading data. See LOAD utility
        unloading data, 259–260
    packages for, 390
    reorganizing table spaces. See REORG util-
        ity
    REPAIR utility, 295–296
    restrictive and advisory states, 299–303
    standalone utilities, 296–299
    statistics. See Statistics
Data manager threshold (DMTH), 593
Data Manipulation Language (DML), 103, 177
Data models, 161
DATA ONLY copy method, 331

Data partitioned secondary indexes (DPSIs),
        156–157
Data retrieval, 178
    column ordering, 180–181
    derived columns, 190–191
    duplicates in, 195–196
    entire tables, 178–180
    functions for, 192–193
    grouping values, 193–194
    multiple rows, 367
    from multiple tables, 182–188
    projecting columns from tables, 180
    restricting, 181–182, 194–195
    searches in, 196–199
    single rows, 367
    sorting output, 189–190
Data sets
    image copies for, 313–314
    log, 307–308
    protection of, 76
Data sharing, 337
    affinity processing and workload manage-
        ment in, 355
    application analysis for, 353
    benefits, 338
    components, 339–344
    current-environment evaluation for, 353–
        354
    data integrity in, 345–351
    distributed processing in, 355–356
    migration issues in, 354–355
    movement to, 353
    performance and processing costs in, 351–
        352
    recovery considerations for, 357–360
    shared data in, 344–345
    sysplex query parallelism in, 356–357
Data-sharing groups, communicating with, 455
Data structures. See Structures
Data System Control Facility (DSCF) address
        space, 24
Data types, 104, 110–111
    conversions with LOAD, 251–252
    date and time, 115–117
    distinct types. See Distinct types
    identity columns, 118–121

numeric, 111–112
selecting, 123–124
string, 112–115
Data Warehouse Edition, 13
Database Administration Server (DAS), 454
Database objects, 103
    data structures, 104–107
    data types for. *See* Data types
    DDL statements for, 108–110
    indexes. *See* Indexes
    materialized query tables, 150–151
    sequence, 134–136
    storage groups, 160
    table spaces. *See* Table spaces
    tables. *See* Tables
    views, 148–149
Database-recovery concepts, 305–306
Database services address space (DSAS), 26
Databases, 107, 159
    attributes in, 162
    concurrency design, 525–526
    creating, 159, 599
    data anomalies in, 165–166
    entities in, 161–162
    logical design, 160–166
    modifying, 159
    monitoring, 565–566
    objects. *See* Database objects
    physical design, 166–167
    privileges for, 79–80
    relationships in, 162–165
    removing, 159
DataJoiner, 451
DataPropagator, 19
DATE data type, 111
    characteristics of, 115–116
    conversions with, 251
DB2
    clients, 10, 13
    commands, 51–53
    data management tools, 19–20
    data types, 110–111
    failures in data sharing recovery, 358–359
    private connections, 65, 452
DB2 Application Client, 13
DB2 Application Development Client, 10

DB2 Connect, 9–11
DB2 Cube Views, 14–15
DB2 Customization Center, 16–17, 37
DB2 Development Center (DB2 DC), 13
    for distributed data, 465
    for stored procedures, 447
DB2 Enterprise Server Edition (DB2 ESE), 5, 7
DB2 Estimator, 18
DB2 Everyplace, 5, 9
DB2 Extenders, 14
DB2 Information Integrator, 9, 11–12
DB2 Information Integrator for Content (EIP), 9,
    12
DB2 OLAP Server, 15
DB2 Personal Developer's Edition, 5, 8
DB2 Personal Edition, 5, 8
DB2 Stored Procedure Address Space (DSNS-
    PAS), 440–441
DB2 UDB for Linux, UNIX, and Windows, 5–7
DB2 UDB for z/OS, 5–6
DB2 Universal Database Express Edition, 8–9
DB2 Visual Explain, 17–18, 552–553
DB2 Warehouse Edition (DWE), 15–16
DB2 Workgroup Server Edition (DB2 WSE), 7–
    8
DB2 Workgroup Server Unlimited Edition (DB2
    WSUE), 8
DB2CERT database, 167
    columns for, 171–172
    DDL for, 599–603
    distinct types for, 171
    keys for, 172–175
    tables for, 168–172
DB2I (interactive program)
    for utilities, 54
    working with, 33–36
DBADM authorization, 87
DBCLOBs (double-byte character large objects)
    characteristics of, 114
    conversions with, 252
    support for, 496
DBCTRL authorization, 87
DBD01 directory table, 64
DBINFO clause, 434–435
DBMAINT authorization, 86

DBPROTOCOL option
    for BIND PACKAGE, 460
    for BIND PLAN, 461–462
    for binding, 65, 395
DCL (Data Control Language), 58, 103
DCLGEN generator, 363
    for host structures, 365–366
    starting, 366
DD (data definition) cards, 56
DD names, 281
DD command, 445
DDF (Distributed Data Facility), 27, 63–67, 449
DDL (Data Definition Language), 57, 103
    for database objects, 108–110
    for DB2CERT database, 599–603
DEADLINE parameter, 272
Deadlocks, 522–524
Debugging stored procedures, 432
DECIMAL data type, 110
    characteristics of, 112
    conversions with, 251
Decision-support systems (DSSs), 233
Declarative RIs with triggers, 481
DECLARE command, 109, 362
DECLARE CURSOR command, 375–376
DECLARE GLOBAL TEMPORARY TABLE
    command, 130, 415
DECLARE TABLE command, 363
DECLARE TEMP command, 159
Declared temporary tables (DTTs), 415–416
    commit options for, 417
    for distributed data, 457
    TEMP database for, 417
    usage considerations for, 416
DEFAULT value
    in identity columns, 421
    in inserted records, 201
DEFAULTIF attribute, 254
DEFER option for binding, 395
Deferred embedded SQL, 384
Defining
    columns, 171–172
    distinct types, 171, 484
    keys, 173–175
    MQTs, 150
    stored procedures, 438–439

    tables, 171–172, 362–363
    views, 362–363
DEGREE option, 395
DELAY parameter, 272
DELETE command, 205–206
    for cursors, 379
    logging, 307
DELETE rules, 127
Delimited loads and unloads, 260
DELIMITED syntax, 260
Delimiters for SQL, 362
Denormalization, 229
Dependent tables, 127
Derived columns, 190–191
DESC keyword, 190
DESCRIBE PROCEDURE command, 436
Design
    example implementation, 167–175
    logical, 160–166
    physical, 166–167
    virtual pool strategies, 594–595
Detail reports, recovery log, 298
Deterministic UDFs, 491
Development Center, 13
    for distributed data, 465
    for stored procedures, 447
DFSMS (Data Facility Storage Management
    Subsystem), 33
DFSMS Concurrent Copy, 316
DFSORT program, 262, 264–267
DIAGNOSE utility, 296
Diagnostic information
    GET DIAGNOSTICS for, 371–375
    Workload Manager for, 445
Direct Access Storage Device (DASD)
    failures in, 358
    shared, 344–345
    storage groups for, 160
Directory, 63–64
    integrity of, 297
    recovering, 319–321
    reorganizing, 280
DIS DDF command, 454
DISABLE option
    for binding, 396
    for CICS, 75

Disaster recovery. *See* Recovery
DISCARDDN parameter, 281
DISCONNECT option
    for BIND PLAN, 460
    for binding, 395
DISPLAY commands for monitoring,
        585–586
DISPLAY DATABASE command, 299–300
DISPLAY DATABASE LOCKS command,
        527–528
DISPLAY FUNCTION SPECIFIC command,
        495
DISPLAY GROUP command, 40
DISPLAY GROUPBUFFERPOOL command,
        350
DISPLAY PROCEDURE command, 440–441
DISPLAY THREAD command, 467
DISPLAY TRACE command, 98, 570
Displaying utilities, 57
DISTINCT clause, 195–196
Distinct types, 121–122, 483
        built-in functions, 485–486
        catalog information for, 486
        creating, 600
        defining, 171, 484
        for LOBs, 499–500
        null values with, 122–123
        operations on, 484–485
        predicate evaluation for, 182
        privileges for, 81–82, 486
        selecting, 123–124
        Unicode support, 124–125
        user-defined functions. *See* User-defined
                functions (UDFs)
Distributed data and environments, 449–450
        communications databases for, 453–454
        communications protocols for, 452–453
        configuration information for, 454–455
        CONNECT for, 458–459
        in data sharing, 355–356
        DRDA, 450–452
        performance with, 466–467
        precompiler options for, 459
        private protocols for, 452
        program preparation for, 459–462

        programming considerations for,
                462–465
        releasing connections for, 459
        savepoints in, 413
        three-part table names for, 456–457
        tuning guidelines for, 467
        update coordination for, 461–462
Distributed Data Facility (DDF), 27, 63–67, 449
Distributed Relational Database Architecture
        (DRDA), 10
        access to, 459–462
        for distributed data, 64–65, 450–452
Distributed requests, 450
Distributed threads, 467
Distributed units of work (DUWs), 11, 450
DM limits, RIDs over, 596
DML (Data Manipulation Language), 103, 177
DMTH (data manager threshold), 593
Double-byte character large objects (DB-
        CLOBs)
        characteristics of, 114
        conversions with, 252
        support for, 496
Double-byte character strings, 114
DOUBLE data type, 111–112
Double-precision floating-point data types, 112
DPSIs (data partitioned secondary indexes),
        156–157
DRAIN ALL option, 271
Drain locks, 520–522
DRAIN WRITERS option, 271
DRDA (Distributed Relational Database Archi-
        tecture), 10
        access to, 459–462
        for distributed data, 64–65, 450–452
DROP command, 109
DROP DATABASE command, 159, 205
DROP INDEX command, 159
DROP PROCEDURE command, 439
DROP SEQUENCE command, 136
DROP STOGROUP command, 160
DROP TABLE command, 133, 205
DROP TABLESPACE command, 147–148, 205
DROP TRIGGER command, 478, 482
DROP VIEW command, 149
Dropping. *See* Removing

DSAS (database services address space), 26
DSCF (Data System Control Facility) address
        space, 24
DSN commands, 50–51
DSN_FUNCTION_TABLE, 548–549
DSN_STATMNT_TABLE, 546–548
DSN1CHKR utility, 297
DSN1COMP utility, 297–298
DSN1COPY utility, 298
DSN1LOGP utility, 298
DSN1MSTR address space, 24
DSN1PRNT utility, 299
DSN1SDMP utility, 299
DSN1SPAS (stored-procedure address space),
        27
DSNACCOR stored procedure, 289
DSNJLOGF (Preformat Active Log) utility, 296
DSNJU003 (Change Log Inventory) utility, 296
DSNJU004 (Change Log Map) utility, 297
DSNSPAS (DB2 Stored Procedure Address
        Space), 440–441
DSNTIAUL program, 259
DSNTIJNE job, 40
DSNTIJTC job, 39
DSNTIJUZ job, 329
DSNTPSMP stored procedure, 446
DSNU Command, 54–55
DSNUM parameter, 313
DSNUTILB stored procedure, 55
DSNUTILS stored procedure, 55
DSNUTILU stored procedure, 55
DSNZPARMs, 41–50
DSSIZE parameter, 139–140, 145
DSSs (decision-support systems), 233
DTTs (declared temporary tables), 415–416
        commit options for, 417
        for distributed data, 457
        TEMP database for, 417
        usage considerations for, 416
Dual image copies, 310
Dual indexes, 503
DUOW (distributed units of work), 11, 450
Duplexed structures in recovery, 360
Duplicates in data retrieval, 195–196
DUWs (distributed units of work), 11, 450
DWE (DB2 Warehouse Edition), 15–16

DWQT threshold, 591–592
Dynamic DSNZPARMs, 49
Dynamic prefetch, 540
Dynamic scrollable cursors, 383
Dynamic SQL
        caching, 557, 598
        for performance, 557–558
        statements, 361, 384–385
Dynamic workload balancing, 443
DYNAMICRULES option, 92, 395, 403

E

Edit input option, 35
EDM (environmental descriptor manager) pools,
        69, 597
Efficiency
        EDM pools, 597
        indexes for, 553–556
EHL (explicit hierarchical locking), 345–346
EIP (Information Integrator for Content),
        9, 12
Elapsed time traces, 568
Embedded dynamic SQL, 384
Embedded UDBs, 5
ENABLE FOR QUERY OPTIMIZATION
        clause, 151
Enable new-function mode (ENFM), 38–40
ENABLE option
        for binding, 396
        for CICS, 75
Encapsulation for stored procedures, 430
ENCODING option, 396
Encryption, 76
ENFM (enable new-function mode), 38–40
ENFORCE CONSTRAINTS option, 254
ENFORCE NO option, 253–254
Enhancements, 6
Enterprise Server Edition, 5, 7
Entities, 161–162
Environment, 23–24
        address spaces, 24–28
        attachments, 28–32
        catalog, 57–63
        commands, 50–53

for data sharing, 353–354
directory, 63–64
Distributed Data Facility, 63–67
installation and migration, 36–40
interfaces, 33–36
parallel sysplex environment, 33
security, 32–33
subsystem pools, 68–70
system parameters, 41–50
utilities, 53–57
z/OS, 24
Environmental descriptor manager (EDM)
    pools, 69, 597
Equal unique indexes, 556
Escalation, lock, 524–525
Estimator, 18
ETL (extract, transform, and load) process, 15
Events, audit, 96–97
Everyplace, 5, 9
Exams, sample, 611–625
Exclusive (X) lock mode
    duration, 517–518
    purpose of, 512–514
EXEC SQL parameter, 258
Execute option, 35
Executing
    external UDFs, 494–495
    utilities, 54–56
Execution authorization for plans, 93, 403
Execution environments for stored procedures,
    440–445
Execution validation in SQL, 368–375
Existence subqueries, 212
EXISTS subqueries, 213–214
Explain facility
    for access paths, 529–530
    gathering data in, 530–531
    for lock monitoring, 526
    output from, 551–553
EXPLAIN option
    for binding, 396
    for rebinds, 401
EXPLAIN_TIME column
    in DSN_FUNCTION_TABLE, 548
    in DSN_STATMNT_TABLE, 547
Explicit clustering indexes, 153

Explicit hierarchical locking (EHL), 345–346
Explicit privileges, 77–83
Expressions
    CASE, 231–233
    nested, 229–230
    row, 233
Extenders, 12, 14
    image, audio, and video, 505–506
    for LOBs, 500–506
    text, 502–505
    XML, 506
External UDFs, 489–491
    creating, 487–488
    executing, 494–495
Externalization
    and checkpoints, 589–592
    and I/O requests, 588–589
    real-time statistics, 288–289
Extract, transform, and load (ETL) process, 15

F

Fact-table detection algorithms, 543–545
Fallback recovery, 323
False lock contention, 348
Fast Log Apply (FLA), 323
FASTSWITCH keyword, 269
FETCH command
    for cursors, 378
    for limited rows, 418–419
    for multirows, 419–420
    for scrollable cursors, 383
    sensitivity clause, 382
FETCH FIRST clause, 418
FIELDPROC clause, 121
FIFO (first-in, first-out) in buffer pools, 588
Filtering
    matching-index scans for, 553–554
    predicates for, 236–241
First normal form (1NF), 163
FIRSTKEYCARD column, 283
Fixed-length character strings, 113
Fixed-list SELECT statements, 384
FLA (Fast Log Apply), 323
FLAG option, 396

Flexibility, packages for, 390–391
FLOAT data type
    characteristics of, 112
    conversions with, 251
FOR BIT DATA clause, 114
FOR EXCEPTION clause, 319
FOR UPDATE clause, 376
FORCE option, 332
Foreign-key constraints, 174
Foreign keys
    defining, 174
    for indexes, 155
    with referential constraints, 126–128
FORMAT DELIMITED syntax, 260
Formatting recovery log, 298
FREE command, 402
FREEPAGE parameter, 145–146, 255
Frequency
    of image copies, 309–310
    of index updates, 504
FREQVAL options, 284
FROM TABLE clause, 273
Full copies, 306, 323, 331
Full image copies, 311–313
Full outer joins, 225–227
FULLKEYCARD column, 283
FULLSELECT for MQTs, 150–151
FUNCTION_NAME column, 549
FUNCTION_TEXT column, 549
FUNCTION_TYPE column, 549
Functional dependence, 162
Functions, 192–193
    built-in, 485–486
    CASE expressions in, 232–233
Fuzzy copies, 315
Fuzzy searches, 503

G

GBPCHKPT threshold, 351
GBPOOLT threshold, 351
Generalized Trace Facility (GTF), 566
GENERATED ALWAYS columns, 118, 121,
    254, 420–422

GENERATED BY DEFAULT columns, 119,
    254, 420–422
GET DIAGNOSTICS command, 371–375
GET INDEX STATUS command, 504
GETPAGE requests, buffer pools for, 586
GETVARIABLE command, 94
GLM (global lock manager) level, 348
Global lock contention, 348
Global lock manager (GLM) level, 348
Global locks, 346
Global transactions, 413
    created temporary tables for, 413–415
    declared temporary tables for, 415–417
Goal mode in Workload Manager, 442
Governor, 566
GRANT command, 77, 82–83, 87
Granting
    authorities, 87–88
    privileges, 82–83
GRAPHIC data type, 111
    characteristics of, 114
    conversions with, 252
GRECP state, 301
Group buffer pools, 349–350
    castout process, 351
    for coupling facility, 341
    in data sharing, 359
    sizing, 350
GROUP BY clause, 193–194
GROUP_MEMBER column
    in DSN_FUNCTION_TABLE, 548
    in DSN_STATMNT_TABLE, 547
    in PLAN_TABLE, 535
Group services in XCF, 344
Grouping values, 193–194
GTF (Generalized Trace Facility), 566

H

Hardware in tuning, 563
Hash tables, lock, 341
HAVING clause, 195
Held cursors, 380
High Performance Unload, 20
HINT_USED column, 536

Hints for access paths, 549–550
Historical statistics, 286
HISTORY keyword, 286
Horizontal deferred write threshold, 591–592
Host structures, SQL, 365–366
Host variables, SQL, 363–364
Hybrid joins, 543

I

I/O
    CPU parallelism for, 558
    and externalization, 588–589
IBM Data Encryption, 20
IBM Debug Tool, 432
IBM_SERVICE_DATA column, 535
ICF (Integrated Catalog Facility) catalog
    for disaster recovery, 328
    synchronizing, 320
ICFs (Internal Coupling Facilities), 339
ICOPY state, 301
ICSF (Integrated Cryptographic Service Facility), 76
Identifiers
    authorization, 77–78
    in security, 77–78
    in sequence names, 423
Identity columns, 118–121, 420–421
    INSERT and UPDATE with, 421–422
    vs. sequence objects, 135–136, 425
    updatable values, 422–423
IFC Selective Dump utility, 299
IFCIDs (Instrumentation Facility IDs), 566, 570–585
Image copies, 309
    access during, 314–315
    COPYTOCOPY for, 310–311
    DFSMS concurrent copies, 316
    for disaster recovery, 328
    dual, 310
    frequency of, 309–310
    full and incremental, 311–313
    index, 317–318
    inline, 315
    MERGECOPY for, 316–317

    for partitions and data sets, 313–314
    vs. tape, 311
Image extenders, 14, 505–506
IMMEDIATE option, 396
Immediate write threshold (IWTH), 593–594
Implicit clustering indexes, 153
IMS (Information Management Systems)
    functions of, 29–30
    in security, 75
IN clause, 199
IN-list index matching, 538
IN-list index scans, 555
IN list subqueries, 212–213
In-use pages in buffer pools, 587
Inactive threads with distributed data, 467
INCLUDE command, 365
INCLUDING IDENTITY clause, 132
INCLUDING IDENTITY COLUMN AT-
    TRIBUTES clause, 121
INCREMENT BY clause, 134, 423
Incremental copy backups, 306, 323
Incremental development, packages for, 390
Incremental image copies
    vs. full, 311–313
    merging, 316–317
INCURSOR parameter, 258
Index-controlled partitioning, 142
Index-only access, 539, 556
Index spaces
    invalid copies, 323
    recovering, 321
Indexable predicates, 237–241
Indexes, 106
    clustering, 153–154
    creating, 151–153, 601–632
    data partitioned secondary, 156–157
    Explain for, 551
    guidelines, 158
    image copies for, 317–318
    integrity of, 291–292
    LOB, 158
    modifying, 158
    nonpartitioning, 106, 156
    null values with, 155–156
    OLAP, 235
    parallel builds, 257–258, 266–267

partitioning, 154
for performance
    avoiding sorts, 556–557
    efficient access, 553–556
PLAN_TABLE columns for, 537–539
removing, 159
reorganizing, 274, 278
screening by, 554
spaces for, 130
for statistics, 287–288
for text extenders, 503–504
unique and nonunique, 154–155
update frequency of, 504
INDEXONLY column, 533, 539, 556
INDEXSPACESTATS table, 287
INDREFLIMIT triggers, 277
INDXVAL phase in LOAD, 247
Information Integrator, 9, 11–12
Information Integrator Classic Federation, 20
Information Integrator for Content (EIP), 9, 12
Information Management Systems (IMS)
    functions of, 29–30
    in security, 75
Inherited privileges, 83, 91
Initialization phase in sort pools, 596
Inline copies, 255, 315
Inline statistics
    benefits of, 286–287
    with LOAD, 255
    with REORG, 272–274
Inline views, 229
Inner joins, 217–218
Inoperative plans and packages, 401
Input data set name option, 35
INSENSITIVE cursors, 382
INSERT command, 200–201, 367
    with identity columns, 421–422
    vs. LOAD, 245
    logging, 307
    for multirows, 419–420
    for sets of values, 202–203
    for specific columns, 201–202
INSERT rules, 127
Inserting
    data, 200–203, 367
    LOBs, 497–499

Installation, 36–40
Installation SYSADM authorization, 83
Installation SYSOPR authorization, 86
Instrumentation Facility IDs (IFCIDs), 566,
    570–585
INTEGER data type, 110
    characteristics of, 111
    conversions with, 251
Integrated Catalog Facility (ICF) catalog
    for disaster recovery, 328
    synchronizing, 320
Integrated Cryptographic Service Facility (IC-
    SF), 76
Integrity, 345
    CHECK utilities for, 290–293
    group buffer pools in, 349–351
    locking in, 345–349
    triggers for, 470
Intent exclusive (IX) lock mode, 512–513
Intent share (IS) lock mode, 512–513
Interactive program (DB2I)
    for utilities, 54
    working with, 33–36
Interactive SQL, 384
Interfaces, 33–36
Internal Coupling Facilities (ICFs), 339
Internal resource lock manager (IRLM), 27
Internal thresholds in tuning, 593–594
INTO clause, 367, 378
INTO TABLE option, 249–250
Invalidations
    in binding, 399
    SQL caches, 285–287
    triggers for, 478–479
Invoking
    traces, 570
    UDFs, 491–493
IRLM (internal resource lock manager), 27
IRLMRWT parameter, 518
IS (intent share) lock mode, 512–513
IS predicate, 198
Isolation levels with locks, 515–516
ISOLATION option for binding, 396
ISPF command, 33
IWTH (immediate write threshold), 593–594
IX (intent exclusive) lock mode, 512–513

J

JDBC (Java Database Connectivity) support, 361–362, 384
Jobs, installation and migration, 37
JOIN_DEGREE column, 534
JOIN_PGROUP_ID column, 534
Join predicates, 236
JOIN_TYPE column, 535
Joins, 185–188, 217
  Cartesian, 545–546
  combining, 227–229
  vs. denormalization, 229
  full outer, 225–227
  hybrid, 543
  inner, 217–218
  left outer, 220–224
  merge-scan, 542–543
  nested loop, 541–542
  outer, 219
  right outer, 224–225
  star, 235–236

K

KEEPDYNAMIC option, 396
Kerberos security, 76
Key-correlation statistics, 283–284
KEYCARD parameter, 284
Keys, 107
  for DB2CERT database, 172–175
  for indexes, 155
  with referential constraints, 126–128

L

L-locks (logical locks), 346–347
Labeled duration operations, 204
Labels for constraints, 129
Language Environment product libraries, 431–432
Large amounts of data, inserting, 202
Large objects. See LOBs (large objects) and LOB columns
Law of diminishing returns, 562

LEAFDISTLIMIT option, 277
LEAFFAR column, 278
LEAFNEAR column, 278
Left outer joins, 220–224
Libraries
  for disaster recovery, 328–329
  for stored procedures, 431–432
LIBRARY option for binding, 396
LIKE clause, 121, 132, 196–197
Limited partition scanning, 540
Limited rows, FETCH for, 418–419
Linguistic indexes, 503
Linkage section for definitions, 362
Links for coupling facility, 343
Linux, UDB for, 6–7
List prefetch, 540
LLM (local lock manager), 348
LOAD utility, 203, 205, 245–247
  concurrent access with, 250–251
  conversions with, 251–252
  cursors with, 258
  free space with, 255
  inline copies with, 255, 315
  inline statistics with, 255
  loading with
    data, 247–248
    LOB columns, 255
    ordered rows, 249
    partitions, 249–250
    ROWID columns, 254
  parallel index builds with, 257–258
  partitioned table spaces with, 258
  PREFORMAT option, 256–257
  rebalancing partitions with, 256
  referential integrity with, 252–254
  replacing data with, 248–249
  SORTKEYS option, 256
Loading LOBs, 497–499
LOBs (large objects) and LOB columns, 114, 496–497
  auxiliary tables for, 131–132
  buffer pools for, 591
  checking, 292–293
  distinct types for, 499–500
  extenders for, 500–506
  indexes for, 158

inserting, 497–499
loading, 255, 497–499
locking, 510–511
recovering, 325–326
table spaces, 107, 142–143
Local copies, 323
Local DB2, 63, 75, 449
Local lock manager (LLM), 348
Local locks, 346
Local predicates, 236
Location names, 66
for BIND PACKAGE, 460
for data-sharing groups, 455
for distributed data, 453
LOCK TABLE command, 413, 511
LOCKMAX option, 524
Locks, 507–508
attributes for, 508
avoiding, 519–520
claims, 520–521
contention in, 348–349
for coupling facility, 340
in data integrity, 345–348
in data sharing recovery, 359
displaying, 527–528
drain, 520–522
durations, 514–518
escalation, 524–525
modes, 512
monitoring, 526–528
promoting, 525
sharing, 413
sizes, 509–510
system parameters for, 518
timeouts and deadlocks with, 522–524
LOG option
for LOB columns, 114
for REORG, 267
LOG NO option, 130
LOG phase for REORG INDEX, 274
Log record sequence number (LRSNs), 307, 357–358
Log table spaces, 600
LOGAPPLY phase in RECOVER, 321–324
Logical database design, 160–166
Logical locks (L-locks), 346–347

Logical terminals (LTERMs), 75
Logical UOWs, 406
LOGLOAD parameter, 589–590
LOGONLY recovery, 359
Logs and logging, 307
bootstrap data sets, 308
in data sharing recovery, 357–358
in disaster recovery, 328
in LOB recovery, 326
log data sets, 307–308
SYSIBM.SYSLGRNX for, 309
LONG VARCHAR data, 251
LONG VARGRAPHIC data, 252
LONGLOG parameter, 272
LPL state, 301
LRDRTHLD parameter, 518
LRSNs (log record sequence number), 307, 357–358
LRU chains in buffer pools, 588
LTERMs (logical terminals), 75
LUNAMEs, 67

M

MAINTAINED BY SYSTEM option, 151
MAINTAINED BY USER option, 151
Maintenance, data. See Data maintenance
Managed System Infrastructure for Setup (msys for Setup), 17, 36–37
Management tools, 19–20
Mapping
attributes, 169
tables, 270
MATCHCOLS column, 532, 538, 553–556
Matching index columns, 538
Matching-index scans, 552–554
Materialized created temporary tables, 415
Materialized query tables (MQTs), 106, 150–151
MAX function, 193
MAXARCH parameter, 308
MAXRO parameter, 271–272
MBCSs (multibyte character sets), 113
MEMBER option, 397
MEMBER CLUSTER option, 153

Memory
in DBMI address space, 26
for pools, 69
MERGE_JOIN_COLS column, 535
Merge phase in SORT pools, 596
Merge-scan joins, 542–543
MERGECOPY utility, 311–312, 316–317
METHOD column, 532, 541–546
Middleware, 9–12
Migration, 36–37
considerations for, 38–40
in data sharing, 354–355
high-level overview, 38
Migration CLIST, 37, 39
MIN function, 193
Minimizing data loss, 329
MIXOPSEQ column, 534
Mobile computing, 5
Modification
databases, 159
indexes, 158
inserting data, 200–203
removing data, 205–206
sequence objects, 136
storage groups, 160
table spaces, 147
tables, 133
updating data, 203–205
Modified locks, 347
MODIFY phase
in MODIFY RECOVERY, 293
in MODIFY STATISTICS, 295
MODIFY RECOVERY utility, 293–294
MODIFY STATISTICS utility, 286, 294–295
MODIFY TRACE command, 570
MOLAP (multidimensional OLAP), 15, 416
Monitoring, 561
DISPLAY commands for, 585–586
locks, 526–528
Performance Monitor for, 565
resource limit facility for, 566
traces for, 566, 569, 574–576
triggers, 479–480
UDFs, 494–495
MQTs (materialized query tables), 106, 150–151

Msys for Setup (Managed System Infrastructure
for Setup), 17, 36–37
Multibyte character sets (MBCSs), 113
Multidimensional OLAP (MOLAP), 15, 416
Multilevel security, 94–95
Multiple conditions in data retrieval, 182
Multiple-index access, 538, 555
Multiple rows
FETCH and INSERT for, 419–420
retrieving, 367
Multiple servers, three-part table names with,
457
Multiple tables, selecting columns from, 182–
188
Multisite updates, 11

N

Name qualifiers, packages for, 391
Names
correlation, 188
in data sharing, 354–355
host variables, 364
schema, 90, 423
tables, 129
unqualified, 92–93
Negative conditions, searching for, 198–199
Nested loop joins, 541–542
Nested table expressions, 229–230
Nesting
joins, 219
stored procedures, 438
Net Search Extender, 14
New function mode (NFM), 38–40
NEXT VALUE FOR expression, 134
NFM (new function mode), 38–40
Ngram indexes, 503
NO ACTION clause, 127
NO CLUSTER option, 154
Non-read-only views, 207–208
Non-SELECT statements, dynamic SQL for,
384
Noncorrelated subqueries, 212
Nonmatching-index scans, 554
Nonpartitioning indexes (NPIs), 106, 156

Nonsargable predicates, 237
Nonscrollable cursors, 381
Nonunique indexes, 154–156
NOPKLIST option, 397, 400
Normalization, 162–165
NOSYSREC option, 265–266
Not deterministic UDFs, 491
NOT NULL columns
    considerations, 122
    inserting data into, 201
NOT NULL foreign keys, 128
NOT predicate, 198–199
NPIs (Nonpartitioning indexes), 106, 156
Null values
    considerations, 122–123
    with indexes, 155–156
    for LOB columns, 132
    searching for, 198
NULLIF attribute, 254
Numeric data types, 111–112
    conversions with, 251
    sequence objects for, 134–136
NUMLKTS parameter, 518
NUMLKUS parameter, 518

O

Object access, 77
    administrative authorities for, 83–88
    authorization identifiers for, 77–78
    catalog table information for, 93
    explicit privileges for, 77–83
    ownership with, 88–93
    plan execution authorization for, 93
    views for, 94
Object Comparison Tool, 19
Object-relational extensions, 482–483
    distinct types, 483–486
    LOBs. See LOBs (large objects) and LOB
        columns
    UDFs. See User-defined functions (UDFs)
Object-relational functionality, 469
Object Restore, 19
Objects
    access to. See Object access

recovering, 322
ODBC (Open Database Connectivity), 361–362,
    384
OFFPOSLIMIT triggers, 277
OLAP (online analytical processing), 233, 235
OLAP Server, 12, 15
OLRs (online reorganizations), 267
    read-only, 268–269
    read/write, 269–272
OLTP (online transaction processing) systems,
    233
ON clause for joins, 218–219
ON COMMIT command, 417
On-demand business, 4–5
One-fetch index access, 556
Online analytical processing (OLAP), 233, 235
Online DSNZPARMs, 49–50
Online reorganizations (OLRs), 267
Online transaction processing (OLTP) systems,
    233
OPEN command for cursors, 377
Open Database Connectivity (ODBC), 361–362,
    384
OPTHINT option
    for binding, 397
    in PLAN_TABLE, 536
Optimization. See Performance; Tuning
OPTIMIZE FOR n ROWS clause
    with distributed data, 466
    with FETCH, 418
Optimizers, 529
OPTIONS command, 56
OPTIONS option
    for BIND PACKAGE, 460
    for binding, 397
OR conditions, 199
ORDER BY clause, 189–191
Ordered rows, loading, 249
Ordering columns, 180–181
Outer joins, 219
    combining, 227–229
    full, 225–227
    left, 220–224
    right, 224–225
Output data set name option, 35
Overloading classes, 487

OWNER option, 89, 92, 397, 402
Ownership
    of plans and packages, 92, 402
    privileges with, 83, 88–93

P

P-locks (physical locks), 346–347
PACKADM authorization, 86
PACKAGE option for binding, 397
Packages
    binding, 389–392
        execution authorization in, 403
        ownership, 402
        package lists in, 400
        rebinding, 399–400
        removing, 402
    ownership for, 92, 402
    privileges for, 79
    for triggers, 478
Page P-locks, 347
PAGE_RANGE column, 535, 540
Page set P-locks, 347
Pages
    in buffer pools, 587–588
    externalized, 588–592
    locks, 347, 510, 514–516
    size of, 587
Parallel index builds
    with LOAD, 257–258
    with REORG, 266–267
Parallelism and parallel sysplex environment,
    33, 337
    in data sharing, 356–357
    for performance, 558–560
    system query, 356–357
    for table access, 546
    in tuning, 592
PARALLELISM_MODE column, 535, 546,
    558–560
PARAMETER STYLE option, 432–435
Parameters
    for stored procedures, 432–435, 445
    system, 41–50, 518
    in tuning, 562

Parent keys, 126–128
PARENT_QBLOCK column, 536
Parent tables, 127
PART clause, 249
PART VALUES clause, 142
PARTITION ENDING AT clause, 142
Partitioned indexes, 106, 154, 156–157
Partitioned table spaces, 107
    creating, 600
    LOAD parallelism, 258
    sorting in, 264–265
    working with, 138–142
Partitions
    image copies for, 313–314
    loading, 249–250
    locking, 509, 515
    rebalancing, 256, 280–281
PassTickets, 75
Passwords in Kerberos, 76
PATH bind option, 483
Path Checker, 20
PATH column, 549
PATH option for binding, 397
PATH special register, 483
Paths, access. *See* Access paths
PCTFREE parameter, 145–146, 255
PE (Personal Edition), 8
Percent characters (%) in string searches, 196–
    197
Performance, 529
    access paths in. *See* Access paths
    in data sharing, 351–352
    with distributed data, 466–467
    dynamic SQL for, 557–558
    Estimator for, 18
    improvement process, 563–564
    indexes for
        avoiding sorts, 556–557
        efficient access, 553–556
    MODIFY RECOVERY for, 294
    MQTs for, 150–151
    query parallelism for, 558–560
    traces for. *See* Traces
    with triggers, 479
    tuning. *See* Tuning
Performance Expert, 19–20

Performance Monitor (PM), 19, 565
Permutations in data retrieval, 180–181
Personal Developer's Edition, 5, 8
Personal Edition (PE), 5, 8
PGFIX feature, 590
PGSTEAL option, 588
Physical database design, 166–167
PIECESIZE clause, 156
PKLIST option, 397, 400
PLAN option, 397
PLAN_TABLE, 530
    columns in, 531–537
    index access in, 537–539
    table access in, 539–546
PLANNO column, 531
Plans
    binding
        options for, 393–398
        purpose and benefits, 389–392
    execution authorization for, 93, 403
    ownership of, 92, 402
    privileges for, 79
    for recovery, 323–324
    removing, 402
PM (Performance Monitor), 19, 565
Point-in-time recovery, 324–326
Points of consistency in UOWs, 407
Policies for coupling facility, 341–343
Polymorphism with UDFs, 493–494
Positioned deletes
    for cursors, 379
    description of, 205
Positioned updates
    for cursors, 378–379
    description of, 203
Precise indexes, 503
Precompiling
    DRDA access options for, 459
    SQL statements in, 388–389
Predicates
    in data retrieval, 181–182
    in filtering, 236–241
    join, 187
PREFETCH column, 534, 540
Prefetching in table access, 540
Preformat Active Log (DSNJLOGF) utility, 296

PREFORMAT option in LOAD, 246, 256–257
Preparation for disaster recovery, 327
Preserved row tables, 220
PREVIEW function, 57
PREVIOUS VALUE FOR expression, 134
PRIMARY_ACCESSTYPE column, 536
Primary authorization IDs, 77
Primary errors, 253
Primary keys, 126
    benefits of, 169
    defining, 173
    for indexes, 155
    with referential constraints, 126–127
Primary partitioning indexes, 154
Printing utility, 299
Priority
    of address space, 28
    Workload Manager for, 443
Private protocols for distributed data, 65–66, 452
Privileges, 77–83
    for distinct types, 81–82, 486
    with ownership, 88–93
    for schema, 483
Processor cost
    in compression, 146
    in data sharing, 351–352
Processors for coupling facility, 339
PROCMS column, 547
PROCSU column, 548
Production environment models, 550–551
PROGNAME column
    in DSN_FUNCTION_TABLE, 548
    in DSN_STATMNT_TABLE, 547
    in PLAN_TABLE, 531
PROGRAM TYPE SUB clause, 444
Programming considerations for distributed da-
    ta, 462–465
Projecting columns, 180
Promoting locks, 525
Propagation, triggers for, 470
Protocols for distributed data
    communications, 452–453
    private, 65–66, 452
PSRBD state, 302

Q

QBLOCK_TYPE column, 536
QBLOCKNO column, 531
QMF (Query Management Facility), 13, 16
Qualified objects, 89–90
QUALIFIER option, 89, 92, 397, 402–403
Qualifiers, packages for, 391
Qualifying rows, 182
Query Management Facility (QMF), 16
Query Monitor, 19
Query parallelism, 558–560
QUERYNO column
    in DSN_FUNCTION_TABLE, 548
    in DSN_STATMNT_TABLE, 547
    in PLAN_TABLE, 531
QUIESCE option, 332
QUIESCE utility, 318

R

RACF (Resource Access Control Facility), 32–33, 74–75
RAISE_ERROR function, 478–479
Random pages in buffer pools, 588
Random processing vs. sequential, 590–591
Ranges, searching for data in, 197
Ratio setting for group buffer pools, 350
RBDP (rebuild pending) condition, 302, 325
RDS limits, RIDs over, 595–596
Read-only OLRs, 268–269
Read-only queries, 552
Read-only views, 149, 207
Read stability (RS) isolation level
    lock avoiding in, 520
    purpose of, 515–516
Read/write OLRs, 269–272
REAL data type, 111–112
Real-time statistics, 287–289
REASON column, 548
Rebalancing partitions, 256, 280–281
REBIND command
    for plans and packages, 92, 393
    statistics for, 290
REBIND PACKAGE command, 399–400
REBIND TRIGGER PACKAGE command, 478

Rebinding, 392–393
    automatic, 400–401
    packages, 92, 399–400
REBUILD INDEX utility, 325
Rebuild pending (RBDP) condition, 302, 325
REBUILDPERCENT keyword, 342
RECOVER utility
    for data sharing, 358
    fast log apply with, 323–324
    for objects, 322
    for point-in-time recovery, 324
    for table spaces, 321
Recoverable Resource Manager Services (RRS)
    component, 413
Recovery, 318
    catalog and directory, 319–321
    CHECK DATA for, 319
    in data sharing, 357–360
    database-recovery concepts, 305–306
    disaster, 327–330
    fallback, 323
    image copies for. See Image copies
    index spaces, 321
    LOBs, 325–326
    logging for, 298, 307–309
    objects, 322
    planning for, 323–324
    point-in-time, 324–326
    system-level, 330–332
    table spaces, 321
Recovery Expert, 19–20
RECP (Recovery Pending) state, 302, 326
RECURHL parameter, 518
Recursive triggers, 479
Reentrant stored procedures, 432
REFERENCE option, 263
REFERENCING clause, 475–476
Referential constraints, 126–128
Referential integrity
    in DB2CERT database, 170–171
    with LOAD, 252–254
REFP state, 303
REFRESH command, 444
REFRESH DEFERRED option, 151
REFRESH TABLE command, 151
Registration of GFP pages, 349

Related privileges, 83
Relational OLAP (ROLAP), 15, 416
Relationships
    anomalies, 165–166
    in DB2CERT database, 170–171
    normalizing, 162–165
RELEASE option
    for BIND PLAN, 460
    for binding, 398
    for locks, 515
RELEASE SAVEPOINT command, 412
Releasing savepoints, 412
RELOAD phase
    in LOAD, 246
    in REORG, 261
REMARKS column, 534
Remote access, 75. *See also* Distributed data and
        environments
Remote servers (RSs), 63, 449
Remote units of work (RUWs), 450
Removing
    check constraints, 129
    data, 205–206, 260
    databases, 159
    indexes, 159
    plans and packages, 402
    sequence objects, 136
    storage groups, 160
    stored procedures, 439
    table spaces, 147–148
    tables, 133
    triggers, 482
    views, 149
RENAME TABLE command, 129
REOPT option, 398
REORG utility, 261–263
    for identity columns, 121
    inline statistics with, 272–274
    LOG option, 267
    NOSYSREC option, 265–266
    for online reorganizations, 267–272
    parallel index builds with, 266–267
    rebalancing partitions with, 280–281
    for removing data, 260
    reorganizing indexes with, 274, 278
    SHRLEVEL option, 263, 281

SORTDATA option, 263–265
SORTKEYS option, 266–267
for table spaces, 278–279
triggers for, 275–280
Reorganizations
    catalog and directory, 280
    REORG for. *See* REORG utility
    and table spaces, 145
REORGANIZE INDEX command, 504
REORP status, 280–281, 303
REPAIR Utility, 295–296
Repeatable read (RR) isolation level
    lock avoiding in, 520
    purpose of, 515–516
REPLACE option
    for binding, 393
    with LOAD, 248–249
RepliData, 20
REPORT parameter, 283, 285
REPORT utility, 317
REPORT RECOVERY utility, 323
REPORTCK phase in CHECK DATA, 291
REPORTONLY feature, 314
Reports
    for lock monitoring, 527
    Performance Monitor, 565
    recovery log, 298
REPRTLOB phase in CHECK LOB, 292
Residual predicates, 237
Resolving restrictive and advisory states, 299–
        303
Resource Access Control Facility (RACF), 32–
        33, 74–75
Resource limit facility, 566
Resource Recovery Services Attachment Facili-
        ty (RRSAF), 31–32, 442
Restart, 332–333
RESTART LIGHT command, 348, 359
RESTORE phase in RECOVER, 321–324
RESTORE SYSTEM utility, 331
Restoring to savepoints, 410–412
RESTP state, 303
RESTRICT clause, 127
Restricted systems for distributed data, 461–462
Restricting data retrieval, 181–182, 194–195
Restrictive states, 299–303

Result sets
   from SELECT, 178, 375
   for stored procedures, 435–437
RESUME keyword with LOAD, 248–249
Retained locks, 348
Retrieving data. *See* Data retrieval
RETURN clause, 489
Reusable stored procedures, 432
REVOKE command, 77, 82–83, 87
Revoking
   authorities, 87–88
   privileges, 82–83
RIDs (row identifiers)
   for indexes, 151
   pools, 69–70, 595–596
Right outer joins, 224–225
Risk in migration, 38
ROLAP (relational OLAP), 15, 416
ROLLBACK command, 407–408
Rollback operations, 306, 405–407
ROLLBACK TO SAVEPOINT command, 410–411
ROLLBACK WORK clause, 410
ROTATE clause, 140–141
Rotated partitioned table spaces, 140–141
ROUTINE_ID column, 537
Routines, privileges for, 82
Row expressions, 233
Row fullselects, 204
Row identifiers (RIDs)
   for indexes, 151
   pools, 69–70, 595–596
Row level security, 94
ROWID columns, loading, 254
ROWID data type, 111
Rows
   locks, 510, 514–516
   maximum, 130
   restricting, 181–182, 194–195
   retrieving. *See* Data retrieval
   triggers for, 475
RR (repeatable read) isolation level
   lock avoiding in, 520
   purpose of, 515–516
RRS (Recoverable Resource Manager Services)
   component, 413

RRSAF (Resource Recovery Services Attach-ment Facility), 31–32, 442
RS (read stability) isolation level
   lock avoiding in, 520
   purpose of, 515–516
RSs (remote servers), 449
Run phase in e-business cycles, 4
Runaway stored procedures, 443
RUNSTATS utility, 281–283
   for catalog, 63, 283, 285
   for inline statistics, 255
   for SQL cache invalidation, 285–287
Runtime clients, 10
RUWs (remote units of work), 450

S

S (share) lock mode
   duration, 517
   purpose of, 512–514
Sample exam, 611–625
Sampling statistics, 283
Sargable predicates, 237
SAVEPOINT command, 408–409
Savepoints, 407–408
   in distributed environments, 413
   establishing, 408–409
   releasing, 412
   restoring to, 410–412
SBCSs (single-byte character sets), 113
SCA (shared communication area), 339–340, 359
Scalar functions, 192, 486–490
SCANTAB phase in CHECK DATA, 291
SCHEMA_NAME column, 549
Schemas
   names for, 90, 423
   for object-relational extensions, 482–483
   privileges for, 81
   for stored procedures, 440
SCOPE option for UDFs, 494
Scrollable cursors, 382–383
SCT02 directory table, 64
SDSNSAMP queries, 63
Searched deletes, 205–206

Searched updates, 203
Searching
    host variables in, 368
    LOB extenders for, 501, 503–504
    for negative conditions, 198–199
    for null values, 198
    in ranges, 197
    for sets of values, 199
    for string patterns, 196–197
Second normal form (2NF), 164
Secondary authorization IDs, 78
Secondary errors, 253
Secondary partitioning indexes, 154
Security
    access. See Access and security
    RACF, 32–33
Segmented table spaces, 107
    benefits of, 137–138
    creating, 599
    unloading, 264
SEGSIZE parameter, 138
SELECT command, 367. See also Data retrieval
    for column projections, 180
    for entire tables, 178–180
Selective partition locking (SPL), 509
SENSITIVE cursors, 382
Sensitivity of cursors, 382
Sequence objects
    creating, 135
    vs. identity columns, 135–136, 425
    modifying, 136
    purpose of, 107, 134–136, 423–425
    working with, 134–135
Sequential detection, 540
Sequential pages in buffer pools, 588
Sequential prefetch, 540
Sequential prefetch threshold (SPTH), 593
Sequential Processing Using File Input (SPUFI)
        option, 35–36
Sequential processing vs. random, 590–591
SET clause, 367
Set closure, 182
SET CONNECTION command, 458
SET CURRENT command, 78
SET CURRENT PATH command, 483
SET LOG command, 332–333, 589

SET NULL clause, 127
SET SYSPARM command, 50
Sets of values
    inserting, 202
    searching for, 199
702 sample exam, 611–625
SFM (Sysplex Failure Management) policy, 342
Shadow copies, 329–330
Share (S) lock mode
    duration, 517
    purpose of, 512–514
Share with intent exclusive (SIX) lock mode,
        512–513
Shared communication area (SCA), 339–340,
        359
Sharing
    data. See Data sharing
    locks, 413
SHRLEVEL parameters
    for image copies, 314–315
    for OLRs, 268
    for REORG, 263, 281
SIGNAL SQLSTATE command, 478–479
Signaling services, 344
Signatures for functions, 493
Simple predicates, 237
Simple table spaces, 107, 137, 264–265
Single-byte character sets (SBCSs), 113
Single-precision floating-point data types, 112
Single-result queries, 212
Single rows, retrieving, 367
SIX (share with intent exclusive) lock mode,
        512–513
Size
    locks, 509–510
    pools
        buffer, 590, 596
        group buffer, 350
        pages in, 587
        pools, 597
        sort, 596
SKCT (skeleton cursor tables) locks, 508
SKPT (skeleton package tables) locks, 508
SMALLINT data type, 110
    characteristics of, 111
    conversions with, 251

SMF (System Management Facility) records, 566
SNA (System Network Architecture)
    for distributed data, 452–454
    for network connections, 66–67
Software in tuning, 563
SORT option in LOAD, 246–247
SORT phase
    in CHECK DATA, 291
    in CHECK LOB, 292
    in REORG, 262
Sort pools, 70, 596
SORTBLD phase, 266–267
SORTC_ columns, 533, 535, 540–541
SORTDATA parameter, 263–265
SORTKEYS option
    for LOAD, 256
    for REORG, 266–267
SORTN_ columns, 533, 535, 540–541
Sorts
    avoiding, 556–557
    output, 189–190
    for table access, 540–541
Sourced functions, 486–487, 489
SPACE keyword, 56–57
SPAS (stored-procedure address space), 27
Spatial Extender, 14
SPEC_FUNC_ID column, 549
Specific IDs, auditing, 97
SPL (selective partition locking), 509
SPT01 directory table, 64
SPTH (sequential prefetch threshold), 593
SPUFI (Sequential Processing Using File Input)
    option, 35–36
SQL, 361–362
    caches in
        invalidating, 285–287
        for performance, 557, 598
    cursors in
        closing, 379
        held, 380
        nonscrollable, 381
        in row retrieval, 375–379
        scrollable, 382–383
        types of, 381
    definitions in, 362–363

delimiting, 362
dynamic, 384–385
    caching, 557, 598
    for performance, 557–558
    statements, 361, 384–385
execution validation in, 368–375
extenders for, 501
host structures in, 365
host variables in, 363–364
inserting and updating data in, 367
retrieving rows in, 367
scalar functions for, 487, 489–490
searching data in, 368
for stored procedures, 445–447
SQL Performance Analyzer, 19
SQLCA (SQL communication area), 368–370
SQLCODE fields, 370–371
SQLERROR option, 93, 398, 460, 463
SQLRULES option
    for BIND PLAN, 461–462
    for binding, 398
SQLSTATE fields, 370–371
SSAS (system services address space), 24–25
Stage 1 predicates, 237–241
Stage 2 predicates, 237–238
Star joins
    for table access, 543–546
    working with, 235–236
Star schemas, 234–235
START DATABASE command, 314, 359
START DB2 command, 51
START FUNCTION SPECIFIC command, 494
START PROCEDURE command, 440
START TRACE command, 97, 567, 570
START WITH setting, 134, 423
Starting traces, 97–98
Statement triggers, 475
Static binding, 390
Static SQL statements, 361
Statistics
    clearing, 294–295
    gathering, 281–285
    inline
        benefits of, 286–287
        with LOAD, 255
        with REORG, 272–274

for lock monitoring, 527
for production environment models, 550–551
real-time, 287–289
for rebinds, 290
for RID pools, 595–596
storing, 287–288
traces for, 567, 584–585
UDF, 495
STATISTICS clause, 273, 287
Status-monitoring services, 344
STDDEV function, 193
Stealing method in tuning, 592
STMT_ENCODE column, 548
STMT_TYPE column, 547
STMTTOKEN column, 537
Stogroups, 160, 599
STOP DB2 command, 332
STOP FUNCTION SPECIFIC command, 495
STOP PROCEDURE command, 440
STOP TRACE command, 98, 570
Stop words for text indexes, 503
Stopping traces, 97–98
Storage groups, 107, 160, 599
Stored-procedure address space (SPAS), 27
Stored procedures, 429
    benefits of, 430–431
    DB2 Development Center for, 447
    defining, 438–439
    for distributed data, 464
    DSNSPAS for, 440–441
    execution environments for, 440–445
    Language Environment product libraries
        for, 431–432
    nesting, 438
    parameters for, 432–435, 445
    removing, 439
    result sets for, 435–437
    schema qualification for, 440
    SQL for, 445–447
    temporary tables for, 414
    units of work for, 437
    Workload Manager for, 441–445
    writing, 431
STOSPACE Utility, 289

String data types
    characteristics of, 112–115
    date, 116
    searching for, 196–197
    time, 117
Strong typing, 121–122
Structures, 104–107
    for coupling facility, 341
    in data sharing recovery, 359–360
    host, 365–366
    table spaces, 107
Subqueries, 211–214
SUBSTR function, 192
Subsystems
    access, 74–76
    pools, 68–70
    privileges for, 80–81
SUM function, 232
Summary recovery log reports, 298
SWITCH phase
    for OLRs, 269
    for REORG INDEX, 274
Synchronized timestamps, 343
Synchronizing ICF, 343
Synchronous reads, 588
Synonyms, 106
SYSADM authorization, 85
SYSCOLUMNS table, 132
SYSCTRL authorization, 84
SYSFUN schema, 440
SYSIBM statistics, 550–551
SYSLGRNX table, 64, 309
SYSOPR authorization, 85
Sysplex Failure Management (SFM) policy, 342
Sysplex query parallelism, 33, 337
    in data sharing, 356–357
    for performance, 560
Sysplex timer, 343
SYSPRINT file, 55
System-level backup and recovery, 330–332
System Management Facility (SMF) records,
    566
System Network Architecture (SNA)
    for distributed data, 452–454
    for network connections, 66–67
System parameters, 41–50, 518

System services address space (SSAS), 24–25
SYSUTILX directory table, 64

T

Table access
    joins for
        hybrid, 543
        merge-scan, 542–543
        nested loop, 541–542
        star, 543–546
    limited partition scanning for, 540
    parallelism usage for, 546
    in PLAN_TABLE, 539–546
    prefetching for, 540
    sorts for, 540–541
    table space scans, 539–540
Table-check constraints, 480–481
Table-controlled partitioning, 142
TABLE_DCCSID column, 537
Table Edition, 20
Table Editor, 20
TABLE_ENCODE column, 537
TABLE keyword, 492
TABLE_MCCSID column, 537
TABLE_SCCSID column, 537
Table spaces, 107
    compressing, 146–147
    creating, 143–145
    free space on, 145–146
    LOB, 142–143
    locks, 509, 513–515
    modifying, 147
    offline, 329
    partitioned. See Partitioned table spaces
    recovering, 321
    removing, 147–148
    reorganizing. See REORG utility
    scans of, 539–540
    segmented, 107
        benefits of, 137–138
        creating, 599
        unloading, 264
    simple, 137
TABLE_TYPE column, 537

Tables, 104, 125
    access to. See Table access
    auditing, 98
    auxiliary
        creating, 602–603
        for LOB data, 131–132
    constraints, 125–129
    copying definitions, 132
    creating, 129–131, 600–602
    for DB2CERT database, 168–171
    defining, 171–172, 362–363
    functions for, 192, 486, 490–491
    locks, 509, 513–514
    modifying, 133
    MQTs, 106, 150–151
    privileges for, 79
    projecting columns from, 180
    removing, 133
    retrieving, 178–180
    temporary, 130, 413–417
    for triggers, 476–477
TABLESPACESET option, 317
TABLESPACESTATS table, 287–288
TABNO column, 532
Tape image copies, 311
Target database names
    for distributed data, 453
    in VTAM, 66
Task control block (TCBs), 32, 568
TCP/IP (Transmission Control Protocol/Internet
        Protocol)
    for distributed data, 452–454
    for networks, 66–67
TEMP database, 159, 417
TEMPLATE command, 56–57
Templates, utility, 56–57
Temporary tables, 130
    CTTs, 413–415
    DTTs, 415–416
TEST_CENTER table, 168
Test Database Generator, 20
TEST table, 168
TEST_TAKEN table, 168
Text extenders, 14
    indexing, 503–504
    for LOBs, 502–503

Third normal form (3NF), 164–165
Threads with distributed data, 467
Three-part names
    for distributed data, 456–457
    table references by, 65–66
Time data types, 115
    characteristics of, 115
    conversions with, 251
    as strings, 117
Time Sharing Option (TSO), 30–31
Timeouts with locks, 522–524
Timers for coupling facility, 343
TIMESTAMP data type, 111
    characteristics of, 115–117
    conversions with, 251
    in PLAN_TABLE, 534
TIMESTAMP_FORMAT function, 117
Timestamps for coupling facility, 343
TNAME column, 532
TO SAVEPOINT clause, 410–412
TOLOGPOINT parameter, 324
Top-down data model design approach, 161
TORBA keyword, 324
Traces, 566
    accounting, 567–568, 570–573
    audit, 95–98, 569, 573
    IFCIDs for, 570–585
    invoking, 570
    monitor, 566, 569, 574–576
    performance, 569, 576–584
    statistics, 567, 584–585
TRACKER SITE option, 329–330
Transactions, 507–508
    global, 413–417
    locking. *See* Locks
Transform phase in e-business cycles, 4
Transition tables for triggers, 476–477
Transition variables for triggers, 475–476
Transmission Control Protocol/Internet Protocol
    (TCP/IP)
    for distributed data, 452–454
    for networks, 66–67
Triggers, 469–470
    activating, 471
    after, 473–474
    before, 474–475

catalog information for, 275–276, 480
    combinations, 477–478
    creating, 471–473
    declarative RIs with, 481
    dropping, 482
    for invalidations, 478–479
    monitoring, 479–480
    packages for, 478
    performance with, 479
    for reorganizations, 275–280
    row and command, 475
    vs. table-check constraints, 480–481
    transition tables for, 476–477
    transition variables for, 475–476
    UDFs for, 481–482
    uses for, 470
TSLOCKMODE column, 533
TSO (Time Sharing Option), 30–31
Tuning. *See also* Performance
    buffer pools, 586–588
    checkpoints and page externalization, 589–
        592
    DISPLAY BUFFERPOOL for, 594–595
    dynamic SQL caching, 598
    environmental descriptor manager pool,
        597
    guidelines for, 562–563
    I/O requests and externalization, 588–589
    internal thresholds in, 593–594
    RID pools in, 595
    scope of, 564
    sort pools, 596
    virtual pool design strategies, 594
Two-phase commits, 461

U

U (update) lock mode
    duration, 517
    purpose of, 512–514
UCS-2 encoding, 124–125
UDB (Universal Database), 5
    clients, 10
    for Linux, UNIX, and Windows, 6–7
    for z/OS, 6

UDFs. *See* User-defined functions (UDFs)
Uncommitted read (UR) isolation level
    lock avoiding in, 520
    purpose of, 515–516
Underline characters (_) in string searches, 196
Unicode support, 124–125
UNION operation, 215–217
Unique constraints, 125–126
Unique indexes, 154–155
Unique keys
    defining, 174
    for indexes, 155
    with referential constraints, 126–128
Unique nonpartitioning indexes, 156
Units of recovery (URs), 407
Units of work (UOWs)
    in commit and rollback operations, 306,
        406–407
    for stored procedures, 437
Universal Database (UDB), 5
    clients, 10
    for Linux, UNIX, and Windows, 6–7
    for z/OS, 6
Universal Database Express Edition, 8–9
UNIX, UDB for, 6–7
UNLOAD EXTERNAL option, 274
UNLOAD phase
    in REORG, 261
    in REORG INDEX, 274
UNLOAD utility, 259–260
Unqualified names, 92–93
Unqualified objects
    in binding, 402–403
    ownership of, 88–89
UOWs (units of work)
    in commit and rollback operations, 306,
        406–407
    for stored procedures, 437
Updatable identity columns values, 422–423
UPDATE command, 203–205
    for cursors, 378–379
    for host variables, 367
    with identity columns, 421–422
    logging, 307
UPDATE INDEX command, 504

Update (U) lock mode
    duration, 517
    purpose of, 512–514
Updated pages in virtual buffer pools, 587
Updating
    data records, 203–205
    distributed data, 461–462
    with host variables, 367
UR (uncommitted read) isolation level
    lock avoiding in, 520
    purpose of, 515–516
URCHKTH parameter, 518
URs (units of recovery), 407
Use privilege category, 81
User-defined data types, 104–105
User-defined functions (UDFs), 192, 486–487,
        530
    catalog information for, 496
    cost information for, 495–496
    executing, 494–495
    external, 487–491
    invoking, 491–493
    monitoring and controlling, 494–495
    polymorphism with, 493–494
    sourced, 489
    SQL scalar, 489–490
    statistics, 495
    table, 490–491
    for triggers, 481–482
User-tailored reports (UTRs), 565
USING clause for storage groups, 160
UTF-8 encoding, 124–125
UTILINIT phase
    in CHECK DATA, 291
    in CHECK LOB, 292
    in LOAD, 246
    in MODIFY RECOVERY, 293
    in MODIFY STATISTICS, 295
    in REORG, 261
    in REORG INDEX, 274
    in UNLOAD, 259
Utilities, 53–57
Utilities Suite V8, 20
UTILTERM phase
    in CHECK DATA, 291
    in CHECK LOB, 292

in MODIFY RECOVERY, 293
in MODIFY STATISTICS, 295
in REORG, 262
in REORG INDEX, 274
in UNLOAD, 259
UTRs (user-tailored reports), 565

V

V8 code, 39
VALIDATE option, 93, 398
Validation
    SQL execution, 368–375
    triggers for, 470
VALUE function, 227
VALUES clause, 201, 367
VARCHAR data type, 113
    conversions with, 251
    size of, 114
VARGRAPHIC data type, 111
    characteristics of, 114
    conversions with, 252
Variables
    host, 363–364
    transition, 475–476
VARIANCE function, 193
Varying-length character strings, 113
Varying-list SELECT statements, 385
VDWQT setting, 592
Verification in bind process, 393
VERSION column, 534
Versioning
    packages for, 390
    plans, 392
Video extenders, 14, 505–506
VIEW_CREATOR column, 549
VIEW_NAME column, 549
Views
    classification of, 206–208
    Cube Views, 12, 14–15
    definitions, 362–363
    inline, 229
    purpose of, 106
    read-only, 149, 207
    removing, 149

in security, 94
    working with, 148–149
Virtual buffer pools
    availability of, 68
    design strategies for, 594
    pages in, 587
virtual pool parallel sequential threshold
        (VPPSEQT), 592
Virtual pool sequential steal threshold (VPSE-
        QT), 590–591
Virtual Telecommunications Access Method
        (VTAM), 66, 453–454
Visual Explain, 17–18, 552–553
VPPSEQT (virtual pool parallel sequential
        threshold), 592
VPSEQT (virtual pool sequential steal thresh-
        old), 590–591
VPSIZE parameter, 590
VPSTEAL threshold, 592
VTAM (Virtual Telecommunications Access
        Method), 66, 453–454

W

Warehouse Edition (DWE), 15–16
Web Query Tool, 20
WEPR state, 303
WHEN_OPTIMIZE column, 535
WHERE clause
    comparison operators in, 181
    with UPDATE, 204
    for views, 148
WHERE NOT NULL option, 155
Wildcard characters in searches, 196–197
Windows, UDB for, 6
WITH CHECK OPTION clause, 149
WITH DEFAULT clause, 121, 201–202
WITH GRANT option, 88
WITH HOLD cursors, 380, 466
WITH RETURN clause, 435–436
WLM. See Workload Manager (WLM)
WORKFILE database, 159
Workgroup Server Edition (WSE), 5, 7–8
Workgroup Server Unlimited Edition (WSUE),
        5, 8

Working-storage section for definitions, 362
Workload balancing, 443
Workload Manager (WLM), 27, 441–442
    benefits, 442
    in data sharing, 355
    for diagnostic information, 445
    environment management for, 444–445
    program types for, 444
    with stored procedures, 443–444
Write thresholds, 591–592
Writing stored procedures, 431
WSE (Workgroup Server Edition), 5, 7–8
WSUE (Workgroup Server Unlimited Edition),
    5, 8

X–Z

X (exclusive) lock mode
    duration, 517–518
    purpose of, 512–514
XCF (Cross System Coupling Facility),
    343–344
XES contention, 348
XLKUPDLT parameter, 518
XML extenders, 14, 506

informIT

YOUR GUIDE TO IT REFERENCE

Articles

Keep your edge with thousands of free articles, in-depth features, interviews, and IT reference recommendations – all written by experts you know and trust.

Online Books

Answers in an instant from **InformIT Online Book's** 600+ fully searchable on line books. For a limited time, you can get your first 14 days **free**.

POWERED BY
Safari
TECH BOOKS ONLINE

Catalog

Review online sample chapters, author biographies and customer rankings and choose exactly the right book from a selection of over 5,000 titles.

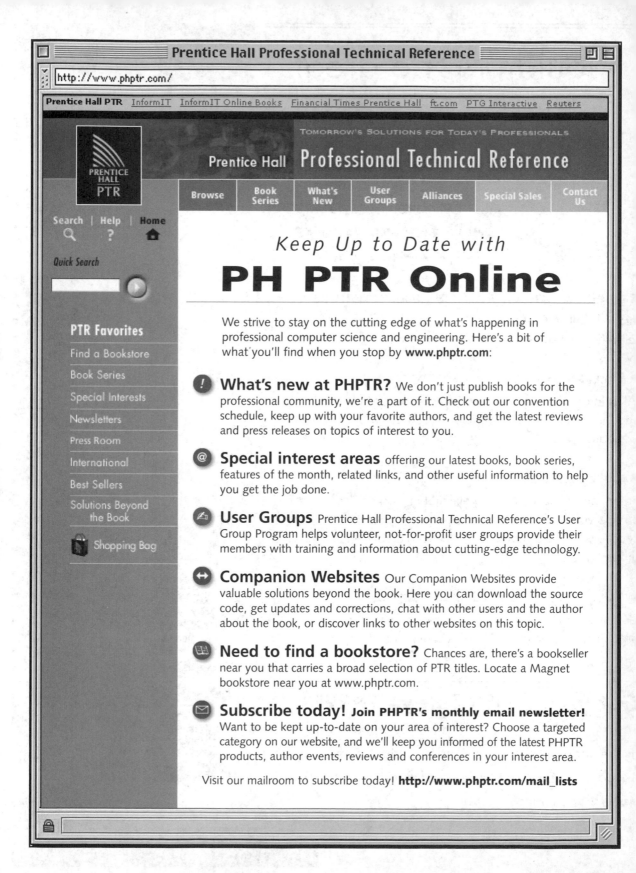